# www.wadsworth.com

*wadsworth.com* is the World Wide Web site for Wadsworth and is your direct source to dozens of online resources.

At *wadsworth.com* you can find out about supplements, demonstration software, and student resources. You can also send email to many of our authors and preview new publications and exciting new technologies.

**wadsworth.com**
Changing the way the world learns®

# SOCIAL PROBLEMS
## *Issues and Solutions*

### FIFTH EDITION

## Charles Zastrow

*University of Wisconsin, Whitewater*

**Wadsworth**
Thomson Learning™

Australia • Canada • Denmark • Japan • Mexico • New Zealand • Philippines
Puerto Rico • Singapore • Spain • United Kingdom • United States

*Publisher:* Eve Howard
*Assistant Editor:* Ari Levenfeld
*Editorial Assistant:* Bridget Schulte
*Executive Marketing Manager:* Diane McOscar
*Marketing Assistant:* Kelli Goslin
*Project Editor:* Jerilyn Emori
*Print Buyer:* Karen Hunt
*Permissions Editor:* Robert Kauser

*Production Service:* Robin Gold/Forbes Mill Press
*Photo Researcher:* Randall Nicholas
*Copy Editor:* Rachel Siegal
*Compositor:* Forbes Mill Press
*Cover Designer:* Yvo Riezebos
*Cover Images:* PhotoDisc
*Cover Printer:* Transcontinental Printing, Inc.
*Printer/Binder:* Transcontinental Printing, Inc.

Printed in Canada
1 2 3 4 5 6 7 04 03 02 01 00

For permission to use material from this text, contact us by
    **Web:** www.thomsonrights.com
    **Fax:** 1-800-730-2215
    **Phone:** 1-800-730-2214

**Library of Congress Cataloging-in-Publication Data**

Zastrow, Charles.
    Social problems : issues and solutions / Charles Zastrow.– 5th ed.
      p. cm.
    Includes bibliographical references and indexes.
    ISBN 0-534-52392-7
    1. Social problems. 2. Deviant behavior. 3. Equality. 4. Social institutions. 5. United States—Social conditions. I. Title.

HN28 .Z37 1999
361.1—dc21
                            99-046729

For more information, contact
**Wadsworth/Thomson Learning**
**10 Davis Drive**
**Belmont, CA 94002-3098**
**USA**
**www.wadsworth.com**

**International Headquarters**
Thomson Learning
290 Harbor Drive, 2nd Floor
Stamford, CT 06902-7477
USA

**UK/Europe/Middle East**
Thomson Learning
Berkshire House
168-173 High Holborn
London WC1V 7AA
United Kingdom

**Asia**
Thomson Learning
60 Albert Street #15-01
Albert Complex
Singapore 189969

**Canada**
Nelson/Thomson Learning
1120 Birchmount Road
Scarborough, Ontario M1K 5G4
Canada

 This book is printed on acid-free recycled paper.

# Contents in Brief

# Contents

---

**PART TWO**             *Inequality Problems*

---

✦✦✦✦✦✦✦✦✦✦✦✦✦✦✦✦✦✦✦✦✦✦✦✦✦✦✦✦✦✦✦✦✦✦✦✦✦✦✦✦✦✦✦✦✦✦✦✦✦✦✦✦✦✦✦✦✦✦✦✦✦✦

## PART FOUR    *Problems of a Changing World*

# Preface

On March 20, 1995, a religious cult in Japan, Aum Shinrikyo ("Supreme Truth"), released the nerve agent *sarin* in the Tokyo subway system. Twelve people were killed, and 5,500 were injured. (A tiny drop of sarin can kill within minutes after skin contact or inhalation of its vapor.) We are increasingly becoming aware that a number of other terrorist groups and a number of countries (including the United States, Iran, Iraq, Syria, Israel, Russia, and China) are developing biological and chemical weapons (which include the use of such biological agents as beriberi, the plague, small pox, anthrax, malaria, and ebola to cause infectious diseases in those who are exposed). The danger of germ warfare attacks are now more likely than that of a nuclear war (see Chapter 14). One of the objectives in studying social problems is to understand the dynamics of group behavior. The threat of biological and chemical weapons being developed and used highlights a number of critical sociological questions. For example, what factors influence terrorist groups and governments to develop biological and chemical weapons? Since the effects of chemical and biological weapons are so inhumane and despicable, what variables influence governments and terrorists to decide to use such weapons? (Some factors that may influence terrorist groups to develop and use such weapons include: huge income disparities between "haves and have-nots," political oppression, religious intolerance, racial and ethnic group discrimination, and glorification of violence in a society.) What actions can societies take to reduce the likelihood of biological and chemical weapons being developed and utilized?

Social problems courses are often among the most stimulating and educational courses taught in colleges and universities. Such courses describe tragic human conditions and personal and social problems faced by every human being. College students are often personally affected by these problems. This text presents material on social problems in a stimulating and educational way.

The book has several goals:

♦ To provide a clear and concise description and analysis of major social problems in America

♦ To present and describe proposed solutions for resolving each of the problems discussed

- To stimulate interest in understanding and doing something about resolving social problems
- To provide an understanding of sociological theories that explain the nature of social problems and also generate proposals to resolve these problems
- To provide an awareness of the importance of sociological research in testing theories and in discovering social facts
- To help readers become aware of the importance of social movements in recognizing and solving social problems
- To instill a sense that problems indeed can be solved, while at the same time tempering this optimism with a realistic understanding of the difficulties involved in achieving this end
- To help readers sort out their values concerning convicted offenders, single parents, abusive parents, people of color, big business, social reformers, the emotionally disturbed, persons with a disability, and others
- To stimulate critical thinking about some of the controversial issues surrounding contemporary social problems

The goals of *Social Problems*—and the specific social problems discussed—were determined in large part by an extensive survey of faculty members who teach social problems courses. Additional information on which problems to include was gathered from sociological writings, opinion polls, and news media coverage. Instead of seeking to explain all social problems from a few theoretical perspectives, this book uses more of an eclectic approach. Theories are presented that best help in understanding each social problem covered, and that promise to generate usable recommendations for alleviating each problem. Repeatedly, it will be demonstrated that sociological research has disproved many "commonsense" beliefs.

A major focus of this text is to present proposals that have been advanced, as well as programs that have been created, to attempt to resolve each of the social problems reviewed. (Most other social problems texts give little attention to describing approaches to resolving social problems.)

The author believes that developing the students' critical thinking capacities is much more important than requiring the learning of unimportant facts to be recited on exams. To the extent possible, jargon-free language is used so that the reader can grasp the material more readily.

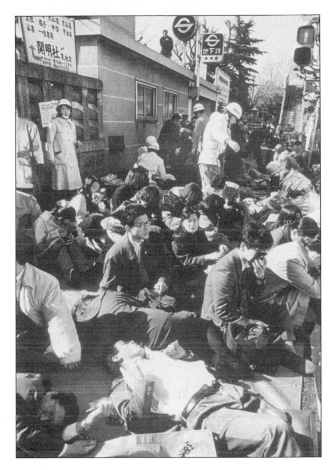

*A commuter is treated by an emergency medical team after being exposed to a lethal gas, nerve agent Sarin, in a Tokyo subway.*

## Plan of the Book

*Social Problems* is structured to cover material in this sequence: first, deviances and social variations experienced by individuals; then, inequality problems experienced by certain groups; next, problems of troubled institutions; and finally, problems of a changing world. This progression from individual problems to more complex problems should assist the reader in grasping and understanding increasingly complex material.

The four parts are preceded by an introduction, "The Sociology of Social Problems," which provides an orientation to the sociological approach to social problems. The components of a social problem are defined, a brief history of investigating social problems is presented, the role of social science in studying social problems is discussed, key sociological terms are defined, and the importance of social movements in resolving problems is described. An overview is given of the role of sociological theory and research in studying social problems.

Part I (Deviance and Social Variations) presents personal problems that involve issues of national concern. Separate chapters cover crime and delinquency, emotional and behavioral problems, drug abuse, and variations in human sexuality. Because so many people are affected by them (e.g., as crime victims or through emotional problems), these *personal* problems are recognized as major *social* problems in the United States.

Part II (Inequality Problems) presents dilemmas of discrimination and unequal distribution of resources. Chapter topics cover racism and ethnocentrism, sexism, ageism, and poverty.

Part III (Troubled Institutions) presents problems confronting key institutions. Chapters cover the family; health care; education; and big business, technology, and work.

Part IV (Problems of a Changing World) presents issues of immense dimensions that affect everyone. Chapter topics cover violence, terrorism, and war; urban problems; population; and environment.

Each chapter presents the following material about a social problem area:

♦ A description of the nature and extent of the problem

♦ Vivid case examples to illustrate the plight of those affected

♦ Sociological theoretical material and research findings on the causes of the problem

♦ Current efforts, programs, and services to resolve the problem

♦ Merits and shortcomings of current efforts to resolve the problem

♦ Controversial contemporary issues surrounding the problem

♦ Proposals to resolve the problem more effectively

The text ends with an epilogue, which summarizes past and present approaches of our society (including the federal government) to combat social problems and describes social trends that provide a view of the future.

*Acknowledgments* The author wishes to express deep appreciation to the following people who assisted in conceptualizing the text and helped in a number of ways with the writing: Vicki Vogel, William Winter, Mathew Zachariah, Robert Scheurell, Lee H. Bowker, and Grafton H. Hull, Jr.

Crime, poverty, racism, sexism, ageism, mental illness, urban problems, pollution, divorce, prostitution, alcoholism, drug abuse, spouse abuse, child abuse, overpopulation—the list of social problems facing us is depressingly long. It is so long that some people, concluding nothing can be done, turn their backs and avoid trying to understand and do something about these problems. Others believe they can be eradicated, or at least reduced, through actions suggested by sociological research and theories. In this text we discuss a number of different social problems and present examples of programs and strategies that sociologists and other professionals have proposed or used to combat them. This chapter:

♦ provides an introduction to the sociological approach to social problems;

♦ defines the components of a social problem;

♦ presents a brief history of the study of social problems;

♦ describes the role of sociology in resolving social problems;

♦ discusses the importance of social movements in resolving problems;

♦ defines key sociological terms;

♦ describes the liberal, conservative, and developmental perspectives on social problems and social programs;

♦ gives a summary of the role of sociological research and theory in studying social problems; and

♦ summarizes three prominent macrosociological theories: functionalism, conflict theory, and interactionism.

## The Sociological Approach

Sociology is the scientific study of human society and social behavior. Sociology has the scientific tools (to conduct case studies, surveys, and experiments) for making sense of social problems. It has the rigorous scientific perspective to develop theories about the causes of social problems and then to develop proposals and programs to reduce the severity and extent of social problems.

Careful sociological study can, by itself, contribute substantially to resolving social problems through clearing up the confusion and misunderstanding surrounding these problems. For example, many people believe most welfare recipients are able to work but would rather remain unemployed and "live it up" on welfare. Yet sociological research shows that only a small fraction of welfare recipients can work. The vast majority are unable to hold a full-time job because they are children or elderly, have a disability, or are mothers with young children.[1]

In addition, public assistance payments barely provide for the basic necessities of food, clothing, shelter and medical care. Therefore welfare recipients are unable to "live it up" on the monthly checks they receive.[2]

## DEFINING A SOCIAL PROBLEM

Most people define a social problem as a social condition that harms, or seems to harm, their own interests. Such a definition is too imprecise and self-centered to determine what is and what is not a social problem. For example, the pro-life movement views abortion as one of our most serious social problems. This movement asserts that abortion degrades human life, threatens survival of the family, leads to a deterioration in moral values, and condones the murder of human beings.

On the other hand, the pro-choice movement views abortion as a needed service and maintains it is certainly *not* a social problem. This movement asserts that making abortions illegal would in fact intensify other social problems. Pro-choice advocates assert that making abortions illegal would result in abortions being performed under unsanitary conditions and would erect a barrier to women achieving control of their lives and of when they want to bear children. The pro-choice movement also asserts that making abortions illegal would hinder women from competing equally with men, increase the number of unwanted births, intensify overpopulation, and increase the number of child-abuse cases because, they assert, unwanted children are more apt to be abused. How, then, can we decide which interpretation of the abortion issue has correctly identified a social problem?

As our guide to studying social problems, we will use the following definition. A *social problem exists when an influential group asserts that a certain social condition affecting a large number of people is a problem that may be remedied by collective action*. Let us examine the four key elements in this definition.

1. *An influential group.* To precisely define and measure whether a group is "influential" is a difficult

task. For our purposes, we will define an influential group as one that appears capable of having a significant impact on social policy at the national level. The pro-life movement, for example, has demonstrated through the voting booth and in legislative activities that it can influence social policy on abortion issues.

On the other hand, groups with little influence have taken positions on social conditions that most people presently do not view as social problems. For example, some groups assert that no one should pay taxes or that parents should not have to send their children to school. These concerns are not considered social problems because these groups presently have little influence.

The degree of a group's influence is measured by three interrelated factors: the *number* of those expressing the concern, the *strength* with which the concern is expressed, and the *power* of those expressing the concern.

For example, a few people have always been concerned about the environment and about equal opportunities for women, but these issues gained recognition as social problems only when the few expressing their concerns were joined by many others.

The strength with which the concern is expressed is another factor. For example, it has been known for decades that living conditions in inner city slums are unhealthy. The federal government did little to improve living conditions until, in the late 1960s, inner city residents in many metropolitan areas violently protested through arson, looting, and rioting. The federal government then responded by providing new programs (costing millions of dollars) to inner-city residents in an effort to improve living conditions. Unfortunately, a few years after the violent protests subsided, the federal government phased out its financial support, and slum living conditions today are no better than they were in the 1960s.[3]

Generating public recognition of a problem is also possible for small groups and individuals with substantial power. In 1954, for example, the nine members of the U.S. Supreme Court stimulated the recognition of racial discrimination as a major social problem in *Brown v. Board of Education,* which ruled that racial segregation in public school is unconstitutional.[4]

In 1985, Rock Hudson, popular film star, publicly announced that he was HIV-positive (he died of complications from this disease on October 2 of the same year). His acknowledgment and subsequent death led our federal government, the news media, and many

other influential segments in our society to recognize that AIDS was a major health and social problem that could adversely affect an enormous and diverse number of individuals and families. Although AIDS had existed for several years prior to 1985, its peril was recognized on a broad scale only after a public figure came forth.

*A view from the Washington monument, Friday, October 11, 1996, shows the huge AIDS Quilt stretching from the monument to the U.S. Capitol.*

It is common for American presidents to use televised speeches and news conferences to convince the public that a condition is a social problem that must be combated through revisions of federal policies and laws, usually accompanied by major expenditures of tax money. Three presidents (Carter, Reagan, and Clinton) used this strategy to define "big govern-

ment" and its attendant unending bureaucratic regulations as a social problem. In 1989, President Bush used the news media to heighten public concern over the drug problem by declaring a "war on drugs."

Individuals and small groups with substantial power may also use their influence to block the definition of a condition, no matter how undesirable, as a social problem. An example is the extensive political lobbying and funding of research institutes and public relations firms by the tobacco industry in an effort to maintain the high volume of cigarette sales and to block the development of a widespread definition of smoking as a health and social problem.

2. *Social condition asserted to be a problem.* The simple existence of an undesirable social *condition* does not make it a social *problem*. To gain recognition as a problem, one or more influential groups must assert it is a problem so that the general public becomes aware of its existence.

The problem of women being physically abused by their mates is an old one, but it received sufficient recognition (partly as a result of concerns expressed by the feminist movement) only in the past thirty-five years, so that services such as shelters for battered women have now been developed (see Box 1.2). We have been polluting our air and water for centuries, but it was only in the past forty years that influential environmental groups formed and convinced many Americans that air and water pollution are serious concerns. (Environmental groups have been aided in their efforts by the increased visibility of pollution as population density increased and by increased awareness of the negative effects of pollution due to publicity about recent scientific studies on pollution.)

3. *Affecting a large number of people.* Social problems affect many people. If undesirable conditions are not widespread, they are unlikely to be defined as social problems. If they affect only isolated individuals, they may be personal problems but not social problems (see Box 1.3). Social problems are social because they are so widespread that they affect society itself. *Widespread* should not be confused with *severe*. A personal problem, such as a baby dying from crib death, can have a much more severe effect on the individuals involved than can broader social problems. However, as severe as such a personal problem may be, it is not always transformed into a social problem.

When do personal problems become social problems? There is no clear-cut answer to the question. Crack, for example, was first widely used in our society a decade or two ago. Only in the past several years, however, has our society recognized that a large number of individuals currently abuse the drug, with tragic consequences to themselves and their families. With this increased recognition, crack abuse is now identified as a social problem.

4. *Remedied by collective action.* Some undesirable social conditions exist that we believe, at the present time, we cannot change. For example, we believe we will die sometime in the future. Dread of dying is a concern held by many people; yet it is not considered a social problem because it is recognized that we do not as yet have the technology to stop the aging process to prevent death.

In our history, conditions such as starvation, mental illness, mental retardation, and poverty were at times viewed as an act of God or an unavoidable feature of life. Viewed as such, these conditions were not considered to be social problems because they were thought to be unchangeable. Furthermore, when social *conditions* are viewed as unchangeable, little effort is expended to reduce or alleviate them.

*Collective action* refers to steps taken by people working together. Such steps include strikes, demonstrations, public service advertising, lobbying, and formation of interest groups. Collective action arises when concerned individuals, realizing they cannot solve problems alone, begin to work together for significant impact on social policy to confront a social condition.

Collective action brings about social and cultural changes. In the past forty years, for example, *overt* racial discrimination appears to have decreased only by collective action. A number of people of all backgrounds joined to publicize and protest discrimination in employment, education, public accommodations (motels, restaurants, and theaters), and so on. Some of these protests have been nonviolent sit-in demonstrations in segregated restaurants, for example. Others have been violent (e.g., the rioting and burning of inner cities in the late 1960s).

## HISTORICAL FOUNDATIONS OF STUDYING SOCIAL PROBLEMS

Origin of the scientific study of social problems is usually traced back to the early 1800s in Europe. During this time, the Industrial Revolution was changing Europe from rural societies to societies that were becoming increasingly urbanized and industrialized. The lifestyles of many people were undergoing drastic changes.

◆ Box 1.2 ◆◆◆◆◆◆◆◆◆◆◆◆◆◆◆◆◆◆◆◆◆◆◆◆◆

# The Creation of the Wife-Beating Problem

Wives have been assaulted by their husbands since the beginning of time. In many societies, physical beatings were perhaps the most important factor in keeping wives in virtual slavery to their husbands. Most Americans would agree today that wife beating is deplorable, but such a view has not always been held. Wife beating was given extensive coverage in the media and received the attention of politicians in the 1970s (not because it had become more frequent or more severe, but because a social movement arose to help battered women).

The battered women movement developed out of existing organizations of feminists and professionals in the fields of social work, law, and mental health. Local chapters of NOW (National Organization for Women) and other grass-roots groups were important in mobilizing support of the movement. After 1976, the media joined in with extensive coverage of the plight of battered women, and government officials responded to this publicity by making statements in support of the movement and by making funds available to battered women's programs. Social service agencies scrambled to make use of available funds for services to battered women. New agencies, such as battered women's shelters, arose and competed for these funds. To date, the movement has succeeded in enhancing the visibility of family violence and has been responsible for the passage of laws and the creation of new organizations to help battered women. The movement has also succeeded in redefining wife beating as a social problem, not just an individual or family problem.

The death of Nicole Brown Simpson in 1994 further heightened the nation's concern about the plight of battered women. Nicole had been abused on several occasions by her husband—O. J. Simpson. Even after she divorced him, the abuse continued. Shortly after her death, O. J. Simpson was charged with her murder and that of Ronald Goldman, an acquaintance of Nicole. The subsequent murder trial was the most publicized in American history and has continued to draw attention to the plight of battered women.

In 1995 a jury in a criminal trial proceeding found O. J. innocent of these two murders. In 1996, a jury in a civil court proceeding found O. J. guilty of committing these two murders, and O. J. was ordered to pay over $30 million in damages to the families of Nicole Brown Simpson and Ronald Goldman.

Box 1.3 ◆◆◆◆◆◆◆◆◆◆◆◆◆◆◆◆◆◆◆◆◆◆◆◆◆◆◆◆◆◆◆◆◆◆

## Is Surrogate Motherhood a Social Problem?

There is a general consensus that social conditions such as poverty, sexism, racism, crime, overpopulation, mental illness, suicide, violence, and incest are social problems. For many social conditions, however, there is considerable controversy as to whether the condition is a social problem. Divorce is viewed by some as a social problem because it breaks up a family unit and often results in adjustment difficulties for spouses and their children; however, divorce is seen by others as a positive step toward ending an unhappy, unfulfilling relationship and as an opportunity for a more satisfying future. Abortion is viewed by some as murder, the taking of human life, whereas others view it as an essential birth-control technique. Premarital sex is viewed by some as morally wrong and as the major cause of births outside of marriage; others view premarital sex as a natural expression of the sex drive and an acceptable way to learn about and express human sexuality.

A social phenomenon that has received extensive publicity is surrogate motherhood. Thousands of married couples unable to reproduce when the wife is infertile have turned to surrogate motherhood. A surrogate, that is, "stand-in," mother gives birth to a baby conceived by artificial insemination, using the sperm of the husband. (Often the surrogate mother is paid a fee for her services.) Upon birth of the baby, the surrogate mother terminates her parental rights, and the child is then legally adopted by the donor of the sperm and his wife.

Couples using the services of a surrogate mother are generally delighted with this medical technique and believe it is a highly desirable solution to their personal difficulty of being unable to bear children. In no way do they view the medical technique as a social problem. However, other groups assert that surrogate motherhood raises a number of moral, legal, and personal issues that justify recognizing the practice as a social problem.

A number of theologians and religious leaders firmly believe God intended conception to occur only among married couples through sexual intercourse. These religious leaders view surrogate motherhood as ethically wrong, because the surrogate mother is not married to the donor of the sperm and because artificial insemination is viewed as "unnatural." Some religious leaders also assert that it is morally despicable for a surrogate mother to accept a fee (often from $5,000 to $10,000). They maintain that procreation is a divine blessing and should not be commercialized.

Surrogate motherhood also raises complicated legal questions of considerable social consequence. For example, surrogate mothers usually sign a nonbinding contract stipulating that the mother will give up the child for adoption at birth. What if the surrogate mother changes her mind shortly before birth and decides to keep the baby? Legally, she may have the right to keep the baby and perhaps even sue the donor of the sperm for child support.[a] In the 1980s and 1990s, there have been some widely publicized court cases in which surrogate mothers sought to keep their babies *after* giving birth. Such court decisions have been inconsistent and have not legally clarified who has parental rights.

Is surrogate motherhood a social problem? Influential groups (such as religious organizations) have asserted that surrogate motherhood is a problem and may be remedied by collective action, but surrogate motherhood does not affect a large number of people at this time. If it becomes as common as abortion, that will be a different story. At the moment, however, we cannot consider surrogate motherhood to be a social problem because it infrequently occurs in American society.

a. Stephen Budiansky, "The New Rules of Reproduction," *U.S. News & World Report* (Apr. 18, 1988): 66–69.

---

For many, urbanization and industrialization brought technological advances and raised the standard of living. It also brought many disruptions. People moved to large communities and became isolated from family and friends. Changes in technology and values destroyed traditional beliefs and customs. Those with emotional or financial needs often had no one to turn to. Urbanization and industrialization brought about dramatic increases in a variety of social problems, including property crime, violence, unemployment, drug and alcohol abuse, and suicide.

During this time period, many European countries were also undergoing dramatic political changes. These changes were intensified by recurrent episodes of social unrest—arson, rioting, and social protests. The French Revolution also contributed to social disruption and shifted political and economic power to new groups.

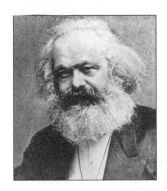

*Early sociologists: Auguste Comte (1798–1857), French; Émile Durkheim (1858–1917), French; Karl Marx (1818–1883), German; Lester Frank Ward (1841–1913), American.*

The extensive turmoil during this period was an important factor in encouraging some scholars to study social instability (and stability) and to develop sociological approaches to studying social problems. Four prominent sociologists of the era were Auguste Comte, Émile Durkheim, Karl Marx, and Lester Frank Ward.

*Auguste Comte* (1798–1857), a Frenchman, has often been called the father of sociology. While a young man, he began developing a science of society, which he labeled *sociology,* to provide insight into France's problems. He believed the most serious social problems in France were the violence and conflict associated with social change and the decline of central social institutions (such as the church and the family).[5] Comte believed that sociologists could resolve social problems through educating people about their causes. He was particularly interested in changing social conditions he felt threatened the stability of French society.

*Émile Durkheim* (1858–1917) used statistical procedures in analyzing social problems. He conducted what is now a classic study of the causes of suicide. Like Comte, Durkheim, also French, was concerned about social conditions that contributed to social instability. He demonstrated that suicide is often a severe consequence of the lack of group involvement (see Box 1.4).

*Karl Marx* (1818–1883) was a German social thinker who approached the social problems of his time from a perspective different from that of Comte and Durkheim, who valued social stability and social order. They sought to change social factors (such as lack of group involvement) that disrupted social stability. In contrast, Marx thought radical societal and political changes were necessary to eliminate social problems. He concluded the social stability advocated by Comte and Durkheim was partially based on the perpetuation of poverty and the exploitation of the working class by the dominant class, composed mainly of land and factory owners. Marx was particularly concerned about inequality and the suffering and degradation that the working class faced (see Box 1.5).

The end of the 1800s saw the beginnings of sociological study in the United States, where dramatic social changes were also brought about by the Industrial Revolution. A number of social problems arose that were similar in nature to problems that Europe was facing—social unrest; increases in crime, suicide and unemployment; and a breakdown in the traditional ways of helping people in need (through the church, family, and neighbors). These social problems stimulated a number of scholars to turn to sociology as a new scientific discipline to study and confront existing social problems.

*Lester Frank Ward* (1841–1913), like Marx, was concerned with inequality and poverty. Unlike Marx, however, Ward did not believe that a workers' revolution and a reorganization of society was the way to resolve such problems.[6] Instead he believed they could be more readily and effectively alleviated through improved occupational and educational opportunities for all people. He advocated that social programs (such as free public education and strong child-labor laws) be developed to achieve these ends. Ward thought that sociologists could solve social problems in the same way that physical scientists attempted to counter undesirable physical conditions such as disease—through first

# An Early Illustration of the Sociological Approach

One of the basic assumptions of the sociological approach is that the personal circumstances of even isolated individuals are always related to the overall social context in which they live. Émile Durkheim—one of the founding fathers of modern sociology—illustrated this principle in his classic study of suicide.[a]

Suicide appears to be an individualistic act, as each victim individually decides to take his or her life. Prior to Durkheim's investigation, theorists were concerned only with the immediate psychological factors associated with taking one's life. They sought to identify the stresses faced by the victim and theorized how such stresses contributed to the decision to stop living. Durkheim thought such individualistic explanations were incomplete and misleading. He sought to identify variables in the social context to help explain suicide.

He compiled statistics on suicide rates, which he found varied significantly among different geographic areas and different population groups. He found that people living alone were more likely to commit suicide than those living in families, that the suicide rate was higher in urban areas than in rural areas, and that deeply religious people were less likely to commit suicide than those who were nonreligious. The common factor he advanced to explain these differences was the degree to which individuals were integrated into social bonds. He theorized that people with strong links to their communities are less apt to take their lives, as the participation serves as a constraint against committing suicide because of its adverse impact on the group. Durkheim coined the term *egoistic suicide* to refer to suicide victims with weak links to their communities.

Durkheim also studied suicide in traditional societies and found rates to be higher in societies that under certain circumstances expected it. In ancient

Rome, for example, people who were disgraced were expected to take their lives; if they did so, they were viewed as having regained their honor. Durkheim thus concluded that people having strong links with a community that expected them in certain circumstances to take their lives would also have high suicide rates. This second type of suicide occurs when persons place group goals and ideals ahead of their own lives. Durkheim called this type *altruistic suicide*, as victims sacrifice their lives for the group. Altruistic suicide helps us understand the Japanese kamikaze pilots in World War II, who made suicidal crashes into American ships; their ties to their families and to their country led them to give up their lives to help their country.

The mass suicides in 1978 in Jonestown, Guyana, in the religious cult headed by Jim Jones can also be better understood by the notion that people with strong ties to their community will commit the ultimate act of suicide. The members of the People's Temple felt so strongly tied to the group that over a thousand took their lives through drinking poison at the urging of Jones. Jones stated it was essential that cult members drink the poison to escape destruction of the cult by outsiders and to be reunited soon in heaven.

The third type of suicide described by Durkheim, *anomic suicide*, differs from both egoistic and altruistic suicide in that the norms of society have broken down—or at least are no longer meaningful to individuals. Although people normally think of the causes of suicide as being located in the victim's personality or immediate environment, anomic suicide demonstrates the way in which disorganization or rapid change in society as a whole can have a significant impact on the behavior of individuals. When people feel that society is breaking down all around them and that the boundary between right and wrong is no longer clear, they may become so despondent that they commit suicide.

a. Émile Durkheim, *Suicide: A Study in Sociology,* John Spaulding and George Simpson, trans. (New York: The Free Press, 1951).

scientifically studying and understanding the problems and then developing and trying out rehabilitative approaches.

Since 1900, there has been an enormous expansion in the development of sociological theories to explain the nature of social problems. A vast number of research studies are conducted to test these theories and to identify the major determinants of social problems. Many of these theories and research studies will be described in this text.

## ROLE OF SOCIOLOGY AND SOCIAL SCIENCE IN RESOLVING SOCIAL PROBLEMS

Sociology has a variety of theoretical approaches for studying and conceptualizing social problems. As will be seen in this text, these different approaches often lead to conflicting views of the causes of social problems and ways to try to resolve them. For example, a few sociological theorists and many politicians advocate that criminals should be severely punished to

Box 1.5 ◆◆◆◆◆◆◆◆◆◆◆◆◆◆◆◆◆◆◆◆◆◆◆

# Karl Marx's Theories of Class Conflict and Communism

**K**arl Marx declared, "This history of all hitherto existing societies is the history of class conflict."[a] Marx assumed that the position a person holds in producing goods and services determines that person's class position. Capitalistic societies, Marx asserted, basically have two classes: the *bourgeoisie*—owners of capital and capital-producing property (e.g., landlords, merchants, and factory owners) and the *proletariat*—those who sell their labor to live (e.g., farm workers, factory workers, laborers of all kinds). The latter, he felt, comprised the larger class.

Marx theorized that these two classes have directly opposing economic interests, as he assumed that the bourgeoisie continually seek to increase their wealth by exploiting the proletariat. Marx believed the basic factor causing the social problems experienced by the working class to be capitalism, an economic system characterized by (a) private ownership of capital goods; (b) investments determined by private decision rather than by state control; and (c) production prices and distribution of goods determined mainly by competition in a free market.

Marx predicted that the workers would become increasingly aware of this exploitation, band together, become involved in a violent conflict with the bourgeoisie, and eventually win this class war and then establish a classless society. Such a society would provide free education and training for all, abolish inheritance and the ownership of private property, and set up a system of producing goods and services for use rather than for profit. He thought that once the basic problem of unequal distribution of power and wealth had been solved and a classless society was created, other social problems (such as crime and poverty) would disappear.

Marx advocated that, after the workers' revolution occurred, a transitional system of socialism should be set up that would be a step toward the ultimate goal of communism. (Socialism is an economic system in which the means of production are owned and controlled by the state, but the distribution of goods and pay is unequal, according to work done.) Communism, according to Marx, would be a classless society, which would have as its basic theme "from each according to his ability, to each according to his need." With this theme, Marx envisioned a society in which people would contribute according to their capacities and abilities and would receive funds and services designed to meet their unique needs.

Marxian theories, of course, have had a major impact on a number of countries that have sought to construct their societies according to the guidelines he outlined. (One should note that most countries—such as Russia and Cuba—that have called themselves communist would be classified by Marx as transitional socialist societies.)

Most countries that were formerly socialistic (such as Russia and Romania) are now moving toward adding capitalistic incentives to their economies and moving away from socialist governing principles toward democratic governing principles. Democracy and capitalism appear to be in ascendance, whereas communism appears to be waning.

---

a. Karl Marx, *Selected Writings in Sociology and Social Philosophy*, T. B. Bottomore, trans. (London: McGraw-Hill, 1964).

---

serve as a warning to deter others from committing crimes. In direct opposition, most sociological theorists working in criminology assert that punishment tends to generate more hostility in prison inmates and thereby leads them to commit additional crimes when they return to society. These theorists therefore recommend a rehabilitative approach to change criminal attitudes and to teach useful vocational trades. Whether crime can best be reduced by increasing punitive measures or by increasing rehabilitative efforts remains a hotly debated issue (see Chapter 2).

Although such conflicting views may be confusing to the general public, they highlight the importance of doing sociological research to test the relative merits of opposing theories. For example, through further study of the consequences of using the punitive approach as compared to the rehabilitative approach, it can be scientifically determined which is more effective in curbing crime.

Sociology offers a variety of suggestions (many untested or only partially tested) about how to reduce the extensiveness and severity of social problems. If proven solutions were available and fully implemented, the scope of current social problems would be greatly reduced. Instead of proven solutions, what we have is a number of unproven suggestions, some of which are conflicting. The conflicting suggestions are usually based on different assumptions about the underlying causes.

Sociology is not the only social scientific discipline that studies social problems. Other disciplines include psychology, psychiatry, geography, political science, social work, cultural anthropology, economics, social biology, and urban planning. Each of these disciplines has made important contributions to increasing our knowledge of the nature of certain social problems and in advancing proposals for alleviating such problems. Psychology and psychiatry, for example, have studied emotional problems and have generated a wide variety of treatment techniques and approaches for those suffering from emotional disturbances.

The role of sociology and other social sciences is to study social problems and to advance social policy recommendations designed to resolve or to reduce the scope of these problems. Once such recommendations are made, it is *not* the role of the social sciences to decide which recommendations to implement. Such decisions are generally made by political bodies (such as federal, state, and local governments). If recommendations are approved and implemented, the social sciences then have the additional role of evaluating the effects of the new programs—assessing their merits and shortcomings.

As current problems are gradually resolved or redefined so they are no longer regarded as social problems, history suggests that new problems will emerge. In the last century, the following problems decreased in severity: racial segregation in public schools, children forced to work long hours, unsanitary working conditions in industry, and barriers that prevent many women and nonwhites from voting in political elections. New problems, however, have gained recognition: ageism, discrimination against persons with a disability, overpopulation, drug abuse, AIDS, and environmental destruction. Most of these conditions have always been with us but gained national recognition as social problems only in the past four decades.

## Social Movements and Social Problems

For a social problem to become recognized, it is essential that a large or influential group publicize the social condition. Groups publicizing a social condition are characterized as social movements. A *social movement* is a large group of people who have joined together to preserve or change a social condition.

Social movements play key roles in identifying social problems, conceptualizing their nature, publicizing the issues, and campaigning for their solutions.

In our society, it is often true that "the squeaky wheel gets the grease." Saul Alinsky, a nationally recognized organizer of social movements, asserted that the only way to force the existing power structure to make social changes is for those suffering from the social condition to unite into a power bloc, to find the weak point in the power structure, and then to use power confrontation tactics to force the power structure to make changes in the desired direction.[7]

Social movements sometimes arise when a number of people are unhappy about a social condition and then band together to attempt to change the condition. The majority of social movements are unsuccessful, partly because they are unable to attract a sufficient number of concerned citizens. Other social movements, however, organize and present their concerns in such a way that they attract many new members. When that occurs, they gain the attention of the news media and the general public. If they are able to persuade a substantial part of the population that changes need to be made, social change is apt to occur.

Spector and Kitsuse (1973) developed a four-stage model through which social movements pass.[8] (Unsuccessful social movements generally fail to progress beyond the first stage.) These stages are agitation, legitimation and co-option, bureaucratization and reaction, and re-emergence of the movement.

## AGITATION

Movements seek to arouse public interest by transforming what are perceived as private troubles into public issues. Failure often occurs at this stage, often for one or more of the following reasons:

♦ claims asserted by the movement may be shown to be heavily biased or erroneous;

♦ the movement may fail to attract sufficient numbers of people or people of influence;

♦ tactics to publicize movement concerns may offend the public;

♦ a more powerful opposition movement may capture the public's support and thus overwhelm the movement; or

♦ powerful business or government entities may undermine the movement to maintain the status quo that serves their interests.

## LEGITIMATION AND CO-OPTION

This stage is reached by winning public support. The legitimacy of the movement's concerns is recognized, and the movement attains "respectability." At the first stage, the leaders are often viewed as agitators—cranks and troublemakers; now they are viewed as responsible reformers. At this point the government becomes aware of the public support and begins to incorporate the movement's recommendations and to co-opt movement leaders into its own policies and programs. Movement leaders may be offered attractive jobs by the government, and government officials gradually may take control of handling movement concerns. How the government handles these concerns often determines whether or not the movement's goals and objectives will be met (see Box 1.6). The government may take direct action and allocate resources to develop programs intended (or at least publicized) as an official attempt to resolve the problem. The government may also attempt to stonewall the issue—by bogging down potential action through referring the movement's proposals to study committees, appointing commissions without adequate resources, holding "do-nothing" conferences to discuss the issues, giving vocal support while claiming resources are presently unavailable, and instituting a small trial project that is poorly funded.

## BUREAUCRATIZATION AND REACTION

As time passes, government departments focus more and more on routine administrative problems rather than on exploring new and innovative programs to accomplish the goals they were originally intended to achieve. (State correctional agencies, for example, now primarily focus on the processing and mechanical aspects of supervising inmates, probationees, and parolees, with very little time spent on developing more effective ways to rehabilitate convicted offenders.) Spector and Kitsuse (1973) note that some organizations reach the point where they spend more time in responding to complaints about their failure to resolve problems than in trying to solve problems directly.

## RE-EMERGENCE OF THE MOVEMENT

At this final stage, the original movement may re-emerge (re-group), or other concerned individuals may seek to form a new movement. Thus, as awareness of the condition as a social problem is rekindled, the movement is apt to be unsatisfied by existing

---

◆ BOX 1.6 ◆◆◆◆◆◆◆◆◆◆◆◆◆◆◆◆◆◆◆◆◆◆

# Participating in a Social Movement Is Often Enjoyable

Saul Alinsky, one of the nation's most noted organizers, was working in the 1960s in the inner city of Chicago with a citizens' group known as the Woodlawn Organization. City authorities had made commitments to this organization to improve several conditions in the neighborhood. However, it became clear that the commitments were not being met by the city. The question arose as to how to find a tactic to pressure the city into making good its promises. An ingenious strategy was selected to pressure city officials by threatening to embarrass the city by tying up all the lavatories at O'Hare International Airport—one of the world's busiest airports. Alinsky describes this effort as follows:

> An intelligence study was launched to learn how many sit-down toilets for both men and women, as well as stand-up urinals, there were in the entire O'Hare airport complex and how many men and women would be necessary for the nation's first "shit-in."
>
> The consequences of this kind of action would be catastrophic in many ways. People would be desperate for a place to relieve themselves. One can see children yelling at their parents, "Mommy, I've got to go," and desperate mothers surrendering, "All right—well, do it. Do it right here." O'Hare would soon become a shambles. The whole scene would become unbelievable, and the laughter and ridicule would be nationwide. It would probably get a front page story in the London *Times*. It would be a source of great mortification and embarrassment to the city administration. It might even create the kind of emergency in which planes would have to be held up while passengers got back aboard to use the toilet facilities.
>
> The threat of this tactic was leaked (again, there may be a Freudian slip here and, again, so what?) back to the administration, and within forty-eight hours the Woodlawn Organization found itself in conference with the authorities who said they were certainly going to live up to their commitments and they could never understand where anyone got the idea that a promise made by Chicago's City Hall would not be observed.[a]

a. Saul Alinsky, *Rules for Radicals* (New York: Vintage Books, 1972), 143–44.

government efforts to resolve the problem. Even though some productive changes may have occurred as a result of efforts of the original movement, the problem is viewed as only partially resolved. The life cycle of the social movement then begins again.

## Consequences of Actions Taken on Social Problems

Often the consequences of actions taken are unexpected, sometimes even ironic or paradoxical. It is generally believed that actions are taken to resolve problems, but at times action is taken simply to reduce the cry for action with no hope of resolving the problem. Consequences of actions taken include resolution of the problem, partial resolution of the problem, confinement of the problem, intensification of the problem, creation of new problems, a shift in focus of the problem, maintenance of the organization formed to resolve the problem, and deflection of public concern.

### RESOLUTION OF THE PROBLEM

Actions may fully resolve the problem. For example, at the turn of the last century, pollution from horse dung was defined as a major problem in urban areas. It was anticipated that as cities grew the problem would intensify. But the invention and widespread use of the automobile fully resolved this problem.

In another example, for several decades prior to the 1950s, polio (poliomyelitis) and its transmission was considered a major health and social problem in the United States. The development of the Salk vaccine by Dr. Jonas Salk in 1953 and its widespread use have practically eliminated this peril.[9]

In the social sciences, however, it is very rare that a specific action fully resolves the problem.

### PARTIAL RESOLUTION OF THE PROBLEM

Most often, legitimate efforts to resolve social problems only partially reduce their extent or severity. Public assistance programs initiated in 1935 and the War on Poverty programs enacted in the 1960s have not eradicated poverty but have reduced somewhat the proportion of our population who are poor and have also provided some financial resources to those who remain in poverty.[10] Programs such as probation and parole

have rehabilitated some offenders, but certainly not all. Psychotherapy has helped some of the emotionally disturbed population, but again, not all. Although shelter homes for battered women help some abused women, spouse abuse remains a serious problem.

### CONFINEMENT OF THE PROBLEM

Some actions are designed simply to confine rather than resolve the problem. Boston, for example, restricted nude dancing and adult bookstores to one geographic area of the city. Although they do not necessarily admit it, a fair number of prison officials have, in practice, given up trying to rehabilitate some hardcore offenders with long histories of criminal offenses. Such prison officials are content merely with keeping them locked up so they cannot commit more crimes. Finally, a few counties in Nevada have legalized prostitution so as to license and monitor brothels.

### INTENSIFICATION OF THE PROBLEM

Some actions have the (unexpected) effect of intensifying the problem. Medical practitioners are especially familiar with this phenomenon. For instance, a physician may seek to cure a sore throat by removing the tonsils, yet, in rare cases the surgery may result in severe throat infection and even death. In the past, lobotomies (surgical incisions into the front part of the brain) were performed on some emotionally disturbed patients in mental hospitals; the operation not only did not help patients recover, it also left them permanently retarded. Long-term stays in mental hospitals often intensify emotional disturbances rather than ease them. Some people with emotional problems who receive professional counseling get worse than people who receive no treatment at all.[11]

Prisons sometimes serve as "schools" for criminals by inadvertently providing opportunity for additional training (from other inmates) in techniques of crime and how to avoid being apprehended, instead of having rehabilitative value. Police decoys and "sting" operations may actually influence some people to commit crimes who would not otherwise have done so. Some of the frail elderly in nursing homes deteriorate instead of improving as a result of being institutionalized.

### CREATION OF NEW PROBLEMS

All too frequently, actions designed to resolve a social problem end up creating new ones. If enough individuals find the new conditions to be problematic, they may create a new social movement to define these conditions as a social problem and to press for new actions to reduce or resolve the problem.

Many states have extended the number of weeks (often up to a year) that unemployed workers are eligible for unemployment compensation. Some critics claim this action has reduced the incentive to work, as some recipients seek to draw as many unemployment checks as they can rather than actively look for work.[12]

No-fault divorce laws have reduced the stigma connected with obtaining a divorce and also made a divorce easier to obtain. No-fault divorces may be a factor contributing to the high divorce rate, which is viewed as a problem by at least some segments of the population.

Developing effective and readily available birth control devices (such as the pill) has reduced the risk of an unwanted pregnancy, but it may also be a factor leading to increased premarital and extramarital sexual relationships, viewed as a problem by some groups.

All of these examples demonstrate that social problems are interconnected and interrelated. For example, poverty is affected by, and also affects, other problems such as alcoholism, mental illness, crime, urban problems, racism, sexism, and family troubles.

## SHIFTING THE FOCUS OF THE PROBLEM

When the civil rights movement escalated in the 1960s, the primary focus of the movement was to lobby for the federal and state governments to enact laws prohibiting racial discrimination in employment practices, housing, use of public accommodations, and educational opportunities. Such legislation was passed, and the focus of the movement then shifted to other areas: enforcing the new legislation, presenting public education programs to sensitize the general public to racial issues, developing work training programs and finding jobs for the unemployed, and establishing programs to heighten educational and business opportunities for people of color.

## MAINTAINING THE ORGANIZATION

Once an organization is created to take action against a problem, its primary objective usually becomes its own survival. This objective almost always takes precedence over efforts to alleviate the problem because staff naturally are interested in keeping their jobs. If the work becomes noticeably slack and their jobs are threatened,

staff are apt to spend more time defending and justifying their positions than serving clients.

Some organizations do successfully eliminate the problem for which they were originally formed. When this occurs, the survival objective is so strong that they will seek another problem to attack in order to perpetuate their existence. After the March of Dimes helped to eliminate polio through raising money for research that led to the discovery of the Salk vaccine, it switched its goal to taking action against diseases in general that cause disabilities in young children.

The need for maternity homes for young single women has nearly dissipated, as it has become more acceptable for such women to remain in their own homes. Moreover, many pregnancies are terminated by abortion. Numerous maternity homes, rather than closing their doors, have re-grouped and now serve as residential treatment facilities for emotionally disturbed youths or as group homes for adolescents unable to live with their parents.

Organizational maintenance as a response to social problems is found not only in formal agencies, but also in self-help groups and other volunteer organizations. Because there is no economic motive involved in the maintenance of these organizations, why do they often resist their dissolution so actively? When people work together to solve a problem, they develop a network of social relations with co-workers, people in other agencies, and others in their communities. They also incorporate this work into their self-images whether they are paid or not. These social relations and self-images are important to volunteers and members of self-help groups, so it is not surprising that they try to maintain them.

## DEFLECTION OF PUBLIC CONCERN

One common reaction to a social movement that proclaims a condition to be a social problem is for government leaders, business executives, and other influential individuals to act to deflect public concern instead of trying to resolve or diminish the extent and severity of the problem. All social problems benefit some people at the expense of others. For example, a large corrections industry benefits extensively from crime and delinquency.

Public concern can be deflected in many ways, some of which have been mentioned earlier in this chapter. The most direct strategy is for influential public figures to announce that the problem has been solved. When former President Reagan said there were no segregated schools left in America, he was using this strategy. It was unsuccessful in that case, however, because opponents of school segregation were quick to bring evidence to the public's attention showing that many private schools remained just as segregated as public schools were in the 1940s.

Another way of deflecting public concern is to create a committee or a commission with many influential people on it. One can then say that the group cannot be rushed, because the problem is such an important one. There must first be extensive research to uncover its causes, nature, and effects. By the time an official report is issued a year or two later, the public may be much less excited about the problem, and the recommendations of the committee or commission may be ignored, rejected, accepted but not implemented, or accepted and only partially implemented with inadequate funding.

## *Perspectives on Social Problems and Social Programs*

The position that politicians take on social issues and social programs are largely determined by whether they are liberal or conservative in orientation. The two prominent political philosophies in the United States are liberalism and conservatism. The Republican Party is considered to be relatively conservative and the Democratic Party is considered to be relatively liberal. This discussion will focus on liberalism and conservatism in their pure forms. In reality, many people espouse a mixture of both views. For example, there are some Democrats who are primarily conservative in ideology and some Republicans who are primarily liberal in ideology.

### CONSERVATIVE PERSPECTIVE

Conservatives (derived from the verb *to conserve*) tend to resist change. They emphasize tradition and believe rapid change usually results in more negative than positive consequences. In economic matters, conservatives feel that government should not interfere with the workings of the marketplace. They encourage the government to support (e.g., through tax incentives) rather than regulate business and industry in society. A free-market economy is thought to be the best way to ensure prosperity and fulfillment of individual

needs. Conservatives embrace the old adage that "that government governs best which governs least." They believe that most government activities constitute grave threats to individual liberty and to the smooth functioning of the free market.

Conservatives generally view individuals as being autonomous, that is, as being self-governing. Regardless of what a person's situation is, or what problems he or she has, each person is thought to be presently responsible for his or her own behavior. People are thought to choose whatever they are doing, and therefore, they are viewed as being responsible for whatever gains or losses result from their choices. People are thought to possess free will, and thus can choose to engage in behaviors such as hard work that help them get ahead, or activities such as excessive leisure that contribute to failing (or being poor). Poverty and other personal problems that people have are seen as being the result of laziness, irresponsibility, or lack of self-control. Conservatives believe that what social welfare programs do is to force the hardworking, productive citizens to pay for the consequences of irresponsible behavior of recipients of social welfare services.

Conservatives generally advocate a residual approach to social welfare programs.[13] The residual view holds that social welfare services should be provided only when an individual's needs are not properly met through other societal institutions, primarily the family and the market economy. Social services and financial aid should not be provided until all other measures or efforts have failed and the individual's or family's resources are fully used up. In addition, this view asserts that funds and services should be provided on a short-term basis (primarily during emergencies) and should be withdrawn when the individual or the family again becomes capable of being self-sufficient.

The residual view has been characterized as "charity for unfortunates." Funds and services are not seen as a right (something that one is entitled to) but as a gift, and the receiver has certain obligations; for example, in order to receive financial aid, recipients may be required to perform certain low-grade work assignments. Associated with the residual view is the belief that the causes of social welfare clients' difficulties are rooted in their own malfunctioning—that is, clients are to blame for their predicaments because of personal inadequacies or ill-advised activities or sins. Under the residual view there is usually a stigma attached to receiving services or funds.

Conservatives believe that dependency is a result of personal failure, and they also believe it is natural for inequality to exist among humans. They assert that the family, religious organizations, and gainful employment should be the primary defense against dependency. Social welfare, they believe, should be only a temporary function that is used sparingly. Prolonged social welfare assistance, they believe, will lead recipients to become permanently dependent. Conservatives believe charity is a moral virtue and that the "fortunate" are obligated to help the "less fortunate" become productive, contributing citizens in a society. If governmental funds are provided for health and social welfare services, conservatives advocate that such funding should go to private organizations, which are thought to be more effective and efficient than public agencies in providing services. Conservatives tend to believe that the federal government is not a solution to social problems but is part of the problem. They assert that federally funded social welfare programs tend to make recipients dependent on the government rather than assisting recipients to become self-sufficient and productive.

Conservatives revere the "traditional" nuclear family and try to devise policies to preserve it. They see the family as a source of strength for individuals, and as the primary unit of society. They oppose: abortion, sex education in schools, rights for homosexuals, public funding of day-care centers, birth control counseling for minors, and other measures that might undermine parental authority or support alternative family forms such as single parenthood.

## LIBERAL PERSPECTIVE

In contrast, liberals believe change is generally good as it usually brings progress; moderate change is best. They view society as needing regulation to ensure fair competition between various interests. In particular, the market economy is viewed as needing regulation to ensure fairness. Government programs, including social welfare programs, are viewed as necessary to help meet basic human needs. Liberals advocate government action to remedy social deficiencies and to improve human welfare. Liberals feel government regulation and intervention is often necessary to safeguard human rights, to control the excesses of capitalism, and to provide equal chances for success. They emphasize egalitarianism and the rights of minorities.

Liberals generally adhere to an institutional view of social welfare. This view holds that social welfare programs are "accepted as a proper legitimate function of modern industrial society in helping individuals achieve self-fulfillment."[14] Under this view, there is no stigma attached to receiving funds or services; recipients are viewed as entitled to such help. Associated with this view is the belief that an individual's difficulties are due to causes largely beyond his or her control (e.g., a person may be unemployed because of a lack of employment opportunities). With this view, when difficulties arise causes are sought in the environment (society) and efforts are focused on improving the social institutions within which the individual functions.

Liberals assert that because society has become so fragmented and complex and because traditional institutions (such as the family) have been unable to meet human needs, few individuals can now function without the help of social services (including such services as work training, job location services, child care, health care, and counseling). Liberals believe that the personal problems encountered by someone are generally due to causes beyond that person's control. Causes are generally sought in that person's environment. For example, a child with a learning disability is thought to only be at risk if that child is not receiving appropriate educational services to accommodate his or her disability. In such a situation, liberals would seek to develop educational services to meet his or her learning needs.

Liberals view the family as an evolving institution, and therefore are willing to support programs that assist emerging family forms—such as single parent families and same sex marriages.

## DEVELOPMENTAL PERSPECTIVE

Liberals for years have criticized the residual approach to social welfare as being incongruent with society's obligation to provide long-term assistance to those who have long-term health, welfare, social, and recreational needs. Conservatives, on the other hand, have been highly critical of the institutional approach as they claim it creates a welfare state, with many recipients then deciding to become dependent on the government to meet their health, welfare, social, and recreational needs—without seeking to work and without contributing in other ways to the well-being of society. Clearly, conservatives will stop the creation of any major new social program that moves our country in the direction of being a welfare society. They have the political power (i.e., the necessary legislative votes) to stop the enactment of programs that are "marketed" to society as being consistent with the institutional approach.

Is there a view of social welfare that can garner the support of both liberals and conservatives? Midgley (1995) contends the developmental view (or perspective) offers an alternative approach that appears to have appeal to liberals, conservatives, and the general public.[15] Midgley defines this approach as a "process of planned social change designed to promote the well-being of the population as a whole in conjunction with a dynamic process of economic development."[16]

This perspective has an appeal to liberals because it supports the development and expansion of needed social welfare programs. The perspective has an appeal to conservatives because it asserts that the development of certain social welfare programs will have a positive impact on the economy (conservative politicians have in the past opposed the development of many social welfare programs as they claimed such programs would have a negative impact on economic development). The general public also would be apt to support the developmental perspective. Many voters oppose welfarism, as they believe it causes economic problems (e.g., recipients choosing to be on the government dole, rather than contributing to society through working). Asserting and documenting that certain proposed social welfare programs will directly benefit the economy is attractive to voters.

Midgley and Livermore (1997) note that the developmental approach, is, at this point in time, not well defined.[17] The developmental approach has its roots in the promotion of the growth of social programs in developing (Third World) countries. Advocates for social welfare programs in developing countries have been successful in getting certain social welfare programs enacted by asserting, and documenting, that such programs will have a beneficial impact on the overall economy of the country. Midgley and Livermore (1997) note, "[t]he developmental perspective's global relevance began in the Third World in the years of decolonization after World War II."[18] The developmental approach was later used by the United Nations in its efforts in developing countries to promote the growth of social programs, as the United Nations asserted such programs had the promise of improving the overall economies of these Third World countries.

What are the characteristics of the developmental approach? It advocates social interventions that contribute positively to economic development, thereby promoting harmony between economic and social institutions. The approach regards economic progress as a vital component of social progress. The approach promotes the active role of the government in economic and social planning, which is in direct opposition to the residual approach, which advocates that the government should seek to minimize its role in the provision of social welfare programs. Finally, the developmental approach focuses on integrating economic and social development for the *benefit of all* members of society.

The developmental approach can be used in advocating for the expansion of a wide range of social welfare programs. It can be argued that any social program that assists a person in becoming employable contributes to the economic well-being of a society.

One can also argue that any social program that assists a person in making significant contributions to his or her family, or to his or her community, contributes to the economic well-being of a society—as functional families and communities are good for businesses, members of functional families tend to be better employees, and businesses desire to locate in communities that are prospering and that have low rates of crime and other social problems.

A few examples will be cited to illustrate how the developmental approach can be used to advocate for the expansion of social welfare programs. One can argue that the following programs will be beneficial for the economy as they will assist unemployed single parents in obtaining employment: job training, quality child-care programs for the children of these parents, and adequate health insurance for these parents and their children so that health care is provided to keep them healthy—which will facilitate the parents being able to work. Furthermore, providing mentoring programs and other social services in school systems will help at-risk children to stay in school and eventually to contribute to society—by their obtaining employment and by their contributions to their families and to the communities in which they live—when they become adults. One can argue that rehabilitative programs in the criminal justice system will help correctional clients in becoming contributing members to society. One can also argue that certain programs will assist those with issues in these areas to better handle these issues, and thereby increase the likelihood of their becoming contributors to the economy and to the well-being of society through, for example, alcohol and other drug abuse treatment programs, domestic violence services, mental health counseling, nutritional programs, eating disorder intervention programs, stress management programs, and grief management programs.

## Sociological Perspectives on Social Problems

All sciences consist of two interrelated elements: theory and research. These elements support and generate each other. Theory guides the direction of research as it identifies areas and variables to be investigated and hypotheses to be tested. Research findings also generate new theoretical formulations, as unexpected findings require new theoretical statements to explain the results.

## PERSONAL TROUBLES OR SOCIAL ISSUES?

Alexander Liazos (1972) has charged that courses on social problems often focus on "nuts, sluts, and 'perverts.'"[19] What Liazos meant was that courses often emphasize the personal troubles faced by individuals rather than focus on the social, economic, and structural forces that contribute to personal troubles.

Oscar Lewis (1966), for example, uses a personal troubles approach to explain poverty as being due to the values held by the poor (see Chapter 9).[20] The values he lists are immediate gratification (the tendency to spend money immediately on personal pleasure rather than to save it for a rainy day), low levels of aspiration, despair, apathy, poor work ethic, and lack of planning. Lewis's explanation is an illustration of the *microsociological* approach, which is primarily concerned with explaining the behavior of individuals and of small groups. Numerous microsociological theories will be described in this text.

On the other hand, a social issues explanation of poverty focuses on the exploitation of the poor by the rich, the high unemployment rate, racial and gender discrimination, and the role of government in maintaining the unequal distribution of wealth and income between the rich and the poor. Such explanations are *macrosociological* theories, which are primarily concerned with explaining the behavior of large groups of people and the workings of entire societies.

Advocates of different theories often disagree with one another. Every theory has certain merits and shortcomings. Some theories are more effective in analyzing a particular social problem, whereas others are more effective in analyzing other problems. Therefore, having a knowledge of all contemporary theories is important for those who study social problems in order to select the theory or theories most effective in analyzing key dynamics of the problem under study. Often, the greatest understanding of a social problem occurs when the insights gained from different theoretical perspectives are combined. This text will seek to present the prominent microsociological and macrosociological theories for the social problems that are analyzed.

## PROMINENT MICROSOCIOLOGICAL THEORIES

Microsociological theories are also known as social psychological perspectives since they focus on the social effects of individual behavior and the psychological effects of social groups. Social psychology is concerned with the behavior of individuals and small groups, and their relationships with one another and with the larger society. Three important categories of microsociological theories that are commonly applied to the study of social problems are biosocial theories, personality theories, and behavioral theories.

*Biosocial Theories*    These theories seek to explain social behavior in terms of biological traits of humans. A century ago biosocial theories were adhered to more strongly than at the present time. At that time much of social behavior was thought to be determined by instincts. For example, "capitalism" was thought to stem from an acquisitive instinct, "warfare" from an aggressive instinct, and "cooperation" from a social instinct. Instinctual theories declined in popularity because research evidence of the existence of the postulated instincts could not be found. Furthermore, there was increasing realization that social phenomena (such as warfare) had numerous causative factors other than instincts—such as complex political, religious, and economic forces.

In recent years, there has been a renewal of interest in biosocial theories. Most sociologists do not now believe that human behavior is fully determined by genetics, but most present day biosocial theorists seek to explain human behavior in terms of the interaction between biological predispositions and the social environment. A number of biosocial theories are described in this text. The morphological theory of criminology (described in Chapter 2) asserts that people with a muscular build are more prone to engage in criminal activity than are people who have a lean build or who are overweight. The medical model approach to mental illness (described in Chapter 3) asserts that the causes of schizophrenia and other psychoses arise from the interaction of biological and social factors. The general theory of alcoholism (described in Chapter 4) asserts that genetics predisposes some people to become alcoholic. Homosexuality is theorized in Chapter 5 to be largely determined by genetics. Chapter 7 suggests that sex role differences between males and females are determined by a complex interaction of biological factors and socialization patterns. Chapter 8 indicates that the process of aging is due to a combination of inherited characteristics and life experiences. Chapter 14 presents a theory that humans have an instinct to conquer and control territory, which often leads to interpersonal conflict.

Some biosocial theories have been highly criticized. For example, Chapter 6 indicates that theories which assert that certain races have genetically determined lower levels of intelligence than whites have been categorized by some authorities as "racist."

*Personality Theories*    Personality refers to the traits and characteristics that distinguish one person from another and that account for differences in individual social behavior. There are a variety of personality theories described in this text. Chapter 2 summarizes psychoanalytic theory (psychoanalytic theory theorizes a personality type, a sociopath, who has no moral constraints against engaging in criminal activity and who will do so whenever it is personally advantageous, even though others may be hurt). Psychodynamic problem-solving theory (also described in Chapter 2) asserts that criminal behavior is determined by various ingredients of the personality, including wishes, drives, fears, internal desires, and codes of ethics. Chapter 6 summarizes the theory that people with an authoritarian personality are apt to be highly prejudiced and also apt to discriminate against other races because they are inflexible, rigid, and have a low tolerance for uncertainty.

Chapter 14 suggests that some witnesses of criminal activity may have a fear of getting involved (a personality characteristic) that prevents them from intervening when they see someone being victimized by crime. Chapter 14 also suggests that all of the following traits contribute to adolescent suicide: the feelings of being helpless and hopeless, of being lonely, and of being impulsive.

*Behavioral Theories*    Behaviorism is a social psychological approach that was founded by Ivan Pavlov, J. B. Watson, B. F. Skinner, and others. The approach seeks to explain behavior in terms of observable and measurable responses. A basic tenet of the approach is that maladaptive behavior patterns are learned and can be unlearned. Behavior, according to this approach, depends on the *reinforcements* the individual receives from his or her actions. If an individual is rewarded (one type of reinforcement) for a certain behavior in a certain situation, he or she is likely to repeat the behavior when the situation recurs. On the other hand, if the individual receives punishment for his or her actions, the behavior is less likely to be repeated. Behaviorists have developed an elaborate set of principles about the many kinds of reinforcements that encourage or discourage the learning of specific behaviors.

Chapter 2 describes differential association, a learning theory that asserts people engage in criminal behavior because they are exposed to more associations with people who favor crime than with those who are opposed to it. Chapter 2 also describes the classical school approach to criminology, that is another variation of learning theory, which asserts that a person decides whether or not to engage in criminal activity based on the anticipated balance of pleasure minus pain. Chapter 6 indicates that a major cause of racial prejudice arises through socialization processes; that is, individuals learn to be prejudiced by the values, norms, and beliefs that are espoused by those in their social environment. Chapter 7 notes that gender stereotypes and traditional sex-role expectations are also learned through socialization processes.

Chapter 14 notes that many sociologists believe violence is learned or acquired through socialization processes. Such socialization processes are varied. Aggressive actions are often rewarded by peers. Television and movies often portray being tough and aggressive as leading to respect from others, exciting romances, and material success. Violent habits are also thought to be learned through modeling: children who observe adults displaying physical aggression and getting what they want learn to use aggression to seek to gratify their desires.

A major trend in behaviorism in the past three decades has been toward a recognition of the role of cognition (thinking processes) in human behavior. Cognitive behavioral approaches assert that the feelings and behaviors of individuals are primarily determined by their thought processes. One of the variations of this approach is self-talk theory, which asserts that what people tell themselves determines their feelings and actions. Self-talk theory is elaborated upon in Chapters 2, 3, 10, and 11.

## PROMINENT MACROSOCIOLOGICAL THEORIES

This section describes the three most prominent macrosociological theories: functionalism, conflict theory, and interactionism. Chapter 9 describes how each of these theories analyzes and views poverty.

*The Functionalist Perspective*   In recent years, functionalism has been one of the most influential sociological theories. The theory was originally developed by Émile Durkheim and refined by Robert K. Merton, Talcott Parsons, and many others. The theory views society as a well-organized system in which most members agree on common values and norms.

Institutions, groups, and roles fit together in a unified whole. Members of society do what is necessary to maintain a stable society because they accept its regulations and rules.

Society is viewed as a system composed of interdependent and interrelated parts. Each part makes a contribution to the operation of the system, thus enabling the entire system to function. The various parts are in delicate balance, with a change in one part affecting the other parts.

A simple way to picture this approach is to use the analogy of a human body. A well-functioning person has thousands of parts, each of which has a specific role to play. The heart pumps blood, the lungs draw oxygen into the body and expel carbon dioxide, the stomach digests food for energy, the muscles move body parts to perform a variety of functions, and the brain coordinates the activities of the various components. Each of these parts is interrelated in complex ways to the others and is also dependent on them. Each performs a vital function without which the entire system might collapse, as in the case of heart failure.

Functionalism asserts that the components of a society, similar to the parts of the human body, do not always work the way they are supposed to work. Things get out of whack. When a component of a society interferes with efforts to carry out essential social tasks, that part is said to be *dysfunctional*. Often, changes that are introduced to correct a particular imbalance in society may produce other imbalances, even when things are going well. For example, as noted earlier, availability of effective birth control devices is instrumental in preventing unwanted pregnancies. However, it may also contribute to increased premarital and extramarital sex.

According to the functionalist perspective, all social systems have a tendency toward equilibrium—maintenance of a steady state, or particular balance, in which the parts of the system remain in the same relationship to one another. The approach asserts that systems have a tendency to resist social change, as change is seen as disruptive unless it occurs at a slow pace. Because society is composed of interdependent and interconnected parts, a change in one part of the system will lead to changes in one or more other parts. The introduction of the automobile, for example, led to drastic changes: the decline in horseback travel, the ability to commute long distances to work, vacation travel to distant parts of the country, the opening of many new businesses (service stations, car dealerships, and such), and sharp increases in air pollution and traffic fatalities.

Some of the functions and dysfunctions of a social system are *manifest,* that is, obvious. For example, a manifest function of police departments is to keep crime rates low. Other functions and dysfunctions are *latent,* that is, hidden and unintended. Sociologists have discovered that when police departments label arrestees with such stigmatizing descriptions as "criminals," "outlaws," and "delinquents," a hidden consequence is that those so labeled may actually commit more crimes over the long run than they would have had they never been arrested in the first place. Thus, police departments in trying to curb crime may unintentionally contribute to its increase.

According to functionalists, social problems occur when society or some part of it becomes disorganized. *Social disorganization* occurs when a large organization or an entire society is imperfectly organized to achieve its goals and maintain its stability. When disorganization occurs, the organization loses control over its parts. Functionalists see thousands of potential causes of social disorganization. However, underlying all these causes is rapid social change, which disrupts the balance of society, producing social disorganization. Technological advances (development of telephones, television, robots, computers, and heart transplants) have occurred with unprecedented rapidity. These advances have led basic institutions (such as the family and the educational system) to undergo drastic changes. Technological advances have occurred at such a pace that other parts of the culture have failed to keep pace. This *cultural lag* between technological changes and our adaptation to them is viewed as a major source of social disorganization.

Other examples of social disorganization abound. The development of nuclear weapons has the potential to destroy civilization. Advances in sanitation and medical technology have sharply lengthened life expectancy but have also contributed to a worldwide population explosion. Advances in artificial insemination have led to surrogate motherhood, which our society has not yet decided whether to encourage or discourage. Technological advances in abortion have led to the capacity to terminate pregnancies safely on request but have also led to a national controversy about the desirability of legalized abortions.

Critics of functionalism assert that it is a politically conservative philosophy, as it takes for granted the idea that society as it is (the status quo) should be preserved. As a result, basic social injustices are ignored. Critics also argue that the approach is value laden, because one person's disorganization is another's organization. For example, some people view divorce as functional, as a legal way to terminate a relationship that no longer works. Others view divorce as dysfunctional as it disrupts one of the basic institutions in our society—the family. Functionalism has also been criticized as being a philosophy that works for the benefit of the privileged social classes, while perpetuating the misery of the poor and those victimized by discrimination.

*The Conflict Perspective* Conflict theory views society as being a struggle for power among various social groups. Conflict is asserted to be inevitable and in many cases actually beneficial to society. For example, most Americans would view the struggle of the "freedom fighters" (England saw them as ungrateful insurgents) during the revolutionary war as being highly beneficial to our society.

The conflict perspective rests on an important assumption: there are certain things (such as power, wealth, and prestige) that members of society value highly, and most of these valued resources are in scarce supply. Because of their scarcity, conflict theory asserts that people—either individually or in groups—struggle with one another to attain them. Thus society is viewed as an arena for the struggle over scarce resources.

Struggle and conflict may take many forms: competition, disagreements, court battles, physical violence, and war. If the struggles routinely involved violence, then nearly everyone would be engaged in violent activities, which is apt to result in the extermination of such a society. Norms have emerged that determine what types of conflict are allowable for which groups. For example, participating in a labor strike or acquiring a higher education is an approved way of competing for the limited money that is available in our society, whereas robbery is not an acceptable way.

From the conflict perspective, social change mainly involves reordering the distribution of scarce goods among groups. Unlike functionalism, which views change as potentially *destructive,* the conflict approach views change as potentially *beneficial*. That is, conflict can lead to improvements, advancements, reduction of discrimination against oppressed groups, and emergence of new groups as dominant forces in society. Without conflict, society would become stagnant.

Another important difference between functionalism and conflict theory must be noted. Functionalists assert that most people obey the law because they believe the law is fair and just, whereas conflict theorists assert that social order is maintained by authority backed by force. The latter assert that the privileged classes hold power legally and use the legal system to make others obey their will. They conclude that most people obey the law because they are afraid of being arrested, imprisoned, or even killed if they do not obey.

Functionalists assert that most people in society share the same set of values and norms. In contrast, conflict theorists assert that modern societies are composed of many different groups with divergent values, attitudes, and norms—and therefore conflicts are bound to occur. The abortion issue illustrates such a value conflict. Pro-life groups and traditional Roman Catholics believe the human fetus at *any* stage after conception is a living human being, and therefore aborting a pregnancy is viewed as a form of murder. In contrast, pro-choice advocates assert that, for *the first few months* after conception, an embryo is not yet a human being because it is unable to survive outside the womb. They also assert that if the state were to forbid a woman to obtain an operation she wanted, the state would be violating her right to control her own life.

Not all conflicts stem from disagreements over values. Some conflicts arise in part *because* people share the same values. In our society, for example, wealth and power are highly valued. The wealthy spend considerable effort and resources to maintain their status quo, whereas the poor and oppressed vehemently advocate for equal rights and more equitable distribution of income and wealth. Labor unions and business owners battle continually over wages and fringe benefits. Republicans and Democrats struggle constantly in the hopes of gaining increased political power.

In contrast to functionalism, which is criticized as being too conservative, conflict theory has been criticized for being too radical. Critics say that if there were as much conflict as these theorists claim, society would have disintegrated long ago. Conflict theory has also been criticized as encouraging oppressed groups to revolt against the existing power structure rather than work within the existing system to address their concerns.

*The Interactionist Perspective* The interactionist approach focuses on individuals and the processes of everyday social interaction among them rather than on larger structures of society, such as the educational system, the economy, or religion. Interactionist theory views behavior as a product of each individual's social relationships. Dorwin Cartwright (1951) has noted:

> How aggressive or cooperative a person is, how much self-respect or self-confidence he has, how energetic

and productive his work is, what he aspires, what he believes to be true and good, whom he loves or hates, and what beliefs or prejudices he holds—all these characteristics are highly determined by the individual's group memberships. In a real sense, they are products of groups and of the relationships between people.[21]

Interactionist theory asserts that human beings interpret or "define" each other's actions instead of merely reacting. This interpretation is mediated by the use of symbols (particularly the words and language a person learns).

Interactionists study the socialization process in detail because it forms the foundation for human interaction. The approach asserts that people are the products of the culture and social relationships in which they participate. Coleman and Cressey (1984) summarize this approach:

> People develop their outlook on life from participation in the symbolic universe that is their culture. They develop their conceptions of themselves, learn to talk, and even learn how to think as they interact early in life, with family and friends. But unlike the Freudians, interactionists believe that an individual's personality continues to change throughout life in response to changing social environments.

The work of the American philosopher George Herbert Mead has been the driving force behind the interactionist theories of social psychology. Mead noted that the ability to communicate in symbols (principally words and combinations of words) is the key feature that distinguishes humans from other animals. Individuals develop the ability to think and to use symbols in the process of socialization. Young children blindly imitate the behavior of their parents, but eventually they learn to "take the role of the other," pretending to be "Mommy" or "Daddy." And from such role taking children learn to understand the interrelationships among different roles and to see themselves as they imagine others see them. Eventually, Mead said, children begin to take the role of a *generalized other*. In doing so, they adopt a system of values and standards that reflect the expectations of people in general, not just those in the immediate present. In this way *reference groups* as well as actual *membership groups* come to determine how the individual behaves.[22]

Some specific social processes will be outlined to illustrate the interactionist perspective. Cooley (1902) observed that measuring most aspects of our self-concept objectively (such as how brave, likable, generous, attractive, and honest we are) is impossible.[23] To gauge the extent to which we have these qualities, we have to rely instead on the subjective judgments of people we interact with. In essence, Cooley asserted, we develop our self-concept through "the looking-glass self process," which means we develop our self-concept in terms of how other people relate to us, as if others were a looking glass or mirror. For example, if a person receives respect from others and is praised for his positive qualities, that person is apt to feel good about himself, will gradually develop a positive sense of worth, will be happier, and will seek responsible and socially acceptable ways to continue to maintain the respect of others. On the other hand, if a person is related to by others as if he is irresponsible, that person is apt to begin to view himself as irresponsible and gradually develop a negative self-concept. With such a view of himself, he decreases his efforts to act responsibly. In both these examples the way that others relate to a person (positively or negatively) becomes a self-fulfilling prophecy.

Another important concept is that social reality is what a particular group agrees it is. Social reality is not a purely objective phenomenon.

Interactionist theory views human behavior as resulting from the *interaction* of a person's unique, distinctive personality and the groups in which he or she participates. Groups are a factor in shaping personality, but the personality is also shaped by the person's unique qualities.

The reality we construct is mediated through symbols. We respond primarily to symbolic reality rather than to physical reality. Sullivan et al. (1980) describe the importance of symbols in shaping our reality:

> Symbols are the principal vehicles through which expectations are conveyed from one person to another. A symbol is any object, word, or event that stands for, represents, or takes the place of something else. Symbols have certain characteristics. First, the meaning of symbols derives from social consensus—the group's agreement that one thing will represent something else. A flag represents love of country or patriotism; a green light means *go*, not *stop*; a frown stands for displeasure. Second, the relationship between the symbol and what it represents is arbitrary—there is no inherent connection. There is nothing about the color green that compels us to use that, rather than red, as a symbol for *go*; a flag is in reality a piece of cloth for which we could substitute anything, as long as we agreed that it stood for country. Finally, symbols need not be tied to physical reality. We can use symbols to represent things with no physical existence, such as justice, mercy, or God, or to stand for things that do not exist at all, such as unicorns.[24]

A direct offshoot of the interactionist perspective is labeling theory, which holds that the labels assigned to a person have a major impact on that person's life. Labels often become self-fulfilling prophecies. If a child is continually called "stupid," that child is apt to develop a low self-concept, anticipate failure in many areas (particularly academic), put forth little effort in school and in competitive interactions with others, and end up "failing." If a teenage female gets a reputation as being promiscuous, adults and peers may label her a "whore," with other young women then shunning her and teenage males ridiculing her or seeking to date her for a "one-night stand." If a person is labeled an "ex con" for spending time in prison, that person is likely to be viewed with suspicion, have trouble finding employment, and be stigmatized as being dangerous and untrustworthy, even though the person may be honest, conscientious, and hardworking. Scheff (1966) has developed a labeling theory to explain why some people develop a "career" of being mentally ill.[25] He asserts that the act of labeling people "mentally ill" is the major determinant of their acting as if they were mentally ill. Once labeled, others interact with them as if they were mentally ill, which leads them to view themselves as being mentally ill, and they then enact this role.

The most common criticism of interactionist theory is that it is so abstract and vaguely worded that it is nearly impossible either to prove or disprove it.

## Research on Social Problems

✕✕✕✕✕✕✕✕✕✕✕✕✕✕✕✕✕✕✕✕✕✕

Consider the following "commonsense" beliefs held by many Americans:

♦ The death penalty has a deterrent effect on serious crimes (such as homicide) being committed.

♦ Most welfare recipients are able to work but would rather "live it up" on welfare.

♦ Mental patients commit higher rates of crime than other people.

♦ Male homosexuals are apt to display "feminine" mannerisms.

♦ Crimes committed by the lower class are the most costly in our society.

As we will see later in this text, all these beliefs have been shown by sociological research to be incorrect. Research demonstrates that a country's adoption of a death penalty generally does not result in a corresponding decrease in homicide rates or in rates of other serious crimes.[26] Only a small fraction of welfare recipients are able to work—the vast majority are unable to work.[27] People labeled mentally ill do not commit more crimes than those considered sane.[28] Male homosexuals are no more apt to be "effeminate" than male heterosexuals.[29] White-collar crime appears to be the most financially costly in our society.[30]

Sociological research seeks to describe and understand what is happening in the social world (see Box 1.7); often, so-called commonsense beliefs are found to be erroneous. Three frequently used sociological research methods are participant observation, the sample survey, and the control group experiment.

## PARTICIPANT OBSERVATION

Suppose you were interested in studying lifestyles in religious cults (a number of cults have developed over the years, such as satanic groups and the Moonies). If you use a participant observation approach you would attempt to participate in the cult's activities. You could either join the group without informing the cult of your scientific purpose (which has serious ethical implications) or inform the leaders of your purpose and ask their permission to observe their activities. In either case, you would seek through observation to obtain data on the group's beliefs, their lifestyles, how they recruit new members, problems encountered, satisfactions derived by members, and so on.

Using the participant observation approach affords the researcher close contact with the subject(s) studied. Participant observation provides rich insights that cannot be obtained from statistics. Statistical reports tend to be dry, whereas case studies provide real-life examples that vividly portray human conditions. Often, a case study (e.g., of a battered woman) has a stronger impact on social policy than pages of statistics on the problem.

Participant observation also has limitations. There is the danger that the setting selected for the study may be atypical, in which case generalizations to apparently similar cases may be invalid. There is also the danger that researchers will add their own conscious or unconscious biases to the final report as they filter the "facts" of the case. Participant observation relies heavily on the abilities and insights of researchers, as well as on the extent to which they can control their biases.

In addition, the people being studied may resent the intrusion of a nosy outsider. If the participant observer hides the purpose of the study and pretends to be a member of the group, there may be pressure to perform an illegal act for the group, in which case the researcher then faces a difficult dilemma.

## THE SAMPLE SURVEY

Compared to participant observation, a sample survey asks a more limited number of questions of a much larger number of people. A sample survey seeks to discover facts or opinions held by members of a population. Because it is often impossible to question everyone, a representative sample is frequently used. There are many survey organizations in the country; two of the best known are the Gallup and Lou Harris polls.

The "population" surveyed may consist of any social category—for example, prostitutes, the elderly in Albuquerque, identical twins, farmers earning over $80,000, or the entire nation. If those sampled are carefully chosen so that they are representative of the entire category, responses can be generalized to the population as a whole. The power of a sample is shown by the fact that a carefully chosen sample of three thousand voters can successfully predict a presidential election outcome within a few percentage points of the final results, despite the fact that some voters change their minds between the interview and the vote.

Suppose you live in a city where an elected judge has recently imposed an unusually light sentence on a twenty-one-year-old male found guilty by a jury for sexually assaulting an eighteen-year-old woman. During the sentencing, the judge indicated that a light sentence was given because the woman was wearing "provocative" clothing. Assume further that groups in the city working to prevent sexual assaults are so incensed by the judgment that they are considering launching an effort to recall the judge. To obtain valuable information on whether a recall effort has a realistic chance for success, you could conduct a survey of public attitudes toward the light sentence and whether the public favors removal of this judge. One way to do this is to construct a questionnaire designed to elicit opinions and then call about three hundred citizens whose names are randomly selected from a telephone directory. (The disadvantage of this method is that people without telephones and those with unlisted numbers will not be included in the sample, so the results will be slightly biased.)

# Key Sociological Concepts

Sociology, similar to other disciplines, has developed its own vocabulary in an effort to describe precisely what it studies. Definitions of some of these terms follow.

*Culture.* The way people live in a certain geographic area. Culture includes nonmaterial items such as norms, beliefs, patterns of thought, values, language, political systems, religious patterns, music, and courtship patterns. Culture also includes material items such as types of dwellings, art, dishes, cars, buses, factories and business offices, and clothes.

*Deviance.* Behavior that does not conform to recognized social norms—usually those norms held by the dominant group in society. Sociologists are careful to avoid making moral judgments when using the term *deviance,* as deviant behavior may be as healthy, enjoyable, and useful to society as behavior prescribed by social norms (or even more so).

*Discrimination.* Negative or unfavorable treatment of people because of their membership in a minority group. Groups that have been victims of discrimination include women, people of color, gays and lesbians, persons with a disability and the elderly.

*Dysfunction.* Something that has negative rather than positive effects on a system. Dysfunctional behavior or arrangements reduce the stability or threaten the survival of a system, whereas functional behavior or arrangements aid the stability of a system.

*Ethnocentrism.* The tendency to view one's own culture and customs as right and superior and to judge other cultures by one's own standards.

*Folkway.* A custom or convention of a society. A folkway is not strongly held by a group. The custom of greeting a friend with "Hi, how are you?" is an example of a folkway. Violation of a folkway (e.g., eating with one's fingers rather than a knife and fork) is only mildly frowned on.

*Group.* A number of individuals who have organized and recurrent relationships with each other. Groups develop their own cultures; and the longer a group is in existence, the more extensive the culture tends to become. For example, each family has its own distinct culture, which is different (even if only slightly) from the cultures of other families. They have special holiday rituals, affectionate nicknames, and so forth.

*Hypothesis.* An idea about reality that one intends to test or that at least is capable of being tested.

*Ideology.* A set of values, beliefs, and ideas that explains and justifies the perceived interests (or more generally, the way of life) of those who hold it. For example, during slavery white landlords viewed blacks as inferior, which served to rationalize their discrimination against blacks.

*Macrosociological theory.* A theory concerned with explaining the behavior of large groups of people and the workings of entire societies.

*Microsociological theory.* A theory concerned with explaining the behavior of individuals and small groups.

*Minority or minority group.* A group that has a subordinate status and is subjected to discrimination. When defining a group as a minority, it is not size but lack of power that is critical. Women, even though in the majority in our society, are a minority according to this definition.

*Mores.* Morally binding customs of a group. Mores are strong norms, violations of which are viewed as morally wrong. Those identified as violating mores are usually punished severely. Examples of violations of mores in our society include murder, assault, rape, and kidnapping. Many mores are encoded in laws.

*Norm.* A formal or informal rule that prescribes what is acceptable in a certain situation and what is not. Norms are usually taken for granted in that we seldom notice them until they are broken. For instance, if a person loudly belches in church, a norm has been violated. Depending on the norm violated (and the circumstances), reaction ranges from mild disapproval (as for picking one's nose in public) to severe punishment (as for rape).

*Power.* The capacity to force others to do something or to protect oneself from being forced by others to do something.

*Prejudice.* A negative attitude toward a group considered different and, without adequate evidence, inferior.

*Role.* A set of expectations and behavior associated with a social position. The sociological use of the term is similar to the theatrical definition of the term *role.*

The term is closely related to status. The distinction is that a person *occupies* a status and *plays* a role. For example, a man may have the *status* of father because he has children, but he does not play the *role* of a father when he and his wife leave the children with a babysitter and go to a movie.

*Social class.* A category of people who have similar shares of items valued in a society. The items that are usually valued in our society include high social status, power, and money. Most Americans today consider themselves to be members of the middle class.

*Social disorganization.* A situation in which a large organization or an entire society is imperfectly organized to achieve its goals and maintain its stability. When disorganization occurs, the organization loses control over its parts.

*Social institution.* A significant practice, relationship, or organization that exists over an extended period of time in a society. The term is somewhat abstract. Common institutions in a society include the family, religion, economics, education, and politics. Social institutions tend to have stable patterns of thought and action and to focus on the performance of important social tasks. The family, for example, functions to raise the children and to provide companionship and emotional support to family members.

*Social movement.* A large group of people who have joined together to change or maintain some social condition.

*Social problem.* A social problem exists when an influential group asserts that a certain social condition affecting a large number of people is a problem and may be remedied by a collective action.

*Social stratification.* The division of a society into social classes that have varying degrees of access to the rewards the society provides.

*Social structure.* The organized, stable patterns of human behavior and social relationships in a society. Social structure includes the ways in which social classes, marriage, and family patterns are organized.

*Socialization.* The process through which individuals learn proper ways (proper as defined by the society) of acting in a culture. The roles, norms, customs, values, language, belief, and most behaviors are learned in the socialization process. Most basic socialization occurs in the early childhood years but some also occurs throughout life.

*Society.* A community, nation, or broad grouping of people having common traditions, institutions, and collective activities and interests.

*Sociology.* The study of human society and social behavior.

*Status.* A person's position or rank in relation to others. Each person has numerous positions in a society—for example, student, woman, daughter, Chicana, Catholic, married, wealthy, and so on. *Ascribed* statuses are inherited from parents, whereas *achieved* statuses are derived from occupation, education, and lifestyle.

*Stereotype.* A standardized mental image of a group that is inappropriately applied to each of its members.

*Subculture.* A culture within a culture characterized by certain unique material and nonmaterial features yet remaining influenced by the larger culture. For example, certain urban areas have subcultures of marijuana smokers, prostitutes, the superrich, the jet set, juvenile gangs, motorcycle riders, and actors.

*Taboo.* A prohibition against behavior considered so despicable it is almost unthinkable. A taboo is the strongest norm. Examples in our society are incest, cannibalism, and infanticide.

*Theory.* A statement that seeks to explain a relationship between concepts or facts. For example, it has been found that a higher percentage of college graduates drink alcoholic beverages than those who do not attend college. One theory to explain this relationship is that graduates learn a set of values while in college that encourages drinking. Another explanation or theory is that graduates earn more and therefore have more money to spend on such nonessentials as alcoholic beverages. Still another theory is that college graduates face more stress as they hold higher pressure jobs, and this higher stress drives them to drink in order to relax. Competing theories such as these can be sorted out by turning them into hypotheses and testing them through research.

*Value.* A belief about what is right, good, and desirable.

*Variable.* A characteristic that can change. Age, social class, and religious affiliation are examples of common social variables.

*1990 U.S. Census taker talks with Hispanic woman in front of her home.*

The sample survey is especially useful for obtaining information about opinions and social characteristics of a population. (The U.S. Census, for example, obtains valuable information about social characteristics of our population every ten years.) Properly selected samples have the advantage (over participant observation) of ensuring that the people studied are not misleading exceptions. Sample surveys, however, do not provide as penetrating an analysis of social problems as participant observation. Another shortcoming of sample surveys is that respondents do not always answer the questions honestly, especially if the questions deal with embarrassing or sensitive areas such as sexual beliefs and behaviors. Surveys can also be fairly expensive to conduct.

There is a danger with surveys, as with participant observation, that researchers may add their biases to the findings. For example, it has been claimed that Shere Hite added her biases about the women's movement to the following description of intercourse in the 1981 *Hite Report on Male Sexuality*. (Over seven thousand men responded to a survey questionnaire in this study, but because they were not randomly selected, the sample is not representative of American men in general.)

> Intercourse is at once one of the most beautiful and, at the same time, the most oppressive and exploitative acts in our society. It has been symbolic of men's ownership of women, for approximately the last 3,000 years. It is the central symbol of patriarchal society; without it there could be no patriarchy. Intercourse culminating in male orgasm in the vagina is the sublime moment during which the male contribution to reproduction takes place. This is the reason for its glorification. And as such, men must love it: Intercourse is a celebration of the male patriarchal society.[31]

## THE CONTROL GROUP EXPERIMENT

An experiment is a rigorously controlled approach for tracing the influence of one variable on another. Although there are many different experimental designs, experimenters prefer to divide their study group into an experimental group and a control group. Both groups are initially tested on the variables to be studied. Then the experimental group is exposed to some information or experience that is not given to the control group. By retesting and comparing the two groups at the end of the experiment, it is then possible to assess what effects (if any) the information or experience being tested had on the experimental group.

For example, you could use the following procedures to test whether exposure to TV violence leads to increased aggression in young children. First, you would divide the children being studied into an experimental group and a control group. (The two groups should be randomly selected or matched on factors that might influence the outcome, such as sex, age, social class, and intelligence.) The experimental group would then be exposed to the variable being tested by viewing a TV program filled with violence.

The control group would not be exposed to violence during this time period. After the experimental group viewed the violent TV program, the two groups would be compared as to the extent to which they display aggressive behavior (e.g., the children could be placed in a room containing punching bags and other toys, and the number of aggressive responses could be tabulated).

The control group experimental method allows of the carefully controlled scientific analysis of problems. With this approach the researcher is able to assess the effects of the variable being studied, while controlling external influences that may distort the results. In a control group experiment, the researcher seeks to manipulate the independent (experimental) variable to show casual connections among phenomena in a field of study. The control group experimental approach is best used in a laboratory. Conducting true social experiments outside the laboratory is extremely difficult because it is nearly impossible to control all the external factors that may influence outcome. For this reason, control group experiments in the real world are rare.

The laboratory itself is a factor that may affect outcome, as subjects are apt to behave differently in a laboratory. Thus watching violent TV programs in a laboratory may well produce different effects from those generated by watching the same programs at home.

## Summary

Sociology is the scientific study of human society and social behavior. A social problem exists when an influential group asserts that a certain condition affecting a large number of people is a problem and may be remedied by collective action. Sociology has a variety of proposals (many unproven) on how to alleviate current social problems; these proposals are usually based on sociological theories. Although some problems are gradually resolved, new problems arise from time to time, and other problems persist over extended periods of time.

Social movements play key roles in making people aware a problem exists, and often they try to resolve social problems. Bringing about social and cultural changes in our society takes collective action. Spector and Kitsuse (1973) have noted that social movements have a four-stage life cycle: agitation, legitimation and co-option, bureaucratization and reaction, and re-emergence of the movement. Actions taken to resolve social problems may result in a variety of consequences: resolution of problem, partial resolution of problem, confinement of problem, intensification of problem, creation of new problems, a shift in focus of the problem, organizational maintenance, and deflection of public concern.

The position that politicians take on social issues and social programs are largely determined by whether they are liberal or conservative in orientation. Liberals generally adhere to an institutional orientation, whereas conservatives adhere to a residual orientation. The institutional orientation holds that social programs are a proper legitimate function of modern industrial society in helping individuals achieve self-fulfillment. The residual orientation holds that social programs should be provided only when an individual's needs are not properly met through other social institutions, primarily the family and the market economy. The developmental perspective of social problems and social programs is an emerging view that appears to have considerable appeal to liberals, conservatives, and to the general public. The developmental perspective advocates social interventions (including social programs) that contribute positively to economic development.

Microsociological theories are concerned with explaining the behavior of individuals and small groups. Three important categories of microsociological theories that are commonly applied to the study of social problems are: biosocial theories, personality theories, and behavioral theories.

Macrosociological theories seek to explain the behavior of large groups of people and the workings of entire societies, focusing on broad social issues. The three most prominent macrosociological theories are functionalism, conflict theory, and interactionism.

Research on social problems is essential to test theories and discover facts about social life. The three most used sociological research methods are participant observation, sample survey, and control group experiment. Sociological research on social problems has discovered that many popularly held beliefs are wrong.

# CHAPTER 2

# *Crime and Delinquency*

*B*eing victimized by crime is the social problem that many Americans are most concerned about. Types of crimes include murder, battery, aggravated assault, burglary, theft, arson, forcible rape, drug trafficking, and white-collar crime. What can be done to prevent these and other offenses?

This chapter:

♦ discusses the nature and extent of crime;

♦ presents various crime causation theories;

♦ describes types of crime;

♦ examines the criminal justice system (the police, the courts, and the correctional system); and

♦ suggests ways to reduce crime and delinquency.

## The Nature and Extent of Crime

A *crime* is an act committed or omitted in violation of a law. A *law* is a formal social rule that is enforced by a political authority. Usually, the state (or the power elite that controls the state) specifies as crimes those acts that violate certain strongly held values and norms. Not all behaviors that violate strongly held norms are prohibited by law; sometimes, informal processes, such as social disapproval, regulate norm violations. For example, a swimmer's failure to aid a drowning person is not a criminal act, although it is usually considered morally wrong.

## WHAT IS CRIME?

Because norms and values change over time, so do laws. There is often a time lag between a change in norms and a change in laws. For example, in some areas obsolete laws remain that still prohibit card playing on Sundays and prohibit sexual intercourse (even among married couples) in any position other than the "missionary position."

Certain norms and values differ among cultures and societies, and therefore so do laws. In many Arab countries the use of alcohol is illegal, whereas the use of marijuana is acceptable;[1] in the United States the reverse is generally the law.

At one time or another, everyone has violated some laws. Whether an offender is convicted depends on a number of factors, including whether the violator is arrested, how forcefully the prosecutor wants to present the case, the legal skills of the defense attorney, whether there are witnesses, and how the offender presents him- or herself in court (including physical appearance, what is said, and the use of nonverbal communication).

With thousands of laws on the books, police, prosecuting attorneys, and judges have considerable discretion over which laws to ignore, which to enforce, and how strongly to enforce them. This discretionary power offers many opportunities for criminal justice officials to choose whom to arrest and whom to release. The act of applying the law often involves issues of political power and favoritism toward certain groups and classes. Because criminal justice power historically

*Reggie, a seventeen-year-old who received a permanent disability in a stolen-car wreck and who was just released from a dentention center was re-arrested after a car chase that resulted in him crashing into a methane gasoline tank. When asked why he did it again, he replied, "Why should I care, nobody else does." He was driving the car using a crutch to brake and accelerate.*

**Table 2.1** *Number of Reported Serious Crimes, 1996*

| Crime | Number |
|---|---|
| Arson | (Statistics unavailable) |
| Murder | 19,650 |
| Forcible rape | 95,770 |
| Robbery | 537,050 |
| Aggravated assault | 1,029,810 |
| Burglary | 2,501,500 |
| Larceny-theft | 7,894,600 |
| Motor vehicle theft | 1,395,200 |
| Total | 13,473,580 |

*Source:* U.S. Department of Justice, *Crime in the United States: Uniform Crime Report, 1996* (Washington, DC: U.S. Government Printing Office, 1997), 61.

**Table 2.2** *Crime Clock: The Occurrence of Reported Crimes According to Time in the United States*

Property crime—one every 3 seconds

Larceny-theft—one every 4 seconds

Burglary—one every 13 seconds

Violent crime—one every 19 seconds

Motor vehicle theft—one every 23 seconds

Aggravated assault—one every 31 seconds

Robbery—one every 59 seconds

Forcible rape—one every 6 minutes

Murder—one every 27 minutes

*Source:* U.S. Department of Justice, *Crime in the United States: Uniform Crime Report, 1996* (Washington, DC: U.S. Government Printing Office, 1997), 4.

has resided with the white middle and upper classes, other groups are often (intentionally or unintentionally) treated more harshly. For example, authorities enforce laws against white-collar crime much less vigorously than they do vagrancy laws in middle-class and upper-class neighborhoods. (The middle-class and upper-class power structure generally seeks to enforce vagrancy laws "to keep bums and other undesirables off the streets, or at least out of respectable neighborhoods.")[2]

## How Extensive Is the Crime Problem?

Crime is one of the most serious problems facing our nation. Former President Richard Nixon remarked on several occasions that crime is our "number one enemy" and that "we must declare war against it." Ironically, President Nixon and many of his top administrative officials later faced criminal charges—with some being imprisoned—in connection with the Watergate affair. (The Watergate affair in the early 1970s involved a break-in at the Democratic Presidential Campaign headquarters, housed in the Watergate Building in Washington, DC, by people who were clandestinely employed to help reelect President Nixon. Nixon and some of his top aides then committed a variety of offenses in an effort to cover up this break-in. President Nixon was eventually forced to resign from the presidency after the coverup was revealed.)

The most comprehensive statistical summary of crime in America is the annual *Crime in the United*

*States: Uniform Crime Report* (UCR), published by the FBI. This report lists the crimes and arrests in this country, as reported by law enforcement agencies. One part of this report is the Serious Crime Index (SCI), which shows the amount of, and trends in, serious crimes. The SCI is composed of four types of property crimes (burglary, larceny-theft, motor vehicle theft, and arson) and four types of crimes against persons (willful homicide, forcible rape, aggravated assault, and robbery).

There are over thirteen million SCI offenses reported annually to law enforcement agencies in the United States.[3] SCI offenses are listed in Table 2.1.

It is generally agreed that serious violent crime has reached alarming proportions in the United States. Many Americans feel unsafe in their own neighborhood at night, and a high proportion own guns, largely for self-protection.[4] Table 2.2 graphically demonstrates why people are so fearful today.

How does the crime rate in the United States compare to the rates in other countries? This question is difficult to answer for a couple of reasons. Different countries define their crimes in somewhat different ways—for example, prostitution is a crime in some countries, but not in other countries. In addition, many other countries do not collect accurate statistics on the extent of crime in their homeland. There is, however, one crime for which every country defines in the same way, and for which they collect accurate data on—murder.

The United States has by far the highest rate of murder of any industrialized nation. The murder rate in the

United States is five times higher than in Canada, and seven-and-a-half times higher than in Europe.[5] Coleman and Cressey (1996) give the following explanation for the high level of violence in the United States:

> The high level of violence in America is often seen as a holdover from the rowdy days of frontier expansion. According to this view, violence became a way of life as an unending stream of settlers fought among themselves and with native peoples for land and profit. . . . Furthermore, America is an extremely wealthy nation, but, compared with other Western countries, it has a bigger gap between the rich and the poor and inferior welfare and social programs. Thus, those at the bottom of the social hierarchy tend to be more frustrated and desperate, and more resentful of those who possess the wealth they are denied.[6]

## WHO IS ARRESTED?

Those who are arrested for crimes are disproportionately likely to be males, young, members of a racial minority, and city residents.

Males are arrested about four times as often as females.[7] (Only in juvenile runaway and prostitution cases are females arrested more often.) There are two major reasons why males are more often arrested. One is sex-role socialization, which encourages males to be more aggressive and daring, whereas females are encouraged to be more passive and conforming to rules and norms. The second reason is the tendency of police officers and the courts to deal more leniently with female offenders.[8] However, it should be noted that in the past two decades crime among females has been increasing faster than that among males,[9] which may be a negative side effect of women's challenging their traditional sex roles.

Young people appear to commit far more than their share of crime, including the crimes that are classified by the FBI as most serious—rape, murder, robbery, arson, burglary, aggravated assaults, auto theft, and larceny. In 1996, 32 percent of all arrests were under the age of twenty-one and 45 percent were under the age of twenty-five.[10] A partial explanation of the high-arrest rate among juveniles and young adults is that they may be less skillful than older adults in avoiding arrest. Also, they tend to commit crimes (such as auto theft) that are highly visible to the police. Even when all these factors are taken into account, the young still commit more crimes than the old.

There are differences in arrest rates among various racial and ethnic groups. Chinese Americans and Japanese Americans have the lowest arrest rates in the country.[11] The arrest rate for African Americans is three times higher than for whites.[12] One reason for this higher rate is that a higher proportion of the African American population is poor or unemployed, and there are high correlations between poverty (and unemployment) and the types of crime classified by the FBI as most serious. An additional reason for the higher arrest among certain minority groups may be racial prejudice. A number of studies have shown that the probability of arrest, prosecution, conviction, and incarceration for an offense decreases as the social status of the offender increases. In one study, judges were given fact sheets on a hypothetical case and asked to recommend an appropriate sentence. The fact sheets contained the following information:

> "Joe Cut," 27, pleaded guilty to battery. He slashed his common-law wife on the arms with a switchblade. His record showed convictions for disturbing the peace, drunkenness, and hit-run driving. He told a probation officer that he acted in self-defense after his wife attacked him with a broom handle. The prosecutor recommended not more than five days in jail or a $100 fine.[13]

Half the fact sheets identified "Joe Cut" as white, and the other half identified him as African American. The judges who thought he was white recommended a sentence of three to ten days, whereas those who thought he was African American recommended a sentence of from five to thirty days.

Kornblum and Julian (1989) describe another factor that contributes to higher arrest rates among African Americans:

> Still another factor that is thought to contribute to high rates of crime among blacks is family disorganization, especially the rapid increase in the number of female-headed families. Such families lack male role models with legitimate jobs, leaving open the possibility that children will be influenced by others in the community, including individuals who engage in criminal activities.[14]

A majority of reported crimes and reported arrests are in large cities, as compared to suburbs and rural areas.[15] Within large cities crime tends to occur in those sections that are changing rapidly and that have a high concentration of low-income and transient inhabitants. Arrest rates are substantially lower in more stable, higher-income, residential areas. Crime is lower in the suburbs than in the cities, and lower still in the rural areas.[16]

## Does Crime Pay? Quite Often!

**V**iolent crimes include murder, rape, robbery and aggravated assault. There are over four million violent crimes committed each year in the United States, but only a tiny fraction of criminals are put behind bars.

For every one hundred violent crimes:

- only forty-two are reported to police
- only seventeen people are arrested
- only five people are convicted
- only four people are sent to prison/jail

*Source:* Ted Gest, "The Real Problems in American Justice," *U.S. News & World Report* (Oct. 9, 1995): 54–55.

## How Accurate Are Official Crime Statistics?

As described earlier, the Federal Bureau of Investigation (FBI) annually compiles the *Uniform Crime Report* (UCR), based on data from law enforcement agencies throughout the country on crimes committed and arrests made. The Serious Crime Index is a part of UCR.

There are a number of problems connected with this index. Actual crime rates are substantially higher than the official rates. Kornblum and Julian (1989) estimate that crimes reported to the police account for about 33 percent of actual offenses and about 50 percent of violent crimes.[17] Victims often do not report crimes to the police because (among other reasons) they feel that nothing can be done.[18] As indicated in Box 2.1, most crimes go unsolved.

The Serious Crime Index focuses on crimes that are more likely to be committed by people of lower social and economic status. It does not reflect the types of crimes typically committed by higher-income groups: fraud, false advertising, corporate price fixing, bribery, embezzlement, industrial pollution, tax evasion, and so on. If white-collar crimes were included in the Serious Crime Index, and if law enforcement authorities were more vigorous in enforcing such laws, the profile of a typical criminal would very likely be older, wealthier, whiter, and more suburban than suggested by the index.

Self-report studies, in which respondents are asked anonymously the details of any crimes they may have committed, reveal that "close to 100 percent of all persons have committed some kind of offense, although few have been arrested."[19] In what way, then, do those who are arrested differ from those who are not? For one thing, those who are not caught tend to commit a crime only rarely, whereas those who are arrested tend to break the law more frequently. Perhaps a better explanation, however, lies in the types of crimes committed. Those arrested may be committing the kinds of crimes that are more strictly enforced by law enforcement agencies. The poor, for example, may be more likely to commit high-risk, low-yield crimes such as larceny, burglary, or robbery. In contrast, the wealthier are more likely to commit low-risk, high-yield crimes, such as income-tax evasion and false advertising.

In the past twenty years, there have been dramatic increases in the number of crimes committed as cited in the Serious Crime Index. Yet, there is uncertainty what this rate increase actually represents. Perhaps crime victims are reporting more offenses. Or perhaps the increase is due to improvements in police-reporting practices; police departments are increasingly using computers, clerical personnel, and statisticians to improve the accuracy of their reports.

Strictly speaking, the Serious Crime Index is not fully comparable among jurisdictions. At times it is even inconsistent from one year to the next within the same reporting unit. A major reason for this difficulty is that each of the fifty states has its own unique criminal code. For example, an offense that is classified as burglary in one state may be classified as larceny or robbery in another; what is classified as sexual assault in one state may be considered a less serious offense in another. Because states occasionally make changes in their criminal codes, inconsistencies may arise from one year to the next within the same reporting unit because of changes in definitions of offenses. Furthermore, individual officers interpret the law differently as they carry out their duties.

Finally, it should be noted that crime statistics are at times manipulated by the police and public officials. Data may be skewed to show higher rates of crime, perhaps to help document the need for a federal or state grant or to politick for a budget increase in personnel or facilities. More often than not, however, police and public officials are under considerable pressure to keep the crime rate low. By manipulating statistics, they can reclassify certain serious crimes into different, less serious categories.

In summary, the Serious Crime Index of the FBI provides an indication of the rates and trends of certain crimes in the United States. Yet these statistics overlook white-collar crime, are affected by police-reporting practices, and must be viewed against the fact that many crimes are unreported. It further appears that the poor, the undereducated, and minorities have been the victims not only of selective law enforcement but also of misleading statistics on crime. Some sociologists have contended that, because higher-income classes are far more involved in white-collar crime (which is often ignored by law enforcement agencies), they may actually have a higher rate of crime than the lower classes.[20]

## Crime Causation Theories

A variety of theories about the causes of crime have been advanced by several disciplines. Space limitations for this text permit only a summary of the more prominent theories. Table 2.3 identifies these prominent theories along with their approximate dates of origin. As you read about each of these theories, ask yourself the following questions: Is this theory helpful in explaining why a person committed a rape (or burglary, murder, drug-trafficking offense, aggravated assault, kidnapping, embezzlement, and so on)? Is the theory useful in suggesting a correctional plan to prevent a recurrence of the offense?

### EARLY THEORIES

Three of the earliest theories on the causes of crime were demonology, the classical/neoclassical theory, and the Marxist-Leninist theory.

*Demonology*  For centuries, many primitive societies conceived of crime as being caused by evil spirits. This belief is commonly referred to as demonology. It was thought that those who engaged in deviant behavior were possessed by the devil. The only way to cure the criminal act was to remove the evil spirit through prayer, through a ritual, or by torture (sometimes to the point of death). This theory is no longer prominent, partly because scientific study has found no evidence that law breakers are possessed by evil spirits. Remnants of the theory remain, however, as seen in satanic cults, rock lyrics with satanic themes, and

**Table 2.3**  *Prominent Theories of Crime*

| Theory | Approximate Date of Origin |
| --- | --- |
| Early theories | |
|   Demonology | Primitive societies |
|   Classical/Neoclassical | 1775 |
|   Marxist-Leninist | 1850 |
| Physical and mental trait theories | |
|   Phrenology | 1825 |
|   Lombrosian | 1900 |
|   Mental deficiency | 1900 |
|   Morphological | 1920 |
| Psychological theories | |
|   Psychoanalytic | 1900 |
|   Psychodynamic problem-solving | 1920 |
|   Frustration-aggression | 1950 |
|   Self-talk | 1975 |
| Sociological theories | |
|   Labeling | 1900 |
|   Differential association | 1939 |
|   Societal control | 1950 |
|   Deviant subcultures | 1955 |
|   Anomie | 1957 |
|   Critical | 1995 |

movies (such as *Friday the 13th* and *The Exorcist*) depicting people possessed by demons.

*Classical and Neoclassical Theory*  The classical and neoclassical schools were based on hedonistic psychology. Classical theory asserted that a person makes a decision about whether to engage in criminal activity based on the anticipated balance of pleasure and pain. Each individual was assumed to have a free will and to act solely on the basis of the anticipated hedonistic calculations. Advocates of this school considered this to be a full and exhaustive explanation of causality. Applied to corrections, this approach urged that clear-cut punishments be assigned to each offense so the prospective offender could calculate anticipated pleasures and pains. The penalties assigned were to be slightly more severe than anticipated pleasures in order to discourage criminal activity. The neoclassical school accepted the basic notion of hedonistic calculations but urged that children and "lunatics" be exempt from punishment because of their inability to calculate pleasures and pain responsibly. Judicial discretion was also urged for certain mitigating circumstances (e.g., an offense now referred to as involuntary manslaughter).

Although correctional systems in the nineteenth century were based primarily on the neoclassical approach, classical and neoclassical theory has waned in popularity. Some elements of it can still be found in our legal and judicial system—particularly the emphasis on using punishment to deter crime. The theory has been severely criticized because it does not allow for other causes of crime and because the punitive approach it advocates has not been successful in curbing further criminal activity. In addition, hedonistic psychology ignores the fact that much human behavior is determined by values and morals, rather than by the pleasure-versus-pain calculation.

*Marxist-Leninist Theory* Marxist-Leninist theory assumes that all crime results from the exploitation of workers and from intense competition among people. Crime disappears, according to neo-Marxists, when society achieves a "classless" status. The basic tenet of communism is "From each according to his ability, to each according to his need." Socialist countries (such as Cuba and North Korea) have in the past sought to formulate their societies on the principles advocated by Karl Marx. Class differentials are much less prominent in socialist countries as compared to capitalist nations. Although Marx asserted that crime would be sharply reduced in socialist countries because there would be less class conflict, substantial criminal activity does occur in these countries. (The extensiveness of criminal activity is difficult to determine, because these countries publish almost no crime-rate reports.) The continued existence of crime in socialist countries is not taken by socialists as evidence that the theory is defective; rather, it is explained as being the result of old capitalistic traditions and ideologies and the imperfect application of Marxist theory. (One should note that many socialist countries in recent years have been discarding Marxist principles and are moving toward incorporating capitalistic incentives into their economies.)

## PHYSICAL AND MENTAL TRAIT THEORIES

You may have noticed in Table 2.3 that the first "physical and mental trait theory," phrenology, actually originated before Marxist-Leninist theory. Although it falls chronologically into the category of

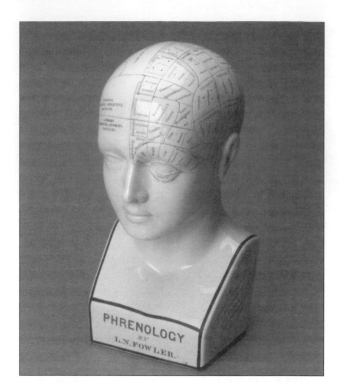

*"Practical phrenologist" L. N. Fowler sold hundreds of busts like this one.*

"early theories," it is more closely related to "trait theories," and will be discussed in this section along with three other trait theories, the Lombrosian, the mental deficiency, and the morphological theories.

*Phrenology* Phrenology was popular until the turn of the twentieth century. Phrenologists maintained that criminal behavior was related to the size and shape of the human skull. They closely scrutinized the grooves, ridges, and number of bumps on a skull. The shape of the brain, which was influenced by the shape of the skull, was thought to be sufficient to predict criminal activity. Although there were isolated incidents in which offenders with "criminal prone" skulls were treated more harshly than other offenders, this approach was not widely incorporated into correctional systems. Scientific studies have found no evidence of correlations between criminal behavior and the shape of the skull.

*Lombrosian Theory* Around the beginning of the twentieth century, biological/constitutional theories were popular. The prototype of such theories was

Cesare Lombroso's theory of the "born criminal." This school maintained that a criminal inherits certain physical abnormalities or stigmata, such as a scanty beard, low sensitivity to pain, distorted nose, large lips, or long arms. The more such stigmata a person had, the more he or she was thought to be predisposed to a criminal career. People with several stigmata were thought to be unable to refrain from criminal activity unless their social environment was unusually favorable. The theory that criminals have distinct physical characteristics was refuted by Charles Goring (1913), who found no significant physical differences in a study comparing several thousand criminals with several thousand noncriminals.[21]

*Mental Deficiency Theory* The mental deficiency theory replaced the Lombrosian school when the latter fell into disrepute. Mental deficiency theory asserted that criminal behavior resulted from "feeble-mindedness," which was alleged to impair the capacity to acquire morality and self-control or to appreciate the meaning of laws. As mental tests became standardized and widely used, it was discovered that many criminals achieved average or above-average intelligence scores. The theory waned in popularity in the 1930s. Neither the Lombrosian nor the mental deficiency approach had a lasting, significant effect on corrections.

*Morphological Theory* Closely related to the mental deficiency and Lombrosian theories is the morphological theory, which asserted that there is a fundamental relationship between psychological makeup and physical structure. The most popular variant of this theory was William Sheldon's, developed in the 1940s. Sheldon described three body categories; endomorph (obese), mesomorph (muscular), and ectomorph (lean). To the mesomorph he ascribed an unusual propensity to criminal activity. Sheldon did not assert that mesomorphs were inherently criminally prone. Rather, he asserted that this physique was associated with a distinctive type of temperament, characterized by such traits as love of physical adventure, abundance of restless energy, and enjoyment of exercise. Mesomorphy thus produced energetic, aggressive, and daring types of individuals, such as generals, athletes, and politicians, as well as criminals. Morphological approaches like Sheldon's are still popular in southern European and South American countries. Scientific studies, however, have found little evidence that muscular people are more likely to commit crimes than people who are lean or overweight.

## PSYCHOLOGICAL THEORIES

Psychological theories about crime attribute its causes to the criminal's thought processes, which are seen as relatively unrelated to overall societal conditions. These theories include the psychoanalytic, psychodynamic problem-solving, frustration-aggression, and self-talk approaches to understanding criminal behavior.

*Psychoanalytic Theory* Psychoanalytic theory is not a single coherent theory but a variety of hypotheses developed by psychoanalysts since the turn of the twentieth century from the pioneering work of Sigmund Freud. Generally, these theories postulated that delinquent behavior results when the restraining forces in the superego (one's conscience and self-ideal) and the ego (mediator among the superego, the id, and reality) are too weak to curb the instinctual, antisocial pressures for the id (source of psychic energy). Human nature was seen as largely determined by id instincts, which were basically antisocial and immoral in character. This theory postulated that current behavior was largely controlled by early childhood experiences. Deviant behavior was viewed as stemming from unconscious conflicts, fixations, and repressed traumatic experiences.

The psychiatric school, of which psychoanalysis is a large component, has had a significant influence on corrections because it asserts that some offenders commit illegal acts because they are insane. Criminal justice systems frequently call on psychiatrists to determine the "sanity" of accused offenders. If someone is judged by the court to be "innocent by reason of insanity," he or she is sent to a mental hospital, instead of to prison, to recuperate.

Psychiatry has also classified individuals into numerous categories in terms of their "mental" functioning. One category, sociopath, has had considerable relevance for corrections. A sociopath is a person who is thought to have no moral constraints against engaging in criminal activity, doing so whenever it is personally advantageous, even though others may be hurt.

Since 1950, Thomas Szasz (1961) and others have seriously questioned the medical-model approach to emotional problems and have asserted that mental illness is a myth.[22] Szasz believes that people have emotional problems, but not a "disease of the mind," as implied by the medical model (see Chapter 3). Courts, however, continue to use the mental illness model.

Psychoanalytic theory is increasingly falling into disfavor. One reason is the finding that people with emotional problems who undergo psychoanalysis are

## Self-Talk Theory: A Presidential Assassination Attempt

On March 30, 1981, President Ronald Reagan was shot in Washington, DC, by a .22 caliber bullet, which pierced the left side of his chest and collapsed his left lung. Also injured was a secret service agent, a Washington policeman, and White House press secretary James Brady. Fortunately, all four men survived. Arrested for this assassination attempt was John W. Hinckley, Jr., 25, the son of a multimillionaire Colorado oil executive.

Born into wealth, John Hinckley has been described as a loner and a drifter, a misfit who craved fame. In high school, Hinckley was an average student but had few friends. He went to college for seven years off and on but never graduated. His father was a self-made millionaire, and his brother was vice president of his father's firm. His family members were known as strong Reagan supporters.

John Hinckley became infatuated with actress Jodie Foster, although they had never met. In the film *Taxi Driver*, Jodie Foster played a teenage prostitute. The film was about a disturbed loser (played by Robert DeNiro) who stalks a political figure. This film appears to have influenced Hinckley's assassination attempt, as he wrote in an unmailed letter to Miss Foster:

> I would abandon this idea of getting Reagan in a second if I could only win your heart and live out the rest of my life with you, whether it be in total obscurity or whatever. I will admit to you that the reason I'm going ahead with this attempt now is because I just cannot wait any longer to impress you. . . .
>
> Jodie, I'm asking you to please look into your heart and at least give me the chance with this historical deed to gain your respect and love.[a]

Apparently, John Hinckley shot the president because he believed that such an action would impress Jodie Foster and lead to a relationship with her.

When attorneys, judges, police officers, and other criminal justice officials search for the motive for an offender committing a crime, they are really searching to identify the cognitions (that is, the self-talk) that led the offender to commit a crime.

---

a. John S. Lang, "John Hinckley—A Misfit Who Craved Fame," *U.S. News & World Report* (Apr. 13, 1981): 26.

no more likely to improve than a comparable group who receive no therapy.[23]

***Psychodynamic Problem-Solving Theory*** Psychodynamic problem-solving theory views deviant behavior as being contrived by the personality as a way of dealing with some adjustment problem. The problem is generally perceived as a conflict among various ingredients of the personality: wishes, drives, fears, strivings, loyalties, codes of ethics, and so on. Situational factors are generally deemphasized.

A serious shortcoming of the theory is that it is often extremely difficult (if not impossible) to determine precisely which wishes, drives, fears, or ethics motivated someone to commit a crime. For example, the following internal desires have all been advanced as motivations for committing rape: unfulfilled sexual desires, a desire for violence, and feelings of inferiority; all are theorized to be temporarily alleviated during rape as the offender feels a sense of power and superiority. When a sexual assault occurs, it is nearly impossible to determine the extent to which each of these internal desires contributed to the assault. Frequently, when using this theory, only speculations can be made about why a crime occurred, as few "tools" exist to check out the accuracy of the speculations.

***Frustration-Aggression Theory*** Frustration-aggression theory asserts that frustration often provokes an aggressive response. Thus, violence is seen as a way to release the tension produced by a frustrating situation. An unemployed husband, unable to pay his bills or find a job, for example, may beat his wife. Some authorities viewed the burning and rioting in our inner cities in the 1960s as being a reaction by African Americans to the frustration of living in a society that promises equality but does not provide it.

Frustration-aggression theory provides an explanation for only violent crimes. It does not attempt to explain other kinds of criminal behavior, such as prostitution, fraud, and forgery.

***Self-Talk Theory*** Self-talk theory is a psychological approach for identifying the underlying motives for committing a crime.[24] According to this theory, the reasons for any criminal act can be determined by examining what the offender was thinking prior to and during the time the crime was being committed (see Box 2.2). A shortcoming of the theory is that, when offenders discuss what they were thinking during a crime, they often seek to slant what they reveal in a socially acceptable way.

## SOCIOLOGICAL THEORY

Sociological theories focus on societal factors that influence people to commit crimes. For ease in understanding these theories, we will examine them out of chronological order (see Table 2.3) as follows: differential association theory, anomie theory, deviant subcultures theory, societal control theory, labeling theory, and critical theory.

*Differential Association Theory* Edwin Sutherland, perhaps the best-known criminologist in contemporary sociology, advanced his famous theory of differential association in 1939. The theory asserts that criminal behavior is the result of a learning process that primarily occurs in small, intimate groups—family, neighborhood peer groups, friends, and so on. In essence, "A person becomes delinquent because of the excess of definitions favorable to violation of law over definitions unfavorable to violation of law."[25] Whether a person decides to commit a crime is based on the nature of present and past associations with significant others. People internalize the values of the surrounding culture. When the environment includes frequent contact with criminal elements and infrequent contact with noncriminal elements, a person is likely to engage in delinquent or criminal activity.

Past and present learning experiences in intimate personal groups thus define whether a person should violate laws; for those deciding to commit crimes, the learning experiences also include choices of which crimes to commit, the techniques of committing these crimes and the attitudes and rationalizations for committing these crimes. Thus, a youth whose most admired person is a member of a gang involved in burglaries or drug trafficking will seek to emulate this model, will receive instruction in committing these crimes from the gang members, and will also receive approval from the gang for successfully committing these crimes.

The theory does little to explain such crimes as arson and embezzlement, in which the offender often has no exposure to others who have committed such crimes.

*Anomie Theory* Robert Merton (1968) applied anomie theory to crime.[26] This approach views criminal behavior as resulting when an individual is prevented from achieving high-status goals in a society. Merton begins by noting that every society has both approved goals (e.g., wealth and material possessions) and approved means for attaining these goals. When certain members of society share these goals but have insufficient access to approved means for attaining them, a state of anomie results. (*Anomie* is a condition in which acceptance of the approved standards of conduct is weakened.) Unable to achieve the goals through society's legitimately defined channels, they then seek to achieve them through illegal means.

Merton asserts that higher crime rates are likely to occur among groups that are discriminated against (i.e., groups that face additional barriers to achieving the high-status goals). These groups include the poor and racial minorities. Societies with high crime rates (such as the United States) differed from those with low crime rates because, according to Merton, high crime rate societies tell all their citizens they can achieve, but in fact they block achievement for some people.

Anomie theory has difficulty explaining why white-collar crime (which is committed primarily by individuals who are seldom discriminated against) is perhaps the most common type of crime committed in this country.[27]

*Deviant Subcultures Theory* Deviant subcultures theory is another explanation for crime. This theory asserts that some groups develop their own attitudes, values, and perspectives, which support criminal activity. Walter Miller (1958), for example, argues that lower-class culture in the United States is more conducive to crime than middle-class culture.[28] He asserts that lower-class culture is organized around six values—trouble, toughness, excitement, fate, smartness (ability to con others), and autonomy—and allegiance to these values produces delinquency. Miller concludes the entire lower-class subculture is deviant in the sense that any male growing up in it will accept these values and almost certainly violate the law.

Albert Cohen (1955), advanced another subculture theory.[29] He contended that gangs develop a delinquent subculture that offers solutions to the problems of young male gang members. A gang gives them the chance to belong, to amount to something, to develop their masculinity, and to fight middle-class society. In particular, the delinquent subculture, according to Cohen, can effectively solve the status problems of working-class boys, especially those who are rejected by middle-class society. Cohen contends that the main problems of working-class boys revolve around status.

As with the previous theories, deviant subculture theories are unable to explain white-collar crime and other crimes committed by the middle and upper classes.

*Societal Control Theory* Control theories ask the question "Why do people *not* commit crimes?" Theories in this category assume that all of us would "naturally"

Box 2.3 ◆◆◆◆◆◆◆◆◆◆◆◆◆◆◆◆◆◆◆◆◆◆◆◆◆◆◆◆◆

# The Saints and the Roughnecks: A Study Showing the Effects of Labeling and the Effects of Expectations of Significant Others

In a dramatic study, William Chambliss examined factors affecting delinquency between two groups of adolescents at the same high school. One group was composed of middle- and upper-class boys (the Saints), and the other was composed of lower-class boys (the Roughnecks). The Saints were often truant from school, openly cheated on exams, harassed citizens and the police, vandalized homes, drank excessively, and drove recklessly. Teachers, school officials, and the police largely ignored their acts, as the Saints were viewed as basically "good boys." They were almost never arrested by the police, and hardly anything negative was written in their school records. These youths were regarded as harmless pranksters, were allowed to "sow their wild oats," and were expected to succeed in life. Interestingly, the success expectations appeared to be a major factor in determining their futures, as practically all of the Saints went on to college and white-collar careers.

On the other hand, the Roughnecks, who committed fewer although similar offenses, were labeled "deviants." Without having cars as the Saints did, the Roughnecks were confined to an area where they were more easily recognized and substantially more often arrested. The police and school officials expected members of the Roughnecks to fail—and they did. They were labeled "delinquents," did poorly in school, and went on to low-status jobs or to criminal careers. This study demonstrates that labeling and the expectations of significant others can have a substantial effect.

One additional factor that led to fewer arrests for the Saints was their apologetic nature whenever they were stopped by a police officer. They were polite, penitent, and pled for mercy when stopped. In contrast, there was a high level of dislike and distrust between the police and the Roughnecks, who, when stopped by police, came across as tough, hostile, and disdainful kids. Consequently, they were arrested more frequently.

*Source:* William Chambliss, "The Saints and the Roughnecks," *Society,* 2 (Nov.-Dec. 1973): 24–31.

commit crime and therefore must be constrained and controlled by society from breaking the law. Control theorists have identified three factors for preventing crime. One is the internal controls that build up through the process of socialization; a strong conscience and a sense of personal morality will prevent most people from breaking the law. A second factor is a strong attachment to small social groups (e.g., the family), which is thought to prevent individuals from breaking the law because they fear rejection and disapproval from the people who are important to them. A third factor (taken from the classical school) is that people do not break the law because they fear arrest and incarceration.

Control theories assume that basic human nature is asocial or evil. Such an assumption has never been proved. Theories that perceive humans as having an evil nature are unable to explain altruistic and other "good" deeds performed by people.

*Labeling Theory*    Labeling theorists, similar to differential association theorists, assert that criminals *learn* to break the law. Labeling theory focuses on the process of branding people as criminals and on the effects of such labeling. Contrary to control theory, this theory holds that labeling a person as a delinquent or a criminal encourages rather than discourages criminal behavior.

Charles Cooley (1902) developed a labeling theory with his "looking glass self-concept."[30] This theory argues that people develop their self-concept (sense of who and what they are) in terms of how others relate to them, as if others were a looking glass or mirror. For example, if a neighborhood identifies a young boy as being a "troublemaker" or "delinquent," neighbors are likely to relate to the youth as if he were not to be trusted. They may accuse him of delinquent acts, and they will label his semidelinquent and aggressive behavior as being "delinquent." This labeling process also results in a type of prestige and status for the boy, at least from his peers. In the absence of objective ways to gauge whether he is, in fact, a "delinquent," the youth will rely on the subjective evaluations of others. Thus, gradually, as he is related to as being a "delinquent," he begins to perceive himself in that way and to enact the delinquent role (see Box 2.3).

Labeling theory is unable to explain why some offenders stop committing crimes after being arrested and convicted or why offenders initially begin to break the law.

*Critical Theory*    This theory argues that the capitalist economic system is the root cause of our crime problem. Supporters of this theory assert capitalism fosters crime by encouraging, and even requiring, the exploitation of one group by another and by promoting the selfish quest for personal gain as if it were the inevitable goal of all human behavior[31] (readers will note the similarities of this theory to Marxist-Leninist theory, which was described earlier). Critical theory fails to explain why crime occurs in communist societies, which do not have a capitalist economic system.

## USEFULNESS OF THEORIES

These theories identify some of the reasons why crime occurs and why crime rates are higher within some groups than others. One of the most important questions in criminology is "Do these theories identify the reasons why an offender committed a specific crime (e.g., an aggravated rape)?" The answer, unfortunately, is that most theories are not very useful in identifying the causes for specific crimes. Also, they are not very useful in explaining why one individual may commit forgery, another may commit rape, and yet another may burglarize someone. Without knowing why a crime occurs, developing an effective rehabilitation approach to curb repeat offenders is extremely difficult.

Theories that attempt to explain all types of crime have a built-in limitation. Crime is a comprehensive label covering a wide range of offenses, including purse snatching, auto theft, rape, check forgery, prostitution, drunkenness, possession of narcotics, and sexual exhibition. Obviously, because the natures of these crimes vary widely, the motives or causes underlying each must vary widely. Therefore, it is unlikely that any theory can adequately explain the causes of all crimes. It may be more productive to focus on developing more limited theories that attempt to identify the causes of specific offenses (e.g., drunkenness, incest, auto theft, rape, or fraud) rather than to develop additional comprehensive theories.

Now we will take a detailed look at specific types of criminal offenses.

## Types of Crimes

We tend to think that crime is a well-defined phenomenon, and we tend to have stereotypical views about who criminals are. Actually, criminal offenses and the characteristics of lawbreakers are almost as varied as noncriminal offenses and law-abiders. Many diverse forms of behaviors are classified as crimes, with the only major common thread being a violation of a criminal statute. Because looking at all crimes is impossible, we will examine the ones that have more of an impact on society. (One should note that the following categories are not mutually exclusive. There is overlap among the categories.)

## ORGANIZED CRIME

Organized crime in the United States is a large-scale operation in which illegal activities are carried out as part of a well-designed plan developed by a large organization that is seeking to maximize its overall profit. Illegal activities that lend themselves to organized crime include illegal gambling, drug dealing, fencing (receiving and selling stolen goods), prostitution, bootlegging, and extortion (in the form of selling protection). Large-scale operations are more cost efficient than small-scale operations in certain illegal activities. For example, in drug trafficking, drugs must be smuggled into a country and distributed on a large scale, with corrupt officials being paid off to reduce the risk of arrest and prosecution.

It appears that most organized crime efforts start on a small scale, generally by developing a small organization to carry on a particular crime, such as extortion or gambling. The group then expands to control this activity within a given neighborhood or city, by absorbing or destroying the competition. Eventually, the organization expands its activities into other crimes and becomes large scale when it operates in a region or even nationwide.

A major characteristic of organized crime is that many of its activities are not predatory (unlike robbery, which takes from its victims). Instead, organized crime generally seeks to provide to the public desired goods and services that cannot be legally obtained. Such goods and services include drugs, gambling, prostitution, and loan money. For its success, organized crime relies on public demand for illegal services.

Organized crime also involves syndicates, which are large-scale, coordinated, illegal operations involving several criminal groups. The exact extent of organized crime is unknown, but authorities agree that organized crime has a large impact on the public in terms of the volume of crimes committed and in terms of the cost to taxpayers. The major organized crime efforts are gambling, drug trafficking, loan sharking, infiltrating legitimate businesses, labor racketeering, and prostitution.

*Gambling*  The extent of and profits from illegal gambling are enormous. Illegal operations include lotteries, off-track betting, illegal casinos, "numbers," and dice games. Such operations can be located practically anywhere—in a restaurant, garage, or tavern; in an apartment complex; or even on business premises.

*Drug Trafficking*  Drug trafficking is an industry that brings in billions of dollars annually in the United States. With such profits it is little wonder that organized crime is involved in the importation and distribution of drugs such as cocaine, heroin, marijuana, crack, amphetamines, and hallucinogens. A recent trend in the illicit drug trade in the United States is the growth of new organizations unassociated with older crime "families." Some of these new organizations have ethnic group identities—such as Colombian, Chinese, Vietnamese, Puerto Rican, Russian, or African American.[32]

*Loan Sharking*  This crime involves lending money at interest rates above the legal limit. Interest rates have been reported to go as high as 150 percent a week.[33] Syndicated crime can ensure repayment by the threat of violence. Major borrowers from loan sharks include gamblers who need to cover losses, drug users, and small business owners who are unable to obtain credit from legitimate sources.

*Infiltrating Legitimate Businesses*  The huge profits from illegal activities provide organized crime with the capital to enter into legitimate operations, including the entertainment industry, banking, insurance, restaurants, advertising firms, bars, the automotive industry, and real estate agencies—to name but a few.

Infiltrating legitimate businesses provides organized crime with tax covers for its members, gives them a certain respectable status in the community, and offers additional profit-making opportunities. With its cash reserves, a syndicate can temporarily lower prices in order to bankrupt competitors. It can also use strong-arm tactics to force customers to buy its goods and services.

*Labor Racketeering*  This activity involves the systematic extortion of money from labor unions and businesses. Racketeers can extort money from union members by forcing them to pay high union dues and fees in order to obtain and secure employment. Racketeers can short-change employees by paying less than union wages and by misusing the union's pension

and welfare funds. Finally, racketeers can extort money from employers by forcing them to make payoffs for union cooperation (e.g., to avoid a strike).

*Prostitution*  Because prostitutes offer a service for which some people are willing to pay high prices, prostitution offers an opportunity for profit making, and organized crime has taken advantage of it. Organized crime draws its profits from being a broker for prostitutes and customers and from providing arrest and prosecution protection for prostitutes by bribing law enforcement officials. Organized crime has also gotten involved in other sex-related forms of crime, such as the illegal distribution of pornographic films and magazines.

*The Structure of Organized Crime*  Because of the obvious emphasis on secrecy in organized crime, only limited information is available about the extent of offenses, the leaders and members of organized crime, or the nature of the internal organization.

Organized crime is thought to be primarily organized around the Mafia (also called the Cosa Nostra). The leadership of the Mafia is Italian American, with the lower ranks drawn from a variety of other ethnic groups. The Mafia largely developed during the 1920s and 1930s, when criminal groups organized to supply illegal alcohol during Prohibition. The Mafia has grown into a loose network of American regional syndicates or groups. These syndicates coordinate their efforts through a "commission," composed of the heads of the most powerful "families." At the head of each family is a "don," who has absolute authority over the family unless overruled by the commission. Each don is assisted by an underboss and a counselor. Next in the hierarchy are "lieutenants," each of whom supervises a group of "soldiers" who are involved in illegal enterprises. Contrary to public opinion, the Mafia is not an international syndicate of Sicilian lawbreakers but is rather a network of syndicates that were developed and organized within the United States. The *Godfather* books and films portray a fairly realistic picture of the structure and operations of organized crime.

The costs to society and to our economy from organized crime are enormous. Through gambling and drug traffic, the lives of many individuals and their families are traumatized. Labor racketeering and infiltration of legitimate businesses lead to higher prices for goods, lower-quality products, the forced closing of some businesses, the establishment of monopolies, the unemployment of workers, misuse of pension and welfare benefits, and higher taxes. Through corruption of public officials (a necessary component of many illegal ventures), organized crime leads to public cynicism about the honesty of public officials and the democratic process. It also leads to higher taxes and mismanagement of public funds.

In the 1980s and 1990s the FBI made immense progress in its battle against organized crime. The heads of many of the nation's Mafia families were indicted, convicted, and incarcerated.[34] In addition, thousands of organized crime members were arrested and convicted of a variety of offenses. Experts credit this breakthrough to a number of factors. The FBI now devotes a significant proportion of its work force to combating organized crime[35] and has been making increased use of electronic eavesdropping. The FBI is also working more closely with state law enforcement authorities and with Italy to curb organized crime. Recently, law enforcement agencies have been successful in getting large numbers of gang members to violate the traditional code of *omertà*—conspiracy of silence. Fearing lengthy stays in prison, where they could be vulnerable to mob ordered murders, many underworld figures are joining a witness-protection effort that provides informants with new identities (including fake biographies) and homes in a different area of the country.

Despite these efforts, no one sees an end to the mob's influence anytime soon. Many of the old leaders are being replaced by a "new breed" of leadership, who have a greater familiarity with the world of high finance and legitimate business. Organized crime is developing new marketplace scams, including counterfeiting consumer credit cards and airline tickets, bootlegging gasoline (thereby avoiding payment of federal and state gasoline taxes), and selling fraudulent tax shelters.[36] In addition, new organizations unassociated with the Mafia are emerging to import and distribute illegal drugs.[37]

## WHITE-COLLAR CRIME

Johnson and Douglas (1973) have noted that the most costly—and perhaps the most frequent—crimes are committed by "respectable" middle-class and upper-class citizens.[38] White-collar crimes are work-related offenses committed by people of high status.[39]

Offenses against customers include false advertising, stock manipulation, violations of food and drug laws, release of industrial waste products into public waterways, illegal emissions from industrial smokestacks, and price-fixing agreements. In the 1980s and early 1990s, there was extensive fraud in the savings and loan industry, which led to the collapse of the savings and loan industry. The federal government had to cover many of the losses. It cost taxpayers an estimated $500 billion, with large amounts of unprotected savings also being lost by individual investors.[40] This savings and loan scandal helps to illustrate that white-collar crimes cost taxpayers more money than all other types of crimes put together.[41]

The case of stock speculator Ivan Boesky provides a classic example of white-collar crime. Boesky personally made over $100 million in illegal insider trading (acting on information not available to the public). Brokers who possess inside information (such as knowledge of an impending corporate merger or a change in the financial condition of a company that will affect the price of its stock) are prohibited from profiting from it themselves or from selling it to others who may be able to profit from it. In 1986, Boesky admitted his illegal activities, paid the Securities and Exchange Commission $100 million in fines and illicit profits and was later convicted of conspiracy to file false documents with the federal government. Boesky's crimes precipitated a wave of additional allegations of insider trading, which have rocked the financial community in recent years. For these multimillion dollar offenses, he was imprisoned only two years.

Embezzlement is an offense in which an employee fraudulently converts some of the employer's funds for personal use through altering the employer's records. Embezzlers who take large sums of money are usually thought to be respectable citizens and trusted employees. A motivating force in the lives of embezzlers is encountering financial problems that their regular income is insufficient to handle—such as gambling debts, financial demands of a lover or spouse, and extensive medical bills for a relative.[42] Sullivan et al. (1980) note:

> Embezzlers rationalize their theft by convincing themselves that they are merely "borrowing" the money, that their employers are really crooks who deserve to lose the money, or that the employers will not miss the funds.[43]

Embezzlement occurs at all levels of business, from a clerk stealing petty cash to the president of a company stealing large investment sums. Many cases go undetected. Even when detected, few are prosecuted. An informal arrangement is often worked out in which the embezzler agrees to pay back the amount

◆◆◆◆◆◆ Box 2.4 ◆◆◆◆◆◆◆◆◆◆◆◆◆◆◆◆◆◆◆◆◆◆◆◆◆

## Dalkon Shield: A Case Example of Corporate Greed

**A**fter the Dalkon Shield, an intrauterine device, killed at least seventeen women in the United States, the manufacturer withdrew it from the domestic market. A. H. Robins, the producer, dumped about 1.7 million devices overseas after the U.S. recall. The largest quantity of Shields was purchased by the U.S. Agency for International Development at a 48 percent discount; these were packaged without being sterilized and were distributed throughout the Third World.

*Source:* P. Beirne and J. Messerschmidt, *Criminology* (New York: Harcourt Brace, 1991).

and seek employment elsewhere—a solution that is often more effective than prosecution for recovering the stolen funds. Because a scandal involving employee dishonesty threatens the employer's public image and hurts future business, employers often seek to handle the offense informally and privately.

Other examples of white-collar crime include income tax evasion, expense-account fraud, misuse of government funds by business organizations, corporate bribes, and computer-related crime (e.g., see Box 2.4). Computer-related crime involves illegal acts in which knowledge of computer technology plays a role. People who have access to a personal computer, a modem, and the correct password can transfer millions of dollars anywhere in the world.

American society, unfortunately, is generally tolerant of white-collar crime. A pickpocket who repeatedly steals small sums of money may well go to prison, whereas someone who repeatedly fails to report large earnings for income tax purposes is unlikely to face prosecution. This tolerance for white-collar crime appears to be largely due to the feeling that the victim is a large, impersonal organization (e.g., the government or a large corporation) that will be unaffected. For example, most people would never think of taking an item from a private home, yet many of these same people steal "souvenirs" (towels, sheets, ashtrays) from hotels.

White-collar crime raises serious questions about our conceptions of crime and criminals. It suggests

crime is not necessarily concentrated among the young, the poor, and racial minorities, and in our inner cities. In our society, burglars and pickpockets are severely punished and stigmatized, whereas white-collar criminals committing offenses that are far more costly are seldom prosecuted or viewed as criminals. Why? Could it be due to the power structure of our society in which the middle and upper classes define their own offenses as being "excusable," whereas offenses committed by powerless groups are viewed as being "intolerable"?

## VICTIMLESS CRIMES

With most crimes, such as embezzlement or robbery, there is an identifiable victim. However, there are several crimes in which no one suffers, except perhaps the person who willfully decides to engage in the illegal activity. Victimless crimes include prostitution, vagrancy, pornography, gambling, drunkenness, curfew violations, loitering, drug abuse, fornication, and homosexuality between consenting adults (some of these are illegal in certain jurisdictions and legal in others). Laws that make such behaviors criminal are designed to regulate people's private lives rather than to protect some citizens from others. These laws exist because powerful groups within society regard these acts as "undesirable."

The United States invests enormous resources in controlling victimless crime, as evidenced by arrest statistics that show that nearly one fourth of all arrests annually involve victimless crimes.[44] Organized crime makes much of its money from victimless crimes by providing illegal goods and services for which certain customers willingly pay. Prohibition is the classic example, as organized crime supplied illegal alcoholic beverages at inflated prices.

Because victimless crimes are considered less serious (by at least some segments of the population) and because these crimes consume excessive money and time that police and courts could devote to reducing more serious crime, there is an effort to decriminalize or repeal some of these laws. Alexander Smith and Harriet Pollack (1971) state:

> For every murderer arrested and prosecuted, literally dozens of gamblers, prostitutes, . . . and derelicts crowd our courts' dockets. If we took the numbers runners, the kids smoking pot, and winos out of the criminal justice system, we would substantially reduce the burden on the courts and the police. . . . Moral laws that do not reflect contemporary mores or that

cannot be enforced should be removed from the penal code through legislative action because, at best, they undermine respect for the law.[45]

Criminal penalties for such crimes may also do more harm than good. For example, treating someone arrested for homosexual activity as a hardened criminal may well damage the person's self concept and status in the community. Criminal penalties may also force the offenders to form a subculture in order to continue their illegal activity with greater safety. Such subcultures, for example with homosexuals and drug users, serve to separate them even further from the rest of society.

## SEX OFFENSES

There are a number of sex offenses, with forcible rape, prostitution, soliciting, statutory rape, fornication, sodomy, homosexuality, adultery, and incest being among the most common.

In most states, only males are legally liable for rape by force. Forcible rape is a highly under-reported crime, with less than one quarter of the victims reporting the rape to the police.[46] Why? It is estimated that in about half of the cases the attacker is a friend or acquaintance of the victim, and therefore some victims think police action will only create more interpersonal problems. Many victims are also reluctant to report the offense because they believe (perhaps realistically) they have nothing to gain and more to lose by making a report, including social humiliation, interrogation by sometimes unsympathetic law enforcement officials, and humiliating public testimony in court about the offense. A danger to society of under-reporting of rape is that the rapist is more apt to seek out other victims because he is less likely to fear apprehension.

Statutory rape involves sexual contact between a male who is of a legally responsible age (usually eighteen years) and a female who is a willing participant but is below the legal age of consent (sixteen years in some states and eighteen years in others). In most states, females are not defined as being liable for committing statutory rape. In some states, a charge of statutory rape can be made on the basis of sexual contact other than sexual intercourse, such as oral-genital contact.

There is considerable variation in homosexuality laws among states. Most states define male homosexual acts between consenting adults as being illegal, although some states have now legalized such relations. Some states that prohibit male homosexuality between consenting adults do not prohibit such acts between adult females (homosexuality is further discussed in Chapter 5).

Increased attention is now being given to sexual abuse of children. Such abuse includes sexual intercourse (genital or anal), masturbation, oral-genital contact, fondling, and exposure. An unambiguous definition of sexual abuse is not available. Sexual intercourse with children is definitely abuse, but other forms of contact are more difficult to judge as being abusive. At some point, hugging, kissing, and fondling become inappropriate. The abusers may include parents, older siblings, extended relatives, friends, acquaintances, or strangers. (Sexual abuse is discussed in greater length in Chapter 5.)

Certain sex offenses (such as incest, rape, and homosexual contact with a minor) incite considerable repugnance among the general public, which results in harsh punishments being assigned to the offender. Unfortunately, less attention is given to helping the victims cope with their exploitation or to rehabilitate the offenders.

## HOMICIDE AND ASSAULT

Criminal homicide involves the unlawful killing of one person by another. Criminal assault is the unlawful application of physical force on another person. Most homicides are unintended outcomes of physical assaults. People get into physical fights because one (or both) is incensed about the other's actions and so retaliates. Initial actions may include ridicule, flirting with the other's spouse or lover, or anger over failure to pay a debt. Getting into a fight is often an attempt by one or both to save face when challenged or degraded. Homicides are often "crimes of passion," occurring during a violent argument or other highly charged emotional situation.

Although most homicides are unintended, some are carefully planned and premeditated, including most gangland killings, killings to obtain an inheritance, and mercy killings. Some homicides are also associated with robberies, in which the robbery victim, the robber, or a law enforcement official is shot.

Contrary to public stereotypes, the vast majority of murders occur between relatives, friends, and acquaintances (e.g., see Box 2.5). People statistically have more to fear in terms of assaults and homicides from people they know than from strangers.[47]

## Murder and the Fall
## of an American Hero

Orenthal James (O. J.) Simpson was born and raised on Connecticut Street in Potrero Hill, a poor neighborhood in San Francisco, which O. J. once described as "your average black ghetto." His father, Jimmy, a custodian and cook, left home when O. J. was five. His mother, Eunice, worked long hours as a hospital orderly to support her four children. As a youth, O. J. joined gangs, picked fights, stole hubcaps, shot craps, and skipped school. After a gang fight at age fifteen landed O. J. briefly in jail, Lefty Gordon, the supervisor of the local recreational center, arranged for Willie Mays (one of baseball's greatest players) to meet with O. J. The meeting left a lasting impression on O. J., who stated, "He made me realize that we all have it in ourselves to be heroes."

O. J. went to work on football. He did not have the grades for a four-year school, so he attended City College of San Francisco, where he set records as a running back. At the start of his junior year, he transferred to the University of Southern California. O. J. led USC to two Rose Bowls, and in his senior year he won the Heisman Trophy, given annually to the best player in college football.

After his triumph at USC, he moved into the pro ranks. In 1973, while playing halfback for the Buffalo Bills, he broke the single-season rushing record held by Jim Brown.

The world of advertising in the 1970s was searching for a "breakthrough black man" who had the right look, the right smile, and the right nickname. O. J. was it. He had a certain magnetic image that brought him several lucrative advertising contracts.

Even before his retirement from pro football after eleven seasons, O. J. started acting in movies and on TV. He also became a sportscaster for NBC and for ABC.

But apparently there was another side to O. J. Simpson. He met Nicole Brown, a very attractive teenager. Shortly after she turned nineteen, they began living together. Eventually they married, had two children, and lived a glamorous life in their West Los Angeles mansion. However, at least eight times police were called to their home to settle domestic fights. In 1989, after one particularly brutal fight, witnesses said O. J. repeatedly screamed, "I'll kill you!" The Los Angeles city attorney filed charges against Simpson for wife beating, and he pleaded no contest.

In 1992, Nicole and O. J. finally divorced but they continued to see each other. O. J. hoped to reconcile. In the spring of 1994, friends say Nicole shattered O. J.'s dreams by telling him she had decided not to reconcile. During the evening of June 12, 1994, Nicole Simpson was brutally stabbed to death outside her condominium. Also brutally stabbed to death was Ronald Goldman, a friend who reportedly was returning the sunglasses Nicole's mother had left in a restaurant earlier in the evening.

A few days later O. J. was arrested and charged with these murders. In 1995, a jury in a criminal trial proceeding found O. J. innocent of these two murders. In 1996, a jury in a civil court proceeding found O. J. guilty of committing these two murders, and O. J. was ordered to pay over $30 million in damages to the families of Nicole Brown and Ronald Goldman.

---

Because of the overt physical damage from assault and homicide, these crimes are among the most feared. The police have a higher success rate (around 70 percent) in making arrests in homicide cases than with any other crime—partly because they devote extensive attention to murders and partly because the questioning of the friends, neighbors, and relatives usually identifies the killer.[48] Alcohol is frequently an important contributing factor in murder and assaults, as slightly over half of all those in prison for violent crimes report they were under the influence of alcohol or other drugs at the time of their offense.[49]

## THEFT

This category of crimes involves the illegal taking of another's property without the person's consent. Offenses under this category range from pickpocketing and burglary to sophisticated forms involving multimillion-dollar swindles. Types of thieves range from grocery store clerks who take small amounts of food to people who concoct highly professional confidence schemes to swindle someone out of thousands of dollars.

The most successful thieves have been labeled professional thieves by the noted criminologist Edwin Sutherland (1937).[50] Professional thieves become involved in confidence games, forgery, expert safe cracking, counterfeiting, extortion (e.g., blackmailing others who are engaging in illegal acts), and organized shoplifting. Most such crimes require that professional thieves appear personable and trustworthy and that they be good actors to convince others they are somebody who they are not. Professional thieves use sophisticated, nonviolent techniques. Their crimes are carefully planned, and they tend to steal as a regular business. They define themselves as thieves, have a value system supportive of their career, and tend to be respected by their colleagues and by law enforcement officials. Because of their cunning and skill, they seldom are arrested. They often justify their activities by claiming that they are simply capitalizing on the fact that all people are dishonest and would probably also be full-time thieves if they had sufficient skills.

Semiprofessional thieves become involved in armed robberies, burglaries, holdups, and larcenies that do not involve much detailed planning. Some semiprofessional thieves work alone, holding up service stations, convenience stores, liquor stores, and the like. Semiprofessional thieves often wind up spending substantial portions of their lives in prison because they commit the types of crimes that are harshly punished by courts. They also tend to be repeat offenders for similar crimes. They often define themselves as products and victims of a corrupt and unjust system, with many starting their careers in low income and ghetto neighborhoods. They adjust fairly well in prison, as other inmates often have similar backgrounds, lifestyles, and views on life. As a group they are apt to return to committing crimes upon their release from prison.[51]

Amateur thieves are individuals who steal infrequently. In contrast to professional and semiprofessional thieves, these individuals generally define themselves as respectable, law-abiding citizens. Their criminal acts tend to be crude and unsophisticated, with some offenders being juveniles. Examples of offenses by this group include stealing from employers, shoplifting, stealing an unguarded bicycle, taking an auto for a joy ride, taking soda from a truck, and breaking into a home to take CDs or beer. Violations of property laws in this group often are opportunistic, unplanned, and amateurish. Nevertheless, businesses and industries suffer substantial losses from amateur thieves who are either employees or customers.

## JUVENILE DELINQUENCY

*Crime among Youth* According to official crime statistics, 19 percent of all people arrested are under the age of eighteen.[52] A fair number of these arrests are for crimes that have already been discussed—thefts, robberies, assaults, and rapes. Yet, one should note that one reason juveniles have such a high arrest rate is that a majority of the arrests are for status offenses—that is, acts that are defined as illegal if committed by juveniles, but not for adults. Status offenses include being truant, having sexual relations, running away from home, being ungovernable, violating curfew, and being beyond the control of parents.

Police arrests of lower-class juveniles are far higher than for middle- and upper-class juveniles.[53] The higher arrest rate for lower-class juveniles is partly due to the fact that police are more inclined to arrest lower-class juveniles than middle- and upper-class juveniles.[54] After reviewing a number of studies on the relationships between delinquency and poverty, Kornblum and Julian (1989) conclude these two variables are interrelated in a complex manner. Middle and upper-class juveniles tend to commit nuisance crimes at rates comparable to lower-class youths, but lower-class youths commit higher rates of serious crimes such as homicide.[55]

*Gangs* Juvenile gangs have existed for many decades in the United States and in other countries. In recent years, there have been increases in the United States in the number of gangs, the number of youths belonging to gangs, gang youth drug involvement, and gang violence. Violent, delinquent urban gang activity has become a major social problem in the United States. The scientific knowledge base about delinquent gangs is very limited. Longres (1990) notes:

> No consensus exists for a definition of a youth gang. In addition, no agreed upon recording system exists, and no data on gang offenses are collected in systematic ways by disinterested agencies. Furthermore, attempts to eradicate gangs through social service and criminal justice programs have met with little success.[56]

The inadequacy of the knowledge base about delinquent gangs is a major obstacle to developing effective intervention strategies with this population. There have been numerous definitions of gangs, but no consensus exists on their distinguishing characteristics.[57] The lack of consensus among investigators is indicated by the numerous and diverse categories that have been used by different investigators to classify gangs: corner group, social club, conflict group, pathological group, athletic club, industrial association, predatory organization, drug addict group, racket organization, fighting-focused group, defensive group, unconventional group, criminal organization, turf group, heavy metal group, punk rock group, satanic organization, skinhead, ethnic or racial group, motorcycle club, and scavenger group.[58]

An illustration of a categorization is provided by Morales (1989), who classified youth gangs into four types: criminal, conflict, retreatist, and cult/occult.[59]

*Criminal gangs* have as a primary goal material gain through criminal activities, including theft of property from people or premises, extortion, fencing, and drug trafficking (especially of rock cocaine).

*Conflict gangs* are turf oriented. They engage in violent conflict with individuals of rival groups that invade their neighborhood or commit acts that they consider degrading or insulting. Respect is highly valued and defended. Latino gangs often fall into this category. Sweeney (1980) notes that the Code of the Barrio mandates that gang members watch out for their neighborhood and be willing to die for it.[60]

*Retreatist gangs* focus on getting "high" or "loaded" on alcohol, cocaine, marijuana, heroin, or other drugs. Individuals tend to join this type of gang in order to secure continued access to drugs. In contrast to criminal gangs that become involved with drugs for financial profit, retreatist gangs become involved with drugs for consumption.

*Cult/occult gangs* engage in devil or evil worship. *Cult* refers to systematic worshiping of evil or the Devil; *occult* implies keeping something secret or hidden, or a belief in supernatural or mysterious powers. Some occult groups place extensive emphasis on sexuality and violence, believing that, by sexually violating an innocent child or virgin, they have defiled Christianity. Not all cult/occult gangs are involved in criminal activity. Unlike the other three gang types, which are composed primarily of juveniles, the majority of occult groups are composed of adults.

Contradictions abound in conceptualizing delinquent gangs. Gangs are believed to be composed largely of ethnically homogeneous adolescents (African American, Latino, and Asian youths); yet some gangs composed of white youths exist. Most gang members are believed to be between the ages of twelve and eighteen, yet, recent evidence indicates some gangs include and may be controlled by adults.[61] Gangs are believed to be composed of males; yet, some gangs have female members, and a few gangs consist exclusively of females.[62] Gangs are believed to be primarily involved in drug trafficking; yet, some delinquent gangs have other illegal foci, such as burglary, robbery, larceny, or illegal drug consumption. Gang activity is thought to be primarily located in large, inner-city, urban areas; yet, gang activity is flourishing in many smaller cities and in some suburbs.[63]

At the present time there is inadequate statistical data on the number of gangs, the number and characteristics of members, and their criminal activities. Longres notes:

> Statistics on gangs and their criminal behavior are not obtained easily. Many cities have gang control units that collect data but do not report them in any systematic way. Even when such data are obtained, they are difficult to interpret because no uniform definition of gang offenses exists, no recording system has been in place long enough to discern trends, and arrest data from police departments may reflect bias. Additionally, no uniform definition of a gang-related offense exists across police jurisdictions even within the same state, city, or county.[64]

Spergel (1995) presents documentation that gangs primarily develop in those local communities that are often socially disorganized, impoverished, or both.[65] Gang members typically come from families where the parents lack effective parenting skills, where the school systems give little attention to students who are falling behind in their studies, where youths are exposed to adult crime groups, and where youths feel there is practically no opportunity to succeed through the legitimate avenues of education and a good paying job. Spergel asserts that youths join gangs for many reasons—security, power, money, status, excitement, and new experiences—particularly under conditions of social deprivation or community inability. In essence, he presents a community-disorganization approach to understanding the attraction of joining a gang.

In a very real sense, a delinquent gang is created because the needs of youths are not being met by the family, neighborhood, or traditional community institutions (such as the schools, police, and recreational and religious institutions). Some useful changes suggested by Spergel are a reduced access to handguns; improved educational resources; access to recreation, job training, jobs, family counseling, and drug rehabilitation; and mobilization of community groups and organizations to restrain gang violence (such as neighborhood watch groups). Social policy changes are also needed at state and national levels in order to funnel more resources to urban centers. Funds are needed to improve the quality of life for city residents, including youths, so that the needs of youths are met in ways other than through gang involvement.[66]

## The Criminal Justice System

The criminal justice system is composed of the police, the courts, and the correctional system. This system is perceived by many Americans as being cumbersome, ineffective, irrational, and unjust because it appears "crime does pay." Some segments of the population are suspicious of the police and fear the police may abuse their powers. Other segments, particularly among the middle and upper classes, believe the police are unduly hampered in their work by cumbersome arrest and interrogation procedures that are designed to protect the civil rights of suspected offenders.

Courts are sharply criticized for their long delays in bringing cases to conclusion and for their sentencing procedures. Many Americans believe that courts are not harsh enough on offenders. Courts are also criticized for (a) varying widely in the harshness of sentences assigned for apparently similar offenses, and (b) giving harsher sentences to "ordinary offenders" but light fines to white collar offenders.

Prisons, too, have been sharply criticized, as they are viewed as failing to prevent those who are incarcerated from committing additional crimes after their release. The rate of recidivism (i.e., a convicted person's return to crime) is alarmingly high. Over half of those released from prison later return after being convicted of committing another crime.[67] Far from rehabilitating offenders, prisons are accused of being schools for crime.

In all societies, criminal justice systems face a conflict between two goals: crime control and due process. The crime control goal involves the need to curb crime and protect society from lawbreakers. It includes an emphasis on speedy arrest and punishment for those who commit crimes. The due process goal involves the need to protect and preserve the rights and liberties of individuals. Some societies are police states that use strong-arm tactics to control their citizens and display little concern for individual rights. At the other extreme are societies in which individuals run wild in breaking the law, with the government having neither the power nor the respect of its citizens in upholding the law. American society seeks to strike a balance between the conflicting goals of crime control and due process. There is a constant struggle between these goals. At times the same individual may seek to have one goal emphasized in one situation but the conflicting goal emphasized in a different setting. For example, a home owner may want speedy justice when his or her home is burglarized (or when a daughter is raped) but may seek to use all the due process protections when accused of income tax evasion.

We will now take a closer look at each of these three components of the criminal justice system.

## THE POLICE

Police officers are the gatekeepers for the criminal justice system. Whom they arrest determines whom the courts and corrections will have to deal with. As we have seen, nearly everyone violates, now and then, laws that have been enacted. Police cannot arrest everyone, as the jails, courts, and prisons would be overloaded and our society would probably collapse. Therefore, police have considerable discretion in which laws they will vigorously seek to enforce and which types of offenders they will seek to arrest. For example, police are more apt to arrest lower-income youths as compared to middle-income youths.

One should note that only a small part of a police department's effort is directly focused on arresting offenders. Police officers classify as "criminal" only about 10 to 20 percent of the calls and incidents they handle on a given day.[68]

David Peterson has noted that the role of a police officer is usually best conceptualized as that of a "peace officer" or even "social worker," rather than as a "law enforcement officer":

> A prominent theme in the literature dealing with the work behavior of the police stresses that the role of the uniformed patrol officer is not a strict legalistic one. The patrol officer is routinely involved in tasks that have little relation to police work in terms of controlling crime. His activities on the beat are often centered as much on assisting citizens as on offenses; he is frequently called upon to perform a "supportive" function as well as an enforcement function. Existing research on the uniformed police officer in field situations indicates that more than half his time is spent as an amateur social worker assisting people in various

ways. Moreover, several officers have suggested that the role of the uniformed patrol officer is not sharply defined and that the mixture of enforcement and service functions creates conflict and uncertainties for individual officers.[69]

Police have such service functions as giving first aid to injured people, rescuing trapped animals, and directing traffic. When police do perform law enforcement functions, they squarely face trying to achieve the proper balance between the crime control model and the due process model. There is considerable pressure to swiftly apprehend certain lawbreakers—murderers, rapists, and arsonists. Yet they are expected to perform according to the due process model so that the legal rights of those arrested are not violated. James Coleman and Donald Cressey note: "Police officers operate more like diplomats than like soldiers engaged in a war on crime."[70]

In many areas of the nation police do not have sufficient resources to do their job effectively. There is also considerable hostility toward police officers. Part of this hostility may result from the fact that everyone commits an occasional crime, and perhaps most are suspicious of police officers because they fear possible apprehension. In addition, some people (particularly the poor and minority group members) are harassed by being picked up for crimes they clearly have not committed, and by being subjected to long "third degree" interrogations. There is also hostility toward the police because of well-publicized incidents of police corruption (e.g., taking bribes), particularly in larger cities.

## THE COURTS

*How the Courts Work*   Criminal justice in the United States is an adversary system. A person is presumed innocent until proven guilty. It is an adversary system in the sense that the prosecuting attorney first presents the state's evidence against a defendant, and the defendant then has an opportunity to refute the charges with the assistance of a defense attorney. There are four key positions in a court: the prosecuting attorney, the defense attorney, the judge, and the jury.

One should note that over 90 percent of the convictions for offenses in the United States, contrary to public opinion, are not obtained in court but through plea bargaining between the prosecuting attorney and the defendant, who is often represented by a defense attorney in the plea-bargaining process.[71] For a plea

of guilty, suspects may receive more lenient sentences, have certain charges dropped, or have the charge reduced to a lesser offense. Plea bargaining is not legally binding in court, but the judge usually goes along with the arrangement. Plea bargaining is highly controversial. It does save taxpayers considerable expense, as court trials are costly. But it may in some cases circumvent due process protections because an innocent person charged with serious offenses may be pressured into pleading guilty to reduced charges.

Prosecuting attorneys have considerable discretionary authority in choosing whether to seek a conviction for those arrested by the police and in choosing how vigorously they will seek to prosecute a defendant. Prosecuting attorneys are either elected or appointed to office and are therefore political figures who must periodically seek reelection or reappointment. As such, they seek to vigorously prosecute those cases they perceive the community is most concerned about. Prosecuting attorneys usually set a focus for police departments about which law violations to enforce, as they decide which arrested people and which law violations will be further processed by the criminal justice system.

Defense attorneys are supposed to represent their clients' interests before the criminal justice system. Impoverished people are provided, at the state's expense, a court-appointed attorney. The skills and competence of the defense attorney are major factors in determining whether a defendant will be found innocent or guilty if there is a trial. The wealthy are able to retain more skilled attorneys and can afford additional resources (such as a private investigator) that help prepare a better defense.

The poor have at times been shortchanged by court-appointed defense attorneys, as such attorneys tend to be young, inexperienced practitioners or less competent, older people who resort to this type of practice in order to survive professionally. Because these defense attorneys depend on the good opinion of their legal colleagues (including judges and prosecuting attorneys) to stay in practice, the client's best interest sometimes receives secondary priority to an emphasis on the attorney's retaining respect from colleagues.[72]

If a prosecuting attorney decides to prosecute a person charged with a minor offense, the case is generally presented before a lower-court judge, without a jury. For a serious offense the defendant first receives a preliminary hearing, which is solely for the benefit of the suspect. At the hearing the prosecuting attorney presents evidence against the suspect, and the judge decides whether the evidence is sufficient to warrant further legal proceedings. If the evidence is insufficient the suspect is discharged. If the evidence is judged sufficient the accused is held over to await a court trial in the future. (Often the held-over cases are decided by plea bargaining before they go to trial.)

Under the bail system, accused people are allowed to deposit money or credit with the court to obtain a release from jail while awaiting the court trial. The amount of bail is set by the court and gives assurance that the suspect will appear for trial. The amount of bail varies according to the offense and partially on the judge's attitudes toward the suspect. The bail system severely discriminates against the poor. Poor people, unable to raise enough money, stay in jail while awaiting trial—which may take several months. Those unable to post bail have less opportunity to prepare a good defense because they are locked up. Also, their case is further prejudiced when they do appear in court because they are brought into the courtroom in handcuffs and have less opportunity to be properly groomed for their court appearance. Being locked up before the court trial is a form of punishment that runs counter to the notion that the suspect is innocent (and should be treated as such) until proved guilty. In some cases a suspect spends more time in jail awaiting trial than she or he spends in jail if found guilty.

After defendants have been found guilty or have pleaded guilty, they return to the courtroom for sentencing. Judges usually have fairly wide discretion in assigning sentences; for example, they can place one murderer on probation, commit another to prison, and, in those states having capital punishment, they can order the execution of a third. Judges base their sentences on such factors as the seriousness of the crime, the motives for the crime, the background of the offender, and their attitudes toward the offender.

Judges vary greatly in the extent to which they send convicted offenders to prison, use probation, or assign fines. Concern about disparities in sentences has grown in recent years. Coleman and Cressey note:

> Judges and other sentencing authorities are on the spot. They are supposed to give equal punishments, no matter what the social status of the defendants involved. Yet they are supposed to give individual punishments because the circumstances of each crime and the motivations of each criminal are always different and a just punishment for one burglar or car thief may be completely inappropriate for another. . . . As judges try to satisfy these conflicting demands, they are bound

to be denounced as unfair. The judge's task, like the police officer's task, is to walk a thin line between the crime control model and the due process model, balancing demands for repressing crime against demands for human rights and freedom.[73]

*Juvenile Courts*  The first juvenile court was established in Cook County, Illinois, in 1899. The philosophy of the juvenile court is that it should act in the best interests of the child, as parents should act. In essence, juvenile courts have a treatment orientation. In adult criminal proceedings, the focus is on charging the defendant with a specific crime, on holding a public trial to determine whether the defendant is guilty as charged, and on sentencing the defendant if he or she is found to be guilty. In contrast, the focus in juvenile courts is on the current psychological, physical, emotional, and educational needs of children, as opposed to punishment for their past misdeeds. Reform or treatment of the child is the goal, even though the child or his or her family may not necessarily agree that the court's decision is in the child's best interests.

Of course, not all juvenile court judges live up to these principles. In practice, some juvenile judges focus more on punishing than on treating juvenile offenders. There is also a danger that court appearances by children can have adverse labeling effects. A Supreme Court decision in the famous *Gault* case of May 15, 1967, restored to juveniles procedural safeguards that had been ignored—including notification of charges, protection against self-incrimination, confrontation, and cross-examination.[74] Because of the adverse labeling effects of court appearances, especially with the increased formality of court procedures, there is currently considerable effort to have juvenile probation officers provide informal supervision for youths who commit "minor" violations. With informal supervision, youthful offenders receive counseling and guidance and do not appear in court.

## CORRECTIONAL SYSTEMS

Current correctional systems in America and throughout the world contain conflicting objectives. Some components are punishment-oriented, whereas others are treatment-oriented. A manifestation of this confusion is the existence, side by side, of correctional programs intended primarily for deterrence and retribution and other programs designed to reform offenders. Only rarely do punitive and treatment

*These pillories furnish amusement for visitors (in Colonial Williamsburg, Virginia) who delight in having photos snapped while they are in the pillory. The jailor is shown here locking up one of the visitors.*

components complement each other. Generally, the two components, when combined, result in a system that is ineffective and inefficient in curbing criminal activity. In the past two decades, correctional systems have moved toward using a more punitive approach.

**The Punitive Approach**   Throughout history various approaches have been used to punish offenders. These methods can be summarized as physical torture, social humiliation, financial penalties, exile, the death penalty, and imprisonment.

*Physical Torture.*   Most societies have at one time or another used this method. Specific examples of corporal (bodily) punishment have included stocks, whipping, flogging, branding, hard labor, confinement in irons and cages, arm twisting, and mutilation of body parts. Corporal punishment was particularly popular during the medieval period. Practically no type of corporal punishment is now assigned by European or U.S. courts.

*Social Humiliation.*   Actions to reduce the social status of an offender are another method of punishment. This approach flourished in the sixteenth and seventeenth centuries, and remnants exist today. Specific techniques included some that also included corporal punishment: the stocks, the pillory, the ducking stool, branding, and the brank. (The brank was a small cage that was placed over the offender's head. The brank had a bar that was inserted into the mouth of the offender to prevent him or her from talking; occasionally this bar had spikes in it.) Some of these methods were temporary—for example, the stocks—whereas others had a permanent effect on the offender—for example, branding. Although one of the objectives of the permanent methods was to deter future crime by publicly humiliating offenders, they frequently had the opposite effect, as they overtly labeled the offender, thereby making it difficult for him or her to secure employment and earn a living in a law-abiding manner.

Deprivation of civil rights is another approach that has been used for centuries to humiliate the convicted offender socially. The principal rights that are taken away from convicted felons by most states in this country are: (a) the right to vote while in prison or while on probation or parole; (b) the right to hold public office; (c) the right to practice certain professions, for example, the right to practice law; and (d) the right to own or possess any firearms.

*Financial Penalties.*   The use of fines in criminal law became widespread in this country about a century ago and is now by far the most frequent court approach to reacting to offenders. More than 75 percent of all penalties imposed at present are fines.[75] The advantages of a fine are: (a) it provides revenue to the state; (b) it costs the state almost nothing to administer, especially in comparison to the cost of imprisonment; (c) the amount of the fine can easily be adjusted to the enormity of the offense, to the reaction of the public, and to the wealth and character of the offender; (d) it inflicts a material type of suffering; and (e) it can easily be paid back if the alleged offender is later found innocent. A serious disadvantage is that it is highly discriminatory toward the poor because they have less ability to pay. Sweden has found a way to curb this discrimination by the creation of day fines in which the offender pays the equivalent of the amount earned in a specified number of days of work rather than a flat amount as a fine.

Courts are also increasingly requiring, in their sentencing decisions, that the offender make restitution payments to the victim that are in line with the amount of injury. This kind of reaction to crime is more treatment oriented, as it attempts to give the offender an opportunity to "make good." Restitution is, of course, also advantageous to the victim. Restitution and reparation are used more frequently for minor offenses. Generally, the offender is placed on probation, with restitution being a condition of probation. Some of the work of probation departments is now concerned with being a collection agency to obtain restitution payments from probationers.

*Exile.* Almost all societies have exiled some offenders, but deportation on a large scale has been used only since about the sixteenth century. Most societies have at times exiled political criminals. The United States has been deporting alien criminals for decades. In addition, many counties and municipalities in the United States give some people accused or convicted of a crime a set number of hours to "get out and stay out" of their jurisdiction.

*Death Penalty.* The extent to which the death penalty has been used has varied considerably in different societies. The methods used to execute offenders have also varied widely and have included hanging, electrocuting, shooting, burning, gassing, drowning, boiling in oil, breaking at the wheel, stoning, poisoning, piercing with a sharp stake or sword, beheading with a guillotine, or enclosing in an iron coffin. In essence, almost every lethal method has at one time or another been used by some society.

The use of the death penalty in America has had an unusual history. In the United States, "witches" in a few communities were burned at the stake in colonial days. While the West was being developed, those who stole a horse or committed certain other crimes could be shot or hanged (sometimes by a lynch mob or a "kangaroo court"). From the time of the Civil War until the recent past, African Americans in the

South who were thought to have committed a serious crime against whites (e.g., rape) were sometimes lynched. Gas chambers, firing squads, lethal injections, hangings, and electric chairs are the current methods of execution used in the United States.

From 1967 to 1977, the death penalty was not used in this country, partly due to U.S. Supreme Court decisions that the penalty was unconstitutional. In October 1976, the Supreme Court changed its position on this issue and ruled that states may execute murderers under certain guidelines. On January 17, 1977, Gary Gilmore was the first person in a decade to be executed. The sensational case attracted national attention. Gilmore was convicted of ruthlessly killing several people. Since 1977, the number of offenders executed annually in the United States has gradually been increasing.[76] The continued use of the death penalty remains a controversial national issue.

The primary argument for using the death penalty for certain crimes is that it is assumed it will have a deterrent effect. This assumption is questionable, as statistics generally do *not* show that when a country adopts a death penalty, there is a corresponding decrease in serious crime rates.[77] Also, there is no clear-cut evidence that when a country discontinues use of the death penalty, there will be an increase in serious crimes.[78] Additional arguments for use of the death penalty are (a) some crimes (such as brutal, premeditated murder) are so abominable that the offender deserves the ultimate punishment, and (b) it is less expensive to society to put hardened criminals to death than to incarcerate them for life. (In reality, executing someone has been more expensive than lifetime incarceration as huge amounts of legal expenses have been incurred due to the appeals that precede an execution.)

Arguments against use of the death penalty are: (a) it constitutes cruel and unusual punishment, as it is the ultimate punishment; (b) if the convicted person is later found innocent, the penalty is irreparable; (c) the "eye for an eye" approach is inconsistent with civilized, humanitarian ideals; (d) the "right to life" is a basic right that should not be infringed on; and (e) the death penalty appears to be assigned in a discriminatory manner, as African Americans and Hispanics are proportionately much more likely to be sentenced to death.

*Imprisonment.* The penal system currently has enormous importance for our society. A large number of people are incarcerated each year. Nationally, the recidivism rate (return to prison some time after release) is estimated to be over 50 percent, which raises questions about its effectiveness in curbing future criminal activity.[79] Since 1970, there have been several large-scale prison revolts (e.g., Attica Prison, New York, in 1971, and New Mexico State Penitentiary in 1980) that have raised the concern of the general public.

Conditions within prisons before the twentieth century were deplorable. Frequently, the young were placed with hardened criminals, and women were not separated from men. Only custodial care was provided, frequently with "hard-labor" work projects. There were a number of prison reform studies from 1700 to 1850 that criticized prison security guards of being intoxicated and personally lewd, having sexual orgies, and gambling. Some prisons confined inmates in solitary confinement for months at a time, and corporal punishment was also frequently used.

Since 1800, prisons have become more specialized. Jails are used for the shorter sentences and for those awaiting trial. Separate institutions have been built for confining the young, for women, and for those labeled as criminally insane. Prisons also have various degrees of security: maximum, medium, and minimum. Special programs have been developed to meet individual needs of inmates: for example, alcohol and drug abuse programs, educational and vocational training, medical and dental programs, and recreational programs.

Prisons are still distasteful and sometimes physically dangerous institutions to be confined in. There is now the danger of HIV being transmitted through sexual assaults in prison. However, in the past one hundred years the horrors of prison life have been somewhat reduced. In addition to rehabilitative programs, improvements have been made in safeguarding civil rights of inmates, in diet, in abandoning long-term solitary confinement, in ventilation, in cleanliness, in physical facilities, in methods of discipline, in promoting contact between inmates and the outside world, in providing libraries, and in reducing the monotony of prison life. Gone are such humiliating approaches as shaving the head, chaining inmates, issuing striped clothing, and using the ball and chain. Also, corporal punishment methods, such as whipping, are no longer officially approved. The most severe punishment that remains for many prisoners is that they live in constant fear of being victimized by their fellow prisoners.

Since 1975, there has been a dramatic increase in the number of people that have been sentenced to prison by courts.[80] Part of this increase is due to increased drug-related convictions, including drug trafficking convictions. Another reason is that our society has become more conservative and is therefore demanding a more punitive approach (imprisonment) to handling convicted offenders. As a result of the increased use of imprisonment, many prisons are currently overcrowded. An alternative to imprisonment that is being used for less serious criminal offenders is home confinement with the use of electronic surveillance monitors to assure that the convicted offenders remain at home.

The first American institution built specifically for housing juvenile offenders was opened in New York City in 1825. There are now over three hundred state and local training schools. From the outset it was contended that such institutions were not prisons, but schools to educate and reform the young. However, until the recent past most were best described as prisons in terms of functions, methods of discipline, and daily routine. Even today a few are still prison oriented. One of the most significant developments in juvenile institutions has been the cottage-type architecture, which provides a more homelike setting. The first were established in Massachusetts and Ohio in 1858. Such settings facilitate, but do not necessarily assure, a treatment orientation.

*Objectives of Incarceration.* The conflict between the punitive approach and the treatment approach to corrections is strikingly clear in our penal system. Until a few centuries ago the purpose of incarceration was to punish an offender. From 1900 to 1970, there was an increased emphasis on treatment and a shift away from punishment. There were several reasons for this shift. Practically all prisoners return to society, and it was concluded that punitive approaches alone do not produce the desired reformation. Locking a person in an artificial environment, without providing rehabilitative programs, does not sufficiently prepare that person to be a productive citizen on his or her return. Moreover, in this era of accountability, the 50 percent recidivism rate is unacceptable, especially because the annual cost of incarceration per inmate is more than $30,000.[81]

In the 1980s and 1990s the pendulum, however, has swung back to using more of a punitive approach in our prison system. Increased concerns about community protection and effects of crime on victims, and an increased emphasis on wanting criminals to pay for their crimes have been factors that have led to a shift away from the treatment approach.

The specific objectives for imprisonment are: (a) to reform offenders so they will no longer commit crimes; (b) to incapacitate criminals so they cannot commit crimes for a period of time, thereby protecting society; (c) to achieve retribution for the victim and, to some extent, for the state; and (d) to serve as a warning to the general public, thereby having a deterrent effect. A major problem with these objectives is that some components conflict with others. The infliction of pain and suffering is aimed at meeting the retribution and deterrence objectives, but most punitive approaches are counterproductive in terms of having reformative value.

There are also some dangers with using imprisonment. Association with other offenders may result in inmates learning additional law-breaking techniques. Moreover, incarceration may label the offender as a "lawbreaker." According to labeling theory, if convicted offenders are related to as "dangerous, second-class citizens who are law violators," they may begin to perceive themselves as being "law violating."[82] Once they perceive themselves as being law violators, labeling theory asserts they will then play that role upon their release.

In addition, as Sutherland and Cressey note, "Hatred of the criminal by society results in hatred of society by the criminal."[83] Relating to criminals as being dangerous, segregating them, and making them keep their distance (both while they are incarcerated and following their release) may force them into a career of criminal activity.

A third danger of long-term imprisonment is "institutionalization." Some prisoners, especially those who have had problems in adjusting to outside society, may eventually prefer prison life over outside society. After several years they may actually feel more comfortable being confined (with their basic needs being met) than having to return to the world outside, which will have undergone substantial change since their entry into prison. They will also have established a circle of friends within the prison from whom they receive respect. If they encounter problems on their return to society (e.g., being unemployed and broke), they may yearn at some level to return to prison.

## The Treatment Approach

There are literally hundreds of treatment programs available in the corrections system. Space limitations prevent an exhaustive coverage of these programs, but a brief summary of major programs will be covered in this section. It is necessary, however, to remember that the punitive approach has the continuous effect of decreasing the efficiency and effectiveness of treatment programs.

The policy of individualized treatment of offenders has been increasingly popular since the nineteenth century. Individualized treatment developed as a reaction to the classical school, which advocated uniform penalties for criminals. Throughout history, however, there has been a dual standard of justice, with the rich and politically influential being (a) much less likely to be charged with a crime; (b) much less likely to be found guilty when accused—because of their "character," their position in society, and better legal representation; and (c) much less likely to receive a severe sentence if found guilty.

*Counseling.* Both one-to-one counseling and group counseling have increasingly been used in prisons and by probation and parole officers in the twentieth century. The aim is to identify the specific problems of each offender (including the reasons that motivated him or her to become involved in criminal activity) and then to develop specific programs for meeting these needs. The needs may cover a wide array of areas, including medical, psychological, and financial issues; drug use and abuse patterns; family and peer relationships; housing; education; vocational training; and employment. Attention is also given to the criminal's attitudes, motives, group and peer relationships, and rationalizations regarding criminality. The effectiveness of counselors (social workers, probation and parole officers, psychologists, and vocational rehabilitation counselors) is somewhat mitigated by their "dual" role perception by offenders. Some offenders view them as people who will be able to assist with a wide variety of needs, whereas others view them as members of a supervision/discipline system who are authority figures in control of rewards and punishments. With the second conception, offenders are reluctant to discuss socially unacceptable needs and motives and reluctant to establish a close relationship for fear that information divulged will be used against them.

*Prison Education.* Education in prisons has two objectives: (a) acquiring for inmates formal academic training comparable to schools, and (b) the broader objective of resocializing inmates' attitudes and behavior. To accomplish these objectives prisons use TV programs, movies, libraries, lectures, classroom instruction in academic subjects (covering elementary, secondary, and sometimes even college-level material), religious programs, group discussions, and recreational programs. One should note, however, that the bitter attitude that most inmates have toward prison and the prison administration is an attitude that continues, even today, to interfere with accomplishing educational objectives.

*Vocational Training.* The objective of these programs is to train inmates in a job skill suitable to their capacities that will prepare them for employment on release. The quality of such programs in institutions throughout the country varies greatly. In many institutions vocational training is defined as the maintenance work of the institution: laundry, cooking, custodial work, minor repairs, and dishwashing. For a period of time, vocational training was considered the main component of rehabilitation, but now rehabilitation is seen as covering many other areas.

*Prison Labor.* Through the history of prisons the idea that prisoners should perform work has existed. Unfortunately, idleness and monotony are generally prevalent. When labor was first introduced in prisons, it was seen as a method of punishment. England, for example, for a long period of time had inmates carry a cannonball on treadmills fixed with meters that measured the number of units of work produced. For each meal inmates had to produce a certain number of units. Additional units were assigned for misconduct.

Currently, there are two conflicting conceptions of work: (a) it should be productive and train inmates for employment on release, and (b) it should be hard, unpleasant, or monotonous for retributive purposes. The second view is still rationalized by some authorities as also having a reformative function, as it is said to teach discipline, obedience, and conformity and to develop an appreciation for avoiding criminal activity.

Convict labor has been used for building roads, running agricultural farms, fighting fires, conducting insect control programs, doing lumber camp work, doing laundry, making state license plates, and a wide variety of other tasks. Huber Law programs in jails and work-release programs in some prisons now allow inmates to work in employment settings in the community during the daytime, while being locked up in the evening.

*Good Time.* Good-time legislation permits a prison review board to release a prisoner earlier if the prisoner has maintained good conduct. Most good-time laws specify that for every month of acceptable behavior, a certain number of days will be deducted from the sentence. Good-time laws are designed to make inmates responsible for their conduct, to provide an incentive for good conduct and rehabilitation efforts, and to reduce discipline problems within prisons.

*A juvenile offender works with a student with a disability at Pace School in BellFlower, California. They are participants in a program in which juvenile offenders work with children with a disability and earn high school credits and work experience.*

Indeterminate sentences, which were first established in the 1800s, have similar objectives. Many sentences are now indeterminate in length, with a minimum and a maximum limit assigned to the amount of time an inmate can be incarcerated. In recent years, however, a movement to return to determinate sentencing has gained considerable support.

*Parole and Probation.* Parole is a conditional release of a prisoner serving an indeterminate or unexpired sentence. Parole is granted by an administrative board (parole board) or an executive. While on parole, parolees are considered "in custody" and are required to maintain acceptable conduct and to avoid criminal activity. Parole is designed both to punish (certain behavior is restricted and there is a threat of return to prison) and to treat the offender (a parole officer is generally assigned to counsel and help the parolee meet his or her needs).

Probation is granted by the courts and involves suspending a prison sentence of a convicted offender and giving him or her freedom during good behavior under the supervision of a probation officer. Probationers are viewed as undergoing treatment. There is, however, the threat of punishment—that is, being sent to prison should the conditions of probation be violated. Similar to parole, probation contains reformation and retribution components.

Probation and parole officers have a "dual" role responsibility: a police role and a rehabilitative role. One of the primary functions of a probation and parole officer is the "police" or authority role of closely monitoring the activities of probationers and parolees to observe whether they are violating laws or violating the conditions of their parole/probation. Those being supervised are continually aware that the probation and parole officer has the authority to initiate procedures to revoke their probation/parole, which will send them to prison. Many probationers and parolees are distrustful of the criminal justice system and are therefore wary of anyone (including probation and parole officers) who is associated with this system. This "police" role conflicts at times with the second primary function of probation and parole officers: the rehabilitative role. For rehabilitation to be most effective, the counselee must trust the counselor, must feel free to reveal socially unacceptable attitudes and activities to the counselor, and must form a close working relationship with the counselor. Obviously, those probationers and parolees who view their supervising officer as primarily having a "police" role are apt to avoid forming a counseling relationship with their supervising officer.

# How to Reduce Crime and Delinquency

✕✕✕✕✕✕✕✕✕✕✕✕✕✕✕✕✕✕✕✕✕

The heading of this section may be inappropriate. Societies have been concerned with reducing crime for centuries and a number of different approaches have been tried, yet the rate of crime seems to fluctuate independently of direct crime suppression efforts. About thirty years ago former President Nixon declared war on crime, and the federal government has since spent billions trying to curb crime, yet the crime rate continues to increase. The prospects for reducing crime in the future remain uncertain, as we do not as yet know enough about how to prevent people from starting to commit crimes or how to reform them if they choose a criminal career. Even though there is uncertainty about whether crime can be reduced, this section will summarize major approaches that have been advanced to improve the situation. (You will note that some of the proposals are contradictory.) We will consider three general areas: increasing or decreasing sentences, reforming the correctional system, and preventing crime in the first place.

## INCREASING OR DECREASING SENTENCES

There are conflicting opinions concerning the appropriateness of various sentences as related to the crime committed. Suggestions to improve the effects of various sentences include shortening the times between arrest, conviction, and punishment; imposing harsher sentences; permanently imprisoning repeat offenders; increasing prosecution of white-collar criminals; creating uniform sentences; decriminalizing victimless offenses; and imposing stricter gun control.

*Instituting Swift and Certain Punishment*  It is generally agreed that the deterrent value of punishment decreases as the time lag between the crime and the eventual punishment increases. Now, only a fraction of those who commit crimes are arrested, and only a fraction of those arrested are ever found guilty. All too often crime does pay—particularly white-collar crime and organized crime. Criminal court proceedings commonly drag on for months and even years, with offenders using due process maneuvers in the hope that public anger over their crimes will dissipate so that they will either be found innocent or have the charges reduced. Swifter action in catching, convicting, and punishing a greater percentage of those who violate laws will, it is argued, lead to greater respect for the law and curb crime. The argument against swifter action is that it would conflict with due-process protections and might result in a higher number of innocent people being arrested, convicted, and incarcerated.

*Imposing Harsher Sentences*  This approach is also based on the assumption that punishment has a deterrent effect. Advocates of this approach demand that punishments be more severe, particularly by lengthening prison sentences and by increasing the use of capital punishment. Advocates also assert that lengthier sentences will reduce crime because criminals obviously cannot victimize citizens when they are locked up.

Opponents of this approach claim that lengthier sentences may well increase crime rates rather than reduce them because practically all people sent to prison return to society, and lengthier sentences may simply increase the bitterness of those serving time, reduce their respect for our laws and criminal justice system, and give them extended training in breaking the law through association with other hardened criminals. Opponents also note that imprisonment is costly to society; it costs more per year to send a person to prison than to send a person to college.

### Separating Repeat Offenders from Society

Crimes of violence (arson, rape, armed robbery, and murder) are of particular concern to a society, as are certain other offenses, such as repeated hard-drug trafficking offenses. Some authorities assert that repeated arrests and conviction for these offenses demonstrate that the offenders are so dangerous to our society that protection of society must become the primary concern. It is further asserted that because past efforts at reformation have not been effective, future efforts are not likely to be either. It is argued that the "key should be thrown away" for repeat offenders of serious crimes. Our courts in fact are heading in this direction by locking up "repeaters" for longer periods of time.

A particular problem with this proposal is that serious crimes of violence are often committed by juveniles. As we have seen, juvenile courts use a "childsaving" approach, as their main focus is not on the nature of the crime but on having a treatment or rehabilitative approach. A number of states have now made provisions for juveniles arrested for homicide and other violent crimes to be charged and tried as adults. In adult court, convicted juveniles can then be given sentences commensurate with the seriousness of their offenses, rather than receiving the lenient treatment of the juvenile court.

Advocating that repeat lawbreakers who commit serious crimes be locked up for long periods is an admission of rehabilitation failure. On the other hand, it is a proclamation that potential victims have rights too and that their rights take priority over the rights of repeaters.

### Getting Tougher on White-Collar Crime

In the early 1970s, many high-ranking officials in the Nixon administration (which was pledged to "law and order") were accused of committing such offenses as illegal wiretapping, tax fraud, destruction of evidence, misappropriation of campaign funds, extortion, bribery, conspiracy to pervert the court of justice, and conspiracy to violate civil rights. These crimes focused considerable attention on white-collar crime. Many of these officials were convicted but received very light sentences (often in special federal prisons referred to as "resorts") in comparison to harsher sentences given to ordinary burglars and thieves. Former President Nixon was pardoned by President Gerald Ford prior to facing criminal charges. The Watergate scandal aroused a major discussion of the mild way in which white-collar crime is handled in our society. Yet today, white-collar crime still is largely ignored or treated more mildly by the police, the courts, and the correctional system. (One should note that organized crime is also increasingly committing white-collar type crimes.) It has been argued that more vigorous arrests, prosecution, and sentencing of white-collar crime and organized crime would lead to increased respect for the law by all citizens and would reduce crime. But in a society in which the white power structure sometimes seems interested only in the vigorous enforcement of laws against such crimes as armed robbery, which are usually committed by members of the powerless groups in our society, some consider it absurd to expect that the white power structure will urge the police and courts to arrest and prosecute its own members.

### Creating Uniform Sentences

As noted earlier, there are wide variations in sentences received by different convicted offenders for the same crime. If justice is to be equal for all, then variables such as the economic status, race, and gender of the offender ought not to influence sentencing. Sentencing one murderer to death while putting another on probation undermines respect for the law and the criminal justice system. One way to reduce the disparity in sentences assigned is to make the sentences subject to appeal; currently, the harshness of a sentence cannot be appealed. A second way is to take legislative action to reduce the latitude that is given to judges in assigning sentences for each type of conviction.

The move toward greater uniformity in sentencing in recent years does somewhat address the need for equality of treatment, but it also reduces the

*Civil rights leaders (left to right: Hosea Williams, the Reverend Jesse Jackson, the Reverend Martin Luther King, Jr., and the Reverend Ralph Abernathy) stand on the balcony of the Lorraine Motel in Memphis, Tennessee, April 3, 1968, the day before Dr. King's assassination at this motel.*

opportunity for individualized justice, which is a hallmark of our system. In addition, more uniform sentences (especially the imposition of mandatory minimums) has increased the average length of stay in prisons and contributed to prison overcrowding.

***Decriminalizing Victimless Offenses***  Prohibition is the classic example of creating problems by outlawing a victimless activity. Prohibition made it a crime to manufacture, distribute, or drink alcohol. Police spent substantial time and resources trying to enforce this law but were largely unsuccessful. Prohibition led to the development of bootlegging and fostered the development of organized crime.

Today, victimless crimes are still with us—gambling, smoking marijuana, premarital and extramarital sex, and prostitution, to name just a few. If such actions were decriminalized, immense resources of money and time could be diverted to confronting the crimes that do have victims. There is some movement to decriminalize certain offenses; for example, Nevada now allows prostitution in a few counties. In the past decade, police departments have been less vigorous in arresting those smoking marijuana, and there are efforts to decriminalize this activity in a number of states. Gambling laws are undergoing change, as many states have now set up legal gambling activities, such as lotteries, gambling casinos, and betting on horse races and dog races.

***Imposing Stricter Gun Control***  In the past forty years, John F. Kennedy, Robert Kennedy, Martin Luther King, Jr., Anwar Sadat, and John Lennon were killed by shootings. In 1981, there were assassination attempts on former President Ronald Reagan and on Pope John Paul XXII. Over nineteen thousand homicides and over five hundred thousand robberies are committed annually in the United States.[84] Many homicides and armed robberies involve the use of a handgun.

There are an estimated sixty million handguns in the United States—one handgun for every two homes and one handgun for every four citizens.[85] More Americans have been killed by handguns than in all the wars fought in the twentieth century.[86] States that have a higher proportion of guns have higher rates of homicides, suicides, and deaths during domestic disputes.[87] A number of special-interest groups have advocated an end to the sale of handguns except for approved and limited purposes.

Apparently, Congress and the federal government are moving in the direction of imposing stricter gun controls. In 1993, the Brady Bill was enacted, which requires that gun buyers wait five business days and undergo a background check by police. (The Brady Bill was named in honor of James Brady, former presidential press secretary who was shot and severely wounded in the 1981 assassination attempt on former President Reagan.) Supporters and opponents of the Brady Bill agree that the enactment of this bill will not stop the majority of criminals from obtaining firearms. In 1994, Congress passed, and President Bill Clinton signed, a crime bill banning nineteen types of assault-style firearms, which are used primarily to rapidly kill a number of people.

The major opposition to passing stricter gun control laws comes from the gun lobby (a coalition of several powerful organizations including the National Rifle Association), which is funded by sports enthusiasts and firearms manufacturers.

## REFORMING THE CORRECTIONAL SYSTEM

Perhaps the first step in improving the correctional system is to clarify the present conflicting objectives, some of which are punitive in nature, whereas others are treatment oriented. When the general public and public officials are confused regarding what the primary objective for incarceration should be, it is obvious prison administration officials and inmates will also become confused, and rehabilitation is unlikely to occur.

If our society decides retribution, deterrence, and vengeance should be our primary goals, then we can expect a continued high rate of recidivism and continued high crime rates, as those being punished are apt to become increasingly bitter and hostile toward society. However, from a society-benefit viewpoint, it would seem the primary objective of a correctional system should be to curb future criminal activity of incarcerated offenders in the least expensive way.

The current prison system is not only ineffectual in preventing recidivism, it is also expensive. The national average per capita cost for institutionalization of adult felons is many times greater than the cost of probation services to adults.

If the correctional system had rehabilitation as its primary objective, there would be a number of changes in the system. For example, sentencing wrong-doers is now primarily based upon the nature of their past deeds. If a convicted person has previously committed serious felonies, a long incarceration is the likely sentence. A reformative approach would, instead, first focus on identifying ways to curb the supervisee's (or offender's) tendency toward breaking the law. Involved in this identification process would be an assessment of the reasons why the person is breaking the law, and a determination of how this person can legally obtain what he or she wants. Needed services would then be specified, and the responsibilities of the supervisee would be identified—such as maintaining or securing employment, enrollment in an educational or vocational program, receiving counseling or family therapy, undergoing medical or drug treatment, or payment of debts, restitution, or both. Removal from society would generally be used only after the supervisee failed to meet requirements of the supervision plan (e.g., restitution) or when the supervisee was a definite threat to society.

Two examples will be used to illustrate this approach. A seventeen-year-old female runs away from home, has very limited employment and educational skills, and therefore turns to prostitution for financial reasons. Instead of assigning fines after each arrest, would it not make more sense to identify her needs (such as financial and educational needs, need for legal employment that pays her more than prostitution, and need to resolve the conflicts with her parents) and then provide her with services to meet these needs? A thirty-two-year-old male is arrested for burglarizing forty-three homes in wealthy neighborhoods over a span of four months. The man is unemployed, and he states he committed the burglaries to support his cocaine habit. Instead of sending him directly to prison at the taxpayers' expense, would it not make more sense to identify his needs (such as job training, employment, and drug treatment) and then provide him with services to meet these needs? As part of such a rehabilitative approach, he would also be required (over a realistic period of time) to make restitution to the victims. He would be informed that additional convictions, after this rehabilitative effort, would result in a lengthy prison sentence. Also, he would be informed that failure on his part to fulfill the terms of the rehabilitative plan would result in a lengthy prison sentence.

With this approach, supervisees would become acutely aware that they have the choice and the responsibility to decide which of two avenues to pursue: continuation of criminal activity (which is apt to result in a lengthy prison sentence) or a more law-abiding, productive, and respectable future. If they choose the latter, they would be informed there are services (e.g., counseling and vocational training) available to assist them, but they would also be made aware that improving their situation requires being a responsible person and putting forth considerable effort.

The choice facing our society appears to be between a punitive system that enacts retribution but does not deter future crimes and a system that seeks to assist offenders in becoming productive citizens. The latter approach is not painless to the offenders, as it requires considerable work and effort. With a punitive approach, however, pain *itself* is the goal and usually does not produce a result that is beneficial to the individual or to society.

With more than one million people behind bars, the United States imprisons a higher proportion of its population than any other nation.[88] Marc Mauer notes:

> The same policies that have helped make us a world leader in incarceration have clearly failed to make us a safer nation. We need a fundamental change of direction, towards proven programs and policies that work to reduce both imprisonment and crime. We've got to stop jailing and start rehabilitating.[89]

*Diversion Programs*    Labeling theory suggests that the criminal justice system perpetuates crime by branding and interacting with offenders as if they were delinquents and criminals. Diversion programs have therefore been developed in a number of communities to divert first-time or minor offenders from entering the criminal justice system; instead, they receive services from community agencies.

One such program is "deferred prosecution," which some communities now provide. Adults who are arrested for the first time for a minor offense (such as shoplifting) are referred by either a judge or a prosecuting attorney to deferred prosecution prior to standing trial for the offense for which they are charged. Deferred prosecution programs provide over a period of several weeks small group sessions that are geared to helping the members refrain from committing additional crimes. The case is dismissed if the defendant (a) pays for any damages; (b) is not re arrested while participating in the program; and (c) attends all the group meetings.

Many diversion programs are focused on keeping juveniles out of juvenile courts and criminal courts by instead referring them to treatment programs handled by community agencies. Juveniles, for example, may be referred for counseling (from social workers, probation officers, or psychologists); they may receive training and help in getting a job; they may receive help for emotional or family problems; or they may receive help with school work.

Many communities have developed "Scared Strait" programs, which were initially developed at Rahway Prison in New Jersey. Juveniles who have committed offenses are taken on a visit to a prison, where inmates harshly describe the realities of prison life. Prison conditions are also observed first-hand. The objective is to expose juveniles to the realities of life in prison so that the threat of going to prison will motivate them to stop breaking the law. It is not yet certain, however, that this exposure has a deterrent effect on juveniles.

*Transitional Programs*    There are a variety of transitional programs. While in jail or prison, a person may be allowed to work in the community during the daytime. School-release programs allow inmates to attend college or a technical school during the daytime. Halfway houses have been used as an alternative to sending a person to prison; they allow residents to work or go to school in their home community. Halfway houses have also been used to help people who have been in prison to adjust to returning to society. If offenders misbehave while in halfway houses, there is the threat of being sent to jail or prison.

With transitional programs, it is hoped that inmates will maintain and develop stronger ties to the noncriminal elements in their home community. The programs seek to reduce or alleviate the negative effects of incarceration and provide opportunities and resources of rehabilitation.

## PREVENTING CRIME

Theoretically, there are four ways to prevent crime:

1. Make the punishment for violating a law so severe that lawbreakers will be deterred from committing crimes. Studies on the use of capital punishment, however, suggest that even this severest penalty does not deter crime.

2. Keep the convicted lawbreakers in prison. Such an approach would be very expensive—especially since practically everyone occasionally commits a crime.

3. Change the economic, social, and political conditions that breed crime. A wide number of proposals, beyond the scope of this text, have been advanced: improve family life; improve the educational system to make education an exciting, growth-producing experience for students; end racial discrimination; provide equal opportunities for achieving success for all citizens, including the poor and minority groups; provide full employment with a decent living wage for all able-bodied

**Table 2.4** *Precautions Against Becoming a Crime Victim*

## Home

♦ Bolt doors and windows and use exterior lighting to frustrate burglary techniques.

♦ Engrave identification numbers on possessions to curb fencing of stolen property.

♦ If you leave home for part of the evening, make it look as though someone is home. Leave some lights and music on. Or leave the television on, keeping it low so that it sounds like muffled voices. To someone outside, it will sound as if people are inside talking or the family is home watching TV.

♦ Double-secure sliding glass doors by placing lengths of metal rod or wooden dowels in the lower tracks to prevent the doors from being opened.

♦ Put in exterior lighting over front and back doors. Also, cut back shrubbery that might be used to hide intruders.

♦ If you hear someone breaking in at night, let the intruder know you have heard the noise, but avoid a confrontation. Chances are the person will leave as fast as possible. If you confront the intruder unexpectedly, you could get hurt. Instead yell, "Get the shotgun!"—even if you are alone; or yell to the neighbors or call the police. One of the best places to have a strong, deadbolt lock is on the inside of your bedroom door.

♦ A dog that barks a lot may deter an intruder. The yapping of the dog will make the intruder wary that someone else will hear the barking, so the intruder will probably exit in a hurry.

♦ Do not leave the key to your home under the doormat, in the mailbox, or on top of the door ledge.

♦ Be cautious about inviting door-to-door salespeople into your home. Many communities now require salespeople to carry an identification card.

♦ Do not leave possessions on lawns or in your driveway at night. If left, bicycles, barbecue grills, power tools, and lawn mowers are easily removed.

♦ Do not leave important papers, expensive jewelry, or large sums of money at home. Rent a bank security deposit box, which not only protects valuables from burglars but also from fires and natural disasters.

♦ When going on an extended vacation arrange for a friend to check your home every few days. Do not let newspapers or mail pile up. The post office will hold your mail at no cost while you are away. Inexpensive timers can be purchased to activate lights, radios, or TVs to give the impression you are home.

♦ When you expect a visitor and are unable to be home, do not leave a telltale note outside: "Welcome—will be back at 8:00 P.M. Walk in and make yourself at home. Door is unlocked." Burglars readily accept such invitations.

♦ Avoid carrying large sums of money. If forced to do so, take along a second wallet containing three or four bills and some expired credit cards, which you can give a thief if confronted.

♦ When in a crowd, place your wallet in a safe place—for example, front pocket, a waist pouch, or a buttoned back pocket to frustrate pickpocketing efforts.

♦ Never leave a purse unattended.

♦ Do not hitchhike or pick up hitchhikers. Hitchhiking has led to a significant number of robberies and assaults. If you cannot avoid hitchhiking, be very selective as to whom you ride with.

## Automobile

♦ Flashy equipment on autos will invite theft or break-ins. If you buy mag wheels, a stereo tape deck, CB radio, fancy wheel covers, and other expensive gadgets, your car will draw attention. The place where you park your car can be an invitation for it to be stolen or broken into. Always lock your car, put valuables in the trunk, and never leave the key in the ignition.

♦ If you leave your car someplace for a few days (e.g., at an airport), it is nearly theft-proof if you pull the center wire out of the distributor in addition to locking the car and taking the keys. (Before pulling the wire, make sure you know how to put it back!)

♦ Remove identification from key chains so that if your keys are lost or stolen, no one knows what they can open.

♦ Women are advised to list only their last name and initials on mailboxes and in phone directories.

## In Public

♦ Avoid going into a dark parking lot. It may be cheaper to call a taxi than risk being mugged.

♦ There are a variety of approaches to avoid becoming a victim of rape, including physical techniques of self-defense (for example, the martial arts) and distasteful approaches (for example, vomiting or urinating on the rapist, informing the potential rapist you have tested positive for HIV, sharply squeezing the genitals of the rapist, and poking your fingers into the rapist's eyes). Women should become familiar with these approaches and select a few that they would be comfortable with and prepared to use should an attack occur.

people; improve housing conditions and the living conditions in our inner cities; and curb alcohol and drug abuse.

4. Educate the general public on how to avoid becoming a victim of crime. This fourth approach will be discussed in some detail and involves reducing the opportunity for crime to occur. This approach is being highlighted because it is an approach that everyone should be aware of and participate in.

Dae Chang describes this approach, which developed from victimology, an area of study in criminology:

> Research shows that much crime—and by far the greatest portion of street crime and burglary—is the result of opportunity and luck rather than of careful and professional planing.
>
> Someone sees an "opportunity"—in an open window, an empty house, a person alone in a dark alley—and acts on it. Muggers look for likely victims, not specific individuals; burglars, for a house they can enter, not a particular address. Preselected targets frequently are chosen precisely because they are seen as "easy marks."
>
> Who is the victim of a crime? What causes crime? Who causes crime? There are some startling answers to these questions. In the majority of cases, the victim contributes, and in some cases is a major cause of a criminal act. All of us are potential victims. We frequently present the criminal or an individual with an invitation to commit a crime. We entice him, advertise to him, coax him, give him the opportunity, and even implant the idea into his head. Through our carelessness, open disregard for our personal possessions, forgetfulness, attitudes, vanity, etc., we frequently invite someone to commit a criminal act either directly at ourselves or to our possessions. We also invite bodily harm upon ourselves by our actions in public and private. Our habits, attitudes, dress, etc. all are signals to the people who would be enticed into crime.[90]

In using this approach effectively one must keep asking oneself, "Is what I'm doing, or failing to do, making me vulnerable to becoming a victim of a crime?" Table 2.4 presents a number of specific precautions to prevent becoming a crime victim.

## Summary

Crime is one of the most serious problems facing our nation. Serious violent crime has reached alarming proportions. In addition, the criminal justice system (the police, the courts, and prisons) are perceived as being relatively ineffective in curbing crime.

Probably everyone, at one time or another, has violated one or more laws. Those arrested for crimes are disproportionately more likely to be male, young, members of a racial minority, and urban residents. If laws against white-collar crime and organized crime were more vigorously enforced, the "typical" criminal would probably be older, white, and a suburban resident.

Official crime statistics are inaccurate because many crimes are unreported. Moreover, police and courts seek vigorous enforcement only for certain crimes, and police reporting practices are sometimes affected by political motives (e.g., reclassifying serious offenses as less serious to show police departments in a favorable light). In terms of number of people victimized and financial cost to society, white-collar crime appears to be our most serious type of crime. Yet laws against white-collar crime are treated less seriously by the police and the courts.

Many theories have been advanced about the causes of crime. These theories identify only some of the reasons crime occurs. We do not as yet have complete explanations for all the reasons why crime occurs. With the crime rate continuing to increase, it is also clear we do not yet know how to reduce crime effectively.

Correctional systems throughout the world currently have conflicting objectives, with some being punishment-oriented and others being treatment-oriented. When combined, generally the two approaches result in a system that is confusing and ineffective in curbing criminal activity. There is a danger that prisons may serve as schools for crime and may have a labeling effect, which leads to future criminal activity.

A number of proposals have been advanced for reducing crime, including swift and certain punishment, imposing harsher sentences, incapacitating repeat offenders who commit serious crimes, getting tougher on white-collar crime, uniform sentencing, decriminalizing victimless offenses, stricter gun control, reforming the correctional system to emphasize the treatment approach, increasing the use of diversion programs and transitional programs, and educating citizens about how to avoid becoming crime victims. Some of these proposals contradict others. Although each proposal is backed by some research, no proposal has conclusively proven valid in reducing crime.

# CHAPTER 3

# *Emotional and Behavioral Problems*

*A*t times, everyone suffers emotional problems, behavioral difficulties, or both. In this century, disciplines such as sociology, psychology, and psychiatry have made important advances in conceptualizing and treating emotional and behavioral problems. This chapter:

♦ describes the nature and extent of such problems;

♦ discusses the concept of mental illness;

♦ presents a theory about the causes of chronic mental illness;

♦ discusses controversial issues in the mental health field;

♦ presents research on the relationship between social structure and the rate of mental illness; and

♦ describes treatment approaches of emotional and behavioral problems.

## The Nature and Extent of Emotional and Behavioral Problems

Emotional and behavioral problems are two global labels covering an array of disorders: depression; excessive anxiety; feelings of inferiority or isolation; alienation; sadism or masochism; marital problems; broken romances; dysfunctional parent-child relationships; hyperactivity; unusual or bizarre acts; being overly critical or overly aggressive; phobias; child or spouse abuse; compulsive or obsessive behavior; guilt; shyness; violent displays of temper; vindictiveness; nightmares or insomnia; sexual deviations; and so on.

For each problem, there are unique and, in many cases, a number of potential causes. Depression, for example, may be caused by loss of a loved one or loss of something else considered highly valuable, by feelings of guilt or shame, by knowledge of a future undesirable impending event (e.g., discovery of a terminal illness), by aggression turned inward, by certain physical phases such as menopause, by feelings of inadequacy or inferiority, and by feelings of loneliness or isolation. Hundreds of thousands of books have been published on causes and ways to treat the wide array of emotional and behavioral problems.

One out of every four Americans experiences some form of emotional or behavioral disorder at some point during any given year.[1] These disorders range from mild depression and anxiety to suicide ideation or a severe eating disorder such as anorexia. Every year more than six million people in the United States receive mental health care.[2] In addition, practically all of us encounter serious emotional difficulties at some time in our lives—for example, a broken romance or divorce, alcohol or drug addiction, failing at a goal, emotional distress associated with a family member being diagnosed with a terminal illness or being victimized by a serious crime, or an eating disorder (see Box 3.1).

## TWO APPROACHES TO MENTAL ILLNESS

Much of the language relating to emotional and behavioral disturbances has become a familiar part of everyday conversation. We use the following terms to express a judgment (often unfavorable) about persons who display unusual behavior or distressing emotions: *crazy, weird, psychotic, neurotic, having a nervous breakdown, insane, sick, uptight, space cadet, mad.* Whatever terms are used, we are apt to have only a vague idea of their meaning. Amazingly, we act as if the label accurately describes the person, and we then relate to the person as if the label were correct and all-encompassing. However, it is impossible to define any of these terms precisely—what, for example, are the specific characteristics that separate a *psychotic* or a *space cadet* from other persons? Probably no one can give a precise answer.

There are two general approaches to viewing and diagnosing emotional disturbances and abnormal behaviors: the medical model and the interactional model.

*Medical Model*   The medical model views emotional and behavioral problems as a mental illness, comparable to a physical illness. The use of mental illness labels involves applying medical labels—schizophrenia, paranoia, psychosis, insanity—to emotional problems. Adherents of the medical approach believe the disturbed person's mind is affected by some generally unknown, internal condition. That condition, they assert, might be due to genetics, metabolic disorders, infectious diseases, internal conflicts, unconscious use of defense mechanisms, or traumatic early experiences that cause emotional fixations and hamper psychological growth.

The medical model has a lengthy classification of mental disorders that are defined by the American Psychiatric Association (see Table 3.1).

Box 3.1 ◆◆◆◆◆◆◆◆◆◆◆◆◆◆◆◆◆◆◆◆◆◆◆◆◆◆◆◆

# Eating Disorders: An Emerging Problem[a]

**E**ating disorders are recognized as very serious afflictions. As many as 20 percent of college females are estimated to have an eating disorder.

The three primary eating disorders are anorexia nervosa, bulimia nervosa, and compulsive overeating. Both anorexics and bulimics have an excessive concern with food and fitness, but their techniques for staying thin vary greatly. On the one hand, an anorexic eats very little food and is near starvation much of the time. Bulimics, on the other hand, binge and purge themselves. Although the average American's food intake is around three thousand calories a day, bulimics eat substantially more. They may devour as much as forty thousand to sixty thousand calories a day. They typically binge on high-calorie junk food, such as sweets and fried foods. Because bulimics also want to stay thin, they purge themselves in a variety of ways, the most common of which is vomiting. Vomiting may be induced initially by putting the fingers down the throat. Some bulimics rely on cotton swabs or on drinking copious amounts of fluids. With practice many bulimics gain control of their esophageal muscles so that they can induce vomiting at will. Although vomiting is the most common bulimic method for purging, other methods include excessive intake of laxatives, fasting, enemas, chewing food and then spitting it out, and compulsive exercise—such as swimming, running, and working out with barbells and weights. Although it is much more common than anorexia, bulimia went unrecognized for so long because the binging and purging cycle is almost always done in secret. Bulimics dread being exposed, so that very few will report their malady.

Bulimics tend to have few friends, as much of their time is spent on secret binging and purging. Bulimics are often overachievers, and in college tend to attain high academic averages. Purging often becomes a purification rite to overcome self-loathing. Through purging, they feel completely fresh and clean again, but these feelings of self-worth are only temporary. They are extremely sensitive to minor insults and frustrations, which are often used as excuses to initiate another food binge.

Anorexia nervosa is a disorder characterized by the relentless pursuit of thinness through voluntary starvation. Anorexics refuse to accept the fact that they are too thin; they will not eat, even when they experience intense hunger. They stubbornly insist they need to lose even more weight from their already emaciated bodies. They have a distorted body image, erroneously believing that they are too fat. They also erroneously believe that having a perfect body (defined by society as a thin body) will ensure happiness and success. Ninety-five percent of all anorexia nervosa cases are females.

Compulsive overeating is the irresistible urge to consume excessive amounts of food; it is the act of eating irrationally, chewing and digesting excessive amounts of food on a long-term basis. Treatment for compulsive overeating is recommended for individuals who weigh more than 20 percent over their recommended weight.

Michael O. Koch, Virginia L. Dotson, and Thomas P. Troast in *Social Work with Groups* describe the relationships among these eating disorders:

> Eating disorders seem to exist on a continuum. On one end are the anorexics, who achieve drastic weight loss by severely restricting food intake. In the middle are the anorexic bulimics, who eat and even binge on occasion, but who still maintain a much lower than normal weight by a combination of strict dieting and purging. Also included are normal-weight bulimics who binge and purge but who are not significantly underweight. These bulimics usually diet when they are not binging and may repeatedly gain and lose ten or more pounds because of their eating behaviors. At the other end of the continuum, the compulsive overeater will repeatedly binge, gaining significant amounts of weight, without engaging in any of the purging behaviors associated with anorexia or bulimia nervosa. Individuals may move back and forth along this continuum, alternatively restricting or binging, depending on their circumstances.[b]

Anorexics and bulimics have some similarities. For example, both are likely to have been brought up in middle-class, upwardly mobile families, where their mothers were overinvolved in their lives and their fathers preoccupied with work outside the home. For the most part bulimics and anorexics were good children, eager to obtain the love and approval of others. Both tend to lack self-esteem, feel ineffective and have a distorted body image that causes them to view themselves as fatter than others view them.

*Even Her Royal Highness, the Princess of Wales, was not immune from affliction with the eating disorder of bulimia.*

on women to be slender and trim than on men. Our socialization practices also overemphasize the importance of women being slender.

Anorexia, bulimia, and compulsive overeating are dangerous health disorders. Anorexics risk starvation, and both bulimics and anorexics risk serious health problems. Fat synthesis and accumulation are necessary for survival. Fatty acids are a major source of energy. When fat levels are depleted, the body must draw on carbohydrates (sugar). When sugar supplies dwindle, body metabolism decreases, which often leads to drowsiness, inactivity, pessimism, depression, dizziness, and fatigue. For compulsive overeaters, as weight increases above the recommended level for one's body type, mortality ratios increase as well. Obesity is a contributing factor to such health problems as hypertension, heart attacks, and diabetes.

Psychotropic drugs (tranquilizers and antidepressants) may affect the bodies of bulimics and anorexics differently due to changes in body metabolism. Abnormalities have been found in the electroencephalograms of people with eating disorders. Chronic vomiting may lead to gum disease and cavities, as a result of the hydrochloric acid content of vomit. Vomiting can also lead to severe tearing and bleeding in the esophagus. Chronic vomiting may result in a potassium deficiency, which then may lead to muscle fatigue, weakness, numbness, erratic heartbeat, kidney damage, and, in severe instances, paralysis.

A variety of treatment programs are available for anorexics, bulimics, and compulsive overeaters. Individual and group therapy programs have been developed to change the psychological thinking patterns that initiated and are sustaining the undesirable eating patterns. For those in whom severe health problems have already developed, medical care is essential. Therapy for eating disorders includes instruction in establishing and maintaining a nutritious diet. Some elementary, secondary, and higher education school systems are now developing preventive programs that inform students about the risks of eating disorders and identify and provide services for students who are beginning to develop an eating disorder.

Anorexics and bulimics differ in that anorexics are generally younger, far less socially competent, and much more isolated from and dependent on the family. Anorexics stay away from food. In contrast, bulimics, during times of stress, turn toward food; they binge and then purge. For the most part, bulimics are able to function in social and work contexts. Their health may be gravely affected by binging and purging, but their lives are not necessarily in imminent danger, as is often the case with anorexics. Anorexics are also *very* thin, whereas bulimics are not so underweight and may even be overweight.

Why are bulimics and anorexics primarily women? One key reason is that our society places more pressure

---

a.  Michael O. Koch, Virginia L. Dotson, and Thomas P. Troast, "Interventions with Eating Disorders" in Charles Zastrow, *Social Work with Groups*, 4th ed. (Chicago: Nelson-Hall, 1997), 463–484.

b.  Ibid., 465–466.

**Table 3.1**  *Major Mental Disorders According to the American Psychiatric Association*

- *Disorders Usually First Diagnosed in Infancy, Childhood or Adolescence.* These include, but are not limited to, mental retardation, learning disorders, communication disorders (such as stuttering), autism, attention-deficit/hyperactivity disorders, and separation-anxiety disorder.

- *Delirium, Dementia, and Amnestic, and other Cognitive Disorders.* These include delirium due to alcohol and other drug intoxication, dementia due to Alzheimer's disease or Parkinson's disease, dementia due to head trauma, and amnestic disorder.

- *Substance-Related Disorders.* This category includes mental disorders related to abuse of alcohol, caffeine, amphetamines, cocaine, hallucinogens, nicotine, and other mind-altering substances.

- *Schizophrenia and Other Psychotic Disorders.* This category includes delusional disorders and all forms of schizophrenia (such as paranoid, disorganized, and catatonic).

- *Mood Disorders.* This category includes emotional disorders, such as depression, and bipolar disorders.

- *Anxiety Disorders.* This category includes phobias, post-traumatic stress disorder, and anxiety disorders.

- *Somatoform Disorders.* This category includes psychological problems that manifest themselves as symptoms of physical disease (e.g., hypochondria).

- *Dissociative Disorders.* This category includes problems in which part of the personality is dissociated from the rest (e.g., dissociative identity disorder, which was formerly called multiple personality disorder).

- *Sexual and Gender Identity Disorders.* This category includes sexual dysfunctions (such as hypoactive sexual desire, premature ejaculation, male erectile disorder, male and female orgasmic disorders, and vaginismus), exhibitionism, fetishism, pedophilia (child molestation), sexual masochism, sexual sadism, voyeurism, and gender identity disorders (such as cross-gender identification).

- *Eating Disorders.* This category includes anorexia nervosa and bulimia nervosa, and compulsive overeating.

- *Sleep Disorders.* This category includes insomnia and other problems with sleep (such as nightmares and sleepwalking).

- *Impulse-Control Disorders.* This category includes the inability to control undesirable impulses (e.g., kleptomania, pyromania, and pathological gambling).

- *Adjustment Disorders.* This category includes difficulty in adjusting to the stress created by such common events as unemployment or divorce.

- *Personality Disorders.* A personality disorder is an enduring pattern of inner experience and behavior that deviates markedly from the expectations of the individual's culture, is pervasive and inflexible, has an onset in adolescence or early adulthood, is stable over time, and leads to distress or impairment. Examples include paranoid personality disorder, antisocial personality disorder, and obsessive-compulsive personality disorder.

- *Other Conditions.* This category covers a variety of "other" disorders that may be a focus of clinical attention. The category includes parent-child relational problems; partner relational problems; sibling relational problems; child victims of physical and sexual abuse, and neglect; adult victims of physical and sexual abuse; malingering; bereavement; academic problems; occupational problems; identity problems; and religious or spiritual problems.

*Source:* The Diagnostic and Statistical Manual of Mental Disorders (DSM-IV), 4th ed. (Washington, DC: American Psychiatric Association, 1994).

---

In the *Diagnostic and Statistical Manual of Mental Disorders* (DSM-IV), numerous mental disorders are defined.[3] A few examples of these disorders are described briefly in the following paragraphs:

*Schizophrenia.* This malady encompasses a large group of disorders, usually of psychotic proportion, manifested by characteristic disturbances of language and communication, thought, perception, affect, and behavior that last longer than six months.

*Delusional disorder.* The essential feature is the presence of one or more delusions that persist at least one month. A delusion is something that is falsely believed or propagated. An example is the persecutory type, in which an individual erroneously believes he or she is being conspired against, cheated, spied on, followed, poisoned or drugged, maliciously maligned, harassed, or obstructed in the pursuit of long-term goals.

*Hypochondriasis.* This is a chronic maladaptive style of relating to the environment through preoccupation with shifting somatic concerns and symptoms, a fear or conviction that one has a serious physical illness, the search for medical treatment, inability to accept reassurance, and either hostile or dependent relationships with care givers and family.

*Bipolar disorder.* This is a major affective disorder with episodes of both mania and depression; formerly called manic-depressive psychosis. Bipolar disorder may be subdivided into manic, depressed, or mixed types on the basis of currently presenting symptoms.

*Phobia.* A phobia is characterized by an obsessive, persistent, unrealistic, intense fear of an object or situation. A few common phobias are acrophobia (fear of heights), algophobia (fear of pain), claustrophobia (fear of closed spaces), and erythrophobia (fear of blushing).

*Personality disorders.* Personality disorders are defined in Table 3.1. Some personality disorders and their characteristics are:

- *Paranoid.* A pattern of distrust and suspiciousness such that others' motives are interpreted as malevolent (see Box 3.2).
- *Schizoid.* A pattern of detachment from social relationships and a restricted range of emotional expression.
- *Schizotypal.* A pattern of acute discomfort in close relationships, cognitive or perceptual distortions, and eccentricities of behavior.
- *Antisocial.* A pattern of disregard for, and violation of, the rights of others.
- *Borderline.* A pattern of instability in interpersonal relationships, self-image, and affects, along with marked impulsivity.
- *Histrionic.* A pattern of excessive emotionality and attention-seeking.
- *Narcissistic.* A pattern of grandiosity, need for admiration, and lack of empathy.
- *Avoidant.* A pattern of social inhibition, feelings of inadequacy, and hypersensitivity to negative evaluation.
- *Dependent.* A pattern of submissive and clinging behavior related to an excessive need to be taken care of.
- *Obsessive-Compulsive.* A pattern of preoccupation with orderliness, perfectionism, and control.

The medical model approach arose in reaction to the historical notion that the emotionally disturbed were possessed by demons, were mad, were to be blamed for their disturbances, and were to be "treated" by being beaten, locked up, or killed. The medical model led to viewing the disturbed as being

Box 3.2 ◆◆◆◆◆◆◆◆◆◆◆◆◆◆◆◆◆◆◆◆◆◆◆

## A Case Example Interpreted in Terms of the Mental Illness Model

Dan Vanda was arrested for fatally stabbing both his parents. He was twenty-two years old and had always been described by neighbors as a "loner." In elementary school, junior high, and high school, he was frequently absent, never had any close friends, and received primarily failing grades. He dropped out of school when he was sixteen. School records showed that teachers had informed protective services on three occasions in his younger years that they believed his parents were abusing and neglecting him. Protective-service records showed his parents were uncooperative. However, insufficient evidence was available to justify placement in a foster home.

At the time of his arrest, Mr. Vanda appeared confused. He stated he was in communication with King David (the biblical David who slew Goliath), who told him to slay his parents because they were "out to get him." Mr. Vanda tended to quote the Bible incoherently and in a rambling fashion. He also stated that cosmic rays were in control of people. At his arrest he appeared to expect congratulations for what he had done, rather than being locked up. The court ordered a ninety-day observation period in a maximum security hospital of the mentally ill to determine if he had a mental disorder.

Neighbors and school officials could add little to explain his actions. Neighbors felt he was "weird" and had ordered their children not to associate with him. They reported they sometimes had seen him butchering birds. When asked why he did this, he stated he had seen the film *The Birds* (directed by the late Alfred Hitchcock) and he was now trying to prevent them from attacking him.

Psychiatrists concluded he was insane and labeled him paranoid schizophrenic. It was felt his insanity was such that he would not be able to understand the nature of court proceedings connected with his offense. With this recommendation, the court committed him indefinitely to a maximum security psychiatric hospital.

in need of help, stimulated research into the nature of emotional and behavioral problems, and promoted the development of therapeutic approaches.

The major evidence for the validity of the medical model approach comes from studies that suggest that some mental disorders, such as schizophrenia, may be influenced by genetics (heredity). The bulk of the evidence for the significance of heredity comes from studies of twins. For instance, in studies, identical twins have been found to have a concordance rate (i.e., if one has it, both have it) for schizophrenia of about 50 percent.[4] The rate of schizophrenia in the general population is about 1 percent.[5] Thus, when one identical twin is schizophrenic, the other is fifty times more likely than average to be schizophrenic. This concordance rate suggests that genes have a causal influence on the development of schizophrenia but that its development is not completely determined by genetics, since concordance for identical twins is only 50 percent, not 100 percent. (One should note the DSM-IV categories are used in the systems of reimbursement from health insurance policies to mental health providers for the provision of psychotherapy to individuals and groups.)

*Interactional Model*   Critics of the medical model approach assert that medical labels have no diagnostic or treatment value and frequently have an adverse labeling effect. In the 1950s, Thomas Szasz was one of the first authorities to assert that mental illness is a myth, that it does not exist.[6] Szasz's theory is interactional; that is, it focuses on the processes of everyday social interaction and the effects of labeling on people. Beginning with the assumption that the term *mental illness* implies a "disease of the mind," Szasz categorizes all of the so-called mental illnesses into three types of emotional and behavioral disorders and discusses the inappropriateness of calling such human difficulties mental illnesses. These three disorders may be summarized as follows:

1. *Personal disabilities.* Examples include excessive anxiety, depression, fears, and feelings of inadequacy. Szasz says such so-called mental illness may appropriately be considered mental (in the sense in which thinking and feeling are considered mental activities), but he asserts they are not diseases.

2. *Antisocial acts.* These include bizarre homicides and other social deviations. (Homosexuality used to be listed in this category but was removed from the American Psychiatric Association's list of mental illnesses in 1974.) Szasz says such antisocial acts are actually social deviations, and he asserts they are neither "mental" nor "diseases."

3. *Deterioration of the brain with associated personality changes.* This category includes the mental illnesses in which personality changes result following brain deterioration from causes such as arteriosclerosis, chronic alcoholism, Alzheimer's disease, AIDS, general paresis, or serious brain damage following an accident. Common symptoms are loss of memory, listlessness, apathy, and deterioration of personal grooming. Szasz says these disorders can appropriately be considered diseases, but are diseases of the *brain,* rather than diseases of the *mind.* Szasz asserts that the notion that people with emotional problems are mentally ill is as absurd as the belief that the emotionally disturbed are possessed by demons:

> The belief in mental illness as something other than man's trouble in getting along with his fellow man is the proper heir to the belief in demonology and witchcraft. Mental illness exists or is "real" in exactly the same sense in which witches existed or were "real."[7]

There are three steps to becoming labeled "mentally ill":

1. The person displays some strange deviant behavior.
2. The behavior is not tolerated by the family or local community and, as a result, the person is referred to a mental health professional.
3. The mental health professional, usually a psychiatrist, happens to believe in the medical model and assigns a mental illness label.

Thomas Scheff and David Mechanic provide evidence that whether the family/community will tolerate the deviant behavior and whether the mental health professional believes in the medical model are more crucial in determining if someone will be assigned a "mentally ill" label than the strange behavior exhibited by the person.[8]

The point that Szasz and many other writers are striving to make is that people *do* have emotional problems, but they *do not* have a mystical mental illness. They believe terms that describe behavior are very useful—for example, depression, anxiety, an obsession, a compulsion, excessive fear, having hallucinations, feelings of being a failure. Such terms describe personal problems that people have. But the medical terms, they assert, are not useful, because there is no distinguishing symptom that would indicate whether a person has or does not have the "illness." In addition, Caplan points out there is considerable variation among cultures regarding what is defined as a mental illness.[9] (Russia, for example, used to define protests against the government as a symptom of mental illness.) The usefulness of the medical model is also questioned because psychiatrists frequently disagree on the medical diagnosis to be assigned to those who are disturbed.[10]

In a dramatic study, psychologist David Rosenhan demonstrated that professional staff in mental hospitals could not distinguish "insane" patients from "sane" patients.[11] Rosenhan and seven "normal" associates went to twelve mental hospitals in five different states claiming they were hearing voices; all eight were admitted. After admission, these pseudopatients stated they stopped hearing voices and acted normally. The hospitals, unable to distinguish their "sane" status from the "insane" status of other patients, kept them hospitalized for an average of nineteen days. All were then discharged with a diagnosis of "schizophrenia in remission."

The use of medical labels, it has been asserted, has several adverse effects.[12] People labeled "mentally ill" believe that they have a disease for which unfortunately there is no known "cure." The label gives people an excuse for not taking responsibility for their actions (e.g., innocent by reason of insanity). Because there is no known "cure," the disturbed frequently idle away their time waiting for someone to discover a cure, rather than assuming responsibility for their behavior, examining the reasons why there are problems, and making efforts to improve. Other undesirable consequences of being labeled mentally ill are that the individuals may lose some of their legal rights; may be stigmatized in social interactions as being dangerous, unpredictable, untrustworthy, or of "weak" character; and may find securing employment or receiving a promotion more difficult.[13]

The question of whether mental illness exists is indeed important. The assignment of mental illness labels to disturbed people has substantial implications for how the disturbed will be treated, for how others will view them, and for how they will view themselves. Cooley's "looking-glass" self-approach crystallizes what is being said here.[14] The "looking glass" says we develop our self-concept in terms of how other people react to us. People are apt to react to those labeled mentally ill as if they were mentally ill. As a result, those labeled mentally ill may well define themselves as being different or "crazy" and begin playing that role.

Authorities who adhere to the interactional model raise a key question, as expectations generally guide behavior: "If we relate to people with emotional and behavioral problems as if they are mentally ill, how can we expect them to act in emotionally healthy and responsible ways?"

Compared to a physical illness, a diagnosis of a mental illness carries a greater stigma. In 1972, Senator Thomas Eagleton was forced to withdraw his candidacy for vice president on the Democratic ticket after it was revealed that he had received electroshock treatments for depression. The leaders of the Democratic Party feared that the public would conclude that someone who had once received psychiatric help would be too "unstable" and "dangerous" to be president. On the other hand, Franklin Roosevelt had a physical disability resulting from polio, but was elected president for four terms.

Szasz also argues that the mental illness approach is used (perhaps unintentionally) as a means of social control over people who do not conform to social expectations.[15] The former Soviet Union had a long history of labeling dissenters (including literary figures and intellectuals who would be respected in this country) as mentally ill and then sending them to concentration camps or to insane asylums. In the past, psychiatrists in Russia often concluded that people who did not accept the Marxist-Leninist philosophy were psychologically impaired. Are some psychiatrists using mental illness labels to control the behavior of nonconformists in our country? Szasz asserts they are, citing as an example homosexuality, which was listed as a mental disorder by the American Psychiatric Association until 1974. As another example, Szasz cites a quote from Dana L. Farnsworth, a Harvard psychiatrist and an authority on college psychiatric services:

> Library vandalism, cheating and plagiarism, stealing in the college or community stores or in the dormitories, unacceptable or antisocial sexual practices (overt homosexuality, exhibitionism, promiscuity), and the unwise and unregulated use of harmful drugs, are examples of behavior that suggest the presence of emotionally unstable persons. . . .[16]

Mental illness labels do have a "boundary" effect, as they define what behaviors a society defines as "sick," with pressures then being put on citizens to avoid such behaviors. Szasz's point is that a number of nonconformists are adversely affected by the use of the medical model to control their behavior.

Adherents to the interactional approach assert that mental illness is a myth. They assert that people are labeled mentally ill for two main reasons—they may have an intense unwanted emotion, or they may be engaged in dysfunctional (or deviant) behavior. Assigning a mental illness label to unwanted emotions or dysfunctional behaviors does not tell us how the

Box 3.3 ◆◆◆◆◆◆◆◆◆◆◆◆◆◆◆◆◆◆◆◆◆◆◆◆◆

# A Case Example Questioning the Usefulness of the Mental Illness Concept

While working at a mental hospital, I was assigned a case involving a twenty-two-year-old male who decapitated his seventeen-year-old girlfriend. Two psychiatrists diagnosed him schizophrenic, and a court found him to be "innocent by reason of insanity." He was then committed to a mental hospital.

Why did he do it? Labeling him "insane" provides an explanation to the general public that he exhibited this strange behavior because he was "crazy." But does such a label explain why he killed this girl rather than killing someone else, or doing something else bizarre? Does the label explain what would have prevented him from committing this slaying? Does the label suggest the kind of treatment that will cure him? The answer to all these questions of course, is no.

What is schizophrenia? A common definition of schizophrenia is a psychotic condition characterized by disturbances of language, communication, thought, perception, affect, and behavior that lasts longer than six months. People who have Alzheimer's disease exhibit all these symptoms. Are they schizophrenic? No. What about the severely and profoundly mentally retarded who have a mental age of less than two? They have the above symptoms but are not considered schizophrenic. What about people who go into a coma following a serious accident? They also fit the definition above but are not considered schizophrenic. Many authorities are now asserting there is no definition of symptoms that separates people who have this "disease" from those who do not.

I generally agree with Albert Ellis's assertion that the reasons for the occurrence of any deviant act can be determined by examining what the offender was thinking prior to and during the time the deviant act was committed.[a] The twenty-two-year-old male who committed the bizarre homicide knew the act was wrong, was aware of what he was doing, was in contact with reality, and told me his reasons for doing what he did. Why was he labeled schizophrenic? After this person described what happened, it was understandable (even though bizarre) why he did what he did. His account also identified the specific problems he needed help with. He described himself as a very isolated person who, except for this girlfriend, had no close relatives or friends. He came from a broken home and was raised by a series of relatives and in foster homes. Because of frequent moves, he attended a number of different schools and made no lasting friends. At age twenty, he met the victim and dated her periodically for two years. She provided the only real meaning that he had in life. He held the traditional vision of marrying her and living happily together thereafter. However, a few months prior to the fatal day, he became very alarmed that he was going to "lose her." She encouraged him to date others, mentioned that she wanted to date others, and suggested that they no longer see as much of each other.

He thought long and hard how he could preserve the relationship. He also realized he had rather intense sexual tensions with no outlet. Putting the two together, he naively concluded, "If I'm the first person to have sexual relations with her, she will forever feel tied to me." Therefore, on several occasions, he tried

---

emotions or behaviors originated, nor does it tell us how to treat such emotions and behaviors. The material presented later in this chapter on rational therapy does both—it gives us an approach for identifying the sources of unwanted emotions and dysfunctional behaviors, and it provides strategies for changing unwanted emotions and dysfunctional behaviors.

## LABELING AS CAUSE OF CHRONIC "MENTAL ILLNESS"

A question frequently raised about Szasz's assertion that mental illness is a myth is: "If you assert mental illness doesn't exist, why do some people go through life as if they are mentally ill?" Thomas Scheff has developed a sociological theory that provides an answer.[17] Scheff's main hypothesis is that labeling is the most important determinant of people displaying a chronic (long-term) mental illness.

Scheff begins by defining how he will determine, for his research purposes, who is mentally ill. Before giving his definition, he notes:

> One source of immediate embarrassment to any social theory of "mental illness" is that the terms used in referring to these phenomena in our society prejudge the issue. The medical metaphor "mental illness" suggests a determinate process which occurs within the individual: the unfolding and development of disease. In order to avoid this assumption, we will utilize sociological, rather than medical, concepts to formulate the problem.[18]

to have coitus with her, but she always managed to dissuade him. Finally, one afternoon during the summer when he knew they would be alone together, he arrived at the following decision. "I *will* have sex with her this afternoon, even if I have to knock her unconscious." He stated he knew such action was wrong, but he said: "It was my last hope of saving our relationship. Without her, life would not be worth living."

He again tried to have sexual relations with her that afternoon, but she continued to dissuade him. Being emotionally excited, he then took a soda bottle and knocked her unconscious. He again attempted to have coitus but was still unsuccessful for reasons related to her physical structure. In an intense state of emotional and sexual excitement, he was unable to consider rationally the consequences of his actions. (All of us, at times, have done things while angry or in a state of intense emotional excitement that we would not have done in a calmer state.) At this point, he felt his whole world was caving in. When asked during an interview what he was thinking, he stated, "I felt that if I couldn't have her, no one else would either." He sought and found a knife, became further carried away with emotions, and ended up slaying her. He knew it was wrong, and he was aware of what he was doing.

From talking with this person (and identifying his thinking prior to and during this bizarre murder), I pinpointed certain factors that help explain why this murder took place, including this man's loneliness and isolation, his feeling that continuing a romantic relationship with this girl was the only source of meaning in his life, his naive thinking that a forced sexual relationship would make the girl feel tied and attracted to him, having no sexual outlet for his sexual drives, and

his jealous and possessive desires to go to extreme lengths to prevent this girl from developing a romantic relationship with anyone else. Such reasons help to explain why the bizarre behavior took place, whereas the label "schizophrenia" does not.

If the problems had been identified and treated prior to the murder, the slaying might have been prevented. What he needed was to find other sources of interest and other meaningful relationships in his life. Joining organizations in the community and developing hobbies may well have helped. An appropriate sexual outlet for his passions probably would have also been helpful. Better control of his passions and other sources of finding meaning might have prevented him from losing control of his emotions that afternoon. Reducing the intensity of his jealous and possessive feelings, along with developing more mature attitudes toward romance and sexuality, might also have been preventive. These specific problems are also the areas in which he needs help while in a mental hospital, rather than with finding a cure for his "schizophrenia." In no way do I feel that this person should be excused for his actions, as implied by the phrase "innocent by reason of insanity." But the person does need help for the specific problems identified. *In ten or fifteen years, he will probably be released and returned to society.* If these problems are not rectified, he will be a danger to society upon his release.

a. For further information on this theory, see Albert Ellis, *Reason and Emotion in Psychotherapy* (New York: Lyle Stuart, 1962).

*Source:* Adapted from Charles Zastrow, "When Labeled Mentally Ill," in *The Personal Problem Solver* (Englewood Cliffs, NJ: Prentice-Hall, 1977).

He states that the symptoms of mental illness can be viewed as violations of social norms and that, for his research purposes, the term *mentally ill* will be used to refer to those assigned such a label by professionals (usually psychiatrists).

Scheff indicates that literally thousands of studies have been conducted that seek to identify the origins of long-term mental disorders. Practically all of these studies have sought to identify the causes as being somewhere inside a person (e.g., metabolic disorders, unconscious conflicts, chemical imbalances, heredity factors). These research efforts have been based on medical and psychological models of human behavior. Yet, despite this extensive research, the determinants of chronic

mental disorder (e.g., schizophrenia) are largely unknown (see Box 3.3).

Scheff suggests that researchers may well be looking in the wrong direction for determinants. He suggests the major determinants lie in social processes (i.e., in interactions with others) rather than inside a person.

Scheff's theory can be briefly summarized as follows. Everyone at times violates social norms and commits acts that could be labeled as symptoms of mental illness. For example, a person may occasionally fight with others, experience intense depression or grief, suffer anxiety, use drugs or alcohol to excess, have a fetish, be an exhibitionist, or commit a bizarre act (see Box 3.4).

Usually, the person who has unwanted emotions or commits deviant acts is not identified (labeled) as

# Desperation Breeds Bizarre Behavior

If you wonder how someone could arrive at a point of doing something as bizarre as taking the life of a loved one, remember it is necessary to attempt to view the situation from the deviant person's perspective. To understand such a perspective, it is essential to try to consider all the circumstances, pressures, values, and belief systems of the deviant person. The following example may help demonstrate that practically anyone will do something bizarre when circumstances become desperate.

Several years ago a passenger plane crashed in the Andes Mountains during the winter. A number of people were killed, but there were nearly thirty survivors. Rescue efforts initially failed to locate the survivors, who took shelter from the cold in the wreckage of the plane. The survivors were without food for over forty days until they were finally rescued. During this time, the survivors were faced with the choice of dying of starvation or cannibalizing those who died. It was a very desperate, difficult situation, in which all but one survivor chose cannibalism; the one who refused died of starvation. Psychologically, many people who commit a bizarre act feel they face a comparable decision.

being mentally ill. Such emotions and deviant actions are typically not classified as symptoms of a mental illness but instead are ignored, unrecognized, or rationalized in some other manner. Occasionally, however, such norm violations are perceived by others as being "abnormal." The offenders are then labeled "mentally ill" and consequently related to as if they were mentally ill. When people are publicly labeled they are highly susceptible to cues from others. They realize they have done something unusual and turn to others for assessment of who they really are. In the absence of objective measures of their sanity, they rely on others for this assessment. If others relate to them as if they are mentally ill, they begin to define and perceive themselves as being mentally ill.

Traditional stereotypes of mental illness define the mentally ill role, both for those who are labeled mentally ill and for people with whom they interact. Those labeled mentally ill are often "rewarded" for enacting the social role of being mentally ill—rewarded with sympathy, attention, being excused from holding a job, from fulfilling requirements of other roles, and from being held responsible for their wrongdoing. In addition, those labeled mentally ill are "punished" for attempting to return to conventional roles; they are viewed with suspicion and implicitly considered still to be insane, and they have considerable difficulty in obtaining employment or a job promotion.

Such pressures and interactions with others gradually lead to changes in their self-concept; they begin to view themselves as different, as being insane. Often a vicious cycle is created: the more they enact the role of being mentally ill, the more they are defined and treated as mentally ill. The more explicitly they are defined and treated as being mentally ill, the more they are related to as if they were mentally ill, and so on. Unless this vicious cycle is interrupted, Scheff suggests, it will lead to a career of long-term mental illness. Scheff's conclusion is that, with this process, labeling is the single most important determinant of chronic mental illness.

If labeling is an important determinant of chronic functional mental illness, significant changes are suggested in diagnostic and treatment practices. Mental health personnel are frequently faced with uncertainty in deciding whether a person has a mental disorder. An informal norm has been developed to handle this uncertainty: when in doubt, it is better to judge a well person ill than to judge an ill person well. This norm is based on two assumptions taken from treating physical illnesses: first, a diagnosis of illness results in only minimal damage to the status and reputation of a person; and second, unless the illness is treated, it will become progressively worse. However, both these assumptions are questionable. Unlike medical treatment, psychiatric treatment can drastically change a person's status in the community; for example, it can remove legal rights that are difficult to regain. Furthermore, if Scheff is right about the adverse effects of mental illness labeling, then the exact opposite norm should be established to handle uncertainty; namely, when in doubt do not label a person mentally ill. This would be in accord with the legal approach that follows the norm, "When in doubt, acquit," or "A person is innocent until proven guilty."

If labeling is indeed a major determinant of mental illness, then certain changes are suggested in treating violators of social norms. One is to attempt to maintain and treat people with problems in their local community without labeling them mentally ill or sending them to a mental hospital where their playing

one flew east
one flew west
one flew over
the cuckoo's nest.

*Thomas Scheff believes that labeling is the most important determinant of people displaying a chronic mental illness. Once labeled, patients are more apt to believe there is something mentally wrong and to then act (for the rest of their lives) as if they are mentally ill.*

the role of the mentally ill is apt to be reinforced. In the past several years the field of mental health has been moving in this direction. Another outgrowth of Scheff's theory would be increasing public education efforts to inform the general population of the nature of emotional and behavioral problems and the adverse effects that result from inappropriate labeling.

## Mental Health Issues

Other issues are at stake in the field of mental health. These include care for the homeless, civil rights of those labeled mentally ill, improper use of the insanity plea to excuse criminals from their actions, the use (or misuse) of drugs in "treating" persons deemed mentally ill, and the merits and shortcomings of managed mental health care systems.

### THE HOMELESS

One of the population groups that has received considerable media attention in recent years is the homeless. Having thousands of homeless people in one of the richest nations in the world is a national disgrace. The number of homeless Americans continues to grow larger. The exact number is unknown, but estimates range from 250,000 to over three million.[19]

Many homeless live on the streets, in parks, in subways, or in abandoned buildings; food is often sought from garbage.

An estimated 25 to 50 percent of the homeless are thought to suffer from serious and chronic forms of mental illness.[20] Discharged from institutions without the support they need, tens of thousands of former patients live on the street in abominable conditions. Instead of providing support services for discharged patients, many states have a deinstitutionalized program of simply drugging people and dumping them into the street. Such an approach is a far cry from what was envisioned years ago when federal authorities embarked on an ambitious program to phase out large state hospitals and move the disturbed to more humane and convenient treatment in communities. Federal, state, and local governments have failed to provide enough housing, transitional care, and job training to integrate patients into society. In many areas of the country, a revolving-door policy prevails whereby patients are discharged from state hospitals only to return because of a lack of community support. It is true that institutional care is not only expensive (over $50,000 per year)[21] but frequently also stifles the intellectual, social, and physical growth of patients. However, the necessary supportive services have not been developed in most communities to serve discharged patients.

Deinstitutionalization of state mental hospitals is one reason for the large increase in the number of

*Two homeless men sleep by a heating vent. This photo was taken the day after the Stock Market panic on October 19, 1987. The economic crisis happened for these men long before the stocks fell.*

homeless. Cutbacks in social services during the Reagan and Bush administrations is another. Urban renewal projects have demolished low-cost housing in many areas. The shift from blue-collar jobs to service and high-tech jobs in our society has reduced sharply the demand for unskilled labor. Another factor has been a growing trend in our society to ignore members unable to fend for themselves. Most of the homeless are destitute because they cannot afford the housing that is available; our country does not have a commitment to a social policy of providing affordable housing to the poor.

Answers to these dismal conditions include low-cost housing, job training and placement programs, and community services for those with emotional problems.

Is our society willing to provide the necessary resources to meet the needs of the homeless? Deplorably, the answer is: "No, not at the present time."

## CIVIL RIGHTS

Involuntary confinement has been a controversial practice for years. State laws permitting involuntary hospitalization in mental health hospitals can be seen as infringement of a person's civil right of liberty. Although state laws differ, in some jurisdictions people may be hospitalized without their consent and without due process.[22] In some jurisdictions, people may be sent to mental hospitals without their consent, based on the statement of a physician.[23]

When this author worked at a hospital for the "criminally insane," there was a patient who was originally arrested on a disorderly conduct charge for urinating on a fire hydrant. Some neighbors thought he might be mentally ill, so the judge ordered that he be sent to a mental hospital for a sixty-day observation period to determine his sanity. The hospital judged him to be "insane" and "incompetent to stand trial" on the charge. He was not considered a harmful threat to himself or to others; but, with the hospital's finding, the judge confined him to a maximum security hospital for the criminally insane. When the author worked there, this patient had already been hospitalized for nine years—for committing an offense for which, if he had been found guilty, he would probably have been required only to pay a small fine.

Today, in most jurisdictions, persons cannot be involuntarily confined unless they commit illegal acts (such as aggravated assaults or suicide attempts) that demonstrate they are a threat either to themselves or to others. Such a policy provides some assurance that emotionally disturbed persons' right to liberty will be safeguarded. But such a policy has been sharply criticized as those emotionally disturbed persons who provide warning signs of doing bodily harm to others cannot be involuntarily confined unless they actually commit an illegal act. As a result, the civil right of others to safety in our society is infringed upon. Striking an acceptable balance between the disturbed person's right to liberty and society's right to safety and protection is a complex issue. Throughout our nation's history, our society's policy on this issue has shifted back and forth on the continuum between these two sets of rights.

In another civil rights area, some mental hospitals provide inadequate treatment. Legally speaking, this is a civil rights violation because in 1964 Congress established a statutory right to treatment in the Hospitalization of the Mentally Ill Act.[24]

Decisions about providing treatments such as electroconvulsive therapy (which has questionable value and may cause brain damage) also raise civil rights questions. The severely disturbed are often unable to make rational choices for their own welfare. Permission of relatives is sometimes obtained, but this still denies patients their fundamental rights.

Problems such as these caused the President's Commission on Mental Health to recommend in 1978 that due process be followed in arriving at decisions involving enforced hospitalization and treatment.[25] Federal court decisions have also reflected these concerns, holding that mental illness is not a sufficient basis for denying liberty and that hospitalized mental patients have a right either to receive adequate treatment or to be released.[26]

## PLEA OF NOT GUILTY
## BY REASON OF INSANITY

In 1979, a San Francisco jury found Dan White not guilty by reason of insanity on charges of the premeditated murder of city mayor George Moscone and city supervisor Harvey Milk. This verdict was rendered even though testimony clearly showed that these murders had been carefully planned and carried out by White.[27] The general public was as shocked by the jury's decision as it was by the crime. With this jury's decision, White was confined in a mental hospital for a few years and then released in 1984.

In 1982, John Hinkley, Jr., was found not guilty by reason of insanity of the attempted assassination of President Reagan a year earlier. Three other people were also injured by Mr. Hinkley in the assassination attempt. Mr. Hinckley is currently receiving treatment in a mental hospital.

Kenneth Bianchi (called the "Hollywood Hillside Strangler") was accused of murdering thirteen women in the Los Angeles area and two more in Washington State. Six different psychiatrists examining Bianchi came to three different conclusions about his mental state: two judged him sane, two judged him insane, and two were undecided.[28]

Such cases have forced the courts and psychiatrists to examine more carefully the plea of not guilty by reason of insanity. As indicated earlier, the terms *mental illness* and *mental health* are poorly defined. Mental illness (insanity) may not even exist. In a num-

ber of trials involving the insanity plea, prosecuting attorneys routinely use as witnesses those psychiatrists who are apt to judge the defendant "sane," whereas the defendant's attorney uses as witnesses those psychiatrists apt to judge the defendant "insane." An authority notes:

> Among psychiatrists, there is nothing remotely approaching a consensus on what constitutes insanity. Moreover, psychiatrists themselves concede that they lack reliable means for determining whether a person was insane in any sense at the time of a crime. All too often, they must rely heavily on the accused's behavior and on what he tells them—two types of data that a shrewd defendant can carefully orchestrate.[29]

Defendants are increasingly aware that they can probably get a psychiatrist to label them insane by "acting crazy," such as by openly performing indecent acts or by claiming to hear voices.

One argument for eliminating the insanity plea is that people are using it literally to get away with murder and other serious felonies. Instead of forcing people to take responsibility for their felonies, the insanity plea excuses them (not guilty by reason of insanity) for their crimes. The plea enables clever defendants (or their defense attorneys) to seek refuge from standard, appropriate retribution for their criminal acts, or both. A person acquitted by reason of insanity is generally sent to a mental institution and, under the law, is kept there until doctors determine and the judge concurs the person is no longer dangerous. Sadly, the measures for determining this judgment are as untrustworthy as those used to assign a mental illness label.

For example, E. E. Kemper III spent five years in a hospital for the criminally insane after murdering his grandparents. Mr. Kemper convinced psychiatrists and the judge that he was cured by giving rational answers to a battery of psychological tests (he memorized the answers prior to the tests) and was released. Three years later, he was again arrested, this time for having brutally killed eight women, including his mother, since his release.[30]

Psychiatrist Lee Coleman urges the insanity defense be eliminated altogether so that courts would be allowed to deal with the guilt or innocence of an individual without interference from psychiatrists. Coleman further urges that the convicted individual who later wishes help for emotional or behavioral problems could then request it.[31]

Because of the controversy over the insanity plea, a number of states have revised their laws surrounding this plea. One approach, which has been adopted by about twenty states, is a two-step process in which the jury first determines whether the defendant is innocent or guilty. If the defendant is found guilty, the jury then decides the defendant's sanity or insanity. If found insane, the defendant is usually sent to a maximum security mental hospital. When finally determined "cured," the defendant may then be required to fulfill the requirements of the original sentence—including time in prison. At least three states—Montana, Idaho, and Utah—have abolished the insanity defense entirely, but there is evidence that those who would have used the plea are now simply found incompetent to stand trial and end up in the same hospitals.

## USE OF PSYCHOTROPIC DRUGS

Psychotropic drugs include tranquilizers, antipsychotic drugs (such as thorazine) and antidepressant drugs. Since their discovery in 1954, the use of psychotropic drugs has been given substantial credit for the marked decrease in the number of patients in state hospitals—from 550,000 in 1955 to about 100,000 at the present time.[32] Psychotropic drugs do not "cure" emotional problems, but they are useful in reducing high levels of anxiety, depression, and stress.

Americans make extensive use of psychotropic drugs, particularly tranquilizers. Valium, Librium, Miltown, and other mild tranquilizers are widely used. Most general practitioners prescribe tranquilizers for the large number of patients who complain of tension and emotional upset. Lithium and Prozac have been found to be effective in reducing depression in a number of clients and are now widely prescribed by physicians. "Popping pills" (both legally and illegally) has become fashionable.

The dangers of excessive drug use include physical and psychological dependence and unwanted side effects. There is also the danger that, because drugs provide temporary symptom relief, users may focus their attention on taking pills rather than making the necessary changes in their lives to resolve the problems causing the anxiety, depression, or stress. Physicians face a dilemma in balancing the benefits of psychotropic drugs against the dangers of abuse, particularly when such drugs are sought by patients for extended periods of time. Because psychotropic drugs provide only temporary relief for patient symptoms such as anxiety and depression, many authorities urge that patients also receive counseling or psychotherapy to help resolve their emotional difficulties.

## MANAGED MENTAL HEALTH CARE

*Managed health care* is a generic term used to describe a variety of methods of delivering and financing health care services that are designed to contain the costs of service delivery while maintaining a defined level of quality of care. At its best, it is a system in which appropriate control, structure, and accountability enable the most efficient use of health resources to achieve maximal health outcome. (To date, there is a lack of agreement as to what is the "best" system.) At its worst, it is a system in which no real dollars are saved, and money is diverted to administrative operations and profits at the expense of needed patient services. Health care delivery is shifting from practice based on fee-for-service to managed care systems. An example of a managed care system is a health maintenance organization (HMO). Most U.S. corporations have now adopted a managed health benefit program to provide health insurance to their employees and their employees' families.

Mental health care has become a component of managed health care, as the health insurance programs offered by employers specify the types of mental health services that will be covered. There are a variety of ways to contain costs in managed health benefit programs for mental health services. Health plans may:

♦ restrict the number of days covered for inpatient care;

♦ limit the number of visits for psychotherapy;

♦ limit the number of dollars per year for mental health care per person;

♦ limit the number of dollars per lifetime for mental health care per person;

♦ increase deductibles;

♦ increase copayments;

♦ require referral by a gatekeeper, such as the primary care physician; and

♦ require approval on a case by case basis by a utilization review mechanism for the types and costs of services provided.

The introduction of managed mental health care has raised many complex issues, including:

♦ To what degree does the design and implementation of a given delivery system work for or against the best interests of the client?

♦ How is quality of care defined, and who defines it?

- What are the provisions for access to care for persons considered at high health risk? For example, there have been instances where a mental health provider has recommended inpatient care for a highly suicidal client, but the utilization review mechanism has denied reimbursement, with the client then subsequently taking his or her life.[33]

- Who has legitimate access to clients' mental health records? More review of care decisions and more computerization mean more prying eyes seeing personal mental health care information.

- Managed care provokes complex confidentiality issues.

- Do managed care efforts to streamline care and keep costs down lead to treating symptoms rather than underlying causes? For example, prescribing drugs that provide symptom relief is cheaper than long-term psychotherapy.

- Does managed care lead to a system in which those therapists who see more people in less time are rewarded, while those therapists who provide longer term care to fewer people are punished?

- Since managed care systems have policies that limit expenses, coverage limits can be a heavy burden for people who need expensive, long-term medication to treat such chronic mental disorders as bipolar disorder.

## Social Structure and Mental Illness

Sociologists have conducted a number of studies examining the relationships between social factors and the rate of mental illness. Questions investigated include:

- Is social class status related to the rate of mental illness?

- Does illness occur more in urban areas, suburbs, or rural areas?

- Which age groups are more prone to be affected?

- Does marital status have any relation to mental illness?

- Are men or women more apt to be affected?

- Does mental illness have any correlation to race?

(As indicated earlier, there is a question whether or not mental illness exists. Consequently, instead of continually repeating this question, the term *mentally ill* will be used in this section to refer to those *labeled* mentally ill.)

## SOCIAL CLASS

A classic study was conducted by Hollingshead and Redlich in New Haven, Connecticut.[34] The study examined the social class status of patients who were treated for a mental illness in hospitals and in private and public agencies. The researchers used a socioeconomic scale ranging from class I (highest) to class V (lowest). Results showed that the rate of mental illness was significantly higher in lower classes than in upper classes. Class V by far had the highest rate, with schizophrenia being eleven times more prevalent for class V than for class I if measured in terms of hospitalization rates. The study also found that the types of treatment and opportunities for rehabilitation for the lower classes were of a lower quality and less satisfactory than for the upper classes.

A second research project, by William Rushing, studied 4,500 males admitted for the first time to mental hospitals in Washington, DC.[35] Hospitalization rates again were found to vary inversely with class.

A third study was conducted in midtown Manhattan in the 1950s by Leo Srole and his associates.[36] The study involved conducting extensive interviews with 1,660 randomly selected people to find out if they had ever had a nervous breakdown, sought psychotherapy, or shown neurotic symptoms. A team of psychiatrists rated each case on the degree of psychiatric impairment. The study found almost 23 percent of the sample were considered "significantly" impaired in mental functioning, including many persons not under treatment. In addition, psychological impairment was found to correlate closely with social class. Nearly one person in every two in the lowest class was considered psychologically impaired, whereas the rate fell to one in eight for the highest class.

These studies clearly suggest that the poor are more apt to be labeled mentally ill. There are, however, a variety of explanations for these results. Perhaps the poor are less likely to seek treatment when emotional problems first begin to develop—thereby becoming mentally ill before receiving help. Perhaps they are under greater psychological stress, which leads to a higher rate. Perhaps their attitudes, values, education, and living conditions make them more susceptible to becoming mentally ill. Perhaps mental illness leads to a lower status. Psychiatrists may have less understanding of the value system of the poor and therefore be more apt to label lower-class behavior as being deviant or mentally ill. And finally, there may be no difference in severity and rate of emotional problems between social classes; it may just be that psychiatrists are less likely to assign a mental illness label to a person of a higher status because of the stigma associated with the label.

A number of studies have also found social class differences in quality of treatment for those labeled mentally ill.[37] Lower-class patients are likely to receive lower quality of care (often just custodial care when hospitalized) and to have lower rates of release when hospitalized in a mental institution.

## URBANIZATION

There is some evidence that cities, particularly the inner city areas, have a higher rate of mental illness than rural areas.[38] One explanation is that in cities (particularly inner city areas) the higher incidence is due to overcrowding and to the deteriorated quality of life—noise, crime, transportation problems, inadequate housing, unemployment, and drugs—which creates a higher level of emotional problems. Another explanation is that the higher rate in cities is due to mental health facilities being located in and around urban areas, which increases the probability that urban dwellers with emotional problems will be identified and treated.

## AGE

The elderly are more likely to have emotional problems, particularly depression (which is partially due to the low status that the elderly have in our society, which leads to a crushing sense of uselessness and isolation). An additional category of mental disorder that the elderly are apt to have is disturbances associated with degeneration of brain cells from such causes as arteriosclerosis and chronic alcoholism.[39]

## MARITAL STATUS

People who are single, divorced, or widowed have higher rates of mental disorder than married people. Unmarried men have somewhat higher rates than unmarried women.[40]

## SEX

Men and women are equally likely to be treated, but the nature of the diagnosis varies. Women are more likely to be diagnosed as suffering from anxiety, depression, and phobias, and are also more likely to be hospitalized in a mental institution. Men are more likely to be diagnosed as having a personality disorder.[41]

The vast majority of psychiatrists are men, and there is evidence that psychiatrists are more apt to consider sexual promiscuity or aggressive behavior in women a mental disorder but to overlook such behavior in men.[42]

## RACE

African Americans are more likely to be diagnosed mentally ill compared to whites, and their rate of hospitalization is substantially higher than the rate for whites.[43] There are several sociological explanations for these trends. African Americans may be under greater psychological pressure due to discrimination. Or, the higher rates may be due to their lower social status, as a greater proportion of people in the lower social classes is diagnosed mentally ill. Or, because most psychiatrists are white, they may have less awareness of the lifestyles of African Americans. This lack of awareness may lead psychiatrists to more readily assign mentally ill labels to African Americans who may differ in class, status, cultural values, and cultural background from whites.

## Treatment

Treatment of the so-called mentally ill, past and present, is fraught with controversy. To see from where we have come and how we got here, we will first consider the history of the various treatments of the emotionally disturbed. Then, after briefly describing current treatment facilities, we will discuss current counseling and psychotherapy approaches (e.g., see Box 3.5).

### HISTORY OF TREATMENT

The history of treatment for the emotionally disturbed is fascinating but also filled with injustices and tragedies. George Rosen documents that most societies have developed unique ways of viewing mental illness and treating those so labeled.[44] In some societies, deviants have been valued highly—even treated as prophets having supernatural powers. In others, the emotionally disturbed have been viewed as evil threats

Box 3.5 ◆◆◆◆◆◆◆◆◆◆◆◆◆◆◆◆◆◆◆◆◆◆◆◆◆◆◆◆

# An Approach to Understanding and Treating Bizarre Behavior

Several years ago, I worked as a counselor at a maximum security hospital for the so-called criminally insane. A number of the residents at this hospital had committed bizarre crimes, due to emotional and behavioral problems. In one case, a twenty-two-year-old male decapitated his seventeen-year-old friend. In another, a married male with four children was arrested for the fourth time for exposing himself. In still another, a male dug up several graves and used the corpses to "redecorate" his home. Another married man was committed after it was discovered he was involved in incestuous relationships with his eleven- and twelve-year-old daughters. Another man was committed after several efforts to deliver sermons in local taverns and after he kept maintaining clouds followed him around in whatever direction he was going. Another brutally killed his father with an axe.

Is there a way to explain why these men did what they did? A variety of interpretations have been offered by different authorities, most of which assert they acted strangely because they are mentally ill.

Albert Ellis, a prominent psychologist, has advanced a different explanation, which offers considerable promise in understanding and treating people who commit bizarre offenses. In a nutshell, Ellis asserts that, through looking at what the offenders were thinking when they committed unusual offenses, we will be able to gain an understanding of: (a) why the bizarre actions occurred; (b) what would have prevented the bizarre actions from happening; and (c) what services are now needed to prevent the offenders from again getting into trouble upon their release.[a]

At the maximum security hospital, Ellis's interpretation was applied to the grave digger's case. The man was forty-six years old when he began digging up graves and redecorating his home. His mother had died three and a half years earlier. Unfortunately, his mother was the only person who had provided meaning to his life. He was shy and had no other friends; the two had lived together in a small, rural community for twenty-two years. After his mother's death, he became even more isolated, with no friends, living by himself. Being very lonely, he wished his mother were still alive. As happens with many people who lose someone close, he began dreaming his mother was still alive. His dreams appeared so real that, upon awakening, he found it difficult to believe his mother was definitely dead. With such thoughts, he began thinking his mother could, in fact, be brought back to life. He concluded that bringing corpses of females to his home would help bring his mother back. (Now, to us, this idea certainly appears irrational; but, being isolated, he had no way of checking what was real and what was not.) Feeling very deeply the loss of his mother, he decided to give the idea a try. He, of course, needed counseling services (then and now) that would help him adjust to his mother's death, that would help him find new interests in life, that would help him become more involved with other people, and that would enable him to exchange thoughts with others to check out what is real and what is not.

---

a. Albert Ellis, *Reason and Emotion in Psychotherapy* (New York: Lyle Stuart, 1962).

and feared as being possessed with demon powers. In medieval times, for example, they were viewed as possessed by demons and "treated" by flogging, starving, and dunking in hot water to drive the devils out. During a brief period in our colonial history, a few of the disturbed were viewed as being witches and burned at the stake. Prior to the nineteenth century, the severely disturbed in the United States were confined in "almshouses," received only harsh custodial care, and were often chained to the walls.[45]

In the nineteenth century, a few mental institutions in France, England, and the United States began to take a more humanitarian approach to treating the disturbed. Although the severely disturbed were still confined in institutions, they began to be viewed as either having an illness or as having an emotional problem. Physical surroundings were improved, and efforts were made to replace the harsh custodial treatment with a caring approach that recognized each resident as a person deserving of respect and dignity. Unfortunately, these humanitarian efforts were not widely accepted, partly because they were considered too expensive. Most of the severely disturbed continued to be confined to overcrowded, unsanitary dwellings with inadequate care and diet.

In 1908, Clifford Bers's book, *A Mind that Found Itself,* was published.[46] Beers had been committed to a mental institution and his book recounted the atrocities he witnessed during his confinement. The book reached a wide audience and sensitized the

# Asylums and Total Institutions

In 1961, Erving Goffman wrote *Asylums,* which described life inside state mental hospitals.[a] Goffman indicates such mental hospitals are "total institutions." (Other total institutions are prisons, boot camps, monasteries, and convents.) In a total institution, a resident is cut off from society for appreciable periods of time and required to lead a regimented life. Inside an asylum, residents are stripped of their possessions and cut off from contact with the outside world. Total institutions seek to fully control residents and to resocialize and remake their lives. In such institutions, the fear of expulsion is a major control mechanism. In asylums, long-term confinement tends to result in people losing their capacity to respond in an adult fashion. Confinement gradually undermines their capacity to cope with the outside world.

Total institutions teach residents to accept the staff's view of right and wrong and erode residents' capacity to think independently. Goffman points out that such actions as raising questions about the therapeutic value of certain mental health programs in a mental institution are not taken as signs of mental stability, but as symptoms of sickness. The "good" patient, from the staff's point of view, is one who is undemanding, docile, and obedient. Such resocialization actually hinders residents from being able to make a successful return to society. The movie *One Flew Over the Cuckoo's Nest* vividly portrays the resocialization process described by Goffman.

---

a. Erving Goffman, *Asylums: Essays on the Social Situation of Mental Patients and Other Inmates* (New York: Doubleday, 1961).

the 1920s to the 1950s, most psychiatrists, social workers, and clinical psychologists accepted Freud's and other psychoanalytic theorists' views in regard to diagnosing and treating the disturbed.

Freud's influence was successful in having the public accept a more humanitarian approach in treating the disturbed. However, in the 1950s, questions began to arise about the effectiveness of the psychoanalytic approach. It was expensive (an analysis took four or five years), and research studies began to appear showing that the rate of improvement for those undergoing analysis was no higher than for those receiving no treatment.[47] Since the 1950s, a variety of counseling approaches has been developed that reject most or all of the concepts underlying psychoanalysis. These newer approaches include behavior modification, rational therapy, reality therapy, transactional analysis, feminist intervention, family therapy, and client-centered therapy.[48]

It should be mentioned that since the nineteenth century certain segments of the medical profession have continued to maintain that mental illness is akin to other physical illnesses. They assert that infectious diseases, genetic endowment, and metabolic disorders are the causes of mental disorders.[49] However, only a few specific organic causes have been identified. General paresis, for instance, which is a progressive emotional disorder, has been linked to syphilis; and pellagra, another disorder, has been found to result from dietary deficiency. The notion that mental disorders are physiological led to certain medical treatments that now appear tragic (see Box 3.6). In the eighteenth century, bloodletting was widely used. In the early twentieth century, prefrontal lobotomies (surgical slashing of the frontal section of the brain) were performed to "remove" the mental illness. Lobotomies have little therapeutic value, cause lasting brain damage, and result in patients becoming docile and retarded.

In the past thirty years, there have been two major developments in the treatment of the severely disturbed. One was the discovery and use of psychoactive drugs—both tranquilizers and antidepressants. The initial hope was that such drugs would cure severe disturbances, but it was soon realized that they provide primarily symptom relief and thereby enable the disturbed person to be more accessible to other therapy programs and approaches.[50] The other development was deinstitutionalization. Mental health practitioners realized that mental hospitals, instead of "curing" the disturbed, were frequently perpetuating disturbed behavior via long-term hospitalization.[51]

public to the emotional trauma experienced by those confined. Under Beers's leadership, mental health associations were formed that advocated the need for improved inpatient care and initiated the concept of outpatient treatment.

Between 1900 and 1920, Sigmund Freud developed psychoanalytic theories about the causes of, and ways to treat, emotional problems. Emotional problems were seen as being mental illnesses, resulting from early traumatic experiences, internal psychological conflicts, fixations at various stages of development, and unconscious psychological processes. From

The disturbed were labeled mentally ill, and through long-term hospitalization would define themselves as "different" and enact the insane role. Also, they became adapted to the relaxed, safe life of a hospital, and the longer they stayed the more they perceived the outside world as threatening.

Mental health professionals now use hospitalization only for those whose emotional problems pose a serious threat to their own well-being or to the well-being of others. Psychotherapy is the main treatment approach used in mental hospitals. (A group psychotherapeutic approach is described in Box 3.7.) In most cases now, hospitalization for an emotional problem is brief. The concept of deinstitutionalization has brought about a significant expansion of services designed to meet the needs of the disturbed in their home community—including community-based mental health centers, halfway houses, rehabilitation workshops, social therapeutic clubs, and foster care services.

A criticism of the deinstitutionalization approach has been that some communities have returned long-term hospitalized patients to society *without* developing adequate community-based support services. The result is that many of the patients discharged are living with families, friends, or on the street, while receiving little or no counseling and medical services. Without support services, the emotional stability of many of these discharged patients is deteriorating, and area residents tend to fear them.

Recent investigations reveal incidents of discharged mental patients living in squalor in unlicensed group homes and low-quality hotels.[52] Many are victims of crime, fire, and medical neglect. Some are fed rancid food and exposed to rats and cockroaches. Sometimes, such former patients set fires, abuse others, or both, and a few commit homicide or suicide.

## TREATMENT FACILITIES—COMMUNITY MENTAL HEALTH CENTERS

Treatment services for emotional and behavioral problems are provided by nearly every direct-service social welfare agency, including public welfare agencies, probation and parole agencies, penal institutions, school social services, family service agencies, adoption agencies, sheltered workshops, nursing homes, and social service units in hospitals. However, in many communities, mental health centers are a primary resource for serving those with emotional problems.

Community mental health centers were given their impetus with the passage by the federal government of the Community Mental Health Centers Act of 1963. This act provided for transferring the care and treatment of the majority of "mentally ill" persons from state hospitals to their home communities. The emphasis is on local care, with provision of comprehensive services (particularly to low-income areas and people).

Other emphases are early diagnosis, treatment, and early return to community; the centers being located near and accessible to the populations they serve; each center being established to serve between seventy-five thousand and two hundred thousand people; the provision of comprehensive care having five basic components—inpatient care; outpatient care; partial hospitalization (e.g., day, night, and weekend care); emergency care; and consultation/education. Services provided are expected to relate to a wide range of problem areas and population groups, such as the disturbed, the elderly, minorities, and those with alcohol and other drug-related problems.

Professionals in a community mental health center may include psychiatrists, social workers, psychologists, psychiatric nurses, specialized consultants, occupational and recreational therapists, and paraprofessionals. Typical services include outpatient care, inpatient care, alcohol and chemical abuse treatment, work evaluation, occupational therapy, family and group therapy, transportation service, counseling, crisis intervention (including twenty-four-hour emergency care), community education, and field training of students in helping professions.

Community mental health services have been criticized by studies that have found some to be ineffective and inadequate.[53] Patients still have high readmission rates and inadequate levels of adjustment to the community.[54] Many centers have been ineffective in dealing with the personal and societal problems of large numbers of poor people, with many of these so-called comprehensive centers providing little more than traditional inpatient and outpatient care for middle-class patients.[55]

On the other hand, proponents of community mental health centers argue that the results of such centers have been impressive. They point out that their programs have reduced the number of people in state and county mental hospitals from 550,000 in 1955 to about 100,000 at the present time.[56]

## COUNSELING AND PSYCHOTHERAPY

The primary therapy approach used to treat people with emotional or behavioral problems is psychotherapy, or

# Group Therapy at a Mental Hospital

Several years ago, while employed as a counselor at a maximum security hospital for the so-called criminally insane, I was requested by a supervisor to develop and lead a therapy group. The following is a first-person account of that group.

Some of the questions I first asked were, "What should be the objective of such a group?" and "Who should be selected to join?" My supervisor indicated those decisions would be mine. He added that no one else was doing any group therapy at this hospital, and the hospital administration thought it would be desirable for accountability reasons for group therapy programs to be developed.

Being newly employed at the hospital and wary because I had never been a leader for a group before, I asked myself, "Who is in the greatest need of group therapy?" I also wondered, "If the group members do not improve—or if they deteriorate—how will I be able to explain this, that is, cover my tracks?" I concluded that I should select those identified as being the "sickest" (those labeled as chronic schizophrenic) to invite as members of the group. Those labeled as chronic schizophrenic are generally expected to show little improvement. With such an expectation, if they did not improve, I felt I would not be blamed. However, if they did improve, I thought it would be viewed as a substantial accomplishment.

My next step was to invite these patients to join the group. I met with them individually and explained the purpose of the group and the probable topics that would be covered. I then invited them to join; eight of the eleven who were contacted decided to join. Some of the eight frankly stated they would join primarily because it would look good on their record and increase their chances for an early release.

In counseling these group members, the therapy approach that was used was based on reality therapy.[a] I began the first group meeting by stating I knew what the "key" was to their being discharged from the hospital, and, I asked if they knew what that might be. This statement got their attention. I indicated the "key" is very simple—they have to learn to "act sane," so that the medical staff thinks they have recovered. At this first meeting the purpose and the focus of the group were again presented and described. It was explained that the purpose was not to review their pasts, but to help them make their present life more enjoyable and meaningful and to help them to make plans for the future. Various topics, it was explained, would be covered, including how to convince the hospital staff they no longer needed to be hospitalized, how to prepare themselves for returning to their home community (for example, learning an employable skill while at the institution), what to do when they felt depressed or had some other unwanted emotion, and what they should do following their release if and when they had an urge to do something that would get them into trouble again. It was further explained that occasional films covering some of these topics would be shown and then discussed, and it was indicated the group would meet for about an hour each week for the next twelve weeks (until the fall, when I had to return to school).

This focus on improving the patients' current circumstances stimulated their interest, but they

---

counseling. (These two terms will be used interchangeably since there does not appear to be a discrete distinction between the two.) Counseling services are provided by practically every direct-service social welfare agency. *Counseling* is a broad term covering individual, family, and group therapy. A skilled counselor has knowledge of interviewing principles and comprehensive and specialized treatment approaches. Material in these two areas is designed to give the reader a flavor of what counseling actually is.

*Interviewing Principles* Counseling someone with personal problems is neither magical nor mystical.

Although training and experience in counseling is beneficial, everyone has the potential of helping another by listening and talking through difficulties. Successful counseling can be done by a friend, neighbor, relative, or the local barber, as well as by social workers, psychiatrists, psychologists, guidance counselors, and the clergy. This is not to say that everyone will be successful at counseling. Professional people, because of their training and experience, have a higher probability of success, but competence and empathy (rather than degrees or certificates) are keys to desirable outcomes.

There are three phases to counseling: building a relationship, exploring problems in depth, and exploring

soon found it uncomfortable and anxiety producing to examine what the future might hold for them. Being informed they had some responsibility and some control of that future also created anxiety. They reacted to this discomfort by stating that they were mentally ill and therefore had some internal condition which was causing their strange behavior and that, unfortunately, a cure for schizophrenia had not yet been found. Therefore, they could do little to improve their situation.

They were informed their excuses were "garbage" (stronger terms were used), and we spent a few sessions on getting them to understand that "chronic schizophrenic" was a meaningless label. I spent considerable time explaining that mental illness is a myth; that is, people do not have a "disease of the mind" even though they may have emotional problems. I went on to explain that what had gotten them locked up was their deviant behavior and that the only way for them to get out was to stop exhibiting their strange behavior and to convince the other staff that they would not be apt to exhibit deviant behavior if released.

The next set of excuses they tried was that their broken homes, or ghetto schools, or broken romances, or something else in their pasts had "messed them up" and therefore they could do little about their situation. They were informed such excuses were also "garbage." True, their past experiences were important to their being in the hospital. But it was emphasized that what they wanted out of the future, along with their motivation to do something about achieving their goals, was more important than their past experiences in determining what the future would hold for them.

Finally, after we had worked through a number of excuses, we were able to focus on how they could better handle specific problems: how to handle being depressed, how to stop exhibiting behavior considered "strange," how to present themselves as being "sane" in order to increase their chances of an early release, how they would feel about returning to their home communities, what kind of work or career they desired upon their release, how they could prepare themselves by learning a skill or trade while at this institution, what they wanted out of the future and the specific steps they would have to take to achieve these goals, why it was important that they should continue to take the psychoactive medication that had been prescribed, and so on.

The results of this approach were very encouraging. Instead of idly spending much of the time brooding about their situation, the participants became motivated to improve their situation. At the end of the twelve weeks, the eight members of the group spontaneously stated that the meetings were making a positive change in their lives and requested that another counselor from the hospital be assigned to the group after I left to continue my college education. This was arranged. Three years later, on a return visit to the hospital, I was informed that five of the eight group members had been released to their home community and two of the others were considered to have shown improvement. The final group member's condition was described as "unchanged." Of course, without a scientific study, there is no way to be sure that the improvements noted were due specifically to participation in the therapy group.

a. See William Glasser, *Reality Therapy* (New York: Harper and Row, 1965) for the basis of this therapeutic approach.

alternative solutions. Successful counseling gradually proceeds from one phase to the next with some overlapping of these phases. For example, in many cases, while exploring problems, the relationship between the counselor and the counselee continues to develop.

In the first phase, *building a relationship,* the counselor should seek to establish a nonthreatening atmosphere in which the counselee feels safe to communicate fully his or her troubles while also feeling accepted as a person. It is important for the counselor to come across as a warm, caring, knowledgeable, and understanding person who may be able to help and who wants to try. The counselor should show respect for the counselee's values and not try to force his or her values on the counselee.

In *exploring problems in depth,* the counselor should help the counselee examine the extent of the problem, how long the problem has existed, what the causes are, how the counselee feels about the problem, and what physical and mental capacities and strengths the counselee has available to cope with the problem—all prior to exploring alternative solutions. Consider, for example, a single teenager who is pregnant. The counselor and counselee need to explore the following questions: How does she feel about being pregnant? Has she seen a doctor? Has she had a

*Anne McGrath of Project Reachout attempts to "build a relationship" with a mentally ill homeless woman on Broadway Street in New York City.*

pregnancy test? About how long has she been pregnant? Do her parents know? What are their feelings and concerns if they know? Has she informed the alleged father? What are his feelings and concerns if he knows? What does she feel is the most urgent situation to deal with first? Answers to such questions will determine the future direction of counseling. The most pressing, immediate problem might be to inform her parents, who may react critically, or it might be to secure medical services.

When a problem area is identified, usually a number of subproblems occur. For example, a single female who discovers she is pregnant may have a number of concerns, such as how to tell her parents, whether to have an abortion, and so on. All of these concerns should be discussed in depth.

The third phase, *exploring alternative solutions,* occurs after a problem is discussed in depth. During this stage the counselor and the counselee jointly explore ways to resolve the problem. Usually, the counselor first asks the counselee what solutions she or he had thought about (or even tried) for resolving the problem. If the counselor knows of some additional strategies, the counselor then presents these. The counselor and counselee then generally explore the merits, shortcomings, and consequences of the various strategies. Initial choices in the previous example include terminating the pregnancy and continuing

the pregnancy to full term. If the teenager decides to continue the pregnancy to full term, possible alternatives for the subproblem of making plans for living arrangements include keeping the child, getting married, seeking public assistance, finding foster care after delivery, filing a paternity suit, placing the child for adoption, and obtaining the assistance of a close relative to help or care for the child.

***Comprehensive and Specialized Counseling Approaches*** In addition to having a good grasp of interviewing principles, an effective counselor needs to have a knowledge of comprehensive counseling theories and of specialized treatment techniques to be able to diagnose precisely what problems exist and decide how to intervene effectively. There are a number of contemporary comprehensive counseling approaches: psychoanalysis, rational therapy, client-centered therapy, Adlerian psychotherapy, behavior modification, Gestalt therapy, reality therapy, transactional analysis, neurolinguistic programming, and encounter approaches. (A good summary of contemporary global counseling approaches is provided in Raymond Corsini and Danny Wedding [eds.], *Current Psychotherapies,* 5th ed. [Itasca, IL: Peacock, 1995]; and Charles Zastrow, *The Practice of Social Work,* 6th ed. [Pacific Grove, CA: Brooks/Cole, 1999]). These therapy approaches generally present theoretical material on (a) personality theory, or how normal psychosocial development occurs; (b) behavior pathology, or how emotional and behavioral problems arise, and (c) therapy, or how to change unwanted emotions and dysfunctional behaviors.

An effective counselor generally has a knowledge of several treatment approaches. Depending on the unique set of problems being presented by the client, the counselor picks and chooses from his or her "bag of tricks" the intervention strategy that is likely to have the highest probability of success. In addition to comprehensive counseling approaches, there are a number of specialized treatment techniques for specific problems, such as assertiveness training for people who are shy or overly aggressive, relaxation techniques for people experiencing high levels of stress, specific sex therapy techniques for such difficulties as premature ejaculation or orgasmic dysfunction, and parent effectiveness training for parent/child relationship difficulties. (A summary of specialized treatment techniques is contained in Charles Zastrow, *The Practice of Social Work*, 6th ed. [Pacific Grove, CA: Brooks/Cole, 1999]). An effective counselor strives to gain a working knowledge of a wide variety of treatment techniques in order to increase the likelihood of being able to help clients.

For illustrative purposes, one comprehensive therapy approach, rational therapy, will be summarized.

***Rational Therapy.*** The two main developers of rational therapy are Albert Ellis and Maxie Maultsby.[57] The approach potentially enables those who become skillful in rationally analyzing their self-talk to control or get rid of any undesirable emotion or any dysfunctional behavior.

It is erroneously believed by most people that our emotions and our actions are determined primarily by our experiences (i.e., by events that happen to us). On the contrary, rational therapy has demonstrated that the primary cause of all our emotions and actions is what we tell ourselves about events that happen to us. *All* feelings and actions occur according to the following format:

*Events*

↓

*Self-talk*

↓

*Emotions*

↓

*Actions*

*Events,* or experiences, are what happens to us. *Self-talk* is the set of evaluating thoughts we give ourselves about these events or experiences. *Emotions* are how we feel about these events and may include simply remaining calm. *Actions* are how we behave in response to the events, our self-talk, and our emotions. The following example will illustrate this process:

*Event*

Cheryl, the five-year-old daughter of Mr. and Mrs. Shaw, knocks over and breaks a lamp while playing with her brother.

↓

*Mr. Shaw's Self-talk*

"That lamp was our favorite; we bought it on our honeymoon—it's irreplaceable. This is awful."

"Spare the rod and spoil the child—some stiff discipline will make her shape up."

"As head of this household, it's my duty to make her shape up. I'll teach her a lesson she'll never forget by giving her the spanking of her life."

"She's always breaking things. I think this might have been intentional! I'll teach her to have respect for me and for our valuable items."

↓

*Emotions*

Anger, disappointment, frustration.

↓

*Actions*

Spanking and yelling at Cheryl, with the severity of the spanking bordering on abuse.

If, on the other hand, Mr. Shaw gives himself different self-talk, his emotions and actions will be quite different, as illustrated here:

*Event*

Cheryl, the five-year-old daughter of Mr. and Mrs. Shaw, knocks over and breaks a lamp while playing with her brother.

↓

*Mr. Shaw's Self-talk*

"This was a lamp we cherished, but I know she didn't break it intentionally. It was an accident. My getting angry at this point won't help."

"I might have prevented this accident by informing Cheryl and our son that they can horse around only in the rec room and in their bedrooms."

"With young children, some accidents are bound to happen."

# A Case Example Using Rational Therapy: The End of a Marriage

A forty-one-year-old college student sought counseling about her deteriorating relationship with her estranged husband and her son. After discussing her feelings in some depth, the counselor instructed her to counter her unwanted emotions by doing a rational self-analysis (RSA). Names and other identifying information have been changed.

Doing an RSA involves writing down:

A. The facts and events that occurred

B. The self-talk a person gives himself or herself

C. The emotions that are experienced

Da. The self-talk statements found in the A section—which should be in the B section (these self-talk statements are identified after looking at the A section to judge whether the statements are factual or whether some are self-talk statements)

Db. Positive and rational self-talk challenges to the negative and irrational self-talk in the B section (this segment is the main therapeutic part of the process)

E. The person's emotional and behavioral goals

The format follows. For this process to be therapeutic, the person must practice replacing the irrational self-talk with rational self-talk.

*Note:* Three weeks after writing this RSA, the student informed her counselor that using these rational debates had helped her immensely in accomplishing her emotional and behavioral goals. However, she added that the process of training her mind to use the rational debates when she was "awfulizing" about the ending of her marriage was much more difficult than she originally anticipated.

---

*A*
*Facts and Events*

On March 14, 1990, I separated from my husband, Blair, because our marriage wasn't working. The marriage was causing me extreme pain, and my husband refused to go to counseling with me. Three weeks after the separation, he filed for a divorce. Since the hearing on April 19, 1990, he has refused to cooperate in following through on his decision to get a divorce. He has refused to have the house and furniture assessed. He has postponed the divorce trial three times. In February 1991 my attorney notified me that my husband has cancer and is in Memorial Hospital. The trial was postponed gain. Both my husband and son blame me for the divorce and for my husband's illness. My son has refused to see me or have any relationship with me since I moved out last March.

---

*Da*
*Camera Check of A*

This is all factual.

**B**
*My Self-Talk*

B-1. "It's not fair. I want out of this marriage. It has dragged on for over a year." (bad)

B-2. "Blair is doing this purposely to keep me from living my own life." (bad)

B-3. "I caused Blair's cancer because I separated from him. It's all my fault." (bad)

B-4. "I'll never see my son again because he blames me for his father's illness." (bad)

B-5. "I have no right to be enjoying myself with Scott. I don't deserve to be happy." (bad)

B-6. "I may never be divorced. If Blair goes into remission, the trial will be rescheduled; if he has a relapse, it will be postponed again. This situation can drag on forever." (bad)

B-7. "I am a bad person for becoming involved with Scott when Blair may be dying." (bad)

B-8. "People will think I'm awful for enjoying myself and my life." (bad)

B-9. "I'm a bad mother because Paul won't see me." (bad)

B-10. "If Blair dies, I won't have maintenance, so I won't have enough money to get through school." (bad)

**Db**
*My Rational Debates of B*

Db-1. "Life isn't always fair. I will make the best of the situation and accept the inconvenience."

Db-2. "Blair may be stalling the divorce, but I can and will live my own life."

Db-3. "I didn't cause the cancer. I'm not that powerful. His illness *isn't* my fault."

Db-4. "I am not seeing my son now, but I don't know what the future may hold. Time heals many wounds."

Db-5. "I have the right to live my own life and to enjoy my relationship with Scott. I deserve a healthy relationship."

Db-6. "I will eventually be free. It may drag on longer than I'd like; however, I doubt it will go on forever."

Db-7. "I am not a bad person. I'm a person who has the right to go forward and develop a new relationship that meets my needs. What is happening to Blair has nothing to do with me."

Db-8. "What people think is not my concern. What is more important is what I think. I think it is okay to enjoy my life and to live it to the fullest."

Db-9. "I'm not a bad mother. I am a good mother. Paul's choice of sides in this divorce has nothing to do with whether I'm a good or a bad mother."

Db-10. "If Blair dies, I'll find other options. I can get more student loans. I could get a full-time job and go to school part-time. I will reach my goals of graduating with a B.S. degree and going to graduate school."

**C**
*My Emotions*

I feel depressed, guilty, hurt, angry, controlled, disappointed, sad, lonely, and frustrated. (very, very bad)

**E**
*My Emotional and Behavioral Goals*

To stop feeling depressed and guilty, and to get rid of my other unwanted emotions;

To feel comfortable in dating Scott;

To feel sufficiently relaxed to concentrate on my studies;

To do whatever is reasonable to restore my relationship with Paul;

To do whatever is reasonable to facilitate the ending of my marriage to Blair.

*Source:* Adapted from Charles Zastrow, "End of a Marriage," in *You Are What You Think* (Chicago: Nelson-Hall, 1993), 32–35.

"The most constructive thing I can do at this point is to say that I understand that it was an accident, that all of us are disappointed that the lamp broke, and that in the future their horsing around should be limited to the rec room and their bedrooms."

↓

*Emotions*

Some disappointment, but overall acceptance and calm.

↓

*Actions*

In an understanding fashion talking to the children and expressing his thoughts in line with his self-talk.

The most important points about this process are that our self-talk determines how we feel and act, and that by changing our self-talk, we can change how we feel and act. Generally, we cannot control events that happen to us, but we have the power to think rationally and thereby change *all* of our unwanted emotions and ineffective actions. According to Maultsby, rational thinking and rational behavior (a) is consistent with the facts; (b) helps you protect your life; (c) helps you achieve your short- and long-term goals more quickly; (d) helps you get out and stay out of significant trouble with other people; and (e) helps you prevent significant unwanted emotions.[58]

The rehabilitative aspect of this conceptualization of self-talk is that any unwanted emotion and any ineffective behavior can be changed by identifying and then changing the underlying self-talk. (The use of rational therapy is demonstrated in Box 3.8.)

## *Summary*

Emotional problems and behavioral problems are two broad labels covering an array of disorders. All of us at times experience emotional and behavioral problems. Serious or severe emotional problems are sometimes labeled "mental illnesses."

The history of treatment for the emotionally disturbed has included many injustices and tragedies. In the past the disturbed have been viewed in a variety of positive and negative ways. Recent major developments are the discovery and use of psychoactive drugs and the trend toward deinstitutionalization.

A major controversy continues over whether mental illness actually exists. Adherents of the medical approach believe the disturbed person's mind is affected by some generally unknown, internal condition. As critics of the medical model, proponents of the interactional model assert that disturbed people display a social deviation or have an emotional problem but do not have a disease of the mind. Further, they assert mental illness labels have no diagnostic or treatment value and frequently have an adverse labeling effect.

Another major mental health issue is civil rights concerns over involuntary confinement, inadequate treatment, and enforced use of treatment approaches that have adverse side effects. In regard to involuntary confinement, it is very difficult to establish a policy that strikes an acceptable balance between the disturbed person's right to liberty and society's right to safety and protection. Other issues include the usefulness of the plea of not guilty by reason of insanity, the extent to which psychotropic drugs should be used, and whether local communities are providing adequate services for the emotionally disturbed who, due to deinstitutionalization, are no longer being sent to state mental hospitals. The emergence of managed mental health care systems raises a number of issues, including the extent to which such systems are restricting the provision of needed services to persons with emotional or behavioral difficulties.

Sociologists have found a number of associations between social factors and mental illness. Higher rates of diagnosed mental illness have been found in the lower socioeconomic classes, in inner cities as compared to rural areas, among the elderly, among unmarried people, and among African Americans as compared to whites. Men and women are about equally likely to receive treatment. Women are more likely to be diagnosed as suffering from anxiety, depression, and phobias and to be hospitalized; men are more likely to be labeled as having a personality disorder. Lower-class patients often receive lower-quality care.

The main therapy approach used to treat people with emotional and behavioral problems is psychotherapy or counseling. *Counseling* is a broad term covering individual, family, and group therapy. A skilled counselor has knowledge of interviewing principles and a variety of comprehensive and specialized treatment approaches. Based on the unique set of problems presented by each client, an effective counselor is able to choose which intervention strategy is apt to have the highest probability of success.

Practically everyone has taken one or more drugs. Most people occasionally have used a drug excessively. A large proportion of our population, as we shall see, is currently abusing one or more drugs. This chapter:

♦ defines drugs and drug abuse;

♦ provides a brief history of our drug-taking society;

♦ presents sociological theories of drug abuse;

♦ describes drug subcultures;

♦ summarizes facts about and effects of commonly used drugs;

♦ describes rehabilitation programs for drug abuse; and

♦ presents suggestions to curb drug abuse in the future.

## *Drugs and Society*

What is generally considered to be a drug, a dangerous drug, or abuse of a drug depends partly on the various norms and traditions of a given society. Our first job, then, is to define the terms *drug* and *drug abuse* as they apply to our study of social problems. Also to be considered is our society's approach to various drugs, sociologists' theories about drug abuse, and the existence and effects of societal subcultures that accept the use of illegal drugs.

### DRUGS AND DRUG ABUSE

Pharmacologically, a *drug* is any substance that chemically alters the function or structure of a living organism.[1] Such a definition includes food, insecticides, air and water pollutants, acids, vitamins, toxic chemicals, soaps, and soft drinks. Obviously, this definition is too broad to be useful. For our purposes, a definition based on context is more useful. In medicine, for example, a *drug* is any substance that is manufactured specifically to relieve pain or to treat and prevent diseases and other medical conditions.

In a social problem approach, a *drug* is any habit-forming substance that directly affects the brain and nervous system. It is a chemical substance that affects moods, perceptions, bodily functions, and consciousness, and that has the potential to be misused as it may be harmful to the user. *Drug abuse* is the regular or excessive use of a drug when, as defined by a group, the consequences endanger relationships with other people, are detrimental to a person's health, or jeopardize society itself. This definition identifies two key factors that determine a society's notion of drug abuse. The first is the actual effects of the drug, and the second is a group's perception of the effects.

Society's perception of the ill effects of a drug is often inconsistent with the actual effects. In our society, moderate use of alcohol is generally accepted; yet moderate use can cause serious accidents and health problems. Aspirin is one of the most widely used drugs in America, extensively used to relieve a variety of real or imagined physical and mental discomforts. Yet excessive dosages of aspirin can cause ulcers, gastrointestinal bleeding, and other ailments. Excessive drinking of coffee (containing caffeine) is accepted in our society, but it can also lead to health problems. In the 1930s, American society was convinced that marijuana was a dangerous drug, as it was thought to cause insanity, crime, and a host of other ills. Now, available evidence suggests it may be no more dangerous than alcohol.[2] The occasional use of heroin has been thought for years to be highly dangerous, even though available evidence indicates occasional users suffer few health consequences and can lead productive lives.[3]

The dominant social reaction to a drug is influenced not only by the actual dangers of the drug, but also by the social characteristics and motives of the groups that use it. Heroin is considered dangerous because its use has been popularly associated with inner-city residents and high crime rates. Society is more accepting of the use of pills for middle-aged people to reduce stress and anxiety, but less accepting of college students using the same pills "to feel good" and "to get high." Surprisingly, legal drugs such as alcohol and tobacco are more often abused and cause more harm in our society than illegal drugs.

Many over-the-counter drugs (available without a physician's prescription) are being abused. Laxatives taken for constipation, for example, can damage the digestive system. Large doses of vitamins A and D are toxic.

Prescription drugs are also frequently abused. Among the most abused prescription drugs are tranquilizers, painkillers, sedatives, and stimulants. Americans are obsessed with taking pills. Many prescription drugs have the potential to be psychologically and physiologically addicting. Drug companies spend millions on advertisements trying to convince consumers there is something wrong with them—that

they are too tense, that they take too long to fall asleep, that they should lose weight, that they are not "regular" enough—and then suggest their medications will solve these problems. Unfortunately, many Americans accept this easy symptom-relief approach and end up dependent on pills, rather than make the necessary changes in their lives to be healthy. Such changes include learning stress reduction techniques, changing diets, and deciding to exercise regularly.

Just because a drug is legal and readily available does not mean it is harmless. Alcohol and tobacco are legal, but both are probably as harmful as marijuana. The rationale determining the acceptability of a drug is often illogical. Drugs favored by the dominant culture (such as alcohol in our society) are generally accepted whereas those favored by a small culture are usually outlawed. In many parts of North Africa and the Middle East, marijuana is legal, although alcohol is outlawed.[4] The United States imposes severe penalties for the use of cocaine, but in certain areas of the Andes Mountains it is legal and widely used.[5]

A characteristic of habit-forming drugs is that they lead to dependence, as the user develops a recurring craving for them. This dependence may be physical, psychological, or both. *Physical dependence* occurs when the body has adjusted to the presence of a drug and then will suffer pain, discomfort, or illness (the symptoms of withdrawal) if the use of the drug is discontinued. With *psychological dependence* the user feels psychological discomfort if use of the drug is terminated. Users also generally develop a tolerance for some drugs, in which case they have to take increasing amounts over time to achieve a given level of effect. Tolerance partly depends on the type of drug, as some drugs (such as aspirin) do not build tolerance.

*Drug addiction* is somewhat difficult to define. In the broadest sense, addiction refers to an intense craving for a particular substance. All of us have intense cravings—such as for ice cream, strawberry shortcake, potato chips, and chocolate. To distinguish drug addition from other intense cravings, some authorities have erroneously defined drug addiction as the physiological dependence that a person develops after heavy use of a particular drug. Most addicts, however, experience periods when they "kick" their physical dependency yet still feel a psychological craving, and they soon return to using their drug of choice. It is therefore more useful to define drug addiction as the intense craving for a drug that develops after a period of physical dependence stemming from heavy use.[6]

Numerous reasons account for why Americans use and abuse drugs: wanting to feel good or get high, wanting to escape reality, wanting relief from pain or anxiety, and wanting to relax or sleep. On a broader level, one should note that many segments of our society encourage and romanticize the use of drugs. Senator Frank Moss, for example, comments on the role played by advertisements and commercials:

It is advertising which mounts the message that pills turn rain to sunshine, gloom to joy, depression to euphoria, solve problems, and dispel doubt. Not just pills; cigarette and cigar ads; soft drinks, coffee, tea, and beer ads—all portray the key to happiness as things to swallow, inhale, chew, drink, and eat.[7]

## A BRIEF HISTORY OF DRUG TAKING IN OUR SOCIETY

When the Pilgrims set sail for America in 1620, they loaded on their ships fourteen tons of water plus ten thousand gallons of wine and forty-two tons of beer.[8] Ever since, Americans have been using—and abusing—drugs.

During and after the Civil War, thousands of injured soldiers were treated with narcotics to relieve their pain, and many became addicted. Narcotics addiction was a serious problem from the 1860s to the first decade of the twentieth century. At the turn of the twentieth century, about 1 percent of the population was addicted to a narcotic drug—the highest rate in our history.[9] At that time, opiates (including heroin and morphine) were easily available for a variety of purposes. They were used to treat minor ailments such as stomach pains and to ease the discomfort of infants during teething. Pharmacies, grocery stores, and mail-order houses did a prosperous business in selling opiates, but this came to a halt in 1914 with passage of the Harrison Narcotics Act. The act required that narcotic drugs be dispensed only through prescriptions by registered physicians.

Tobacco was widely chewed in colonial times. After 1870 it was also frequently smoked and since then it has been commonly used and abused. For a brief time shortly after 1900, its sale was prohibited in fourteen states, as it was thought to be a stepping-stone to using alcohol and also believed to lead to sexual deviance, insanity, and impotence. The laws proved ineffective in banning the sale and were repealed after World War I. Today, we are becoming increasingly aware of the health hazards of smoking.

Marijuana has been used throughout American history. In the mid-nineteenth century, it was often smoked by writers and artists in the larger cities. Shortly after the turn of the twentieth century, it began to be smoked by African Americans and Mexican Americans. The drug was then thought to lead to "unruly" behavior, and the first laws prohibiting its use and distribution were rapidly passed in southern states. The rest of the states soon enacted similar legislation. In 1937, the director of the Federal Bureau of Narcotics claimed marijuana was the "assassin of youth." The mass media jumped on this campaign and began publishing stories stereotyping marijuana users as "crazed drug fiends." Later, to continue receiving funds for his narcotics bureau, the director asserted that marijuana was dangerous because it was a stepping-stone to using narcotic drugs.[10] In the 1960s and 1970s, marijuana became increasingly used by youths, college students, drug subcultures, and by the general population. Its use and effects remain controversial issues.

The use of alcohol has continued unabated ever since the Pilgrims landed. The first governor of Massachusetts complained of excessive drunkenness in his colony, and since that time there have always been segments of American society that viewed its use as a social problem. The American Temperance Society was formed in the early 1800s. It was later joined by the Women's Christian Temperance Society, the Anti-Saloon League, and many other temperance organizations. Alcohol was blamed for many social ills: crime, the collapse of the family, and unemployment. Immigrants, the poor, and certain minority groups were the major consumers of alcohol at this time. Under such pressure, several states passed legislation in the latter half of the nineteenth century prohibiting the sale and distribution of alcoholic beverages. By the start of World War I, nearly half the population resided in "dry" areas.

The Eighteenth Amendment to the Constitution, which prohibited the sale of alcohol, became law in 1920. Despite Prohibition, people continued to drink, and the law was nearly unenforceable. This lack of regard for the law gave organized crime its impetus to become involved in bootlegging. Speakeasies (places where illegal alcoholic beverages were sold) flourished. Prohibition became a political embarrassment and a laughingstock around the world. In 1933, the Eighteenth Amendment was repealed. Following Prohibition, the use of alcohol became more widespread.[11] The middle- and upper-middle classes also began drinking it on a rather large scale. No longer was it viewed as the scourge of society. Interestingly, narcotics made a transition from respectability to disrepute in the past one hundred years, while alcohol made exactly the opposite transition.

## SOCIOLOGICAL THEORIES OF DRUG ABUSE

There are numerous biological, psychological, and sociological theories of drug abuse. Summarizing all of these theories is beyond the scope of this text. Three sociological theories are presented for illustrative purposes: anomie theory, labeling theory, and differential association.

*Anomie Theory*   Anomie theory was developed by Émile Durkheim[12] and Robert Merton.[13] Merton used anomie to explain deviant behavior. As you will recall from Chapter 2, Merton viewed deviance as occurring when there is a discrepancy between socially approved goals (such as making considerable money) and the availability of socially approved means of achieving them (such as high-paying jobs). Applied to drug abuse, this theory asserts that if people are prevented from achieving their goals, they may be driven to drink or to use other drugs. According to this theory, drugs may be used as an escape to avoid the suffering caused by failing to achieve goals, or they may be used as a substitute to experience the "highs" and "feeling good" that users originally hoped to experience from successfully accomplishing their goals.

Merton asserts that drug abuse can be reduced by having society set realistic goals that people can attain, and by society then establishing legitimate means, which are available to everyone, for attaining these goals. One should note that anomie theory fails to explain drug abuse by people who appear to be achieving goals.

*Labeling Theory*   Labeling theory was developed by a variety of theorists[14] who view drug abuse as due largely to the process in which some occasional users are labeled "abusers." Initially, occasional users indulge in drug use that is disapproved by others—such as getting drunk or smoking marijuana. These users do not at this point view themselves as abusers. However, if their use is discovered and made an issue by significant others (parents, police, or teachers), and if they are then publicly labeled as "drunkards," "pot heads," or "addicts," they are more closely watched. Under closer surveillance, if they continue using drugs, the label is gradually confirmed. If these significant others begin to relate to them in terms of the label, the occasional users may come to identify with that label. When this happens, the occasional user is apt to embark on a "career" as a habitual drug abuser.

Labeling theory asserts drug abuse can be reduced by avoiding labeling; that is, by refusing to treat occasional drug users as if they were abusers. One should note that labeling theory fails to explain drug abuse among "closet alcoholics" and others who abuse drugs before being labeled as such.

*Differential Association*   The theory of differential association was developed by Edwin Sutherland.[15] Applied to drug abuse, differential association theory asserts people are apt to learn and take on the drug use norms of the small, intimate groups with which they associate. These groups include family, neighborhood peer groups, and religious and social groups. Differential association has been used to explain differences in alcoholism rates among ethnic groups and among religious groups. For example, marked differences exist between the alcohol use patterns of the Irish compared to Italians and Jews in the United States. Italians (both in Italy and this country) widely accept the moderate use of alcohol, particularly at mealtimes, during which wine is part of the dietary customs in which even the young participate. Excessive drinking, however, is frowned upon. As a result, even though alcohol is widely used in the Italian community, drunkenness and alcoholism are relatively rare.[16] Similarly, the Jewish community uses alcohol widely, including it in religious rituals. As with Italian families, the use of alcohol in controlled social settings minimizes its potential negative effects. And because there are strong norms against drunkenness and abuse, alcoholism among American Jews is also rare.[17] By contrast, the Irish subculture tolerates periodic episodes of excessive drinking, particularly by single males. Such drinking is seen as a way to relieve tension and frustration. With such norms, there is a relatively high rate of alcoholism among Irish American males.[18]

It is possible, of course, for people to be resocialized into the drug use norms of another subculture. For example, a teenager raised in a family that opposes use of marijuana may become attracted to a high school group that places a high value on smoking marijuana. This teenager may then, through the principles of differential association, become resocialized by this new group into using marijuana.

However, differential association theory primarily explains the reasons drug abuse varies among groups, rather than identifying the numerous causes of drug abuse. There are many other theories (including psychological and biological ones) that explain the causes of drug abuse.[19] No single theory of drug abuse sufficiently identifies all the causes, and each theory may or may not apply in a given case.

## DRUG SUBCULTURES

A decision to use a drug depends not only on personality characteristics and family background, but also on the views of peers. Peer opinion plays an important role in how often drugs are used, the amount used at any one time, and other activities that will be engaged in when drugs are used.

A group of peers who advocate the use of one or more drugs can be called a *drug subculture*. Drug use usually occurs in a social group that approves the use of the drug. In a classic study, "Becoming a Marijuana User," Howard Becker found that the peer group plays crucial roles in learning to smoke marijuana.[20] The group introduces the novice to smoking and teaches the new smoker to recognize the pleasant experiences associated with a "high." Membership in this group also encourages further drug use and instructs the newcomer to reject established norms against using marijuana and instead to accept the norms of the drug subculture.

Drug subcultures appear to play similar roles in learning to use other drugs. Drug subcultures are more apt to develop around the use of illegal drugs than with legal ones. Alcohol use among teenagers, as well as use of marijuana, heroin, LSD, PCP, and cocaine and crack, often occurs in drug subcultures. In many U.S. cities, a number of youth gangs have become involved in widespread use and distribution of illegal drugs. Frequently, gang members also become involved in other crimes (such as thefts and burglaries) to support their drug habits.

Although drug subcultures are often dysfunctional for society, they do serve important functions for the user. They provide instructions on how to use the drug and provide guidelines on the safety limits of dosages. They help handle adverse effects, assist in obtaining the drug, and provide protection from arrest. They also provide a party atmosphere to help a person enjoy the effects of the drug (see Table 4.1 for a listing of the facts and effects of these drugs as well as some other commonly used drugs).

## Facts about and Effects of Commonly Used Drugs

◆◆◆◆◆◆◆◆◆◆◆◆◆◆◆◆◆◆◆◆◆◆◆◆

### DEPRESSANTS

In this section we will examine the following drugs classified as depressants: alcohol, barbiturates, tranquilizers, Quaaludes, and phencyclidine (PCP).

*Alcohol*   Alcohol, a depressant, is the most abused drug in American society. Yet, the use of alcohol is so accepted that relatively few Americans view it as a serious social problem (e.g., see Box 4.1). Social drinking is highly integrated into social customs. In many areas the local pub, community taverns, and nightclubs are the center of meeting and socializing with friends and neighbors, and entertaining dates and business partners. Going out and "getting high" is a favorite pastime of college students. Movies and television programs glamorize drinking. Songs ("Scotch and Soda," "Tiny Bubbles," and "Kisses Sweeter Than Wine") highlight drinking. Businesses "wine and dine" customers. In some communities, it is customary to have "a second church service" at a local watering hole following the weekly church service.

Alcohol is a colorless liquid that is in beer, wine, brandy, whiskey, vodka, rum, and other intoxicating beverages. Americans over the age of twenty-one consume an average of 33.2 gallons of beer, 2.7 gallons of wine, and 2.0 gallons of hard liquor a year.[21] The vast majority of American teenagers and adults drink.

Drinking has become so entrenched in our customs that those who do not drink are sometimes viewed as "weird," "stuck-up," or "killjoys" and are often assumed to have something wrong with them.

**Table 4.1**  *Drugs of Abuse: Facts and Effects*

| Drug | Dependence Potential | | Tolerance | Duration of Effects (in hours) | Usual Methods of Administration | Possible Effects | Effects of Overdose | Withdrawal Symptoms |
| --- | --- | --- | --- | --- | --- | --- | --- | --- |
| | Physical | Psychological | | | | | | |
| *Narcotics* | | | | | | | | |
| Opium | High | High | Yes | 3 to 6 | Oral, smoked | Euphoria; drowsiness; respiratory depression; constricted pupils; nausea | Slow and shallow breathing; clammy skin; convulsions; coma; possible death | Watery eyes, runny nose, yawning, loss of appetite, irritability, tremors, panic, chills and sweating, cramps, nausea |
| Morphine | | | | | Injected, smoked | | | |
| Heroin | | | | | Injected, sniffed | | | |
| *Depressants* | | | | | | | | |
| Alcohol | High | High | Yes | 1 to 12 | Oral | Slurred speech; disorientation; impaired coordination; impaired reactions | Shallow respiration; dilated pupils; weak and rapid pulse; coma; possible death | Anxiety, insomnia, tremors, delirium, convulsions; possible death |
| Barbiturates | High | High | Yes | 1 to 16 | Oral, injected | | | |
| Tranquilizers | Moderate | Moderate | Yes | 4 to 8 | Oral | | | |
| Quaaludes | High | High | Yes | 4 to 8 | Oral | | | |
| *Stimulants* | | | | | | | | |
| Caffeine | High | High | Yes | 2 to 4 | Oral | Increased alertness; excitation; euphoria; dilated pupils; increased pulse rate and blood pressure; insomnia; loss of appetite | Agitation; increase in pulse rate and blood pressure; loss of appetite; insomnia | Apathy, long periods of sleep, irritability, depression, disorientation |
| Cocaine | Possible | High | Yes | 2 | Injected, sniffed | | Agitation, increase in body temperature; hallucinations; convulsions; possible death; tremors | |
| Crack | Possible | High | Yes | 2 | Smoked | | | |
| Amphetamines | Possible | High | Yes | 2 to 4 | Oral, injected | | | |
| Butyl Nitrate | Possible | ? | Probable | Up to 5 | Inhaled | Excitement; euphoria; giddiness; loss of inhibitions; aggressiveness; delusions; depression; drowsiness; headache; nausea | Loss of memory; confusion; unsteady gait; erratic heartbeat and pulse; possible death | Insomnia; decreased appetite; depression; irritability; headache |
| Amyl Nitrate | Possible | ? | Probable | Up to 5 | Inhaled | | | |
| *Hallucinogens* | | | | | | | | |
| LSD | None | Degree unknown | Yes | Variable | Oral | Illusions and hallucinations; poor perception of time and distance | Longer, more intense trip episodes; psychosis; possible death | ? |
| Mescaline and Peyote | | | | | Oral, injected | | | |
| Psilocybin-Psilocin | | | | | Oral | | | |
| PCP | | | | | Oral, injected, smoked | | | |
| *Cannabis* | | | | | | | | |
| Marijuana | Degree unknown | Moderate | Yes | 2 to 4 | Oral, smoked | Euphoria; relaxed inhibitions; increased appetite; disoriented behavior; increased heart and pulse rate | Fatigue; paranoia; possible psychosis; time disorientation; slowed movements | Insomnia, hyperactivity, and decreased appetite reported in a limited number of individuals |
| Hashish | | | | | | | | |
| Nicotine (Tobacco) | High | High | Yes | 2 to 4 | Smoked, chewed | Increased alertness; excitation; euphoria; dilated pupils; increased pulse rate and blood pressure; insomnia; loss of appetite | Agitation; increase in pulse rate and blood pressure; loss of appetite; insomnia | Apathy, long periods of sleep, irritability, depression |

**Table 4.2** *Percentage of Alcohol in the Blood and Its Effects*

| Percent Alcohol | Effects |
| --- | --- |
| .05 | Lowered alertness and a "high" feeling |
| .10 | Decreased reactions, reduced coordination (legally drunk in most states) |
| .20 | Massive interference with senses and motor skills |
| .30 | Perceptions nearly gone, understanding nearly gone |
| .40 | Unconsciousness |
| .50 | Possible death |

*Source:* Adapted from Oakley S. Ray, *Drugs, Society and Human Behavior* (St. Louis, MO: Mosby, 1972), 86, and Erich Goode, *Drugs in American Society* (New York: Knopf, 1972), 142–143.

The serving of alcoholic beverages is expected at many rituals and ceremonies for adults (weddings, birthday parties, Christmas parties, graduations, and the like). Some formal religious rites also serve alcohol (e.g., wine as the blood of Christ). However, it is not the use of alcohol at rituals and ceremonies that causes most alcohol problems. Most alcohol use is informal and relatively uncontrolled and therefore can easily become excessive.

The type of alcohol found in beverages is ethyl alcohol (also called grain alcohol, as most of it is made from fermenting grain). Many drinkers believe alcohol is a stimulant, as it lessens sexual and aggressive inhibitions, seems to facilitate interpersonal relationships, and usually leads those who have a few drinks to talk more. It is, however, very definitely a depressant to the central nervous system, as its chemical composition and effects are very similar to those of ether (an anesthetic used in medicine to induce unconsciousness).

Alcohol slows mental activity, reasoning ability, speech ability, and muscle reactions. It distorts perceptions, slurs speech, lessens coordination, and slows memory functioning and respiration. In increasing quantities it leads to stupor, sleep, coma, and finally death. A hangover (or aftereffects of too much alcohol) includes having a headache, thirst, muscle aches, stomach discomfort, and nausea.

The effects of alcohol vary with the percentage of alcohol in the bloodstream as it passes through the brain. Generally, the effects are observable when the concentration of alcohol in the blood reaches one-tenth of 1 percent. Five drinks (with each drink being one ounce of 86-proof alcohol, twelve ounces of beer, or three ounces of wine) in two hours for a 120-pound person will result in a blood alcohol concentration of one-tenth of 1 percent. (The heavier a person, the more drinks it takes to increase the level of alcohol in the blood.) Table 4.2 shows the effects of increasing percentages of alcohol in the blood.

In 1990, scientists discovered that women's stomachs are less effective than men's at neutralizing alcohol, and, as a result, women generally become intoxicated more quickly. Men have substantially more dehydrogenase (an enzyme) in their stomachs than women. This enzyme breaks down much of the alcohol in the stomach before it reaches the bloodstream. This finding may also help explain why women alcoholics develop medical complications more rapidly than alcoholic men, including cirrhosis of the liver, anemia, and gastrointestinal bleeding.[22]

*Who Drinks?* Several factors relate to whether an individual will drink and how much. These include socioeconomic factors, gender, age, religion, urban-rural residence, and geographic region.[23]

In terms of *socioeconomics,* college-educated persons are more apt to drink than those with only high school educations. Young men at the highest socioeconomic level are more apt to drink than young men at lower socioeconomic levels. However, drinkers at the lower socioeconomic levels are more apt to drink more than those at higher socioeconomic levels.

As for *gender,* men are more apt to use and abuse alcohol than women. Yet recent decades have seen a dramatic increase in alcoholism among adult women. One explanation is that cultural taboos against heavy drinking among women have weakened. Another is that increased drinking is related to the changing roles of women in our society.

As for *age* breakdown, older people are less likely to drink than younger people, even if they were drinkers in their youth. Heavy drinking is most common at ages twenty-one to thirty for men, and ages thirty-one to fifty for women.

*Religion* is another factor. Nonchurchgoers drink more than regular churchgoers. Heavy drinking is more common among Episcopalians and Catholics, whereas conservative and fundamentalist Protestants are more apt to be nondrinkers or light drinkers.

In terms of *residence,* urban residents are more apt to drink than rural residents.

Prior to the 1980s, courts tended to be very lenient with drunk drivers who get involved in serious traffic accidents. Societal values, then, were that being intoxicated was viewed as a condition that, to a considerable extent, excused drunk drivers from being held responsible for the damage they caused. There has been a major change in the 1980s and 1990s on this issue.

For example, Larry Mahoney was a thirty-four-year-old father who was described by a friend as "somebody who wouldn't hurt anybody for the world." On Sunday evening, May 14, 1988, while drunk, Larry climbed into his pickup and drove the wrong way down a Kentucky interstate. He had 0.24 percent alcohol in his blood, more than twice Kentucky's statutory level. He slammed head-on into an old school bus carrying sixty-seven passengers, mainly teenagers, on a church outing from Radcliff,

Kentucky. Twenty-four teenagers and three adults were killed in this crash. This was the worst alcohol-related traffic accident in U.S. history. Larry Mahoney was charged with "capital murder," which carries the death penalty. In December 1989, he was found guilty of twenty-seven counts of second-degree manslaughter, twenty-seven counts of first-degree wanton endangerment, twelve counts of first-degree assault, fourteen counts of second-degree wanton endangerment, and one count of drunken driving. He was sentenced to sixteen years in prison. This conviction and lengthy prison sentence is one more indication that the court system is taking a tougher stand on drunk driving. Many states have enacted legislation to immediately suspend drivers' licenses for offenders and have mandated jail terms for repeat offenders. Many states now also mandate instant suspension of the driver's license for individuals failing or refusing to take a breath test.

*Source:* "Kentucky's Textbook Case in Drunk Driving," *U.S. News & World Report* (May 30, 1988): 7–8; and "Man Sentenced in Fatal Church Bus Accident," *Wisconsin State Journal* (Feb. 24, 1990): 3A.

---

*Geographical region* plays a part in who drinks and how much. People who live in the Northeast and along the West Coast are more apt to drink than people who live in the South and Midwest.

In the last two decades, there has been a decline in American drinking patterns, especially of hard liquor.[24] For example, some business executives have switched from martini luncheons to jogging and working out. The federal government has put considerable financial pressure on states to raise the drinking age to twenty-one; if a state has a drinking age lower than twenty-one, federal highway funds are withheld. Many secondary schools, colleges, and universities have initiated alcohol awareness programs. Businesses and employers have developed employee assistance programs designed to provide treatment services to alcoholics and problem drinkers.

Many states have passed stricter drunk driving laws, and police departments and the courts are more vigorously enforcing them (see Box 4.2). Organizations such as Mothers Against Drunk Driving (MADD) and Students Against Drunk Driving (SADD) have been fairly successful in creating greater public awareness of the hazards of drinking and driving. A cultural norm is emerging in

many segments that it is stylish *not* to drink too much. Despite these promising trends, rates of alcohol use and abuse in the United States remain extremely high.

*Reasons for Drinking.* As discussed earlier a major reason for alcohol use is that our social patterns influence people to drink socially in a wide variety of situations. Happy hours, a cocktail or beer before and after dinner, and parties where alcoholic beverages are served are common.

There are also individual reasons for drinking. For some people drinking acts as a "social lubricant" in that it relaxes them so that they feel more at ease in interacting with others. Others use alcohol as a kind of anesthetic to dull the pain of living and to take their minds off their problems. Some excessive drinkers seek a continual "buzz" to avoid facing life. Others occasionally drink to be "high." Some insomniacs drink in order to sleep (often they pass out). Alcohol has a tranquilizing effect, and drinking prior to flying is common for those who have fears about flying.

People often drink to get rid of unwanted emotions, including loneliness, anxiety, depression, feelings of inadequacy, insecurity, guilt, and resentment.[25]

*Alcoholism.* Since there is no clear-cut distinction between a problem drinker and an alcoholic, *alcoholism* is a rather imprecise term. An imprecise but useful definition is *the repeated and excessive use of alcohol to the extent that it is harmful to interpersonal relations, to job performance, or to the drinker's health.*

Whether a person is labeled "alcoholic" depends to a large extent on the reactions of employers, family, friends, associates, and community. For example, the "drier" the community in which one lives, the less alcohol and the fewer the problem incidents involving alcohol it takes for someone to be defined as an alcoholic.

People's reactions to drinking also vary considerably. Some can drink large amounts regularly and appear sober—although their driving and other reactions and perceptions are actually affected and they may have a high likelihood of becoming alcoholic in the future. Some can drink large amounts and not experience hangovers—although hangovers are functional, as they inform people when they have ingested to much alcohol and discourage further binges. As suggested before, generally the more the drinker weighs, the more he or she can consume before becoming intoxicated. Many alcoholics who want to stop drinking have to refrain *totally* from drinking, because if they start again they will have a compulsive, uncontrollable urge to drink excessively. Because of this, Alcoholics Anonymous assumes "once an alcoholic, always an alcoholic." There is some (highly controversial) evidence that a few alcoholics can, after treatment, return to social drinking.[26] This finding has been highly criticized by a number of treatment organizations as it has led some alcoholics who quit drinking to try to drink lightly, with the result that they immediately returned to excessive drinking.

There are over fifteen million alcoholics in America, and each one affects at least four other people close to him or her—including spouse, family, employer, or all three. Approximately two out of three alcoholics are male, but the proportion of female alcoholics has risen sharply in the past twenty years.[27] Contrary to popular stereotypes, only an estimated 5 percent of alcoholics are "skid-row bums,"[28] most are ordinary people. In fact, one out of ten social drinkers becomes an alcoholic.[29]

Some people become alcoholic quite soon after they start drinking. Others may drink for ten, twenty, or thirty years before becoming addicted. An alcoholic may be only psychologically dependent on alcohol, but a sizable number are also physically dependent.

*Alcohol and Health.* Alcoholics have a life expectancy that is ten to twelve years less than nonalcoholics.[30] Several reasons account for this. One is that over an extended period of time, alcohol gradually destroys liver cells and replaces the cells with scar tissue. When the scar tissue is extensive, a medical condition occurs called cirrhosis of the liver, which is the eighth most frequent cause of death in America (about twenty-five thousand deaths per year).[31] Also, although it has no healthy food value, alcohol contains a high number of calories. As a result, heavy drinkers have a reduced appetite for nutritious food and thus frequently suffer from vitamin deficiencies and are more susceptible to infectious diseases. Heavy drinking also causes kidney problems, contributes to a variety of heart ailments, is a factor leading to sugar diabetes, and also appears to contribute to cancer. In addition, heavy drinking is associated with over eight thousand suicides annually.[32] Death may also result from drinking an excessive amount of alcohol—for example, from depression of the respiratory system or from the drinker choking on vomit while unconscious.

Interestingly, for some yet unknown reason, the life expectancy for light-to-moderate drinkers exceeds that for nondrinkers.[33] Perhaps an occasional drink helps people to relax and thereby reduces the likelihood of life-threatening stress-related illnesses.

Combining alcohol with other drugs can have disastrous, and sometimes fatal, effects. Two drugs taken together may have a *synergistic* interaction—that is, they interact to produce an effect much greater than either would cause alone. For example, sedatives like barbiturates (often found in sleeping pills) or Quaaludes taken together with alcohol can so depress the central nervous system that a coma or even death may result.

Other drugs tend to have an *antagonistic* response to alcohol; that is, one drug negates the effects of the other. Many doctors now caution patients not to drink while taking certain prescribed drugs, as the alcohol may reduce, or even totally negate, the beneficial effects of these drugs.

Whether dugs will interact synergistically or antagonistically depends on a wide range of factors: the properties of the drugs, the amounts taken, the amount of sleep the user has had, the kind and amount of food eaten, and the user's overall health and tolerance. The interactive effects may be minimal one day and extensive the next.

When used by pregnant women, alcohol may gravely affect the unborn child by causing mental retardation, deformities, stunting of growth, and

## Fetal Alcohol Syndrome

**P**rior to the 1940s, it was thought that the uterus was a glass bubble that totally separated the fetus from the outside world and fully protected it from whatever drugs the mother happened to be using. Since the 1940s, medical science has learned that chemical substances are readily transferred from the mother's uterine arteries, across the placental membrane, into the baby's umbilical vein, and then to the baby's entire body.

When a pregnant woman drinks any alcoholic beverage (including beer and wine), the alcohol easily crosses the placenta, and the fetus attains blood-alcohol levels that are similar to those in the mother. Heavy alcohol consumption by pregnant mothers can cause a variety of malformations in the new baby that have been labeled the fetal alcohol syndrome. These malformations include mental retardation and developmental delays, overall growth retardation before and after birth, and various congenital malformations of the face, head, skeleton, and heart. Such babies also are more apt to be born premature, have a low birth weight, be hyper-irri-

table, and have neurological defects and poor muscle tone. Such babies have a higher infant mortality rate. The chances are also much higher for the occurrence of microcephaly (a condition in which the baby has a small brain and skull and is mentally retarded).

The more alcohol a pregnant woman ingests, the higher the chances that her baby will have fetal alcohol syndrome. Studies suggest that if a pregnant woman has five or more drinks at any one time, her baby has a 10 percent chance of having fetal alcohol syndrome. Also, if she drinks lightly over a prolonged period, the syndrome may also occur. An average of 1 ounce of alcohol once a day results in a 10 percent risk, and an average of 2 ounces a day results in a 20 percent risk.

The U.S. Public Health Service recommends that pregnant women should not drink alcohol. Just as a mother would not give a glass of wine to her newborn, she should not give it to her unborn baby. It is not just alcohol but also the use of other drugs (such as tobacco, marijuana, cocaine, and heroin) during pregnancy that endangers the unborn child.

*Source:* Diane E. Papalia and Sally W. Olds, *Human Development*, 6th ed. (New York: McGraw-Hill, 1995), 76.

---

other abnormalities. This effect has been named the fetal alcohol syndrome (see Box 4.3).

Withdrawal from alcohol, once the body is physically addicted, may lead to the DTs (delirium tremens) and other unpleasant reactions. The DTs include rapid heartbeat, uncontrollable trembling, severe nausea, and profuse sweating.

*Drinking and Driving.*   Alcohol is a significant contributing factor in approximately half of all fatal automobile accidents and in serious automobile accident injuries.[34] Each year, over a million people in the United States are arrested for driving under the influence of alcohol.[35] (One of the most noted persons to die in an alcohol-related accident was Diana, Princess of Wales, who died in August 1997 at the age of thirty-six. The driver of the car, Henri Paul, was legally drunk when the car crashed in a tunnel in Paris, France.) Mothers Against Drunk Driving (MADD) is having considerable success in getting states to enact and enforce stricter drunkdriving laws. In addition, the news media in recent years have been airing more programs and announcements that seek to inform the public that driving after drinking is life threatening.

*Alcohol and Crime.*   About one-eighth of arrests for minor crimes are alcohol related. These include public drunkenness, violations of liquor laws, disorderly conduct, and vagrancy.[36] Alcohol is a contributing factor in many major crimes. In a majority of homicides, aggravated assaults, sexual crimes against children, and sexually aggressive acts against women, the offender had been drinking.[37] This is not to say that alcohol is the main cause of these crimes; rather, its use appears to be a contributing factor that increases the likelihood of such crimes occurring.

*Effects on the Family.*   In the past, a problem drinker in the family was almost always the husband. Traditionally, social customs have encouraged drinking among men and discouraged drinking among women. These customs are slowly changing. Although it is still statistically apt to be the husband who drinks, it frequently also may be the wife or one or more of the teenagers.

Heavy drinking is a contributing factor to many family problems: child abuse, child neglect, spouse abuse, parent abuse, financial problems, unemployment, violent arguments, and unhappy marriages.

Marriage to an alcoholic often ends in divorce, separation, or desertion. Children of an alcoholic parent have higher rates of severe emotional and physical illnesses.[38]

Sharon Wegscheider indicates that family members in alcoholic families tend to assume roles that protect the chemically dependent person from taking responsibility for his or her behavior, and that actually serve to maintain the drinking problem. She identifies several roles which are typically played by family members. In addition to the chemically-dependent person, there is the chief enabler, the family hero, the scapegoat, the lost child, and the mascot.[39]

The chief enabler's main purpose is to assume the primary responsibility for family functioning. The abuser typically continues to lose control and relinquishes responsibility. The chief enabler, on the other hand, takes more and more responsibility and begins making more and more of the family's decisions. A chief enabler is often the parent or spouse of the chemically dependent person.

Conditions in families of chemically dependent people often continue to deteriorate as the dependent person loses control. A positive influence is needed to offset the negative. The family hero fulfills this role. The family hero is often the perfect person who does well at everything he or she tries. The hero works very hard at making the family look like it is functioning better than it is. In this way the family hero provides the family with self-worth.

Another typical role played by someone in the chemically dependent family is the scapegoat. Although the alcohol abuse is the real problem, a family rule mandates that this fact must be denied. Therefore, the blame must be placed elsewhere. Frequently, another family member is blamed for the problem. The scapegoat often behaves in negative ways (e.g., gets caught for stealing, runs away, becomes extremely withdrawn), which draws to him or her much attention. The scapegoat's role is to distract attention from the dependent person and onto something else. This role helps the family avoid addressing the problem of chemical dependency.

Often there is also a lost child in the family. This is the person who seems rather uninvolved with the rest of the family, yet never causes any trouble. The lost child's purpose is to provide relief to the family from some of the pain it is suffering. At least there is someone in the family who neither requires much attention nor causes any stress. The lost child is just simply there.

Finally, chemically dependent families often have someone playing the role of mascot. The mascot is the person who probably has a good sense of humor and appears not to take anything seriously. Despite how much the mascot might be suffering inside, he or she provides a little fun for the family.

In summary, chemical dependency is a problem affecting the entire family. Each family member is suffering from the chemical dependency, yet each assumes a role in order to maintain the family's status quo and to help the family survive. Family members are driven to maintain these roles, no matter what. The roles eventually become associated with the survival of the family.

*Alcohol and Industry.*    Alcoholism costs businesses and industry billions of dollars annually. This figure reflects losses incurred by sick leave, absenteeism, missed or late work assignments, and on-the-job accidents. It is further estimated that 6 to 10 percent of the work force experiences drinking problems to such a degree that it affects job performance.[40]

*Alcoholism Gene Theory.*    Alcoholism has long been assumed to be caused by both environmental and genetic factors. There has been considerable controversy in recent years as to whether alcoholism is caused primarily by environmental factors or genetic factors. This section summarizes the evidence for the alcoholism gene theory.

Alcoholism has been found to run in families. In addition, children whose biological parents were alcoholics and who were adopted at an early age have a significantly higher chance of becoming alcoholic than do children in the general population.[41]

In 1990, researchers reported having pinpointed a gene in people prone to alcoholism, which adds weight to the argument that alcoholism is a disease and not a moral weakness or willful misconduct.[42] The researchers, Noble and Blum, reported a particular gene on a chromosome previously linked with alcoholism to be far more common in alcoholics than in nonalcoholics. Previous research implicated three chromosomes as possibly contributing to alcoholism, but no one had isolated a gene on these chromosomes as the culprit. (Chromosomes are threadlike structures of thousands of individual genes, the "fingerprints" of DNA—deoxyribonucleic acid—that carry each cell's hereditary blueprint. A person's traits are determined by the nearly one hundred thousand genes in each cell.)

The gene pinpointed by Noble and Blum has two alternative forms, each of which produces one form of a type of nerve cell called the *dopamine D2 receptor,* believed to play a key role in experiencing pleasure. The researchers looked at both alternative forms of the gene—the *A-1 allele* and the *A-2 allele*—in brain matter from the cadavers of seventy subjects (thirty-five alcoholics and thirty-five nonalcoholics). The A-1 allele was found to have a high association with alcoholism, and the A-2 allele was found to be associated with nonalcoholism. The A-1 allele was present in 69 percent of the alcoholics, but in only 20 percent of nonalcoholics. (The study suggests, but does not conclusively prove, the existence of an alcoholism gene. In addition, because there is not a 100 percent association between the A-1 allele and alcoholism, the results suggest other factors—including environment—also play a role in causing alcoholism.)

Noble and Blum conclude that the rare form of the gene may make people more prone to alcoholism, but they remain cautious about the implications.

Previous studies suggesting an association between genes and diseases (such as manic depression and schizophrenia) have not held up to further scrutiny. If the dopamine D2 receptor does turn out to be linked to alcoholism, a test for the A-1 allele could identify individuals at high risk before they become addicted to alcohol. The disease may be brought on by a number of genes; having identified one of them would allow scientists to map the chemical pathways to alcoholism and to devise drugs to alter them. Such drugs, for example, could reduce the craving for liquor, thereby affording alcoholics a means of recovery.

One should note that a study published in late 1990 failed to replicate the results reported by Noble and Blum. The study, conducted by the National Institute on Alcohol Abuse and Alcoholism, found that the dopamine D2 receptor gene was present in approximately the same proportion of alcoholics as nonalcoholics.[43] These conflicting results lead to the conclusion that the extent to which genetic composition is a contributing factor to alcoholism is unclear.

*Seeking Treatment for Alcoholism.*   Many alcoholics (perhaps the majority) do not seek help because they deny having a drinking problem. They seek to prove they can drink like any other person and wind up sneaking drinks, excusing their drinking behavior, or blaming others ("If you had a job like mine, you'd drink too!"). There are many reasons alcoholics deny having a drinking problem. Alcoholism is highly stigmatized, so alcoholics do not like to admit they have a drinking weakness and are different from others.

Alcoholism is viewed as a disease, and they do not want to acknowledge that they have this illness. Drinking often becomes the central interest of their life. They socialize through drinking and are also able to relax, fall asleep, or escape from their problems. For them to acknowledge that they have a drinking problem means they would have to stop drinking. Because they believe drinking is essential to their lives, they often choose to keep drinking even though they are aware it is ruining their health, destroying their reputation in the community, getting them fired from a variety of jobs, and breaking up their family. Many alcoholics believe that the freedom to continue to drink is the most important need in their lives, and they will sacrifice their marriage, children, career, and health to alcohol. In many ways, alcohol becomes their best friend, which they refuse to abandon—even if it kills them.

If an alcoholic is to be helped, the problem of denial must be confronted. (We will discuss denial further in the section on rehabilitation programs.)

**Barbiturates**   Barbiturates, derived from barbituric acid, depress the central nervous system. Barbiturates were first synthesized in the early 1900s, and there are now over twenty-five hundred different varieties. They are commonly used to relieve insomnia and anxiety. Some are prescribed as sleeping pills, and others are used during the daytime to relieve tension and anxiety. They are also used to treat epilepsy and high blood pressure and to relax patients before or after surgery. Barbiturates are illegal, unless obtained by a physician's prescription.

Taken in sufficient doses, barbiturates have effects similar to strong alcohol. Users experience relief from inhibitions, have a feeling of euphoria, feel "high" or in good humor, and are passively content. However, these moods can change rapidly to gloom, agitation, and aggressiveness. Physiological effects include slurred speech, disorientation, staggering, appearance of being confused, drowsiness, and reduced coordination.

Prolonged heavy use of barbiturates can cause physical dependence, with withdrawal symptoms similar to those of heroin addiction. Withdrawal is accompanied by body tremors, cramps, anxiety, fever, nausea, profuse sweating, and hallucinations. Many authorities believe barbiturate addiction is more dangerous than heroin addiction, and it is considered more resistant to treatment than heroin addiction. Abrupt withdrawal can cause fatal convulsions. One forensic pathologist noted: "Show me someone who goes cold turkey [the sudden and complete halting of drug use] on a bad barbiturate habit, and I'll show you a corpse."[44]

Barbiturate overdose can cause convulsions, coma, poisoning, and sometimes death. Barbiturates are particularly dangerous when taken with alcohol because alcohol acts synergistically to magnify the potency of the barbiturates (see Box 4.4). Accidental deaths due to excessive doses are frequent. One reason for this is that the user becomes groggy, forgets how much has been taken, and continues to take more until an overdose level has been reached. Barbiturates are also the number one suicide drug. A number of famous people, such as Marilyn Monroe, have fatally overdosed on barbiturates.

Barbiturates are generally taken orally, although some users also inject them. Use of barbiturates, like use of alcohol, may lead to traffic fatalities.

*Tranquilizers*   Yet another depressant is the group of drugs classified as tranquilizers. Common brand names are Librium, Miltown, Serax, Tranxene, and Valium (see Box 4.5). They are sedatives that reduce anxiety and relax muscles. Users have moderate potential of becoming physically and psychologically dependent. Tranquilizers are usually taken orally, and the effects last four to eight hours. Side effects include slurred speech, disorientation, and behavior resembling intoxication. Overdoses are possible, with the effects including cold and clammy skin, shallow respiration, dilated pupils, weak and rapid pulse, coma, and possibly death. Withdrawal symptoms are similar to those from alcohol and barbiturates: anxiety, tremors, convulsions, delirium, and possibly death.

*Quaaludes and PCP*   Both Quaaludes and phencyclidine (PCP) are depressants. (PCP also produces effects similar to those of hallucinogens.)

Methaqualone (better known by its patent name Quaalude) has effects similar to barbiturates and alcohol, although it is chemically different. It has the reputation of being a "love drug," because users believe it enhances sexual pleasure. It probably does so because, like alcohol and barbiturates, it lessens inhibitions. Quaaludes also reduce anxiety and induce euphoria. Users can become both physically and psychologically dependent. Overdose can result in convulsions, coma, delirium, and even death. Most deaths occur when the drug is taken together with alcohol, which vastly magnifies the drug's effects. Withdrawal symptoms are severe and unpleasant. Quaalude abuse may also cause hangovers, fatigue, liver damage, and temporary paralysis of the limbs.

PCP was developed in the 1950s as an anesthetic, a medical use that was soon terminated as patients displayed symptoms of severe emotional disturbance after receiving the drug. PCP is used legally today to tranquilize elephants and monkeys, because apparently they do not experience the adverse side effects.

PCP's streetname is *angel dust,* and is primarily used by young people who are unaware of its hazards. It is usually smoked, often after being sprinkled on a marijuana "joint." It may also be sniffed, swallowed, or injected. PCP is a very dangerous drug in that it distorts the senses, disrupts the sense of balance, and leads to an inability to think clearly. Larger amounts can cause paranoia, lead to aggressive behavior (in some cases it has led to committing violent murder), and cause the user temporarily to display symptoms of severe emotional disturbance. Continued use can lead to the development of a prolonged emotional disturbance. Overdose can result in coma or death. Research has not yet concluded whether it induces physical or psychological dependence. The drug has a potential to be used (and abused) extensively because it is relatively easy to prepare in a home laboratory and because the ingredients and recipes are widely available. An additional danger of PCP is that even one-time users sometimes have flashbacks in which the hallucinations are reexperienced, even long after use. It may be that many accidents and unexplained disasters may be due to inadvertent use of PCP or some other undetectable hallucinogen.

## Date-Rape Drugs

In the mid-1990s, Rohypnol became known as the date-rape drug. A number of women were sexually assaulted after the drug was slipped into one of their drinks (both alcoholic and nonalcoholic drinks). Rohypnol often causes blackouts, with complete loss of memory. Female victims of being slipped the drug, and then raped, often cannot remember any details of the crimes.

Rohypnol is a sedative, related to Valium, but ten times stronger. Rohypnol is legally available in more than sixty countries to treat severe insomnia. It is illegal in the United States. Much of the illegal Rohypnol in the United States is smuggled in from Mexico and Colombia.

Rohypnol is also popular with teens and young adults, both males and females, who like to combine it with alcohol for a quick punch-drunk hit. Another reason for its popularity is that it's relatively inexpensive, often being purchased on the street for $1 to $5 per pill. In some jurisdictions, drivers are now being tested for Rohypnol when they appear drunk, but register a low alcohol level. (One should note that Rohypnol is also addictive, and there is a potential for lethal overdosing.)

Because of the ease through which Rohypnol can be slipped into a drink, rape crisis centers are urging women to *never* take their eyes off their drink. In 1997, the marketer of Rohypnol, Hoffman-La Roche, announced it intended to sell only a new version of Rohypnol—one that would cause any liquid that it is slipped into to have a blue color. Even with this change being made, people (particularly women) need to beware—other sedatives have similar effects.

Gamma hydroxy butyrate (GHB) is another drug that is increasingly being used as a date-rape drug. GHB is a central nervous system depressant that is approved as an anesthetic in some countries. It can be readily made at home from chemicals purchased in stores. Just one gram of this liquid home brew provides an intoxicating experience equivalent to twenty-six ounces of whiskey. GHB, like Rohypnol, is slipped into the drink of the intended victim.

## STIMULANTS

In this section we will examine the following drugs classified as stimulants: caffeine, amphetamines, cocaine, crack, amyl nitrate, and butyl nitrate.

*Caffeine*  Caffeine is a stimulant to the central nervous system. It is present in coffee, tea, cocoa, cola drinks, and many other soft drinks. It is also available in tablet form (e.g., stay awake pills). Caffeine is widely used; practically all Americans use it on a daily basis. It reduces hunger, fatigue, and boredom and improves alertness and motor activity. The drug appears addictive, because many users develop a tolerance for it. A further sign that it is addictive is that heavy users (e.g., habitual coffee drinkers) experience withdrawal symptoms of mild irritability and depression.

Excessive amounts of caffeine cause insomnia, restlessness, and gastrointestinal irritation. Surprisingly, excessive doses can even cause death. Because caffeine has the status of a "nondrug" in our society, users are not labeled criminals, there is no black market for it, and no subculture gives support in obtaining and using it. Because caffeine is legal, its price is low compared to other drugs. Users are not tempted to resort to crime to support their habit.[45]

*Amphetamines*  Amphetamines are called *uppers* because of their stimulating effect. When prescribed by a physician they are legal. Some truck drivers have obtained prescriptions to stay awake and more alert while making a long haul, with a few becoming addicted. Dieters have received prescriptions to help them lose weight and have also found that the pills tend to buoy their self-confidence. College students have used them to stay awake and more alert while studying. Others who have used amphetamines to increase alertness and performance for relatively short periods of time include athletes, astronauts, and executives. Additional nicknames for this drug are *speed, ups, pep pills, black beauties,* and *bennies.*

Amphetamines are synthetic drugs. They are similar to adrenalin, a hormone from the adrenal gland that stimulates the central nervous system. The better known amphetamines include Dexadrine, Benzedrine, and Methedrine. Physical reactions to amphetamines are extensive. Consumption of fat stored in body tissues is accelerated, heartbeat is increased, respiratory processes are stimulated, appetite is reduced, and insomnia is common. Users feel euphoric, stronger, and have an increased capacity to concentrate and to express themselves verbally. Prolonged use can lead to irritability, deep anxiety feelings, and an irrational persecution complex that can lead to sudden acts of violence.

Amphetamines are usually taken orally in tablet, powder, or capsule form. They can also be sniffed or injected. "Speeding" (injecting the drug into a vein) produces the most powerful effects and can also cause the greatest harm. An overdose can cause coma, with possible brain damage; in rare cases death may occur. There are other dangers, as speeders may develop hepatitis, abscesses, convulsions, hallucinations, delusions, and severe emotional disturbances. Another danger is that when sold on the street, the substance may contain hazardous impurities.

An amphetamine high is often followed by mental depression and fatigue. Continued amphetamine use leads to psychological dependence. It is unclear whether amphetamines are physically addicting, because the withdrawal symptoms are uncharacteristic of withdrawal from other drugs. Amphetamine withdrawal symptoms include sleep disturbances, apathy, decreased activity, disorientation, irritability, exhaustion and depression. Some authorities believe such withdrawal symptoms indicate that amphetamines may be physically addicting.[46]

One of the legal uses of certain amphetamines is the treatment of hyperactivity in children. Hyperactivity (also called hyperkinesis) is characterized by short attention span, extensive motor activity, restlessness, and shifts in moods. Little is known about the causes of this condition. When children become older, the symptoms tend to disappear even without treatment. Interestingly, some amphetamines (Ritalin is a popular one) have a calming and soothing effect on hyperactive children; the exact opposite effect occurs when Ritalin is taken by adults. It should be noted that treating "uncontrollable" children with amphetamines in the past has frequently been abused. Some of the children for whom Ritalin is prescribed are not really hyperactive. They are normal children who simply refuse to submit to what their teachers and parents consider appropriate childhood behavior. As a result, these children are labeled as problem children and are forced to take a mood-altering drug every day.

One amphetamine that has had increasing illegal use in recent years is methamphetamine hydrochloride (Desoxyn), known on the street as *meth* or *ice*. In liquid form it is often referred to as *speed*. Under experimental conditions, cocaine users often have difficulty distinguishing cocaine from methamphetamine hydrochloride. There is a danger this drug may increasingly be abused, as its "high" lasts longer than a cocaine "high,"

and the drug can be synthesized relatively easily in laboratories from products that are sold legally in the United States. Methamphetamine hydrochloride is legally used to treat obesity as one component of a "last resort" weight reduction regimen. A serious side effect when using this drug for weight reduction is that the user's appetite returns with greater intensity after use of the drug is discontinued.

***Cocaine and Crack***  Cocaine is obtained from the leaves of the South American coca plant. It has a chic status in this country and is rapidly replacing other illegal drugs in popularity. Although legally classified as a narcotic, it is in fact not related to the opiates from which narcotic drugs are derived. It is a powerful stimulant and antifatigue agent.

In America, cocaine is generally taken by sniffing and is then absorbed through the nasal membranes. The most common method is sniffing through a straw or a rolled-up bank note (snorting). It may also be injected intravenously, and in South America the natives chew the coca leaf. It may be added in small quantities to a cigarette and smoked. Cocaine has been used medically in the past as a local anesthetic, but other drugs have now largely replaced it for this purpose.

Cocaine constricts the blood vessels and tissues and thereby leads to increased strength and endurance. It also is thought by users to increase creative and intellectual powers. Other effects include a feeling of euphoria, excitement, restlessness, and a lessened sense of fatigue. It is claimed by some that use of cocaine heightens or restores their virility and enables them to extend the sex act for long periods.[47]

Larger doses or extended use may result in hallucinations and delusions. A peculiar effect of cocaine abuse is *formication*—the illusion that ants, snakes, or bugs are crawling on or into the skin. Some abusers have such intense illusions that they literally scratch, slap, and wound themselves trying to kill these imaginary creatures.

Physical effects of cocaine include increased blood pressure and pulse rate, insomnia, and loss of appetite. Heavy users may experience weight loss or malnutrition due to appetite suppression. Physical dependence on cocaine is considered to be a low to medium risk. However, the drug appears to be psychologically habituating; terminating use usually results in intense depression and despair, which drives the person back to taking the drug.[48] Additional effects of withdrawal include apathy, long periods of sleep, extreme fatigue, irritability, and disorientation. Serious tissue damage to the nose can occur when large quantities of cocaine are sniffed over a prolonged time period. Regular use may result in habitual sniffling and sometimes leads to an anorexic condition. High doses can lead to agitation, increased body temperature, and convulsions. A few people who overdose may die if their breathing and heart functions become too depressed.

Crack (also called *rock*) is obtained from cocaine by separating the adulterants from the cocaine by mixing it with water and ammonium hydroxide. The water is then removed from the cocaine base by means of a fast-drying solvent, ether being the most common. The resultant mixture resembles large sugar crystals similar to rock sugar (thus the name rock). Crack is highly addictive. Some authorities claim that one use is enough to lead to addiction.

Crack is usually smoked, either in a specially made glass pipe or mixed with tobacco or marijuana in a cigarette. The effects are similar to cocaine, but the "rush" is more immediate and the drug gives an intensified high and has an even greater enhancement effect on orgasms.

An overdose is more common when crack is injected than when it is smoked. Withdrawal effects include an irresistible compulsion to have it, as well as apathy, long periods of sleep, irritability, extreme fatigue, depression, and disorientation.

Communal use of needles spreads AIDS. Cocaine and crack can have serious effects on the heart, straining it with high blood pressure, with interrupted heart rhythm, and with raised pulse rates. Cocaine and crack may also damage the liver. Severe convulsions can cause brain damage, emotional problems, and sometimes death. Smoking crack may also damage the lungs (see Box 4.6).

*Amyl Nitrate and Butyl Nitrate*  Amyl nitrate (*poppers*) is prescribed for patients who risk forms of heart failure. It is a volatile liquid that is sold in small bottles. When the container is opened, the chemical begins to evaporate (similar to gasoline). If the vapor is sniffed, the user's blood vessels are immediately dilated, and there is an increase in heart rate. These physical changes create feelings of mental excitation ("head rush") and physical excitation ("body rush"). The drug is supposedly sold only by prescription, but as with many other drugs the illicit drug market distributes it.

Butyl nitrate is legally available in some states without a prescription and has an effect similar to amyl nitrate. Trade names under which it is sold are Rush and Locker Room. It is available at some sexual aid and novelty stores. As with amyl nitrate, the vapor is sniffed.

Both these drugs have been used as aphrodisiacs and as stimulants to enhance the enjoyment of dancing. The drugs have some short-term, unpleasant side effects that may include fainting, headaches, and dizziness. A few deaths have been reported as a result of overdoses.

## NARCOTICS

The most commonly used narcotic drugs in the United States are the opiates (such as opium, heroin, and morphine). The term *narcotic* means sleep inducing. In actuality, drugs classified as narcotics are more accurately called analgesics, or painkillers. The principal effect produced by narcotic drugs is a feeling of euphoria.

The opiates are all derived from the opium poppy, which grows in many countries. Turkey, Southeast Asia, and Colombia have been major sources of the opiates. The centuries-old drug opium is the dried form of a milky substance that oozes from the seed pods after the petals fall from the purple or white flower.

Morphine, the main active ingredient of opium, was first identified early in the 1800s and has been used extensively as a painkiller. Heroin was first synthesized from morphine in 1874. It was once thought to be a cure for morphine addiction but later was also found to be addicting. Heroin is a more potent drug than morphine.

Opium is usually smoked, although it can be taken orally. Morphine and heroin are either sniffed (snorted) or injected into a muscle or a vein (mainlining), which maximizes the drugs' effects.

Opiates affect the central nervous system and produce feelings of tranquility, drowsiness, or euphoria. They produce a sense of well-being that dissipates pain, anxiety, or depression. Tony Blaze-Gosden notes:

> It has been described as giving an orgasmlike rush or flash that lasts briefly but memorably. At the peak of euphoria, the user has a feeling of exaggerated physical and mental comfort and well-being; a heightened feeling of buoyancy and bodily health; and a heightened feeling of being competent, in control, capable of any achievement, and being able to cope.[49]

Overdoses can cause convulsions and coma and, in rare cases, death by respiratory failure. All opiates are now recognized as being highly addicting.

Heroin is the most widely abused opiate. In addition to the above-mentioned effects, heroin slows the

# Crack Babies

In recent years, crack cocaine use by pregnant women has sharply increased. As a result, hundreds of thousands of babies have been born adversely affected by their mothers' use of crack cocaine.

Cocaine causes blood vessels in a pregnant woman to constrict, thus reducing the vital flow of oxygen and other nutrients to the fetus. Because fetal cells multiply swiftly in the first months, an embryo deprived of a proper blood supply by a mother's early and continuous use of cocaine is apt to be adversely affected cognitively. Such babies tend to look quite normal, but are apt to be undersized, and the circumference of their heads tends to be unusually small—a trait associated with lower IQ scores. Only the most intensive care after birth will give these babies a fighting chance to have a "normal" life.

In rare cases during the latter months of pregnancy, heavy crack use can create an embolism (a clot) that lodges in a fetal vessel and completely disrupts the blood supply to an organ or a limb. The result is a deformed arm or leg, a missing section of an intestine or kidney, or some other deformity.

Cocaine exposure affects brain chemistry as well. The drug alters the actions of neurotransmitters, the messengers that travel between nerve cells and help control a person's mood and responsiveness. Such changes may help explain the behavioral problems, including impulsiveness and moodiness, seen in cocaine-exposed children as they mature.

Mothers who, while pregnant, repeatedly used crack cocaine in combination with other drugs, can adversely impact the fetus in a variety of ways. (The other drugs that are used can also damage the fetus.) The children born to pregnant mothers who used crack cocaine have become known as "crack babies" and "crack kids." A few such children have severe physical deformities from which they will never recover. In others, the damage can be more subtle, showing up as behavioral problems that may sabotage their schooling and social development. Many of these children look and act like other children, but their early exposure to cocaine makes them less able to overcome negative influences, such as a disruptive home life.

Crack children often ring up huge bills for medical treatment and other care. Some grow up in dysfunctional families and increasingly display behavioral and emotional disorders. The injury during gestation is often compounded after birth by an environment of neglect, poverty, and violence. Even after mothers give birth to drug-impaired children, their addiction to crack cocaine is so strong that many tend to continue using the drug.

How can such children be helped? What does seem to work is a combination of the social services carrot and the legal stick. The best way to rescue a crack child is to rescue the mother as well. The most successful programs for addicted mothers offer a variety of assistance, which begins with detoxification, then extends to pediatric services for the child,

---

functioning parts of the brain. The user's appetite and sex drive tend to be dulled. After an initial feeling of euphoria, the user generally becomes lethargic and stuporous. Contrary to popular belief, most heroin users take the drug infrequently and do not as a rule become addicted,[50] although frequent use is highly addicting.

Opiate addiction occurs when the user takes the drug regularly for a period of time. Whether addiction will occur depends on the opiate drug taken, the strength of the dosages, the regularity of use, the characteristics of the user, and the length of time taken—sometimes use for as little as a few weeks can cause addiction. Users rapidly develop a tolerance and may eventually need a dose that is up to one hundred times stronger than a dose that would have been fatal during the initiation to the drug.[51]

Withdrawal symptoms may include chills, cramps, sweating, nervousness, anxiety, running eyes and nose, dilated pupils, muscle aches, increased blood pressure, severe cramps, extreme nausea, and fever. Most addicts are obsessed with securing a fix to avoid these severe withdrawal symptoms.

Most opiate addicts are under the age of thirty, of low socioeconomic status, and poorly educated. A disproportionate number are African Americans. Distribution and addiction to narcotic drugs primarily occur in large urban centers.

When first discovered in the late 1800s, heroin was used for three purposes: as a painkiller, as a substitute for people addicted to morphine, and as a drug taken by many to experience euphoria. A fair number of people became addicted, and in the early 1900s laws were passed to prohibit its sale, possession, and distribution.

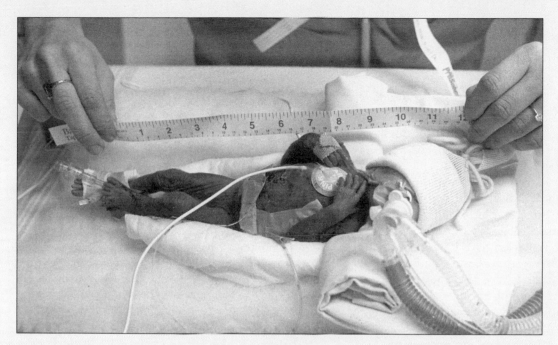

*A very tiny baby—the mother used crack while she was pregnant.*

to psychological and job counseling for the mother, and to extensive parenting classes. These crack children often need extensive medical services, social services, and specialized educational services. All of these services need to be backed up with the threat of legal intervention, including the threat of removal of the child to foster care through the protective services system.

Some studies have shown that cocaine-exposed infants can catch up in weight, length, and head circumference by one year of age.[a] They may also be able to catch up in other ways. So it is important for people who care for such children and for policymakers not to give up on them—they can be helped after birth.

a. Diane E. Papalia and Sally W. Olds, *Human Development*, 6th ed. (New York: McGraw-Hill, 1995), 77–78.

Heroin abuse continues to be regarded by some Americans as our most serious drug problem. This stereotype does not appear warranted because only a tiny fraction of the United States population has ever tried heroin, and the number of people addicted to heroin is minuscule compared to the number addicted to alcohol or tobacco. In addition, drugs such as alcohol and barbiturates contribute to many more deaths.

One reason heroin has the reputation it does is because users are thought to be "dope fiends" who commit violent crimes and reject the values of contemporary society. Addicts, however, are unlikely to commit violent crimes such as rape or aggravated assault. They are more apt to commit crimes against property (shoplifting, burglary, pickpocketing, larceny, and robbery) in order to support their habit.[52] Prostitution is also common among addicts. Because

the severe withdrawal symptoms begin about eighteen hours after the last fix, addicts who have experienced these symptoms will do almost anything to avoid them.

Unsanitary injections of heroin may cause hepatitis and other infections. Communal use of needles can spread AIDS. Also, the high cost of maintaining a heroin habit—often over $100 daily—may create huge financial problems for the user.

Because the price of illicit narcotic drugs is so high, organized crime has made huge profits in the smuggling and distribution of these drugs. Often, they are diluted with dangerous impurities, which poses serious health hazards for the users. Unfortunately, addicts are often forced for economic reasons into illegal activities to maintain their daily supply to avoid the withdrawal symptoms.

# HALLUCINOGENS

Hallucinogens, popular as psychedelic drugs in the late 1960s, distort the user's perceptions, creating hallucinations consisting of sensory impressions of sights and sounds that do not exist. The four hallucinogens most commonly used in this country are Mescaline (peyote), psilocybin, psilocin, and LSD. All are taken orally in capsule form, on a sugar cube, or licked from the back of a stamp.

Peyote is derived from a cactus plant. Mescaline is the synthetic form of peyote. Psilocybin and psilocin are found in approximately ninety different species of mushrooms that have been called magic mushrooms. Both peyote and psilocybin have long been used by certain Native American tribes. Members of the Native American church have won the legal right to use peyote on ceremonial occasions.[53] By far the most popular hallucinogen is lysergic acid diethylamide (LSD). LSD is a synthetic material derived from a fungus (ergot) that grows on rye and other plants. It is one of the most potent drugs known; a single ounce will make up to three hundred thousand doses.

The effects of LSD vary a great deal depending on the expectations and psychological state of the user and the context in which it is taken. A person may experience differing reactions on different occasions. The effects that can be experienced include the "seeing" of sounds, "hearing" of colors, colors seeming unusually bright and shifting kaleidoscopically, exaggerations of color and sound, and objects appearing to expand and contract. Users become highly suggestible and easily manipulated; seduction of males and females alike becomes easier.

Bizarre hallucinations are common. The experience may be peaceful or may result in panic. Some users have developed severe emotional disturbances that resulted in long-term hospitalization.[54] Usually a "trip" will last eight to sixteen hours. Physical reactions include increased heartbeat, goose bumps, dilated pupils, hyperactivity, tremors, and increased sweating. Aftereffects include acute anxiety or depression. Flashbacks sometimes occur after the actual drug experience and may happen at any time and place, with no advance warning. If the user is driving a car when a flashback occurs, a life-threatening condition is present for the user and for others in the vicinity.

There is no evidence of physical or psychological dependence on LSD by users. Users do develop tolerance to the drug very rapidly; effects can be achieved in the future only by taking larger doses. Cessation of use, even for a few days, will restore sensitivity to the drug, enabling the user to take smaller quantities to experience the effects.

The effects and dangers of mescaline, psilocybin, and psilocin are similar to those of LSD. LSD is, however, the most potent of these hallucinogens.

# TOBACCO

The use of tobacco is recognized as one of the most damaging drug habits in America. Smoking causes emphysema, cancer of the mouth, ulcers, and lung cancer and reduces life expectancy. It significantly increases the risk of strokes and heart disease, particularly in women who use birth control pills.[55] Smoking by a pregnant woman sometimes leads to a miscarriage, a premature birth, or the child being born underweight. Despite these widely publicized hazards, about 25 percent of the adult population continues to smoke.[56]

Tobacco is the number one killer drug. It contributes to far more deaths than all other drugs combined.[57] Tobacco is estimated to contribute to four hundred thousand deaths per year in the United States.[58] This is more than double the number of deaths to which alcohol abuse contributes, and hundreds of times the number of deaths to which cocaine contributes.[59] Most of the deaths are the result of diseases such as heart disease and lung cancer from cigarette smoking. However, over two thousand deaths per year result from fires caused by smoking.[60] There is also substantial evidence that "passive smoking" (breathing the smoke from others' cigarettes, cigars, or pipes) is also hazardous to health. One source of evidence for this is that young children whose parents smoke have a higher incidence of pneumonia and other respiratory disorders than young children whose parents do not smoke.[61]

The attitudes of Americans toward tobacco use are gradually becoming more negative. In the 1990s, a movement developed that increasingly views tobacco as a dangerous drug, and nonsmokers are increasingly treating smokers as pariahs. Some authorities are now predicting that cigarettes will some day be outlawed in many countries.

In 1988, the U.S. Surgeon General C. Everett Koop declared that tobacco is as addictive as heroin or cocaine.[62] Koop noted that people addicted to tobacco are drug addicts.

Tobacco is highly habit forming. Nicotine, the primary drug in tobacco, has remarkable capacities, as it

*Medicinal uses for marijuana: San Francisco's Cannabis Buyer's Club.*

can act as a depressant, a stimulant, or a tranquilizer. Smokers quickly develop a tolerance for nicotine and tend to gradually increase consumption to one or two packs or more a day.

There are special clinics and a variety of other educational and therapeutic programs to help people quit smoking. Tobacco is a habit-forming drug. Withdrawal from use leads people to become restless, irritable, and depressed and to have an intense craving to smoke. Studies show that only a minority of smokers who make determined efforts to quit actually succeed.[63]

In the biggest civil settlement in U.S. history, tobacco companies agreed in 1998 to pay over $240 billion to the 50 states to settle claims against the industry for health-care costs blamed on tobacco-related illnesses. The payments to the states are distributed over 25 years (payments began in 2000). Some of the funds will go to a foundation to study how to reduce teen smoking. A major objective of the deal is to discourage children from smoking by restrictions on advertising and by imposing sharp limits on the ways that cigarettes are marketed.[64]

## MARIJUANA

Marijuana (*grass,* or *pot*) comes from the hemp plant *Cannabis sativa.* Cannabis grows throughout the world, and its fibers are legally used to produce rope, twine, paper, and clothing.

The main use of the plant now, however, centers on its dried leaves—marijuana—and on its dried resin—hashish. Both may be taken orally but are usually smoked. Hashish is several times more potent than marijuana.

The effects of marijuana and hashish vary, as with any other drug, according to the mood and personality of the user, the circumstances, and the quality of the drug. The effects are rather complicated and may induce a variety of emotions. Many of the effects are produced because marijuana has sedative properties and creates in the user a sense of relaxed well-being and freedom from inhibition. There may also be mild hallucinations that create a dreamy state in which the user may experience fantasies. Smokers become highly suggestible and may engage in actions (such as sexual activities) in which they may not otherwise be involved. The drug may induce feelings of joyousness, hilarity, and sociability. It may lead to talkativeness, disconnected ideas, a feeling of floating, and laughter. It may also intensify sensory stimulation, create feelings of enhanced awareness and creativity, and increase self-confidence. A person may gradually experience some of these emotions, followed by others.

The threat of physical dependence is rated low; the threat of psychological dependence is rated as moderate. Withdrawal, however, may be very unpleasant, with the user suffering from insomnia, hyperactivity, and loss of appetite.

The short-term physical effects of marijuana are minor: reddening of the eyes, dryness of the throat and the mouth, and a slight rise in heart rate. There is some evidence that continued use by teenagers will result in their becoming apathetic and noncompetitive.

Frequent users may have impairments of short-term memory and concentration and of judgment and coordination. They may find it difficult to read, to understand what they read, or to follow moving objects with their eyes. Users may feel confident that their coordination, reactions, and perceptions are quite normal while they are still experiencing the effects of the drug; under these conditions activities such as driving a vehicle may have tragic consequences to them and to others. Marijuana use by pregnant women may also be a contributing factor to malformations in fetuses, much like the effects of alcohol use.

An overdose of the active ingredients of cannabis can lead to panic, fear, confusion, suspiciousness, fatigue, and sometimes aggressive acts. One of the most voiced concerns about marijuana is that it will be a stepping-stone to using other drugs. About 60 percent of marijuana users "progress" to using other drugs.[65] However, other factors such as peer pressure are probably more crucial determinants of what mind-altering drugs people will "progress" to use.

The attempt to restrict use of marijuana through legislation has been described as a "second Prohibition"[66] and has had similar results; a large number of people are using the drug in disregard of the law. The unfortunate effect of laws that attempt to regulate acts (crimes as defined by law) without victims is that they criminalize the private acts of many otherwise law-abiding people. Such laws also foster the development of organized crime and the illicit drug market.

For years, heated debates have raged about the hazards of long-term marijuana use. Some studies claim it may cause brain damage, chromosome damage, irritation of the bronchial tract and lungs, and a reduction in male hormone levels. These findings have not been confirmed by other studies,[67] and the controversy rages on.

In 1982, the National Academy of Sciences completed a fifteen-month, extensive study on marijuana. The study found no evidence that marijuana causes permanent changes in the nervous system and concluded that the drug probably does not break down human chromosomes. It also found that marijuana may be useful in treating glaucoma, asthma, certain seizure disorders and spastic conditions, and in controlling severe nausea caused by cancer chemotherapy. The study warned, however, that the drug presents a variety of short-term health risks and justifies "serious national concern." One of the reversible, short-term health effects is impairment of motor coordination, which adversely affects driving or machine-operating skills. The drug also impairs short-term memory, slows learning abilities, and may cause periods of confusion and anxiety. The study also found evidence that smoking marijuana may affect the lungs and respiratory system in much the same way that tobacco smoke does and may be a factor in causing bronchitis and precancerous changes. Thus the study found some evidence that marijuana may lead to certain adverse, long-term health problems. The major recommendation was that "there be a greatly intensified and more comprehensive program of research into the effects of marijuana on the health of the American people."[68]

In 1996, voters in California and Arizona approved the medical use of marijuana to treat, for example, symptoms of AIDS, cancer, and other diseases. However, the Clinton administration threatened sanctions against doctors who prescribed it. In 1997, a panel of experts who convened at the National Institutes of Health stated that marijuana shows promise in treating painful symptoms of some diseases and urged further study of its medical use.[69] The controversy continues.

## ANABOLIC STEROIDS

Anabolic steroids are synthetic male hormones. Although steroids have been banned for use by athletes in sporting competition, steroids are still being used by some athletes, body builders, and teenagers who want to look more muscular and brawny. From early childhood, many boys have been socialized to believe that the ideal man looks something like Mr. Universe. Such well-known athletes as Olympic sprinter Ben Johnson and Seattle linebacker Brian Bosworth are known to have taken the steroid short-cut to be more muscular and to increase running speed.[70]

Many adolescents who use steroids want to be sports champions. Steroids are derivatives of the male hormone testosterone. Some young male body builders who use steroids to promote tissue growth and to endure arduous workouts routinely flood their bodies with one hundred times the testosterone they produce naturally.[71] Most steroid users are middle-class and white.

Steroid-enhanced physiques are a hazardous prize. Steroids can cause temporary acne and balding, upset hormonal production, and damage the heart and kidneys. Doctors suspect they may contribute to liver cancer and atherosclerosis.[72] For teens, the drugs can stunt growth by accelerating bone maturation. Male steroid users have also experienced shrinking of the testicles, impotence, yellowing of the skin and eyes, and development of female-type breasts. In young boys, steroids can have the effect of painfully enlarging the sex organs. In female users, the voice deepens permanently, breasts shrink, periods become irregular, the clitoris swells in size, and hair is lost from the head but grows on the face and body.

Steroid drug users are prone to moodiness, depression, and irritability. Users are apt to experience difficulty in tolerating stress. Some males who had been easygoing prior to steroid use experience raging hostility after prolonged use; such hostility is displayed in a variety of ways—ranging from being obnoxious to continually provoking physical fights. Some users become so depressed that they commit suicide.

Steroid users generally experience considerable difficulty in terminating steroids after prolonged use. One reason is that bulging biceps and hamhock thighs soon fade when steroid use is discontinued. Concurrent with the decline in muscle mass is the psychological feeling of being less powerful and less "manly." Most users who try to quit wind up back on the drug. A self-image that relies on a steroid-enhanced physique is difficult to change.

## *Rehabilitation Programs*

Rehabilitation programs for alcohol abuse are very similar to rehabilitation programs for most other drugs. We will begin by looking closely at the treatment of alcoholism.

### ALCOHOL TREATMENT PROGRAMS

As mentioned earlier, before an alcoholic may be helped, the alcoholic's denial of the problem must be confronted. If the alcoholic cannot or does not confront the situation, the confrontation can be done by family members, friends, employers, counselors, or by all of these together. Tim Bliss briefly describes guidelines for this confrontation:

In confronting the alcoholic, documentation of incidents that occurred while drinking becomes extremely important. This is particularly important because the alcoholic may have blackouts. These are periods of amnesia as opposed to passing out or unconsciousness. Both are due to excessive drinking. Many times during confrontation it is important that the entire family be present to reinforce the incident. In documenting the incident, one should be instructed to write down the date and time and to be as specific as possible in describing the situation. The counselor can be present during this confrontation to act as a facilitator; however, the primary responsibility in breaking through denial is with the spouse, family, or employer.

Many times, the practicing alcoholic has been threatened with divorce, job discipline, and so on. It is important not to continue these threats; action must occur if the alcoholic continues to drink after confrontation.[73]

If the alcoholic continues to deny that a problem exists, there are some guidelines for what family members should and should not do. "Nagging" the alcoholic will only increase family arguments and may provoke the alcoholic into verbally or physically abusing someone, particularly when he or she is inebriated. Family members often make the mistake of assuming they are responsible for getting the alcoholic to stop drinking and feel guilty or frustrated if the person continues to drink. They, however, do not *own* the drinking problem—the alcoholic is the one responsible for his or her drinking and is the one that determines whether he or she will stop drinking. When a person is drunk, yelling and screaming at him or her will accomplish nothing; it usually results in the other family members becoming more upset. More productive for the other family members is to isolate themselves from the alcoholic when she or he is drunk—perhaps by going shopping, taking a walk, or, if need be, locking themselves in a room.

There are two self-help groups that family members can attend. Al-Anon is for spouses and other family members of alcoholics. The program reaches out to people affected by another person's drinking, whether or not the alcoholic recognizes a drinking problem. It helps members learn the facts about alcoholism and about how to cope with an alcoholic. Alateen is for teenaged children of alcoholics and helps teenagers to understand alcoholism and to learn effective ways of coping.

If the alcoholic does acknowledge a drinking problem, there are many treatment programs available. The best known and most successful is Alcoholics Anonymous (see Box 4.7).

Box 4.7 ◆◆◆◆◆◆◆◆◆◆◆◆◆◆◆◆◆◆◆◆◆◆◆◆◆

# Alcoholics Anonymous

In 1929, Bill Wilson was a stock analyst. When the stock market crashed that year, he lost most of his money and "took to the bottle." A few years later his doctor warned him that his continued drinking was jeopardizing his health and his life. Bill underwent what he perceived as a spiritual experience and made a commitment to stop drinking. He also discovered that discussing his drinking problem with other alcoholics helped him to remain sober. One of the people with whom he discussed his problem was Robert Smith, an Ohio doctor and also an alcoholic. Together they formed Alcoholics Anonymous (AA) a self-help group composed of recovering alcoholics.

AA stresses a *confession* by the member to the group that he or she has a drinking problem, a *testimony* by the member to the group recounting past experiences with the drinking problem and plans for handling the problem in the future, and a *call* to another member of the group when suffering an intense urge to drink. The other member will do whatever possible to keep the person "dry," including staying with the person until the urge subsides.

Today, AA has chapters in over one hundred countries, providing services to hundreds of thousands of recovering alcoholics. (The term *recovering* is used because AA believes there is no such thing as a permanently recovered alcoholic.) Local chapters (around twenty-five persons per chapter) meet once or twice a week for discussion sessions. These group sessions resemble traditional group therapy meetings without a trained professional leader.

Bill W. and Dr. Bob, as they were known within AA, remained anonymous until their deaths. Local chapters still follow similar treatment procedures—the sharing of experiences in order to abstain from "the first drink that is too many and the thousand drinks that are not enough."

AA is still widely recognized as the treatment approach that has the best chance of helping an alcoholic. Testimony to its value is that hundreds of other self-help groups having treatment principles based on the AA model have now been formed to deal with other personal problems—Weight Watchers, Prison Families Anonymous, Parents Without Partners, Debtors Anonymous, Gamblers Anonymous, Emotions Anonymous, Emphysema Anonymous, and many more.

There appear to be several reasons why such self-help groups are successful. The members have an internal understanding of the problem, which helps them to help others. Having experienced the misery and consequences of the problem, they are highly motivated and educated to find ways to help themselves and fellow sufferers. Participants also benefit from the "helper therapy principle"; that is, the helper gains psychological rewards by helping others.[74] Helping others leads the helper to feel good and worthwhile and also enables the helper to put his or her own problems into perspective by seeing that others have problems that are as serious or even more serious. From the viewpoint of the new member who is still drinking, having people around who have successfully stopped provides role models of abstinence and gives them reason to believe that they too can break the grip of alcohol abuse.

At one time, intoxicated people simply were just thrown in jail to sober up. (Unfortunately, this is still happening in some communities.) Many communities, however, have now switched to a treatment approach, and most alcohol treatment facilities offer both inpatient and outpatient programs. Outpatient treatment usually serves clients who can still live at home. If the client is unable to live at home or does not show potential to stop using alcohol, inpatient treatment is usually recommended. Those going through an inpatient program will receive later follow-up treatment on an outpatient basis. Inpatient treatment can last anywhere from a few days to three months, depending on the patient's problems and the treatment program. Inpatient treatment is usually intense, including one-on-one therapy, group therapy, an orientation to AA, and occupational and recreational therapy. Outpatient treatment is not as intense, usually lasts from three to six months, and offers the same forms of treatment.

Outpatient and inpatient services are provided in some medical hospitals, in drug rehabilitation centers, and in community mental health centers. Many communities also have halfway houses that serve the alcoholic who is unable to live with family members and who is not yet ready to live alone.

Most larger companies now sponsor alcohol treatment programs for their employees (called employee assistance programs). These programs seek to identify problem drinkers in their early stages and then to intervene before severe problems arise. Such programs refer problem drinkers to appropriate community resources. If the employee uses such help, there are no adverse work consequences. However, there is considerable pressure on the employee to participate, as there is the threat of eventual discharge if the employee refuses help and continues to demonstrate lowered work productivity due to drinking.

Most therapists now believe that drinking is being used to meet some need or needs of the alcoholic— the need for socialization, relaxation, escapism, and so on. If treatment is to be successful, it must find alternatives for meeting these needs—by helping the alcoholic to find a new circle of friends, to learn other ways to relax, to learn to handle life's problems better—whatever may be the unique needs of the drinker. This is known as the theory of functional need equivalents and has been applied to other addictions as well as to alcohol abuse.

## OTHER DRUG TREATMENT PROGRAMS

The stereotype "once an addict, always an addict" has hampered efforts to rehabilitate those who are drug dependent. Although past statistical evidence tended to confirm this myth, more recent evidence suggests those dependent on drugs can successfully kick the habit. Kasindorf found, for example, that with effort American soldiers addicted to heroin during the Vietnam War could successfully terminate use on returning home to a nonheroin culture.[75]

Physical dependence on practically any drug can be ended with detoxification programs. Generally, the user will undergo intense and painful withdrawal symptoms for the first few days or even for a few weeks. Psychological dependence, however, is often more difficult to end. Users of drugs receive certain rewards (feelings of relaxation, euphoria, more alertness, less pain, and escape from reality and their problems). The psychological needs met by taking a drug are often individual to each user.

Because drugs meet psychological needs, they are functional. To end psychological dependence, it is necessary for drug treatment programs to discover what psychological needs are being met for each user and then to teach the user new ways (drug-free ways) to meet such needs.

*Inpatient Programs*  Community mental health centers, specialized chemical abuse rehabilitation centers, and some medical hospitals provide inpatient treatment programs. Detoxification lasts from twenty-four hours to three weeks depending on the severity of withdrawal. Additional inpatient care lasts two to three more weeks in a chemically free environment.

Inpatient care is designed for those chemically dependent individuals who are unable to end the dependence while remaining in the community.

*Outpatient Programs*  Outpatient care is usually not as intense as inpatient care and generally lasts three to six months. Outpatient care serves people who no longer need to be hospitalized and also people who have a fair chance of terminating their habit without having to become an inpatient. Outpatient care consists of counseling, medical services, and vocational services. Outpatient services are provided by community mental health centers, specialized rehabilitation centers for treating chemical abuse, medical hospitals, and outpatient clinics for chemical abuse.

*Self-Help Programs*  There are many self-help programs for abusers that are modeled after Alcoholics Anonymous. Such programs include Narcotics Anonymous, Synanon, Potsmokers Anonymous, Pills Anonymous, Delancey Street Foundation, and Renaissance Project.[76]

*Therapeutic Communities*  Therapeutic communities are long-term residential treatment programs, with patients usually staying from twelve to eighteen months. Therapeutic communities focus on making lifestyle changes so that the person will find rewards for staying drug-free and will also function more appropriately in society (see Box 4.8). Tim Bliss further describes the focus:

> The environment [of therapeutic communities] is one of constant confrontation that aims at breaking down walls that cover up the real person. An individual might, for example, come on as a "tough guy" as a result of leading the street life. Actually, this image needs to be broken down. Feelings that are painful (for example, loneliness, fear, depression) are allowed to be expressed, eventually allowing the individual to be honest with him/herself, and thus not needing to wear a mask. Many graduates of therapeutic communities remain in close contact for support purposes. It is difficult to measure the success of these programs, because there is a high rate of dropouts. However, for those that graduate, there is evidence they are successful in obtaining employment and remaining chemical-free.[77]

*Halfway Houses*  Halfway houses assist those who have been hospitalized (and detoxified) to gradually reenter the community at their own pace. Halfway houses also serve those who are psychologically

Box 4.8

# Therapy with a Heroin Addict

Tim Bliss, a drug counselor, describes the efforts made to treat a heroin addict:

Many times, the drug counselor feels he or she isn't making any progress in the recovery process of the heroin addict. Counseling the heroin addict takes a special type of counselor—one who can walk the walk and talk the talk, so to speak. To counsel, first off, it takes an extreme amount of dedication, concentration, and effort.

The client I worked with was a thirty-year-old black married male with three children. The history was as follows. The client will be referred to as Bob. Bob was raised in an urban area; he was the middle child and seemingly led a normal childhood. As he reached his early teens, he got more and more involved with drinking and drugs. He graduated from high school and went into the army soon after graduation. This is where many problems arose. Bob had several bouts with the army ranging from insubordination to disorderly conduct. He started chipping (occasionally using) heroin and became quite involved in the drug culture overseas in Germany. He then married a white German woman and brought her back to the United States, where they have lived for the past ten years. Bob then became involved in an armed robbery and claimed he was innocent; yet he spent three years in prison. After his prison time ended, Bob secured a job at a local factory; this lasted approximately one and one-half years, at which time he was fired for excessive absenteeism. The excessive absenteeism was a result of episodic drinking and drug use.

Prior to Bob's going to prison, he was involved in the Black Panthers [a militant black separatist organization]. What was interesting was that he was married to a white, which had to be a conflict with Bob.

In general, Bob seemingly had quite a conflict being black. He wanted at times to be white, and yet at other times [he] wanted to be married to a black instead of a white.

Bob became increasingly involved with drugs, and in time [he] developed a habit with heroin. This led to his involvement in both the criminal justice system and treatment.

Fortunately, there was a federal grant at this time that could divert criminal justice clients to alcohol or drug treatment centers. Bob became involved in a local alcohol treatment center while on probation. However, due to the fact that he was a heroin addict, treatment was ineffective. Within a very short period of time after discharge, Bob was back to "junk." He was then involved in another armed robbery and this time was facing seven to ten years for several counts of armed robbery and burglary. At this point, I became involved with the client. Bob was out on bond and was awaiting his court date. Throughout this time period, Bob was seen on an outpatient treatment basis. Urine drug screens were taken, and all turned up negative for opiates for about four weeks. Then Bob started chipping (using heroin on occasion). A therapeutic community which treated heroin addicts had been contacted to arrange an intake interview with Bob. The therapeutic community was a six- to nine-month intensive inpatient treatment program. [Its] philosophy was that the drug of choice was only a symptom, and what needed to be changed was the lifestyle.

The court date was finally reached, and it was time for Bob to "face the music." The therapeutic community had interviewed Bob, and he was accepted into their program. I had arranged for a psychologist to run a series of tests on Bob to determine statistically his chances of succeeding in treatment. The results of this testing were that Bob would have one-third of a chance of succeeding in

---

dependent and want to kick a habit but do not need to be hospitalized. Halfway houses provide counseling services (both one-to-one and group) to help residents remain drug-free and to work on resolving other personal problems. Residents also receive vocational training, assistance in finding a job, and room and board. Many halfway houses employ staff who are former addicts. Recovered drug abusers are often more effective than professional staff in relating to the residents and in breaking down the barriers of denial, anger, isolation, and hostility that addicts feel. Former addicts also provide a model that addiction is a curable disease. Halfway houses emphasize the importance of residents assuming responsibility for their actions and behavior.

*Treatment Using Drugs* Similar to the Antabuse used by alcoholics (see Box 4.9), some chemicals are used in therapeutic programs to treat certain drug

treatment, one-third of not succeeding, and one-third of no change at all. Obviously, statistics were against Bob; but in outpatient treatment, he had demonstrated that he was sincere and did want to change. So with that, this author and Bob's probation officer felt treatment was the best alternative, rather than incarceration. The presiding judge was approached with this alternative, and he accepted it. However, Bob was found guilty, so the judge imposed a stayed sentence of seven years to be served if Bob did not successfully complete treatment.

The following week, Bob was transferred to the therapeutic community. He stayed there approximately six months, at which time the community voted that he be terminated, unsuccessfully completing treatment. Bob was voted out for a number of reasons: (a) he wasn't following instructions when reprimanded by staff; (b) overall, he was an extremely bad influence on the rest of the community, as he was always "gaming" people, not being able to be honest with himself or others; [and] (c) he was breaking cardinal rules, which meant that, when he would get angry, other members of the community were actually afraid to be around him, as they were afraid he might get physically violent. The incident that resulted in Bob's termination was that he was reprimanded for an action that involved a female client. Supposedly, Bob had intercourse with the female, and the female admitted this to the staff in one of the community's "cop to" groups. (A "cop to" simply means people in the community that have done something wrong, or are feeling guilty, talk about it in one of these groups.)

The staff told Bob he was on a communication ban (no talking) the following day; they also requested he wear a five-foot sign with some writing on it. This kind of reprimand might seem ineffective or silly to some of us; however, it is quite effective in an atmosphere like a therapeutic community, especially on a long-term basis. Bob didn't

follow through the next day, a vote was taken, and he was transferred to the county jail, where he would await a decision by the probation officer, the judge, and the original referring agent.

We had decided Bob was still amenable to treatment. However, this would entail a more highly structured treatment environment, a facility that dealt more with the hard-core heroin addict.

Meanwhile, Bob was becoming increasingly bitter, sitting in jail thinking about what had occurred, and also becoming anxious due to the fact he was facing seven years in prison.

The probation officer and original treatment staff involved with Bob found a treatment facility that would be most favorable to any kind of successful treatment for Bob. The judge also went along with this.

Bob, after about two weeks of sitting in jail, was transferred on a Friday afternoon to this treatment facility. Friday evening, he called his wife and absconded from treatment. He has not been heard of since, and consequently his probation has been revoked, and, when caught, he will be sent to prison.

I have heard unofficial reports he is still around, back to heroin in his old way of life.

This is not a success story, obviously, but all too often that's all we ever hear. The field is challenging; however, this case history is also a real part of treatment—that oftentimes a therapist has to realize his or her own limitations and accept reality as it is. Not everyone is a success, and no matter what you do, *you* can't change that. All we can do is seek as much knowledge about the field as possible and utilize every tool available to motivate clients in changing their behavior. Only after this can we say, "I gave it my best shot, and that's all there is."

*Source:* Tim Bliss, "Drugs—Use, Abuse, and Treatment," in Charles Zastrow, ed., *Introduction to Social Welfare Institutions,* 2nd ed. (Homewood, IL: Dorsey Press, 1982), pp. 315–316.

addictions. Methadone, sometimes used to treat heroin addiction, has by far received the most publicity.

Methadone is a synthetic narcotic and is sufficiently similar to heroin to satisfy the addict's physical craving. It prevents the anguish of heroin withdrawal symptoms without inducing a high. Methadone thus allows a heroin addict to function fairly normally in a community. (It usually is not effective for heroin users who seek to become high.)

Methadone itself is addictive. It also does not cure a heroin addict of addiction to heroin. It simply *maintains* heroin addicts in their communities without having them actually use heroin. Methadone is controversial because some authorities object to treating heroin addicts simply by having them become dependent on another drug.

Methadone is only legally available through approved programs. In the first few weeks of treatment,

Box 4.9

## Antabuse Treatment

Antabuse is a drug that is useful in helping an alcoholic stay sober. When taken it makes a patient's system react adversely to even small quantities of alcohol. Shortly after a person drinks an alcoholic beverage, antabuse causes the person to become intensely flushed, the pulse to quicken, and the person to feel intensely nauseated, often to the point of regurgitation.

Antabuse was developed in Copenhagen in 1947. Before Antabuse is administered, the patient is detoxified. Treatment then begins when the drug is given to the patient for several consecutive days, along with small doses of alcohol. The small amounts of alcohol are used to help the patient recognize the strong and uncomfortable effects that will occur while drinking.

Antabuse is not a cure-all for drinking because the reasons for drinking still remain. An alcoholic, if she or he chooses, can simply stop taking Antabuse and resume drinking. Antabuse, however, is useful as part of a comprehensive treatment program involving counseling, vocational and social rehabilitation, and AA. By taking Antabuse a person is forced to remain sober and is thereby more apt to respond to other therapies.

addicts are usually required to report daily to the treatment center to receive the drug. As with any other drug that is in demand, an illicit market has also developed in methadone. Some heroin addicts use it to tide them over when they cannot obtain heroin, and other heroin addicts sometimes seek to treat themselves by taking methadone instead of heroin. As with heroin, an overdose of methadone can result in death.

Some opiate (morphine and heroin) addicts have a psychological craving to become euphoric. Scientists have also developed narcotic antagonists, which prevent opiate users from experiencing euphoria. Two of the best known opiate antagonists are Naloxone and Cyclazocine. These drugs prevent opiate addicts from experiencing pleasurable sensations when taking opiates and thereby help addicts who are motivated to kick the habit.

***Understanding and Treating Codependency*** Codependent people are so trapped by a loved one's addiction that they lose their own identity in the process of obsessively managing the day-to-day trauma created by the addict. Codependency is unhealthy behavior learned amid chaos. Some codependents are as dysfunctional as the addict, if not more so. Living with addiction triggers excessive caretaking, suppression of one's needs, a feeling of low self-worth, and strained relationships. The life and identity of a co-dependent becomes "enmeshed" with the everyday problems of living with an addict.

Many codependents grow up in a dysfunctional family. (Some are adult children of alcoholics.) They marry or become romantically involved with someone who abuses alcohol or some other drug. To some extent, the addict fills the needs of the codependent—the need to care for someone, to remain lonely, or to engage in destructive behavior such as excessive partying and thrill seeking. Codependency can be viewed as a normal reaction to abnormal stress.

If the addict terminates the use of his or her drug of choice, the codependent's dysfunctional behaviors generally continue unless he or she receives treatment. There are a variety of treatment approaches for codependents—individual psychotherapy, self-help groups (such as Al-Anon and Adult Children of Alcoholics), and codependency therapeutic groups. For many codependents, treatment involves recognition that they have a life and an identity separate from the addict; that the addict alone is responsible for his or her drug abuse; and that his or her life and the addict's will improve if he or she terminates the caretaking and enabling behaviors. Through treatment, many codependents regain (or gain for the first time in their life) their own identity. Treatment is designed to banish the self-destructive habits that sabotage the codependent's happiness.

## Suggestions for Curbing Drug Abuse in the Future

Although it is important to treat current drug abusers, perhaps even more important is a prevention approach designed to keep nonabusers from becoming abusers. We will consider six approaches: educational programs, prevention of illegal drug trafficking across borders, employee drug-testing programs, stricter laws and enforcement, decriminalization, and the British approach.

## EDUCATIONAL PROGRAMS

More programs are gradually appearing that give students and the general public a realistic understanding of drug use and abuse. Quality programs inform people of:

- the nature and effects of commonly used drugs;
- how to recognize signs of abuse;
- how to counter negative peer pressure to use drugs;
- how to help someone who overdoses;
- how to help friends and relatives who are abusing drugs;

- what treatment resources and programs are available in the community;
- what to do if you believe you may have a drug problem;
- what to do if a relative or friend refuses to acknowledge the existence of a drug problem; and
- how to help abusers learn drug-free ways to meet the psychological needs they are now attempting to satisfy through drug use.

Educational programs of the past tried to use scare tactics—showing pictures of fatal automobile crashes after drug use, suggesting drug users would end up on "skid row," and indicating experimenting in small quantities with drugs would drive such users crazy and forever ruin their lives. Such scare tactics are now viewed as ineffective. The young see their parents, other adults, and peers using drugs (particularly alcohol) with generally no tragedies occurring. Such alarmist approaches wound up destroying the credibility of the educators.

Fortunately, there are now books, curriculum guides for teachers, and audiovisual materials that are available to give a more realistic approach to drug use and abuse. Hopefully, the ineffective scare approach is on its way out.

In the past two decades, major prevention efforts directed toward drunk driving, alcohol abuse, hazards of smoking tobacco, and illegal drug use have been undertaken through the media and in the schools. Extensive drug abuse prevention programs are now under way in elementary schools, middle schools, high schools, and colleges. These programs, which are tailored to the age level of the students at which they are targeted, include McGruff, the Crime Dog, at the kindergarten level; D.A.R.E. (Drug Abuse Resistance Education), a police-sponsored program, at the elementary school level; and various clubs, retreats, and lock-ins at middle- and high-school levels. They use a variety of approaches, including pointing out the risks of drug use, providing accurate information on drugs and their effects, providing instructions on how to say "no" assertively to peer pressure to use drugs, providing enjoyable drug-free activities, and enhancing students' self-esteem.

With drug and alcohol abuse increasingly presented in the media and in the schools as risky and dangerous rather than glamorous and fashionable, overall drug and alcohol use among adults appears to be declining.[78] It is highly unlikely that the United States will ever become drug free. Certain drugs do have considerable valid medical use. Drugs also meet certain psychological needs. But the abuse of drugs can certainly be curbed.

One reason the United States has one of the highest rates of drug abuse of any country is the erroneous view that "There's a pill for everything." Americans tend to believe that medical technology can solve every ill the body encounters, a belief that can sometimes be used to absolve people of the responsibility of living a healthy lifestyle. At the same time, the tendency to self-medicate is a common response to feelings of worthlessness, to being "stressed out," and to

being mistreated by society. In a society where medication is so much the norm (a view boosted by advertising from the massive alcohol, pharmaceutical, and tobacco industries), it is easy to turn to drugs, alcohol, or smoking as a way of relieving stress or forgetting about one's all-too-real problems. Public education is definitely needed to convey that drug use does not *solve* life's problems; it *intensifies* such problems.

## PREVENTION OF ILLEGAL DRUG TRAFFICKING ACROSS BORDERS

Small drug dealers are rich, middlemen are millionaires, and the top drug barons are billionaires. Illegal drug trade across borders is a big, highly profitable business. One way to combat drug trafficking across borders would be for countries of the world to agree to treat it as an international crime, indictable under international law.

An international court could be established to administer this law. This court, possibly as a division of the United Nations, could have an investigative force that would have the authority to enter drug-producing countries to gather evidence about the drug barons masterminding the production, manufacture, and distribution of illegal drugs across borders. Countries would be expected to arrest and extradite for trial to this international court those indicted as masterminding drug trafficking across borders. Those found guilty could be penalized with a life sentence, with no chance of parole. The United Nations could be empowered to impose trade sanctions against any country that refused to arrest and extradite indicted drug barons. (No country can survive nowadays without international trade and finance.) Gradually, stiffer trade sanctions could be levied against countries that make little or no effort to arrest and extradite indicted drug barons. In addition, armed forces of the United Nations could be made available to those governments too weak to combat the private armies employed by some notorious drug barons.

The United States and other countries have spent millions of dollars trying to prevent illegal drugs from being smuggled across borders. A few drug shipments have been confiscated, and a few transporters of drugs have been arrested. But drug barons are generally successful in finding creative ways to smuggle drugs across borders. If allowed to do business in drug-producing countries, drug barons will continue to find ways to smuggle drugs across borders. If drug trafficking across borders is to be stopped, other actions need to be taken.

## EMPLOYEE DRUG-TESTING PROGRAMS

In 1986, the President's Commission on Organized Crime recommended that both government and private industry should launch drug-testing programs of employees. The commission asserted that such examinations would help curb a drug abuse epidemic that drains billions of dollars annually from American society and erodes the nation's quality of life.[79]

A number of major U.S. companies already require applicants or employees to submit to urinalysis to detect use of cocaine, marijuana, heroin, and morphine. Tests are also given in the military, a few sensitive federal agencies, and in many drug treatment facilities.

Many local governments now require random drug testing of employees in certain job categories, such as bus drivers.

Professional baseball, basketball, and football organizations also have drug-testing programs. For example, the National Football League requires all players to take a mandatory urine test prior to the start of the regular season and two unscheduled tests during the regular season. A player who tests positive is first required to receive treatment. If a player relapses twice (as identified by three positive tests over a period of time), he is permanently banned from the league. The National Basketball Association and the National Football League already have banned several players from playing in their leagues for repeated drug violations.

Drug-testing programs are being recommended in the interest of safety, in the interest of health, and in the interest of increased productivity. These programs are a clear signal that companies are serious about addressing the hazards caused by drugs. Those detected are generally given an opportunity to enter treatment programs. If further drug tests show the use of illegal drugs is continuing, such employees are discharged.[80]

## STRICTER LAWS AND ENFORCEMENT

It is clear from public-opinion polls that the most popular approach to curbing drug abuse is enactment of stricter laws and more enforcement activity against violations involving drug abuse. In the past two decades, a variety of stricter laws involving drugs have

*Neighborhood participation and discussion with police are imperative to stopping and helping prevent drug activity in communities. This concerned parent wants solutions to drug sales near the local junior high school.*

been passed. In 1984, federal legislation was passed that placed considerable pressure on states to raise the minimum drinking age to twenty-one. States that did not comply risked losing federal matching funds for highways. Most states have reduced the alcohol levels required for conviction of drunken driving and toughened the penalties for driving while under the influence. In regard to smoking tobacco, most states have passed "clean indoor air" laws, requiring non-smoking areas in restaurants and, in many cases, entirely banning smoking in numerous public places. In regard to illegal drugs, a policy was established for confiscating property such as cars or boats if they were used to carry or store drugs, even small amounts of marijuana for personal use. Drug testing in the workplace, as discussed earlier, has been encouraged and is becoming more widespread.

Have such efforts worked? Drug, alcohol, and tobacco use appear to be down in our society, but it is hard to tell how much of the current decline is due to stricter laws and enforcement, and how much is due to increased awareness of the risks of drug and alcohol abuse and smoking.

## DECRIMINALIZATION OF DRUG USE

During the past century, a number of laws have been enacted prohibiting the use of a variety of drugs. Penalties have also become harsher. Yet, the proportion of the population using drugs remains high. In every jail and prison are numbers of people who have been arrested for drug law violations. Drug legislation makes possession of illegal drugs a crime with penalties in some cases equivalent to or in excess of those for such criminal acts as grand larceny and second-degree murder. In the recent past, states have sentenced people for up to twenty-five years, even life, for selling or giving small quantities of marijuana to another person. Such harshness discredits the criminal justice system and is a factor leading to disrespect for the law.

Until recently, drug legislation in this country has been designed to punish users rather than treat drug abuse or prevent use of drugs. Does it really do any good to arrest and jail (sometimes weekly) habitual drunks?

The public's general lack of accurate information about drugs has led to irrational fears about drug use and abuse. For example, there is the fear that use of marijuana will always be a stepping-stone to use of narcotic drugs. There are unwarranted fears about the negative effects of such drugs as heroin and opium. These irrational fears have led citizens to demand that stiff legislation be passed to attempt to curb the use of drugs.

However, it is increasingly recognized that punitive legislation often does not work. Prohibition demonstrated that outlawing alcohol would not end its use. Analogous to the results of laws prohibiting the use of alcohol, laws prohibiting the use of other drugs have been largely responsible for the enormous growth of organized crime and the illicit drug trade. Because prison wardens cannot keep drugs out of their own prisons, it is clear that punitive drug legislation cannot stop drug abuse.

A number of authorities are now urging that drug laws be revised to emphasize treatment rather than punishment of addicts and to make the penalties for the possession of drugs more consistent with the actual dangers. It seems irrational to send to prison (at huge expense to taxpayers) a person who possesses one joint of marijuana (a drug that may be less dangerous than alcohol).

Changes in certain drug laws in the past two decades have been emphasizing rehabilitation and the reduction of harsh penalties for the sale and possession of certain drugs. Many of these revisions have centered on marijuana.

In 1972, the National Commission on Marijuana and Drug Abuse recommended changes in state and federal laws regarding marijuana. The commission urged that the private possession of marijuana for personal use and the distribution of small amounts without profit to the distributor no longer be considered offenses.[81] Since this 1972 report, a number of states have passed laws decriminalizing the use of marijuana.[82]

Laws have also been passed mandating that those arrested for public drunkenness receive treatment rather than simply being thrown into jail. In some areas of the country, individuals who acknowledge that they are addicted to a hard drug (such as heroin) are now given treatment rather than arrested or incarcerated. Such programs are experimental and often controversial.

One of the countries that has decriminalized drugs is the Netherlands, which did so in 1976. Drug users and small-time dealers are not prosecuted, whereas large drug dealers and those who sell to minors are. Since 1976, the consumption rate of marijuana and hashish in the Netherlands has declined, and the use of other drugs has not increased.[83] The Netherlands has fewer hard-core drug addicts than other Western European countries.[84] It has a much smaller drug problem, and a lower death rate from drug overdose, than does the United States.[85] The Netherlands also has a very low incidence of AIDS among intravenous drug users.[86] It treats drug addiction as a health problem instead of a crime. This approach creates an atmosphere in which addicts can openly acknowledge their drug abuse and seek treatment for their addiction and associated health problems.

Whether the approach used in the Netherlands would work in this country is questionable. A value system has developed in the Netherlands which tolerates moderate use of drugs and which encourages those with a serious drug problem to seek treatment. There is a danger that if we decriminalize illegal drugs in the United States, many more people would experiment with hard-core drugs. If we did not develop a value system that urged drug abusers to seek treatment (as is done in the Netherlands), then there is an imminent danger that use and abuse of currently illegal drugs would sharply increase.

## THE BRITISH APPROACH

As noted, the United States in the twentieth century has primarily used a punitive approach with anyone found guilty of possessing or using prohibited drugs. In contrast, the British for many years have avoided labeling drug users as criminals and have viewed drug use as a disease that should be treated. Because of this rehabilitative emphasis, the British have formulated a very different set of laws and government policies to curb drug abuse. The British regard narcotic addicts as "sick" instead of "criminal." Rather than sending narcotic addicts to prison, they allow them to buy drugs at a low cost. If the addict cannot pay, she or he is given the drug free of charge. The system does not allow the addict to have an unlimited supply of narcotics. Extensive precautions are taken to carefully regulate the distribution of narcotic drugs.

The British program applies to heroin, morphine, and cocaine. (It does not involve marijuana, barbiturates, amphetamines, or hallucinogens.) To qualify, the narcotics user must demonstrate to a physician certified by the government that she or he is an addict. The person is then officially registered as an addict and receives a steady supply of the drug. The dosage is not enough to produce a "high" but is sufficient to prevent withdrawal symptoms. There is a central registry, so it is difficult for addicts to register with more than one clinic to obtain duplicate supplies. If a registered addict is discovered to be receiving a narcotic drug from more than one source, she or he is prosecuted. Also, anyone found possessing a narcotic who is not a registered addict is also prosecuted. Efforts are made to rehabilitate the addicts. For example, with heroin addicts the amount of heroin that is given is gradually decreased or the addicts are switched to methadone.

The British approach appears to be working well for them. The rate of addiction is far lower than in the United States, and the illicit market is far smaller and less profitable. British addicts do not require vast amounts of money to support their habits, and as a result they commit fewer property crimes. Organized crime has little profit incentive to smuggle narcotics into the country, so there are few narcotics available for nonaddicts to experiment with. Because the prescription drug is of uniform strength and is distributed in small dosages, narcotics overdosing is rare.

The prescription drug does not contain impurities, thereby minimizing drug fatalities and other health hazards. In addition, a higher percentage of British addicts (compared to American addicts) are able to keep their jobs and be productive.[87]

Whether the British system would work in this country is questionable. The idea of giving heroin and other drugs to addicts runs counter to American values that people should not be drug dependent, that users should be punished to deter others, and that the government should not be involved in distributing potentially harmful drugs. With organized crime's strong position in this country, there is also the danger that it could gain access to the government's supply of drugs and sell them to nonaddicts at inflated prices. However, because the British system is so successful, it certainly warrants careful consideration about whether or not to adapt it here.

## *Summary*

A *drug* is any substance that directly affects the central nervous system; it affects moods, perceptions, bodily functions, and/or consciousness. Habit-forming drugs are those which produce either psychological dependence, or physical dependence, or both. Drug abuse is the regular or excessive use of a drug when, as defined by a group, the consequences endanger relationships with others, are detrimental to a person's health, or jeopardize society itself. The dominant social reaction to a drug is influenced not only by the actual dangers of the drug, but also by the social characteristics and motives of the groups that use it. Legal drugs are more often abused and cause more harm in our society than illegal drugs. Alcohol is the most widely abused drug in our society. Often, users develop a "tolerance" for a drug; that is, the need for steadily increasing dosages.

Social costs of drugs include property crime (generally committed to support a habit), automobile accidents, economic losses, health problems, disrespect for the law, family disruption, spouse and child abuse, financial crises for users, and adverse psychological effects upon individuals.

Our society romanticizes and encourages the use of several drugs through commercials, films, books, and TV programs. Widely advertised drugs include alcohol, tobacco, caffeine, and over-the-counter medications.

Treatment programs for drug abuse include inpatient and outpatient services provided by community mental health centers, some medical hospitals, and specialized chemical abuse rehabilitation centers. Additional programs include self-help groups, halfway houses, and therapeutic communities.

Drug abuse will probably never cease in this country, but the extent of the abuse can certainly be reduced. Punitive laws, as Prohibition demonstrated, do not deter drug use for many people and often encourage the development of organized crime and an illicit drug market. Suggestions for curbing abuse include expansion of quality educational programs that give accurate information about drugs, prevention of illegal drug trafficking across borders, employers using employee drug-testing programs, stricter laws and more enforcement activity against violations involving drug abuse, decriminalization to encourage a treatment approach rather than a punitive approach, and the British approach, which views drug abuse as a disease, rather than a crime.

I regard sex as the central problem of life . . . sex lies at the root of life, and we can never learn to reverence life until we know how to understand sex.

—*Havelock Ellis[1]*

Amazingly, we were able to put a person in space before we understood the physiology of sexual orgasms.[2] This chapter first considers how attitudes about what constitutes socially accepted sex vary from culture to culture and through history. The chapter then summarizes key formal studies of sex. We will learn about the concept of sex variances, noting which "variances" are generally tolerated—or perhaps even accepted—by American society today.

We will then learn about:

♦ asocial sex variances (such as incest and rape), which are highly disapproved of in our society;

♦ structural sex variances (such as prostitution and pornography), which are also disapproved of by some persons in our society but have supportive social structures;

♦ personal sexual concerns (such as premature ejaculation and failure to reach orgasm), which may be considered social problems from the standpoint that society often stigmatizes these problems, making it difficult to seek help.

## Sex in History and in Other Cultures

Practically every conceivable sexual activity has been socially acceptable to some degree, at least to some people. Sex only for procreation, oral-genital relations, premarital sex, adultery, anal intercourse, monogamy, polyandry (more than one husband), polygyny (more than one wife), homosexuality, and lifelong celibacy—each has been a sexual activity that has been socially approved by some human community. Not even incest, the most widely prohibited sexual relationship, has been universally tabooed. For example, some ancient cultures encouraged incest among royal families to maintain the wealth and power among a small number of people and to ensure purity of the royal line. In 1976, a government committee in Sweden urged that all laws prohibiting incest be dropped, as the committee concluded incest causes little social or genetic harm.[3] (The conclusions reached by this committee may be erroneous, as there is some evidence that children born from inbreeding do significantly worse in school performance, on tests of physical performance, on intelligence tests, and on some measures of health.[4])

There is also a wide range of attitudes toward homosexuality in various cultures. At one extreme are societies that strongly disapprove of homosexual behavior for people of any age. In contrast, some societies

*Cultures vary greatly in their attitudes toward sexuality. In this Gimi play in New Guinea, a newly married couple lie in the garden sharing intimacies. The groom's younger brother arrives on the scene to find out how babies are made. He tries to distract his elder brother by poking the lovers with his walking stick. The performers who play the couple are both male. In New Guinea, when plays are risqué, the sexes do not act together.*

tolerate homosexual behavior for children but disapprove of it for adults. Still other societies actively force all their male members to engage in some homosexual behavior, usually in conjunction with puberty rites.[5] For example, male and female homosexuality in ancient Greece was not only acceptable but encouraged. No matter how a particular society views homosexuality, the behavior always occurs in some individuals; thus, homosexuality is found universally in all societies.[6]

Societies differ considerably in their rules regarding premarital sex. Inhabitants of the Tobriand Islands encourage premarital sex because it is thought to be an important preparation for marriage (see Box 5.1). Some societies permit young boys and girls to play husband and wife even before puberty. In Asia, the Lepcha society believes that girls need sexual intercourse in order to mature.[7] In contrast, in many Muslim and South American cultures, premarital chastity for women is highly revered: a female who has premarital sex is likely to be shamed and ostracized. However, in some other developing countries, some low-income parents sell their adolescent daughters as prostitutes, particularly to tourists.

In some cultures rape is practically nonexistent. For example in the Arapesh culture of New Guinea, males are socialized to be peaceful and nonaggressive. In contrast, in the Gussi tribe in Kenya, the rate of rape is at least five times higher than in the United States. In this tribe, both men and women are socialized to be aggressive and competitive so that women often resist sexual relations, even with their husbands.[8] It has also been fairly common throughout history for soldiers to rape the women of the societies they conquered.

In the past, white slave owners often prohibited their slaves from marrying, and some attempted to determine the characteristics of African-American children by mating female slaves with an African American male considered to have "desirable" characteristics. In Nazi Germany in the 1930s and 1940s, Hitler mated women with certain soldiers to produce offspring with the characteristics he considered desirable. Some of the persons with a cognitive disability in various societies were sterilized to prevent them from reproducing.

Eskimos practice a social custom that encourages husbands to offer male guests the privilege of spending the night with their wives, and it is considered a serious insult for guests to refuse. In Sirono, Bolivia, a male is permitted to have sex with his wife's sisters and his brother's wife and her sisters.[9]

## Sexuality in Mangaia

**M**angaia is an island in the South Pacific. The Mangaians have elaborate rituals that promote sex for pleasure and procreation.

Around the age of seven or eight, Mangaian boys are instructed on how to masturbate. At around age thirteen they undergo a superincision ritual of manhood (in which a slit is made on the full length of the skin on the top part of the penis). During this ritual they are also instructed in how to kiss, suck breasts, perform cunnilingus, and bring a female partner to orgasm several times before having their own orgasm. Approximately two weeks following this ritual, each boy is introduced to sexual intercourse with an experienced woman. She introduces him to intercourse in various positions and further instructs him on how to delay ejaculation in order to have simultaneous orgasm with his partner.

Mangaian girls also receive sexual instruction from adult women. Following such instruction, Mangaian boys and girls actively seek each other out, and many have coitus nearly every night. Teenage girls are brought up to believe virility in a male is proof of his desire for her. In particular, a male is valued who is able to vigorously continue in-and-out action of intercourse for fifteen to thirty minutes or longer while the female moves her hips back and forth. A male unable to perform this act is considered an unworthy sexual partner.

By age twenty, the average male is likely to have had ten or more girlfriends, whereas the average female will have had three or four successive boyfriends. Mangaian parents encourage such sexual experience, as they want their daughters and sons to find a marriage partner with whom they are sexually compatible. At around age eighteen, Mangaians typically have sex every night. Men are brought up to believe that bringing their partner to orgasm is one of the chief sources of male sexual pleasure.

*Source:* Donald S. Marshall, "Too Much in Mangaia," in D.S. Marshall and R.C. Suggs, eds. *Human Sexual Behavior* (New York: Basic Books, 1971), 147–163.

Some subcultures in Europe consider it appropriate for fathers to have intercourse with their daughters to teach them about sexuality (at least, that is the rationale which is given). Although there exists a myth in our society that the elderly never engage in sexual activity, some elderly in nursing homes are sexually active and in some instances have more than one sexual partner.

Although sex-change operations have been occurring since the early 1930s, they became publicized in 1952 with Christine Jorgensen's sex-change operation. Such operations were initially met with widespread disapproval. Nonetheless several thousand people have since undergone them.[10]

## JUDEO-CHRISTIAN TRADITION

Clearly what is defined as acceptable or nonacceptable sexual behavior varies from culture to culture and from one time period to another. A major influence on what is acceptable has been the Judeo-Christian tradition. The Old Testament generally restricted sexual intercourse to partners married to each other, although there were a few exceptions. For example, Hebrew law required a younger son to have sex with his brother's wife if the brother was first heir in the family and had died before leaving a male heir. Also, if a wife was barren, the husband was allowed to produce an heir with another woman (usually a servant), which he and his wife would then raise as their own. The only purpose of intercourse, it was asserted, should be to conceive children. Masturbation, homosexuality, and all other sexual expressions outside marriage were viewed as sinful.

Early organized Christianity held an even more conservative attitude toward sex, regarding it as evil and degrading and to be indulged in only by married couples for the purpose of procreation. (The Roman Catholic Church still officially asserts that sexual intercourse should occur only among married couples for the purpose of procreation, although many of its members take a more permissive view.)

The Protestant Reformation that began in the sixteenth century advocated a strict and repressive sexual code. The espoused Protestant ethic emphasized the importance of hard work and asserted it was morally wrong to engage in pleasurable activities. Denial of sexual interests and refraining from sexual activities (except to procreate) were seen as virtues. The Puritans, a major immigrant group that began colonizing America in the seventeenth century, rigidly adhered to this ascetic life.

Views promulgated by the Protestant ethic became incorporated into what has become known as *Victorian morality,* a name derived from the reign of Queen Victoria of England, who sought to establish an atmosphere of suppressed sexual expression. Victorian morality was prominent in the nineteenth and early twentieth centuries. Gagnon and Henderson describe Victorian morality as follows:

> The Puritan-dominated sex ethic became that of penny-pinching Adam Smith. . . . The moral values of the new middle classes, with their belief in hard work, delayed gratification, and avoidance of pleasure, including the sexual, were to triumph during the Victorian age, not only in England but in most of Western Europe.[11]

Victorian morality all but banished sexuality from discussion in respectable relationships. Modesty was stressed to the point of extreme prudery. In polite conversations, simple anatomical terms such as legs or breasts were taboo and instead were referred to as limbs and bosoms. The "limbs" of tables were often covered by long tablecloths so that sexual interest would not be aroused! Women did not "get pregnant"; they were "in a family way" and were expected to remain at home during their "condition." In Philadelphia in the early 1900s, men and women were not allowed to visit art galleries together for fear their modesty might be offended by classical statues. Plaster fig leaves were added to the genital areas of the statues to minimize their offensiveness.[12]

Middle- and upper-class women, prior to marriage, were expected to be virgins. There were considered to be two types of single women: "good" and "bad." The good were virgins, so-called undamaged property, who were fit to marry. The bad or "fallen" women were those who had had sex without being married. They were pitied but not consoled, because their "fall" was attributed to their own weakness. They were no longer considered fit to marry but were nevertheless acceptable for nonmarital relations with men.

A popular myth throughout this Victorian period held that men were inherently more sexual than women. This led to the development—still prevalent today—of the so-called double standard of behavior. Although it was hoped they would remain chaste, men were thought to have "animal natures." Therefore they seldom were criticized for having premarital and extramarital relations. Furthermore, it was thought that prostitutes and lower-class women were proper outlets for those excessive sexual urges that were too beastly to impose on their wives. Palen notes:

> From this division of women—good and bad, mothers and whores—came the double standard that implicitly allowed men to be sexually active but that forbade "nice girls" even to think about such things. Overt sexuality

*Switched gender play activities are increasing.*

was condemned, while covert premarital or extra-marital sex among men was tolerated as a necessary evil, given the male's more pressing sexual urges.[13]

(Researchers have since found that the female's sex drive is as strong as the male's.)

Interestingly, even during the repressive Puritan and Victorian eras, certain segments always advocated more liberal expressions of sexuality. For example, there was a profitable Victorian trade in erotic drawings and novels.

## CURRENT VIEWS ON SEXUALITY

Since the early 1900s there have been dramatic changes in sexual attitudes and behaviors. For example, recent surveys indicate that most males and females in the United States have engaged in premarital intercourse by the age of nineteen, and that most young women between the ages of eighteen to twenty-four are not virgins at marriage.[14] One of the most striking features of the sexual revolution of the last few decades is the increased popularity of mouth-genital (oral-genital) sex.[15]

The 1970s in the United States were viewed as a time of sexual permissiveness and experimentation during which many people engaged in sexual behaviors that were previously uncommon. Since then there

has been a partial reversal of this permissive trend, with a general movement toward fewer partners, more emphasis on long-term relationships, and a more gradual development of the sexual aspects of a relationship. This reversal has been attributed to a general dissatisfaction with sexual behavior divorced from intimacy, as well as to the very real threat of increased susceptibility to sexually transmitted diseases for persons who have sexual contact with multiple partners.[16] In the 1980s and 1990s, there was substantial publicity about seemingly new epidemics of sexually transmitted diseases, particularly genital herpes and AIDS. The AIDS epidemic has been likened to a modern-day plague. Cures have not yet been found for either genital herpes or AIDS. Publicity about AIDS and the realization that prevention cannot be guaranteed short of sexual abstinence or sexual monogamy with an uninfected partner have led millions of people to shift their patterns of sexual behavior by taking precautions (e.g., using condoms). Several of the tenets of the sexual revolution, such as the belief that sexual intercourse between relative strangers could be enjoyed purely for recreational pleasure and without consequences, are being rejected in the face of new challenges.

At present, ambiguity and confusion abound over what ought to be the sexual code and behavior of Americans. On the conservative end of the spectrum

## Learning Sexual Behavior Via Scripts

Social scientists have made a major contribution to an understanding of human sexuality by asserting that sexual behavior (as well as most other human behavior) is developed through learning "scripts." *Scripts* (as in the theater) are plans that we learn and then carry around in our heads. These scripts enable us to conceptualize where we are in our activities and provide us with direction for completing our activities and accomplishing our goals. Scripts are also devices for helping us to remember what we have done in the past.

Sexual scripts result from elaborate prior learning in which we acquire an etiquette of sexual behavior. According to this script approach, little in sexual behavior is spontaneous. Scripts tell us who are appropriate sexual partners, what sexual activity is expected, where and when the sexual activity should occur, and what should be the sequence of the different sexual behaviors.

Scripts vary greatly from one culture to another. Hortense Powdermaker provides the following description of a script about female masturbation generally held by the Lesu of the South Pacific:

> A woman will masturbate if she is sexually excited and there is no man to satisfy her. A couple may be having intercourse in the same house, or near enough for her to see them, and she may thus become aroused. She then sits down and bends her right leg so that her right heel presses against her genitalia. Even young girls of about six years may do this quite casually as they sit on the ground. The women and men talk about it freely, and there is no shame attached to it. It is a customary position for women to take and they learn it in childhood. They never use their hands for manipulation.[a]

a. Hortense Powdermaker, *Life in Lesu* (New York: Norton, 1933), 276–277.

are groups such as the Catholic Church and some fundamentalist religious organizations. They advocate that sex be for procreation only and restricted to heterosexual, married people. Such groups express alarm that increased sexual permissiveness will destroy the moral fiber of the family and ultimately result in the destruction of our society.

At the liberal end of the spectrum are groups and individuals holding that sex can legitimately be enjoyed for recreation as well as for procreation. They assert that the ways in which sexuality is expressed should be of no concern except to those consenting adults who participate.

Repercussions of this liberal attitude are visible throughout society. Sexual topics are presented frankly and openly by the mass media, including television, magazines and newspapers. Nudity is displayed in movies, in magazines, and on television. No longer are women who have premarital sex considered unfit for marriage. One factor that appears to have led to the increases in premarital and extramarital relations is the increased availability of birth control devices, particularly the Pill.[17]

Because of the widely conflicting codes advocated by parents, peers, and other pressure groups in our society, many individuals go through considerable turmoil in arriving at a personal code of sexual behavior—one that they can be comfortable with and seek to live by.

## FORMAL STUDY OF SEX

Prior to the twentieth century there were practically no scientific studies of human sexuality. Since about 1900, the work of four social scientists has had profound effects on our understanding of human sexuality: Sigmund Freud, Alfred C. Kinsey, and the team of William Masters and Virginia Johnson.

*Freud*   Sigmund Freud was a psychoanalyst who theorized in his writings (from 1895 to 1925) that the sex drive was a fundamental part of human life. Freud realized that many people had sexual conflicts. He made sexuality a central focus of his theories and defined most emotions and behaviors as being primarily sexual in nature. He defined sexuality broadly, as he thought it included physical love, affectionate impulses, self-love, love for parents and children, and friendship associations. Among a number of Freud's controversial theories was his assertion that everyone, from birth on, has sexual interests. He stated that, around age three, boys fall sexually in love with their mother and fear their father will discover this interest and then castrate them. Thus he believed boys at this age suffer from castration anxiety. Girls, on the other hand, at about the same age fall sexually in love with their father. Freud asserted the girls discover they do not have a penis, and their desire to have one leads to penis envy. Girls conclude they lost their penis at an earlier age when their mother discovered their developing sexual interest in their father. Young girls believe their mother "castrated" them because of their love for their father. Girls, Freud believed, also suffer from castration anxiety, but the source and nature of their anxiety is different from that of boys. Girls have castration anxiety because they believe having been castrated makes them inferior to males.

Freud's notion that sexuality was a critical part of human development initially provoked shock and outrage. Before his time it was thought that sexual interests played only a minor role in human development. Gradually his theories had a liberating effect, as sexuality slowly became recognized as playing a key role in personality development. Freud's theories also led to increased communication about sexuality and stimulated scientific investigations of this topic. Perhaps Freud's greatest contribution was this liberating effect on sexuality. Unfortunately, Freud developed a number of hypotheses and advanced them as "truths" without scientifically testing their validity. Consequently, some of his specific hypotheses about sexuality have been hotly disputed and widely challenged—for example, his hypotheses involving castration anxiety in boys, and his hypotheses about castration anxiety and penis envy in girls.

In recent years, feminists have strongly criticized Freudian theory. Feminists are particularly offended by Freud's assumption that the female is biologically inferior to the male because she lacks a penis. They ask what is so intrinsically valuable about a penis that makes it better than a clitoris, a vagina, or a pair of ovaries? Feminists argue that psychoanalytic theory is essentially a male-centered theory that has adverse effects on women because it asserts that females are biologically inferior to males.

*Kinsey*    In 1948, Alfred C. Kinsey, an American zoologist, published *Sexual Behavior in the Human Male,* which was based on interviews with 5,300 white American men. This study investigated sexual practices and found that the sexual behavior of males differed substantially from the stated moral values of the time. For instance, one-third of the respondents had had at least one homosexual experience since puberty, 83 percent had had premarital relations, 50 percent of married respondents had had extramarital affairs, and 92 percent had masturbated to orgasm.[18]

Five years later, in 1953, Kinsey published *Sexual Behavior in the Human Female,* based on interviews with 5,940 white American women.[19] This study showed, to some extent, that the double standard was still operating. It also found that women were not as asexual as was commonly thought. More than half of these respondents had had premarital relations, and one-fourth of married respondents had had extramarital relations.

Kinsey's findings, widely publicized by the mass media, directly confronted many people for the first time with the wide gaps that existed between sexual *mores* and sexual *practices*. Kinsey's studies may have led people to become freer in their sexual behavior—or at least to feel less guilt about sexual behavior that was inconsistent with traditional sexual mores. The studies certainly challenged the belief that women were basically uninterested in sex.

*Masters and Johnson*    In 1957, William Masters and Virginia Johnson began their study of the physiology of human sexual response, which culminated in the publication of their classic text *Human Sexual Response*.[20] Their findings have generally stood the test of others' replications. Masters and Johnson were the first to provide accurate information about the physiology of human sexual response based on laboratory observation of people's responses rather than on their personal reports. Their findings destroyed a number of myths. For example, Freud had asserted that vaginal orgasm was superior to clitoral orgasm. Masters and Johnson found that the clitoris had the most nerve endings and therefore was the area of greatest pleasure for women. Because the clitoris was essentially the main area being stimulated in both clitoral and vaginal orgasms, there were no physiological differences between these orgasms. This finding enhanced the sex lives of many women who futilely sought the vaginal orgasm—many of whom felt that they were inadequate or missing out on something. Other important findings were that men and women are able to enjoy sexual activity into advanced age, and that some women enjoy multiple orgasms.

On completion of this research, Masters and Johnson began to treat people with sexual dysfunctions, such as premature ejaculation in males and failure to achieve orgasm in females. They departed radically from the prevailing thinking of the day, which viewed sexual dysfunctions as a by-product of other individual or relationship problems. They identified the relationship of the two partners as the client, rather than one person or the other, and indeed required both partners to participate in the process of therapy. They did what many others had thought untenable—they dealt primarily with the sexual problem and treated people in short-term (two-week) therapy. Extremely successful results were achieved, and their methods and outcomes were subsequently published in *Human Sexual Inadequacy*.[21] They also demonstrated there is no evidence that relief of a sexual problem led (as Freud asserted) to the formation of a replacement problem. Most contemporary forms of sex therapy are based on Masters and Johnson's original work.

## Sex Variances Rather Than Sex Problems

Human beings are capable of expressing their sexuality in an amazing variety of ways, as a result of both biological determinants and learning. Everyone has some form of a sex drive, but how it is expressed is shaped by biological predispositions, rituals, acceptable role models, trial and error as to what is pleasurable and what is not, and the attitudes of others (parents, peers, teachers, and so on). Gagnon and Henderson note that the learning of ways to express our sexuality is closely related to the process of forming our gender identity (our self-concept of maleness or femaleness):

> We assemble our sexuality beginning with gender identity, and we build upon that the activities we come to think of as fitting to ourselves. Our belief in what is correct and proper results more from our social class, religion, style of family life, and concepts of masculinity and femininity than from the specifically sexual things that we learn.[22]

One approach to studying the wide variety of sexual behaviors is the social problems approach. This approach seeks to classify as social problems all sexual behaviors that differ from a norm to such an extent that a significant number of people (or a number of significant people) feel that something should be done about it. Using this approach requires delineation of the code or norm of acceptability. However, there is no consensus about which sexual expressions are acceptable and which are not. In addition, as the Kinsey study showed, there is a vast difference between the purported sexual norms of society and people's actual sexual behavior.

Another shortcoming in using the social problems approach is that those acts that would be identified as social problems would then be stigmatized as "sick," "degenerate," or "perverted." During the Victorian era our society suffered too much from the efforts of some to make value judgments about what is inappropriate sexual behavior. This text will not attempt to force any specific sexual code onto readers—too many other groups are still trying to do this. Instead of the term *social problems,* the term *sex variances* will be used to refer to sexual expressions that are of concern to certain segments of our society.

Definitions of acceptable and nonacceptable sexual behavior tend to change over time. Some behaviors that were once widely condemned are now generally accepted. Masturbation, for example, once viewed as sinful, immoral, and unhealthy is widely practiced and is recommended by sex therapists as a way to learn about one's sexuality. Not long ago, oral sex was considered immoral or wrong, but today a large majority of young people engage in oral sex.[23]

It may be argued that laws in a society can be used to determine acceptable and unacceptable sexual expressions. Any sexual acts that are legally prohibited could therefore be identified as unacceptable. However, many of our present laws relating to sexual behaviors were enacted during the Victorian era and remain highly conservative. There is a considerable time lag between changes in laws relating to sexuality and changes in attitudes and norms about sexuality. Acts that are currently still illegal in at least some states include premarital sex, oral sex, masturbation, extramarital sex, cohabitation, and intercourse in any position other than the missionary position. Historically, severe penalties were imposed for those found guilty of "sex crimes." For example, the seventeenth-century Puritans made extramarital sex a crime punishable by death. Some states continue to have severe penalties for "sex crimes." For example, a Georgia statute specifies oral sex between consenting adults as being a felony, punishable by not less than one year, or more than twenty years, in jail.[24]

Laws, to some extent, are an indicator of how societies feel about certain sexual behaviors. For example, the stiff penalties for rape and child molestation suggest strong disapproval. Yet, for the reasons cited above, laws cannot be used as the only measure of prevailing views about acceptable sexual behavior in a society.

## TYPES OF SEXUAL VARIANCES

A useful classification of sexual variances is provided by William Kornblum and Joseph Julian, who identify three categories: tolerated sex variance, asocial sex variance, and structural sex variance.[25] Asocial sex variances are behaviors that our society strongly

*Some Americans object strongly to this kind of play because they view it as being immoral. Others see this as an unsophisticated way of exploring sexuality.*

disapproves of and that do not have supportive social structures. Behaviors in this category include incest and rape. Structural sex variances are generally disapproved of by some people in our society, yet have supportive social structures. This category includes homosexuality, prostitution, and pornography.

## Tolerated Sex Variance

Included in this category are masturbation, premarital intercourse, sex between consenting adults in a variety of positions, and heterosexual oral-genital contact. A few groups (such as certain fundamentalist religious groups) assert such acts are immoral and ought to be prohibited, and laws in some states prohibit such sexual behavior—although they are seldom enforced. Most segments in our society, however, tolerate these acts. Because these sexual behaviors are generally tolerated and are of lesser concern to our present society, this chapter will move on to examine disapproved sexual variances.

## Asocial Sex Variance

Asocial sex variances include acts that elicit widespread strong disapproval and that do not have supportive social structures. Acts in this category include child molesting, incest, rape, exhibitionism, and voyeurism. People who engage in these illegal behaviors usually act alone—that is, they do not have a social group that encourages and rewards such acts.

## CHILD MOLESTING

Child molesting occurs when an adult sexually abuses a child. Sexual abuse includes genital or anal sexual intercourse, oral-genital contact, fondling, exposing one's genitals to a child, and photographing or viewing a child for the molester's erotic pleasure. While legal definitions of various forms of sexual contact between older and younger persons are clearly delineated in statute books, the central feature which makes the behavior abusive is that the sexual act is designed for the erotic gratification of the older, more powerful person. In child sexual abuse, the child is used as an object for the immediate gratification of another person, generally with no regard for the short- or long-term consequences for the child.

Child molestation is generally regarded as one of the most despicable sexual offenses in our society. The public fears—rightly—that this type of sexual abuse will destroy the innocence of the child and may lead to severe psychological trauma, interrupting the child's (and subsequent adult's) normal sexual development.

How extensive is child molestation? Many studies have been done to determine the incidence of child sexual abuse, and they indicate that approximately one in three girls and one in six boys has experienced sexual abuse.[26]

More than 90 percent of child molesters are males.[27] A number of factors partially explain this gender imbalance. Men in our culture are socialized more toward seeing sexuality as focused on sexual acts rather than toward seeing sexuality as part of an emotional relationship. Men are also socialized to be more aggressive and to believe that appropriate sexual partners are smaller and younger than themselves. In contrast, women are socialized to think that appropriate partners are larger and older than they are. Finally, women in this culture are much more often caregivers of children and therefore are more attuned than are men to children's emotional needs. A person who is closely involved since a child's birth with caring for him or her is less likely to view the child in sexual ways than is someone who has had more incidental contact.

In the past few decades there have been several well-publicized cases of child molestation. In 1979, John Gacy was arrested and convicted in Chicago for enticing thirty-three male adolescents into his home, sexually assaulting them, and then killing and burying them under his home. He was executed for these crimes in 1994. On March 11, 1977, Roman Polanski (a noted film director) was arrested in Los Angeles and charged with unlawful sexual intercourse, child molestation, supplying a minor with the drug Quaalude, oral copulation, sodomy, and rape via the use of drugs. A teenage girl was the alleged victim of these acts. As part of a plea bargain, he confessed to and was found guilty of only the first charge. While awaiting sentencing, he fled the United States. Fearing a prison sentence, he has never returned. More recently, scores of fathers, stepfathers, Boy Scout leaders, child care workers, and persons from all walks of life have been found to be child molesters. In 1991 in Milwaukee, Jeffrey Dahmer (who was on probation for molesting a thirteen-year-old boy in 1988) confessed to sexually assaulting, murdering, and dismembering seventeen males, some of whom were teenagers. In 1993, Michael Jackson, the immensely popular singer, was accused of prolonged sexual contact with a thirteen-year-old boy; in 1994 the boy's parents withdrew a civil lawsuit for damages against Jackson after he paid them several million dollars.

Who are child molesters? The stereotype is that a molester is a stranger who lurks in the dark, waiting to pounce on a child who is walking or playing alone. The fact is that in most cases the offender is an acquaintance, friend, or relative.[28] (If the offender is a relative, the abuse is called incest.) Force is rarely used. Rather, the abuser generally gains sexual access to the child by manipulation and enticement. The nature of the abuse ranges from inappropriate touching to actual intercourse. In a small proportion of cases, the child may even initiate the contact. However, such initiation does not justify the adult's becoming an active participant and almost always indicates that the child has been sexually abused previously. (It is *always* the adult's responsibility for any abuse that occurs, and never the child's.)

A. Nicholas Groth has identified two categories of child molesters: fixated and regressed.[29] A *fixated* child molester's primary sexual object choice is children and, as such, he would always prefer a child as a sexual partner over an adult. A *regressed* child molester is a person whose usual sexual interest is in adult partners, but when faced with massive stress (marital difficulty, loss of job, death in family, and so on), he "regresses" emotionally (becomes a psychologically younger person) and acts out sexually toward children to meet his needs. Regressed male child molesters generally seek female children as partners; fixated male molesters are generally interested in male children. Most incest perpetrators are of the regressed type; they generally function well in society, are in a stable heterosexual relationship, but manage stress inappropriately by acting out sexually toward children. For some, molesting children is only one of a large variety of inappropriate sexual behaviors, including voyeurism ("Peeping Tom"), exhibitionism, and even rape of adult women.[30] They apparently exercise little control over their sexual impulses, and when a child becomes available, he/she becomes a victim. Incest offenders tend to view males as entitled to sexual privilege. They view children as sexually attractive and sexually motivated, and they minimize the harm caused to children from incest.

While the most attention in the media and among protective service workers is given to the sexual assault of girls in families (primarily incestuous relationships), recent research indicates that child molesters who abuse boys outside the home tend to victimize numerous boys. In an innovative study, Abel and his colleagues discovered that child molesters of boys reported a mean of 150 victims, whereas child molesters of girls reported a mean of 20 victims.[31] If this is the case, why is there less attention to sexual abuse of boys as compared to girls? The most significant reason is that girls are far more likely to report sexual victimization than are boys, as boys often view being molested a sign of some unmasculine weakness in themselves. It is thought by many authorities that child molestation of boys is the most underreported major crime in America.

How traumatic is the molesting for the child? The factors that affect the emotional impact on the child (even into adulthood) seem to include (a) the relationship between the child and the molester (it is more damaging to the further development of trust to be abused by someone you are close to than by a stranger); (b) the frequency and duration of the abuse; (c) the actual sexual behaviors engaged in; (d) whether the child is abused by multiple perpetrators; (e) the reactions of persons if the abuse is revealed; (f) the child's general mental and emotional health and coping strategies; and (g) the availability and use of professional intervention by the abuser, the victim, and others (such as the parents). The most helpful interventions following child sexual abuse are for all significant parties (professionals, parents, siblings, etc.) to believe the child's report, for the perpetrator to take full responsibility for his/her actions, and for the child to have a forum at various stages in his/her development in which to understand and heal from the assault.

## INCEST

Incest is defined as sexual relations between blood relatives. Typically, the definition is extended to include sex between certain nonblood relatives, such as between a stepparent and a child. In the past, families generally attempted to hide this type of abuse, and it usually was not reported. Now, with an increasing openness about human sexuality, there is a rising willingness by family members to seek professional help.

In the largest proportion of incest cases reported to the police, the sexual abuse is between father or stepfather and daughter.[32] However, most incest cases are never reported to the police. Brother-sister incest is actually the most common form of incest.[33] This may or may not be sexual abuse. If the children are approximately the same age and the sexual activity is mutual and not coerced, this type of incest may be considered normal sexual experimentation. However, if the children are more than a few years apart in age, the potential exists for the younger child to be coerced into activity she or he is not comfortable with. At that point consent no longer exists, and nonconsenting sex is sexual abuse.

It is extremely difficult to determine the true incidence of child sexual abuse. The incest taboo has been extremely effective in preventing its widespread reporting but much less effective in preventing its occurrence.

Most often incest occurs in the child's home. The child is usually enticed or pressured, rather than physically forced, to participate. The age range of the abused child is from several months to adulthood, although most reports involve teenagers.[34] Children are unlikely to report sexual abuse because they often have loyalties toward the abuser and realistically fear the consequences for themselves, for the abuser, and for the family.

*Causes of Incest*  Why does incest occur? Experts in sexology have long known that people frequently use sexual behavior to achieve nonsexual rewards. For example, a teenage boy might wish to have intercourse with his girlfriend (sexual behavior) not primarily because he loves her or for the sexual gratification, but rather to enhance his status with his friends, and therefore his ego (nonsexual reward).

Adults who are threatened by and fearful of the rejection of other adults often turn to children, who are nonthreatening and generally unconditionally loving, for reassurance. This need for acceptance can develop into the adult initiating sexual behavior (especially if the adult was sexually abused as a child, as is often the case), since many people view sexual behavior as the ultimate acceptance and ego validation. Most child molesters intend no harm to their victims; they are psychologically needy people who use children in their own battle for emotional survival.

*Effects of Incest*  Blair and Rita Justice have studied the consequences of incest at three different points in time: while the incest is going on, when the incest is discovered, and the long-term effects in future years.[35] It is important to bear in mind that incest is a symptom of a disturbed family system.

First, we will look at the effects while the incest is occurring. A daughter who has sex with her father often gains special power over him; she controls the power of a very important secret. The daughter can receive special privileges from the father, which makes the other siblings (and even the mother) jealous. Role confusion often occurs. The daughter is still a child, but at times she is a lover and an equal to her father. Victims are deprived of the opportunity to explore and discover their sexuality by themselves or with a peer partner of their choice. Instead, this normal sexual development is violated by an adult imposing his exploitative behavior. The daughter often does not know if her father is going to act as a parent or as a lover, so she is confused about when or whether she should respond to her father as a child or as a partner. The mother may become both a parent and a rival to her daughter. Siblings may also become confused about who is in charge and how to relate to their sister who is receiving special privileges. Fathers in an incestuous family may become jealous and overpossessive of their daughters.

As the daughter grows older, she wants to be more independent and to spend more time with other teenagers. Often, she grows more resentful of her father's possessiveness. To make a break from the father she may run away or tell someone about the incest. Or, she may passively resist the father's rules by, for example, staying out later at night than the time he sets. In a small number of cases incest is discovered when the daughter becomes pregnant. (Genetically, incest may have adverse consequences as it leads to inbreeding. The offspring are more apt to have a lower intelligence, physical performance difficulties, and genetic defects).[36] At times the incest is discovered by the mother, who then may try to stop it by reporting it to the police. (Sometimes the mother discovers the incest but remains quiet.)

If the incest is reported to the police and criminal charges are filed against the father, the entire family is usually caught up in a traumatic, time-consuming, confusing, and costly legal process. When there is legal involvement, questions that the daughter is asked often result in embarrassment and humiliation. The daughter feels, at times, that her account of the incest is not believed. Or she may feel blame is being placed on her rather than on her father. Once she is recognized as a victim of incest, she may, at times, be approached sexually by other men who now view her as "fair game."[37] Often she is removed from the home to prevent further abuse. In addition, the mother and father suffer considerable embarrassment and humiliation. Their marriage may become so contentious that it ends in divorce.

The long-term effects of incest vary from child to child. Younger children usually do not as fully realize the significance of the sexual behavior and tend to suffer less guilt than adolescent victims. However, with young children there is always the danger that as they grow older and recognize that society condemns incest, they may start blaming themselves for having participated. Possible long-term effects on the daughter include low self-esteem, guilt, depression, and fear.[38]

The daughter may also become angry at times with both parents for not protecting her and angry at the father for exploiting her. Moreover, she may believe she is somehow to blame for what happened; she may feel tainted by the experience and see herself as worthless, or as "damaged goods." Because of her guilt and anger, she may in future years develop sexual difficulties and experience difficulty in relating to men. She may also have difficulty in trusting men, since she was betrayed and severely hurt by her father whom she deeply trusted. Some victims seek to blot out their pain and loneliness through self-destructive behavior such as prostitution, drug abuse, or suicide.

If the incest is ongoing and unreported and the victim is an older child, she may attempt to avoid the abuser by running away from home. If she does run, there is an increased chance that she will become a prostitute (to support herself) and also become addicted to drugs, in part because she has been taught dysfunctionally that her sexuality is valued by men. She may also come to believe—erroneously—that her sexuality is her most valuable asset. She is likely to abuse drugs to escape the situation she is trapped in.

Some victims during their childhood years seek to deny or suppress the traumas associated with incest. When such victims become adults they are apt to experience difficulties in developing relationships with others. Since relationships are founded on trust, and since the victims' fundamental trust in others (and therefore their ability to trust their own judgment of others) has been fundamentally violated, they often fear the pain and disappointment that can result from making commitments to others. Many of these adult victims finally acknowledge the traumas they experienced as children. Therapy is strongly recommended for these adult victims to help them come to terms with these traumas and the fact that they were violated by someone they trusted.

***Treatment of Incest*** Because incest is but one symptom of a disturbed family, treating these families is difficult and complex. In the past when incest was reported, the victim (usually a teenaged girl) was generally placed in a foster home, thus further victimizing her. Such action was likely to expose the sexual abuse to the local community. Often, neighbors, relatives, and friends expressed shock and began shunning all members of the family. The disruption usually intensified the marital conflict between husband and wife and generally led to permanent dissolution of the family. In some communities the husband was also prosecuted, which even further intensified the family conflicts.

In recent years a number of social service agencies have been seeking to keep the family intact, particularly when all three of the members involved (husband, wife, and victim) express a desire to maintain the family. A typical intervention requires the father's removal from the home for a period of six months to a year, during which time all family members are involved in individual and group treatment. During this time the incest perpetrator must acknowledge to his wife and daughter that he was entirely responsible for the sexual abuse, that he is sorry it happened, and that he will make the necessary lifestyle and value changes to ensure that the abuse will not recur. The nonabusing parent (typically the mother) is taught assertiveness. Intervention with the mother and daughter is also geared to improving their relationship, which is usually very damaged. The victim (typically the daughter) is helped in processing her anger, guilt, and confusion. Eventually all family members are seen in therapy together to help them build, perhaps for the first time, a healthy, functional family system.

## RAPE

Forced intercourse is a commonly committed violent crime in the United States. More than ninety thousand cases are reported annually, and many more cases go unreported.[39] Victims of rape are hesitant to report cases for a variety of reasons. They feel that reporting the case will do them no good because they already have been victimized. They fear they may be humiliated by the questions the officer will ask. They are reluctant to press charges because they fear the reactions of the general public and of people close to them, including their friends or husbands. Many fear that if they report the offense, the attacker will be more likely to attack them again. Some try to forget about it by not thinking or doing anything about it. Others fail to report it because they do not want to testify in court. But perhaps the most common reason why women fail to report sexual assault victimization is because they feel—usually wrongly—that they somehow contributed to the rape occurring. This is especially true in the most frequent type of rape, that between acquaintances.

In many states rape is defined as a crime that only males can commit, but this is not necessarily true. Although the great majority of male rape victims are raped by men (frequently in prison settings), a few men are raped by women.[40] Research shows that men may respond with an erection in emotional states such as anger and terror,[41] and this is what allows the rape to occur. Research also indicates men who have been raped by women experience a rape trauma syndrome that is very similar to the rape trauma syndrome (soon to be described) for female victims.

A highly unusual case of a woman raping a man occurred in Seattle. Mrs. Mary Kay Letourneau was a highly respected, thirty-four-year-old elementary school teacher. She was married and the mother of four children. In 1997, she pleaded guilty to raping a thirteen-year-old boy who was a former student of hers. She acknowledged that she had had a six-month affair with this young teenager, become pregnant by him, and delivered a baby girl. In November 1997, a judge sentenced her to six months in jail and to three years participation in an outpatient sex offender treatment program for committing second-degree rape of a child. (A few months later she violated the rules of probation by having contact with the teenager and was sentenced by a judge to prison for over seven years.)

There is no profile that fits all rapists. Rapists vary considerably in terms of motivations for committing the rape, prior criminal record, education, occupation, marital status, and so on. In a majority of cases the rapist and his (or her) victim know each other on a first-name basis. Contrary to the myth of the rapist who is a stranger, a significant proportion of rapes are date rapes.

Rape is first an aggressive and second a sexual act. Rape is a sexual expression of aggression, not an aggressive expression of sexuality. Many people wrongly believe rape occurs because the rapist manages his sexual arousal poorly or because he is "oversexed." Rape is, instead, the mismanagement of aggression where the rapist's gratification (if any) comes not from the sexual act but rather from the expression of anger or control through the extreme violation of another's body.

There are a number of typologies for classifying rapists, which depend on numerous variables. One straightforward model was developed by A. Nicholas Groth,[42] who describes rapists as falling into one of three categories: the anger rapist, the power rapist, and the sadistic rapist.

The *anger rapist* performs his act to discharge feelings of pent-up anger and rage. He is brutal in the commission of his assault, using far more force than is necessary to gain sexual access to his victim. His aim is to hurt and debase his victim; forced sex is his ultimate weapon in degrading his victim.

The *power rapist* is interested in possessing his victim sexually, not harming her. He acts out of underlying feelings of inadequacy and is interested in controlling his victim. He uses only the amount of

Box 5.3

## Gang Rapist Fraternities

Anthropologist Peggy Sanday analyzed a number of fraternity gang rapes that have been reported to the authorities. She concludes such gang rapes have two consequences: 1) they promote strong bonds among the male offenders, and 2) they debase the female victims and establish dominance over them. Usually the victim is drunk or is secretly drugged so that she is barely conscious. (When the gang rape occurs, many of the fraternity members are also intoxicated.) Sanday further concludes that fraternities in which gang rapes occur are essentially a subculture that socializes their members to have sexist attitudes toward women and creates an environment in which gang rape is apt to occur. In such fraternities, the members are socialized to prize loyalty to the group over their own values and mores. Sometimes, when cases of gang rape go to court, the male offenders state they had no idea that their activities were wrong or illegal.

In one fraternity investigated by Sanday, the intoxicated victims were raped successively by a series of members of the XYZ (name has been changed for confidentiality reasons) fraternity who stood in line to take their turn just as one car follows another as a train passes. The members called this practice the "XYZ express," referring to an express train. Sanday concludes, "Social ideologies, not human nature, *prepare men to abuse* women" (p. 12).

*Source:* Peggy R. Sanday, *Fraternity Gang Rape*, New York: New York University Press, 1990.

force necessary to gain her compliance. Sometimes he will kidnap his victim and hold her under his control for a long period of time, perhaps engaging in sexual intercourse with her numerous times.

The *sadistic rapist* eroticizes aggression; that is, aggressive force creates sexual arousal in him. He is enormously gratified by his victim's torment, pain, and suffering. His offenses often are ritualistic and involve bondage and torture, particularly to the sexual organs.

We live in a society that promotes aggression and represses sexuality. In the United States, males are socialized to be aggressive, including in seeking sexual gratification. Men, for example, are often expected to play the "aggressive" role in sex. In our culture, sex and aggression are frequently confused and combined.

In Swedish culture, where sexual information is readily available in the media but depictions of aggression are not, the rate of rape offenses is low. According to Janet Hyde, the confusion of sex and aggression in socialization practices may lead males to commit rape.

> It may be, then, that rape is a means of proving masculinity for the male who is insecure in his role. For this reason, the statistics on the youthfulness of rapists make sense; youthful rapists may simply be young men who are trying to adopt the adult male role, who feel insecure about doing this, and who commit a rape as proof of their manhood. Further, heterosexuality is an important part of manliness. Raping a woman is a flagrant way to prove that one is a heterosexual.[43]

*Date Rape* A study by Struckman-Johnson of female college students found that 22 percent stated they had been victimized by at least one incident of forced sexual intercourse on a date.[44] The study demonstrates that date rape is not a rare occurrence.

In some cases date rape seems to result from the mistaken belief on the part of the man that, if he spends money on the woman, he is entitled to (or she is implicitly giving consent to) sex. The traditional view in dating relationships has been that if the woman says "no," she really means "yes." Unfortunately, media depictions of this misinformation abound, from John Wayne-type movies to such classics as *Last Tango in Paris* and *Gone With the Wind*. The underlying message is that real men obtain power, status, and sexual gratification by violating women sexually—a very dangerous message indeed!

Leon, a college student, describes the thinking processes that led him to rape a date:

> It's time for me to make my move. Tonight her every dream will come true when I show her what it's like to be with a real man. It'll be the perfect ending to an evening she'll never forget. I knew that she was after more than dinner and dancing from the moment that I picked her up. I mean check out that dress she's wearing, those fancy jewels, that sexy perfume. And those looks she has been giving me are unmistakable. Now that she has agreed to a nightcap at my place, we can end the evening in style. I'll just slide a little closer to her on the couch, slip my arm around her shoulder, and kiss her neck. . . . Does she really think that moving away and saying "No!" will stop me? I guess all women play that game. I dropped a bundle on this date and now it's time for her to pay up. Boy, the guys will be impressed to know that I scored with such a classy number. Even if she wanted to, she couldn't stop

someone as powerful as me. Besides, everyone knows that when a woman says "No!" she really means "Yes!"

The vast majority of date rapes go unreported. In fact, many of the female victims of sexual assault do not interpret the assault as such.[45] Because many of the victims view themselves as being "in love" with the perpetrator, there is a tendency to view the rape as within the realm of acceptable behavior.

Kanin studied seventy-one unmarried college men who were self-disclosed date rapists and compared them to a control group of unmarried college men.[46] The date rapists tended to be sexually predatory. When asked how frequently they attempted to seduce a new date, 62 percent of the rapists said "most of the time," compared with 19 percent of the controls. The date rapists were also much more likely to report a variety of manipulative techniques with their dates, including falsely professing over, getting them high on alcohol or other drugs, and falsely promising going steady or becoming engaged.

Date rape educational programs are needed in elementary, secondary, and higher education settings. Laws against date rape need to be more vigorously enforced. The entertainment industry and our society need to stop glamorizing rape and start portraying it as a serious crime that has potentially devastating effects on victims. People (especially men) need to be instructed that it is vastly better to ask a woman they are dating if she wants to become sexually intimate than to force themselves on her. Men also need to learn that "no" means "no."

***Effects of Rape on Victims*** Burgess and Holmstrom have found that rape is generally a severe crisis for the victims, and that adjustment effects often persist for six months or longer.[47] They analyzed the reactions of ninety-two victims of rape and found them to undergo a series of emotional changes that researchers labeled the "rape trauma syndrome."[48]

Rape trauma syndrome occurs in two phases: an acute phase and a long-term reorganization phase. The *acute phase* begins immediately after the rape (or attempted rape) and may last for several weeks. Victims have an expressive reaction in which they are apt to cry and feel anger, fear, humiliation, tension, anxiety, and a desire for revenge. During this phase victims also usually have periods of controlled reaction in which they mask or deny their feelings and appear calm, composed, or subdued. Victims also experience many physical reactions during this phase,

such as stomach pains, nausea, headaches, insomnia, and jumpiness. In addition, some women who were forced to have oral sex reported irritation or damage to the throat. Some who were forced to have anal intercourse reported rectal pain and bleeding. Two feelings were predominant: fear and self-blame. Many women feared future physical violence, or continued to suffer from the fear of being murdered during the attack. Self-blame is related to the tendency on the part of the victim (and others) to "blame the victim." Such women often spent hours agonizing over what they thought they had done to cause the attack or what they could have done to fight off the attacker. Common self-criticisms are, "If only I hadn't walked alone," "If only I had bolt-locked the door," "If only I hadn't worn that tight sweater," "If only I hadn't been dumb enough to trust that guy."

During the *long-term reorganization phase,* which follows the acute phase, victims may experience a variety of major disruptions. These disruptions vary among victims. For example, some women who were raped outdoors may develop fears about going outdoors, whereas those raped indoors may come to fear being indoors. Some are unable to return to work, particularly if the rape occurred at work. Some victims quit their jobs and remain unemployed for a long time. Many, fearing the rapist will find them and assault them again, move (sometimes, several times), change their telephone number, or get an unlisted number. Some develop sexual phobias that preclude or delay return to a regular sexual lifestyle. In some cases it takes several years before the victim returns to her previous lifestyle.

In addition, if the victim reports the rape, the police investigation and the trial (if there is one) are further crises to be faced. Police and the courts have a history of abusive and callous treatment of rape victims. At times the police have implied that the victim may be fabricating the assault or suggested she consented but then changed her mind. The police often ask embarrassing questions about the details of the assault, without showing much sensitivity. In court it is common for the defense attorney to imply that the victim seduced the defendant and then decided to call it rape. Victims are sometimes made to feel as if *they* are on trial. Fortunately, many police departments recently have developed more sensitive crime units with specially trained officers to intervene in cases of rape and child sexual assault. With such units, victims are less likely to be further victimized by authorities. Also, a number of states have enacted "shield" evidence laws, which prohibit defense attorneys from asking questions about the

# How to Attempt to Prevent Rape

There have been a number of suggestions to help women prevent rape and fight off an attacker. These suggestions include having and using secure locks on doors, not walking alone at night, and learning self-defense measures such as judo, aikido, tae kwon do (Korean karate), or jujitsu. Presenting oneself in an assertive fashion may be another way to stop a potential rape from occurring; being assertive when saying "no" to unwanted sexual advances is particularly useful in preventing acquaintance rape.[a] Exercising regularly and keeping in shape are also recommended to give the potential victim the strength to fight back and the speed to run fast. Some experts recommend poking an attacker in the eyes or snapping a knee into his groin. Other experts recommend every woman should have a psychological strategy to use if attacked, such as telling the rapist that she has cancer of the cervix or has a contagious venereal disease (e.g., the AIDS virus). If other preventive measures fail, some experts urge dissuading the attacker by regurgitating on him, which can be accomplished by sticking one's finger in one's throat. Another last-ditch strategy is to urinate on him. *It is important that each woman have a strategy or set of defensive measures she would seek to use if an attack occurred.* No one set of advice can apply to all situations, because the rapist may respond quite differently to the victim fighting back, depending on whether he is primarily a power, anger, or sadistic rapist. Therefore, any woman who physically survives a rape should be viewed as having utilized a successful strategy.

On a broader, sociological level, feminists urge certain sex-role socialization practices be changed so that attacks would seldom, if ever, occur. Margaret Mead has noted rape does not occur in certain societies where males are socialized to be nurturant rather than aggressive.[b] To sharply reduce rape, Janet S. Hyde recommends the following changes in socialization practices:

> . . . If little boys were not so pressed to be aggressive and tough, perhaps rapists would never develop. If adolescent boys did not have to demonstrate that they are hypersexual, perhaps there would be no rapists. . . .
>
> Changes would also need to be made in the way females are socialized, particularly if women are to become good at self-defense. Weakness is not considered a desirable human characteristic, and so it should not be considered a desirable feminine characteristic, especially because it makes women vulnerable to rape. . . . While some people think that it is silly for the federal government to rule that girls must have athletic teams equal to boys' teams, it seems quite possible that the absence of athletic training for girls has contributed to making them rape victims. . . .
>
> Finally, for both males and females, we need a radical restructuring of ideas about sexuality. As long as females are expected to pretend to be uninterested in sex and as long as males and females play games on dates, rape will persist.[c]

a. Janet S. Hyde, *Understanding Human Sexuality*, 5th ed. (New York: McGraw-Hill, 1994), 496.

b. Margaret Mead, *Sex and Temperament in Three Primitive Societies* (New York: Morrow, 1935).

c. Hyde, *Understanding Human Sexuality*, 498.

victim's previous sexual experience (except with the alleged rapist). In the past, defense attorneys at times sought to imply that the victim was promiscuous and therefore probably seduced the defendant.

Burgess and Holmstrom urge immediate counseling for victims, with the following objectives:

♦ to provide support and allow the victims to ventilate their feelings;

♦ to lend support and guidance during the medical tests and police questioning;

♦ to be similarly supportive during the trial;

♦ to provide follow-up extended counseling.[49]

Burgess and Holmstrom also note that because a majority of rapes are not reported, many of the nonreporters have a *silent rape reaction*.[50] These nonreporters not only fail to report the rape to the police but many tell no one about it. Although nonreporters are apt to experience the same adjustment problems as victims who report, the trauma for nonreporters is often intensified as they have no way of expressing or venting their feelings. Some nonreporters eventually seek professional counseling for other problems such as depression, anxiety, or inability to reach orgasm. Often such problems are then found to stem from the rape. Women with secret rape experiences should be gently urged to talk about the rape experience so they can gradually learn to deal with it. A number of communities now have rape crisis centers that provide victims with counseling, medical services, and legal services.

## EXHIBITIONISM AND VOYEURISM

Exhibitionists and voyeurs are frequently referred to respectively as "flashers" and "Peeping Toms." They are often considered nuisances rather than serious threats to society or to individuals. There is, of course, more alarm and disdain when exhibitionists disrobe in front of children. Having someone peek into our homes is also alarming. Of greater concern is research that shows exhibitionists and voyeurs are also apt to engage in more assaultive sex offenses, such as sexual molestation of children and rape.[51] This finding contradicts the traditional view that exhibitionists and voyeurs are unlikely to commit more harmful sexual acts.

To some extent all of us have probably become involved in displaying our bodies to others. Nude swimming (skinny-dipping) has been popular for a long time. Some people go to beaches to display their physiques. A number of years ago streaking (running nude on college campuses and other places) was popular. "Mooning" (displaying one's buttocks in public) has been a common fad among high school and college students. However, the exhibitionist obtains a great deal of sexual arousal by exposing his genitals to unwitting strangers. The exhibitionist may be unable to become aroused by more normal expressions of sexuality and is often quite compulsive in his exposure behaviors. For him, exposure is not an occasional lark with the guys, but a planned and frequently repeated activity.

Voyeurism is defined as watching persons undress, viewing them in the nude, and observing them performing sexual acts without their knowledge or consent. To some extent most of us have found enjoyment in at least one of the following: looking at magazines containing pictorials of people who are nude or seminude, going to night clubs featuring nude dancers, going to X-rated movies, watching our sex partner undress, and observing the attractive physiques of others out in public. Again, it should be noted that invasion-of-privacy voyeurism is demeaning and threatening to an unwilling victim.

Exhibitionism and voyeurism involve behaviors that differ in degree from the kinds of showing and looking that are considered "normal" in our society.

## Structural Sex Variance

Behaviors in this category include prostitution, pornography, and homosexuality. As in the previous category (asocial sex variance), sexual behaviors in this category run counter to prevailing norms and legal statutes. The differences are that the behaviors in this category have supportive social structures and are participated in by substantial numbers of persons.

## PROSTITUTION

Prostitution, "the world's oldest profession," is promiscuous, paid sexual activity. Prostitution is seen as a social problem by people who view it as immoral. It involves using sex to make money rather than as a way to express love or to reproduce. Many who view it as immoral are also concerned about prostitution violating the value of monogamy (sharing sex with only one partner).

Others view prostitution as a social problem to the extent that it facilitates the spread of sexually transmitted diseases, allows the prostitute and accomplices to rob or blackmail their clients, and provides an enterprise for organized crime. A number of people view prostitution as a social problem because of its effects within the community, such as:

- promoting solicitation and loitering on the streets;
- attracting undesirables (clients of disreputable characteristics and crime figures);
- making it difficult for non-prostitutes to walk in the neighborhood without being solicited and harassed by potential clients;
- having adverse effects on children in the area;
- making it difficult for men to walk in the area without being solicited or harassed;
- attracting to the area the kinds of businesses that will lower property values and often lead to deterioration of buildings.

Prostitution is illegal in every state in the United States, with the exception of some counties in Nevada. Yet prostitution has been flourishing for decades in our country and for thousands of years in the world.

U.S. prostitution is presently undergoing two apparently conflicting trends. On the one hand, advertising for prostitution is becoming more open: streetwalkers in central cities are soliciting more openly. At the same time, the actual number and use of prostitutes appear to be declining. Estimates of the number of prostitutes is difficult to obtain, but there is some evidence there may be only half as many as there were forty years ago.[52] Obtaining information about the number of prostitutes is difficult, as prostitutes do not reveal to the government their occupation because of its illegal nature. Also, there are a number of part-time prostitutes, some of whom have a full-time position or attend high school or college. In 1948, Kinsey found that 69 percent of all white males had had some experience with prostitutes.[53] A 1994 study by the University of Chicago's National Opinion Research Center found the percentage of males who have paid for sex has dropped to 16 percent since the Kinsey study.[54]

A major reason for the declining use of prostitutes has been a change in sexual mores in which the stigma attached to women having premarital relations has been sharply reduced. With increased sexual outlets for both nonmarried and married people, many men no long patronize prostitutes. Palen quotes an older prostitute in this regard: "Why should a john [customer] pay a professional for it when college girls are giving it away for free?"[55] Another reason for the decline is the fear of AIDS. (Prostitutes are at a higher risk of having the AIDS virus as they have multiple sex partners.) About 40 percent of street prostitutes in the United States are estimated to have been exposed to the AIDS virus; a major reason for this high exposure rate is that some of their lovers tend to be intravenous drug users.[56] Recent research indicates that prostitutes are increasingly trying to get customers to use condoms, but many customers refuse to do so. Research also indicates that an increasing number of HIV-positive men continue to frequent prostitutes, particularly prostitutes who are streetwalkers.[57]

*Forms of Prostitution*   To the general public, prostitution means "sex for sale." There are some problems with this definition. Is a woman or man who marries for money a prostitute? Is a person who accepts a job promotion in exchange for sexual favors a prostitute? If a person moves in with a lover who pays the major expenses, is that prostitution? To avoid such difficulties, we will limit the definition of a prostitute to one who uses prostitution as a major source of income, accepts a number of customers, and feels no emotional attachment to them. At least five forms of prostitution fall within this definition, as discussed in the following paragraphs.

*Call girls* have the highest status and earnings in the profession. Generally they are in their twenties, dress well, and live a luxurious lifestyle. Call girls, as their name suggests, make most appointments by phone and can be selective in choosing their clients. Most of their appointments are "regulars" who have been introduced through the private recommendations of other customers. Some charge several hundred dollars for an evening, whereas others are maintained by a wealthy client as a mistress and set up in an apartment; a few eventually marry such a client. Life at the top of this profession is often glamorous, exciting, and well paying.

A cut below call girls, *bar girls* work out of hotel lounges, bars, and the like. Many have an arrangement with bartenders, bar managers, security officers, or pimps to make contacts with clients. Bar girls have some selectivity in clients. They charge less than call girls and "turn more tricks" a night. Some bar girls are former call girls who have aged or otherwise lost appeal.

*House girls* work and sometimes live in a brothel (brothels or houses of prostitution are declining in number but are legal in some Nevada counties). The owner of a brothel, a *madam,* often is an older retired prostitute. The madam hires, trains, and supervises the house girls; takes a high percentage of each trick; and soon fires those girls unable to attract clients. Organized crime has been especially active in brothels, as it is necessary (except in legal Nevada brothels) to pay off police and politicians to protect the establishment from harassment. In most cities, brothels are being replaced by massage parlors and private "health clubs."

*Streetwalkers* solicit customers directly on the street, take them to a cheap hotel or rooming house, or possibly service them in the customer's vehicle. Streetwalkers may turn a trick quickly and be back on the street in a half-hour or so. They sometimes are prostitutes who have seen better days, or they are young runaways; some are only fourteen or fifteen. Streetwalkers make the least money and are likely to be harassed and arrested by the local vice squad. They are generally regarded as a public nuisance. Most streetwalkers have an association with a pimp, which will be discussed later.

*Male prostitutes* are less common than female prostitutes. Many prostitution statutes apply to women only. Heterosexual male prostitution is even rarer, as most male prostitution is homosexual. Some men are supported by women as gigolos. There is evidence that with the development of escort services, some male escorts also provide sexual favors to women.

There are several types of male homosexual prostitutes. The *hustler* has the lowest status and is usually an adolescent who solicits customers on the streets. Most hustlers view themselves as heterosexual and view their solicitation as simply a way to make money. The *bar hustler,* generally an adult, solicits clients in gay bars. In some larger cities the *house boy* works, but generally does not live, in a house of male prostitution. (The term house boy is often used differently in gay society to mean "live-in" housekeeper, often with implied sexual responsibilities as well.) A *kept boy* is similar to a mistress, as he is maintained in an apartment or home by a wealthy man. The *call boy,* similar to a call girl, has the highest status and works out of an apartment or hotel room for a select group of clients.

Prostitutes are generally thought to come from lower-class and lower-middle-class backgrounds. Although studies are few, there is evidence of an absence of warmth between the girl and her parents, particularly the father, who is often alcoholic, violent, or absent. Many come from broken homes, with some having been placed in foster homes. During adolescence, many appear to have been loners, without close friends. They may have held low-paying jobs prior to turning to prostitution (e.g., nurse's aide, salesclerk, waitress). Some have low self-esteem, which may be a factor in choosing a profession that is highly stigmatized. Many prostitutes were promiscuous during adolescence, and many were victims of sexual abuse during their childhood years.[58]

Entry into prostitution appears to be a slow transition from promiscuity to eventually defining oneself as a prostitute; it is not an abrupt decision. Teenagers, particularly runaways, are apt to drift into the business because they often have no alternatives for making money. Slowly they start taking money for sex (often to buy food or clothes), and gradually they start turning more tricks. Some women are recruited through contact with another prostitute who teaches them skills of the trade—how to solicit, how to handle rowdy customers, how to recognize vice officers, and the like. Some are recruited by a "pimp," a male who usually manages several women. He finds clients for his women, makes room arrangements for the encounters, protects the women from assault by customers, pays bail when they are arrested, and collects a portion of their fees.

Some prostitutes, particularly call girls, enjoy their work. They find the life exciting, glamorous, and less demanding than other jobs. For example, according to a call girl who works the travel-business executive circuit in Philadelphia and New York:

I got to the point where I was living in a fairy tale. I was telling myself, "Well, you just need the money, and then you'll get out of it and get back to a career or something . . . you're not like the other girls who make a life out of this."

After about a year, I got to the stage where I was able to admit openly to myself that I liked it. I don't know; it has a style to it—a zing that I really enjoy. You're moving with really classy people. Some girls hate the marks they service. I don't. I can really get into the give-and-take of the situation. I like the sex, and I like the personal contact. It's not just an assembly line with me. A couple months ago, one guy took me on a five-day trip to Puerto Rico. OK, it was a business arrangement but it was also great fun, and we both enjoyed it.

Of course, you do get some weirdos or kinky guys every now and then, that happens in all jobs. A lot of girls aren't able to admit how much they like it. Something inside doesn't want to let it surface. It sort of has to roll around inside you, and then it breaks out, and you see it and can say, "I really do enjoy this."[59]

Kingsley Davis has stated that a truly puzzling question is why more women do not become prostitutes, because it offers good pay, association with glamorous people, and a chance to form a romantic relationship. Many women instead chose tedious, lower-paying jobs, such as waitressing or secretarial work.[60] A major reason, of course, why more women do not become prostitutes is because many consider it morally wrong or distasteful. They also dislike the stigma and the offensive clients. "Prostitute" is a poor reference on a job application of a "straight" position when one's physical features begin to fade. In addition, as mentioned, prostitutes are at great risk of acquiring the AIDS virus.

Of course, hustling on the streets is neither as glamorous or rewarding as other forms of prostitution. Some streetwalkers are addicted to alcohol or other drugs and use prostitution to support their habits.[61]

Because prostitution is highly stigmatized, prostitutes have a problem in maintaining their self-respect. Norman Jackman et al. found that prostitutes claim to be no more immoral than others.[62] They view themselves as being less hypocritical than respected men who cheat on their wives. They also view themselves as needed, as indicated by the following comment:

We got 'em all. The kids who are studying to be doctors and lawyers and things, and men whose wives hate the thought of sex. And men whose wives are sick or have left them. What are such men going to do? Pick on married women . . . or run around after underage girls? They're better off with us. That's what we're here for.[63]

Jackman and his associates found three types of prostitutes.[64] One type identified with pimps, racketeers, other prostitutes, and hustlers. This type viewed the rest of society with contempt, as being square, hypocritical, and boring. Prostitutes of this type generally enjoyed their work and their sexual activities.

Another type identified with the values of middle-class America. They separated their work from the rest of their lives, identified strongly with their families, and associated little with other prostitutes. They generally did not enjoy the sexual acts in which they engaged and did not want to discuss sex at all.

A third type, categorized as "alienated," were apathetic, identified with no one, and were often addicted to alcohol or other drugs. They had low self-images and made little effort to find a rationale to justify their occupation.

Much has been written about the relationships between streetwalkers and pimps. An erroneous notion is that pimps always use physical force to get prostitutes to work for them. Furthermore, it is not true that they generally control their women by getting them addicted to heroin, as addicts are not viewed very highly by potential customers.

It is true, however, that pimps exploit their women financially and sexually. It is also true that the women derive something they feel they need from this relationship. As noted earlier, pimps make many of the arrangements with potential customers and provide protection from rowdy customers and, to some degree, from law enforcement officials. Sometimes a prostitute and a pimp are lovers, with the pimp providing a sense of belonging, a sense of family and of being cared for. The relationship between a pimp and a prostitute can be construed as analogous to the traditional husband-wife relationship, with the economic roles reversed: the prostitute makes money, and the pimp gives her a sense of security and family.

*Reasons for Prostitution*   As already mentioned, prostitution offers the lure of high earnings for relatively few work hours. For the higher-status prostitutes, there is also the glamour, the opportunity to wine and dine with noted people, live in luxury, and travel.

For clients, prostitution offers sexual gratification at relatively low costs. Clients receive sexual variety while avoiding the troublesome obligations of more socially acceptable relationships. Older men or men with a physical disability may find prostitution to be the only opportunity for a sexual encounter with an attractive young woman. Prostitution offers convenient sexual gratification. Many prostitutes argue their clientele are in marriages in which sexual relationships have gone sour, but the men do not have to dissolve their marriages to have gratifying sexual encounters. (Feminists decry all of these reasons, noting that prostitution exploits women and treats them as sex objects. They also point out that prostitution is an expression of the double sexual standard and of the efforts of males to dominate our society.)

Kingsley Davis takes the position that prostitution is highly functional for society.[65] His argument begins with the need for a family system to rear and socialize children. Such rearing takes about two decades. Many people, according to Davis, are unable to satisfy their sexual needs within the family structure. Single men and widowers have no legally approved sexual outlet. Some married men seek sexual variety, whereas others are in a marriage where their sexual relations are no longer fully satisfying. Others, such as salesmen and members of the armed forces, are absent from home for long periods of time. Without the brief, impersonal, non-obligating relationships afforded by prostitutes, many marriages would dissolve, as men would seek to form personal sexual relationships with other women. Davis points out that, if most marriages dissolve, there would be no effective means of socializing children, and society would therefore tend to collapse.

Davis argues further that the only society in which prostitution would be phased out would be a fully sexually permissive society. In such a society, the sexual freedom would destroy the family and make it impossible to raise children. Prostitution, in Davis's argument, is therefore less threatening to a society than moving toward a society that is fully sexually permissive. (It should be noted Davis's argument was written in 1937 and now appears sexist in its view of women. Yet his argument that prostitution has some functional aspects is probably an explanation of why prostitution is found in cultures throughout the world. It should be added that prostitution also has many dysfunctional aspects, including considerable pain and anguish. Prostitutes are susceptible to violence, sexually transmitted diseases, human degradation, and unwanted pregnancies. In addition, considerable marital strife usually occurs if and when a wife discovers her husband has had sexual contact with a prostitute.)

### Decriminalization or Legalization of Prostitution

On Mother's Day in 1972 a group of San Francisco prostitutes formed COYOTE (Cast Out Your Old Tired Ethics), an organization aimed at improving conditions of prostitutes. Similar organizations have emerged in other cities, such as PONY (Prostitutes of New York). Two goals of such groups are decriminalization or legalization of prostitution and the unionization of prostitutes. The feminist movement generally has supported such goals and organizations.

Decriminalization involves changing prostitution from a crime punishable by incarceration to a misdemeanor offense punishable by fines. One reason for decriminalizing prostitution is the high cost attached to arresting prostitutes. In San Francisco, for example, it costs the city more than $1,000 for each arrest, and the prostitute is soon back on the street soliciting.[66]

Many arguments have been offered in support of legalization. A 1971 Nevada statute reaffirmed the right of counties in the state to license houses of prostitution. It is claimed that prostitution serves a needed function and will always exist, regardless of laws. Legalization would make prostitutes' income taxable and thereby provide a source of revenue for the government. Licensing fees would provide another source of revenue. Legalization could reduce the involvement of organized crime in prostitution. Medical examinations at regular intervals could be given to prostitutes to reduce the spread of AIDS and other sexually transmitted diseases. Legalization of brothels, it is claimed, would reduce streetwalking, which tends to disturb neighborhood residents. It is also argued that it is senseless to have victimless crimes (such as prostitution) in which both the customer and seller willingly participate with few complaints. Because prostitution laws are regularly violated, proponents of legalization assert it is harmful to have laws that people routinely violate, as it leads to disrespect for other laws.

In Nevada, legalized prostitution appears to be working well. The brothels do a profitable business, bring in substantial tax revenues, and are well accepted in the communities; and the prostitutes are regularly examined by physicians.[67]

## PORNOGRAPHY

*Pornography* may be defined as pictorial or written matter designed to excite the viewer or reader sexually. It is interesting to note that the general public appears to be more concerned with pornography than with prostitution, probably because pornography is more widespread and visible. There appears to be a general consensus that there has been an increase in the amount of material designed to arouse people sexually—including nude magazines, X-rated movies, adult book stores, sex on television (particularly on soap operas and on certain cable channels), and erotic books.

Although pornography is designed for heterosexual males, there is also a significant business in gay pornography and pornographic material geared toward heterosexual females.

There are several types of pornography. *Soft-core magazines* seek to display nudity in "tasteful" photographs. *Hard-core magazines* have a no-holds-barred approach, showing photographs that may include everything from vaginal to anal intercourse, bondage, sadomasochism, and sex with animals. Hard-core films also have a no-holds-barred approach. One type of hard-core film, called a *loop,* is a short film set up in coin-operated projectors in private booths, usually in adult bookstores. *X-rated videocassettes* of hard-core films also are now available. *Live sex shows* with male or female strippers are another part of the sex industry. *Telephone porn* (commercial telephone numbers) enables customers to dial for erotic phone calls. *Kiddie porn* features pictures or films of sexual acts involving children. Some authorities assert that *sex in advertising* represents another form of pornography; in such advertisements subtle and obvious sexual suggestions are used to sell a wide variety of products. Some *private cable television systems* have extended the consumption of explicitly sexual materials. Pornographic material is also increasingly available on the *Internet.*

Most adults—as well as adolescents—have viewed sexually explicit material. In general, the likelihood of exposure is greater for the well-educated than the poorly educated, and for men than women. About one-fifth to one quarter of the adult male population has regular exposure to sexually explicit material. Young adults do not generally patronize adult bookstores; the typical customer is white, married, middle-aged, and middle class.[68]

### Effects of Pornography

There is general agreement that frequent exposure to pornography will have an effect on human tastes and development. To argue otherwise would be equivalent to arguing that no experience affects human development—that is, no learning is possible.

The arguments surrounding the pornography issue instead revolve around *what* the effects will be.

Opponents of pornography argue that it presents a disgusting, tasteless view of human beings and sexuality and that it promotes sex crimes and contributes to the spread of sexual deviances. Feminists point out that it portrays women in a demeaning, dehumanizing fashion. Some opponents make a distinction between harmless pornography and pornography that is potentially harmful. The later category includes child pornography, which may be harmful to the children involved. Harmful pornography may also include depictions of forced rape, representations of violent sex that include criminal acts—stabbing and murder—and other forms that show sex as being cruel and vindictive. There is a danger that violent depictions of sexual acts may be a factor in triggering real-life sexual violence.

Defenders of pornography agree that some material may be distasteful to some audiences, but they assert it is harmless. Furthermore, they assert that pornography (at least nonviolent pornography) actually reduces, rather than advances, the number of sex crimes, as it serves as a substitute for prohibited sexual acts. Defenders also assert that pornography enhances appropriate sexual expression (such as enlivening marital sex). James McCary has noted adults hold a variety of beliefs about pornography:

> The attitude of American men and women to pornography is varied indeed. Many consider it informative or entertaining; others believe that it leads to rape or moral breakdown, or that it improves the sexual relationship of married couples, or that it leads to innovation in a couple's coital techniques, or that it eventually becomes only boring, or that it causes men to lose respect for women, or that it serves to satisfy normal curiosity. More people than not report that the effects on themselves of erotica have been beneficial. Among those who feel pornography has detrimental effects, the tendency is to see those bad effects as harming others—but not one's self or personal acquaintances.[69]

Research results suggest that nonviolent pornography does not appear to have much of a long-term effect on sexual behavior. (There may be some short-term increases in arousal lasting from a few minutes to an hour.) For example, Brown et al. found there was no significant increase in sexual activity in the week following exposure by male subjects to sexually explicit slides; however, the males did show a large increase in masturbation on the day of exposure.[70]

The effects of aggressive pornography on aggressive behavior, however, is a different story. Violent porn appears to increase aggressive behavior in viewers and also to affect attitudes and perceptions of violence toward women. Viewing aggressive pornography appears to have a "triggering effect" as viewers display more aggressive acts over an extended period of time, as compared to non-viewers. Research has also found that viewing pornography of male sexual aggression toward females with "positive" consequences (e.g., the women eventually becoming aroused by the aggressive sex) leads males to an increased acceptance of interpersonal violence against women and increases their acceptance of rape myths.[71] One of the most dangerous themes in pornography is that women enjoy being sexually overpowered.

There is also considerable concern about kiddie porn, as the child models are often adversely affected.[72] Children, by virtue of their developmental level, cannot give true informed consent to participate. The potential is significant for their participation to cause long-term psychological (and physical) damage. As a result, many states have passed legislation that makes it illegal to photograph or sell pornographic material involving children.

Another danger of many forms of pornography is that they tend to degrade women. Pornographic material often erroneously depicts women as sexual objects who are anonymous, dehumanized, panting playthings whom "macho" males should use, abuse, and then discard. The danger of such depictions is that it may be a factor in socializing some males to seek to exploit females and to treat them as sexual objects.

*Censorship*  The pornography issue also raises questions about censorship. The First Amendment to the Constitution guarantees freedom of speech and expression. Some Americans who find certain pornographic material offensive are reluctant to urge that the material be censored. Censorship deprives citizens of the right to make up their own minds about what is tasteless and what has value. Even more important is the danger that censorship will be abused. History is filled with examples of artistic works, now recognized as classics, being censored. Books that have been censored in communities include *Alice in Wonderland, Huckleberry Finn, On the Origin of Species, Robinson Crusoe,* and even the Bible. Plays of William Shakespeare have been banned in the past in some schools because they were thought to be obscene. It now seems ridiculous that some museums, less than a century ago, put plaster fig leaves over the genital areas of classic Roman and Greek sculptures.

The courts have generally taken the position that pornographic material is not protected by the First Amendment and therefore pornographic and obscene or repulsive material can be censored. The courts have defined material as pornographic or obscene when it meets *each* of three criteria: (1) The "average person" finds that it appeals to "prurient interests" (*prurient* means arousing lewd or lustful thoughts and desires); (2) it depicts or describes sexual conduct "in a patently offensive way"; and (3) taken as a whole, it "lacks serious literary, artistic, political, or scientific value."[73] Although each of these criteria is difficult to apply, the three together seem to allow for the establishment of "community standards" while protecting freedom of speech. It is far easier, however, to define pornography and obscenity in the abstract than to decide whether a particular film or book is obscene. Former Supreme Court Justice Potter Stewart provided the common working definition when he stated, "I know it when I see it."[74] A Washington observer has quipped that pornography is "whatever turns the Supreme Court on."[75]

Clearly, however, what is judged to be pornographic is in the eye of the beholder. On one end of the continuum is material such as *Alice in Wonderland,* which few people would claim is obscene. At the other end are magazines showing explicit sexual acts between children and adults and "snuff films" which appeared in the mid-1970s. (These short films began with portraying a woman and a man having sex, followed by the woman being murdered and dismembered on the screen.) In addition, the guideline "local community standards" could mean just about anything, depending partly upon who is allowed to define those standards. Perhaps the standards should only include questions of whether the material teaches behavior that would hurt another individual.

One possible guideline is to censor pornographic material that has adverse effects. Nonviolent pornographic material may not have serious adverse effects, but there is substantial evidence that kiddie porn and violent porn do. Hyde summarizes the results of research studies:

> In sum, then, we can conclude that exposure to nonviolent pornography does not have much of an effect on people's sexual behavior or aggressive behavior. However, exposure to aggressive pornography does increase males' aggression toward women, as well as affecting males' attitudes, making them more accepting of violence against women.[76]

One dilemma that might be provoked by the outlawing of certain types of pornography is the development of a black market for the forbidden materials.

## HOMOSEXUALITY*

A homosexual is a person whose sexual or erotic orientation is towards members of his or her same sex. We use this term to refer to an orientation, rather than occasional sexual experimentation with someone of the same gender. Teenagers, in experimenting with sexuality, may, for example, have some homosexual experiences. People isolated from the other gender (in prisons, segregated schools, sailors at sea, juveniles in correctional schools) often have sexual experiences with members of their own sex when members of the other gender are not available.

On the other hand, it is possible to be a homosexual without practicing homosexual behavior—by ignoring one's homosexuality, denying it, or simply pretending to be heterosexual.

It is important to note that most Americans disapprove of homosexuality. Surveys have found that a majority of Americans regard homosexuality as "very obscene and vulgar" and as being a "curable disease."[77] Being gay or lesbian is also often viewed as being harmful to American life. The negative view of homosexuality in this country is indicated by the array of derogatory slang terms for gays and lesbians. (It should be noted that similar attitudes and different derogatory terms have been applied in the past to various ethnic minorities including the Irish, Italians, African Americans, and Hispanic Americans.) Gay or lesbian persons have frequently been the victims of anti-gay hate crimes. Many heterosexuals are *homophobic*—they feel personal anxiety and disgust for gay or lesbian persons, and seek to avoid contact with them.

---

*By discussing homosexuality together with prostitution and pornography, the author is not making a judgment as to the desirability or undesirability of homosexuality. Whether homosexual behavior is "natural" or "unnatural" has not as yet been scientifically determined. Instead of viewing homosexuality as a social problem, we will discuss it as a sexual variation. Engaging in prostitution or pornography appears to have primarily sociological and psychological determinants. In contrast, research is increasingly confirming that sexual orientation is determined very early in life (before age five) and may be biologically driven. Similar to masturbation, homosexuality has been viewed negatively by some segments of our society, yet recent research suggests that both are natural expressions of sexual drives.

**Table 5.1**    *Kinsey's Conception of Homosexuality and Heterosexuality as Variations on a Continuum*

| 0 | 1 | 2 | 3 | 4 | 5 | 6 |
|---|---|---|---|---|---|---|
| Exclusively heterosexual | Mostly heterosexual with incidental homosexual experience | Heterosexual with substantial homosexual experience | Equal heterosexual and homosexual experience | Homosexual with substantial heterosexual experience | Homosexual with incidental heterosexual experience | Exclusively homosexual |

*Source:* Adapted from Alfred C. Kinsey et al., *Sexual Behavior in the Human Male* (Philadelphia, PA: W.B. Saunders, 1948), 638. Adapted by permission of the Kinsey Institute for Research in Sex, Gender, and Reproduction, Inc.

Such negative attitudes can have considerable psychological impact upon gay and lesbian persons. It can be devastating to learn that a majority of Americans consider your natural interests and behaviors to be vulgar. It is distressing for a gay or lesbian person to realize that a majority of Americans consider him/her vulgar and obscene. Some gays and lesbians therefore seek to hide their sexual orientation, and they live in constant fear of discovery. Some believe (often correctly) that discovery will result in their being fired from their job or ostracized by friends and relatives. Tragically, some gay and lesbian youth become so despondent that they commit suicide. The suicide rate for homosexual adolescents is significantly higher than that for heterosexual teenagers. This is a sad and extreme example of the ultimate costs of bigotry.

Erroneous myths about homosexuality include the following:

*Myth 1:* People are either homosexual or heterosexual.

*Fact:* Alfred Kinsey found that homosexuality and heterosexuality are not mutually exclusive categories. Most people have had sexual thoughts, feelings, and fantasies about members of both sexes. Kinsey proposed a seven-point rating scale to categorize sexuality, with exclusive heterosexuality at one end and exclusive homosexuality at the other (Table 5.1). Kinsey noted:

> The world is not divided into sheep and goats. . . . Only the human mind invents categories and tries to force facts into pigeonholes. The living world is a continuum in each and every one of its aspects. The sooner we learn this concerning human sexual behavior, the sooner we will reach a sound understanding of the realities of sex.[78]

*Myth 2:* Homosexuality is universally disapproved of in all cultures.

*Fact:* Some cultures accept homosexuality, and others encourage it. A young boy in ancient Greece was sometimes given a boy slave who served as a sexual partner until the boy was old enough to marry a woman. It was common for older Greek married men to form a homosexual relationship with a young boy. Today, all males among the Siwans of North Africa are expected to engage in homosexual relationships throughout their lives. Among the Aranda of Central Australia, there are relationships between young boys and unmarried men, with these liaisons generally ending at marriage.[79]

*Myth 3:* Male homosexuals are generally "effeminate," and female homosexuals are generally "masculine." The erroneous stereotype is that male homosexuals are limp-wristed, talk with a lisp, and have a "swishy" walk, whereas lesbians are erroneously believed to have short hair and wear clothes normally worn by males.

*Fact:* Most gay or lesbian persons are indistinguishable in appearance and mannerisms from heterosexuals.[80] This myth probably comes from confusing homosexuality with transvestism—wearing the clothing of the opposite sex for sexual arousal. Transvestism and homosexuality are in fact quite different. Most transvestites are heterosexual. Interestingly, although our culture erroneously associates male homosexuality with effeminacy, ancient Greeks and Romans associated homosexuality with aggressive masculinity (as among the Spartan warriors).[81]

Janet Hyde notes:

> The belief that gay men are feminine and that lesbians are masculine represents a confusion of two important concepts: *gender identity* (sense of maleness or femaleness) and *sexual orientation* (heterosexual or homosexual). The gay person differs from the majority in who the erotic and emotional partner is, but the gay person does not typically differ from the majority in gender identity. That is, the gay man chooses a partner of the same gender, but his identity is quite definitely mascu-

line. He thinks of himself as male and has no desire to be a female. The same holds true for the lesbian; although her erotic and emotional orientation is toward other women, she is quite definitely a woman and typically has no desire to be a man.[82]

*Myth 4:* Homosexuals are "sick" and different in personality characteristics from heterosexuals.

*Fact:* Clinical projective tests do not reliably distinguish between homosexuals and heterosexuals. Studies of homosexuals and heterosexuals have found no differences between the two groups in personality traits or in general adjustment.[83] The only difference is their sexual orientation.

Homosexuality was listed as a mental disorder by the American Psychiatric Association until 1973. For a number of years preceding 1973, gay and lesbian persons demonstrated at psychiatric conventions, demanding that homosexuality no longer be considered a mental disorder. In 1973, after several years of heated controversy, the Board of Trustees of the American Psychiatric Association voted to strike homosexuality from its official list of mental diseases. Thomas Szasz (a psychiatrist) had asserted around this time that psychiatrists and others who labeled homosexuality as an illness were merely taking the place of the church in labeling gays and lesbians as being "deviant" and then punishing them for their "deviant" sexual behavior.[84]

*Myth 5:* One partner in a homosexual liaison generally plays the "active" or masculine role in sexual activity and the other plays the "passive" or feminine role.

*Fact:* Most gay and lesbian persons play both roles and (like heterosexuals) experiment with a variety of arousal techniques. There is no single form of homosexual expression or identity. In reality there is as wide a divergence among homosexuals as among heterosexuals. Some married homosexuals enjoy intercourse with their spouses; a few are genuinely bisexual, enjoying the sex act with either male or female partners. Most married homosexuals are more comfortable in homosexual relationships but are married for the sake of domestic stability, companionship, and respectability. Some gay or lesbian persons candidly acknowledge their sexual orientation and live their homosexuality openly. Others are not willing to "come out," as they fear they may then be discriminated against. Some gay or lesbian persons refuse to view themselves as being homosexual, primarily from abhorrence at being identified with a socially outcast minority.

The question is sometimes asked: "What do gay or lesbian persons do in bed?" Most of their activities are similar to those in which heterosexuals engage. Foreplay generally includes kissing, hugging, and petting. Gay men may engage in mutual masturbation, oral-genital sex, interfemoral intercourse (in which one man's penis moves between the thighs of the other), and anal intercourse. Lesbians may engage in mutual masturbation, oral-genital sex, and, more infrequently, tribadism (one partner lying on top of the other and making thrusting movements so that both receive genital stimulation); a rarer practice among lesbians is the use of a dildo by one female to stimulate the other.

*Myth 6:* Male homosexuals primarily seek out young boys.

*Fact:* Gay and lesbian persons are no more attracted to children than are heterosexuals, and homosexual child molesting is less common than its heterosexual counterpart. Most child molesting is done by heterosexual men and involves young girls.[85] Strangely, people who worry that gay teachers will try to seduce young boys in a school do not seem to worry that heterosexual male teachers will try to seduce young girls—and it is the latter that occurs much more frequently.

*Myth 7:* Gays and lesbians are to blame for AIDS, which is a punishment from God for their behavior.

*Fact:* Although gay males are a high-risk group for contracting the AIDS virus in our society, very few cases have been reported among lesbians.[86] (Gay men are at high risk for acquiring AIDS because of the transfer of body fluids that occurs during anal intercourse.) AIDS is a life-threatening disease not only for gay men; AIDS is currently spreading most quickly among heterosexuals.[87]

Gay and lesbian persons are not the cause of AIDs. Blaming this deadly disease on the group that, in the United States, has suffered and died most disproportionately from it is a classic and regrettable case of blaming the victims. Although it is true that the largest single risk group of people with AIDS is gay men, it is ludicrous to assume this group caused this health crisis. AIDS is caused by a virus. It is even more ludicrous to assert that gay men would want to deliver the disease on the world after first spreading it among themselves. Quite to the contrary, the gay male community in the United States has been in the forefront of educating people about behavior that minimizes the transmission of the disease. Gay men have radically altered their sexual behavior patterns, as evidenced by a substantial drop in the rate of transmission of this disease among this group in the past few years. (Expanded material on AIDS is presented in Chapter 11.)

*Incidence of Homosexuality*   Determining the extent of homosexuality is difficult. First, there are definitional problems, as most people are not exclusively heterosexual or homosexual. Second, because of the stigma attached to homosexuality, some people are reluctant to acknowledge their homosexual thoughts, feelings, or acts.

A 1994 study of 3,432 Americans by the University of Chicago's National Opinion Research Center found that 2.8 percent of men and 1.4 percent of women identify themselves as homosexual or bisexual. The study also found that 9 percent of men and over 4 percent of women have had a sexual experience with someone of the same sex since puberty.[88] Other studies have resulted in similar estimates.[89] After reviewing several studies, Janet Hyde concludes:

> [The question] How many people are homosexual?— is complex. Probably about 80 percent of men and 90 percent of women are exclusively heterosexual. About 2 percent of men and 1 percent of women are exclusively homosexual. And the remaining group have had varying amounts of both heterosexual and homosexual experience.[90]

The Ten Percent Society, a gay and lesbian organization, asserts that the incidence of homosexuality is 10 percent. Hyde notes:

> This statistic comes from no single study, but rather from an amalgamation of many. It represents those people whose orientation is predominately homosexual, although they may have had some heterosexual experience. In view of the most recent surveys, the 10 percent figure may be a bit high, but it is probably not too far off.[91]

*Causes of Homosexuality*   People are often curious about what causes homosexuality; that is, why are some persons erotically attracted to the same gender and others attracted to the other? Social, behavioral, and biological scientists have examined and argued this question for decades. Let us see what they have learned.

First, you cannot study the question of why one *becomes* homosexual without studying the larger question of what *determines* sexual orientation. Why do certain people become aroused by a woman, or a woman with particular attributes, or a man of a certain body type? Is this a learned response? Are we born with a "script" that determines our sexual object choice?

Many researchers and theoreticians have advanced hypotheses to explain this complex and important question. Some believe that the biology of an individual determines heterosexuality or homosexuality. Some studies have shown chemical differences between these two groups, but it is impossible to determine causation from the results of these studies. In other words, are the chemical differences between people responsible for this behavior, or does their behavior somehow alter their body chemistry?

Other theorists posit that childhood experiences determine heterosexuality or homosexuality. Here we have the causation question again. If we determine that a certain child had more sex play with a child of the same gender and grew to be a homosexual in adult life, can we say that this sex play led to homosexuality? Perhaps the increased sex play grew out of an inborn desire and erotic potential toward gratification from such play; that is, the behavior grew out of a predisposition toward homosexuality.

The most comprehensive study of this question to date was undertaken by researchers at the Alfred C. Kinsey Institute for Sex Research.[92] The researchers, Alan P. Bell, Martin S. Weinberg, and Sue Kiefer Hammersmith, studied 979 homosexual and 477 heterosexual men and women, gathering information about their lives to determine critical and statistically significant differences between the groups. They analyzed their data using a method called *path analysis,* which enabled them to examine a large number of independent variables (such as parental traits, parent and sibling relationships and gender conformity) to determine causation of sexual orientation, and not merely association between variables. They made three significant findings:

1. By the time boys and girls reach adolescence, their sexual orientation is likely to be already determined, even though they may not yet have become sexually very active.

2. The gay and lesbian persons in the study were not particularly lacking in heterosexual experiences during their childhood and adolescent years. They were distinguished from their heterosexual counterparts, however, in finding such experiences ungratifying.

3. Among both the men and women in the study, there was a powerful link between gender nonconformity and the development of homosexuality. (*Gender nonconformity* refers to children who prefer activities generally associated in this culture with the other gender, for example, boys playing with dolls.) This factor of gender nonconformity

*Sexual variances now openly invoke support from family and friends in a way that was unheard of years ago.*

freely choose who or what "turns us on." The question of what causes a person's sexual orientation to be set (either as homosexual or heterosexual) before birth or at a very early age has not as yet been answered. (Some people are naturally left-handed and others are naturally right-handed; it appears that some people are naturally heterosexual in orientation and others are naturally homosexual.)

The possibility that sexual orientation is more a matter of nature than nurture got a boost in a 1991 study that reported differences between the brains of gay men and heterosexual men. The research focused on the hypothalamus, the region of the brain thought to control sexual behavior. The results were striking. Certain groups of nerve cells in the hypothalamus were more than two times larger in heterosexual men than in gay men. The hypothalami of gay men appear to be closer in structure to those of heterosexual women than to those of heterosexual men.[93]

Studies in 1991 and 1993 (at the Boston University School of Medicine) of separated twins found a greater likelihood of twins both being homosexual if they are identical—that is, they share the same genes—than if they are fraternal—that is, they do not share exactly the same genes.[94] In another 1993 study, additional evidence was found that suggests homosexuality is genetically determined. Evidence of a gay gene was found when researchers studied the X chromosome in forty pairs of gay brothers. The researchers found thirty-three shared identical genetic markers in the tip of the X chromosome, which suggested with more than 99 percent certainty that the sexual orientation of the men was genetically influenced.[95]

was more significant for males than for females, with variables related to family relationships more important for females.

What do thee findings suggest? First, they show that sexual orientation is established early in life, perhaps long before adolescence. Although every person has the potential to behave sexually in the manner they choose, true sexual orientation may be set before birth or at a very early age, and then no longer be influenced by the environment. Many homosexually oriented persons behave as if they are heterosexual because of societal sanctions against homosexuality. However, their true orientation and preferred sexual partner, in the absence of these negative sanctions, would be someone of the same gender. Human beings certainly have the ability to respond sexually to persons who are not their most preferred sexual partners, but to do so requires going against the current of their innermost inclinations. We can freely choose various behaviors; we cannot

***Life as a Gay or Lesbian Person*** Homosexual behavior between males is illegal in many states. Lesbianism is prohibited in fewer states than is male homosexuality. There appear to be several reasons for this. Fewer females are homosexual than males. Lesbians, unlike gay men, keep their sexual behavior more hidden and are not as likely to form obvious homosexual communities. In addition, most legislators have been males and perhaps see male homosexuality as more of a threat to them than female homosexuality.

The gay liberation movement seeks to change negative attitudes and end discriminatory acts toward homosexuals. Yet many people still view homosexuals as being psychologically "sick." (Until 1973 the American Psychiatric Association defined homosexuality as a mental illness.)

The gay liberation movement is a coalition of groups such as the Gay Liberation Front, the National Gay Task Force, and the International Union of Gay Athletes. The movement contends (along with many social scientists) that homosexuality is not a perversion or sickness but simply a different lifestyle. Their arguments have met with mixed reactions. For instance, some states have repealed antihomosexual legislation, whereas several cities have passed civil rights ordinances that prevent discrimination against police officers, teachers, and other city employees on the basis of sexual orientation. Other municipal and state governments have rejected bills that sought to ban discrimination against gay and lesbian persons.

When Bill Clinton was running for President of the United States in 1992, he promised to reverse the fifty-year-old policy aimed at keeping gay and lesbian persons out of the military. After his inauguration in 1993, he tried to lift the ban by executive order and encountered strong resistance from both the Pentagon and Congress. After months of hearings and negotiations, Congress passed, and Clinton signed, a policy that has been called "Don't ask, don't tell." New recruits to the military can no longer be asked by military personnel if they are homosexual; however, anyone who openly engages in homosexual conduct can be discharged. As part of the policy, the Pentagon promised to end purges of military personnel who keep their homosexuality private. (Some gay activists consider this new policy to be as onerous as the original prohibition.) A legal battle is raging over the "Don't ask, don't tell" policy. Federal courts have split on the issue and a Supreme Court test case seems inevitable.

In 1996, Congress passed, and President Clinton signed, the Defense of Marriage Act, which allows states to refuse to recognize gay marriages. (At the time of this writing, no state has passed legislation which legally recognizes same-sex marriages.) The Defense of Marriage Act prevents one partner in a homosexual relationship from claiming social security, veteran's or other federal benefits in the event of the other's death or disability. It also bars gay and lesbian couples from filing joint income-tax returns, even if they live under the same roof and share everything else.

Courts are increasingly hearing cases involving gay rights issues. Some judges are supportive of gay rights issues, whereas others are not, as illustrated by the following two conflicting decisions (both of which were made in 1993). A federal judge in Virginia denied a lesbian mother custody of her son solely because of her sexuality; he awarded custody to the boy's grand-mother. However, in Boston a state supreme court ruling made two lesbians the first gay couple to win approval to adopt a child in Massachusetts.[96]

Job discrimination against gays is legal in most states in the United States.[97] Such discrimination exists even though more than 80 percent of the public believe (in survey polls) that gays should be protected from employment discrimination.[98]

Because of negative attitudes and discriminatory acts, some gay or lesbian persons go to extensive lengths to hide their sexual behavior. They fear discrimination and even loss of employment. They also fear the stigma and embarrassment that they and their families would receive if they "came out" (publicly acknowledged their sexual orientation). Some gay or lesbian persons marry someone of the opposite sex and may even hide their homosexual encounters from their spouses. Leading a double life, with fear of criminal penalties if one's sexual orientation were discovered, is stress producing.

Many larger cities now have homosexual communities that provide an escape from the pressures of leading such a double life. These communities may offer recreational and leisuretime activities and may serve to socialize new entrants into the homosexual subculture. They are often located in a certain geographical area of a city and generally have shops, restaurants, and hotels that are owned and patronized primarily by homosexual customers. The "gay bars" are perhaps the most visible establishments in such communities. Gay bars provide opportunities for their clientele to drink, socialize, and find a sexual partner or a lover. Some gay bars look just like any other bar from the outside, while others have names (such as The Gay Closet) that indicate to the alert who the clientele is.

Unlike other minority-group members, gay and lesbian youths grow up as minorities even within their own families. People of color, for example, are socialized—trained—by their parents, older siblings, and relatives about functioning in a society that is likely to discriminate against them. Gay and lesbian youths have no such training ground, as most are raised in heterosexual families. This makes homosexually identified institutions (the most visible and approachable of which is the gay bar) very important in the life of the young gay or lesbian adult. Most homosexuals patronize these gay bars for only a brief period (primarily while they are formulating their gay or lesbian identity). After this phase, they generally prefer social contact with other gay or lesbian persons in environments where the focus is not on alcohol and superficial interactions.

It should be noted that there is a wide variation in homosexual lifestyles, as is true for heterosexuals. Also, lesbians and gay men differ somewhat in their sexual attitudes and practices. Lesbians are more likely to equate sex with love. They tend to engage in sex with fewer partners than do gay men. Their relationships tend to last longer and to be based more on love and affection. Lesbians may be less likely to acknowledge their sexual orientation publicly and to participate in a homosexual community.[99]

Lesbians are better able to conceal their sexual orientation because the public is less suspicious of two women living together or otherwise being close to each other. Most lesbians have had sexual relationships with men. Jack H. Hedblom notes: "The female homosexual does not prefer sex with a woman because she has had no experience with a man."[100]

A bisexual is a person whose sexual orientation is toward both women and men—that is, toward members of the other gender and members of the same gender. The proponents of bisexuality argue that being bisexual has advantages, as it allows more variety in one's sexual and human relationships than either exclusive homosexuality or exclusive heterosexuality. On the other hand, some heterosexuals may devalue those who are known to be bisexual. In addition, persons who are bisexual may be viewed with suspicion or downright hostility by the gay community.[101] Some gays and lesbians view persons who are bisexual as "fence sitters" who betray the gay and lesbian movement because they can pretend to be "straight" when it is convenient, and gay (or lesbian) when it is convenient.[102] There is a diversity of bisexuals. Some bisexuals (referred to as 50:50 bisexuals) have equal preferences for men and for women. Some bisexuals have a preference for one gender but are accepting of sex with the other gender. Some are sequentially bisexual; they have only one lover at a time, sometimes a man and sometimes a woman. Some are simultaneously bisexual; they have both a male and a female lover at the same time. Some bisexuals are transitory bisexuals, as they are passing through a bisexual phase on the way to becoming exclusively heterosexual or homosexual. Some are enduring bisexuals, as they maintain their bisexual preferences throughout their lifespan.

The specter of AIDS has had a tremendous impact on gay and lesbian communities, particularly on gay men. Gay and lesbian communities have been active in encouraging federal and state governments to (a) recognize the dangers of AIDS; (b) provide research funds to develop treatments for those who are infected

with the AIDS virus; and (c) provide research funds to develop approaches to prevent the spread of AIDS.[103] Gay and lesbian communities have also been advocates of safer sex practices, and many gay men have made responsible and dramatic changes in their sexual practices. Gay and lesbian communities have also developed support systems for people who have AIDS. (Unfortunately, the larger society has been slow in developing services and programs for people who have AIDS. People with AIDS are often shunned and victimized by discrimination in our society.)

*Current Issues*  As mentioned earlier, a major issue is whether civil rights laws should be enacted to protect gay and lesbian persons from discrimination in housing, employment, military service, and other areas. Gay and lesbian persons argue that they are refused jobs in teaching, the military service, and in many private corporations. They also note they are commonly the targets of blackmailers who know of their sexual orientation. They assert that legal protection for gay rights will not turn heterosexuals (e.g., school children) into homosexuals. They maintain they have been the victims of abuse and exploitation, and now want the same protection other minorities receive.[104]

Opponents of civil rights laws for gay and lesbian persons assert that homosexuals are not like other minority groups discriminated against based on physical characteristics (people of color, women, persons with a physical disability). It is argued that gay and lesbian persons, by contrast, *choose* their sexual behavior, which can be changed if they so desire. Another objection is that legislation to protect gay rights would indicate approval of what opponents assert is unnatural behavior. Permitting gays and lesbians to teach in school, it is asserted, would unwisely expose children to homosexual attitudes and activities, and probably lead to increased homosexual experimentation. Because most members of society are heterosexual, and many are confused or threatened by their lack of information and understanding of homosexuality, many heterosexuals view homosexuality as being morally wrong and socially damaging. They believe that if sanctions against homosexuality were relaxed, such behavior would flourish, the stability of the family would be threatened, birthrates would fall drastically, and society would be severely damaged. Of course, this is highly unlikely because with or without social sanctions, gay and lesbian persons compose only a small minority of any society. And social support is unlikely to significantly increase behavior so integral to one's being as his or her sexual orientation.

As can be seen, arguments on both sides of this issue are intense, and other issues further complicate the controversy. For example, some churches are now marrying couples who are gay or lesbian. These marriages are recognized by certain religious groups but not by state laws, which still prohibit homosexuals from marrying one another. Proponents of such marriages assert that gay and lesbian persons ought to be permitted to receive the same personal gratifications and financial advantages through marriage that are available to heterosexuals. Opponents assert that such marriages are sacrilegious, a violation of the purpose of marriage, and a threat to the stability of the traditional family.

Related issues involve whether married gay or lesbian couples ought to be allowed to adopt children and whether gay fathers or lesbian mothers ought to be allowed to retain custody of their children after divorce. In some court cases lesbian mothers have won custody of their children after divorce. In other cases courts have decreed that lesbian behavior is sufficient evidence that a person is unfit to be a parent. At issue in many homosexual adoptions and custody battles is whether gay men and lesbian women would pass on their sexual orientation to the child. Initial findings from studies suggest that this is unlikely to occur.[105] Our society continues to be confused about whether and how sexual orientation might influence other important aspects of life, such as child rearing or work performance.

In the past, psychotherapists who counseled gay and lesbian persons generally had the goal of changing their sexual orientation to heterosexuality. This goal was almost never achieved.[106] Such gay or lesbian clients often became more anxious and uncomfortable about their sexual orientation, but continued to maintain homosexual behavior. The counseling emphasis has shifted in recent years. Most therapists now seek to have gay and lesbian clients examine their concerns and arrive at a sexual identity they can be comfortable with. Most choose to continue their homosexual behavior, and counseling is then geared to helping them deal with discrimination they may face and concerns they have (such as whether to inform their relatives or employer, and whether to come out in other ways).

A number of issues involving homosexuality have been debated for decades, and undoubtedly will continue to be national issues. Over time, our society has become more tolerant of homosexuality. Thirty-five years ago efforts to suppress homosexuality were so strong that no newspaper even dared to print the word *homosexual*.

Homosexuality is no longer an unmentionable deviancy. It is discussed on the airwaves, in newspapers, in movie theaters, and in political debates. Openly gay candidates are increasingly being elected to political office in the United States. Officially sanctioned support groups for gays are being established in high school. Domestic partnerships between gay couples are recognized officially in dozens of cities, and increasingly corporations are granting partners of their homosexual employees the same benefits heterosexual spouses receive. Discrimination on the basis of sexual orientation is now illegal in several states and in nearly one hundred cities and countries.

## Personal Sexual Concerns

At one time or another everyone has sexual concerns. The kinds of sexual concerns are probably infinite, so only a few will be listed:

♦ A teenager may wonder whether to become sexually involved with someone he or she is dating.

♦ A male who had sex with a prostitute may be concerned he has contracted the AIDS virus.

♦ Adolescents may feel guilty about masturbating.

♦ A wife may feel guilty about having had an extramarital affair.

♦ Men may worry about premature ejaculation, failure to have an erection, or failure to become sexually aroused.

♦ Some women are concerned because they seldom have an orgasm.

♦ Persons married or dating over an extended period of time may become alarmed because their sex life appears to be becoming boring and routine.

♦ Some people may be unhappy with various sexual techniques and approaches used by their partners.

♦ Victims of rape or incest may still have unwanted emotions related to what happened to them.

♦ An admirer of someone of his or her own sex may wonder if this attraction has homosexual elements.

Box 5.5 ◆◆◆◆◆◆◆◆◆◆◆◆◆◆◆◆◆◆◆◆◆◆◆◆◆◆

## Case Example: Sex Counseling for Seeking Meaning in Life Through Sex

Cassie, a nineteen-year-old fast-food restaurant employee, revealed to Maria Ricardo (social worker at a Planned Parenthood clinic) that she felt guilty and despondent upon "being used by men." She indicated that she had had a series of "one-night stands" and always felt guilty and depressed afterwards. Ms. Ricardo probed into her feelings of guilt, and Cassie gradually revealed the thoughts underlying her guilty feelings, including: "I am promiscuous, which my religion says is immoral"; "I am letting men who don't love me use my body"; "I am giving myself to men whom I don't love, which is wrong"; and "I'm a bad person, a whore, for doing this."

They also explored why Cassie felt depressed after sex. The thoughts that underlay her depression were: "No one really cares about me as a person, only about my body"; "I am leading the kind of life I really don't want to lead"; "I'm putting myself at risk for getting AIDS, or some other STD (sexually transmitted disease)"; and "I give everything I have to these guys, and they don't even ask me out for a date afterwards."

When asked by Ms. Ricardo to identify the thoughts that lead her to engage in intercourse, Cassie gradually revealed: "At times I really like it, and enjoy and want sex"; and "Sex is the one way I can get a guy interested in me." After being asked by Ms. Ricardo to reflect on these reasons, Cassie concluded that she was using her sexuality as the primary way to attract men which was leading to "one-night stands", putting her at risk for an STD, and resulting in her feeling guilty and depressed. Ms. Ricardo asked Cassie if her current way of seeking meaning in life was through dating and whether she was using sex to get dates. Cassie thought about this and gradually agreed. Ms. Ricardo then asked Cassie whether such a strategy was getting her what she wanted in life. Cassie replied, "Definitely not—it is leading to one-night stands, which result in me feeling guilty and depressed."

Ms. Ricardo asked Cassie to do a homework assignment prior to the next time they talked, which involved Cassie brainstorming and writing down a list of options (including some she might have little interest in pursuing) for how to feel better about herself, and to identify other ways of finding meaning in life. Cassie came back the next week with the following list:

1. Wait until marriage to next have sex.
2. Wait to have sex until I meet someone I love—and who also loves me.
3. Take courses at the local community college in an effort to find, and prepare for, a career I'm interested in.
4. Volunteer at the nursing home that my grandmother is living in.

Ms. Ricardo explored these options with Cassie and indicated that the option or options Cassie selected were up to her, as she was in the best position to know which would best suit her values, her current lifestyle, and her goals in life. For each option, Ms. Ricardo also discussed with Cassie how she was apt to feel about herself if she were to pursue that option. After considerable discussion, Cassie decided to pursue options two and three. She seemed to feel good about her decisions.

Ms. Ricardo then asked Cassie if she would be interested in having a test for HIV. Cassie said that she was interested in doing so. She had the test, and the results came back negative two weeks later. Ms. Ricardo also discussed safer sex practices (such as using a condom) that Cassie might use in the future when she became romantically involved with someone. Ms. Ricardo suggested that Cassie have another HIV test in about six months, just in case she had been recently exposed to the AIDS virus. (For a person infected with HIV, it generally takes up to six months before enough antibodies are produced to be detected by an AIDS test. AIDS tests do not directly detect the virus, but only the antibodies a person's immune system develops to fight the virus.) The additional AIDS test was scheduled for six months in the future.

◆ Middle-aged people may fear losing their sexual capacities.

◆ Some may find intercourse painful.

◆ Some know their current sexual partner has had previous sexual experiences with others and feel angry or hurt.

A major reason why personal sexual concerns are include in this social problems text is because personal sexual concerns (similar to emotional difficulties) are encountered by so many people that the subject becomes a societal problem.

Sexual counseling and sex therapy are designed directly to resolve personal sexual concerns. *Sexual counseling* is short-term, often crisis-oriented counseling directed toward the alleviation of some immediate sexual concern. *Sex therapy,* on the other hand, is somewhat longer term and tends to focus more on resolving specific sexual dysfunctions (such as premature ejaculation and erectile difficulties in men and failure to achieve orgasm and painful intercourse in women). Sex therapy involves several stages: problem identification, taking a sexual physical examination, information giving, history about the concern, assigning sexual exercises designed to resolve the dysfunction, and ongoing evaluation.[107] In actual counseling the distinctions between sexual counseling and sex therapy are not clear-cut. Sexual counseling and sex therapy treatment programs are now provided by private sex therapy centers in many communities. At most social service agencies, counselors and psychotherapists occasionally treat clients with sexual concerns.

Jack Annon has developed an extremely useful conceptual scheme for treating personal sexual concerns.[108] Having found that very few persons with sexual concerns need intensive sex therapy, he advances a model of four levels of intervention:

1. Permission
2. Limited information
3. Specific suggestions
4. Intensive therapy

Most people can be treated at one of the first three levels of intervention.

The largest number of people can be treated at the first level simply by the helping professional giving accurate, well-placed "permission." *Permission* involves a kind of professional reassurance, letting clients know they are all right, normal—not sick or perverted. Many people at this level are not bothered by the sexual behavior they are engaging in but are more concerned about what other people think. These concerns may include masturbation, oral-genital sex, and sexual fantasies. It is important to note that permission involves helping clients first to understand it is to their benefit to engage in sexual activities they desire as long as they do not hurt themselves or infringe on the rights of others, and then to assure them of their right *not* to engage in sexual behaviors that other people are urging. Lloyd Sinclair gives the following example of counseling at the permission level:

The client reports, "My wife and I hear a lot about oral sex. We just aren't interested in doing that. Do you think there's something wrong with us?" The counselor

can give permission: "Sex is best when you're doing things you *both* want to do, not because of somebody else's expectations. I would encourage you to do what you both like, and if at some point you want to try oral sex, fine. But if you don't, that's fine too."[109]

The second largest number of people need *limited information,* that is, specific factual information, to alleviate their sexual concerns. Lloyd Sinclair gives an example of providing limited information and its effects:

A sixty-eight-year-old client . . . had believed for as long as he could remember that human beings were capable of a certain number of orgasms in life, and no more. So he had *rationed* them, always confining orgasm to a single intercourse experience each weekend. The therapist informed him that what he had believed was incorrect. In fact, he could enhance his ability to respond sexually by maintaining a frequency and regularity of response. Since this client received this information, he has been making up for a great deal of lost time.[110]

The third level of intervention is *specific suggestions.* A smaller number of clients can benefit at this level than at each of the preceding levels. Prior to giving suggestions, the therapist first takes a brief sexual history about the concern, including: a description of the current concern, a description of the onset and course of the concern, the client's views of the cause and maintenance of the concern, past treatment efforts and outcome, and current goals and expectations from treatment.[111]

Brief sexual histories are taken at this level to identify precisely the nature of the concern and to determine specifically the client's treatment goals. Such background information is very useful in determining which specific suggestions are apt to be the most useful in alleviating the sexual distress.

Specific suggestions are often given to treat performance difficulties. For example, a woman who finds intercourse painful due to lack of sexual arousal and lack of lubrication may benefit from suggestions encouraging the couple to spend more time on foreplay, helping her to communicate to her partner those behaviors that are pleasurable to her, and advising her not to proceed to intercourse until she is lubricating.

For a male suffering from premature ejaculation, a specific suggestion is to briefly stop the stimulation in order to decrease the erection and thereby delay the orgasm. Another suggestion is for him or his partner to squeeze the penis in certain areas during an erection to decrease the erection and delay the orgasm. Yet another suggestion is to use touching experiences with one's partner without proceeding to intercourse, so that the male learns to enjoy such touching experiences and thereby delays orgasm.[112]

Annon's final level of intervention, *intensive therapy,* is needed by a very small number of persons with sexual concerns. At this level, the concerns are fairly complicated and involved. An example would be a married couple who no longer is having sexual intercourse, largely because the wife has never experienced orgasm and because the husband is now having difficulty maintaining an erection. Descriptions of intensive therapy[113] are beyond the scope of this text. Intensive therapy involves having clients receive physical examinations, taking an extensive sexual history of both partners, helping the partners to communicate better with each other, conveying accurate information to the clients about the physiology of sex, assigning sexual exercises designed to resolve the concerns, and evaluating efforts being made to resolve the concerns.

## Summary

Practically every conceivable sexual activity is socially acceptable to some groups of people. What is defined as acceptable and unacceptable sexual behavior varies from culture to culture and from one time period to another. Judeo-Christian values, the Puritan influence, and Victorian morality have sought to repress sexual expression. Currently there is ambiguity and confusion about what the sexual behavior of Americans ought to be. For the past several decades our society has been undergoing a revolution in sexual values and mores.

Three formal studies have made immense contributions to improving our understanding of sexuality—those of Freud, Kinsey, and the team of Masters and Johnson.

This text uses a social variance approach to examining sexual concerns, rather than a social problems approach, as there as yet is no general consensus as to which sexual acts are acceptable and which are not. Four categories of sexual concerns are tolerated sex variance, asocial sex variance, structural sex variance, and personal sexual concerns.

Tolerated sex variance includes masturbation, premarital intercourse, and heterosexual oral-genital contact between consenting adults.

Asocial sex variance includes those acts that elicit strong disapproval and at the same time do not have a social structure that supports them. Acts in this category include incest, child molestation, rape, voyeurism, and exhibitionism.

Structural sex variance refers to those acts that run counter to prevailing norms and legal statutes but at the same time have supportive social structures. Sexual variances in this category include prostitution, pornography, and homosexuality. There is considerable debate over whether our society should take a more tolerant, or a more repressive, approach toward these three activities.

Almost everyone experiences personal sexual concerns. For example, men may worry about premature ejaculation, and women may experience painful intercourse. A useful model for counseling people with sexual concerns was developed by Jack Annon. This model has four levels of intervention: permission, limited information, specific suggestions, and intensive sex therapy.

In the past century our country has made a number of changes in what are acceptable sexual attitudes and sexual behaviors.

# CHAPTER 6

# Racism and Ethnocentrism

Nearly every time we turn on the evening news we see ethnic and racial conflict—riots, beatings, murders, and civil wars. From Northern Ireland to Bosnia, from Iraq to Israel, and from the United States to South America, clashes have resulted in bloodshed. Practically every nation with more than one ethnic group has dealt with ethnic conflict. Oppression and exploitation of one ethnic group by another is particularly ironic in democratic nations that claim to cherish freedom, equality, and justice. In reality, rarely does the dominant group agree to share (equally) its political and economic power and its wealth with other ethnic groups.

Supposedly our country was founded on the principle of human equality. The Declaration of Independence and the Constitution assert equality, justice, and liberty for all. Yet, in practice, America has always been racist; inequality and racial prejudice and discrimination have always existed. From its earliest days, our society has singled out certain minorities for unequal treatment. (A *minority* can be defined as a group that has a subordinate status and is being subjected to discrimination.) Even Abraham Lincoln, who is recognized as the key person in abolishing slavery in the United States, held racist views, as indicated in the following speech he delivered in 1858 in Charleston, Illinois:

> I will say, then, that I am not, nor ever have been in favor of bringing about in any way the social and political equality of the white and black races; that I am not, nor ever have been, in favor of making voters or jurors of Negroes, nor of qualifying them to hold office, nor to intermarry with White people . . . and inasmuch as they cannot so live, while they do remain together there must be the position of superior and inferior, and I as much as any other man am in favor of having the superior position assigned to the White race.[1]

The categories of people singled out for unequal treatment have changed somewhat over the years. In the late 1800s and early 1900s, people of Irish, Italian, and Polish descent were discriminated against, but that discrimination has been reduced substantially. In the first half of the nineteenth century, Americans of Chinese and Japanese descent were severely discriminated against, but for many decades this also has been declining.

As time passes, new minorities become recognized victims of discrimination. For example, women, people with disabilities, and homosexuals have always been discriminated against, but only in the past thirty-five years has there been extensive national recognition of this discrimination. This chapter:

♦ defines and describes ethnic groups, ethnocentrism, racial groups, racism, prejudice, discrimination, oppression, and institutional discrimination;

♦ outlines the sources of prejudice and discrimination;

♦ summarizes the effects and costs of discrimination and oppression;

♦ presents background material on specific racial groups (African Americans, Hispanic Americans, Native Americans, and Asian Americans);

♦ outlines strategies to advance social and economic justice for populations victimized by discrimination; and

♦ forecasts the pattern of race and ethnic relations in the United States.

## Ethnic Groups and Ethnocentrism

An ethnic group has a sense of togetherness, a conviction that its members form a special group, and a sense of common identity or "peoplehood." Coleman and Cressey define an ethnic group as "a group whose members share a sense of togetherness and the conviction that they form a distinct group or 'people.' "[2] Practically every ethnic group has a strong feeling of ethnocentrism. *Ethnocentrism* means "the tendency to view the norms and values of one's own culture as absolute and to use them as a standard against which to judge and measure all other cultures."[3] Ethnocentrism leads members of ethnic groups to view their culture as superior, as being the one other cultures should adopt. Ethnocentrism also leads to prejudice against so-called foreigners, who may be viewed as barbarians, heathens, uncultured people, or savages.

Feelings of ethnic superiority within a nation are usually accompanied by the belief that political and economic domination by one's own group is natural, morally right, in the best interest of the nation, and perhaps also "God's will." Ethnocentrism has been a factor in some of the worst atrocities in human history—such as Adolf Hitler's mass executions of an estimated six million European Jews and Gypsies, and the European colonists' attempt to exterminate Native Americans.

In interactions between nations, ethnocentric beliefs sometimes lead to wars and serve as justification for foreign conquests. In the past several centuries at least a few wars between nations occurred because one society sought to force its culture on another. Until recently, the United States and the Soviet Union struggled to extend their influence over other cultures. Also in the past few decades, Israel and the Arab countries have been involved in a bitter struggle in the Middle East. China and Taiwan are in conflict. Countries in Southeast Asia (such as Cambodia and Vietnam) have been in conflict.

## RACE AND RACISM

Although a racial group is often also an ethnic group, the two groups are not necessarily the same. A *race* is believed to have a common set of physical characteristics. Even so, members of a racial group may or may not share the sense of togetherness or identity that holds an *ethnic group* together. A group that is both a racial group and an ethnic group is Japanese Americans, as they are thought to have some common physical characteristics and also a sense of "peoplehood." On the other hand, white Americans and white Russians are of the same race, but they hardly have a sense of togetherness. In addition, some ethnic groups are composed of a variety of races. For example, a religious group (such as Muslims) is sometimes considered an ethnic group although it is composed of members from diverse racial groups.

In contrast to ethnocentrism, racism is more apt to be based on physical differences than on cultural differences. Racism is "a belief in racial superiority that leads to discrimination and prejudice toward those races considered inferior."[4] However, like ethnocentric ideologies, most racist ideologies assert that members of other racial groups are inferior.

## *Prejudice, Discrimination, and Oppression*
xxxxxxxxxxxxxxxxxxxxxx

*Prejudice* means to prejudge, to make a judgment in advance of due examination. The judgment may be unduly favorable or negative. In terms of race and ethnic relations, however, prejudice refers to negative prejudgments. Gordon Allport defines prejudice as "thinking negatively of others without sufficient justification."[5] His definition has two elements: an unfounded judgment and a feeling of scorn, dislike, fear, and aversion. In regard to race, prejudiced people apply racial stereotypes to all, or nearly all, members of a group according to preconceived notions of what they believe the group to be like and how they feel the group will behave. Racial prejudice results from the belief that people who differ in skin color and other physical characteristics also differ in behaviors, values, intellectual functioning, and attitudes.

The phrase *to discriminate* has two very different meanings. It may have the positive meaning "to be discerning and perceptive." However, in minority group relations it refers to making categoric differentiations based on a social group being ranked as inferior, rather than judging an individual on his or her merits. Racial discrimination involves denying to members of minority groups equal access to opportunities, certain residential housing areas, membership in certain religious and social organizations, certain political activities, access to community services, and so on.

*Prejudice* is a combination of stereotyped beliefs and negative attitudes, so that prejudiced individuals *think about people* in a predetermined, usually negative, categorical way. *Discrimination* involves physical actions, such as unequal *treatment of certain people* because they belong to a category rather than because of their beliefs and attitudes. Discriminatory behavior often derives from prejudiced attitudes. Robert Merton, however, notes prejudice and discrimination can occur independently of each other. Merton describes four different "types" of people:

1. The *unprejudiced nondiscriminator,* in both belief and practice, upholds American ideals of freedom and equality. This person is not prejudiced against other groups and, on principle, will not discriminate against them.

2. The *unprejudiced discriminator* is not personally prejudiced but may sometimes, reluctantly, discriminate against other groups because it seems socially or financially convenient to do so.

3. The *prejudiced nondiscriminator* feels hostile to other groups but recognizes that law and social pressures are opposed to overt discrimination. Albeit reluctantly, this person refrains from translating that prejudice into action.

4. The *prejudiced discriminator* does not believe in the values of freedom and equality and consistently discriminates against other groups in both word and deed.[6]

*Members of the Ku Klux Klan in Delaware join the USA Nationalists, a neo-Nazi group, at a "Gaybash" in Washington Crossing's Park near New Hope, Pennsylvania. Extreme ethnocentrism leads to the formation of these intolerant groups who believe their culture is superior to all others.*

An example of an unprejudiced discriminator (or type 2) is the unprejudiced owner of a condominium complex in an all-white middle class suburb who refuses to sell a condominium to an African American family because the sale might reduce the value of the remaining units. An example of a prejudiced nondiscriminator (type 3) is a personnel director of a fire department who believes Chicanos are unreliable and poor firefighters but complies with affirmative action efforts to hire and train Chicano firefighters.

It should be noted it is very difficult to keep personal prejudices from eventually leading to some form of discrimination. Strong laws and firm informal social norms are necessary to break the causal relationship between prejudice and discrimination.

Discrimination is of two types: de jure and de facto. *De jure discrimination* is legal discrimination. The so-called Jim Crow laws in the South gave force of law to many discriminatory practices against blacks, including denial of the right to trial, prohibition against voting, and prohibition against interracial marriage. Today, in the United States, there is practically no de jure discrimination, as such laws have been declared unconstitutional and have been removed.

*De facto discrimination* refers to discrimination that actually exists, whether legal or not. Acts of de facto discrimination often result from powerful informal discriminatory norms. Marlene Cummings gives an example of this type of discrimination and urges victims to confront such discrimination assertively:

> Scene: department store. Incident: Several people are waiting their turn at a counter. The person next to be served is a black woman; however, the clerk waits on several white customers who arrived later. The black woman finally demands service, after several polite gestures to call the clerk's attention to her. The clerk proceeds to wait on her after stating, "I did not see you." The clerk is very discourteous to the black customer; and the lack of courtesy is apparent, because the black customer had the opportunity to observe treatment of the other customers. De facto discrimination is most frustrating. . . . Most people would rather just forget the whole incident, but it is important to challenge the practice even though it will possibly put you through more agony. One of the best ways to deal with this type of discrimination is to report it to the manager of the business. If it is at all possible, it is important to involve the clerk in the discussion.[7]

Oppression is the unjust or cruel exercise of authority or power. Members of minority groups in our society are frequently victimized by oppression from segments of the white power structure. Oppression and discrimination are closely related, as all acts of oppression are also acts of discrimination.

## RACIAL AND ETHNIC STEREOTYPES

Racial and ethnic stereotypes involve attributing a fixed and usually inaccurate or unfavorable conception to a racial or ethnic group. Stereotypes may contain some truth but generally are exaggerated, taken out of context, or distorted. Stereotypes are closely related to the way we think, as we seek to perceive and understand things in categories. We need categories in which to group things that are similar in order to study them and to communicate about them. We have stereotypes about many categories, including mothers, fathers, teenagers, Communists, Republicans, schoolteachers, farmers, construction workers, miners, politicians, Mormons, and Italians. These stereotypes may contain some useful and accurate information about a member in any category. Yet each member of any category will have many characteristics that are *not* suggested by the stereotypes and may even have some characteristics that run *counter* to some of the stereotypes.

Racial stereotypes involve differentiating people in terms of color or other physical characteristics. For example, Native Americans were erroneously stereotyped as rapidly becoming intoxicated and irrational when using alcohol. This belief was then translated into laws that for a number of years prohibited Native Americans from buying and consuming alcohol. Another stereotype is that African Americans have "natural rhythm" and therefore have greater natural ability to play basketball and certain other sports. At first glance such a stereotype appears complimentary to African Americans, but it has broader negative implications. The danger with this stereotype is that, if people believe the stereotype, it may well suggest to them that other abilities and capacities (such as intelligence, morals, and work productivity) are also determined by race. In other words, believing this "positive" stereotype increases the probability that people will also believe negative stereotypes.

## RACIAL AND ETHNIC DISCRIMINATION AS THE PROBLEM OF WHITES

Gunnar Myrdal points out that minority problems are actually majority problems.[8] The white majority determines the "place" of nonwhites and other ethnic groups in our society. The status of different minority groups varies in our society because whites apply different stereotypes to various groups; for example, African Americans are viewed and treated differently from Japanese Americans. Elmer Johnson notes, "Minority relationships become recognized by the majority as a social problem when the members of the majority disagree as to whether the subjugation of the minority is socially desirable or in the ultimate interest of the majority."[9] Concern about discrimination and segregation has also received increasing national attention because of rising aspirations among minority groups who demand equal opportunities and equal rights.

Our country was supposedly founded on the principle of human equality. The Declaration of Independence and the Constitution assert equality, justice, and liberty for all. Yet, in practice, our society has always discriminated against minorities.

From its earliest days, our society has singled out certain minorities to treat unequally. Barker defines a *minority* as "a group, or a member of a group, of people of a distinct racial, religious, ethnic, or political identity that is smaller or less powerful than the community's controlling group."[10]

## RACE AS A SOCIAL CONCEPT

Ashley Montague considers race to be one of the most dangerous and tragic myths in our society.[11] Race is erroneously believed by many to be a biological classification of people. Yet there are no clearly delineating characteristics of "race." Throughout history, the genes of different societies and racial groups have occasionally been intermingled, so that no one so-called racial group has any unique or distinctive genes. In addition, biological differentiations of racial groups have gradually been diluted through sociocultural factors such as changes in preferences of characteristics in mates, effects of different diets on those who reproduce, and other variables such as wars and diseases in selecting who will live and reproduce.[12]

Despite definitional problems, it is necessary to use racial categories in the social sciences, as race has important (though not necessarily consistent) social meanings for people. In order to have a basis for racial classifications, a number of social scientists have used a social, rather than a biological, definition. A social definition is based on the way members of a society classify each other by physical characteristics. For

Photographer Margaret Bourke-White captured an American irony with this photo of Louisville flood victims, taken during the Great Depression.

example, a frequently used social definition of a black person in America is anyone who either displays overt black physical characteristics or is known to have a black ancestor.[13] The sociological classification of races is indicated by different definitions of any one race among various societies. For example, in the United States, anyone who is not "pure white" and is known to have a black ancestor is considered black, whereas in Brazil, anyone who is not "pure black" is classified as white.[14]

Race, according to Ashley Montague, becomes a dangerous myth when it is assumed that physical traits are linked with mental traits and cultural achievements.[15] Every few years, it seems, some noted scientist stirs the country by making this erroneous assumption. For example, Herrnstein and Murray asserted that whites, on the average, are more intelligent, as IQ tests show that whites average scores of 10 to 15 points higher than African Americans.[16] Herrnstein and Murray's findings have been sharply criticized by other authorities as falsely assuming that IQ is largely genetically determined.[17] These authorities contend that IQ is substantially influenced by environmental factors, and it is likely that the average achievement of African Americans, were they given similar opportunities to realize their potentialities, would be the same as whites. Also, it has been charged that IQ tests are racially slanted. The tests ask the kinds of questions that whites are more familiar with and thereby more apt to answer correctly.

Elmer Johnson summarizes the need for an impartial, objective view of the capacity of different racial groups to achieve:

> Race bigots contend that, the cultural achievements of different races being so obviously unlike, it follows that their genetic capacities for achievement must be just as different. Nobody can discover the cultural capacities of any population or race . . . until there is equality of opportunities to demonstrate the capacities.[18]

Most scientists, both physical and social, now believe that, in biological inheritance, all races are alike in every significant way. With the exception of several very small, inbred, isolated primitive tribes, all racial groups appear to show a wide distribution of every kind of ability. All important race differences that have been noted in personality, behavior, and achievement appear to be due to environmental factors.

(It should be noted that many Americans classify themselves as "mixed-race" or "multiracial," as they have one parent of one race and the other parent of another race. Tiger Woods, for example, a noted golfer, has a multiracial background, with Caucasian, African American, Native American, and Asian heritage.)

## CAUSES OF RACIAL DISCRIMINATION

No single theory provides a complete picture of why racial discrimination occurs. By studying the variety of theories presented in the following sections, the reader should at least be better sensitized to the nature and sources of discrimination. Sources of discrimination are both internal and external to those who are prejudiced.

*Projection*   *Projection* is a psychological defense mechanism, in which one attributes to others characteristics that one is unwilling to recognize in oneself. Many people with personal traits they dislike in themselves have an understandable desire to get rid of such traits, but this is not always possible. Therefore, they may "project" some of these traits onto others (often to some other group in society), thus displaying the negative feelings they would otherwise direct at themselves. In the process, they then reject and condemn those onto whom they have projected the traits.

For example, a minority group may serve as a projection of a prejudiced person's fears and lusts. That is, people who view African Americans as lazy and preoccupied with sex may be projecting their own internal concerns about their industriousness and their sexual fantasies onto another group. It is interesting to note that, whereas some whites view African Americans as promiscuous and sexually indiscreet and immoral, historically it was white men who sexually exploited African-American women (particularly slaves). It appears many white males felt guilty about these sexual desires and adventures and dealt with their guilt by projecting their own lusts and sexual conduct onto African-American males.

*Frustration-Aggression*   Another psychic need satisfied by discrimination is the release of tension and frustration. All of us at times become frustrated when we are unable to achieve or obtain something we desire. Sometimes we strike back at the source of frustration, but many times direct retaliation is not possible—for

example, we are apt to be reluctant to tell our employers what we think of them when we feel we are being treated unfairly, as we fear repercussions.

Some frustrated people displace their anger and aggression onto a scapegoat. The scapegoat may not be limited to a particular person but may include a group of people, such as a minority group. Like people who take out their job frustrations at home on their spouses or family pets, some prejudiced people vent their frustrations on minority groups. (The term *scapegoat* derives from an ancient Hebrew ritual in which a goat was symbolically laden with the sins of the entire community and then chased into the wilderness. It "escaped"; hence the term *scapegoat*. The term was gradually broadened to apply to anyone who bears the blame for others.)

*Insecurity and Inferiority*   Still another psychic need that may be satisfied by discrimination is the desire to counter feelings of insecurity or inferiority. Some insecure people seek to feel better about themselves by putting down another group, as they then can tell themselves that they are "better than" these people.

*Authoritarianism*   One of the classic works on the causes of prejudice is *The Authoritarian Personality* by T. W. Adorno et al.[19] Shortly after World War II, these researchers studied the psychological causes of the development of European fascism and concluded there was a distinct type of personality associated with prejudice and intolerance. The *authoritarian personality* is inflexible and rigid and has a low tolerance for uncertainty. This type of personality has a great respect for authority figures and quickly submits to their will. Such a person highly values conventional behavior and feels threatened by unconventional behavior of others. In order to reduce this threat, such a personality labels unconventional people as being "immature," "inferior," or "degenerate," and thereby avoids any need to question his or her own beliefs and values. The authoritarian personality views members of minority groups as being unconventional, degrades them, and tends to express authoritarianism through prejudice and discrimination.

*History*   There are also historical explanations for prejudice. Charles F. Marden and Gladys Meyer note that the racial groups now viewed by white prejudiced persons as being second-class are groups that have been either conquered, enslaved, or admitted into our society on a subordinate basis.[20] For example, blacks were imported as slaves during our colonial period and stripped of human dignity. Native Americans were conquered, and their culture was viewed as inferior. Mexican Americans were allowed to enter this country primarily to do seasonal, low-paid farm work.

***Competition and Exploitation*** Our society is highly competitive and materialistic. Individuals and groups are competing daily with one another to acquire more of the available goods. These attempts to secure economic goods usually result in a struggle for power. In our society, whites have historically sought to exploit nonwhites. As previously mentioned, they have either conquered, enslaved, or admitted nonwhites into our society on a subordinate basis. Once the white group achieved dominance, they then used, and are still using, their powers to exploit nonwhites through cheap labor—for example, as sweatshop factory laborers, migrant farm hands, maids, janitors, and bellhops.

Members of the dominant group know they are treating the subordinate group as inferior and unequal. To justify such discrimination, they develop an ideology (set of beliefs) that their group is superior and that it is right and proper that they have more rights, goods, and so on. Often, they assert that God divinely selected their group to be dominant. Furthermore, they assign inferior traits to the subordinate group (lazy, heathen, immoral, dirty, stupid) and conclude that the minority need and deserve less because they are biologically inferior.

***Socialization Patterns*** Prejudice is also a learned phenomenon and is transmitted from generation to generation through socialization processes. Our culture has stereotypes of what different racial group members "ought to be" and the ways racial group members "ought to behave" in relationships with members of certain out-groups. These stereotypes provide norms against which a child learns to judge persons, things, and ideas. Prejudice, to some extent, is developed through the same processes by which we learn to be religious and patriotic, or to appreciate and to enjoy art, or to develop our value system. Racial prejudice, at least in certain segments in our society, is thus a facet of the normative system of our culture.

***Belief in the One True Religion*** Some people are raised to believe that their religion is the one true religion—and that they will go to heaven, while everyone who believes in a different religion is a heathen who

*Fundamentalist religious group members at an abortion protest expressing belief that their religion is the one true religion.*

will go to eternal damnation. A person with such a belief system comes to the conclusion that he or she is one of "God's chosen few"—which leads that person to value himself or herself over "heathens." Feeling superior to others often leads such a person to devalue "heathens" and then to treat them in an inferior way. The influence of the "one true religion" has led to many wars between societies who each thought their religion was superior. Such societies thought they were justified in spreading their chosen religion through any possible means, including physical force.

An excellent question to ponder is "If a person believes his or her religion is the one true religion, can that person fully accept as equals those who are members of some other religious faith?" The belief in the one true religion may be one of the most crucial determinants in developing an attitudinal system of racial prejudice.

*In the Eye of the Beholder*　No one of these theories explains all the causes of prejudice, which has many origins. Taken together, however, they identify a number of causative factors. It should be noted that all these theories assert that the causative factors of prejudice are in the personality and experiences of the person holding the prejudice, not in the character of the group against whom the prejudice is directed.

A novel experiment documenting that prejudice does not stem from contact with the people toward whom it is directed was conducted by Eugene Hartley. He gave his subjects a list of prejudiced responses to Jews and African Americans and to three groups that did not even exist: Wallonians, Pireneans, and Danireans. Prejudiced responses included such statements as "All Wallonians living here should be expelled." The respondents were asked to state their agreement or disagreement with these prejudiced assertions. The experiment showed that most of those who were prejudiced against Jews and African Americans were also prejudiced against people whom they had never met or heard anything about.[21]

## INSTITUTIONAL RACISM AND INSTITUTIONAL DISCRIMINATION

In the last three decades, institutional racism has become recognized as a major problem. Institutional racism refers to discriminatory acts and policies against a racial group that pervade the major macro systems of society, including the legal, political, economic, and educational systems. Some of these discriminatory acts and policies are illegal, while others are not. Barker defines institutional racism as "those policies, practices or procedures embedded in bureaucratic structures that systematically lead to unequal outcomes for people of color."[22]

In contrast to institutional racism, Barker defines individual racism as "the negative attitudes one person has about all members of a racial or ethnic group, often resulting in overt acts such as name-calling, social exclusion, or violence."[23] Carmichael and Hamilton make the following distinction between individual racism and institutional racism:

> When white terrorists bomb a black church and kill five black children, that is an act of individual racism, widely deplored by most segments of society. But when in the same city . . . five hundred black babies die each year because of the lack of proper food, shelter, and medical facilities, and thousands more are destroyed and maimed physically, emotionally, and intellectually

because of conditions of poverty and discrimination in the black community, that is a function of institutional racism.[24]

Institutional discrimination is "prejudicial treatment in organizations based on official policies, overt behaviors, or behaviors that may be covert but approved by those in power."[25]

Discrimination is built, often unwittingly, into the structure and form of our society. The following examples reflect institutional racism:

- A family counseling agency with branch offices assigns its less skilled counselors and thereby provides lower-quality services to an office located in a minority neighborhood.

- A public welfare department encourages white applicants to request funds for special needs (e.g., clothing) or to use certain services (e.g., day care and homemaker services), whereas nonwhite clients are not informed (or are less enthusiastically informed) of such services.

- A public welfare department takes longer to process the requests of nonwhites for funds and services.

- A police department discriminates against nonwhite staff in terms of work assignments, hiring practices, promotion practices, and pay increases.

- A real estate agency has a pattern of showing white home-buyers houses in white neighborhoods, and African American home-buyers houses in mixed or predominantly African American areas.

- A bank and an insurance company engage in redlining, which involves refusing to make loans or issue insurance in areas with large minority populations.

- A probation and parole agency tends to ignore minor rule violations by white clients but seeks to return nonwhite parolees to prison for similar infractions.

- A mental health agency tends to label nonwhite clients "psychotic" while ascribing a less serious disorder to white clients.

- White staff at a family counseling center are encouraged by the executive board to provide intensive services to clients with whom they have a good relationship (often white clients) and are told to give less attention to those clients "they aren't hitting it off well with" who may be disproportionately nonwhite.

And what are the results of institutionalized racism? The unemployment rate for nonwhites has consistently been over twice that for whites. The infant mortality rate for nonwhites is nearly twice as high as for whites. The life expectancy for nonwhites is several years less than for whites. The average number of years of educational achievement for nonwhites is considerably less than for whites.[26]

There are many examples of institutional racism in school systems. Schools in white suburbs generally have better facilities and more highly trained teachers than schools in minority neighborhoods. Minority families are, on the average, less able to provide the hidden costs of "free" education (higher property taxes in the neighborhoods where the best schools are located, transportation, class trips, clothing, and supplies), and therefore their children become less involved in the educational process. Textbooks generally glorify the white race and give scant attention to minorities. Jeannette Henry writes about the effects of history textbooks on Native American children.

> What is the effect upon the student, when he learns from his textbooks that one race, and one alone, is the most, the best, the greatest; when he learns that Indians* were mere parts of the landscape and wilderness which had to be cleared out, to make way for the great "movement" of white population across the land; and when he learns that Indians were killed and forcibly removed from their ancient homelands to make way for adventurers (usually called "pioneering goldminers"), for land grabbers (usually called "settlers"), and for illegal squatters on Indian-owned land (usually called "frontiersmen")? What is the effect upon the young Indian child himself, who is also a student in the school system, when he is told that Columbus discovered America, that Coronado "brought civilization" to the Indian people, and that the Spanish missionaries provided havens of refuge for the Indians? Is it reasonable to assume that the student, of whatever race, will not discover at sometime in his life that Indians discovered America thousands of years before Columbus set out upon his voyage; that Coronado brought death and destruction to the native peoples; and that the Spanish missionaries, in all too many cases, forcibly dragged Indians to the missions.[27]

*The term *Indian* was originally used by early European settlers to describe the native populations of North America. Because of its nonnative derivation and the context of cultural domination surrounding its use, many people, particularly Native Americans, object to the use of the word. The term *Native American* is now generally preferred.

Even in school districts that use busing to attempt to achieve integration, institutional discrimination may occur. One method of discriminating is to use a track system. Most white children are placed in an "advanced" track, receiving increased educational attention from teachers, while most nonwhite children are placed in a "slower learner" track, receiving less educational attention.

Our criminal justice system also has elements of institutional racism. The justice system is supposed to be fair and nondiscriminatory. The very name of the system, *justice*, implies fairness and equality. Yet in practice there is evidence of racism. Although African Americans constitute only about 12% of the population, they make up nearly 50% of the prison population. (There is considerable debate about the extent to which this is due to racism as opposed to differential crime rates by race.) The average prison sentence for murder and kidnapping is longer for African Americans than for whites. Nearly half of those sentenced to death are African Americans.[28] Police departments and district attorneys' offices are more likely to vigorously enforce the kinds of crimes committed by lower-income groups and minority groups than those by middle- and upper-class white groups. Poor people (a disproportionate number of nonwhites are poor) are substantially less likely to be able to post bail. As a result, they are forced to remain in jail until their trial, which may take months or sometimes more than a year to come up. Unable to afford the expenses of a well-financed defense (including the prices charged by the most successful criminal defense teams) they are more likely to be found guilty.

## EFFECTS AND COSTS OF DISCRIMINATION AND OPPRESSION

Racial discrimination is a barrier in our competitive society to obtaining the necessary resources to lead a contented and comfortable life. Being a victim of discrimination is another obstacle which has to be overcome. Being discriminated against due to race makes it more difficult to obtain adequate housing, financial resources, a quality education, employment, adequate health care and other services, equal justice in civil and criminal cases, and so on.

Discrimination also has heavy psychological costs. All of us have to develop a sense of identity—who we are and how we fit into a complex, swiftly changing world. Ideally, it is important that we form a positive self-concept and strive to obtain worthy goals. Yet, as we have noted before, according to Cooley's "looking glass self," our idea of who we are and what we are is largely determined by the way others relate to us.[29] When members of a minority group are treated by the majority group as if they are inferior, second-class citizens, it is substantially more difficult for such members to develop a positive identity. Thus, people who are the objects of discrimination encounter barriers to developing their full potential as human beings.

Young children of groups who are the victims of discrimination are likely to develop low self-esteem at an early age. African American children who have been subjected to discrimination have a preference for white dolls and white playmates over black.[30]

Pinderhughes has noted that the history of slavery and oppression of African Americans, combined with racism and exclusion, have produced a "victim system."

> A victim system is a circular feedback process that exhibits properties such as stability, predictability, and identity that are common to all systems. This particular system threatens self-esteem and reinforces problematic responses in communities, families and individuals. The feedback works as follows: Barriers to opportunity and education limit the chance for achievement, employment, and attainment of skills. This limitation can, in turn, lead to poverty or stress in relationships, which interferes with adequate performance of family roles. Strains in family roles cause problems in individual growth and development and limit the opportunities of families to meet their own needs or to organize to improve their communities. Communities limited in resources (jobs, education, housing, etc.) are unable to support families properly and the community all too often becomes an active disorganizing influence, a breeder of crime and other pathology, and a cause of even more powerlessness.[31]

Discrimination also has high costs for the majority group. It impairs intergroup cooperation and communication. Discrimination also is a factor in contributing to social problems among minorities—for example, high crime rates, emotional problems, alcoholism, and drug abuse—all of which have cost billions of dollars in social programs. Albert Szymanski argues that discrimination is a barrier to collective action (e.g., unionization) among whites and nonwhites (particularly people in the lower income classes) and, therefore, is a factor in perpetuating low-paying jobs and poverty.[32] Less affluent whites who could benefit from collective action are hurt.

The effects of discrimination are even reflected in life expectancy. The life expectancy of nonwhites is six years less than that of whites in the United States.[33] Nonwhites tend to die earlier than whites because they receive inferior health care, food, and shelter.

Finally, discrimination in the United States undermines some of our nation's political goals. Many other nations view us as hypocritical when we advocate human rights and equality. In order to make an effective argument for human rights on a worldwide scale, we must first put our own house in order by eliminating racial and ethnic discrimination. Few Americans realize the extent to which racial discrimination damages our international reputation. Nonwhite foreign diplomats to America often complain about being victims of discrimination, as they are mistaken for being members of American minority groups. With most of the nations of the world being nonwhite, our racist practices severely damage our influence and prestige.

## Background of Racial Groups
✗✗✗✗✗✗✗✗✗✗✗✗✗✗✗✗✗✗✗✗

The largest racial group in the United States is the white race, which is the majority group, both in numbers (about 76% of the population)[34] and in power. African Americans compose about 12% of the population,[35] and Latinos compose about 9% of the population.[36] The other nonwhite groups constitute about 3% of our population and primarily include Native Americans and people of Japanese, Chinese, and Filipino descent. There are also small numbers of the following nonwhite groups: Aleuts, Asian Indians, Eskimo, Hawaiians, Indonesians, Koreans, and Polynesians. In educational attainment, occupational status, and average income, most of these nonwhite groups are clearly at a disadvantage as compared with the white groups. (The two major nonwhite groups that now approach whites in socioeconomic status are Japanese Americans and Chinese Americans.)

### AFRICAN AMERICANS

The United States has always been a racist nation. Although our country's founders talked about freedom, dignity, equality, and human rights, the economy of the United States prior to the Civil War depended heavily on slavery.

Many slaves came from cultures that had well-developed art forms, political systems, family patterns, religious beliefs, and economic systems. However, because their culture was not European, slave owners viewed it as being of "no consequence" and prohibited slaves from practicing and developing their art, language, religion, and family life. For want of practice, their former culture soon died in the United States.

The life of a slave was harsh. Slaves were viewed not as human beings but as chattel to be bought and sold. Long, hard days were spent working in the field, with the profits of their labor going to their white owners. Whippings, mutilations, and hangings were commonly accepted white control practices. The impetus to enslave blacks was not simply racism; many whites believed that it was to their economic advantage to have a cheap supply of labor. Cotton growing, in particular, was thought to require a large labor force that was cheap and docile. Marriages between slaves were not recognized by the law, and slaves were often sold with little regard to marital and family ties. Throughout the slavery period and even afterward, African Americans were discouraged from demonstrating intelligence, initiative, or ambition. For a period of time it was even illegal to teach them to read and write.

Some authorities have noted that the opposition to the spread of slavery preceding the Civil War was due less to moral concern of human rights and equality than to the North's fears of competition from slave labor and the rapidly increasing migration of free blacks to the North and West.[37] Few whites at that time understood or believed in the principle of racial equality.

Following the Civil War, the federal government failed to develop a comprehensive program of economic and educational aid to African Americans. As a result, most of them returned to being economically dependent on the same planters in the South who had held them in bondage. Within a few years, laws were passed in the southern states prohibiting interracial marriages and requiring racial segregation in schools and public places.

A rigid caste system in the South hardened into a system of oppression known as "Jim Crow." The system prescribed how African Americans were supposed to act in the presence of whites, asserted white supremacy, embraced racial segregation, and denied political and legal rights to African Americans. Those who opposed Jim Crow were subjected to burnings, beatings, and lynchings. Jim Crow was used to "teach" African Americans to view themselves as inferior and to be servile and passive in interactions with whites.

World War II opened up new employment opportunities for African Americans, who migrated to the North in large numbers. Greater mobility afforded by wartime conditions led to upheavals in the traditional caste system. Awareness of disparity between the ideal and the real led many people to try to improve race relations, not only for domestic peace and justice, but also to answer criticism from abroad. With each gain in race relations, more African Americans were encouraged to press for their rights.

A major turning point in civil right history was the 1954 U.S. Supreme Court decision in *Brown* v. *Board of Education,* which ruled that racial segregation in public schools was unconstitutional. Since then there have been a number of organized efforts by both African Americans and certain segments of the white population to secure equal rights and opportunities for minorities. Attempts to change deeply entrenched racist attitudes and practices have produced much turmoil: the burning of our inner cities in the late 1960s,* the assassination of Martin Luther King, Jr., and clashes between militant black groups and the police. There have also been significant advances. Wide-ranging legislation has been passed, protecting civil rights in areas such as housing, voting, employment, and the use of public transportation and facilities. During the riots in 1968 the National Advisory Commission on Civil Disorders warned that our society was careening "toward two societies, one black, one white—separate and unequal."[38]

America today is not the bitterly segregated society that the riot commission envisioned. African Americans and whites now more often work together and lunch together—yet few really count each other as friends.

Four out of five African Americans now live in metropolitan areas, over half of them in our central cities.[39] American cities are still largely segregated, with African Americans primarily living in African-American neighborhoods. In recent years, the main thrust of the civil rights movement among African Americans has been economic equality. The economic gap between African Americans and whites continues to be immense. African-American families are three times as likely as white families to fall below the poverty line.[40] Since the early 1950s, the African-American unemployment rate has been approximately twice that for whites. Unemployment is an especially

---

*On April 4, 1968, Martin Luther King, Jr., was killed by a white assassin's bullet. His death helped trigger extensive rioting in forty cities; in many places whole blocks were burned down.

severe problem for African-American teenagers, whose rate of unemployment is substantially higher than for white youth and has run as high as 50 percent.[41]

We, as a nation, have come a long way since the U.S. Supreme Court's decision in 1954. But we still have a long way to go before we eliminate African American poverty and oppression. Living conditions in African American inner cities remain as bleak as they were when our inner cities erupted in the late 1960s. Dissatisfaction with living conditions in the 1960s led African Americans in many inner city areas to torch and burn down numerous buildings—buildings largely owned by white absentee landlords.

Two developments have characterized the socio-economic circumstances of African Americans in the past thirty years. A middle class has emerged that is better educated, better paid, and better housed than any group of African Americans that has gone before it. However, as comparatively well-off middle-class African Americans move to better neighborhoods, they leave behind those who are living in poverty. This group that has been left behind generates a disproportionate share of the social pathology that is associated with the inner city—including high rates of crime, unemployment, drug abuse, school dropouts, births outside of marriage, and families receiving public assistance.

Over half of all African-American children are being raised in single-parent families.[42] However, many African-American children living in single-parent families are living in family structures composed of some variation of the extended family. Many single-parent families move in with relatives during adversity, including economic adversity. In addition, African-American families of all levels rely on relatives to care for their children while they work.

While it is a reality that many African-American families are headed by single mothers, it would be a serious error to view such family structures as inherently pathological. A single parent with good parenting skills, along with a supportive extended family, can lead to healthy family functions.

Schaefer summarizes five strengths identified by the National Urban League that allow African American families to function effectively in a racist society:

1. *Strong kinship bonds.* Blacks are more likely than whites to care for children and the elderly in an extended family network.

2. *A strong work orientation.* Poor blacks are more likely to be working, and poor black families often include more than one wage earner.

3. *Adaptability of family roles.* In two-parent families, the egalitarian pattern of decision making is the most common. The self-reliance of black women who are the primary wage earners best illustrates this adaptability.

4. *A high achievement orientation.* Working-class blacks indicate a greater desire for their children to attend college than working-class whites. Even a majority of low-income African Americans desire to attend college.

5. *A strong religious orientation.* Black churches since the time of slavery have been the source of many significant grassroots organizations.[43]

Solomon notes that "black culture contains elements of 'mainstream' white culture, elements from traditional African culture, and elements from slavery, reconstruction and subsequent exposure to racism and discrimination."[44] Subcultures of African Americans have vocabularies and communication styles that differ from those of dominant white culture. Young children raised in these subcultures often have difficulty understanding the English spoken in schools. African-American dialects appear to be the result of a creolized form of English that was at one time spoken on Southern plantations by slaves.[45] (A *creolized* language is a speaker's native language that is based on two or more other languages.) Present-day African-American English is a combination of the linguistic remnants of its Southern plantation past and a reflection of the current African-American sociocultural situation. As such, it is important to recognize it as a dialect in its own right, not as just a distortion of standard English. Most adult African Americans are bicultural, being fluent in an African-American dialect and in standard English.

Religious organizations that are predominantly African American have tended to focus not only on spirituality, but also on social action efforts to combat racial discrimination. Many prominent African American leaders, such as Martin Luther King, Jr., and Jesse Jackson, have been members of the clergy. African-American churches have served to develop leadership skills. They have also functioned as social welfare organizations to meet basic needs, such as clothing, food, and shelter. These churches have been natural support systems for troubled black individuals and families.

Many African Americans have had the experience of being negatively evaluated by school systems, social welfare agencies, health care institutions, and the justice system. Because of their past experiences, African

Box 6.1 ◆◆◆◆◆◆◆◆◆◆◆◆◆◆◆◆◆◆◆◆◆◆

# The Africentric Perspective and Worldview

An emerging perspective on African-American culture is the *Africentric perspective*.[a] African-American culture has numerous components. It has elements from traditional African culture; elements from slavery, reconstruction, and subsequent exposure to racism and discrimination; and elements from "mainstream" white culture. The Africentric perspective acknowledges African culture, the expression of African beliefs, and the validity of African values, institution, and behavior. It recognizes that African Americans have retained, to some degree, a number of elements of African life and values.

The Africentric perspective asserts that the application of Eurocentric theories of human behavior to explain the behavior and ethos of African Americans is often inappropriate. Eurocentric theories of human behavior reflect concepts of human behavior that were developed in European and Anglo-American cultures. Eurocentric theorists have historically vilified people of African descent and other people of color. Such theorists have explicitly or implicitly claimed that people of African descent were pathological or inferior in their social, personality, or moral development.[b]

The origins of this denigration can be found in the slave trade, as slave traders and owners were pressed to justify the enslavement of Africans. The fallout of Eurocentric theories is the portrayal of the culture of African peoples as "uncivilized" and as having contributed practically nothing of value to world development and human history.

The Africentric perspective seeks to dispel the negative distortions about people of African ancestry by legitimizing and disseminating a *worldview* that goes back thousands of years and that exists in the hearts and minds of many people of African descent today. The concept of worldview involves one's perceptions of oneself in relation to other people, objects, institutions, and nature. It focuses on one's view of the world and one's role and place in it. The worldviews of African Americans are shaped by unique and important experiences, such as racism and discrimination, an African heritage, traditional attributes of the African-American family and community life, and a strong religious orientation.

The Africentric perspective also seeks to promote a worldview that will facilitate human and societal transformation toward moral, spiritual and humanistic ends and that seeks to persuade people of different cultural and ethnic groups that they share a mutual interest in this regard. The Africentric perspective rejects the idea that the individual can be understood separately from others in his or her social group. It emphasizes a collective identity which encourages sharing, cooperation, and social responsibility.

The Africentric perspective also emphasizes the importance of spirituality, which includes developing morally and attaining meaning and identity in life. The Africentric perspective views the major sources of human problems in the United States as oppression and alienation. Oppression and alienation are not only generated by prejudice and discrimination, but also by the European worldview that teaches people to see themselves primarily as material, physical beings seeking immediate gratification of their physical, material or sexual desires. This perspective further asserts that this European worldview discourages spiritual and moral development.

The Africentric perspective has been used to explain the origins of specific social problems. For example, violent crimes by youths are thought to be a result of the limited options and choices they have to advance themselves economically. Youths seek a life of street crime as a logical means to cope with, and protest against, a society that practices pervasive employment discrimination (as manifested by minimum wages, layoffs, lack of opportunities for education or training, and a wide gap between the rich and the poor). These youths calculate that they can make more money from a life of street crime than from attending college or starting a legitimate business with little start-up capital. The turn to a life of crime is also thought more likely to occur in a society employing the European worldview that deemphasizes spiritual and moral development, as individuals then have little or no awareness of collective and social responsibility.

The Africentric perspective values a more holistic, spiritual and optimistic view of human beings.

---

a. W. Devore and E.G. Schlesinger, *Ethnic-Sensitive Social Work Practice*, 4th ed. (Needham Heights, MA: Allyn and Bacon, 1996.)

b. J. H. Schiele, "Africentricity: An Emerging Paradigm in Social Work Practice," *Social Work* 41 (May, 1966): 284–94.

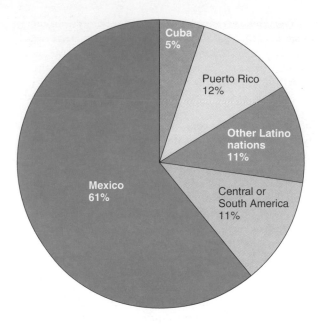

**Figure 6.1** *Percentage Distribution of Latinos in the United States by Type of Spanish Origin*

Source: Richard T. Schaefer, *Racial and Ethnic Groups,* 6th ed. (Boston: Little, Brown, 1996), p. 253.

Americans are likely to view such institutions with apprehension. Schools, for example, have erroneously perceived African Americans as being less capable of developing cognitive sills. These perceptions often become a self-fulfilling prophecy. If African-American children are expected to fail in school, teachers may put forth less effort in challenging them to learn. The children may then also put forth less effort to learn, resulting in a lower level of achievement.

## LATINOS

Latinos are Americans of Spanish origin. They constitute diverse groups bound somewhat together by their language, culture, and ties to Roman Catholicism. This broad categorization includes Mexican Americans (Chicanos), Puerto Ricans, Cubans, people from Central and South America and the West Indies, and others of Spanish origin (Figure 6.1). The Latino population is growing at five times the rate of the rest of the population.[46] There are three main reasons for this large growth: a tendency to have large families, a continual inflow of immigrants (particularly from Mexico), and the high proportion of Latinos in this country who are of childbearing age.

*Mexican Americans*   The largest Latino group in the United States is Mexican Americans. Although many Americans are unaware of the fact, Mexican Americans have had a long history of settlement and land ownership in what is now the United States. In the 1700s and 1800s there were a number of small Latino communities in what later became the American Southwest—in areas that have since gained statehood (including Texas, Arizona, New Mexico, and California). These early Latinos were generally small landholders. In the 1800s, whites moved into these regions, and competition for good land became fierce. Many Mexican Americans had their land taken away by large white-owned cattle and agricultural interests. Texas was once part of Mexico. In 1836 the settlers (including many of Spanish descent) staged a successful insurrection against the Mexican government and formed an independent republic. In 1845 Texas was annexed to the United States. As a consequence, many of the Mexican settlers became U.S. citizens.

Since the 1850s there has been a steady migration of Mexicans to the United States, with a number of immigrants entering this country illegally. The average income in Mexico is much lower than in the United States, so the quest for higher wages and a better life has lured many Mexicans to this country.

Relations between whites and Mexican Americans have on occasion become vicious and ugly. Similar to black/white confrontations, there have been many riots between whites and Mexican Americans.

Many Mexican Americans live in barrios (Spanish-speaking sections of U.S. cities that become ghettos) in such cities as Los Angeles, Denver, and Chicago. Although some are moving up in socioeconomic status, most are employed in low-paying occupations.

A smaller number of Mexican Americans are employed in temporary, seasonal work, largely on farms. Some migrate north in the summer to be farm laborers and return to the Southwest in the fall. In rate of acculturation and assimilation, these migrant workers are among the least "Americanized" of all ethnic groups.[47] They are reluctant to seek help from social agencies, partly because of their pride and partly because of language and cultural barriers.

An increasingly large segment of this ethnic group is becoming involved in the "Chicano" movement. Chicanos are Americans of Mexican origin who resent the stereotypes that demean Mexican Americans—particularly the image of laziness—because many are performing some of the hardest physical labor in our society. The origin of the word *Chicano* is not clear, but until the last generation it was a derogatory term whites used for Mexican Americans. Now the word and the people have come full circle, and *Chicano* has taken on a new, positive meaning. The Chicano movement asserts that social institutions must become more responsive to the needs of Chicanos. Chicano studies programs have been developed at a number of universities.

The civil rights activities of African Americans have provided encouragement for the Chicanos' militant stance. In addition, second- and third-generation Mexican Americans have fewer ties to Mexico than did their elders, and they are oriented more toward the majority American culture in terms of aspirations and goals. Yet, similar to African Americans, Mexican Americans generally have low-paying jobs, high rates of unemployment, and high levels of poverty. They also have high rates of infant mortality, low levels of educational attainment, and high levels of substandard housing. Their standard of living is no better than that of African Americans.

Chicano men, as contrasted to Anglo men, have been described as exhibiting greater pride in their maleness.[48] *Machismo*—a strong sense of masculine pride—is highly valued among Chicano men and is displayed by males to express dominance and superiority. Machismo is demonstrated differently by different people. Some may seek to be irresistible to women and to have a number of sexual partners. Some resort to weapons or fighting. Some interpret machismo to mean pride in one's manhood, honor, and ability to provide for one's family. Others boast of their achievements, even those that never occurred. Recent writers have noted that the feminist movement, urbanization, upward mobility, and acculturation are contributing to the decline of machismo.[49] Chicanos also tend to be more "familistic" than Anglos. Familism is the belief that the family takes precedence over the individual. Schaefer notes:

> Familism is generally regarded as good . . . as an extended family provides greater emotional strength at times of family crisis. The many significant aspects of familism include: (1) the importance of the *compadrazo* (godparent-godchild relationship); (2) the benefits of financial dependency on kin; (3) the availability of relatives as a source of advice; and (4) active involvement of the elderly within the family.[50]

In the 1970s and 1980s, César Chávez unionized migrant workers in California, organized several strikes, and led successful nationwide boycotts of fruit and vegetables picked by underpaid workers. Powerful white economic interests made several violent attempts to break these strikes. Chávez's campaigns provided an example and incentive for other collective action by Chicanos. The future is likely to see Chicanos becoming an increasingly powerful political force with which to be reckoned.

***Puerto Ricans*** After World War II large numbers of Puerto Ricans migrated to the mainland United States, largely because of population pressure and insufficient job opportunities on the island. Although they are found in all the states, they have settled mainly in New York City, New Jersey, Illinois, Florida, California, Pennsylvania, and Connecticut. Those migrating from Puerto Rico were from the higher socioeconomic classes in their home society. Although their earnings on the mainland are higher than in Puerto Rico, they have experienced lower job status than Anglos and many live in substandard housing.

For Puerto Ricans the Spanish culture has been dominant, but they have also been influenced by the Taino, American, African, and European cultures. In Puerto Rico, status is based on culture or class, not skin color, and interracial marriages are common. On entering the mainland United States, many Puerto Ricans, understandably, become puzzled by the greater emphasis given to skin color here.

The island of Puerto Rico is in a commonwealth arrangement with the United States, and citizenship was extended to Puerto Ricans living on the island by the Jones Act of 1917.[51] Because it is a commonwealth, its people have privileges and rights different from those on the mainland. They are subject to military service, selective service registration, and all federal laws. Yet they cannot vote in presidential elections and have no voting representation in Congress. Puerto Ricans pay a local income tax but no federal income tax. There is currently considerable controversy in Puerto Rico as to whether the island should seek independence from the United States, seek statehood, or remain a commonwealth.

Richard Schaefer summarizes the current status of Puerto Ricans:

> The Puerto Rican people share many problems with other subordinate groups: poor housing, inadequate health care, weak political representation, and low incomes. Like Chicanos, they have a language and cultural tradition at variance with that of Anglo society. The dominant society has removed some barriers to achievement by Spanish-speaking people in the United

States but public concerns grow about bilingual and bicultural programs. Chicanos and Puerto Ricans are poorly represented among key decision makers in both corporate offices and governmental agencies. Both Chicanos and Puerto Ricans, however, are close to or are actually in their home country, a situation that facilitates maintaining a rich cultural tradition. Hispanics' ability to maintain their original identity and solidarity means they have not been as compelled as European immigrants to assimilate White American customs and values.

The situation of Puerto Ricans is unique. Those on the island must resolve the issues of its political relationship to the mainland and the proper pace and emphasis of economic development. Those migrating to the mainland must adapt to a social definition of race different from that on the island and adjust to a system that leaves some Puerto Ricans in an ambiguous social position.[52]

*Cubans*  Most Cuban Americans are recent migrants to the United States. Many are political refugees, having fled Cuba following the takeover of the government by Fidel Castro in 1959. Many of these Cuban Americans are well educated and have managerial or professional backgrounds. Large numbers have settled in southern Florida, particularly in the Miami area.

In 1980, Castro opened the doors of his socialist island, and over 100,000 more Cubans fled to this country. Many of these latest arrivals were from the lower class, some of whom had been imprisoned in Cuba for a variety of crimes. (Castro apparently sent them to the United States to reduce the costs of the correctional system in Cuba.) Many of these most recent arrivals have also settled in southern Florida, where they have experienced confrontations with Euro-Americans, a high rate of crime, and other adjustment problems.

## NATIVE AMERICANS

When Columbus first came to America in 1492, there were about a million Native Americans grouped into more than 600 distinct societies.[53] Tribal wars between groups were common, and there were wide variations among tribes in customs, culture, lifestyles, language, and religious ceremonies. The whites gradually expanded their settlement, moving westward and slowly usurping native land. Colonists and pioneers adopted a policy that amounted to deliberate extermination of Native Americans. The saying "The only good Indian is a dead Indian" became popular. Whites

took their lands away, depleted the buffalo herds on which many tribes depended for survival, slaughtered tribes, and indirectly killed many others by leading forced marches in freezing weather and bringing diseases and famine.[54] Unable to mobilize a common defense, all native tribes were defeated by 1892.

In 1887, Congress passed the General Allotment Act, which empowered Congress unilaterally to revise treaties made with Native Americans. This action opened the way for land-hungry whites to take productive native land. From 1887 to 1928, the land held by Native Americans decreased from 137 million acres to 50 million acres, with most of the remaining property being some of the least productive real estate in the country.[55]

Contact with the white culture has undermined Native Americans' traditional living patterns. It has been said that "the buffalo are gone"—meaning that Native Americans can no longer sustain themselves through hunting and fishing. Segregation to reservations has further damaged their pride and sense of self-worth. Government programs now attempt to meet subsistence needs, but they also serve to pauperize Native Americans. Native Americans on reservations have high rates of suicide, alcoholism, illiteracy, poverty, homicide, child neglect, and infant mortality.

Earlier in this century, the plight of Native Americans was largely ignored because of their isolation on remote reservations. Through the Bureau of Indian Affairs (BIA) they received the most paternalistic treatment by the government to all minorities. For many years the BIA had programs designed to destroy Native American culture, religion, and language. Today the bureau has become a symbol of frustration and despair.[56]

In the 1960s and 1970s the plight of the Native Americans received national attention, and many whites became actively involved in their problems. In the past, films depicted the "glorious" victories of the whites over "savages." Now we know that early white settlers exploited the Native Americans by taking away their land and destroying their way of life.

During most of the twentieth century, Native Americans have not been very active in civil rights activities. However, in the 1960s and 1970s there were some organized efforts to make changes. Like African Americans and Chicanos, Native Americans staged some widely publicized demonstrations, such as one at Wounded Knee, South Dakota, in the 1970s.

In 1978 the U.S. Congress enacted the Indian Child Welfare Act (PL 95-608), which seeks to protect Native

American families and tribes. Recognizing that Native American children are the most important resource of the tribes, the act establishes federal standards for involuntary removal of Native American children from their families and provides a legal mechanism for tribes to assume jurisdiction over Native American children who have been involuntarily removed by state and local authorities. The act is therefore designed to promote the security and stability of Native American families and tribes. When a child is removed from a Native American family, the tribe must be notified, and preference must be given to placing the child with relatives, tribal members, or other Native American families. Despite this critical piece of federal legislation, many Native American children continue to be placed in foster care or for adoption with non-Native American families.[57] A significant hindrance to the implementation PL 95-608 is the lack of awareness of social workers concerning the act's mandates.

High rates of poverty and other social problems continue among Native Americans. Schaefer notes:

> Another enemy of the Native American people is their disunity: full-bloods are pitted against mixed-bloods, reservation residents against city dwellers, tribe against tribe, conservative against militant. This disunity reflects the diversity of cultural backgrounds and historical experiences represented by the people collectively referred to as Native Americans. This disunity is counterproductive when it comes to confronting a central government.[58]

Some tribes are taking legal action to recover land that was illegally usurped from them. The Nonintercourse Act of 1870 stated that any land transaction between Indians and others not approved by Congress is null and void. Many such transactions were not ratified by Congress. Some tribes have brought legal claims for land and for rights to minerals and rivers, and some of these claims have already been upheld. Two tribes in Maine have won their claim to half the land in the state. In Alaska, Native Americans have been awarded $1 billion and 40 million acres of land in compensation for illegal seizures of their territory in the past.[59]

In recent years, a number of Native American tribes have opened gambling casinos in many states. These casinos have become very popular and highly profitable. (Recent court decisions about federal treaties with Native Americans permit substantial tax breaks on these profits.) Many Native American tribes who were operating casinos are using some of the profits to fund social and educational programs for their tribal members.

## ASIAN AMERICANS

Asian Americans in the United States include the Japanese, Chinese, Filipinos, Koreans, Burmese, Indonesians, Guamanians, Samoans, South Vietnamese, Hmongs, and Thais. A large number of South Vietnamese immigrated to this country in the mid-1970s following the end of the Vietnam War. Contrary to a popular stereotype, Asians are not homogeneous. Each ethnic group has its own history, religion, language, and culture. These Asian American groups also differ in terms of group cohesion, levels of education, and socioeconomic status. Just as it is wrong to view all Europeans as being the same, it is an error to view all Asians as a single entity.

Like other disenfranchised groups, Asian Americans are victimized by discrimination. Immediate problems include housing, education, income maintenance, unemployment and underemployment, health care, and vocational training and retraining. Because of language and cultural barriers, many needy Asians (particularly new immigrants and the elderly) do not seek out services to which they are entitled. The two most prominent Asian groups in this country are Japanese Americans and Chinese Americans.

*Japanese Americans* Until 1900 few Japanese migrants came to the United States, partly because of legal restrictions against their migration and partly because of the unfriendly reception they received in this country.

After the turn of the century, Japanese migration increased. Immigrants settled primarily on the West Coast. By 1941 (when Peal Harbor was attacked), there were few distinctive Japanese American settlements outside the West Coast other than in New York City and Chicago. During World War II, Japanese Americans' loyalty was viewed with intense suspicion, and they severely felt the impact of prejudice, war hysteria, and the denial of certain civil rights. On March 2, 1942, the commander of the Western Theater of Operations established "relocation centers" (concentration camps) to which Japanese Americans living on the West Coast were sent. The confused policies of our nation during this war are indicated by the fact that 33,000 Japanese Americans served in the armed forces for the United States, while 110,000 Japanese Americans were confined in concentration camps.[60]

Not only were their civil rights violated, but they also were forced to sell their property. (In comparison, Americans of German or Italian descent were not similarly persecuted, even though the war was fought against Germany and Italy as well as Japan.) Following the war, the return of Japanese Americans to the West Coast met with some initial opposition, but among whites a counteraction soon developed that emphasized fair play and acceptance.

Since 1946, Japanese Americans have settled in other parts of the country, and their socioeconomic status is now approaching that of whites. Japanese Americans now have a higher level of educational achievement than white Americans.[61]

An act of Congress in 1988 granted $20,000 to each of the Japanese Americans who were interned during World War II. This act is a hopeful signal of greater intergroup cooperation in the future.

*Chinese Americans*   In the 1800s the Chinese were encouraged to immigrate to the United States to do mining, railroad construction, and farm work. These immigrants soon encountered hostility from some whites, particularly in Western states, because of their willingness to work for low wages. Their racial and cultural distinctiveness also made them targets for scapegoating, especially during periods of high unemployment. Charles Henderson et al. describe the extent to which Chinese Americans were subjected to racism during this time period:

> Racism against Asians is shown in the 1854 decision of the California Supreme Court in *The People* vs. *Hall*. The appellant, a white Anglo-American, had been convicted of murder upon the testimony of Chinese witnesses. Was such evidence admissible? The judge ruled that Asians should be ineligible to testify for or against a white man. This ruling opened the floodgate for anti-Chinese abuse, violence, and exploitation. Group murders, lynchings, property damage, and robbery of the Chinese were reported up and down the West Coast. Because of the harsh treatment of the Chinese, any luckless person was described as not having a "Chinaman's chance."[62]

In the early 1900s, Chinese Americans were concentrated largely on the West Coast, but since the 1920s they have tended to disperse throughout the nation. They have settled in large cities, and many live in Chinatowns in such cities as Los Angeles, San Francisco, New York, Boston, and Chicago.

The struggles of China against Japan before and during World War II brought about a more favorable image of Chinese Americans. Nevertheless, some discrimination continues. They have been subjected to less discrimination in Hawaii than on the mainland, as Hawaii is much closer to being a pluralist society than the rest of the country. Chinese Americans now have a higher level of educational achievement than white Americans.[63] Although Chinese Americans still tend to intramarry, they are now more likely to marry a member of another racial group than was true in the past. An increasing number are also moving out of Chinatowns to live in suburbs and in other areas.

## *Strategies for Advancing Social and Economic Justice*

Social justice is an ideal condition in which all members of a society have the same basic rights, protection, opportunities, obligations, and social benefits.[64] Economic justice is also an ideal condition, in which all members of a society have the same opportunities for attaining material goods, income, and wealth. A wide range of strategies have been developed to reduce racial and ethnic discrimination and oppression, thereby advancing social and economic justice. These strategies include the following: mass media appeals, strategies to increase interaction among the races, civil rights laws, activism, school busing, affirmative action programs, confronting racist remarks and actions, and developing minority-owned businesses.

### MASS MEDIA APPEALS

Newspapers, radio, and television at times present programs that are designed to explain the nature and harmful effects of prejudice and promote the harmony of humanity. Mass media are able to reach large numbers of people simultaneously. By expanding public awareness of the existence of discrimination and its consequences, the media may strengthen control over racial extremists. But mass media are limited in what they can do to change prejudiced attitudes and behaviors; they are primarily providers of information and seldom have a lasting effect in changing deep-seated prejudices through reeducation. Broadcasting platitudes such as "all people are brothers and sisters" and "prejudice is un-American" is not very effective. For one thing, highly prejudiced persons are often unaware of their own prejudices. Even if they are aware, they generally ignore mass media appeals as irrelevant or dismiss them as propaganda. It should be noted, however, that the mass media probably have had a significant impact in reducing discrimination through showing how nonwhites and whites work harmoniously in commercials, on news teams, and on TV shows.

## GREATER INTERACTION AMONG THE RACES

Increased contact among races is not in itself sufficient to alleviate racial prejudice. In fact, increased contact may, in some instances, highlight the differences and thus exacerbate suspicion and fear. Simpson and Yinger reviewed a number of studies and concluded that prejudice is likely to be increased when contacts are tension laden or involuntary.[65] Prejudice is apt to subside when individuals are placed in situations where they share characteristics in nonracial matters; for example, as co-workers, fellow soldiers, or classmates. Equal-status contacts, rather than inferior—superior-status contacts, are also more apt to reduce prejudice.[66]

## CIVIL RIGHTS LAWS

In the past thirty years, equal rights have been legislated in areas of employment, voting, housing, public accommodation, and education. A key question is how effective laws are in changing prejudice.

Proponents of civil rights legislation make certain assumptions. The first is that new laws will reduce discriminatory behavioral patterns. The laws define what was once "normal" behavior (discrimination) as now being "deviant" behavior. Through time it is expected that attitudes will change and become more consistent with the forced nondiscriminatory behavior patterns.

A second assumption is that the laws will be applied. Civil rights laws were enacted after the Civil War but were seldom enforced and gradually were eroded. Unfortunately, it is also true that some official will find ways of evading the intent of the law by eliminating only the extreme overt symbols of discrimination without changing other practices. Thus the enactment of a law is only the first step in the process of changing prejudiced attitudes and practices. However, as Martin Luther King, Jr., noted, "The law may not make a man love me, but it can restrain him from lynching me, and I think that's pretty important."

## ACTIVISM

Activism attempts to change the structure of race relations through direct confrontations with discrimination and segregation policies. Activism has thee types of politics: the politics of creative disorder, the politics of disorder, and the politics of escape.[67]

The *politics of creative disorder* operates on the edge of the dominant social system and includes school boycotts, rent strikes, job blockades, sit-ins (for example, at businesses that are alleged to discriminate), public marches, and product boycotts. This type of activism is based on the concept of nonviolent resistance. A dramatic illustration of nonviolent resistance began on December 1, 1955, when Rosa Parks of Montgomery, Alabama, refused to give up her seat on a bus to a white person (see Box 6.2).

The *politics of disorder* reflects alienation from the dominant culture and disillusionment with the political system. Those being discriminated against resort to mob uprisings, riots, and other violent strategies.

In 1969 the National Commission on Causes and Prevention of Violence reported that two hundred riots had occurred in the previous five years, when our inner cities erupted.[68] In the early 1980s there were again some riots in Miami and in other inner cities. In 1992 there were devastating riots in Los Angeles, following the acquittal of four white police officers who had been charged with using excessive force in arresting Rodney King, an African American. The brutal arrest had been videotaped. The focus of most of these riots has been minority group aggression against white-owned property.

The *politics of escape* engages in passionate rhetoric about how minorities are being victimized. However, because the focus is not on arriving at solutions, the rhetoric is not productive, except perhaps for providing an emotional release.

The principal value of activism or social protest seems to be the stimulation of public awareness of certain problems. The civil rights protests in the 1960s made practically all Americans aware of discrimination against nonwhites. Due to this awareness at least some of the discrimination has ceased, and race relations have improved. Continued protest beyond a certain (although indeterminate) point, however, appears to have little additional value.[69]

Box 6.2 ◆◆◆◆◆◆◆◆◆◆◆◆◆◆◆◆◆◆◆◆◆◆◆◆◆◆◆◆◆◆◆

## Rosa Parks' Act of Courage Sparked the Civil Rights Movement in 1955

On December 1, 1955, Rosa Parks was in a hurry. She had a lot of things to do. When the bus came to the boarding area where she was standing, she got on without paying attention to the driver. She rode the bus often and was aware of Montgomery's segregated seating law which required blacks to sit at the back of the bus.

In those days in the South, black people were expected to board the front of the bus, pay their fare, then get off and walk outside the bus to reboard on the back. But she noted the back was already crowded, standing room only, with black passengers even standing on the back steps of the bus. It was apparent to Rosa that it would be all but impossible to reboard at the back. Besides, bus drivers sometimes drove off and left black passengers behind, even after accepting their fares. Rosa Parks spontaneously decided to take her chances. She paid her fare at the front of the bus, then walked down the aisle and took a seat toward the back but still in the area reserved for whites. At the second stop after she boarded, a white man got on and had to stand.

The bus driver saw the white man standing and ordered Rosa Parks to move to the back. She refused, thinking "I want to be treated like a human being." Two police officers were called, and they arrested Rosa. She was taken to City Hall, booked, fingerprinted, jailed, and fined. Her arrest and subsequent appeal—all the way to the U.S. Supreme Court—were the catalyst for a year-long boycott of Montgomery, Alabama's buses by blacks, who composed 70 percent of the bus riders. The boycott inspired Martin Luther King, Jr., to become involved. The boycott ended when the Supreme Court declared Montgomery's segregated seating laws unconstitutional. Rosa Parks' unplanned defiance of the segregated seating law sparked the Civil Rights Movement. This Civil Rights Movement has not only promoted social and economic justice for African Americans, but has also served to inspire other groups to organize to advocate for their civil rights. These groups include other racial and ethnic groups, women, the elderly, persons with a disability, and gays and lesbians.

*Source:* Marie Ragghianti, "I Wanted to Be Treated Like a Human Being," *Parade Magazine,* Jan. 19, 1992, 8-9

## SCHOOL BUSING

Housing patterns in many large metropolitan centers have led to de facto segregation; that is, blacks and certain other nonwhites live in one area, and whites live in another. This segregation has affected educational opportunities for nonwhites. Nonwhite areas have fewer financial resources; as a result, the educational quality is often substantially lower than in white areas. In the past three decades, courts in a number of metropolitan areas have ordered that a certain proportion of nonwhites must be bused to schools in white areas and that a certain proportion of whites must be bused to schools in nonwhite areas. The objectives are twofold: to provide equal educational opportunities and to reduce racial prejudice through interaction. In some areas school busing has become accepted and appears to be meeting the stated objectives. In other areas, however, the approach is highly controversial and has exacerbated racial tensions. Busing in these areas is claimed to be highly expensive; to destroy the concept of the "neighborhood school" in which the facility serves as a recreational, social, and educational center of the community; and to result in lower-quality education. A number of parents in these areas feel so strongly about busing that they send their children to private schools. In addition, some have argued that busing increases "white flight" from neighborhoods where busing has been ordered.[70] As a result, in some communities, busing programs that once carried black students to white schools now simply move them from a black neighborhood to a predominantly black school system.[71]

Busing children a long distance is very costly and uses funds that could otherwise be spent to improve the quality of education. Busing lessens local control and interest in schools, and it makes it less practical for parents to become involved in school affairs because the school is less accessible.

Surveys indicate a majority of Americans (including a large number of African Americans) oppose busing for integration purposes.[72] The main reason for the growing opposition toward busing is that it often has not raised educational achievements of students of color.[73] As a result, it is unlikely there will be a resurgence of political support for expanding efforts to promote busing for integration purposes.

School busing to achieve integration was vigorously pursued by the court system and the Justice Department in the 1970s. In 1981, the Reagan administration stated that it would be much less active in advocating busing as a vehicle to achieve integration. The Bush and Clinton administrations have also been fairly inactive in promoting school busing. In the past decade there has been less emphasis in many communities on using busing to achieve integration. In 1991 the U.S. Supreme Court ruled that busing to achieve integration, when ordered, need not be continued indefinitely. The ruling allows communities to end court-ordered busing by convincing a judge they have done everything reasonable to eliminate discrimination against African Americans. School busing for integration purposes is discussed further in Chapter 12.

## AFFIRMATIVE ACTION PROGRAMS

Affirmative action programs provide preferential hiring and admission requirements (for example, admission to medical schools) for minority applicants. The programs apply to all minority groups, including women. They require employers to (a) make active efforts to locate and recruit qualified minority applicants; and (b) in certain circumstances, have hard quotas under which specific numbers of minority members must be accepted to fill vacant positions (for example, a university with a high proportion of white, male faculty members may be required to fill half of its faculty vacancies with women and members of other minority groups). Affirmative action programs require that employers demonstrate, according to a checklist of positive measures, that they are not guilty of discrimination.

A major dilemma with affirmative action programs is that preferential hiring and quota programs create reverse discrimination, in which qualified majority group members are sometimes arbitrarily excluded. There have been several successful lawsuits involving reverse discrimination. The best-known case to date has been that of Alan Bakke, who was initially denied admission to the medical school at the University of California, Davis, in 1973. He alleged reverse discrimination because he had higher grades and higher scores on the Medical College Admissions Test than several minority applicants who were admitted under the university's minorities quota policy. In 1978 his claim was upheld by the U.S. Supreme Court in a precedent-setting decision.[74] The Court ruled that strict racial quotas are unconstitutional, but it did not rule out the use of race as one among many criteria in making admissions decisions.

Charles Henderson et al. summarize some of the views of whites and minority groups about affirmative action:

> The minority worker in white agencies often asks himself: "Why have I been hired?" . . . The worker may meet resistance from white colleagues if he or she is a product of "affirmative action," seen by some white people as simply "reverse discrimination." Whites may be quick to say that competence is what counts. Blacks perceive this as saying that they are not competent. Considering the many ways in which whites have acquired jobs, blacks wonder why competence is now suggested as the only criterion for employment. For every white professional who may dislike affirmative action to compensate for past exclusions and injustices, there is a black professional who feels that it is tragic that organizations have had to be forced to hire minorities.[75]

Supporters of affirmative action programs note that the white majority expressed little concern about discrimination when its members were the beneficiaries instead of the victims. They also assert that there is no other way to make up rapidly for past discrimination against minorities, many of whom may presently score slightly lower on qualification tests simply because they did not have the opportunities and the quality of training that the majority group members have had.

Affirmative action programs raise delicate and complex questions about achieving equality through preferential hiring and admissions policies for minorities. Yet no other means has been found to end obvious discrimination in hiring and admissions.

Gaining admission to educational programs and securing well-paying jobs are crucial elements in the quest for integration. The history of immigrant groups that have "made it" (such as the Irish, the Japanese, and the Italians) suggests that equality will be achieved only when minority-group members gain middle- and upper-class status and thus become an economic and political force to be reckoned with. The dominant groups then become pressured into modifying their norms, values, and stereotypes. For this reason, a number of authorities have noted that the elimination of economic discrimination is a prerequisite for achieving equality and harmonious race relations.[76] Achieving educational equality among races is also crucial because lower educational attainments lead to less prestigious jobs, lower incomes, lower living standards, and the perpetuation of racial inequalities from one generation to the next.

In the mid-1990s the future of affirmative action became a hotly debated national issue. In the 1996 presidential campaign, several Republican presidential hopefuls urged that affirmative action programs be ended. A *Wall Street Journal/NBC News* survey found that two out of three Americans were opposed to affirmative action.[77] The assault on affirmative action gathered strength from a slow-growth economy, stagnant, middle-class incomes, and corporate downsizing, all of which make the question of who gets hired—or fired—more volatile. Minority candidates who receive positions that are perceived by other workers as being the result of affirmative action are often viewed with suspicion by the other workers—which sometimes results in toxic tension in the workplace. Critics claim that such tension has not brought us a color-blind society (which was the hope) but instead has brought us an extremely color-conscious society. Critics assert that, as a result, affirmative action is now a highly politicized and painful remedy that has stigmatized many of those it was meant to help. Affirmative action is now perceived by many as a system of preferences for the unqualified. Critics further assert that while affirmative action may have been necessary thirty years ago to make sure that minority candidates received fair treatment to counter the social barriers to hiring and admission that stemmed from centuries of unequal treatment, such programs are no longer needed. They assert it is wrong to discriminate against white males for the sole reason of making up for the injuries that somebody's great-grandfather may have done to somebody else's great-grandfather. They assert it is wrong for the daughter of a wealthy African-American couple to be given preference in employment over the son of a homeless alcoholic who happens to be white.

Supporters of affirmative action argue that "if we abandon affirmative action, we return to the old boys' network." They assert that affirmative action has helped a number of women and people of color to attain a good education and higher paying positions, and thereby to remove themselves from the ranks of the poor. They also assert that in a society where racist and sexist attitudes remain, it is necessary to have affirmative action in order to give women and people of color a fair opportunity to attain a quality education and well-paying jobs.

In 1996, voters in the state of California passed Proposition 209, which explicitly rejects the idea that women and other minority group members should get special consideration when applying for jobs,

government contracts, or university admission. This affirmative action ban became law in California in August 1997. In addition, a number of lawsuits have been filed objecting to reverse discrimination. If the courts rule in favor of those filing the lawsuits, the power of affirmative action programs will be sharply reduced. In November 1997, the U.S. Supreme Court rejected a challenge to the California law that ended racial and gender preferences in that state. This Supreme Court action clears the way for other states and cities to ban affirmative action.

Is there a middle ground for the future of affirmative action? Zuckerman recommends:

> The vast majority of Americans would probably accept a return to the original notion of affirmative action—an aggressive outreach to minorities to make sure they have a fair shot. They would probably see a social benefit in accepting that racial justice might be relevant in a tiebreaker case, or might even confer a slight advantage. The goal must be a return to policies based on evenhandedness for individuals rather than for groups. Then employers can concentrate on whether a minority applicant is the right person for the job rather than being moved by whether the applicant looks litigious. All employees could take it for granted that they had a fair shot.[78]

## CONFRONTING RACIST AND ETHNIC REMARKS AND ACTIONS

Race-related jokes and sarcastic remarks help shape and perpetuate racist stereotypes and prejudices. It is important that both whites and nonwhites tactfully but assertively indicate they do not view such remarks as humorous or appropriate. It is also important that people tactfully and assertively point out the inappropriateness of racist actions by others. Such confrontations make explicit that subtle racist remarks and actions are discriminatory and harmful, which has a consciousness-raising effect. Gradually, it is expected that such confrontations will reduce racial prejudices and actions.

Noted author, lecturer, and abolitionist Frederick Douglass stated:

> Power concedes nothing without a demand—it never did, and it never will. Find out just what people will submit to, and you've found out the exact amount of injustice and wrong which will be imposed upon them. This will continue until they resist, either with words, blows, or both. The limits of tyrants are prescribed by the endurance of those whom they oppress.[79]

## MINORITY-OWNED BUSINESSES

Many people aspire to run their own business. Running one's own business is particularly attractive to many members of minority groups. It means an opportunity to increase one's income and wealth. It is also a way to avoid some of the racial and ethnic discrimination that occurs in the work world, such as the "glass ceilings" that block the promotion of qualified minority workers.

Since the 1970s, federal, state and local governments have attempted to assist minority-owned businesses in a variety of ways. There are programs that have provided low-interest loans to minority-owned businesses. There are set-aside programs that stipulate that a minimum proportion of government contracts, usually 10 to 30 percent, must be awarded to minority-owned businesses. Some large urban areas have created enterprise zones, which encourage employment and investment in blighted neighborhoods through the use of tax breaks. The number of minority-owned businesses has slowly been increasing, yet only a small fraction of the total number of people classified as minorities has benefited from government support of minority-owned businesses.

## The Future of American Race and Ethnic Relations

◆◆◆◆◆◆◆◆◆◆◆◆◆◆◆◆◆◆◆◆◆

The 1980s and 1990s were a struggle for minorities as they tried to hold onto past gains in the face of reactions against minority rights. Vowing to take "big government" off the back of the American people and to strengthen the economy by giving businesses the incentive to grow and produce, President Reagan and his administration (1980–88) largely removed the federal government from its traditional role as initiator and enforcer of programs to guarantee minority rights. President Bush and his administration (1988–92) continued to follow a similar strategy. The federal government under the Reagan and Bush administrations asserted that private businesses were in the best position to correct the problems of poverty and discrimination. (Because businesses generally profit from paying low wages, most companies in the 1980s and early 1990s did not aggressively seek to improve the financial circumstances and living conditions of minorities.) Perhaps because of the federal government's shift in policies, minorities were less active in the 1980s and 1990s (as compared to the 1960s and 1970s) in using the strategy of activism. In the 1980s and 1990s, minority groups were experiencing difficulties in maintaining the gains they had achieved two decades earlier in the job market through affirmative action and Equal Employment Opportunity programs. Bill Clinton, elected president in 1992, ran on a platform that promised a more active role by the federal government in promoting social and economic justice for all racial and ethnic groups in this country.

Bill Clinton's views on resolving social problems are consistent with a moderate (middle-of-the-road) to liberal orientation. His liberal proposals that would have benefited populations-at risk included a universal health insurance program for all Americans and significantly expanded educational and training programs for individuals on welfare in order to help them become self-supporting.

The move toward liberalism in the early 1990s may, however, have been short lived. In the congressional elections of 1994, the Republicans (most with a conservative orientation) won majority control of both the Senate and the House of Representatives. (This was the first time in forty years that Republicans held a majority in the House.) These Republicans have a conservative political agenda that includes such components as shifting spending from crime prevention to prison construction, eliminating affirmative action programs, reducing spending for many social welfare programs, and reducing the amount of taxes paid by high-income individuals. Such proposals, if enacted into law, will probably widen the income gap between the rich and the poor, and result in a severe reduction of services to populations-at-risk.

It is clear that minorities will assertively, and sometimes aggressively, pursue a variety of strategies to change racist attitudes and actions. Counteractions by certain segments of the white dominant society are also likely to occur. (Even in the social sciences, every action elicits a reaction.) For example, in recent years there has been increased membership in organizations that advocate white supremacy (such as the Ku Klux Klan).

Minorities have been given the hope of achieving equal opportunity and justice, and it is clear that they will no longer submit to a subordinate status. Obviously we will see continued struggles to achieve racial equality.

What will be the pattern of race relations in the future? Milton Gordon has outlined three possible

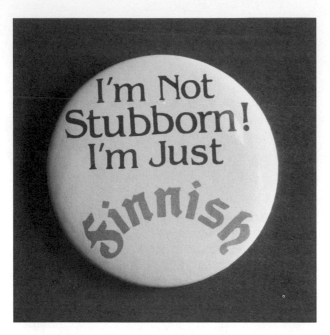

*Many racial and ethnic groups take pride in their culture and heritage.*

patterns of intergroup relations: Anglo-conformity, the melting pot, and cultural pluralism:

> *Anglo-conformity* assumes the desirability of maintaining modified English institutions, language, and culture as the dominant standard in American life. In practice, "assimilation" in America has always meant Anglo-conformity, and the groups that have been most readily assimilated have been those that are ethnically and culturally most similar to the Anglo-Saxon group.
>
> The *melting pot* is, strictly speaking, a rather different concept, which views the future American society not as a modified England but rather as a totally new blend, both culturally and biologically, of all the various groups that inhabit the United States. In practice, the melting pot has been of only limited significance in the American experience.
>
> *Cultural pluralism* implies a series of coexisting groups, each preserving its own tradition and culture, but each loyal to an overarching American nation. Although the cultural enclaves of some immigrant groups, such as the Germans, have declined in importance in the past, many other groups, such as the Italians, have retained a strong sense of ethnic identity and have resisted both Anglo-conformity and inclusion in the melting pot.[80]

Members of some European ethnic groups (such as the British, French, and Germans) have assimilated the dominant culture of the United States and are now integrated. Other European ethnic groups (such as the Irish, Italians, Polish, and Hungarians) are now nearly fully assimilated and integrated.

Cultural pluralism appears to be the form that race and ethnic relations are presently taking. There has been a renewed interest on the part of a number of ethnic European Americans in expressing their pride in their own customs, religions, and linguistic and cultural traditions. We see slogans like "Kiss me, I'm Italian," "Irish Power," and "Polish and Proud." African Americans, Native Americans, Latinos, and Asian Americans are demanding entry into mainstream America—but not assimilation. They want to coexist in a plural society while preserving their own traditions and cultures. This pride is indicated by slogans such as "Black is beautiful" and "Red power." These groups are finding a source of identity and pride in their own cultural backgrounds and histories.

Some progress has been made toward ending discrimination since the *Brown* v. *Board of Education* Supreme Court decision in 1954. Yet equal opportunity for all people in the United States is still only a dream, as Martin Luther King, Jr., noted in his famous speech in 1963:

> I say to you today, my friends, though, even though we face the difficulties of today and tomorrow, I still have a dream. It is a dream deeply rooted in the American dream. I have a dream that one day this nation will rise up, live out the true meaning of its creed: "We hold these truths to be self-evident, that all men are created equal."
>
> I have a dream that one day on the red hills of Georgia sons of former slaves and the sons of former slave-owners will be able to sit down together at the table of brotherhood. I have a dream that one day even the state of Mississippi, a state sweltering with the heat of injustice, sweltering with the heat of oppression, will be transformed into an oasis of freedom and justice.
>
> I have a dream that my four little children will one day live in a nation where they will not be judged by the color of their skin, but by the content of their character.
>
> When we allow freedom to ring—when we let it ring from every city and every hamlet, from every state and every city, we will be able to speed up that day when all of God's children, black men and white men, Jews and Gentiles, Protestants and Catholics, will be able to join hands and sing in the words of the old Negro spiritual, "Free at last, Free at last, Great God Almighty, We are free at last."[81]

# Summary

XXXXXXXXXXXXXXXXXXXXX

Our country has always been racist and ethnocentric, but there has been progress in the past few decades in alleviating prejudice and discrimination. Yet we cannot relax. Discrimination continues to have tragic consequences for its victims. Individuals who are targets of discrimination are excluded from certain types of employment, educational and recreational opportunities, certain residential housing areas, membership in certain religious and social organizations, certain political activities, access to some community services, and so on. Discrimination is also a serious obstacle to developing a positive self-concept and has heavy psychological and financial costs. Internationally, racism and ethnocentrism severely damage the United States' credibility in promoting human rights.

Race is primarily a social rather than a biological concept. No "racial" group has any unique or distinctive genes. A social definition is based on the way members of a society classify each other by physical characteristics.

Prejudice is an attitude whereas discrimination involves actions. Discrimination is often based on prejudice, although either may exist independently of the other. Oppression is the unjust or cruel exercise of authority or power.

Racial and ethnic discrimination is largely a social problem of whites, who tend to be the primary discriminators in power. (This does not mean, however, that only whites must work to end discrimination; the effort must be an interracial one.)

Theories about the sources of discrimination and oppression include: projection, frustration-aggression, insecurity and inferiority, authoritarianism, historical explanations, competition and exploitation, socialization processes, and the belief that there is only one true religion. Institutionalized racism is pervasive in our society and involves discrimination that is built into societal institutions, such as the legal system, politics, employment practices, health care, and education.

There are numerous white and nonwhite groups in our nation, each with a unique culture, language, and history and with special needs. This uniqueness needs to be understood and appreciated if we are to progress toward racial and ethnic equality.

Strategies for advancing social and economic justice include mass media appeals, increased interaction among races, civil rights legislation, protests and activism, school busing, affirmative action programs, minority-owned businesses, and confronting racist and ethnic remarks and actions.

Three possible patterns of intergroup race relations in the future are Anglo-conformity, melting pot, and cultural pluralism. Cultural pluralism is the form that race and ethnic relations are presently taking and may well take in the future.

# CHAPTER 7

## *Sexism*

Women who work full time are paid only about three-fourths as much as men who work full time.[1] Jobs held mainly by women (such as nurse or elementary school teacher) are paid at rates that average 20 percent less than those for equivalent jobs held mainly by men.[2] The average woman college graduate is paid about the same as the average male high school graduate.[3] The average working white woman is paid less than the average working African-American man, and the average working African-American woman (subjected to double discrimination) earns least of all.[4] In families, with female householder, no spouse present, 37 percent live below the poverty line, compared to 12 percent of all families.[5]

This chapter:

♦ Presents a history of sex roles and sexism

♦ Defines sexual harassment

♦ Examines whether there is a biological basis for sexism and describes traditional sex-role expectations and socialization practices

♦ Examines the consequences of sexism on males as well as females

♦ Describes the sex-role revolution in our society and presents strategies for achieving sexual equality

## The History of Sexism

In almost every known society, women have a lower status than men.[6] Women have been bound by more social restrictions and have consistently received less recognition for their work than men. Women have been regarded differently from men—not only biologically but emotionally, intellectually, and psychologically. Double standards have existed for dating, marriage, and social and sexual conduct.

Most traditional religious doctrines (including Judeo-Christian, Hindu, and Islamic) ascribe an inferior status to women. This tradition continues today in most countries, even though women tend to attend places of worship more often, hold firmer religious beliefs, pray more often, and be more active in religious programs.[7] Many societies have concluded that it is divinely ordained that women shall play a secondary, supportive role to men. In many Christian religions, women cannot become ministers or priests. Some Orthodox Jewish men offer a daily prayer of thanks for *not* being a woman. In almost all religious sectors, God is referred to as "He."

So-called primitive hunting and gathering societies provide insight into the processes that have resulted in women being assigned a lower status. Such societies usually lived in small tribes consisting of several married couples and their dependents. Men generally were the hunters, and women were the gatherers (of nuts, plants, and other foods). There are several explanations for this differentiation. Males tended to be better suited to hunting as they were physically stronger and could run faster. Also, the infant mortality rate was very high in these tribes, so it was necessary for the women to be pregnant or nursing throughout most of their childbearing years to maintain the size of the tribe. The need to tend children largely prevented women from leaving the camp for days at a time to hunt large game. Even though women often gathered more food than men could obtain through hunting, the male's hunting activities were viewed as being more prestigious—perhaps the first example of sexism.

Because women were pregnant or nursing infants for much of their adult lives, they stayed at home, where the tasks of raising children, cooking, serving, and washing became their responsibilities. Thus these sex-role distinctions came to be seen as "natural" and practical behavior for men and women.

Gradually, more behavior patterns were added to these sex-role distinctions. Because they were trained at hunting, men came to be recognized as the defenders of their tribe against attack from other tribes. Child-rearing patterns emerged to teach boys to be aggressive leaders. Girls, on the other hand, were assigned supportive roles and taught to be more passive and dependant.

Before the Industrial Revolution, practically all societies had come to assign distinct roles to men and women. Women were generally involved in domestic and child-rearing activities, whereas men were involved in what were then considered to be the productive functions (such as hunting and providing economic support) and protective functions for the family. The use of the term *productive* indicates the higher status assigned to the male role. In actuality, the roles of women were often as, or more, "productive" in completing the essential tasks that needed to be performed. It should be noted that in preindustrial societies women were also involved in food producing and economic support, such as making clothes, growing and harvesting garden crops, and helping on the farm.

# The Ideal Wife, According to Buddhism

**M**ost traditional religions assert that women should have a submissive and supportive role to men. For example, Buddhism asserts the ideal wife should be:

> . . . like a maid-servant. She serves her husband well and with fidelity. She respects him, obeys his commands, has no wishes of her own, no ill-feeling, no resentment, and always tries to make him happy.[a]

---

a. *The Teaching of Buddha* (Tokyo, Japan: Kosaido Printing Co., 1966), 448.

---

However, their specific responsibilities were often viewed as being inferior and requiring fewer skills.

During the nineteenth century the Industrial Revolution brought about dramatic changes in sex roles. Men, instead of working on small farms, went outside the home to work in factories or other settings to provide economic support. Women's economic role declined, as they were less likely to perform economically productive tasks. The roles of women became increasingly defined as child rearing and housework. Yet for several reasons the amount of time required to perform these roles declined. Families had fewer children. With mass education, older children went to school. Gradually, labor-saving devices and mass production reduced the time needed to perform certain domestic tasks (for example, baking bread, canning vegetables, and washing). As their traditional roles began to change, some women began to pursue outside employment, which traditionally had been the domain of men. With these changes, the distinctions between sex roles began to blur.

## THE FIGHT FOR WOMEN'S RIGHTS

The struggle for women's rights in America has been going on for nearly two centuries. In the early nineteenth century, women working for the abolition of slavery became aware that they too were denied many rights, such as voting. (An 1840 antislavery conference even refused to seat women, although male delegates gave impassioned speeches about the moral rightness of ending slavery.)

In 1848 two feminists, Susan B. Anthony and Elizabeth Cady Stanton, organized the first women's rights caucus, held in New York.[8] They demanded suffrage (the vote for women) and the reform of many laws that openly discriminated against women. It took over seventy years to pass the Nineteenth Amendment to the Constitution, which in 1920 gave the vote to women. The movement was marked by fierce controversy and jailings of feminist militants. Unfortunately, the struggles led many women leaders to believe that sexual equality went hand in hand with the right to vote. After the 1920 "passage," the women's movement was virtually dormant for forty years.

In the early 1900s modern birth-control techniques became available, which granted women greater freedom from the traditional roles of child rearing and housework.

During World War II, for the first time large numbers of women were employed outside the home to take the places of men who had been drafted into the military. At this time over 38 percent of all women sixteen years old and over were employed, causing a further blurring of traditional sex roles.[9]

In the 1960s there was a resurgence of interest in sex-role inequality. This occurred for a variety of reasons. The civil rights movement had a consciousness-raising effect in that people became more sensitive to the general issue of inequality. The movement to curb racial discrimination through social action also served as a model to a number of women concerned with alleviating sexual discrimination. More women were attending college and thereby becoming more aware of inequalities. As women moved into new occupational positions, they became increasingly conscious of discriminatory practices. There was an explosion of research suggesting sex-role differences were not innately determined but were in fact the result of socialization patterns, and that the effects of such sex roles were often discriminatory against women.

One such study was conducted in 1955 by Money, Hampson, and Hampson on hermaphrodites.[10] A hermaphrodite is a person born with both male and female sexual characteristics but is called either a male or a female at birth and then related to as being of that labeled sex. These researchers did *not* find a significant correlation between physical characteristics and hermaphrodites' own feelings about their sexual identities. Hermaphrodites were fulfilling the sex-role expectations of their labeled gender, although their observable

## Female Genital Mutilation: An Extreme Example of Sexism

Female circumcision, or more accurately female genital mutilation (FGM), is commonplace among women in more than half of Africa's countries and in parts of the Middle East. The details of FGM vary somewhat from culture to culture and from region to region, but the basics are the same.

Shannon Brownlee and Jennifer Seter describe FGM as follows:

Some time between infancy and adulthood, all or part of a girl's external genitalia is cut away with a knife or razor blade, usually with no anesthetic. In most cases, the clitoris and the labia minora are removed. In the most extreme form, known as infibulation, the external labia are also scraped and stitched together with thread or long thorns, leaving only a tiny opening for urine and menstrual blood. The opening must be widened on the woman's wedding night.

The pain of this "surgery" lasts far longer then the operation itself. Many of the 85 million to 110 million women who have endured FGM suffer ill effects, ranging from reduced or lost sexual sensation to infections, persistent pain, painful intercourse, infertility, and dangerous childbirth. The purpose is to diminish sexual appetite in order to maintain a girl's virginity—and thus her marriageability.[a]

Anthropologists believe that the first clitoridectomies were, like chastity belts, a means for husbands to ensure that their children were truly their own, since FGM reduces a woman's interest in sex and thereby the chances that she'll be interested in sex with other men. Now, young women in many African countries who have not undergone the procedure are shunned as oversexed, unmarriageable, and unclean. Currently, FGMs are usually performed by select older women, who are held in high esteem in their societies.

Although feminist organizations in the Western world tend to view FGM as an extreme form of gender oppression, most international human rights organizations have been slow to advocate against the practice. Some observers argue that people living in one culture should not interfere with other people's cultural practices.

a. Shannon Brownlee and Jennifer Seter, "In the Name of Ritual," *U.S. News & World Report*, Feb. 7, 1994, 56–58.

---

sex characteristics often tended to place them in the "other" category. This research raised questions about the biological determination of sex roles.

Other studies have found dramatic differences in socialization patterns between males and females. Boys are given more sports equipment and task-oriented toys (like construction sets) to play with, whereas girls are given dolls and other toys relating to marriage and parenthood.[11] During the first few months of life, girls receive more distal stimulation (looking and talking) from their parents, whereas boys receive more proximal stimulation (rocking and handling).[12] Fathers tend to play more aggressively with sons than with daughters. American sex-role socialization practices are not universal, however. For example, in some Middle Eastern societies males are reared to be more emotional and sensitive than females, whereas females tend to be more impassive and practical.[14] In Sweden most heavy-machinery operators are women.[15] In Russia most physicians are women.[16]

In her 1963 book *The Feminine Mystique*, Betty Friedan provided the ideological base for the resurgence of the women's movement.[17] By the term *feminine mystique*, Friedan referred to the negative self-concept, lack of direction, and low sense of self-worth among women. The book served as a rallying point for women and in 1966 led Friedan to form the National Organization for Women (NOW). Today, NOW is the largest women's rights group in this country and an influential political force. NOW and other women's groups have been working to end sexual discrimination, to achieve sexual equality, to end sexual double standards, and to improve women's self-identity.

## WOMEN'S RIGHTS IN THE LAW

The Civil Rights Act of 1964, primarily intended to end racial discrimination, also prohibited discrimination on the basis of sex. However, a number of states have laws that discriminate against women and reinforce prejudices against them. For example, some states still have statutes that assign longer sentences to women than men for the same crimes, on the assumption that female offenders require more rehabilitation.[18] Conversely, many states treat women offenders more leniently than men on the assumption

## Traditional Stereotypes of a Businessman and a Businesswoman

- ◆ He's aggressive; she's pushy.

- ◆ He's good at details; she's picky.

- ◆ He loses his temper because he's so involved in his job; she's bitchy.

- ◆ When he's depressed (or hungover), everyone tiptoes past his office; when she's moody, it's just her time of the month.

- ◆ He follows through; she doesn't know when to quit.

- ◆ He's confident; she's conceited.

- ◆ He stands firm; she's hard.

- ◆ He has judgments; she's prejudiced.

- ◆ He's a man of the world; she's been around.

- ◆ He drinks because of excessive job pressure; she's a lush.

- ◆ He isn't afraid to say what he thinks; she's mouthy.

- ◆ He exercises authority diligently; she's power-mad.

- ◆ He's close-mouthed; she's secretive.

- ◆ He's a stern taskmaster; she's hard to work for.

- ◆ He climbed the ladder to success; she slept her way to the top.

that women require the state's protection—for example, in many states women must volunteer for jury duty or they will not be called.[19] Such laws and practices are forms of reverse discrimination.

In 1972 the Equal Rights Amendment (ERA) received congressional approval but required ratification by three-fourths of the states (thirty-eight) to become the Twenty-Seventh Amendment to the Constitution. According to ERA, "Equality of rights under the law shall not be denied or abridged by the United States or any state on account of sex." Time ran out on ERA in 1982 when, after ten years of extensive political action, it narrowly failed to gain support of enough states to be ratified.

Emotions ran high on both sides of the question of ERA ratification. Proponents asserted ERA would eliminate numerous state laws that are discriminatory toward women.[20] Opponents argued that passage of ERA would mean that women could be drafted into the armed forces; that women would lose preferential treatment in divorce actions; that parents would be equally liable for alimony, child support, and spouse support; that certain labor laws, which give preferential treatment to women would have to be revised (such as the amount of weight women may lift on the job); and that "maternity leaves" would have to be made available to husbands who want to stay home with a newborn child.[21] A number of women felt ERA would be more detrimental than beneficial to women and actively opposed its passage.

Even though ERA failed to be ratified, a variety of statutes have been passed to prevent sex discrimination. The federal Equal Pay Act of 1963 and a number of similar state laws require equal pay for equal work. The Civil Rights Act of 1964 outlaws discrimination on the basis of race, color, sex, or religion. Executive Order 11246, as amended by Executive Order 11375 on October 13, 1967, forbids sex discrimination by federal suppliers and contractors and provides procedures for enforcement. In addition, numerous court decisions have set precedents establishing the illegality of sex discrimination in hiring, promotion, and rate of pay.[22] Several landmark decisions have required employers to pay female employees millions of dollars to compensate for past wage discriminations.[23] For example, in 1988 the State Farm Insurance Company in California agreed (in a multimillion-dollar settlement) to pay damages and back pay to thousands of women refused jobs as insurance sales agents over a thirteen-year period. The women had been told that a college degree was required for sales agents even though men were hired without degrees.[24]

The Equal Credit Act of 1974 bars discrimination on the basis of marital status or sex in credit operations. A number of states have passed laws prohibiting discrimination against pregnant women in hiring, training, and promotion.[25] Despite these laws, acts, and precedents, substantial illegal sex discrimination still occurs, which women often have to fight on a case-by-case basis. For example, some high schools prohibit pregnant or married girls from attending, but permit unmarried fathers or married boys to attend.

Affirmative action programs apply to women as well as to certain racial minorities. These programs originate in the 1964 Equal Employment Opportunity Act forbidding discrimination on account of race, color, religion, sex, or national origin by employers and organizations who receive federal funds. This act created the Equal Employment Opportunity Commission (EEOC) to administer the law. The commission then proceeded to develop affirmative action programs to implement the act. The following employers are required to have affirmative action programs:

♦ Government contractors and suppliers

♦ Recipients of government funds

♦ Businesses engaged in interstate commerce

Affirmative action primarily applies to job *vacancies*. Employers must demonstrate active efforts to locate and recruit minority applicants (defined to include women); demonstrate positive effort to increase the poll of qualified applicants (for example, special training programs for minorities); give preference to hiring minority applicants; and in some cases set hard quotas that specify numbers of minority members who must be accepted (regardless of qualifications) to fill vacant positions. The clout of the EEOC is the threat of loss of government funds if employers do not have effective affirmative action programs. (As noted in Chapter 6, presently there is an active backlash movement that threatens to curtail affirmative action programs.)

## Sexual Harassment

Sexual harassment may be defined as repeated and unwanted sexual advances. Sexual harassment has recently become recognized as a form of sex discrimination, most victims of which are women. Horton et al. identify some of the victims of sexual harassment:

> Sexual harassment is an ancient practice. Attractive female slaves were routinely bought as sex playthings, and domestic servants were often exploited. If the Victorian housemaid denied her bed to a lecherous master, he dismissed her; if she admitted him, she soon became pregnant and disgraced, and his wife dismissed her. Either way, she lost!
>
> Sexual harassment can be found anywhere, but is likely to be a problem only where men have supervisory or gatekeeper power over women. The "casting couch" is a well-known feature of show business, and women in many occupations can escape unwelcome attentions only by quitting their jobs, often at a sacrifice. Sexual harassment on the campus has also surfaced, with many female graduate students claiming that senior professors claimed sexual privileges as the price for grades, degrees, and recommendations.[26]

*Sexual harassment scene—the woman is stopping the man's advances.*

The definition of what is and what is not sexual harassment is somewhat vague. Repeated, unwanted touching is certainly harassment. A 1986 U.S. Supreme Court decision broadened the definition. Today a hostile work environment in which a woman feels hassled or degraded because of constant unwelcome flirtation, lewd comments, or obscene joking *may* be sufficient grounds for a lawsuit.[27] A number of colleges and universities in recent years have defined sexual harassment to include consenting sexual relationships between faculty and adult students. The rationale is that students are in a lower power position and may suffer adverse consequences if they refuse.

Sexual harassment (see Box 7.4) is distinct from flirtation, flattery, request for a date, and other acceptable behavior occurring in the workplace or the classroom. It is also distinct from other forms of harassment that do not involve conduct of a sexual

# Types of Sexual Harassment

Sexual harassment falls into three categories: verbal, non-verbal, and physical. The following examples may represent sexual harassment if the behavior is clearly unwelcomed and not reciprocated.

## Verbal

♦ Sexual innuendo. ("So you're majoring in packaging? I love your packaging.")

♦ Suggestive comments. ("Those jeans really fit you well.")

♦ Sexual remarks about a person's clothing, body, or sexual activities. ("I noticed you lost weight. I'm glad you didn't lose your gorgeous chest too.")

♦ Sexist insults or jokes or remarks that are stereotypical or derogatory to members of the opposite sex. ("Women should be kept barefoot, pregnant, and at the edge of town.")

♦ Implied or verbal threats concerning one's grades or job. ("It's simple. If you want to pass this course, you have to be nice to me, and sex is the nicest thing I can think of.")

♦ Sexual proposition, invitations, or other pressures for sex. ("My office hours are too limited; why don't you drop by my house tonight? We'll have more privacy and time to get to know each other.")

♦ Using employment position to request dates or sexual favors.

## Nonverbal

♦ Visual sexual displays; unwanted display of pornographic pictures, posters, cartoons, or other materials.

♦ Body language (such as leering at one's body or standing too close).

♦ Whistling suggestively.

♦ Mooning or flashing.

♦ Obscene gestures.

♦ Actions that involve gender-directed favoritism or disparate treatment.

## Physical

♦ Patting, pinching, and any other inappropriate touching or feeling.

♦ Bra-snapping.

♦ Brushing against the body.

♦ Grabbing or groping.

♦ Attempted or actual kissing or fondling.

♦ Coerced sexual intercourse.

♦ Attempted or actual sexual assault.

---

nature. Sexual harassment is a type of sexual coercion that relies on the power of the perpetrator to affect the victim's economic or academic status and does not necessarily involve physical force. According to U.S. law, sexual harassment is a form of sexual discrimination in employment and education that is prohibited by Title VII of the Civil Rights Act of 1964. Sexual harassment is defined as:

> Unwelcome sexual advances, requests for sexual favors, and other verbal or physical conduct of a sexual nature constitute sexual harassment when 1.) submission to such conduct is made either explicitly or implicitly a term or condition of an individual's employment; 2.) submission to or rejection of such conduct by an individual is used as a basis of employment decisions affecting such individual; or 3.) such conduct has the purpose or effect of unreasonably interfering with an individual's work performance or creating an intimidating, hostile, or offensive working environment.[28]

Sexual harassment almost always involves elements of unequal power and coercion. Although most victims are women, sexual harassment can be directed at either males or females. Repeated incidents of sexual harassment generally results in a hostile, intimidating, or anxiety-producing work or educational environment.

Those found guilty of sexual harassment are subject to reprimand, dismissal, demotion, and other consequences at their place of employment. Unfortunately, even a successful protest sometimes further victimizes the victim. She must endure the unpleasantness of pursuing the complaint, and she may be viewed by some as having invited the advances. Some women who protest eventually are forced to seek a new job because of the discomfort they feel in the old workplace.

In recent years corporate America has received several wake-up calls on sexual harassment. For example, in 1994 a San Francisco jury awarded a legal secretary $7.1 million in punitive damages after finding that her former employer failed to stop an attorney in the firm from harassing her.

In 1998 Astra AB in Boston agreed to pay nearly $10 million to more than 70 women to settle claims that its president and other executives replaced older female employees with beautiful, young, single women who were then pressured into having sex.

Also in 1998 Mitsubishi Motors agreed to pay a record $34 million to 350 women to settle allegations that women on the assembly line at its Illinois factory were groped and insulted and that managers did nothing to stop it.

In June 1998 the U.S. Supreme Court ruled than an employer could be held liable when a supervisor sexually harasses a worker, even if the employee's job is not harmed. (However, if a company has a strong program in place to prevent and discipline harassment, that company has, according to the Supreme Court, some measure of protection from sexual harassment lawsuits.)

## *Sex Roles and Sexism: Biology or Socialization?*
XXXXXXXXXXXXXXXXXXXX

The women's movement has made remarkable advances in the past twenty-five years. Yet substantial sex discrimination and restrictive sex-role stereotyping still remain. For centuries it was erroneously assumed that men are innately superior to women. The domination of one social group by another is always supported by a set of beliefs that justifies the distinction. Typically this ideology becomes so pervasive that even the subordinate group largely accepts it. (For example, peasants in the Middle Ages believed in the right of aristocrats to rule them.) Until recently, most women believed their role was to be secondary and supportive to men.

### BIOLOGICAL EXCUSES FOR SEXISM: FACT OR FICTION?

Sexist ideology assumes that the differences between men and women are due to their biological differences. It assumes that anatomy equips men to play an active and dominant role in the world and equips women to play a passive and secondary role.

Of course, there are the obvious anatomic sexual and reproductive differences between the sexes. There are also differences in hormone levels. Each sex has both male and female hormones, but women have higher levels of female hormones and males have higher levels of male hormones. Research (which may or may not be applicable to humans) on some animal species has shown that when male hormones are injected into females, the females have a heightened sex drive and become more aggressive.[29] Scientists, however, believe this hormone difference plays only a minor role in humans, because human behavior patterns are almost entirely learned, whereas behavior patterns of lower animals are more influenced by hormonal factors.[30]

On the average, men are taller and heavier than women and have greater physical strength. Women can tolerate pain better and have greater physical endurance.[31] In most respects, women are physically healthier.[32] Women are less susceptible to most diseases and, on the average, live longer. Males have higher rates of fetal and infant mortality. Male fetuses can inherit a greater number of sex-linked weaknesses—over thirty disorders have been exclusively found among males, including hemophilia, certain types of color blindness, and webbing of the toes.

Soon after birth, female babies tend to be more content and less physically active.[33] As children develop, other differences appear; but it has not been determined yet whether these identified differences are due to inherited or learned factors. For example, girls learn to talk and read at an earlier age. Also, girls become more docile and dependent and seem more intellectually mature (most remedial education classes have a large majority of boys). More boys are superior in tasks based on spatial, mechanical, and analytic ability, whereas more girls are superior at tasks involving verbal capacities and numerical computation.[34] Whether these differences are learned or innate is uncertain. For example, girls may be better at reading and language because they are encouraged to spend more time with adults and to read more rather than being urged to become involved in competitive sports.

Considerable research supports the position that sex-role differences are primarily due to socialization patterns. John Money and associates examined cases in which parents wanted a girl so badly that they raised a male child to be a girl, or vice versa.[35] The study found that children learn to play the role they are socialized to learn, rather than the genital role outlined by traditional sex-role expectation. Money concluded that children are "psychosexually neuter at birth" and that sex role is independent of physiological sex.

## Sex-Role Expectations Are Culturally Determined

In the classic study *Sex and Temperament in Three Primitive Societies*, Margaret Mead refuted the notion that sex-role expectations are biologically determined. The study was conducted in the early 1930s in three tribes in New Guinea. Mead demonstrated that many characteristics Americans classify as typically female or male are classified differently in these tribes.

Both sexes among the Arapesh would seem "feminine" to us. Both men and women are gentle, nurturant, and compliant. The personalities of males and females are not sharply differentiated by sex. Girl and boys learn to be unaggressive, cooperative, and responsive to the needs and wants of others. Behaviors of husband to wife parallel the traditional behaviors of mother to child in our society, with the Arapesh husband often seeing his role as providing training to his much younger wife.

In contrast, among the Mundugamors, both sexes would seem "masculine" to us. Men and women are headhunters and cannibals, are nonnurturant and aggressive, and actively initiate sexual involvement.

The most interesting finding involved the Tchambuli society, which virtually reverses our traditional sex-role expectations and stereotypes. The men spend much more time than the women in grooming and decorating themselves. Also, the men spend much of their time painting, carving, and practicing dance steps. In contrast, the women are efficient, impersonal, unadorned, managerial, and brisk. The women are the traders and have most of the economic power.

Mead concludes:

> We no longer have any basis for regarding such aspects of behavior as sex linked. . . . Standardized personality differences between the sexes are . . . cultural creations to which each generation, male or female, is trained to conform.[a]

---

a. Margaret Mead, *Sex and Temperament in Three Primitive Societies* (New York: Morrow, 1935), 190–92.

---

The fact that there are wide variations in sex-role expectations among cultures also suggests sex roles are learned rather than biologically determined. (If there were a biological basis for sex-role distinctions, all cultures would tend to define sex-role expectations in a similar way.) For example, most cultures expect women will do most of the carrying of heavy objects, whereas in the United States and most European cultures men are expected to do most of the lifting and carrying of heavy objects. Some societies, also contrary to ours, have the men do most of the cooking. Not so long ago in Europe, males as well as females wore stockings, perfume, and silk. Men in Scotland still wear kilts (skirts). In the societies of the Maoris and the Trobrianders (located on islands in the Pacific Ocean) it is the women who are expected to take the initiative in sexual activity.[36]

In a classic study, Margaret Mead examined sex-role expectations in three tribes in New Guinea.[37] One tribe required males and females to behave in a way *we* would define as "masculine," a second required both to behave in a way *we* would define as "feminine," and the third required females to behave in a way *we* would call "masculine" and the males in a way *we* would regard "feminine." Mead concluded sex-role expectations are primarily determined by cultural learning experiences (see Box 7.5).

## TRADITIONAL SEX-ROLE EXPECTATIONS

As we have seen, *sex roles* are learned patterns of behavior expected of each sex in a particular society. Sex-role expectations define how men and women are to behave and to be treated by others. Sex-role expectations are largely based on stereotypes. Stereotypes make it easier for discrimination to occur.

American women traditionally are expected to be affectionate, passive, conforming, sensitive, intuitive, dependent, and "sugar and spice and everything nice." They are supposed to be primarily concerned with domestic life, to be nurturing, to instinctively love caring for babies and young children, to be deeply concerned about their personal appearance, and to be self-sacrificing for their family. Similarly, they should not appear ambitious, aggressive, competitive, or more intelligent than men. They are expected to be ignorant of and uninterested in sports, economics, and politics. In relationships with men, supposedly they should not initiate a relationship and are expected to be tender, "feminine," emotional, and appreciative.

There are also a number of traditional sex-role expectations for males in our society. A male is expected to be tough, fearless, logical, self-reliant, independent, and aggressive. He is expected to have definite opinions about the major issues of the day and to make authoritative decisions at work and at home. He is expected to be strong and never to be depressed, vulnerable, or anxious. He is not to exhibit "sissy" or "feminine" traits. He is expected not to cry or display so-called feminine emotions. He is expected to be the provider and to be competent in all situations. He is supposed to be physically strong, self-reliant, and athletic; to have a "manly" air of confidence and toughness; to be daring and aggressive, to be brave and forceful; to be always in a position to dominate any situation—in effect, to be a "Rambo" or a Clint Eastwood.[38] He is supposed to initiate relationships with women and be dominant in relationships with them. Men who are supported by their wives—or who earn less than their wives—are apt to be criticized and to feel embarrassed and inadequate.

Even young boys are expected to be "masculine." Parents and relatives are far more concerned when a boy is a "sissy" than when a girl is a "tomboy." A tomboy is expected to outgrow her "masculine" tendencies, but it is feared a sissy will never fare well in our competitive society and may even become homosexual. (The right of a boy to wear his hair long had to be won in many court battles in this country, but hardly anyone is concerned when a girl wears her hair short.)

## SEX-ROLE SOCIALIZATION

In this country, sex-role socialization starts shortly after birth. Baby girls are dressed in pink; baby boys, in blue. Babies are given sex-role–related toys. Boys are bounced on the knee and handled roughly, whereas girls are cooed over. At a very early age, a child becomes aware he is a "boy" or she is a "girl" long before becoming aware of anatomical differences between the sexes.[39] Lawrence Kohlberg notes that children make basic decisions (based on what others tell them) that they are boys or girls and then select those activities that significant others (that is, people they view as important to them) say conform to this self-concept.[40]

Parents go to great lengths to socialize their offspring during the childhood years according to sex-role expectations. Little boys are given toy trucks to play with, and girls are given dolls. Boys are encouraged to play ball, and girls are urged to play house. Ruth Hartley notes:

Girls gain approval . . . by doing the rather undemanding things that are expected of them. . . . A girl need not be bright as long as she is docile and attractive. . . .

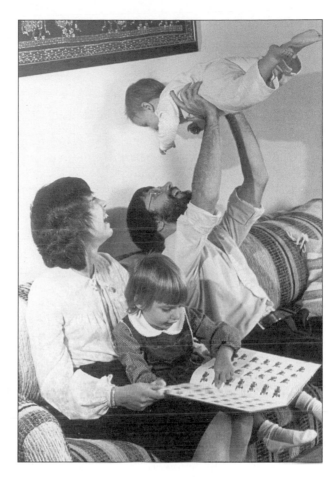

*Traditional gender role stimulation: distal stimulation (looking and talking) with young girl by a parent, and proximal stimulation (rocking and handling) of infant boy by the other parent.*

This kind of treatment is likely to produce rather timid, unventuresome, unoriginal, conformist types.[41]

According to Hartley, the early socialization of boys is quite different:

Almost from birth, the boy has more problems to solve autonomously. In addition, he is required to limit his interest at a very early age to sex-appropriate objects and activities, while girls are permitted to amble their way to a similar status at a more gradual and natural pace. . . . He is challenged to discover what he should do by being told what he should *not do*, as in the most frequently employed negative sanction, "Don't be a sissy!" . . . Interest in girlish things is generally forbidden and anxiety-provoking in American boyhood. . . . The boy is constantly open to a challenge to prove his masculinity. He must perform, adequately and publicly, a variety of physical feats that will have very little utility in most cases in adulthood. He is constantly under pressure to demonstrate mastery over the environment and, concomitantly, to suppress expression of emotion.[42]

Young children are at an impressionable age. Such sex-role stereotyping often becomes self-fulfilling prophecy. As we have noted several times previously in this text, people tend to view themselves as others relate to them.[43] Boys are discouraged from showing overt affection and are taught to seek material rewards; to be dominant in dating and marital relationships; to seek respect, power, and prestige; not to cry, and to keep their concerns within themselves—to be "macho." In contrast girls are taught to be more passive, nurturing, and maternal. In many families, young girls are still raised by their parents to be mothers and homemakers and/or encouraged to seek lower-status employment for lower pay. Research shows some females are taught actually to fear success and achievement and to "play dumb" to "boost the male ego."[44] Females are expected to be "feminine" by displaying softness, helplessness, tenderness, and understanding. Adolescent and adult females are put in a double bind due to "femininity-achievement incompatibility."[45] There is a traditional view in our society that a woman cannot be both feminine *and* an achiever; achievement is somehow perceived as reducing femininity, and the truly feminine female is erroneously thought to be someone who does not seek to be an achiever. (Of course this traditional view is an arbitrary rule leading women to play a submissive role; there is nothing intrinsically incompatible about femininity and achievement.) In summary, males are encouraged to be outgoing and aggressive, whereas females are encouraged to be passive and reserved.

A significant part of the socialization process occurs in school. Girls are often channeled into sewing, typing, and cooking classes, whereas boys are channeled into such classes as woodworking, printing, and mechanics. Although 83 percent of grade-school teachers are female, close to 90 percent of principals are male.[46] Thus, children see men in superior, decision-making positions and women in subordinate positions.

A review of more than 100 studies by the American Association of University Women found that:

♦ Although girls and boys start school with similar levels of skill and confidence, by the end of high school girls trail boys in test scores in science and math.

♦ Teachers pay less attention to girls than to boys.

♦ Reports of sexual harassment of girls are increasing.

♦ Textbooks still ignore or stereotype women and girls and omit discussion of pressing problems such as sexual abuse.

♦ Some tests are biased against females and thereby limit their chances of obtaining scholarships.

♦ African-American girls are particularly likely to be ignored or rebuffed in schools.[47]

Since boys are given more encouragement to be independent and assertive, boys are more likely to act up and get into trouble.[48] Perhaps for this reason, studies of teacher-student interaction have found that boys get more attention from teachers than do girls.[49] Myra Sadker and associates put it this way: "Boys are the central figures . . . and girls are relegated to second-class participation."[50] Partly because of such socialization practices in school systems, males are much more apt when they enter college to major in such fields as science, mathematics, and engineering; fields that are most likely to lead directly to high-paying careers.

Textbooks in preschool, elementary, junior high, and high school portray female characters as being more passive and dependent and less creative than males.[51]

Guidance counselors generally advise students to pursue careers not just on the basis of their abilities, but also on the basis of traditional sex-role expectations. For example, a young girl who excels at math may be encouraged to be a teacher, whereas a young boy with equal skills may be urged to consider engineering. Janet Chafetz comments on such counseling practices:

Counselors defend such practices on the basis of what youngsters may "realistically" expect to face in the future: marriage, child care, and a lack of opportunity in a number of career fields for females, and the need to support a family at the highest income and status levels possible for males. "Realism," however, has always been an excuse for maintaining the status quo, and it is no different in the case of sex role stereotypes. If, for instance, females do not prepare to enter previously masculine fields, such fields will remain male-dominated, allowing another generation of counselors to assure girls that females can't work in them. In addition, it is questionable whether counselors' notions of "reality" in fact keep pace with reality. There is undoubtedly a lag between expanding opportunities and changing sex role definitions on the one hand, and counselors' awareness of these phenomena on the other.[52]

Even contemporary theories in psychology describe women as being more passive and emotional, lacking in abstract interests, and as having an instinctive tenderness for babies.[53] Even though masculinity and femininity are largely learned roles, contemporary psychological theories subtly imply (erroneously) that sex-role differences are genetically determined. Sigmund Freud's theory of the development of the female personality is probably the most sexist and outrageous. According to Freud, young girls discover that their genitals differ from boys', which leads them to have "penis envy." Because of this difference, girls conclude that they are biologically inferior to males and then develop a passive, submissive personality as a way to adjust to interactions with males, whom they view as superior.[54]

There are many sexist implications built into the English language. The words we select to use greatly influence our interpretation of reality. The use of sexist language in our society has been a significant factor in defining and maintaining the position of males as being dominant in our society, with females then being assigned a supportive or submissive role. The following words and phrases portray males as having the dominant position: mankind, manned, manpower, chairman, congressman, businessman, mailman, salesman, foreman, policeman, the best man for the job, and man and wife.

There are other examples of how sexism has infiltrated the English language. Books tended in the past (there has been considerable improvements in recent years) to use the pronoun "he" to refer in a generic sense to a person when the gender is unspecified. On reaching adulthood, a man becomes a "Mr." for the remainder of his life; this is a polite term that makes no reference to the status of a man's personal life. On the other hand, a woman starts as a "Miss," and then becomes a "Mrs." upon marriage, which clearly identifies her marital status. In addition, traditional customs assume a woman will, upon her marriage, use her husband's last name (instead of her maiden name).

The mass media, particularly in advertising, also play an important role in sex-role socialization. Women are frequently portrayed in commercials as being wives, mothers, or sex objects or as being obsessed with getting a date. They used to be portrayed as invariably less intelligent and more dependent than men and were hardly ever shown in executive positions. Some TV ads still depict women in traditional sex-role stereotypes such as delighting in waxing their floors or in discovering a new detergent to get their families' white clothes whiter. Fortunately, changes are occurring in the mass media's portrayal of women, reflecting changes in our society. Many commercials are now even reversing traditional roles. Because the mass media are important

socialization vehicles, they can assist in changing attitudes about "proper" sex roles in the future.

## Consequences of Sexism

XXXXXXXXXXXXXXXXXXXXX

Sexism is prejudice or discrimination against women. Although women are a numerical majority in our society, they are considered a minority group because they are victims of discrimination on many fronts and have unequal access to valued resources.

### OCCUPATION AND INCOME

Jobs held by women tend to be concentrated at the bottom of the occupational hierarchy, as indicated by Table 7.1. Women tend to be concentrated in lower-paying

| Position | Percentage Held by Women |
|---|---|
| Dental assistants | 99.1 |
| Secretaries | 98.6 |
| Child-care workers | 97.1 |
| Receptionists | 96.9 |
| Typists | 94.8 |
| Cleaners, servants | 93.6 |
| Registered nurses | 93.3 |
| Teachers' aides | 92.1 |
| Hairdressers, cosmetologists | 91.1 |
| Bookkeepers | 91.1 |
| Telephone operators | 90.5 |
| Bank tellers | 90.1 |
| Elementary schoolteachers | 83.3 |
| Librarians | 82.7 |
| Maids, housemen | 81.8 |
| General office clerks | 80.8 |
| Cashiers | 78.1 |
| Waiters, waitresses | 77.9 |
| File clerks | 77.6 |
| Social workers | 68.5 |
| Psychologists | 61.4 |
| Food service workers | 56.6 |
| Authors | 54.1 |
| Financial managers | 54.0 |
| College teachers | 43.5 |
| Natural scientists | 29.3 |
| Lawyers, judges | 29.0 |
| Physicians | 26.4 |
| Architects | 16.7 |
| Police officers | 15.8 |
| Dentists | 13.7 |
| Engineers | 8.5 |
| Firefighters | 2.1 |

Table 7.1  *Employment Positions Held by Women*

*Source:* U.S. Bureau of the Census, *Statistical Abstract of the United States, 1997* (Washington, DC: U.S. Government Printing Office 1997).

positions (secretaries, child-care workers, receptionists, typists, nurses, hairdressers, bank tellers, cashiers, file clerks). Men tend to be concentrated in higher-paying positions (lawyers, judges, engineers, accountants, college teachers, physicians, dentists, sales managers). As noted earlier, full-time working women are paid about three-fourths of what full-time working men are paid.[55] Even though sex discrimination laws have been passed, job discrimination continues to be found in a number of studies.[56]

Women hold fewer than 10 percent of the nation's elective offices.[57] There has never been a woman president or vice president in the United States. The vast majority of senators and representatives in Congress are men. It is a rarity when a woman is elected governor in a state. Men still control the political processes to nominate candidates and to campaign for their election. The potential political clout of women, however, is immense, because they constitute a majority of the nation's voters.[58]

Women hold only 2 percent of the top management positions in American corporations, and just 6 percent of the seats on corporate boards of directors.[59] Even successful female executives often complain about an invisible "glass ceiling" that seems to lock them out of the key positions of power. One study, based on interviews with 100 male and female executives from three major U.S. corporations, concluded that there was a clear double standard in promotions and that women had to perform significantly better than their male counterparts to get ahead.[60]

About two-thirds of the women who work outside the home in the United States are employed in the "women's ghetto" positions of housekeepers, secretaries, receptionists, telephone operators, clerks, and so on.[61] And, overall, women earn less income than men in practically every job category.[62] Even in the armed forces, where pay levels are standardized, it is less likely that women will receive additional "flight pay," "combat pay," or "hazardous duty pay."[63] It is true that differences in income between men and women by job category are due partly to seniority (men earn more because they've held their jobs longer), but studies taking seniority into account have found that women tend to receive less pay for doing the same job.[64]

There are probably many reasons for these occupational and income differences between men and women. Female children are socialized to seek lower-paying occupations and careers. For example, boys are encouraged to be lawyers and doctors, whereas girls are encouraged to be teachers and secretaries. Men and

*A fifteen-year-old mother comforts her daughter in a public high school classroom for pregnant teens and young parents in Northern California that encourages high school graduation.*

women are also "sex typed" for various jobs: Males seeking employment are encouraged by prospective employers to apply for higher-status positions, whereas women are encouraged to apply for lower-level positions.[65] Then there is the tendency for our society to assign lower pay to job categories in which women are concentrated: receptionists, secretaries, and typists. Nonetheless, lower pay for women holding the same jobs as men indicates that there are discriminatory practices occurring even after women are hired.

Paul Horton and Gerald Leslie provide additional reasons, stemming from sex-role socialization, of the job and income disparity between men and women:

> Motivation for career advancement is difficult to measure, and rash generalization is dangerous. Yet there are good reasons to suspect that intense career ambitions have been less common among women than among men. Beginning in early socialization, most girls are trained to please and charm others; most boys are trained to impress and outdistance others. Boys are trained to dominate and lead; girls, to submit and follow. Boys are taught to make demands upon others; girls learn to serve others' needs. Boys are praised for their strength; girls, for their prettiness and graciousness. As adults, men in our society are evaluated primarily according to their career success ("Meet my son, the doctor"), while women have been evaluated primarily according to

their skill in human relationships ("She has a handsome husband and three darling children"). Husbands who knowingly neglected their families to pursue career advancement (moonlighting, night school, weekends working at the office) were praised for their ambition, while wives who allowed their careers to interfere with family life were scolded and scorned. A woman's spectacular success might alienate men, and much has been written about the avoidance-of-success syndrome in women. . . . This all has contributed to a lower level of career expectation among women than among men.[66]

## HUMAN INTERACTIONS

The effects of sexism on human interactions are immense. Some examples will be briefly described.

Parents place more social restrictions on teenaged daughters than on teenaged sons. Daughters cannot stay out as late, their friends are more closely monitored, they are less likely to obtain the family car for going out, and they are discouraged from involvement in athletic activity.

There are extensive pressures on women to have the "Miss America" look—well-developed busts, shapely figures, and attractive features. Practically all women find it difficult to maintain such features. Unfortunately, women who according to current American stereotypes are judged less attractive, receive less attention from males, find it more difficult to obtain dates, and may find it more difficult to obtain higher-status employment. The psychological costs are particularly severe when a woman reaches middle age. Socialized into believing her main function is the rearing of her family and that her main asset is her physical attractiveness, she often watches with despair as both her children and her youth leave her.

There are many double standards for male and female social interactions. Sexually active teenage males are viewed as "studs," but sexually active teenage females may be called derogatory names. To a greater extent, males are allowed to be aggressive and to use vulgar language. There are social retributions that discourage women from entering certain nightclubs and other places of entertainment. Married women who have an affair are usually subjected to more disapproval than are married men who do.

In interactions between males and females, there is a tendency for the male to seek to be dominant and for the female either to seek an equalitarian relationship or to be manipulated into being submissive. For example, the male usually is expected to ask the female for a date and to select what they will do on a date. Also, males often try to be "macho"; some females find that to receive positive reinforcement and social acceptability, they must play along by being submissive, passive, or "feminine." When both husband and wife work, there is a tendency for the wife to follow her husband to a new geographic area if his job location changes.[67]

Often, there are power struggles between males and females related to sex-role expectations. Males may seek to be dominant, whereas females are more likely to seek equalitarian relationships. Marriage counselors are now seeing many couples in which the husband wants his wife to play a traditional role—stay at home, raise the children, and do the housework. If a wife does work, the husband often demands that the job not interfere with her doing the domestic tasks and wants the job to be viewed as "second income" rather than "career." Wives who want equalitarian relationships and who are becoming increasingly aware of the negative effects of sex-role stereotyping are apt to engage in power struggles with husbands who want them to fulfill the traditional wife role.

Women more than men experience depression and dissatisfaction in marriage.[68] Women are expected to make most of the adjustments necessary to keep the marriage intact. Middle-aged women frequently suffer severe depression when many of their tasks as mothers and homemakers are phased out—especially if they do not have outside jobs.[69] Research demonstrates that employed wives are happier than full-time homemakers.[70] Women who are extensively battered by their husbands, yet continue for years to live in these circumstances, sadly document the extent to which some women are trapped by social arrangements that perpetuate their dependence and submission.

Horner found that many women are motivated to avoid success as they fear the more ambitious and successful they appear, the less feminine they will appear in their interactions with men.[71]

Sex-role stereotypes probably also play a role in women being treated only as sex objects by some men, and in women being sexually harassed at work, at school, and in other settings.

It is not only female stereotypes that cause human interaction difficulties. Males also experience problems in living up to the Clint Eastwood image of a model man, as described earlier. It is almost impossible for any male to live up to this image. Yet there are considerable pressures on males to try—or suffer the consequences. Take the example of Senator Edmund Muskie in the 1968 Democratic presidential primary campaign. Senator Muskie was the leading candidate for the nomination when a newspaper in New England made some derogatory accusations about his wife and Muskie reacted by "breaking down and crying" in public. Very quickly the American public concluded that Muskie did not have the emotional stability to be president, and his popularity plummeted in the polls. David and Brannon describe another example:

> A friend explained to me that he broke down and cried in front of a colleague at the office after some personal tragedies and office frustrations. He explained, "the news of my crying was all over the office in an hour. At first, no one said anything. They just sort of looked. They couldn't handle the situation by talking about it. Before this, only girls had cried. One of the guys did joke, 'Hear you and Sally been crying lately, eh?' I guess that was a jibe at my masculinity, but the 'knowing silence' of the others indicated the same doubts. What really hurt was that two years later, when I was doing very well and being considered for a promotion, it was brought up again. My manager was looking over my evaluations, read a paragraph to himself, and said, 'What do you think about that crying incident?' You can bet that was the last time I let myself cry."[72]

Ruth Hartley notes that sex-role socialization of boys inevitably leads to personal conflicts in later years:

The boy is not adequately socialized for adulthood. . . . The boy is conditioned to live in an all-masculine society, defining his own self-image by rejecting whatever smacks of femininity. In adulthood, he will have to adjust to a heterosexual work world, perhaps even take orders from a female, a species he has been taught to despise as inferior. Finally, the emphasis on repression of the emotions, the high value of stoicism, leaves the boy wholly unprepared for the emotional closeness and intimate personal interaction now more and more expected of a lover and spouse.[73]

Men frequently feel they must put their careers first, and thereby sharply limit the interactions and satisfactions of being husbands or fathers. In contrast, women are urged by traditional expectations to put their roles as wives and mothers first and thereby limit their growth, capacities, and satisfactions in other areas.

Men in this country are disadvantaged in the eyes of the law in several areas. In some jurisdictions, husbands are legally required to provide financial support for their families, and failure to do so is grounds for divorce by the wife. If a marriage breaks up, there is a tendency for the court to grant custody of the children to the wife. In child-custody battles the father bears a heavier burden of proof that he is a fit parent than does the mother, and only in cases in which the mother is demonstrably negligent is the father's claim seriously considered. Alimony is much more frequently awarded to wives, even if both spouses can support themselves. Several men's groups have now formed in various regions of the country to advocate for equal treatment of men in these legal areas.

Sex-role stereotyping probably also plays a key role in the following statistics.[74] Men are four times more likely than women to commit suicide, substantially more likely to be involved in violence, and commit more crimes. Alcoholics and drug addicts are primarily men. Males also have higher rates of stress-related illnesses, such as heart disease, ulcers, and hypertension. The life expectancy for men in our society is several years less than for women. Could this shorter life expectancy be partially because of pressures on men to succeed financially and because they're socialized not to ventilate their emotions? Men may experience greater psychological stress, which leads to higher rates of stress-related illnesses. Some of those illnesses may result in a shorter life span of men.

Because of male stereotypes, many men view themselves as failures when they cannot meet the financial needs of their families. Some are badly beaten in fights they felt they could not walk away from and still be "real men." Many women find it frustrating to interact with men unable to be honest and open about their feelings. Not being able to live up to the model man image makes many men unhappy, depressed, and unfulfilled. Thus sex-role stereotyping imposes huge costs (financial, social, and personal) not only for women, but also for men.

## Recent Developments and the Future

〔xxxxxxxxxxxxxxxxxxxxx〕

A sex-role resolution in our society is under way and women are becoming aware of the negative effects of sex-role distinctions. Increasingly, courses on this topic are taught in high schools, vocational schools, and colleges. More and more women are entering the labor force. The proportion of employed females to employed males is about 45 percent to 55 percent.[75]

### CHANGES IN SEX-ROLE STEREOTYPES

Women are becoming more involved in athletics and are entering certain types of competition previously confined to males (basketball, football, softball, and volleyball). Increasing numbers of women compete in track and field events, swimming, boxing, wrestling, weight lifting, golf, tennis, and stock-car racing.

In 1981 Sandra Day O'Connor was the first woman appointed to the United States Supreme Court. In 1984 Geraldine Ferraro was the first woman selected to be a vice presidential candidate for a major political party.

Women are also pursuing a number of professions and careers that previously were male dominated: the military, engineering, law, the judiciary, fire fighting, medicine (physicians, dentists), accounting, administration, law enforcement (police officers), management. The number of female midlevel managers in businesses is increasing. Entering such new careers often has obstacles. Glassman, for example, reports that women who have become police officers receive stares from other citizens and often are viewed with suspicion by male partners.[76] (Male police partners fear that women may break under pressure, may not be able to subdue and handcuff a resisting offender, and may not be able to handle disorderly males and other violent situations. Male officers tend to feel both hostile and protective toward patrolwomen, and one woman's failing is often held up as an indictment against all the rest.)

There are also changes in human interactions, with more women being assertive and seeking out equalitarian relationships with males. To some extent, men are also (more slowly) beginning to realize the negative effects of sex-role distinctions. Men are gradually realizing that the stereotyped model man role limits their opportunities in terms of emotional expression, interpersonal relationships, occupations, and domestic activities. Coleman and Cressey note:

Advocates of the men's movement argue that current gender roles are just as harmful to men as they are to women, but in different ways. They particularly object to the ideal of masculinity that holds that "real" men must always be strong, self-controlled, and successful. The effort to live up to this impossible ideal (or at least to appear to live up to it) leaves many men feeling anxiety-ridden and isolated.[77]

A men's movement is slowly becoming more prominent in our society. Some men are concerned that women tend to see them as "success objects," as women are substantially more apt than men to believe that a well-paying job is an essential requirement for selecting a spouse.[78] Men also are concerned that when a divorce occurs, many courts routinely assume that the mother will make the better parent. As a result the mother is usually given custody of the children, with the father having to pay to support them, and often only given limited visitation rights in return. The men's movement also asserts that some feminists have a tendency toward "male bashing"; they claim such feminists perpetuate negative stereotypes of men and blame men for problems that are actually created by historical forces beyond the control of any person or group.

Sex-role stereotypes have been costly to society. They have prevented a number of people from assuming more productive roles and have resulted in the expenditure of substantial resources on emotional and physical problems generated by these stereotypes.

Men also are taking on new roles and entering new careers. It is becoming increasingly common for men to accept equal responsibility for domestic tasks and for child rearing. In addition, we are now seeing more male nurses, secretaries, child-care workers, nursery school teachers, and flight attendants.[79]

In the past three decades, millions of Americans have begun to change their ideas about the "naturalness" of sex roles. Traditional discriminations are coming to be perceived as an irrational system that threatens women with lifelong inferiority and wasted potential and restricts men to the role of always being competitive, aggressive, and emotionally insensitive.

Our society is slowly moving toward gender equality, but as we have seen earlier in this chapter, substantial gender inequality continues to exist. If men and women achieve sexual equality in our society, what will be the effects? Kornblum and Julian speculate:

One obvious answer is that society's supply of talent in every segment of the work force would increase. More men would participate in traditionally female fields. . . . Breaking down the occupational barriers

## Strategies for Achieving Sexual Equality

Sexual equality does not mean achieving a *unisex* society. Advocates of sexual equality do not urge using the same public bathroom facilities, nor do they urge dressing the same or playing professional football and hockey together. What they *are* advocating is equal treatment of the sexes (e.g., in employment) and the end to traditional sex-role stereotyping. They are advocating that no role, behavior, aptitude, or attitude should be limited to one sex alone. True sexual equality simply means that people would be free to be whatever they want to be.

To achieve sexual equality will require action in many areas, some of which are summarized below:

◆ An end must be put to the motherhood myth, which holds that women are most fulfilled as mothers.

◆ Fathers must share equally in the process of child raising and in domestic tasks. This guideline does not mean men should do exactly half of each domestic task but that husband and wife communicate with each other about how best to allocate family responsibilities. Women cannot compete equally with men in the work world if they also are required to assume all of the traditional child-rearing and homemaker responsibilities.

◆ Additional day-care provisions are needed for working mothers and fathers, particularly for one-parent families. Unless quality day-care arrangements are available, many mothers who want to work will be prevented from doing so.

◆ Laws preventing sex discrimination need to be enforced, and laws need to be enacted where legal discrimination still exists. (For example, sometimes women have a more difficult time obtaining a bank loan.) Sex discrimination laws for men are also needed in certain areas (such as alimony and child custody).

◆ Dysfunctional sex-role socialization practices should be ended. Children should be reared to take on the roles, attitudes, and behaviors they desire and in which they have capacities, rather than boys being raised to be "masculine" and girls to be "feminine." Parents and teachers should learn to relate to each child as an *individual*, rather than as a *male* or *female*.

◆ Assertiveness training programs should be used more widely to help men and women express themselves effectively and gain skills in countering sex-role stereotypes.

◆ Advertisers who still portray women only as homemakers or as sex objects should start giving equal treatment to men and women.

◆ Consciousness-raising groups need to be expanded to reach more men and women. Self-help groups are now being held largely with women to help them become more aware of sex-role stereotypes, establish a better self-concept, and foster contact with others working to end sexism.

◆ Continued development of services such as shelters for battered women, rape crisis centers, abortion counseling, family planning, and marriage and sexual counseling is needed if people are to develop their capacities fully.

◆ School counselors and teachers should help students make career decisions based on their abilities, not their gender.

◆ Girls and boys should be encouraged to take whatever vocational courses (cooking, shop, typing, printing) they desire without regard to gender.

◆ Publishers should continue to put an end to sex-role stereotyping and portray females and males in a variety of roles (e.g., males performing domestic tasks and women piloting airplanes and performing surgery).

◆ Laws should be enacted demanding that both governmental and private business organizations abide by the principles of comparable worth. Women have the right to receive equal pay or have pay equity for doing work comparable to that which men traditionally do. (This concept is described more fully at the end of this chapter.)

that separate women and men would also help them relate to each other as equals. Also, because fewer men would be the sole support for their families, there would be more flexibility in working life: Men and women would be freer to leave their jobs if they were unhappy with them, and in general there would be greater sharing of economic and homemaking responsibilities. This would reduce the pressures that exist for men to "succeed" and for women to remain dependent. The most important result of true sexual equality, then, may be simply that people would be free to be themselves.[80]

*Pro-Choice—a woman's legal right to have an abortion—is an important issue in the women's rights movement. Here women demonstrate at a rally organized by the Feminist Majority Foundation.*

Some feminists and social scientists have urged that men and women be socialized to be flexible in their role playing and to express themselves as human beings rather than in traditional feminine or masculine ways.[81] This idea is called "androgyny," from *andro* (male) and *gyne* (female). The notion is to have people explore a broad range of role-playing possibilities and to choose to express emotions and behaviors without regard to sex-role stereotypes. People thus are encouraged to pursue tasks and careers at which they are most competent and with which they are most comfortable and to express the attitudes and emotions they really feel. If a male wants to be a cook or an elementary school teacher and a female wants to be a soldier or an athlete—and they're good at it—then it is functional for society if both develop their talents and are allowed to achieve everything they're capable of.

## FUTURE DIRECTION OF THE WOMEN'S MOVEMENT

Within the women's movement there is currently much debate over policy directions. Coleman and Cressey note:

> As in other social movements, all feminists do not agree on the best ways to win their objectives. The *liberal feminists* are the largest group in the movement, and their approach is the predominant one in the National

Organization for Women (NOW). Drawing on the values of freedom and individual liberty that are central to the liberal tradition, these feminists call for a vigorous government attack on all forms of prejudice and discrimination. The liberal feminists nonetheless have their critics both inside and outside the movement. To the left are the *socialist feminists,* who argue that the exploitation of women arises from the capitalist system and that only fundamental changes in our economic institutions can liberate women. *Radical feminists* focus more on the social arena, calling for a "women-centered" culture to replace the current pattern of patriarchal (male-dominated) society. At the same time, all feminists are criticized by those who feel that they are undermining the family and traditional social values.[82]

The conservative trend of the 1980s and early 1990s jeopardized some of the progress that feminists made during the 1960s and 1970s. Both President Ronald and Nancy Reagan, as well as most members of the Reagan cabinet, opposed the Equal Rights Amendment, and it eventually failed to be ratified. The conservative movement and the Reagan and Bush administrations put less emphasis on enforcing affirmative action programs and actively opposed the concept of setting quotas for the percentage of minorities that must be hired by employers. There also were cuts in a number of social programs that the women's movement vigorously supported, such as funding for public day care, sex education, and contraception.

Bill Clinton, who was elected president in 1992, and reelected in 1996, has a more liberal orientation than Reagan and Bush. His wife, Hillary, has been very active in policymaking decisions and is viewed by many as being a role model for contemporary women. President Clinton has appointed a number of feminists to high-level government positions and has supported the feminist position on several social issues, such as the abortion debate and universal health insurance coverage.

The National Organization for Women (NOW) has been united in its determination to fight efforts to prohibit abortions. The women's movement views access to abortions as a basic right of women to decide what happens to their bodies and to their lives.

Women burdened by unwanted children often become dependent on their partners or on public assistance and find it very difficult to compete with men in the job market. In a key 1989 abortion decision, *Webster v. Reproductive Health Services,* the U.S. Supreme Court gave indications that it may be backing away from its previous position, passed down in *Roe v. Wade* in 1972, which held that women had a right to obtain an abortion in the first trimester of their pregnancy.[83] This 1989 decision gave states the right to pass certain laws regulating abortions. The broader effect of the Court's decision is to throw this hot political issue back to state legislatures. Feminists are hopeful that Clinton will have the opportunity to appoint justices with "pro-choice" views to the Supreme Court, thereby preserving the basic provisions of *Roe v. Wade.*

There is a debate in the women's movement about whether traditional roles held by women should be devalued. Advocates for modern roles emphasize equality and careers, yet some leaders of NOW assert that the role of homemaker should be given equal respect.

One of the directions that the women's movement is taking is to seek help for single-parent families, particularly low-income, female-headed families. There has been a feminization of poverty in this country, and an increasing proportion of poor people are women. It is almost impossible for single mothers to be "financially equal" to males in the job market when day care is highly expensive and when women who work full time are paid considerably less than men who work full time. The women's movement is certain to continue to advocate for increased financial support by the federal government for child care.

The women's movement has also been advocating for "comparable worth." Comparable worth involves the concept of "equal pay for comparable work" rather than "equal pay for equal work." Comparable worth asserts that the intrinsic value of different jobs, such as that of a secretary or plumber, can be measured. Those jobs that are evaluated to be of comparable value should receive comparable pay. If implemented, it is believed that the concept will reduce the disparities in pay between women and men who work full time. Jobs held mainly by women pay an average of 20 percent below equivalent jobs held mainly by men.[84] Some states (such as Wisconsin and Washington) have initiated efforts to develop comparable worth programs for state employees.

Another direction that the women's movement is taking is to encourage and support female candidates for public offices at federal, state, and local levels. The women's movement recognizes that achieving social equality depends partly on moving toward political equality.

The women's movement has made important gains in improving the status of women in our society in the past three decades. It is clear that its general thrust toward equality will continue.

## Summary

In almost every known society, women have had a lower status than men. Women have traditionally been assigned housework and child-rearing responsibilities and have been socialized to be passive, submissive, and "feminine." The socialization process and sex-role stereotyping have led to a number of problems. There is sex discrimination in employment, with men who work full time being paid substantially more than women who work full time. There are double standards for male and female conduct. There are power struggles between males and females, because men are socialized to be dominant in interactions with women, whereas women are more likely to seek equalitarian relationships. Sex-role stereotyping and the traditional female role have caused many women to be unhappier in marriage and to be more depressed than men.

Sex-role stereotyping is pervasive in our society, with aspects found in child-rearing practices, the educational system, religion, contemporary psychological theories, our language, mass media, the business world, marriage and family patterns, and our political system. Scientific evidence indicates that sex-role differences in our society are based primarily on socialization patterns, not on biological differences between males and females.

It is almost impossible for a woman to fill the traditional model woman role—to have the "Miss America" look, to be "feminine," passive, submissive, expressive, and to be "sugar and spice and everything nice." Trying to fill such stereotypes has led to considerable unhappiness and distress for many women.

The women's movement that had a resurgence in the 1960s is revolutionizing sex-role stereotypes and the socialization process. A number of laws forbidding sex discrimination have been enacted. Women (as well as men) are pursuing new careers and taking on roles and tasks that run counter to traditional sex stereotypes. The notion of androgyny (people exploring a broad range of role-playing possibilities and choosing to express emotions and behaviors without regard to sex-role stereotypes) is gaining momentum.

The women's movement also has many payoffs for males. Males find it extremely difficult to fulfill the stereotypes of the "model man" role—always dominant, strong, and never depressed or anxious; to hide emotions, be the provider, and be self-reliant, aggressive, and brave; and never to cry. Men are gradually realizing that this stereotype limits their opportunities for interpersonal relationships, occupations, emotional expression, and domestic activities. Sex-role stereotyping has huge costs for women, for men, and for society. True sexual equality simply means that people would be free to be themselves.

# CHAPTER 8

# *Ageism*

The plight of the elderly is finally recognized as a major social problem in the United States. The elderly face a number of personal problems: high rates of physical illness and emotional difficulties, poverty, malnutrition, lack of access to transportation, low status, lack of a meaningful role in our society, and inadequate housing. A "recently discovered" minority group, the elderly are victimized by job discrimination, excluded from the mainstream of American life based on supposed group characteristics, and subjected to prejudice based on erroneous stereotypes.

This chapter:

♦ Gives an overview of the treatment of the elderly and what being "elderly" means

♦ Explains specific problems faced by the elderly and the causes of these problems

♦ Describes current services to meet these problems and service gaps

♦ Proposes social and political changes to improve the status of the elderly

## An Overview

Throughout time, some tribal societies have abandoned their enfeebled old. For example, the Crow, Creek, and Hopi tribes built special huts away from the tribe where the old were left to die. Eskimos left incapacitated elderly in snowbanks or had them paddle away in a kayak. The Siriono of the Bolivian forest simply left them behind when they moved on in search of food.[1] Even today, the Ik of Uganda leave the elderly and disabled to starve to death.[2] (Generally such societies are forced to abandon their elderly because of scarce resources.)

Although Americans might consider such customs barbaric and shocking, have we not also abandoned our elderly? We encourage them to retire when many are still productive. All too often, when a person retires, he or she suffers a loss of status, power, and self-esteem. Also, we seldom have physical space for large numbers of older people. Community facilities—parks, subways, libraries—are oriented to serving children and young people. Most housing is designed and priced for the young couple with one or two children and an annual income in excess of $30,000. If the elderly are not able to care for themselves (and if their families are unable unwilling to care for them), we store them away in nursing homes.

Our abandonment of the elderly is further indicated by our taking little action to relieve their financial problems; one-fifth have incomes close to or below the poverty line.[3] (In one sense, our abandonment of the elderly is more unethical than that of tribal societies forced by survival pressures to abandon the aged. We do not have such serious survival problems.)

## A "RECENTLY DISCOVERED" MINORITY GROUP

The elderly are a "recently discovered" minority group, whose treatment has come to be viewed as a major social problem.

It is now recognized that, like other minority groups, they are subjected to various discriminations—for example, job discrimination. The most striking example of age-based job discrimination was mandatory retirement, under which people were forced to leave their jobs once they reached a certain age. Mandatory retirement at age sixty-five had been the norm until 1978, when Congress enacted legislation that raised the age to seventy for most jobs. In 1986 Congress, recognizing that mandatory retirement overtly discriminated against the elderly, outlawed most mandatory retirement policies.

The elderly are discriminated against in many other ways as well. For example, older workers are erroneously believed to be less productive. Unemployed workers in their fifties and sixties have greater difficulty finding new jobs and remain unemployed much longer than younger unemployed workers. Ours is a youth-oriented society, which devalues growing old, glorifies the body beautiful and physical attractiveness, and thereby shortchanges the elderly. The elderly are viewed as "out of touch with what's happening," and therefore their knowledge is seldom valued. It is also erroneously believed that intellectual ability declines with age, even though research shows intellectual capacity, barring organic problems, remains essentially unchanged until very late in life.[4]

The elderly are erroneously thought to be senile, conservative, resistant to change, inflexible, incompetent workers, and a burden on the young. Given opportunities, elderly individuals usually prove such prejudicial concepts to be wrong. They generally react to prejudice against them in the same way that racial and ethnic minority groups react, by displaying self-hatred and by being self-conscious, sensitive, and defensive about their social and cultural status.[5] As mentioned previously, individuals who frequently

Box 8.1 ◆◆◆◆◆◆◆◆◆◆◆◆◆◆◆◆◆◆◆◆◆◆

# The Best Years of Your Life

This is Tom Townsend. He was with the iron works plant forty-two years. Being promoted to foreman sixteen years ago had fulfilled his dreams, and there was nothing he desired more than to be on the job and managing his crew. He has been married to Laura for the past thirty-seven years. At first, their marriage had some rough moments, but Laura and Tom grew accustomed to and comfortable with each other over the years. They have a traditional view of the role of women in society. Her main job over the years has been to manage the home. They have two grown children who have moved away and now have homes of their own.

The factory was Tom's life. He didn't have time to develop other hobbies and interests, nor was he interested in picnics or socials. He spent time off from work repairing things around home and "tooling up" for getting back to work. Television replaced talk in his home, and Tom usually spent weekends watching a variety of sports programs.

When Tom turned seventy, he retired. The company marked the occasion with a dinner that was well attended. Tom and Laura were there along with their children and their families, the members of Tom's crew and their wives, and the company manager and their wives. At first everyone was a little anxious, as these people did not often get together socially. The dinner, however, went fairly well. Tom was congratulated by everyone, received a gold watch, and made appropriate remarks about his positive feelings about the company. After a few more cocktails, everyone went home. Tom was feeling sentimental but also good about himself, because everyone was acknowledging his contributions.

Tom awoke at seven o'clock the next morning, his usual time for getting ready for work. Then it hit him. He was retired, with nowhere to go and no reason for rising. His life at the plant was over. What to do now?

He spent the next week following Laura around the house, getting on her nerves. At times he complained about feeling useless. Twice he commented he wished he were dead. He went back to the plant to see his men, but they were too busy to talk. Besides, there was Bill, who had been promoted to foreman and who enjoyed showing Tom how the department's productivity had increased and boring Tom with his plans for making changes to further increase production.

Long walks didn't help much either. As he walked, he thought about his plight and became more depressed. How could he occupy his time meaningfully? He looked into a mirror and saw his receding hairline and numerous wrinkles. More and more, he started to feel a variety of aches and pains. He thought to himself, "I guess I'm just a useless old man." He wondered what the future would hold. Would his company pension keep pace with increasing bills? Would he eventually be placed in a nursing home? What was he going to do with the remainder of his life? He just didn't know.

---

receive negative responses from others eventually come to view themselves negatively.

## DEFINITIONS OF LATER ADULTHOOD

Kornblum and Julian describe some of our myths and stereotypes about the elderly:

> Popular culture characterizes old people as senile, lacking in individuality, tranquil, unproductive, conservative, and resistant to change. These beliefs persist despite abundant evidence to the contrary.[6]

On the other hand, the mass media sometimes portray retired people as able to travel and play golf, in good health, sunning themselves in warm climates in the winter, and free of money worries. For the "young aging," particularly those in upper-income groups, there is some validity to this stereotype. But this is not the experience of most of the elderly in our society.

Giving attention to the social and physical needs of the elderly is a relatively recent phenomenon. In early societies, few persons survived to advanced ages. Life expectancy has increased dramatically in America since the turn of the century—up from forty-nine years in 1900 to seventy-six years at the present time.[7] Also, in most other societies, in contrast to ours, the elderly had meaningful roles to perform—as arbitrators and advisers, as landowners and leaders, as repositories of the wisdom of the tribe, as performers of tasks within their capabilities.

Members of primitive tribes often do not know how old they are; in contrast, chronological age is very important to us. Our passage through life is partially governed by chronological age, which controls when we go to school, drive a car, marry, or vote. Our society also regards sixty-five as the beginning of old age.

In primitive societies, old age is generally determined by physical and mental conditions rather than

# Old Does Not Equal Over

Age need not be a barrier to making major contributions to life. Here are some impressive examples of this frequently unrecognized truth:

- At age 77, Ronald Reagan was president of the United States.
- At 80, George Burns received his first Motion Picture Academy Award, for his role in *The Sunshine Boys.*
- At 81, Johann Wolfgang von Goethe finished writing *Faust.*
- At 81, Benjamin Franklin mediated the compromise that led to the adoption of the U.S. Constitution.
- At 82, Leo Tolstoy wrote *I Cannot Be Silent.*
- At 82, Winston Churchill finished his four-volume text, *A History of the English-Speaking Peoples.*
- At 84, W. Somerset Maugham wrote *Points of View.*
- At 88, Konrad Adenauer was chancellor of Germany.
- At 88, Michelangelo designed the Church of Santa Maria degli Angeli.
- At 88, Pablo Casals was giving cello concerts.
- At 89, Arthur Rubinstein gave a critically acclaimed recital in Carnegie Hall.
- At 89, Mary Baker Eddy headed the Christian Science Church.
- At 89, Albert Schweitzer directed a hospital in Africa.
- At 90, Pablo Picasso still produced engravings and drawings.
- At 91, Eamon de Valera was president of Ireland.
- At 91, Adolf Zukor was chairman of the board of Paramount Pictures.
- At 93, George Bernard Shaw wrote a play entitled *Farfetched Fables.*
- At 94, Bertrand Russell headed international peace drives.
- At 100, Grandma Moses was still painting. (In fact, she didn't *begin* painting until she was 78.)

psychological factors may retard or accelerate the physiological changes.

The process of aging is called *senescence,* the normal process of bodily change that accompanies aging. Senescence affects different persons at different rates. Also, the rates of change in various body processes affected by aging vary among persons. Visible signs of aging include the appearance of wrinkled skin, graying and thinning of hair, and stooped or shortened posture from compressed spinal discs.

As a person ages, blood vessels, tendons, the skin, and connective tissue lose their elasticity. Hardening of blood vessels and stiffening of joints occur. Bones become brittle and thin. Hormonal activity slows, and reflexes become slower. Many of the health problems faced by the elderly result from a general decline of the circulatory system. Reduced blood supply impairs mental sharpness, interferes with balance, and reduces the effectiveness of the muscles and body organs. The probability of strokes and heart attacks also increases.

As a person ages, the muscles lose some of their strength, and coordination and endurance become more difficult. There is also a decline in the functioning of body organs such as the lungs, kidneys, and, to a lesser extent, the brain. As senescence proceeds, hearing and vision capacities decline, food may not taste the same, the sense of touch may become less perceptive, and there may be some loss of memory. Fortunately, the degree to which one's body loses its vitality can be influenced by one's lifestyle. People who are mentally and physically active throughout their younger years remain more alert and vigorous in their later years.

A key notion to remember about senescence is that no dramatic decline need take place at one's sixty-fifth birthday or at any other age. We are all slowly aging throughout our lives; the rate at which we age depends on many factors. Unfortunately, describing the process of aging tends to give the impression that physical and mental functions are reduced to a minimal level. Although somewhat reduced, these functions are sufficient to allow most elderly to remain physically active and mentally alert.

Growing evidence demonstrates that many of the effects of aging are neither irreversible nor inevitable. Many of the supposed effects are largely due to inactivity that is often associated with aging. Learning to reduce stress, as well as taking appropriate exercise, and following proper diet can reverse, or at least hold in abeyance, many of the effects thought to be caused by aging. In one study, a group of seventy-year-old inactive men participated in a daily exercise program;

by chronological age. Primitive societies' definition of *old age* is more accurate than ours. Everyone is not in the same mental and physical condition at age sixty-five. Aging is an individual process that occurs at differing rates in different people, and social-

**Table 8.1**    *Composition of U.S. Population Aged 65 and Older, 1900–2000*

|                                     | 1900 | 1950 | 1970 | 1980 | 1990 | 2000 (projected) |
|-------------------------------------|------|------|------|------|------|------------------|
| Number of older people (in millions) | 3    | 12   | 20   | 25   | 31   | 35               |
| Percent of total population          | 4    | 8    | 9.5  | 11   | 12   | 13               |

*Source:* United States Bureau of the Census. *Statistical Abstract of the United States, 1997* (Washington, DC: U.S. Government Printing Office, 1997).

at the end of a year they had regained the physical fitness levels normally associated with forty-year olds.[8]

In defining *old age*, the federal government generally uses a chronological cutoff point—age sixty-five—to separate elderly adults from others. There is nothing magical or particularly scientific about age sixty-five. In 1883 the Germans set age sixty-five as the criterion for the world's first modern social security system for the elderly.[9] When our Social Security Act was passed in 1935, the United States also selected age sixty-five as the eligibility age level for retirement benefits, based on the German model. It should be noted that the elderly are an extremely diverse group, spanning a range of thirty to thirty-five years. This wide age range by itself leads to considerable diversity. Just as there are substantial differences between people age twenty and those age fifty, there are substantial differences between sixty-five-year-olds and ninety-five-year olds.

## AN INCREASING ELDERLY POPULATION

There are now over ten times as many people age sixty-five and older than there were at the turn of the century. (See Table 8.1.)

Several reasons account for the phenomenal growth of the older population. The improved care of expectant mothers and newborn infants has reduced the infant mortality rate. Vaccinations have prevented many life-threatening childhood illnesses, thus extending longevity. New drugs, better sanitation, and other medical advances have increased the life expectancy of Americans.

Another reason for the increased elderly population is the declining birthrate—fewer babies are being born, whereas more adults are reaching old age. A post–World War II baby boom, roughly from 1947 to 1960, saw the fastest rise in birthrates ever recorded in our society. These births flooded our schools in the 1950s and 1960s. Today these births are crowding the labor market. By the year 2000 this generation will have reached retirement. After 1960, there was a baby bust, a sharp decline in birthrates. (The average births per woman went from a high of 3.8 in 1957 to the current rate of about 2.0.)[10]

Increased life expectancy, and the baby boom followed by the baby bust will significantly increase the median age of Americans in future years. The long-term implications of this increasing median age will be considerable, as the United States will undergo a number of cultural, social, and economic changes.

## THE FASTEST-GROWING AGE GROUP: "OLD OLD"

As our society achieves more success in treating and preventing heart disease, cancer, strokes, and other killers, an increasing percentage of the elderly live into their eighties, nineties, and beyond. People age eighty-five and over—the "old old"—constitute the fastest-growing age group in the United States.

The older population is getting older. In 1995 the 65–74 age group (18.8 million) was eight times larger than in 1900, but the 75–84 group (11.1 million) was fourteen times larger and the 85+ group (3.6 million) was twenty-nine times larger.[11]

We are witnessing "the graying of America," also called "the aging of the aged." This population revolution is occurring rather quietly in our society.

Those who are age 85 and over will present a number of problems and difficult decisions for our society. Alan Otten notes:

> It is these "oldest old"—often mentally or physically impaired, alone, depressed—who pose the major problems for the coming decades. It is they who will strain their families with demands for personal care and financial support. It is they who will need more of such community help as Meals on Wheels, homemaker services, special housing. It is they who will require the extra hospital and nursing-home beds that will further burden federal and state budgets.

BOX 8.3

## Later Adulthood Is the Age of Recompense

The following case example illustrates that how we live in our younger years largely determines how we will live in our later years:

LeRoy was a muscular outgoing teenager. He was physically bigger than most of his classmates and starred in basketball, baseball, and football in high school. In football he was selected an all-state linebacker in his senior year. At age sixteen he began drinking at least a six pack of beer each day, and at seventeen he began smoking. Since he was an athlete, he had to smoke and drink on the sly. Since LeRoy was good at conning others, he found it fairly easy to smoke, drink, party, and still play sports. That left little time for studying, but LeRoy was not interested in that anyway. He had other priorities. He received a football scholarship and went on to college. He did well in football and majored in partying. His grades suffered, and when his college eligibility for football was used up he dropped out of college. Shortly after dropping out, he married Rachel Rudow, a college sophomore. She soon became pregnant and dropped out of college. LeRoy was devastated after leaving college. He had been a jock for ten years, the envy of his classmates. Now he couldn't obtain a job with status. After a variety of odd jobs, he obtained work as a road-construction worker. He liked working outdoors and also liked the macho-type guys he worked, smoked, drank, and partied with.

He had three children with Rachel, but he was not a good husband. He was seldom home, and when he was, he was often drunk. After a stormy seven years of marriage (including numerous incidents of physical and verbal abuse) Rachel moved out and got a divorce. She and the children moved to Florida with her parents so that LeRoy could not continue to harass her and the children. LeRoy's drinking and smoking increased. He was smoking over two packs a day, and sometimes also drank a quart of whiskey.

A few years later he fathered an out-of-wedlock child for whom he was required to pay child support. At age thirty-nine he married Jane, who was only twenty. They had two children together and stayed married for six years. Jane eventually left because she became fed up with being belted around when LeRoy was drunk. LeRoy now had a total of six children to help support and seldom saw any of them. LeRoy continued to drink and also ate to excess. His weight went up to 285 pounds, and by age forty-eight he was no longer able to keep up with the other road-construction workers. He was discharged by the construction company.

The next several years saw LeRoy taking odd jobs as a carpenter. He didn't earn much, and he spent most of what he earned on alcohol. He was periodically embarrassed by being hauled into court for failure to pay child support. He was also dismayed because he no longer had friends who wanted to get drunk with him. When he was sixty-one, the doctor discovered he had cirrhosis of the liver and informed him he wouldn't live much longer if he continued to drink. Since LeRoy's whole life centered around drinking, he chose to continue to drink. LeRoy also noticed that he had less energy and frequently had trouble breathing. The doctor indicated that he probably

And it is they whose mounting needs and numbers already spark talk of some sort of rationing of health care. "Can we afford the very old?" is becoming a favorite conference topic for doctors, bioethicists and other specialists.[12]

Many of the old old suffer from a multiplicity of chronic illnesses. Common medical problems include arthritis, heart conditions, hypertension, osteoporosis (brittleness of the bones), Alzheimer's disease, incontinence, hearing and vision problems, and depression.

The older an elderly person becomes, the higher the probability that she or he will become a resident of a nursing home. Although only about 5% of the elderly are currently in a nursing home, nearly one out of four of those age 85 and over are living in nursing home.[13] The cost to society for such care is high—more than $30,000 a year per person.[14]

Despite the widespread image of families dumping aged parents into nursing homes, most frail elderly still live outside institutional walls, with a spouse, a child, or a relative being the chief caretaker. Some middle-aged people are now encountering simultaneous demands to put children through college and to support an aging parent in a nursing home. (The term

had damaged his lungs by smoking and now had a form of emphysema. The doctor lectured LeRoy on the need to stop smoking, but LeRoy didn't heed that advice either. His health continued to deteriorate, and he lost 57 pounds. At age sixty-four, while drunk, he fell over backward and fractured his skull. He was hospitalized for three and one-half months. The injury permanently damaged his ability to walk and talk. He now is confined to a low-quality nursing home. He is no longer allowed to smoke or drink. He is frequently angry, impatient, and frustrated. He no longer has any friends. The staff detests working with him; his grooming habits are atrocious, and he frequently yells obscenities. LeRoy frequently expresses a wish to die to escape his misery.

ElRoy's early years were in sharp contrast to his brother LeRoy's. ElRoy had a lean, almost puny muscular structure, and did not excel at sports. LeRoy was his parents' favorite and also dazzled the young females in school and in the neighborhood. ElRoy had practically no dates in high school and was viewed as a prude. He did well in math and the natural sciences. He spent much of his time studying and reading a variety of books and liked taking radios and electrical appliances apart. At first, he got into trouble because he was not skilled enough to put them back together. However, he soon became known in the neighborhood as someone who could fix radios and electrical appliances.

He went on to college and studied electrical engineering. He had a zero social life, but graduated with good grades in his major. He went on to graduate school and obtained a masters degree in electrical engineering. On graduation he was hired as an engineer by Motorola in Chicago. He did well there, and in four years was named manager of a unit. Three years later he was lured to RCA with an attractive salary offer. The group of engineers he worked with at RCA made some significant advances in television technology.

At RCA ElRoy began dating a secretary, Elvira McCann, and they were married when he was 36. Life because much smoother for ElRoy after that. He was paid well and enjoyed annual vacations with Elvira to such places as Hawaii, Paris, and the Bahamas. ElRoy and Elvira wanted to have children, but could not. In ElRoy's early forties, they adopted two children, both from Korea. They bought a house in the suburbs and also a sailboat. ElRoy and Elvira occasionally had some marital disagreements, but generally got along well. In their middle adult years, one of the adopted sons, Kim, was tragically killed by an intoxicated automobile driver. That death was a shock and very difficult for the whole family to come to terms with. But the intense grieving gradually lessened, and after a few years Elroy and Elivira put their lives back together.

Now, at age sixty-seven, Elroy is still working for RCA and loving it. In a few years he plans to retire and move to the Hawaiian island of Maui. ElRoy and Elvira have already purchased a condominium there. Their surviving son, Dae, has already graduated from college and is working for a life insurance company. ElRoy is looking forward to retiring so he can move to Maui and get more involved in his hobbies of photography and making model railroad displays. His health is good, and he has a positive outlook on life. He occasionally thinks about his brother and sends him a card at Christmas and at his birthday. Since ElRoy never had much in common with LeRoy, he seldom visits him.

*sandwich generation* has recently been coined to refer to middle-aged parents who are caught in the middle of trying to meet the needs of both their aging parents and their children.)

With people retiring at age 65 or 70 and then living to age 85 or 90, the number of years spent in retirement can be considerable. To maintain the same standard of living after retiring will require immense assets.

Rising health care costs and superlongevity have ignited controversy of whether to ration health care to the very old. For example, should people over age 75 be prohibited from receiving liver transplants or kidney dialysis? Discussion of euthanasia (the practice of killing individuals who are hopelessly sick or injured) has also been stirring increased debate. In 1984 Governor Richard Lamm of Colorado made the controversial statement that the terminally ill have a duty to die. Dr. Eisdor Fer stated:

> The problem is age-old and across cultures. Whenever society has had marginal economic resources, the oldest went first, and the old people bought that approach. The old Eskimo wasn't put on the ice floe; he just left of his own accord and never came back.[15]

*Sandwich generation: Middle-aged parents caught between meeting the needs of their children and their elderly parents.*

## Problems Faced by the Elderly

We have a personal stake in improving the status and life circumstances of the elderly. The elderly are what we are becoming—someday we will be elderly too. If we do not face and solve the problems of the elderly now, we will be in dire straits in the future. Some of these problems are discussed in the following sections.

### LOW STATUS

The elderly suffer because we have generally been unsuccessful in finding something important or satisfying for them to do. In most earlier societies, the old were respected and viewed as useful to their people to a much greater degree than is the case in our society. Industrialization and the growth of modern society have robbed our elderly of high status. Prior to industrialization, older people were the primary owners of property. Land was the most important source of power; therefore the elderly controlled much of the economic and political power. Now people primarily earn their living in the job market, and the vast majority of the elderly own little land and are viewed as having no labor value.

In earlier societies, the elderly were also valued for their knowledge. Their experiences enabled them to supervise planting and harvesting and to pass on knowledge about hunting, housing and craft making. They also played key roles in preserving and transmitting the culture. The rapid advances of science and technology, however, have limited the value of technological knowledge of the elderly; books and other memory-storing devices have resulted in the elderly being less valuable as storehouses of culture and records.

The low status of the elderly is closely associated with *ageism,* a term that refers to having negative images of and attitudes toward people simply because they are old. Today, many people react negatively to the elderly. Ageism is like sexism or racism because it involves discrimination and prejudice against all members of a particular social category.

In the past two hundred years, the status of the elderly has declined, for several reasons. The elderly no longer hold positions of economic power. Children no longer learn their future profession or trade from their parents—instead, such skills are learned through institutions, such as the school system. In addition, the children of the elderly no longer depend on their parents for their livelihood, as they generally are capable of making a living through a trade or profession that is independent of their parents. Finally, the elderly no longer perform tasks viewed as essential by society—often the older worker's skills are viewed as outmoded even before he or she retires.

# High Status for the Elderly in China, Japan, and Other Countries

For many generations the elderly in Japan and China have experienced higher status than the elderly in the United States. In both of these countries the elderly are integrated into their families much more than in the United States. In Japan, more than 75 percent of the elderly live with their children, while in the United States most of the elderly live separately from their children.[a] The elderly in Japan are accorded respect in a variety of ways. For example, the best seats in a home are apt to be reserved for the elderly, cooking tends to cater to the tastes of the elderly, and individuals bow to the elderly.

However, Americans' images of the elderly in Japan and China are somewhat idealized. The elderly, although more revered than in the United States, are not as revered as idealized in the stereotypes that Americans have of elderly Chinese and Japanese. Japan is now becoming more urbanized and Westernized—as a consequence, the proportion of the elderly living

with their parents is decreasing, and the elderly there are now often employed in lower-status jobs.[b]

What factors are associated with whether the elderly are accorded a position of high status in a culture? Five factors have been identified as predicting high status for the elderly in a culture:

1. Older persons are recognized as having valuable knowledge.

2. Older persons control key family and community resources.

3. The culture is more collectivistic than individualistic.

4. The extended family is a common family arrangement in the culture, and older persons are integrated into the extended family.

5. Older persons are permitted and encouraged to engage in useful and valued functions as long as possible.[c]

a. John W. Santrock, *Life-Span Development*, 5th ed. (Madison, WI: Brown & Benchmark, 1995).

b. Ibid., p. 562.

c. Ibid., p. 562.

*Many Asian cultures accord high respect to the elderly.*

Prejudice against the elderly shows up in everyday language—"old buzzard," "old biddy," "old fogey." From a rational view, ageism makes no sense: those who delight in discriminating against the elderly will one day be old themselves. If you believe that "old age is ugly," then you probably are guilty of ageism.

## EARLY RETIREMENT

Maintaining a high rate of employment is a major goal in our society. In many occupations, the supply of labor exceeds demand. An often-used remedy for the oversupply of available employees is early retirement. Forced retirements often create financial and psychological burdens that retirees usually face without much assistance or preparation.

Many workers forced to retire early supplement their pension by obtaining another job, usually of a lower status. Nearly 90 percent of Americans age sixty-five and older are retired, even though many are intellectually and physically capable of working.[16]

Our massive Social Security program supports early retirement, as retirement can come as early as age sixty-two. Some company pension plans and craft unions make it financially attractive to retire as early as fifty-five. Perhaps an extreme case is the armed forces, which permits retirement on full benefits as early as age thirty-eight after twenty years' service.

Early retirement has some advantages to society, such as reducing the labor supply and allowing younger employees to advance faster. But there are also some serious disadvantages. The total taxpayer bill of retirement pensions is already huge and still growing. For the retiree, it means facing a new life and status without much preparation or assistance. Although our society has developed educational and other institutions to prepare the young for the work world, it has not developed comparable institutions to prepare the elderly for retirement. Being without a job in our work-oriented society is often a reality shock for older people.

Our society still views people's worth partly in terms of their work. Individual self-image often is developed in terms of occupation—"I am a teacher," "I am a barber," "I am a doctor." Because the later years generally provide no exciting new roles to replace the occupational roles lost upon retirement, retirees cannot proudly say "I am a . . ." Instead they must say "I *was* a . . ." The more a person's life revolves around work, the more difficult retirement is apt to be.

Retirement often removes people from the mainstream of life. It diminishes their social contacts and their status and places them in a *roleless role*. People who were once valued as salespeople, teachers, accountants, barbers, or secretaries are now considered noncontributors in a roleless role on the fringe of society.

Several myths about the older worker have been widely believed by employers and the general public. For example, they are thought to be less healthy, clumsier, more prone to absenteeism and accidents, more forgetful, and slower in task performance.[17] Research has shown these beliefs to be erroneous. Older workers have lower turnover rates, produce at a steadier rate, make fewer mistakes, have lower absenteeism rates, have a more positive attitude toward their work, and have lower on-the-job injury rates than do younger employees.[18] However, when older workers do become ill, they usually take longer to recover.[19]

Even though employers can no long force a worker to retire, many exert subtle pressures on their older employees to retire. Adjustment to retirement varies for different people. Retirees who are not worried about money and who are healthy are happier in retirement than those who miss their income and do not feel well enough to enjoy their leisure time. Many recent retirees relish the first long stretches of leisure time they have had since childhood. After a while, however, they may begin to feel restless, bored, and useless. Schick found that the most satisfied retirees tend to be physically fit people who are using their skills in part-time volunteer or paid work.[20]

Retirement appears to have little effect on physical health, but it sometimes affects mental health. Bossé, Aldwin, Levenson, and Ekerdt found that retirees are more likely than workers to report depression, obsessive-compulsive behavior, and physical symptoms that had no organic cause.[21] Workers who are pressured to retire before they want to may feel anger and resentment, and may feel out of step with younger workers. Also, workers who defer retirement as long as possible because they enjoy their work may feel no longer working is an immense loss when they are pressured to retire.

On the other hand, some people's morale and life satisfaction remain stable through both working and retirement years. The effect of retirement on the lives of people has positive consequences for some, and negative consequences for others.

The two most common problems associated with retirement are adjusting to a reduced income and missing one's former job. Those who have the most difficulty in adjusting tend to be rigid or overly identify with their work by viewing their job as their

Box 8.5 ◆◆◆◆◆◆◆◆◆◆◆◆◆◆◆◆◆◆◆◆◆◆◆◆

## Disengagement Theory: Response of Individuals and Society to Aging

In 1961 Elaine Cumming and William E. Henry coined the term *disengagement* to refer to a process whereby people respond to aging by gradually withdrawing from the various roles and social relationships they occupied in middle age.[a] Such disengagement is claimed to be functional for the individual, as he or she is thought to gradually lose the energy and vitality to sustain all the roles and social relationships held in younger years.

The term *societal disengagement* has been coined to refer to the process whereby society withdraws from the aging person.[b] It is claimed it is functional for our society—which values efficiency, competition, and individual achievement—to disengage from the elderly, who have the least physical stamina and the highest death rate. Societal disengagement occurs in a variety of ways: older people may not be sought out for leadership positions in organizations, their employers may seek to encourage them to retire, their children may no longer involve them in family decisions, and the government may be more responsive to the needs of younger people. To be fair, societal disengagement is often unintended and unrecognized by society. A number of the elderly do not handle forced role losses well. Some even try to escape through alcohol, drugs, or suicide.

With reference to the two terms just explained, *disengagement theory* thereby hypothesizes a mutual disengagement or withdrawal between the individual and society. Disengagement theory has stimulated considerable interest and research. There is controversy regarding whether disengagement is functional for the elderly and for our society. Research has found some people undeniably disengage voluntarily as they grow older. Yet disengagement is neither a universal nor an inevitable response to aging. Contrary to disengagement theory, most older persons maintain extensive associations with friends. Most also maintain active involvements in voluntary organizations (church groups, fraternal organizations, unions). Some elderly develop new interests after retiring, expand their circle of friends, do volunteer work, and join clubs. Others *rebel* against society's stereotypes and refuse to be treated as if they had little to offer. Many of these people are marshaling political resources to force society to adapt to their needs and skills.

A severe criticism of societal disengagement theory is that it may be used to justify society's failure to help the elderly maintain meaningful roles and thus promote ageism. Disengagement theory may at best be merely a description of the age/youth relationships (and reactions to them), which we should combat as we try to combat ageism.

In contrast to the disengagement theory of aging is the *activity theory*. It asserts that the more physically and mentally active the elderly are, the more successfully they will age. There is considerable evidence that being physically and mentally active will help maintain the physiological and psychological functions of the elderly. In contrast to disengagement theory, which expects the elderly to "slow down," activity theory urges the elderly to remain physically and mentally active.

a. Elaine Cumming and W. E. Henry, *Growing Old: The Process of Disengagement* (New York: Basic Books, 1961), 6.

b. Robert C. Atchley, *Society Forces and Aging*, 7th ed. (Belmont, CA: Wadsworth, 1994).

---

primary source of satisfaction and self-image. Those who are happiest are able to replace job prestige and financial status with values stressing self-development, personal relationships, and leisure activities.

The "golden age" of leisure following retirement appears to be largely a myth. Lawton found that life in retirement is likely to be sedentary, with TV viewing and sleep outranking such traditional leisure-time activities as gardening, sports, clubs, and other pastimes.[22] Many of the elderly are poorly educated, which makes them less likely to enjoy reading or activities that focus on learning or self-improvement. A sharp reduction in income, fear of crime, lack of transportation, and reduced mobility also contribute to the sedentary lifestyle of the elderly.

It would seem far better if workers who are still productive could stay on the job longer on a part- or full-time basis rather than being pensioned off or forced to take another job of a lower status. (This perspective will be expanded on later in this chapter.)

## EMPHASIS ON YOUTH

Our society fears aging more than most other societies. Our emphasis on youth is illustrated by our dread of getting gray hair and wrinkles or becoming

*An elderly man running with his son in the Boston Marathon.*

required "brute" strength, energy, and stamina. Competition has always been emphasized and has been reinforced by Darwin's theory of evolution, which highlighted survival of the fittest and the need to struggle to exist.

## HEALTH PROBLEMS AND COST OF CARE

Later adulthood is a social problem partly because of the high costs of health care. Most of the elderly have at least one chronic condition, and many have multiple conditions. The most frequently occurring chronic conditions are: arthritis, hypertension, hearing impairments, heart disease, orthopedic impairments, sinusitis, cataracts, diabetes, visual impairments, and tinnitus.[23] Older persons see their doctors more frequently, spend a higher proportion of their income on prescribed drugs, and once in the hospital, they stay longer. As might be expected, the health status of the old old (eighty-five and over) is worse than that of the young old.

The medical expenses of an elderly person average more than four times more than those of a young adult.[24] One of the reasons medical costs are higher is because the elderly suffer much more from long-term illnesses—such as cancer, heart problems, diabetes, and glaucoma.[25]

The physical process of aging (senescence) is one reason why the elderly have a higher rate of health problems. However, research in recent years has demonstrated that social and personal stresses also play a major role in causing diseases. The elderly face a wide range of stressful situations: loneliness, death of friends and family members, retirement, changes in living arrangements, loss of social status, reduced income, and a decline in physical energy and physical capacities. Medical conditions may also result from substandard diets, inadequate exercise, cigarette smoking, and excessive alcohol intake. Flynn notes:

> Studies of long-living peoples of the world show that neither heredity nor low prevalence of disease is a significant determinant of longevity. Four other factors are much more likely to predict long-term survival: (1) a clearly defined and valued role in society; (2) a positive self-perception; (3) sustained, moderate physical activity; and (4) abstinence from cigarette smoking. Studies in this country indicate that secure financial status, social relationships, and high education are also important.[26]

(Health care for the elderly is further discussed in Chapter 11.)

bald, and by our being pleased when someone guesses our age to be younger than it actually is. More than other societies, we place a higher value on change and new programs. European societies, on the other hand, have tended to place a higher value on tradition and preserving customs and lifestyles from the past.

Our society places a high value on youthful energy and action. We like to think we are doers. But why this emphasis on youth in our society? The reasons are not fully clear. Industrialization resulted in a demand for energetic, agile, and strong laborers. Rapid advances in technology and science have made obsolete past knowledge and certain specialized work skills (for example, that of a blacksmith). Pioneer living and the gradual expansion of our nation to the West

## Inadequate Income

Many elderly live in poverty. A fair number lack adequate food, essential clothes and drugs, and perhaps a telephone. One-fifth of the elderly have incomes close to or below the poverty line.[27] Only a small minority of the elderly have substantial savings or investments.

Financial problems of the elderly are compounded by the high cost of health care, as previously discussed. Another factor is inflation, especially devastating to those on fixed incomes. Most private pension benefits do not increase after a worker retires. For example, if annual living costs rise at 7 percent, a person on a fixed pension would in twenty years be able to buy one-fourth as many goods and services as she or he could at retirement.[28] Fortunately, in 1974 Congress enacted an "automatic escalator" clause in Social Security benefits, providing a 3 percent increase in payments when the Consumer Price Index (CPI) increased a like amount. However, it should be remembered that Social Security benefits were never intended to make a person financially independent—it is nearly impossible to live comfortably on monthly Social Security checks.

Subgroups of the elderly that have high proportions of members living in poverty include: African Americans, Hispanics, women, and those living alone or with nonrelatives.[29]

The importance of financial security for the elderly is emphasized by Sullivan et al. as follows:

> Financial security affects one's entire lifestyle. It determines one's diet, ability to seek good health care, to visit relatives and friends, to maintain a suitable wardrobe, and to find or maintain adequate housing. One's financial resources, or lack of them, play a great part in finding recreation (going to movies, plays, playing bridge or bingo, etc.) and maintaining morale, feelings of independence, and a sense of self-esteem. In other words, if an older person has the financial resources to remain socially independent (having her own household and access to transportation and medical services), to continue contact with friends and relatives, and to maintain her preferred forms of recreation, she is going to feel a great deal better about herself and others than if she is deprived of her former style of life.[30]

## The Social Security System

The Social Security system was never designed to be the main source of income for the elderly. It was originally intended as a form of insurance that would *partially* supplement other assets when retirement, disability, or death of a wage-earning spouse occurred. Yet many elderly do not have investments, pensions, or savings to support them in retirement, and therefore Social Security has become their major source of income.

The U.S. Social Security system was developed in 1935. The system was fairly solvent until recently. During its first few decades, more money was paid into the system from Social Security taxes imposed on employer and employees than was paid out. This was largely due to the fact that life expectancy was only about sixty years of age. The life expectancy rate, however, has gradually increased to seventy-six.[31] There is a danger that the Social Security system will soon be paying out more than it is taking in. Social Security taxes have increased sharply in recent years, but with the old old being the fastest-growing age group and with the proportion of the elderly increasing in our society, the system may go bankrupt. Some projections have the fund being depleted around 2020.

The *dependency ratio* is the ratio between the number of working people and the number of nonworking people in the population. With the elderly proportion of the population increasing, nonworkers will represent a ballooning burden on workers. Authorities predict that by the year 2020 the dependency ratio will decline from the current level of about 3 workers for every nonworking person to a ratio of about 2 to 1.[32]

Clearly, serious problems exist with the system. First, as already noted, the benefits are too small to meet the financial needs of the elderly. With payments from Social Security, an estimated 80 percent of retirees now live on less than half of their preretirement annual incomes. The monthly payments from Social Security are generally below the poverty line.[33] Second, it is unlikely that the monthly benefits will be raised much, because the amount of Social Security taxes paid by employees is already quite high.

The nation faces some hard choices about how to keep the system solvent in future years. Benefits might be lowered but this would even further impoverish recipients. Social Security taxes might be raised, but there is little public support for this, as the maximum tax rate has already increased more than tenfold since 1970 (about $400 in 1970 to about $5,000 at the present time per employee).[34]

## Loss of Family and Friends

Single elderly generally are less well-off than married elderly. The longer life span of women has left nearly

# Alzheimer's Disease

Tony Wilkins is sixty-eight years old. Two years ago his memory began to falter. As the months went by, he even forgot what his wedding day to Rose had been like. His grandchildren's visits slipped from his memory in two or three days.

The most familiar surroundings have become strange to him. Even his friends' homes seem like places he has never been before. When he walks down the streets in his neighborhood, he frequently becomes lost.

Tony is now quite confused. He has difficulty speaking and can no longer perform such elementary tasks as balancing his checkbook. At times Rose, who is taking care of him, is uncertain whether he knows who she is. All of this is very baffling for Tony. Until he retired three years ago, he had been an accountant and had excelled at remembering facts and details.

Tony has Alzheimer's disease. Although the disease sometimes strikes in middle age, most sufferers are over sixty-five. Estimates of its prevalence range from 2 to 10 percent of all people over sixty-five and from about 13 to 50 percent of people eighty-five and over.[a] The statistics indicate the disease affects the old old to a greater extent than the younger old.

Alzheimer's disease is a degenerative brain disorder that causes gradual deterioration in intelligence, memory, awareness, and ability to control bodily functions. In its final stages, Alzheimer's leads to progressive paralysis and breathing difficulties. The breathing problems often result in pneumonia, the most frequent cause of death for Alzheimer's victims. Other symptoms include irritability, restlessness, agitation and impairments of judgment. Although most of those affected are over sixty-five, the disease occasionally strikes people in middle age.

Over a period lasting from as few as five years to as many as twenty, the disease destroys brain cells. The changes in behavior displayed by those afflicted show some variation. Brownlee notes:

> One sufferer refuses to bathe or change clothes, another eats fried eggs without utensils, a third walks naked down the street, a fourth has the family's beloved cats put to sleep, while yet another mistakes paint for juice and drinks it. The outlandish acts committed by Alzheimer's patients take as many forms as there are people who suffer the disease. Yet in every case, the bizarre behavior serves as a sign that the sufferer is regressing towards unawareness, a second childishness.[b]

The most prominent early symptom of Alzheimer's is memory loss, particularly for recent events. Other early symptoms (which are often overlooked) are a reduced ability to play a game of cards, reduced performance at sports, and sudden outbreaks of extravagance. More symptoms then develop—irritability, agitation, confusion, restlessness, and impairments of concentration, speech, and orientation. As the disease progresses, the symptoms become more disabling. Caregivers eventually have to provide twenty-four-hour supervision—which is a tremendous burden. As the disease progresses in its final stages, a nursing home placement is often necessary. Near the end, the patient usually cannot recognize family members, cannot understand or use language, and cannot eat without help.

Brownlee describes the mental and physical trauma that caregivers and family members of those afflicted experience:

> They live in a private hell, one that cannot be discussed with neighbors and friends in too much detail because the details are so devastating. They grieve even as their loved ones plunge them into a maelstrom of unreality, where mothers streak through the living room wearing nothing but a

---

60 percent of women over age sixty-five without a spouse.[35] Gordon Moss and Walter Moss comment about the value of marriage for older persons:

> They now have much more time for and are more dependent upon each other. Some marriages cannot handle this increased togetherness, but those that can become the major source of contentment to both partners. A good marriage, or a remarriage, provides the elderly person with companionship and emotional support, sex, the promise of care if he is sick, a focus for

daily activities, and frequently greater financial independence. Sex roles often blur, and the husband actively helps in household chores.[36]

The elderly person's life becomes more isolated and lonely when close friends and relatives move away or die. Latter adulthood, of course, is a time when close friends are most apt to die.

The needs of aging parents can present some painful dilemmas for their children, especially if the parents are poor or in ill health. The children may

shower cap and garter belt and grandfathers try to punch their baby granddaughters.[c]

In addition, the patient's inability to reciprocate expressions of caring and affection robs relationships of intimacy.

Diagnosing the disease is difficult because the disorder has symptoms that are nearly identical to those of other forms of dementia. The only sure diagnosis at the present time is observation of tissue deep within the brain, which can be done only by autopsy after death. Doctors usually diagnose the disease in a living person by ruling out other conditions that could account for the symptoms.[d]

Researchers in recent years have made tremendous strides in identifying the causes of Alzheimer's disease. As of 1997 three different genes have been identified as being linked to causing the disease. There may be additional genes that are associated with the disease. Yet, having one or more of these genes does not always result in the development of this disorder. Therefore researchers believe there must be some yet-unidentified "triggers." Possible triggers are such variables as viral infections, biochemical deficiencies, high levels of stress, toxic poisons, exposure to radiation, and nutritional deficiencies. Scientists are now aware that genetic tendencies are a contributing factor as relatives of Alzheimer's patients have an increased risk of having the disease in the future.[e]

Scientists are now investigating a number of hypotheses as to what triggers Alzheimer's. One intriguing clue comes from the finding that victims of Down's syndrome (a severe form of mental retardation due to a chromosome defect) who survive into their thirties frequently develop symptoms indistinguishable from those of Alzheimer's. Another recent clue is the discovery of fragments of amyloid in brains of persons who died from the disorder. Amyloid is a very tough protein that in normal amounts is necessary for cell growth throughout the body. Some researchers hypothesize that abnormal patches of this protein in the brain set up a chain reaction that progressively destroys brain cells. This amyloid protein is an abnormal product formed from a larger compound called amyloid precursor protein, or APP.

Researchers are now seeking to develop a test to detect Alzheimer's disease in its early stages. If Alzheimer's disease can be detected in its early stages, people will be better able to plan for their future care and make arrangements for their families while they still retain control of their mental faculties. Furthermore, if in fact Alzheimer's disease results from an accumulation of the amyloid protein, and if the early accumulation of this protein can be detected, then it is likely that drugs can be developed to treat the disorder by blocking the formation of amyloid in the brain.[f]

At the present time there is no cure for the disease. Patients with Alzheimer's receive some relief from drugs that reduce depression and agitation and help them sleep. Both vitamin E and selegiline (a drug used against Parkinson's disease) seem to slow the progress of Alzheimer's disease. Exercise, physical therapy, proper nourishment, and proper fluid intake are also beneficial. Memory aids assist somewhat in everyday functioning. Especially helpful to patients and their families are emotional and social support provided by groups and professional counseling.

a. Diane Papalia and Sally W. Olds. *Human Development.* 6th ed. (New York: McGraw-Hill, 1995), 541.

b. S. Brownlee, "Alzheimer's: Is There Hope?" *U.S. News & World Report*, Aug. 12, 1991, 40–49.

c. Brownlee, "Alzheimer's: Is There Hope?," 48.

d. L. L. Heston and J. A. White, *Dementia* (New York: Freeman, 1983).

e. Papalia and Olds, *Human Development*, 539–42.

f. S. S. Sisodia, E. H. Koo, K. Beyreuthe, A. Unterbeck, and D. L. Price. "Evidence That B-Amyloid Protein in Alzheimer's Disease Is Not Derived by Normal Processing," *Science*, 248 (Apr. 27, 1990), 492–95.

have families of their own, requiring heavy responsibilities on their time and finances. For children on tight budgets, deciding how to divide their resources among their parents, their own children, and themselves can be agonizing. Some children face the difficult question of whether to maintain a parent within their home, to leave the parent living alone, to place the parent in a nursing home, or to place the parent in some other housing for the elderly (such as a group home).

## HOUSING

We hear so much about nursing homes that few people realize 95 percent of the elderly do not live in nursing homes or in any other kind of institution.[37] About 77 percent of all elderly males are married and live with their wives.[38] Because females tend to outlive their spouses, about 40 percent of women over age 65 live alone.[39] Nearly 80 percent of older married couples maintain their own households—in

Box 8.7

# Triple Jeopardy: Being Female, African American, and Old

The poverty rate for elderly females is almost double that of elderly males.[a] Many immigrant ethnic groups in our society traditionally have relegated the woman's role to family maintenance. Younger, female African Americans have been victimized by both sexism and racism. Despite their positive status in the African-American family and the African-American culture, African-American women over the age of seventy are the poorest population group in the United States.[b]

Three out of five elderly African-American women live alone; most of them are widowed.[c] The poverty rate of this age group is related to ageism, sexism, and racism. In the past these women tended to hold very low-paying jobs—some of which were not even covered by Social Security, or, in the case of domestic service was not apt to be reported by the employer even though the reporting is legally required.

Even though many of these women are struggling (financially, socially, and physically), Edmonds notes that they have shown remarkable adaptiveness, resilience, coping skills, and responsibility.[d] Extension of family networks helps them cope with the bare essentials of living, and gives them a sense of being loved. African-American churches have provided avenues for meaningful social participation, social welfare services, feelings of power, and a sense of internal satisfaction. These women have also tended to live together in ethnic minority communities, giving them a sense of belonging. These women have also tended to adhere to the American work ethic, and have viewed their religion as a source of strength and support. Nonetheless, the income and health of older African-American women (as well as that of other ethnic minority individuals) are important concerns in our aging society.

---

a. John W. Santrock, *Life-Span Development*, 5th ed. (Madison, WI: Brown & Benchmark, 1995), 560.

b. Ibid., 560.

c. Ibid., 560.

d. M. Edmonds, "The Health of the Black Aged Female." In Z. Harel, E. A. McKinney and M. Williams (eds.) *Black Age* (Newbury Park, CA: Sage, 1990).

---

apartments, mobile homes, condominiums, or their own houses.[40] When the elderly do not maintain their own households, they most often live in the homes of relatives, primarily one of their children.

The elderly who live in rural areas generally have a higher status than those in urban areas. People living on farms can retire gradually. Also, people whose income is in land, rather than in a job, can retain importance and esteem to an advanced age.

However, about three-quarters of our population reside in urban areas, where the elderly often live in poor-quality housing.[41] At least 30 percent of the elderly live in substandard, deteriorating, or dilapidated housing.[42] Often the urban elderly live in inner-city hotels or apartments with inadequate living conditions. Their neighborhoods may be decaying and crime-ridden, which makes them easy prey for thieves and muggers.

Fortunately, many mobile-home parks, retirement villages, assisted living residences, and apartment complexes geared to the needs of the elderly have been built throughout the country. Such housing communities provide a social center, security/protection, sometimes a daily hot meal, and perhaps a little help with maintenance.

## TRANSPORTATION

Owning and driving a car is a luxury only the more affluent and physically vigorous elderly can afford. The lack of convenient, inexpensive transportation is a problem faced by most elderly.

## CRIME VICTIMIZATION

Having reduced energy, strength, and agility, the elderly are vulnerable to being victimized by crime, particularly robbery, aggravated assault, burglary, larceny, vandalism, and fraud. Many of the elderly live in constant fear of being victimized, although reported victimization rates for the elderly are lower than rates for younger people. The actual victimization rates for the elderly may be considerably higher than official crime statistics indicate, because many of the elderly feel uneasy about becoming involved with the legal and criminal justice systems. Therefore, they may not report some of the crimes they are victims of. Some of the elderly are afraid of retaliation from the offenders if they report the crimes, and some of the elderly dislike the legal processes they have to go through if they press charges.

Some of the elderly are hesitant to leave their homes for fear they will be mugged or for fear their homes will be burglarized while they are away.

## SEXUALITY IN LATER ADULTHOOD

There is a common misconception that older people lose their sexual drive. If an older male displays sexual interest he is labeled a "dirty old man." When two older people exhibit normal heterosexual behavior, someone is apt to comment "Aren't they cute?" Yet many older people have a strong sexual interest and a satisfying sex life.[43] Sexual capacities, particularly in women, show little evidence of declining with age, and a large percentage of both elderly men and women are capable of sexual relations.[44]

William Masters and Virginia Johnson see no reason why sexual activity cannot be enjoyed by the elderly.[45] If sexual behavior does decline, it probably is due more to social reasons than to physical reasons. According to Masters and Johnson, the most important deterrents to sexual activity when one is older are the lack of a partner, overindulgence in drinking or eating, boredom with one's partner, attitudes toward sex (such as the erroneous belief that sex is inappropriate for the elderly), poor physical or mental health, attitudes toward menopause, and fear of poor performance.[46]

The attitudes of the "younger generation" frequently create problems for the elderly. A widow or widower at times faces strong opposition to remarrying from other family members. Negative attitudes are often strongest when an elderly person becomes interested in someone younger who will become an heir if the older person dies. The elderly are sometimes informed that they should not be interested in members of the opposite sex, and that they should not establish new sexual relationships when they have lost a mate.

Fortunately, the attitudes toward sexuality in late adulthood are changing. Merlin Taber notes:

> With the changing attitudes of younger people to alternatives to the traditional family, some older people are finding informal arrangements for living together attractive. The couple who do not have a marriage ceremony can share all the companionship and sexual satisfactions without upsetting inheritance rights and retirement benefits. When they become aware of it, their children may accept such a pattern because they find it preferable to remarriage. We have no idea of the numbers that are involved, but the old as well as the

*Romance and sexual interest does not necessarily decline as people grow older*

young have new options as societal norms change. The popularity of living together without marriage will probably increase.[47]

## MALNUTRITION

The elderly are the most uniformly undernourished segment of our population.[48] There are a number of reasons for chronic malnutrition among the elderly: transportation difficulties in getting to grocery stores; lack of knowledge about proper nutrition; lack of money to purchase a well-balanced diet; poor teeth and lack of good dentures, which greatly limit one's diet; lack of incentives to prepare an appetizing meal when one is living alone; and inadequate cooking and storage facilities.

## EMOTIONAL PROBLEMS

The older person is often a lonely person. Most people seventy years of age or older are widowed, divorced, or single. When someone has been married for many years and his or her spouse dies, a deep sense of loneliness usually occurs that seems unbearable. The years ahead often seem full of emptiness. It is not surprising, then, that depression is the most common emotional problem of the elderly. Symptoms of depression include feelings of uselessness, of being a burden, of being unneeded, of loneliness, and of hopelessness. Somatic symptoms of depression include loss of weight and appetite, fatigue, insomnia, and constipation. It is often difficult to determine whether such somatic symptoms are due to depression or to an organic disorder.

Depression can alter the personality of an elderly person. Depressed people may become apathetic, withdrawn, and show a slowdown in behavioral actions. An elderly person's reluctance to respond to questions is apt to be due to depression rather than to the contrariness of old age.[49]

Those who have unresolved emotional problems in earlier life will generally continue to have them when older. Often, these problems will be intensified by the added stresses of aging.

Two major barriers to good mental health in the late years are failure to bounce back from psychosocial losses (such as the death of a loved one) and failure to have meaningful life goals. Later adulthood is a time when there are drastic changes thrust on the elderly that may create emotional problems: loss of a spouse, loss of friends and relatives through death or moving, poorer health, loss of accustomed income, and changing relationships with children and grandchildren.

Unfortunately, there is an erroneous assumption that *senility* and *mental illness* are inevitable and untreatable. On the contrary, the elderly respond well to both individual and group counseling.[50] In addition, even many ninety-year-olds show no sign of senility. Senility is by no means an inevitable part of growing old.

Elderly males have the highest suicide rate of any age group in the United States.[51] Although the elderly make up about 13 percent of the population, about 25 percent of reported suicides occur in this age group.[52] The suicide rate of white men in their eighties is three times that of men in general.[53] There are a variety of reasons why the elderly have a high rate of suicide, including: declining health, loss of status, reduced income, and lack of relationships with families and friends. The higher suicide rate for elderly males is thought to be due to the fact that males are more apt than females in our society to make work the central focus of their lives; once they retire, many no longer see a reason for living.

## DEATH

Preoccupation with dying, particularly with the circumstances surrounding it, is an ongoing concern of the elderly. For one reason, they see their friends and relatives dying. For another, they realize they've lived many more years than they have left.

The elderly's concern about dying is most often focused upon dreading the disability, the pain, and long periods of suffering that may precede death.[54] They generally would like a death with dignity in their own homes, with little suffering, with mental faculties intact, and with families and friends nearby. The elderly are also concerned about the costs of their final illness, the difficulties they may cause others by the manner of their death, and whether their resources will permit a dignified funeral.

In our society, we tend to wall the dying off with silence. One of the reasons we do this is it helps us avoid acknowledging our own mortality. We often force people to die alone. In hospitals, great efforts are made to separate the dying from the living. Dying patients are sometimes moved into separate rooms. Sometimes the medical staff attempts to shield the dying person from becoming aware of impending death. Families, too, also begin to treat the patient differently when they know the end is near. (Being treated differently by medical staff and family often subtly informs the dying that death is imminent.)

In modern America most deaths occur in nursing homes or hospitals, with the dying surrounded by medical staff.[55]

Fortunately the hospice movement has developed in an attempt to allow the terminally ill to die with dignity—to live their final weeks in the way they want to. Hospices have their origin among European religious groups in the Middle Ages who welcomed travelers who were sick, tired, or hungry.[56]

Hospices view the *disease* as terminal, not the patient. Hospices emphasize helping patients to use their time left, rather than trying to keep people alive as long as possible. Many hospice programs are set up to assist patients to live their remaining days in the home of their family. In addition to medical and visiting nurse services, hospice volunteers help the patient and family with counseling, transportation, filling out insurance forms and other paperwork, and respite care (that is, staying with the patient to provide temporary relief for family members). Pain relievers are used extensively so that the patient can live out final days in relative comfort.

## PARENT ABUSE

Parent abuse refers to elderly parents who are abused by children they live with or depend on. This problem is described in more depth in Chapter 10.

## Current Services

Present services and programs for the elderly are primarily maintenance in nature, as they are mainly designed to meet basic physical needs. Nonetheless, there are a number of programs, often federally funded, to provide services needed by the elderly. Before we briefly review many of these programs, we will look at the Older Americans Act of 1965, which has set objectives for programs that serve the elderly.

## OLDER AMERICANS ACT OF 1965

The Older Americans Act of 1965 created an operating agency (Administration on Aging) within the Department of Health, Education, and Welfare (as of 1980, the Department of Health and Human Services). This law and its amendments are the basis for financial aid by the federal government to assist states and local communities to meet the needs of the elderly. The objectives of the act are to secure for the elderly:

♦ An adequate income

♦ Best possible physical and mental health

♦ Suitable housing

♦ Restorative services for those who require institutionalized care

♦ Opportunity for employment

♦ Retirement in health, honor, and dignity

♦ Pursuit of meaningful activity

♦ Efficient community services

♦ Immediate benefit from research knowledge to sustain and improve health and happiness

♦ Freedom, independence, and the free exercise of individual initiative in planning and managing their own lives[57]

Although these objectives are commendable, in reality these goals have not been realized for many of the elderly. However, some progress has been made. Many states have state offices on aging, and some municipalities and counties have established community councils on aging. A number of universities have established centers for the study of gerontology, which focus on research on the elderly and training of students for working with the elderly in such disciplines as nursing, psychology, medicine, sociology, social work, and architecture. (Gerontology is the scientific study of the aging process from the physiological, pathological, psychological, sociological, and economic points of view.) Government research grants are being given to encourage the study of the elderly and their problems. Publishers are now producing books and pamphlets to inform the public about the elderly, and a few high schools are beginning to offer courses to help teenagers understand the elderly and their circumstances.

A number of programs, often federally funded and administered at state or local levels, provide funds and services needed by the elderly. A few of these are listed in Box 8.9.

## NURSING HOMES

Because of the national attention given to nursing homes, we will take a closer look at them. Nursing homes were created as an alternative to expensive hospital care and are substantially supported by the federal government through Medicaid and Medicare. More than 1.6 million older people now live in extended-care facilities, making nursing homes a billion-dollar industry.[58] There are more patient beds in nursing homes than in hospitals.[59]

Nursing homes are classified according to the kind of care they provide. At one end of the scale are residential homes that provide primarily room and board, with some nonmedical care (such as help in dressing). At the other end are nursing-care centers that provide skilled nursing and medical attention twenty-four hours a day. The more skilled and extensive the medical care, the more expensive the home. The cost per resident averages more than $3,000 per month.[60] Although only about 5 percent of the elderly live permanently in homes, many spend some time convalescing in them.

One scandal after another characterizes care in some nursing homes. Patients have been found lying in their own feces or urine. In some nursing homes the food is so unappetizing that some residents refuse to eat it. Some homes have serious safety hazards. In some homes, boredom and apathy is common among staff as well as residents.

A number of nursing homes fail to meet food sanitation standards and have problems administering drugs and providing personal hygiene for residents.[61]

Donald Robinson conducted a nationwide investigation of nursing homes and concluded: "I learned that the majority of nursing homes are safe, well-run institutions that take good care of the sick people entrusted to them. Some are superb."[62] Robinson

# Ethical Issue: Should Assisted Suicide Be Legalized?

The technology of life-support equipment can keep people alive almost indefinitely. Respirators, artificial nutrition, intravenous hydration, and so-called miracle drugs not only sustain life but also trap many of the terminally ill in a degrading mental and physical condition. Such technology has raised a variety of ethical questions. Do people who are terminally ill and in severe pain have a right to die by refusing treatment? Increasingly, through "living wills," patients are able to express their wishes and refuse treatment. However, does someone in a long-term coma who has not signed a living will have a right to die? How should our society decide when to continue and when to stop life-support efforts? Courts and state legislatures are presently working through the legal complexities governing death and euthanasia.

Should assisted death, or assisted suicide, be legalized? As of 1999 only the Netherlands permitted physicians to give qualifying terminally ill patients a lethal dose of drugs. There is considerable controversy about assisted suicide in the United States. Hemlock Society founder Derek Humphrey has written a do-it-yourself suicide manual that has become a bestseller. (The Hemlock Society promotes active voluntary euthanasia.) Michigan doctor Jack Kevorkian has made national news by building a machine to help terminally ill people end their lives and by assisting a large number of them to do so.

In the Netherlands an informal, *de facto* arrangement made with prosecutors more than twenty-five years ago allows physicians there to help patients die, as long as certain safeguards are followed. The patient, for example, has to be terminally ill, in considerable pain, and mentally competent; she or he must also repeatedly express a wish to die.

Oregon's Death with Dignity Act was passed by voters in 1994. It allows doctors to prescribe lethal drugs at the request of terminally ill patients who have less than six months to live. Doctors may only prescribe a lethal dose, not administer it.

People in favor of assisted suicide argue that unnecessary, long-term suffering is without merit and should not have to be endured. They argue that people have a right to a death with dignity, which means a death without excessive emotional and physical pain and without excessive mental, physical, and spiritual degradation. They see assisted suicide as affirming the principle of autonomy—upholding the individual's right to make decisions about his or her dying process. Allowing the option of suicide for the terminally ill is perceived as the ultimate right of self-determination.

Opponents assert that suicide is unethical and is a mortal sin for which the deceased cannot receive forgiveness. They view assisted suicide as assisted murder. They assert that modern health care can provide almost everyone a peaceful, pain-free, comfortable, and dignified end to life. Opponents believe that most terminally ill persons consider suicide not because they fear death but because they fear dying—pain, abandonment, and loss of control—all of which the hospice is designed to alleviate. Horror stories of intense suffering are most often the tragic results of medical mismanagement, they feel. Moreover, assisted-suicide legislation could easily result in the philosophy that the terminally ill have a *duty* to die, in order to avoid being a financial and emotional burden to their families and to society.

---

also noted a number of horrors and abuses in some of the homes. The abuses included giving new and unapproved drugs to patients without their consent, giving patients heavy doses of tranquilizers to keep them docile, stealing funds from patients, submitting phony cost reports to Medicare, and charging patients thousands of dollars to gain admission to a home; there were also instances of sexual abuse of patients by staff members.[63]

At present, people of all ages tend to be prejudiced against nursing homes, even those that are well run. Frank Moss describes the elderly person's view of nursing homes: "The average senior citizen looks at a nursing home as a human junkyard, as a prison—a kind of purgatory, halfway between society and the cemetery—or as the first step of an inevitable slide into oblivion."[64] To some degree there is reality to the notion that nursing homes are places where the elderly wait to die.

The cost of care for impoverished nursing home residents is largely paid by the Medicaid program (described in chapter 11). Since the federal government has set limits on what will be reimbursed under Medicaid, other problems may arise. There may be an effort to keep salary and wage levels as low as possible and the number of staff to a minimum. A nursing home may postpone repairs and improvements. Food is apt to be inexpensive such as macaroni and cheese,

A health care system intent upon cutting costs could give subtle, even unintended, encouragement to a patient to die. Relatives of a terminally ill person receiving expensive medical care may put pressure on the person to chose physician-assisted suicide to avoid eroding the family's finances. There is concern that, if competent people are allowed to seek death, the pressure will grow to use the treatment-by-death option with adults in comas or with others who are mentally incompetent (such as the mentally ill and those who have a severe cognitive disability). Finally, many people worry that, if the "right to die" becomes recognized as a basic right in our society, then it can easily become a "duty to die" for the elderly, the sick, the poor, and others devalued by society.

Some authorities have sought to make a distinction between active euthanasia (assisting in suicide) and passive euthanasia (withholding or withdrawing treatment). In many states it is legal for physicians and courts to honor a patient's wishes to not received life-sustaining treatment.

A case of passive euthanasia involved Nancy Cruzan. On January 11, 1983, when this Missouri woman was 25, her car overturned. Her brain lost oxygen for 14 minutes following the accident, and for the next several years she was in a "persistent vegetative state," with no hope of recovery. A month after the accident, her parents, Joyce and Joe Cruzan, gave permission for a feeding tube to be inserted. In the months that followed, however, the parents gradually became convinced there was no point in keeping Nancy alive indefinitely in such a hopeless condition.

In 1986 they were shocked when a Missouri state judge informed them that they could be charged with murder for removing the feeding tube. The Cruzans appealed the decision all the way to the U.S. Supreme Court, requesting the Court to overturn a Missouri law that specifically prohibits withdrawal of food and water from hopelessly ill patients. In July 1990 the Supreme Court refused the Cruzans' request that their daughter's tube be removed but ruled that states could sanction the removal if there is "clear and convincing evidence" that the patient would have wished it. Cruzan's family subsequently found other witnesses to testify that Nancy would not have wanted to be kept alive in such a condition.

A Missouri judge decided that the testimony met the Supreme Court's test. The tube was disconnected in December 1990, and Nancy Cruzan died several days later, on December 26.

At the present time, 10,000 Americans are in similar vegetative conditions, unable to communicate. Many of these individuals have virtually no chance to recover. Right-to-die questions will undoubtedly continue to be raised in many of these cases.

In June 1997 the U.S. Supreme Court ruled that terminally ill people do not have a constitutional right to doctor-assisted suicide. The Court upheld laws in New York and Washington State that make it a crime for doctors to give life-ending drugs to mentally competent but terminally ill patients who no longer want to live. The judges in their ruling made it clear that their decision does not permanently attempt to resolve the assisted suicide issue, and they in fact urged that debate continue about this issue.

Do you believe that the terminally ill have a right to die by refusing treatment? Do you believe that assisted suicide should be legalize? If you had a terminally ill close relative who was in intense pain and asked you to assist her or him in acquiring a lethal dose of drugs, how would you respond? Would you be willing to help? Or would you refuse?

which is high in fat and carbohydrates. Congress has mandated that every nursing home patient on Medicaid is entitled to a monthly personal spending allowance. The homes have control over these funds, and some homes keep this money.

A danger of nursing home care is the potential abuse of the residents by staff members. In a telephone survey of 577 nurses and nurses' aides, Pillemer and Moore heard many instances of abuse by staff.[65] More than one-third of the respondents stated they had seen other staff members physically abusing patients—pushing, shoving, pinching, hitting, or kicking them; throwing things at them; or restraining them more than necessary. Ten percent acknowledged committing one or more of these acts themselves. Psychological abuse was even more common, with 81 percent of the respondents indicating they had seen other staff members yelling at patients, insulting them, swearing at them, isolating them unnecessarily, threatening them, or refusing to give them food. Forty percent of the respondents acknowledged committing such abuse themselves!

Complaints about the physical facilities of nursing homes include not enough floor space or too many people in a room. The call light by the bed may be difficult to reach, or the toilets and showers may not be conveniently located. And the building may be in a state of decay.

Box 8.9

# Programs for the Elderly

- *Medicare:* Helps pay medical and hospital expenses (described in Chapter 11).

- *Old Age, Survivors, and Disability Insurance:* Provides monthly payments to eligible retired workers (described in Chapter 9).

- *Supplemental Security Income:* Provides a minimum income for indigent elderly (described in Chapter 9).

- *Medicaid:* Pays for most medical expenses for low-income people (described in Chapter 11).

- *Food Stamps:* Offsets some of the food expenses for low-income people who qualify (described in Chapter 9).

- *Nursing Home Ombudsman Program:* Investigates and acts on concerns expressed by residents in nursing homes.

- *Meals on Wheels:* Provides hot and cold meals to house-bound recipients incapable of obtaining or preparing their own meals but able to feed themselves.

- *Senior-citizen centers, golden-age clubs, and similar groups:* Provide leisure and recreational activities.

- *Special bus rates:* Reduced bus transportation costs.

- *Property tax relief:* Available to the elderly in many states.

- *Protective services for adults:* Serve adults who are neglected or abused, or whose physical or mental capacities have substantially deteriorated.

- *Special federal income tax deduction:* For people over sixty-five.

- *Housing projects for the elderly:* Built by local sponsors with financing assistance by the Department of Housing and Urban Development (HUD).

- *Reduced rates at movie theaters and other places of entertainment:* Often offered voluntarily by individual owners.

- *Home health services:* Provide visiting-nurse services, physical therapy, drugs, laboratory services, and sickroom equipment.

- *Nutrition programs:* Provide meals for the elderly at group "eating sites." (These meals are generally provided four or five times a week and usually are luncheon meals. These programs improve the nutrition of older adults and offer opportunities for socialization.)

- *Homemaker services:* Provided in some communities to take care of household tasks that the elderly no longer can do for themselves.

- *Day-care centers:* Provide activities that are determined by the needs of the group. (This service relieves the family from around-the-clock care. Programs such as home health services, homemaker services, and day-care centers prevent or postpone institutional care.)

- *Telephone reassurance:* Provided by volunteers, often other older persons, who telephone elderly people who live alone. (Such calls provide meaningful social contact for both parties and also monitor for accidents or other serious problems requiring emergency attention.)

- *Nursing homes:* Provide residential care and skilled nursing care when independence is no longer practical for the elderly or their families.

---

While the quality of nursing home care ranges from excellent to awful, nursing homes are needed, particularly for those requiring round-the-clock health care for an extended time. If nursing homes were abolished, other institutions such as hospitals would have to serve the elderly. Life in nursing homes need not be bad. Where homes are properly administered, residents can expand their life experiences.

The ideal nursing home should be lively (with recreational, social, and educational programming), safe, hygienic, and attractive. It should offer stimulating activities and opportunities to socialize with people of both sexes and all ages. It should offer privacy so that (among other reasons) residents can be sexually active. It should offer a wide range of therapeutic, social, recreational, and rehabilitative services. The best-quality care tends to be provided by larger nonprofit facilities that have a high ratio of nurses to nurse's aids.[66]

At present only 5 percent of the elderly population reside in nursing homes. However, it is estimated that one out of every five of us who live beyond age sixty-five will spend part of our life in a nursing home.[67]

## The Future

In spite of all the maintenance programs that are now available for the elderly, the key problems of the elderly remain to be solved. A high proportion of the elderly do *not* have "meaningful" lives, respectful status, adequate income, adequate transportation, good living arrangements, adequate diet, or adequate health care.

## THE ELDERLY AS A POWERFUL POLITICAL FORCE

Most programs for the elderly are designed to maintain them at their current level of functioning, rather than to enhance their social, physical, and psychological well-being. In spite of all the maintenance programs available for the elderly, key problems remain to be solved. A high proportion of the elderly do not have meaningful lives, respected status, and adequate income, transportation, living arrangements, diet, or health care.

The elderly are victims of ageism—prejudice and discrimination against the elderly. How can we defend urging people to retire when they are still productive? How can we defend the living conditions within some of our nursing homes? How can we defend our restrictive attitudes toward sexuality among the elderly? How can we defend providing services to the elderly that are limited to maintenance and subsistence, while a wide range of services are being provided to help younger people live gratifying and fulfilling lives? According to Gordon and Walter Moss: "Just as we are learning that black can be beautiful, so we must learn that gray can be beautiful, too. In so learning, we may brighten the prospects of our own age."[68]

In the past, prejudice was most effectively combated when those being discriminated against joined together for political action. Therefore, it seems apparent that, if major changes are to take place in the elderly's role in our society, it will have to be done through political action.

Older people are in fact becoming increasingly involved in political activism and, in some cases, even radical militancy. Two prominent organizations are the American Association of Retired Persons (AARP) and its affiliated group, the National Retired Teachers Association (NRTA). These groups, among other projects, are lobbying for the interests of the elderly at local, state, and federal levels of government.

An action-oriented group that has caught the public's attention is the Gray Panthers. The organization argues that a fundamental flaw in our society is the emphasis on materialism and on the consumption of goods and services, rather than on improving the quality of life for all citizens (including the elderly). The Gray Panthers seek to end ageism and to advance the goals of human freedom, human dignity, and self-development. This organization emphasizes using social action techniques, including getting the elderly to vote as a block on issues that concern them. The founder of the group, Maggie Kuhn, stated: "We are not mellow, sweet old people. We have got to effect change, and we have nothing to lose."[69]

There are clear indications that the politics of age have arrived. The elderly are rapidly becoming one of the most politically organized and influential groups in America. The past thirty-five years have seen some significant steps toward securing a better life for the elderly: increased Social Security payments, enactment of Medicare and Medicaid programs, the emergence of hospices, and the expansion of a variety of other programs for the elderly. With this population segment becoming a powerful political bloc, we are apt to see in future years a number of changes to improve the status of the elderly in our society.

## FINDING A SOCIAL ROLE FOR THE ELDERLY

The elderly face a variety of problems. Following retirement, their income drops, often to below poverty levels. Health care expenses rise considerably, as the elderly are more susceptible to chronic illnesses. With reduced income, their living standard drops dramatically. With less money, the elderly often reduce their physical and mental activities, which accelerates the aging process. The life expectancy of the elderly is increasing, with the old old being the fastest growing age group in our society. The elderly depend on the Social Security system for a large amount of their income; yet the monthly payments are inadequate, and with the increasing number of recipients, the system may go bankrupt. Young people today can no longer count on the Social Security system being their primary source of income when they grow old and retire. The elderly have a roleless role in our society, and are the victims of ageism. How can these problems be combated?

*Maggie Kuhn is co-founder of the Gray Panthers. Ms. Kuhn was 81 when this photo was taken.*

It would seem essential to find a meaningful productive role for the elderly. At the present time early retirement programs that many businesses have and society's stereotypical expectations of the elderly often result in the elderly being unproductive, inactive, dependent, and unfulfilled. To develop a meaningful role for the elderly in our society, the productive elderly should be encouraged to continue to work, and the stereotypical expectations of the elderly should be changed.

The elderly who want to work and are still performing well should be encouraged to continue working past age sixty-five or seventy. Also, if an elderly person wants to work half-time or part-time, this should be encouraged. For example, two elderly persons working half-time could fill a full-time position. New roles might also be created for the elderly to be consultants after they retire in the area where they possess special knowledge and expertise. For those who do retire, there should be educational and training programs to help them develop their interests and hobbies (such as photography) into new sources of income.

Working longer in our society would have a number of payoffs for the elderly and for society. The elderly would continue to be productive, contributing citizens. They would have a meaningful role. They would continue to be physically and mentally active. They would have higher self-esteem. They would begin to break down the stereotypes of the elderly being unproductive and a financial burden on society. They would be paying into the Social Security system, rather than drawing from it.

What is being proposed here is a system for the elderly to have a productive role, either as paid workers or as volunteers. In our materialistic society perhaps the only way for the elderly to have a meaningful role is to be productive. The elderly face the choice (as do younger people) between having adequate financial resources through productive work or inadequate financial resources by not working.

Objections to such a system may be raised by those who maintain some of the elderly are no longer able to be productive. This may be true, but some young people are also unproductive. What is needed to make the proposed system work is jobs having realistic, objective, and behaviorally measurable levels of performance. Those at any age who do not meet the performance levels would first of all be informed about the deficiencies, and would be given training to meet the deficiencies. If the performance levels still were not met, discharge processes should be used as a last resort. For example, if a tenured faculty member was deficient in levels of performance—as measured by student-course evaluations, peer faculty evaluations of teaching, record of public service, record of service to the department and to the campus, and record of publications—that faculty member should first of all be informed of the deficiencies. Training and other resources to meet the deficiencies should be offered. If the performance did not improve to acceptable standards, then dismissal proceedings would be initiated. Some colleges and universities are now moving in this direction.

In the productivity system that is being suggested, the elderly would have an important part to play. They would be expected to continue to be productive within their capacities. By being productive, they would serve as examples to counter the current negative stereotypes of the elderly.

Another objection that has been voiced about this new system is that the elderly have worked most of their lives and therefore deserve to retire and live in leisure with a high standard of living. It would be nice if the elderly had this option. It would be nice if no one had to work, yet had a high standard of living. However, that is not realistic. Most of the elderly do not have the financial resources, after retiring, to maintain a high standard of living. The fact is that when most of the elderly retire, their income and their standard of living are both sharply reduced. The choice in our society is really between working and thereby maintaining a high standard of living or retiring and having a lower standard of living.

We are already seeing a number of the elderly heading in this productive direction. Most members of the U.S. Supreme Court and many members of Congress are over age seventy. In addition, a number of organizations have been formed to promote the productivity of the elderly. Three examples of these organizations are: Retired Senior Volunteer Program, Service Corps of Retired Executives, and Foster Grandparent Program.

The *Retired Senior Volunteer Program* (RSVP) offers people over age sixty the opportunity of doing volunteer service to meet community needs. RSVP agencies place volunteers in hospitals, schools, libraries, day-care centers, courts, nursing homes, and a variety of other organizations.

The *Service Corps of Retired Executives* (SCORE) offers retired businessmen and businesswomen an opportunity to help owners of small businesses and managers of community organizations who are having management problems. Volunteers receive no pay but are reimbursed for out-of-pocket expenses.

The *Foster Grandparent Program* employs low-income older people to help provide personal, individual care to children who live in institutions. (Such children include those who have a severe cognitive disability, those who are emotionally disturbed, and those who have a developmental disability.) Foster grandparents are given special assignments in child care, speech therapy, physical therapy, and as teacher's aides. This program has been shown to be of considerable benefit both to the children and to the foster grandparents.[70] The children served become more outgoing and have improved relationships with peers and staff. They have increased self-confidence, improved language skills, and decreased fear and insecurity. The foster grandparents have an additional (although small) source of income, increased feelings of vigor and youthfulness, an increased sense of personal worth, a feeling of being productive, and a renewed sense of personal growth and development. For society, foster grandparents provide a vast pool of relatively inexpensive labor to do needed work in the community.

The success of these programs illustrates that the elderly can be productive in both paid and volunteer positions. In regard to using elderly volunteers in agencies, Atchley makes the following recommendations to further successful outcomes:

First, agencies must be flexible in matching the volunteer's background to assigned tasks. If the agency takes a broad perspective, useful work can be found for almost anyone. Second, *volunteers must be trained*. All too often agency personnel place unprepared volunteers in an unfamiliar setting. Then the volunteer's difficulty confirms the myth that you cannot expect good work from volunteers. Third, a variety of placement options should be offered to the volunteer. Some volunteers prefer to do familiar things; others want to do *anything but* familiar things. Fourth, training of volunteers should not make them feel that they are being tested. This point is particularly sensitive among working-class volunteers. Fifth, volunteers should get personal attention from the placement agency. There should be people (perhaps volunteers) who follow up on absences and who are willing to listen to the compliments, complaints or experiences of the volunteers. Public recognition from the community is an important reward for voluntary service. Finally, transportation to and from the placement should be provided.[71]

A 1990 study found a surprisingly large number of recent retirees who say they would like to be back at

## Community Options Program: Providing Alternatives to Nursing-Home Placement

**W**isconsin's Community Options Program (COP) is an innovative program that provides alternatives to nursing-home placement. COP is funded by state and federal monies and administered by county social service departments.

To qualify for the program a person must have a long-term or irreversible illness or disability and be a potential or current resident of a nursing home or facility for persons with a developmental disability. The person must also have income and assets that are below the poverty line. If these eligibility guidelines are met, a social worker and a nurse assess applicants for their social and physical abilities and disabilities to determine the types of services needed.

If an alternative to nursing-home placement is available, financially feasible, and, most important, acceptable to an applicant, a plan for services is drawn up and a start date for in-home or in-community services is determined.

A wide variety of alternative services may be provided, including homemaker services, visiting-nurse services, home-delivered meals, adult foster care, group home care, and case management. COP is a coordinated program that makes use of a number of resources from a variety of agencies. Wisconsin is finding that the program is not only cost effective compared to the high cost of nursing-home care but also preferred over nursing-home care by service recipients.

should lessen the fear of growing old. For those of modest means who have prepared thoughtfully, later adulthood can be a period, if not of luxury, then at least of reasonable comfort and pleasure.

Our lives largely depend upon our goals and our motivations to achieve those goals. How we live prior to retiring will largely determine whether later adulthood will be a nightmare or fulfilling and gratifying. There are a number of areas we should attend to in our younger years:

*Health*   A sound exercise plan and periodic health examinations are critical to the prevention of chronic health problems. Also critically important in maintaining health is learning and using approaches to reduce psychological stress (see Chapter 11).

*Finances*   Saving money for later years is important and so is learning to manage or budget money wisely.

*Interests and Hobbies*   Psychologically, people who are traumatized most by retirement are those whose self-image and life interests center around their work. People who have meaningful hobbies and interests look forward to retirement in order to have sufficient time for them.

*Self-Identity*   People who are comfortable and realistic about who they are and what they want out of life are better prepared, including in later years, to deal with stresses and crises that arise.

*Looking Toward the Future*   A person who dwells in the past or rests upon past achievements is apt to find the older years depressing. On the other hand, a person who looks to the future generally has interests that are alive and growing and is thereby able to find new challenges and new satisfactions in later years. Looking toward the future involves planning for retirement, including deciding where you would like to live, in what type of housing and community, and what you look forward to doing with your free time.

*Effective Problem Solving*   If a person learns to cope effectively with crises in younger years, these coping skills will remain when a person is older. Involved in effective coping is learning to approach problems realistically and constructively.

work.[72] Half are satisfied, one-quarter are unable to work because of health or family situations, and one-quarter (about two million) say they prefer working again over retirement.

## PREPARING FOR LATER ADULTHOOD

Growing old is a lifelong process. Becoming sixty-five does not destroy the continuities between what a person has been, is, and will be. Recognition of this fact

## Summary

Aging is an individual process that occurs at differing rates in different people. Chronological age is not an accurate measure of how physically fit and mentally alert an elderly person is.

People sixty-five and older now compose over one-tenth of our population. The old old are now the fastest growing age group in our society. The elderly encounter a number of problems in our society: low status, lack of a meaningful role, the emphasis on youth in our society, health problems, inadequate income, loss of family and friends, inadequate housing, transportation problems, restrictive attitudes about expressing their sexuality, malnutrition, crime victimization, and emotional problems (such as depression and concern with circumstances surrounding dying). A majority of the elderly depend on the Social Security system as their major source of income. Yet monthly payments are inadequate, and the system is no longer financially sound.

A wide array of services are available to the elderly, but these are primarily geared to maintaining them, often at or only slightly above a subsistence level of existence. Services provided in many of our nursing homes are inadequate, and the level of care in some of these homes has been sharply criticized. Nursing homes have also been criticized as being "storage centers" for the elderly so that young members of our society can avoid coming face to face with their own mortality.

Although the level of care needs to be substantially improved in some of them, nursing homes are needed for the elderly who cannot take care of themselves and/or for those whose families can no longer provide care. Most elderly, however, do not need nursing homes for permanent care or shelter (95 percent of the elderly live independently or with relatives, not in nursing homes).

In many ways the elderly are victims of ageism. Increasingly, the elderly are becoming politically active and organized to work toward improving their status. Gradually, the composition of the elderly population will change; aging people will become better educated and a more powerful political bloc. In the future there are apt to be a number of social, economic, and political changes that will improve the status of the elderly.

# CHAPTER 9

# *Poverty*

overty has always been one of the most serious problems in our country. In most other countries, it is even more severe.) In our modern society, more than 36 million Americans, about 14 percent of our population, are estimated to be living below the poverty line.[1] (The poverty line is the level of income that the government considers sufficient to meet the basic requirements of food, shelter, and clothing.) In other words, nearly one out of seven Americans is poor.

This chapter:

♦ Presents a brief history of U.S. response to poverty

♦ Defines poverty and considers its effects and extent, including the income and wealth gaps between the rich and the poor in this country

♦ Summarizes the causes of poverty

♦ Outlines current programs to combat poverty and discusses their merits and shortcomings

♦ Suggests possible strategies to reduce poverty in the future

## Poverty in the United States

xxxxxxxxxxxxxxxxxxxxx

Throughout our history, a significant proportion of our population has always been impoverished. Yet poverty has seldom been recognized as a major social problem. Prior to the 1960s the topic of poverty was seldom discussed in social problems textbooks and was practically nonexistent in sociological literature.[2]

## HISTORY OF OUR RESPONSE TO THE POOR

One of the problems faced by our societies is to develop ways to meet the needs of those who are living in poverty. The way a society cares for its needy reflects its values. Prior to the Industrial Revolution, this responsibility was usually assumed by extended-family members, the church, and neighbors. One of the values of the Judeo-Christian religion throughout history has been humanitarianism, that is, ascribing a high value to human life and benevolently helping those in need.

From the mid-eighteenth through the nineteenth centuries, the Industrial Revolution flourished in Europe and America. A major reason for its development was a series of technological advances, such as the development of the steam engine. But the revolution was also made possible by the so-called *Protestant ethic* and the *laissez-faire* economic view. These two themes had important effects on the poor. The Protestant ethic emphasized *individualism,* the view that one is responsible for one's actions and conditions in life. Hard work and acting in one's self-interest were highly valued. An overriding goal resulting from the practice of the Protestant ethic was to acquire material goods. People tended to be judged not so much on the basis of their personalities and other attributes as on how much wealth they had acquired. To be poor was thought to be due to one's own deficiencies.

The laissez-faire economic theory asserted that the economy and society in general would best prosper if businesses and industries were permitted to do whatever they desired to make a profit. Any regulation of business practices by the government (for example, setting safety standards, passing minimum wage laws, prohibiting child labor) was discouraged. Many businessmen used the Protestant ethics and laissez-faire economics to justify such business practices as cutthroat competition, formation of monopolies, deplorable safety and working conditions, and exploitation of the working class through low pay, long hours, and child labor.

The implications of the Protestant ethic for the poor reached an inhumane apex in the theory of *Social Darwinism,* which was based on Charles Darwin's theory of the evolution of species. Darwin theorized that higher forms of life evolved from lower forms through survival of the fittest. He had seen in the animal world a struggle for survival that rewarded those best fitted to their environment and produced evolutionary change. Herbert Spencer, extending this theory to society, thought struggle and survival of the fittest to be essential to progress in human society. The theory stated, in its most inhumane form, that the strong (the wealthy) survived because they were superior, whereas the weak (the needy) *should* perish and that it would be a mistake to help the weak survive. Although leaving the weak to perish was never advocated widely, the theory did justify our society making very few efforts to develop programs to help the poor.

Around 1800 various segments of the population became aware of the evils of unlimited competition and abuses by those with economic power. It became clear that a few captains of industry were becoming very wealthy while the standard of living for most of the population remained static and only slightly above subsistence. One leader of this new social view was

# The Ideology of Individualism

In this country, wealth is generally inherited. There are few individuals who actually move up the social status ladder. Having wealth opens up many doors (through education and contacts) for children of the wealthy to make large sums of money when they become adults. For children living in poverty there is little chance to escape when they become older. Yet the individualism myth is held by many. It states that the rich are personally responsible for their success and that the poor are to blame for their failure. The main points of this individualism myth are:

♦ Each individual should work hard to succeed in competition with others.

♦ Those who work hard should be rewarded for their success (such as wealth, property, prestige, and power).

♦ Because of extensive employment opportunities and because of equal opportunity legislation, those who work hard will in fact be rewarded with success.

♦ Economic failure is an individual's own fault and reveals lack of effort and other character defects.

The poor are blamed for their circumstances in our society. Blaming the poor has led to a stigma attached to poverty, particularly to those who receive public assistance (welfare).

*Source:* Philip R. Popple and Leslie H. Leighninger, *Social Work, Social Welfare, and American Society* (Boston, MA: Allyn and Bacon, 1990), 28–30.

---

Lester Ward, who in *Dynamic Sociology* (1883) drew a sharp distinction between purposeless animal evolution and human evolution.[3] Ward asserted that everyone could benefit from improving environmental conditions and from social and economic controls. This new thinking was in direct opposition to Social Darwinism and the laissez-faire economic view. It called on the federal government to take on new functions: regulation of business practices through legislation and provision of programs for the poor. As a result, around 1900 there was an awakening to social needs, with the federal government allocating limited funds to programs such as health, housing, and slum clearance.

The Great Depression of the 1930s brought profound changes in programs for the poor. Until this time America still largely subscribed to the doctrine of individualism (see Box 9.1). The depression severely tested this belief. With an estimated 15 million people unemployed in the middle and upper classes, it became clear that events beyond individual control could cause deprivation, misery, and poverty. In addition, it became obvious that private social work agencies, which up until then had been a major source of financial assistance to the poor, did not have the resources to meet the needs of the large numbers of unemployed and poor. Therefore, the federal government was called on to fill this new role.

In 1935 the Social Security Act was passed, which formed the basis of most of the current public programs to help the poor. (These programs are described later in this chapter.) The basic intent of the Social Security Act was to provide a decent standard of living to every American. President Franklin Roosevelt, the main architect of this act, believed that financial security (including public assistance) should not be a matter of charity but a matter of justice. Not only did he believe every individual has a right to a minimum standard of living in a civilized society, he believed liberty and security were synonymous. He believed people without financial security would eventually despair and revolt. Therefore, he believed, the very existence of a democratic society depended on the health and welfare of its citizens.

After 1935 our country's economy slowly began to recover, and some who lived in poverty began to enjoy a more affluent lifestyle (although many others remained living in poverty). Unfortunately, the latter were left behind and forgotten. Public concern switched to World War II in the early 1940s and then to issues such as the Korean War and halting the spread of communism. From the 1940s through the 1950s, poverty was no longer recognized as a major problem, although large segments of the population continued to live in abject poverty.

In 1960 John Kennedy saw large numbers of people in many states living in degrading human circumstance due to poverty. He made poverty an issue in his national presidential campaign, so that once again poverty was targeted as a major social problem. In 1962 Michael Harrington published *The Other America,* which graphically described the plight of the

20 percent or one-fifth of our population who lived in poverty.[4] The media publicized the poverty issue, and public concern increased dramatically.

In 1964 President Lyndon Johnson initiated the War on Poverty with the stated hope of eradicating poverty and creating the Great Society. Eliminating poverty became one of our nation's highest priorities. A variety of programs were established to wipe out poverty: Head Start, VISTA (Volunteers in Service to America), Job Corps, Title I Educational Funding, Community Action Program, Youth Corps, and Neighborhood Legal Services.

Although these programs reduced poverty somewhat, the optimism of the early 1960s of being able to eradicate poverty was far from successful. The Vietnam War in the late 1960s drained resources that might otherwise have been spent on domestic programs; it also distracted attention away from poverty.

In the early 1970s, after the end of the Vietnam War, for several years the turmoil of the late 1960s was replaced with relative calm on both the foreign and domestic fronts. In contrast to the hope of the 1960s that government programs could cure our social ills, an opposing philosophy emerged that assumed many problems were beyond the capacity of the government to alleviate. Hence the liberalism of the 1960s that resulted in the expansion and development of new social programs was replaced by a more conservative approach in the 1970s and 1980s. Practically no new, large-scale social welfare programs were initiated.

During President Jimmy Carter's administration (1976 to 1980) there was increased recognition that the federal government simply did not have the power—no matter how much money it spent—to eliminate poverty and other social ills. Instead of a recognition that the government could partially allay *many* of these problems, there appears to have been a 180-degree turn in which many citizens began despairing and demanding that government should sharply reduce the amount of tax money spent on social welfare programs.

In 1980 Ronald Reagan was elected president on a platform that called for (1) sharp cuts in individual and corporate taxes, (2) large increases in military spending, and (3) drastic cuts in social welfare programs. Reagan was successful in accomplishing all three of these objectives. His massive cutback in federal support for social welfare programs was the first large-scale reduction in federal support of such programs in our country's history. Practically every social program was cut back, and some were eliminated. In 1988 George Bush was elected president on a conservative platform, and he continued the social welfare policies of the Reagan administration.

The Reagan and Bush administrations endorsed an economic program that cut taxes and government spending, eliminated cumbersome federal regulations and red tape that restricted the growth of business and industry, and provided incentives to the private sector for expansion and greater employment. The stated objective was to create a period of prosperity that "trickles down" to the lowest stratum so that everyone benefits. The result, however, was that the gap between the rich and the poor widened, with the poor failing to benefit from the improved financial circumstances of the rich.[5] The people hurt the most by cutbacks in funding of federally financed social welfare programs were present and former recipients.

What have been the longer-term effects of these cutbacks? Many of our present social problems have intensified: The proportion of people living in poverty has increased, more citizens are hungry, the income gap between the rich and the poor has widened, efforts to reduce racial discrimination have slowed, prisons are overflowing, many of the chronically mentally ill have been released from mental hospitals and now live in squalor without receiving supportive services, the plight of inner-city people is as bleak as when our inner cities erupted in the 1960s, and single-parent families continue to increase in number. More and more we hear alarming stories of people living in poverty and despair. In some cities the unemployed stand in food lines for free meals provided by voluntary organizations. The number of homeless and hungry continues to grow.

Bill Clinton was elected president in 1992. During his campaign Clinton promised "to end welfare as we know it." He was referring specifically to federal entitlement programs, particularly AFDC (Aid to Families of Dependent Children). AFDC was a major component of the so-called social safety net of measures designed to prevent poverty from turning into starvation and abject destitution. The conservative sweep of both houses of Congress in 1994 and President Clinton's endorsement of welfare reform legislation prior to the 1996 presidential election were important political steps toward the most far-reaching changes in support for poor families and individuals since the 1930s. The 1996 welfare reform legislation (also known as the Personal Responsibility and Work Opportunity Reconciliation Act) ended the sixty-year-old AFDC program.

## Personal Income Disparities Are Astounding

In some countries in the world the average per capita income is less than $500 per year. In the United States, more than 36 million people (nearly 14 percent of the population) are living in poverty. (In 1996, the poverty threshold for a family of four was $16,036.)

In fall 1997, Kevin Garnett signed a six-year deal for $123 million with the Minnesota Timberwolves (a professional team in the National Basketball Association). The deal of $17.3 million annual average was (at the time) the richest long-term sports contract. Kevin Garnett was only twenty years old when he signed the contract—he joined the NBA after high school, without ever attending (or playing basketball in) college.

From 1996 to 1997, according to *Forbes* magazine, Bill Gates's net worth more than doubled in one year. His net worth in October 1997 was $39.8 billion. During this one-year time period he made an astounding average of $400 million per week, which is more than $50 million per day! Bill Gates is chair of the Microsoft Corp.

*Sources:* U.S. Bureau of the Census, *Statistical Abstract of the United States, 1997* (Washington, DC: U.S. Government Printing Office), 1997; Randolph E. Schmid, "Census Bureau: Poor Lose, Rich Win," *Wisconsin State Journal*, September 30, 1997, 2A; and Eric R. Quinones, "Rich get Richer: Forbes Lists 170 Billionaires," *Wisconsin State Journal*, Oct. 14, 1997, 2A.

legislation asserts single mothers (and fathers) now have an obligation to work for a living.

What will be the long-term effects of this recent welfare to work legislation? Will the legislation harm poor people, particularly poor children? It is too early to tell, but even conservative critics of the old welfare system are worried that drastic cuts in welfare benefits and the new punitive measure will create additional social problems and a potential backlash against the 1996 welfare reform legislation.[6]

Kornblum and Julian note:

Welfare critics on the liberal or left side of the political spectrum have been asking with increasing frequency why it is that the public and political leaders have been so determined to attack AFDC since it was a relatively small federal program. It never cost more than about 1 percent of the federal budget, and fewer than 5 million people are on the rolls, a number that has not changed appreciably since the 1970s. One answer is that beginning in the early 1980s, the welfare poor have been targeted as examples of the failure of liberal antipoverty policies. To afford tax cuts and budget reductions it has been necessary to cut programs for the most vulnerable and politically powerless segments of the population. The poor are foremost among those groups. So are immigrants, whose benefits are also scheduled for cuts under the new policies being formulated in many states. The idea that some people could subsist on payments that transferred funds from the more well-to-do to the poor, and that in some cases they could live that way for years without any work requirement, became an easy target for those who wished to decrease federal spending.[7]

The 1996 welfare reform legislation, and other programs to combat poverty, are discussed in greater detail later in this chapter.

## THE RICH AND THE POOR

Throughout most countries in the world, wealth is concentrated in the hands of a few individuals and families. Poverty and wealth are closely related in that abundance for a few is often created through deprivation of others.

There are two ways of measuring the extent of economic inequality. *Income* refers to the amount of money a person makes in a given year. *Wealth* refers to a person's total assets—real estate holdings, cash, stocks, bonds, and so forth.

The distribution of wealth and income is highly unequal in our society. Like most countries, the United States is characterized by *social stratification;*

Under 1996 welfare reform legislation, parents whose household incomes fall below a given level (depending on the size of the household) are *no* longer entitled to federal funds administered through state and country welfare agencies. Instead, states now receive block grants (that is, large sums of money earmarked for assistance to the poor) from the federal government. Federal requirements of these block grants specify that recipients of financial benefits cannot receive more than two years of financial assistance without working, and there is a five-year limit of benefits for adults. In 1935 when the AFDC program was enacted as a component of the Social Security Act, it was thought it was best for single mothers to stay at home to raise their children. The 1996 welfare reform

that is, it has social classes, with the upper classes having by far the greatest access to the pleasures that money can buy.

Although this chapter focuses on poverty in the United States, it is important to note that there is a growing gap between the rich and the poor in most countries. In the world today there are about 170 billionaires and about 2 million millionaires, but there are approximately 100 million homeless people.[8] Americans spend about $5 billion per year on diets to lower their caloric intake while 400 million people around the world are undernourished to the point of physical deterioration.[9] Kornblum and Julian note:

> These growing disparities between rich and poor throughout the world have a direct bearing on the situation of the poor in the United States because American jobs are being "exported" to areas where extremely poor people are willing to accept work at almost any wage. World poverty also contributes to environmental degradation, political instability, and violence—all problems that drain resources that could be used to meet the nation's domestic needs.[10]

In the United States, the wealthiest 1 percent of all households hold about 34 percent of all personal wealth.[11] (Net worth refers to the value of all assets minus debts; assets include savings and checking accounts, automobiles, real estate, and stocks and bonds.) The distribution of income is also unequal. The wealthiest 20 percent of households in the United States receive nearly 50 percent of all income, whereas the poorest 20 percent receive less than 5 percent of all income.[12]

In the words of a pastoral letter issued by a committee of Roman Catholic bishops, "The level of inequality in income and wealth in our society . . . must be judged morally unacceptable."[13] Paul Samuelson, an economist, provides a dramatic metaphor of the disparity between the very rich and most people in the United States:

> If we made an income pyramid out of a child's blocks, with each layer portraying $1,000 of income, the peak would be far higher than the Eiffel Tower, but almost all of us would be within a yard of the ground.[14]

Given the enormous wealth of the richest 20 percent, it is clear that a simple redistribution of some of the wealth from the top one-fifth to the lowest one-fifth could easily wipe out poverty. Of course, that is not politically acceptable to members of the top fifth, who have the greatest control of the government. It should also be noted that many of these rich families avoid paying income taxes by taking advantage of tax loopholes and tax shelters.

An estimated 30 million Americans are hungry, due to lack of financial resources, at least some period of time each month.[15] Millions of those who go hungry in the United States are children.

Hunger can have devastating effects on young children, including causing mental retardation. The brain of an infant grows to 80 percent of its adult size within the first three years of life. If supplies of protein are inadequate during this period, the brain stops growing, the damage is irreversible, and the child will be permanently retarded.[16]

Coleman and Cressey describe the respective effects of wealth and poverty:

> The economic differences between the rich, the poor, and the middle class have profound effects on lifestyles, attitudes toward others, and even attitudes toward oneself. The poor lack the freedom and autonomy so prized in our society. They are trapped by their surroundings, living in run-down, crime-ridden neighborhoods that they cannot afford to leave. They are constantly confronted with things they desire but have little chance to own. On the other hand, wealth provides power, freedom, and the ability to direct one's own fate. The wealthy live where they choose and do as they please, with few economic constraints. Because the poor lack education and money for travel, their horizons seldom extend beyond the confines of their neighborhood. In contrast, the world of the wealthy offers the best education, together with the opportunity to visit places that the poor haven't even heard of.
>
> The children of the wealthy receive the best that society has to offer, as well as the assurance that they are valuable and important individuals. Because the children of the poor lack so many of the things everyone is "supposed" to have, it is much harder for them to develop the cool confidence of the rich. In our materialistic society people are judged as much by what they have as by who they are. The poor cannot help but feel inferior and inadequate in such a context.[17]

## THE PROBLEM OF POVERTY

In 1997, more than 36 million people, about 14 percent of our population, were living below the poverty line.[18] (The poverty line is the level of income that the federal government considers sufficient to meet basic requirements of food, shelter, and clothing.) A cause for alarm is that the rate of poverty is higher now than it was in 1980, and the poverty rate in 1997 was nearly as high as it was in 1966.[19]

# Wealth Perpetuates Wealth, and Poverty Perpetuates Poverty

The following summaries of the life experiences of two people illustrate that in the United States wealth perpetuates wealth, and poverty perpetuates poverty.

Tim Mills is the son of wealthy parents (both of whom also had parents in the upper social class). Tim Mills's mother, Suzanne, is a successful stock broker; his father, David, is a successful attorney. (Their household income is in excess of $300,000 per year.) After Tim was born, he was always dressed in the finest clothes money could buy, and his parents focused on providing extensive early stimulation and on providing the highest quality educational experiences.

He attended expensive private schools in kindergarten, elementary school, middle school, and high school. The schools had low student-to-teacher ratios, so Tim Mills received extensive attention from his teachers. The parents of Tim always were highly involved in the parent-teacher associations in the school systems, which encouraged the teachers to give Tim extra attention, and also to frequently praise him, which contributed to Tim developing a positive self-concept and a high level of self-confidence.

Tim's parents liked to travel to other countries two or three times a year, and they always took Tim along, which helped Tim learn to understand and appreciate diversity and other cultures. It also led Tim to understand that he needed to attain a college education in order to secure a high-paying position in order to have the privileges that money can buy.

Tim's mother and father had friends who were also in the power elite in their community. Tim was introduced to this higher circle, and made friends with the children of the parents in the power elite. In this sphere of the power elite, he acquired skills and confidence in his ability to socialize and to increasingly participate in the decisions being made by this power elite. After graduating from high school, he attended a prestigious private college on the East Coast, and many of his high school friends attended the same college. Upon graduation from the four-year college, he attended a prestigious law school, and graduated with honors. His father's connections helped him join a distinguished law firm, as a corporate attorney, upon receiving his law degree. A year after graduating from law school, he married Virginia DeMarco, a lawyer whom he met while in law school—who had a similar upper-class background. Five years later, their household income per year was in excess of $500,000.

In contrast, the following summary of Marcee Calvello's life describes how poverty and dismal living conditions lead to despair, hopelessness, and failure.

Marcee Calvello was born and raised in New York City. Her father had trouble holding a job because he was addicted to cocaine, and her mother was an alcoholic who divorced her husband when Marcee was three years old. Marcee's mother at first sought to provide a better home for Marcee and her three brothers. She worked part-time and also went on AFDC. However, her addiction to alcohol consumed most of her time and money. Neighbors reported the children were living in abject neglect, and Protective Services removed Marcee and her brothers to foster care. Marcee was placed in a series of foster homes—a total of seventeen different homes. In one of these homes her foster father sexually assaulted her, and in another a foster brother assaulted her. Being moved from foster home to foster home resulted in frequent school changes. Marcee grew distrustful of the welfare system, schoolteachers and administrators, males, and anyone else who sought to get closer to her.

When she turned eighteen, the state no longer paid for her foster care. She got a small efficiency apartment that cost her several hundred dollars a month. Because she dropped out of school at age sixteen, she had few marketable job skills. She worked for a while at some fast-food restaurants. The minimum wage she received was insufficient to pay her bills. Eight months after she moved into her apartment she was evicted. Unable to afford another place, she started living in the subway system of New York City. She soon lost her job at McDonald's because of poor hygiene and an unkempt appearance.

Unable to shower and improve her appearance, she has not been able to secure another job. For the past two years she has been homeless, living on the street and in the subway. She has given up hope of improving her situation. She now occasionally shares IV needles and has been sexually assaulted periodically at night in the subway by men. She realizes she is at high risk for acquiring the AIDS virus but no longer cares very much. Death appears to be, to her, the final escape from a life filled with victimization and misery.

Poverty does not mean simply that poor people in the United States are living less well than those of average income. It means that the poor are often hungry. Many are malnourished, with some turning to dog food or cat food for nourishment. Poverty may mean not having running water, living in substandard housing, and being exposed to rats, cockroaches, and other vermin. It means not having sufficient heat in the winter and being unable to sleep because the walls are too thin to deaden the sounds from the neighbors living next door. It means being embarrassed about the few ragged clothes that one has to wear. It means great susceptibility to emotional disturbances, alcoholism, and victimization by criminals, as well as having a shortened life expectancy. It means lack of opportunity to advance oneself socially, economically, or educationally. It often means slum housing, unstable marriages, and few chances to enjoy the finer things in life—traveling, dining out, movies, plays, concerts, and sports events.

The infant mortality rate of the poor is almost double that of the affluent.[20] The poor have less access to medical services and receive lower-quality care from health care professionals. The poor are exposed to higher levels of air pollution, water pollution, and unsanitary conditions, They have higher rates of malnutrition and disease. Schools in poor areas are of lower quality and have fewer resources. As a result, the poor achieve less academically and are more likely to drop out of school. They are also more likely to be arrested, indicted, and imprisoned, and they are given longer sentences for the same offenses committed by the nonpoor. They are less likely to receive probation, parole, or suspended sentences.[21]

Poverty also often leads to despair, low self-esteem, and stunted growth—including physical, social, emotional, and intellectual growth. Poverty hurts most when it leads to a view of the self as inferior or second-class.

We like to think that the United States is a land of equal opportunity and that there is considerable upward class mobility of those who put forth effort. The reality is the opposite of the myth. Extensive research has shown that poverty is almost "escape proof." Children raised in poor families are likely to live in poverty in their adult years. Most people have much the same social status their parents had. Movement to a higher social status is an unusual happening in practically all societies—including the United States.[22]

## DEFINING POVERTY: A POLICY PROBLEM

Despite all the research on poverty, we as yet have not agreed on how to define the condition. A family of four living on a farm that earns $15,000 per year may not view themselves as being "poverty stricken," especially if they have no rent to pay, are able to grow much of their own food, and are frugal and creative in securing essential needs. On the other hand, a family of four earning $20,000 per year in a city with a high cost of living may be deeply in debt, especially if they pay high rent and are confronted with unexpected medical bills.

The usual definitions of poverty are based on lack of money, and annual income is the measure most commonly applied. There are two general approaches to defining poverty: the absolute approach and the relative approach.

The *absolute approach* holds that a certain amount of goods and services is essential to an individual's or family's welfare. Those who do not have this minimum amount are viewed as poor. The fundamental problem with this approach is that there is no agreement as to what constitutes "minimum" needs. Depending on the income level selected, the number and percentage of the population who are poor change substantially, along with the characteristics of those defined as poor.

A serious problem with the absolute definition of poverty is that it does not take into account the fact that people are poor not only in terms of their own needs, but also in relation to others who are not poor. That is, poverty is relative to time and place. Those Americans labeled poor today would certainly not be poor by the standards of 1850; nor would they be viewed as poor by standards existing in India or in other less-developed countries. In the 1890s no one felt particularly poor because of not having electric lights; yet today a family without electricity is usually considered poor.

It is important to realize that the experience of poverty is based on conditions in one's own society. People feel poor or rich with reference to others around them, not with reference to very poor or very rich people elsewhere in the world. To the poor in the United States it is of little comfort for them to be informed that they would be regarded as well-off (according to their income and wealth) if they were living in Ethiopia (or some other impoverished country).

*Almost 15 percent of the U.S. population continues to live in poverty in one of the richest countries in the world.*

The *relative approach* states, in essence, that a person is poor when his or her income is substantially less than the average income of the population. For example, anyone in the lowest one-fifth (or tenth, or fourth) of the population is regarded as poor. By defining poverty in these terms, we avoid having to define absolute needs, and we also put more emphasis on the inequality of incomes. With a relative approach, poverty will persist as long as income inequality exists. The major weakness with a relative approach is that it tells us nothing about how badly, or how well, the people at the bottom of the income distribution actually live. With poverty measures, ideally, we want to know not only how many people are poor but also how desperate their living conditions are.

The federal government has generally chosen the absolute approach in defining poverty. The poverty line is raised each year to adjust for inflation. In 1996 the government set the poverty line at $16,036 for a family of four.[23]

## THE POOR

An encouraging trend is that the proportion of the population below the poverty line has gradually decreased in the past 100 years. Prior to the twentieth century a majority of Americans lived in poverty. In 1937 President Franklin D. Roosevelt stated: "I see one-third of a nation ill-housed, ill-clad, ill-nourished."[24] In 1962 the President's Council of Economic Advisors estimated that one-fifth of the population was living in poverty.[25] In 1996 about 14 percent of the nation was estimated to be below the poverty line. An alarming concern is that, since 1978, there has been an increase in the proportion of the population that is poor.[26]

Poverty is concentrated in certain population categories, including one-parent families, children, the elderly, large-sized families, and people of color. Educational level, unemployment, and place of residence are also factors related to poverty.

*One-Parent Families*   Most one-parent families are headed by a female, and 37 percent of female-headed families are in poverty, compared to 12 percent for two-parent families.[27] Single mothers who are members of a racial minority (e.g., African Americans, Latinos, Native Americans) are particularly vulnerable to poverty, as they are subjected to double discrimination (race and sex) in the labor market.

Women who work full time are paid on the average only about 75 percent of what men who work full time are paid.[28] Many single mothers are unable to work due to lack of transportation, the high cost of day-care facilities, and inadequate training. Of the families living in poverty, approximately half are headed by a single mother.[29] About one out of every five children in this country is now living apart from one parent, and, because of increasing divorce rates, separations, and births outside marriage, it is estimated that nearly one of two children born today will spend part of the first eighteen years in a family headed by a single mother.[30] Single-parent families now constitute more than 20 percent of all families in the United States.[31] The increase in one-parent families has led to an increase in the feminization of poverty.

*Children*   Twenty percent of children under the age of eighteen are living in poverty, and nearly 40 percent of the poor are children under sixteen.[32] More than one-half of these children live in families with an absentee father.[33] When the 1996 welfare reform legislation was passed, two-thirds of the nation's welfare recipients were children.[34] The 1996 welfare reform legislation focuses on putting adult welfare recipients to work. With two-thirds of the recipients being children, concerns are now being raised as to what will happen to the children in those families in which the parents use up their eligibility for benefits and yet do *not* obtain employment that provides sufficient income to support them and their children.

*The Elderly*   Many of the elderly depend on Social Security pensions or public assistance (in the form of Supplemental Security Income) for their basic needs. Since the initiation of the 1964 War on Poverty programs, the population group that has benefited most has been the elderly. Programs such as Medicare and Supplemental Security Income, as well as increases in monthly payments under the Old Age, Survivors, Disability, and Health Insurance Program, have reduced the poverty rate among the elderly from over 25 percent in 1964 to around 11 percent at the present time.[35]

*Large Families*   Large families are more likely than smaller ones to be poor, partly because more income is needed as family size increases. It now costs an estimated $161,000 to raise a child from birth to age eighteen in low-income families.[36]

*People of Color*   Contrary to popular stereotypes, most poor people (over 60 percent) are white.[37] But members of most minority groups are disproportionately likely to be poor. African Americans, for example, constitute about 12 percent of the total population, but more than 25 percent of all the poor.[38] One out of every three African Americans is poor, compared with one out of ten white persons.[39] Approximately one-third of Native American families live below the poverty line, and about one out of every three Latinos live in poverty.[40] Racial discrimination is a major reason why most racial minorities are disproportionately poor.

*Education*   Attainment of less than a ninth-grade education is a good predictor of poverty. A high school diploma, however, is not a guarantee that one will earn wages adequate to avoid poverty, as many of the poor have graduated from high school. A college degree is an excellent predictor of avoiding poverty; only a small proportion of those with a college degree are impoverished.[41]

*Employment*   Being unemployed is of course associated with being poor. However, being employed is not a guarantee of avoiding poverty; more than 1.5 million family heads work full time, but their income is below the poverty level.[42] The general public (and many government officials) wrongly assumes that employment is the key to ending poverty. However, jobs alone cannot end poverty.

*Place of Residence*   People who live in rural areas have a higher incidence of poverty than those in urban areas. In rural areas, wages are low, unemployment is high, and work tends to be seasonal. The Ozarks, Appalachia, and the South have pockets of rural poverty with high rates of unemployment.[43]

People who live in urban slums constitute the largest geographical group in terms of numbers of poor people. The decaying cities of the Northeast and Midwest have particularly large urban slums. Poverty is also extensive on Native American reservations and among seasonal migrant workers.

All these factors indicate that some people are more vulnerable to poverty than others. Michael Harrington, who coined the term *other America* for the poor in the United States, notes that the poor made the simple mistake of:

> being born to the wrong parents, in the wrong section of the country, in the wrong industry, or in the wrong racial or ethnic group. Once that mistake has been made, they could have been paragons of will and morality, but most of them would never even have had a chance to get out of the other America.[44]

## CAUSES OF POVERTY

There are a number of possible causes of being poor:

- High unemployment
- Poor physical health
- Physical disabilities
- Emotional problems
- Extensive medical bills
- Alcoholism
- Drug addiction
- Large families
- Job displacements due to automation
- Lack of an employable skill
- Low educational level
- Female head of household with young children
- No cost-of-living increases for people on fixed incomes
- Racial discrimination
- Being labeled "ex-convict" or "crazy"
- Living in a geographic area where jobs are scarce
- Divorce, desertion, or death of a spouse
- Gambling
- Budgeting problems and mismanagement of resources
- Sex discrimination
- Being a crime victim
- Holding anti-work-ethic values
- Underemployment
- Low-paying jobs
- Mental retardation
- Being beyond the age of retirement

This list is not exhaustive. However, it serves to show there are many causes of poverty, that eliminating the causes of poverty would require a wide range of social programs, and that poverty interacts with almost all other social problems—such as emotional problems, alcoholism, unemployment, racial and sex discrimination, medical problems, crime, gambling, and mental retardation. The interaction between poverty and these other social problems is complicated. As indicated, these other social problems are contributing causes of poverty. Yet, for some social problems, poverty is also a contributing *cause* of those problems (such as emotional problems, alcoholism,

and unemployment). Being poor intensifies the effects (the hurt) of all social problems.

***The Culture of Poverty*** To some extent, poverty is passed on from generation to generation in a cycle of poverty (see Figure 9.1). Why? Some authorities argue that the explanation is due to a "culture of poverty." Oscar Lewis, an anthropologist, is a chief proponent of this cultural explanation.[45]

Lewis examined poor neighborhoods in various parts of the world and concluded the poor are poor because they have a distinct culture or lifestyle. The culture of poverty arises after extended periods of economic deprivation in highly stratified capitalistic societies. Such economic deprivation is brought about by high rates of unemployment for unskilled labor and low wages for those employed. Such economic deprivation leads to the development of attitudes and values of despair and hopelessness. Lewis describes these attitudes and values as follows:

> The individual who grows up in this culture has a strong feeling of fatalism, helplessness, dependence, and inferiority, a strong present-time orientation with relatively little disposition to defer gratification and plan for the future, a high tolerance for psychological pathology of all kinds.[46]

Once developed, this culture continues to exist, even when the economic factors that created it (e.g., lack of employment opportunities) no longer exist. The culture's attitudes, norms, and expectations serve to limit opportunities and prevent escape. A major reason the poor remain locked into their culture is that they are socially isolated. They have few contacts with groups outside their own culture and are hostile toward the social services and educational institutions that might help them escape poverty. They reject such institutions because they perceive them as belonging to the dominant class. Furthermore, because they view their financial circumstances as private and hopeless, and because they lack political and organizational skills, they do not take collective action to resolve their problems.

The culture of poverty theory has been controversial and widely criticized. Eleanor Leacock argues that the distinctive culture of the poor is not the *cause* but the *result* of their continuing poverty.[47] She agrees that the poor tend to emphasize "instant gratification," which involves spending and enjoying one's money while it lasts. But she argues instant gratification is a result of being poor, because it makes no

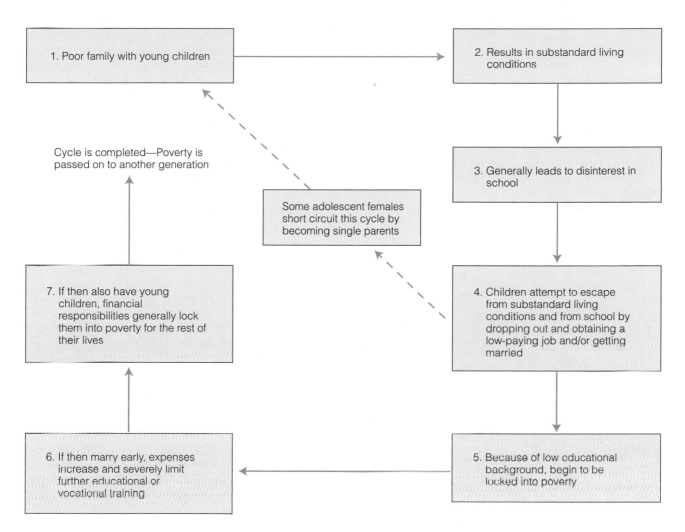

**Figure 9.1**  *Cycle of Poverty*

sense to defer gratification when a person is pessimistic about the future. Deferred gratification is a rational response only when one is optimistic that postponing pleasures today by saving the money will reap greater benefits in the future. (Interestingly, studies have found that, when ghetto residents obtain stable, well-paying jobs, they then display the middle-class value of deferred gratification.[48]) Because of poverty, Leacock argues, the poor are forced to abandon middle-class attitudes and values, because such values are irrelevant to their circumstances. If they had stable, well-paying jobs, they would likely take on the values of the middle class.

In an even stronger indictment, William Ryan criticizes the culture of poverty theory as simply being a classic example of "blaming the victim."[49] Blaming

the poor for their circumstances is a convenient excuse, according to Ryan, for refusing to endorse the programs and policies thought necessary to eradicate poverty. The real culprit is the social system that allows poverty to exist. Ryan says bluntly that the poor are not poor because of their culture, but because they do not have enough money.

Pro and con arguments for the culture of poverty theory continue to persist. There are many reasons, both external and internal, why a person may be poor. External reasons include high rates of unemployment and underemployment; racial discrimination; automation, which throws people out of work; lack of job training programs; sex discrimination; a shortage of antipoverty programs; and inflation. Internal reasons include physical or mental impairment, alcoholism, obsolete job skills, early parenthood, dropping out of school, and lack of interest in taking available jobs.

***The Functions of Poverty*** Obviously poverty is dysfunctional, mainly to the poor themselves, but also to the affluent. However, the realization that poverty also has some functions in society can help us understand why some decision makers are not actively seeking to eradicate poverty.

Eleven functions are provided by the poor to affluent groups:

1. They are available to do the unpleasant jobs no one else wants to do.

2. Their activities subsidize the more affluent (for example, domestic service for low pay).

3. They help create jobs (for example, jobs for social workers who provide services to the poor).

4. They purchase poor-quality goods that otherwise could not be sold.

5. They serve as examples of deviance that are frowned on by the majority and that thereby support dominant norms.

6. They provide an opportunity for others to practice their "Christian duty" of helping the less fortunate.

7. They make mobility more likely for others because they are removed from the competition for good education and good jobs.

8. They contribute to cultural activities (for example, by providing cheap labor for the construction of monuments and works of art).

9. They create cultural forms (e.g., jazz and the blues) that are often adopted by the affluent.

10. They serve as symbolic opponents for some political groups and as constituents for others.

11. They often absorb the costs of change (e.g., by being the victims of high levels of unemployment that result from technological advances).[50]

Also, denigrating the poor has the psychological function for some Americans of making them feel better about themselves.

Partly because poverty is functional, our society makes only a halfhearted effort to eradicate—or at least reduce—it. To eliminate it would mean a redistribution of income from the rich to the poor, a policy generally seen as undemocratic (sometimes communistic) even by the not-so-affluent. Because the rich control the political power, proposals that would eliminate poverty (such as guaranteed annual income programs) have generally met with opposition. Gans emphasizes this point:

> Legislation in America tends to favor the interests of the businessman, not the consumers, even though the latter are a vast majority; of landlords, not tenants; of doctors, not patients. Only organized interest groups have the specific concerns and the time, staff, and money to bring their demands before government officials. . . . The poor are powerless because they are a minority of the population, are not organized politically, are often difficult to organize, and are not even a homogeneous group with similar interests that could be organized into a single pressure group. . . . Given the antagonism toward them on the part of many Americans, any programs that would provide them with significant gains are likely to be voted down by a majority. Legislative proposals for a massive antipoverty effort . . . have always run into concerted and united opposition in Washington.[51]

Our government has the resources to eliminate poverty—but not the will. Our country in the present century has been able to find billions of dollars in resources within a few months when we go to war (which has happened several times), but our country has not been willing to allocate similar funds to improve living conditions for the homeless and millions of other people who are living in poverty in this country.

## ADDITIONAL PERSPECTIVES ON CAUSES OF POVERTY

This section will conclude with a discussion of three perspectives—functionalist, conflict, and interactionist—on the causes of poverty and how to combat the problem. (A fuller discussion of the theoretical frameworks of each of these perspectives is contained in Chapter 1.)

***The Functionalist Perspective*** Functionalists view poverty as being due to dysfunctions in the economy. A wide range of dysfunctions have been identified, some of which will be mentioned here. Rapid industrialization has caused disruptions in the economic system. For example, people who lack job skills are forced into menial work at low wages. Then when automation comes, they are discharged, without having work, money, or marketable job skills. Some products produced by industry also become outdated— such as steam engines, milk bottles, and horse-drawn carriages—causing workers to lose their jobs. In addition, work training centers and apprenticeship programs may continue to produce graduates whose skills are no longer in demand. For example, there no longer is a job market for people trained to repair adding machines and manual typewriters. Also, direct telephone dialing is sharply reducing the need for telephone operators.

Functionalists also note the welfare system, intended to solve the problem of poverty, has a number of dysfunctions. Social welfare programs are sometimes established without sufficient funds to meet the needs of potential clients. Some providers of services are more concerned about their personal life than the well-being of their clients. Some bureaucrats are sometimes reluctant to bend their complex rules to help a deserving family that is "technically" ineligible for assistance. Social welfare programs at times have design dysfunctions in meeting the needs of recipients. For example, in the past, mothers of young children in some states were eligible for public assistance only if the fathers were out of the home. Consequently, some unemployed men were forced to desert their families so their children could be fed and sheltered.

Additional problems in the welfare system are caused by inadequate information systems that fail to inform the poor about benefits to which they are entitled (in addition to the deliberate withholding of information due to prejudice). Job training and educational programs sometimes train people for positions in which there are no employment openings.

According to functionalists, the best way to deal with poverty is to make adjustments to correct these dysfunctions.

It should be noted that many functionalists view some economic inequality (that is, poverty) as being functional. Because the poor are at the bottom of the stratification system, they receive few of society's material and social rewards. Functionalists view the threat of being at the bottom of the heap as an important mechanism for motivating people to perform their proper roles. According to functionalists, poverty becomes a social problem when it no longer performs the function of motivating people to make productive contributions to society.

*The Conflict Perspective*   Conflict theorists assume because there is such enormous wealth in modern societies, no one in such societies should go without their essential needs being met. These theorists assert poverty exists because the power structure wants it to exist. They assert that the working poor are being exploited, paid poverty-level wages so that their employers can reap higher profits and live more affluent lives.

The unemployed are also seen as being the victims of the power structure. Wealthy employers oppose programs to reduce unemployment (such as educational and job training programs), as they do not want to pay the taxes to support them.

Wealthy people are apt to cling to the ideology of individualism, as they tend to view unemployment and poverty as stemming from a lack of effort rather than from social injustice or from other circumstances beyond the control of the individual. As a result, the wealthy ignore the economic and political foundations of poverty, and instead get involved in charitable efforts to the poor, which leaves them feeling they have done "good deeds." Charity and government welfare programs are seen as being a force in perpetuating poverty and economic inequality, as such programs quell political protest and social unrest that threaten the status quo. Conflict theorists also assert that many poor people eventually come to accept the judgments passed on them by the rest of society, and adjust their aspirations and their self-esteem downward.

Conflict theorists do not see poverty as either essential or functional but as arising because some groups benefit from seeing to it that the poor have less. From the conflict perspective, poverty becomes a social problem when some group feels the existing distribution of resources is unfair and unjust and that something should be done about it.

Conflict theorists believe poverty can best be dealt with by the poor becoming politically aware and active so that they organize themselves to reduce inequality through government action. These theorists view poor people's adjustments to poverty as being a set of chains that must be broken. Most conflict theorists believe poverty can be significantly reduced only through political action by poor people—action that receives at least some support from concerned members of the power structure.

*The Interactionist Perspective*   Interactionists emphasize the subjective nature of poverty, viewing it as being relative, depending on what it is compared to. Most poor people in the United States presently have a higher standard of living than middle-class people did two hundred years ago. Poor people in this country are also substantially better off than poor people in Third World countries.

*Most poor people live in urban areas, though many live in rural environments. The older cities of midwestern and northeastern states have large urban economically depressed areas.*

The main reference for poor people in this country is their poor neighborhoods. A successful person in some neighborhood is someone who knows where the next meal is coming from, and a "big success" may be someone who gets a job on an assembly line. People with such attitudes become trapped in their own beliefs, as they have low-level goals and put forth little effort to improve their circumstances. Another value they acquire that keeps them in the poverty trap is instant gratification; they are not inclined to defer immediate rewards so that long-range goals (such as a college education) can be reached.

Interactionists also emphasize the psychological effects of being poor in a wealthy society. Through comparing themselves to people with wealth, many come to believe they are failures and attribute their failure to personal shortcomings rather than to social forces that are beyond their control. With such a failure identity, they may withdraw from society, develop emotional problems because of their perceptions of self, turn to drugs to escape, or turn to delinquency and crime to obtain material goods illegally that they are unable to obtain legally.

Interactionists view poverty as a matter of shared expectations. The poor are negatively judged by influential groups. Those who are the objects of such labeling are stigmatized and may begin to behave in accordance with those expectations. Interactionists emphasize that poverty is not just a matter of economic deprivation but involves a person's self-concept. For example, a third-generation welfare recipient is apt to view himself much more negatively than a person working his way through college, even though both may have the same income.

To resolve the poverty problem, interactionists urge that the stigma and negative definitions associated with poverty be eliminated. Positive changes in the poverty problem will not occur until the poor are convinced that they no longer are doomed to live in poverty. The poverty trap can be sprung with public assistance programs that bring the poor up to an adequate standard of living, *combined* with programs that open up opportunities to move up the socioeconomic ladder, and programs that encourage the poor to redefine more positively their social environment.

## Programs to Combat Poverty

Because poverty interacts with nearly every other social problem, almost every existing social service to some extent combats poverty (such as

Alcoholics Anonymous, health care programs, vocational rehabilitation, Parents Without Partners, foster care, adoption, day care, Head Start, housing programs, urban renewal, community action programs). Such programs indirectly reduce poverty by alleviating other social problems that happen to interact with poverty. These programs are too numerous to describe fully in this text. This section will instead describe income-maintenance programs, which are directly designed to alleviate poverty. Income-maintenance programs include social insurance programs and public assistance programs.

## Two Conflicting Views

Present programs are substantially influenced by the past. Currently there are two conflicting views of the role of poverty programs in our society.[52] One of these roles has been termed *residual:* a "gap-filing" or "first-aid" role. This view holds that poverty programs should be provided only when an individual's needs are not properly met through other societal institutions, primarily the family and the market economy. With the residual view, it is thought that social services and financial aid should not be provided until all other measures or efforts have failed, after the exhaustion of the individual's or family's resources. In addition, this view asserts, funds and services should be provided on a short-term basis (primarily during emergencies) and withdrawn when the individual or the family again becomes self-sufficient.

The residual view has been characterized as "charity for unfortunates."[53] Funds and services are seen not as a right but as a gift, with the receiver having certain obligations; for example, to receive financial aid, recipients may be required to perform certain menial work assignments. Associated with the residual view is the belief that the causes of most poor people's difficulties are rooted in their own malfunctioning; that is, they are to blame for their predicaments because of personal inadequacies, ill-advised activities, or "sins." Under the residual view, there is usually a stigma attached to receiving services or funds.

The opposing point of view, termed *institutional,* holds that poverty programs are to be accepted as a legitimate responsibility of modern society in helping people achieve self-fulfillment. Under this view, there is no stigma attached to receiving funds or services. Recipients are viewed as being entitled to such help. Associated with this view is the belief that an individual's difficulties are due to

causes largely beyond his or her control (for example, the reason a person is unemployed may well be due to a lack of employment opportunities). With this view, when difficulties arise causes are sought in the environment (society), and efforts are often focused on improving the social institutions within which the individual functions.

Adherents of the residual view of public assistance generally hold the following opinions, as summarized by Samuel Mencher:

◆ Assistance should be made as unpleasant as possible as a deterrent to its use. This is to be accomplished by giving relief in kind rather than money, by threatening prosecution, by continuous reevaluation of need, by making it only temporary, stopping it if illegitimacy is involved, and removing children from their own homes when these homes do not come up to standard.

◆ Relief should be made unpleasant by requiring recipients to work for it regardless of the nature of the work, how depressed the wage, or whether the requirements would be used as means for securing cheap labor; and, notwithstanding, income from this work is still labeled relief.

◆ Assistance should be discouraged by making payments too low for anyone to really want it. It is argued by advocates of this approach that assistance in amounts greater than would be received by the lowest paid, most menial worker would encourage individuals to seek assistance in lieu of employment.

◆ Outsiders should be prevented from seeking help by extending emergency aid for only short periods of time.

◆ People should be forced to remain on their jobs or return to employment by denying assistance to anyone who is guilty of a "voluntary quit."[54]

In contrast, the institutional view of public assistance, as described by Skidmore and Thackeray, assumes or advocates as follows:

◆ [Government should provide] an income floor for all citizens and the elimination of hunger and destitution, or their threat, as an instrument of social policy.

◆ [Government should extend] relief to applicants who can qualify under eligibility requirements, that is, remove it from subjective, biased, and capricious considerations. Relief should be based on need as it is determined to exist by objective, rather than subjective, criteria and as a legally determined right.

♦ It is assumed that workers, generally, prefer income from employment to public welfare and that motivations to work are built into the economy in the form of social, cultural, and economic advantages to the employed man or woman.

♦ Psychological and social barriers sometimes stand in the way of rehabilitation and employment. Counseling and other services may be needed to restore certain individuals to economic and social self-sufficiency.

♦ Preservation of the independence and self-respect of the applicant for the assistance is a prime consideration in the administration of programs for relief.

♦ A punitive approach defeats the purpose for which assistance is used; namely, the restoration of the individual to normal functioning. It deepens feelings of inadequacy and dependency, causes embarrassment and humiliation, and brings destructive psychological defenses into play.

♦ There are many pulls in society that tend to make work more appealing than public welfare—a higher standard of living, the prestige and sense of importance one receives from work, tenure, emoluments [rewards] of society and others.[55]

## SOCIAL INSURANCE PROGRAMS

Social insurance programs are largely based on the institutional view. They include Social Security, Medicare, unemployment insurance, and workers' compensation insurance.

The residual approach characterized poverty programs from our early history to the Great Depression of the 1930s, since which time both approaches have been applied to poverty programs, some programs being largely residual in nature and others being more institutional in design and implementation.

This section will describe social insurance programs, and the next section will describe public assistance programs. (Social insurance programs are financed by taxes on employees, or on employers, or on both employees and employers. Public assistance program benefits are paid from general government revenues.)

*Old Age, Survivors, Disability, and Health Insurance (OASDHI)*  OASDHI was created by the 1935 Social Security Act. Usually referred to as Social Security by the general public, it is the largest income insurance program and is designed to partially replace income lost when a worker retires or becomes disabled. Cash benefits are also paid to survivors of "insured" workers.

Payments to beneficiaries are based on previous earnings. Rich as well as poor are eligible if insured. Benefits are provided to fully insured workers at age sixty-five or older (age sixty-two if somewhat smaller benefits are taken). Dependent spouses over sixty-two and dependent children under eighteen (no age limit on disabled children who become disabled before eighteen) are also covered under the retirement benefits.

Participation in this insurance program is compulsory for most employees, including the self-employed. The program is generally financed by a payroll tax (FICA—Federal Insurance Contributions Act) assessed equally to employer and employee. The rate has gone up gradually. Eligibility for benefits is based on the number of years in which Social Security taxes have been paid and the amount earned while working.

A major concern has been the financial soundness of OASDHI. Since 1935, the Social Security (FICA) tax has led to a buildup in the trust fund for OASDHI. But the liberalization of benefits and the increase in recipients in recent years have raised concern about the system paying out more than it takes in. In times of high unemployment and recession, the number of workers paying into OASDHI is decreased. The decline in the birthrate, with a steadily increasing retired population, may jeopardize the financial soundness of the program, as the number of recipients is increasing at a faster rate than the number of payers into the system. If OASDHI is to remain financially sound, benefits may have to be scaled back, FICA taxes increased, or both.

*Medicare*  In 1965 Congress enacted Title XVIII (Medicare) to the Social Security Act. Medicare provides two coordinated programs of health insurance for those over sixty-five. Plan A provides for hospitalization and extended care. It is financed on a self-supporting basis by an additional surcharge on the Social Security Act. All recipients of OASDHI retirement benefits are eligible. Plan B is a voluntary insurance plan for medical services, especially physicians' charges. Medicare is a public health insurance program and is more fully described in Chapter 11.

*Unemployment Insurance*   This program was also created by the 1935 Social Security Act and provides benefits to workers who have been laid off or, in certain cases, fired. Unemployment insurance is financed by a tax on employers. The weekly benefit amount of which the unemployed are eligible, along with the number of weeks, varies from state to state. In many states, the unemployed are eligible for benefits for about a year. In most states, to be eligible a person must have worked a certain number of weeks in covered employment; be ready, willing, and able to work; file a claim for benefits and be registered in a public employment office; and demonstrate that unemployment is due to a lack of work for which the employee is qualified.

Unemployment insurance benefits help individuals and families who become unemployed due to a lack of work. In our society, where employment is valued highly, being without work can be a demeaning experience. In the past two decades, the unemployment rate has ranged from 4 to 11 percent of able-bodied workers. Such high rates clearly indicate a lack of available jobs. On the other hand, the unemployment insurance program has been sharply criticized by claims that some of the unemployed would rather collect insurance benefits than make a concerted effort to obtain employment.

*Workers' Compensation Insurance*   Workers' compensation, financed by a tax on employers, provides both income and assistance in meeting medical expenses for injuries sustained on a job. This program was enacted after a series of lawsuits by injured employees against employers—the only recourse employees had. The first workers' compensation program was the Federal Employees Compensation Act in 1908. Individual states gradually passed workers' compensation laws modeled after the program for federal employees. By 1920 all but six states had such laws; but it was not until 1948 that all states had adequate coverage.[56] Cash benefits are paid for total or temporary disability or death. Medical benefits cover hospital and doctors' fees. Rehabilitation benefits are also available for those needing aftercare and retraining to become employable again.

## PUBLIC ASSISTANCE PROGRAMS

Public assistance is sometimes viewed by the general public as being synonymous with welfare; yet there are hundreds of other social welfare programs.

Public assistance has primarily residual aspects, and applicants must undergo a "means test," which reviews their assets and liabilities to determine eligibility for benefits.

Distinguishing features of public assistance programs are:

- *Means test.* Individuals applying for assistance must have their income and assets examined to determine whether their financial needs meet eligibility requirements. The means test is designed to ensure that individuals receiving assistance do not already have sufficient resources for subsistence. Resources that are examined include both earned and unearned income. Earned income is money in the form of salary or wages. Unearned income includes benefits from other public and private financial programs, gifts, life insurance annuities, stock dividends, rental income, inheritances, support payments from relatives, and so on.

- *Review.* Applications are reviewed on a case-by-case basis for eligibility and benefit levels. Although there are federal, state, and local guidelines on eligibility and on how much is allowable as a benefit for eligible persons, members of the various staffs administering public assistance have substantial discretion in deciding whether a client will receive special allowances in addition to basic benefits. Staff also have discretion in deciding which social services and other resources might be mobilized on behalf of a client. Eligibility determination, along with level of benefit determination, is a cumbersome and lengthy process involving extensive review of documents.

- *Benefits as charity.* In contrast to social insurance benefits to which recipients are usually viewed as legally entitled, public assistance benefits are viewed as charity. In this country, poor persons are not viewed as having a constitutionally established right to a minimum income. (In comparison, some foreign countries—Great Britain for example—recognize the right of those in poverty to be maintained and protected by the government.)

- *Funding.* Program benefits are paid from general government revenues. Public assistance benefits at the federal, state, and local levels are financed through taxes on personal income and on property.

The main public assistance programs include Supplemental Security Income, General Assistance, Medicaid, food stamps, housing assistance, and the

Personal Responsibility and Work Opportunity Reconciliation Program (which was enacted in 1996 to replace Aid to Families with Dependent Children).

*Supplemental Security Income (SSI)*   Under SSI, the federal government pays monthly checks to people in financial need who are sixty-five years of age and older, or who are blind or disabled at any age. To qualify for payments, applicants must have no (or very little) regular cash income, own little property, and have little cash or few assets that could be turned into cash (such as stocks, bonds, jewelry, and other valuables).

The SSI program became effective January 1, 1974, and replaced the following programs that were created by the 1935 Social Security Act: Old-Age Assistance, Aid to the Blind, and Aid to the Permanently and Totally Disabled. SSI is the first federally administered assistance program. All other public assistance programs are administered through state and local governments. The word *Supplemental* in the term *Supplemental Security Income* is used because in most cases payments *supplement* whatever income may be available to the claimant. Even OASDHI benefits are supplemented by this program.

SSI provides a guaranteed minimum income (an income floor) for the aged, the legally blind, and the disabled. To be "legally blind" is to have vision no better than 20/200 (even with glasses) or to have tunnel vision. To be "disabled" is to have a physical or mental disability that prevents a person from doing any substantial gainful work and is expected to last at least twelve months or result in death.

Administration of SSI has been assigned to the Social Security Administration. Financing of the program is through federal tax dollars, primarily income taxes.

*General Assistance (GA)*   The General Assistance (GA) program is supposed to serve those needing temporary, rather than long-term, financial support. It is designed to provide financial help to those in need who are ineligible for any other income-maintenance program. No clearly stated eligibility requirements exist for general assistance. GA is the only public assistance program that receives no federal funds. It is usually funded by property taxes. In some large cities the state contributes substantially toward meeting the costs of GA. In most localities, however, the program is financed and administered at the local level, through the county or township or by a village or city. In many local governmental units, a political official has arbitrary jurisdiction over whether an applicant receives help. Most expenditures for GA are for medical care. In-kind payments (food, medical care, clothes, and other items other than money) are frequent. Whenever feasible, communities usually attempt to move GA recipients into federally funded public aid programs in order to reduce local expenses.

Payments for GA tend to be minimal and grudgingly made to discourage people from applying and from becoming dependent on welfare. With in-kind and voucher payments, GA conveys to recipients the suspicion that they are incapable of managing their own affairs. Because able-bodied unemployed men and women sometimes find it necessary to seek GA benefits, GA has been viewed as a public assistance program for the "undeserving poor." In some parts of the country, GA has demoralizing effects because many local program directors hold—and convey to recipients—a negative attitude about providing assistance.

In recent years some states and counties have terminated their GA program.

*Medicaid*   This program provides hospital and medical care to certain poverty-stricken people. Those eligible are individuals who have very low income and few assets. Because Medicaid is a joint federal/state program, the laws governing eligibility and benefits vary in different geographic areas. Generally, recipients of SSI and other public assistance programs are eligible. In addition, states have the option to include people who are able to provide for their own daily living but whose income and resources are not sufficient to meet all their medical costs.

Medicaid is administered by the states, with financial participation by the federal government. Direct payments are made to providers of services. As is required for every public assistance program, Medicaid applicants must undergo a means test.

*Food Stamps*   Tragically, an estimated 30 million people in the United States (the most powerful and one of the richest countries in the world) do not have enough food to eat.[57] Many of those with inadequate diets are poor. Not only does insufficient diet affect the individual, but research suggests that severe nutritional deficits in expectant mothers also may lead to irreversible brain defects in their children.

The food stamp program is designed to combat hunger. Food stamps are available to public assistance recipients and to other low-income families. These stamps are then traded in for groceries. With millions of Americans going hungry, the food stamp program is obviously underfunded.

*Housing Assistance* Similar to food stamps and Medicaid, housing assistance is an "in-kind" program, rather than a cash program. Generally, such assistance is provided in the form of public housing, usually large housing projects that are owned and operated by the government. In a public housing project, the tenants have lower, subsidized rents. Because they pay less than the market value of their apartments, they are effectively receiving an income transfer.

There are also housing assistance programs for low-income people who are renting and even buying their homes and apartments in the private market. In these programs, the rent or mortgage payment is reduced, with the Department of Housing and Urban Development (HUD) making up the difference.

*Aid to Families with Dependent Children (AFDC)*
With the passage of the 1996 welfare reform legislation, this program has been phased out, and replaced by the Personal Responsibility and Work Opportunity Reconciliation Program. In order for readers to have an understanding of the difference between these two programs, AFDC will be described here.

The AFDC program was created by the 1935 Social Security Act. It was originally titled Aid to Dependent Children (ADC), and a few decades later renamed AFDC. When first enacted, one of ADC's objectives was to enable mothers with young children to remain at home so that their children would be raised well. Since 1935 our values surrounding working mothers have changed. There now is the expectation that single mothers (and single fathers) should obtain gainful employment. (The Personal Responsibility and Work Opportunity Reconciliation Program was largely created in 1996 to emphasize this change in expectation from welfare to work.)

The precise parameters of eligibility for AFDC varied from state to state. Payments were made for both the parent (or parents) and the children in eligible families. To be eligible, the children must have been deprived of parental support or care because of a parent's death or continued absence from the home (through desertion, divorce, or separation) or because the parent was never married. AFDC payments were also made to low-income two-parent families in which both parents were unemployed. In this situation the breadwinner (or breadwinners) had to agree to seek

*One of the public assistance programs for individuals and families who are poor is Food Stamps.*

work actively, to register with the state unemployment service, and to participate in job-training programs. Most AFDC families were headed by a single parent, usually the mother and usually because the father was absent from the home.

Financing and administration of the AFDC program were shared by federal and state governments. In many states, counties also participated in the financing and administration. The federal government, through the Department of Health and Human Services, wrote regulations to implement the Social Security laws. States, and often counties, then wrote their own regulations, within federal guidelines, relating to eligibility criteria, benefit standards, and qualifications of public assistance staff.

Decisions about eligibility criteria for AFDC benefits were made by the executive, legislative, and judicial branches of government and at federal, state, and local levels. As a result, the program was cumbersome, slow to change to meet emerging needs, and heavily bogged down by red tape and bureaucratic processes.

AFDC became the most stigmatized public assistance program. The general public's concept of welfare was the AFDC program. More money was spent on AFDC than on any other public assistance program. Concern arose about the fact that many adult recipients of AFDC had parents who were also recipients; AFDC was criticized as being a "way of life" for some people who chose to be on welfare rather than working.[58] Also it was found that the longer a family received AFDC, the higher the rate of social problems their children manifested in their teenage years (births outside marriage, early marriage, emotional problems, truancy delinquency, and dropping out of school).[59] Some authorities asserted it was not AFDC, per se, that led to an increase in social problems displayed by some recipients, but due to the fact that AFDC recipients were often stigmatized and viewed as "second-class citizens."[60] The program was also criticized for keeping most recipients in poverty by inadequate assistance grants that averaged well below the poverty level.[61]

***AFDC Myths versus Facts*** One of the main reasons that the AFDC program was discontinued in 1996 was that a number of erroneous myths had arisen about the program. This section summarizes these myths, and presents the facts that refute the myths. The myths and facts are summarized by Coleman and Cressey, and by Kornblum and Julian.[62]

*Myth 1:* Most welfare children are "illegitimate."

*Fact:* A sizable majority of the children who received AFDC benefits were "legitimate." (This author strongly objects to labeling any child "illegitimate." The marital status of one's parents has nothing to do with one's value as a human being.)

*Myth 2:* Welfare makes it profitable for women to have illegitimate babies.

*Fact:* Because it costs more than $160,000 to raise a child from birth to age 18, the "profit" from AFDC that a mother might expect to realize from having an additional child was minuscule, even if she minimized all expenditures for the child. Having more babies makes a family poorer.

*Myth 3:* Give them more money and they'll spend it on alcohol and drugs.

*Fact:* When AFDC families received extra funds (which rarely occurred) they almost always spent it on essentials.

*Myth 4:* Most welfare recipients are cheaters and frauds.

*Fact:* If fraud is defined as a deliberate and knowing attempt by a client to deceive the agency, then the incidence of fraud is remarkably low. A national survey found that one out of every twenty AFDC recipients received checks for which he or she was ineligible. Less than half of 1 percent of welfare cases were referred for prosecution for fraud.[63] Because determining eligibility was a cumbersome, complex process, most of these errors were identified as honest mistakes made by state and local public assistance bureaucrats or by recipients. Contrasted with tax fraud, the welfare system was squeaky clean. The Internal Revenue Service estimates a 20 to 25 percent error rate in payment of income taxes—most of which is attributable to underreporting of income by taxpayers.[64]

*Myth 5:* The welfare rolls are soaring out of control.

*Fact:* Most caseload growth in the AFDC program occurred before 1973, with dramatic increases between 1970 and 1973. From early 1976 to 1996 the number of people on AFDC only increased minimally each year.

*Myth 6:* Welfare is just a money handout—a dole.

*Fact:* Most families on AFDC received one or more social services designed to meet personal and social problems and to make them self-supportive. Available social services varied widely from area to area. Possible services included health care, financial counseling, counseling on home management, employment counseling, day care, vocational rehabilitation, homemaker services, consumer education, assistance in child rearing, Head Start, job training, and marriage counseling. The provision of social services to low-income families was one of the three programs enacted by the 1935 Social Security Act.

*Myth 7:* People on welfare are able-bodied loafers.

*Fact:* Contrary to public opinion, few able-bodied persons received assistance; the vast majority of AFDC recipients were children. Less than 1 percent of welfare recipients were able-bodied, unemployed males. The largest group of able-bodied adults was composed of AFDC mothers, most of whom headed families in which no able-bodied male was present. Many of these mothers already were working or were actively seeking work, were receiving work training, or were waiting to be called back after a payoff. Other AFDC mothers faced serious barriers to obtaining employment: very young children to rear, lack of money for child care, lack of job skills, and lack of extensive medical or rehabilitative services to become employable.

Contrary to the stereotype of the "welfare mother" as shiftless, lazy, and unwilling to take a job, even long-term AFDC mothers continued to have a strong work ethic but lacked skills and confidence to obtain a job.

*Myth 8:* Most welfare families are African American.

*Fact:* The number of white families receiving AFDC was approximately the same as the number of African-American families. Because African Americans constituted about 12 percent of the U.S. population and over 45 percent of all AFDC recipients, the stigma attached to AFDC may have been associated with racial prejudice.

*Myth 9:* "Why work when you can live it up on welfare?"

*Fact:* In most states AFDC payments were below the established poverty level. Living in poverty is not "living it up."

*Myth 10:* Once on welfare, always on welfare.

*Fact:* In the early 1990s only 10 percent of the households received AFDC benefits for ten years or longer. Half the families on welfare had been receiving assistance for twenty months or less and two-thirds for less than three years.

*Myth 11:* Welfare is eating up tremendous chunks of our tax money, causing inflation, and "bleeding the country dry."

*Fact:* At a federal level about 1 percent of the federal budget was allocated to AFDC. The largest single item in the national budget is defense spending.

*Myth 12:* Welfare is only for the poor.

*Fact:* The United States pays out much more to the rich than to the poor. These payments are not called welfare but research grants, training grants, tax loopholes, compensation, low-interest loans, and parity. Dale Tussing notes that the United States has two welfare systems:

> Two welfare systems exist simultaneously in this country. One is well known. It is explicit, poorly funded, stigmatized and stigmatizing, and is directed at the poor. The other, practically unknown, is implicit, literally invisible, is nonstigmatized and nonstigmatizing, and provides vast but unacknowledged benefits for the nonpoor. . . . Our welfare systems do not distribute benefits on the basis of need. Rather, they distribute benefits on the basis of legitimacy. Poor people are viewed as less legitimate than nonpoor people . . . by and large, welfare programs for the poor are obvious, open and clearly labeled, and those for the nonpoor are either concealed (as in tax laws, for instance) and ill understood, or are clothed in protective language. . . .

Whether or not a person is poor can often be determined by the names of his welfare programs. If his programs are called "relief," "welfare," "assistance," "charity," or the like, he is surely poor; but if they are called "parity," "insurance," "compensation," or "compulsory saving," he is surely a member of the large majority of nonpoor persons who do not even think of themselves as receiving welfare payments.[65]

Eleanor Clift adds:

> If one counts a broad range of federal spending and tax programs, an average upper-income person will get more than a typical poor person.
>
> It's no secret that middle- and upper-income families enjoy the benefit of tax breaks and entitlement programs like social security. But such families, many of whom complain bitterly these days that government is ignoring them, may be surprised to learn how much more they get than their poorer counterparts. In some ways, such benefits remain the holiest of sacred cows.[66]

***Personal Responsibility and Work Opportunity Reconciliation Program*** Author Charles Murray proposed in 1986 in his controversial book *Losing Ground* that the government should eliminate welfare benefits for all working-age adults.[67] He contended that court decisions, bureaucratic reforms, and antipoverty programs in our society have actually made the poor worse off by creating a dependency. In essence, he asserted people on welfare decide that being on the government dole is better than working.

Murray was especially critical of the AFDC program. He asserted that it provided an incentive for single women to want to have children in order to receive welfare payments. He also asserted that increases in crime and drug abuse, poor educational performance in schools, and deteriorating conditions in inner cities stem largely from the increase in single-parent families, which he attributed to government programs that support such families. His solution to overhauling the AFDC program was simple: "If you want to cut illegitimate births among poor people, . . . I know how to do that. You just rip away every kind of government support there is."[68]

Critics of this approach were horrified. They argued that Murray's plan would make innocent children suffer for their parents' inadequacies, which seems doubly unfair, given that two out of three AFDC beneficiaries were children. If the AFDC program were eliminated without any program to replace it, many more children undoubtedly would end up homeless and hungry. Murray's response was that single mothers who are unable to care for their children should place them for adoption. He further asserted that terminating the AFDC program would force single women to think twice about getting pregnant and would force more low-income males to refrain from fathering children outside of marriage.

Although there was little support for eliminating the AFDC program without replacing it, political decision makers in the early 1990s became more interested in replacing AFDC with a program that forced unemployed single mothers (and single fathers) to take a job.

In the 1994 elections, Republicans (mostly conservatives) won a majority of seats in the House of Representatives for the first time in forty years, and had control of both houses of Congress. The new House speaker, Newt Gingrich, proposed there be no AFDC benefits unmarried teens and their children. In addition, he proposed that AFDC recipients be prohibited from receiving benefits for more than five years, with states having the option of reducing the time limit for welfare benefits to two years.

When Bill Clinton was campaigning for the presidency in 1992, he promised to "end welfare as we know it." In 1994 he proposed attacking the costly national problem of welfare dependency with a plan that would force growing numbers of young welfare mothers into public or private jobs. The objective of the plan was to make young single mothers self-sufficient by giving them money and child care while they receive job training—but then to cut off their cash benefits after no more than twenty-four months. Those who were unable to find jobs would be given temporary tax-subsidized work, usually at the minimum wage, either in the private sector or in community service.

In 1996, President Clinton, and the Democrats and Republicans in Congress, compromised on welfare reform, and passed the Personal Responsibility and Work Opportunity Reconciliation Act. Key provisions of this act are:

♦ The federal guarantee of cash assistance for poor families with children (under the AFDC program) is ended. Each state now receives a capped block grant (lump sum) to run its own welfare and work programs. These block grants to states are now called Temporary Aid to Needy Families (TANF) funds.

♦ The head of every family has to work within two years, or the family loses its benefits. After receiving welfare for two months, adults have to perform

community service unless they have found regular jobs. (States can choose not to have a community service requirement.)

♦ Lifetime public welfare assistance is limited to five years. (States can establish stricter limits.) Hardship exemptions from this requirement are available for up to 20 percent of recipients in a state.

♦ States can provide payments to unmarried teenage parents only if a mother under eighteen is living at home or in another adult-supervised setting and attends high school or an alternative educational or training program as soon as the child is twelve weeks old.

♦ States are required to maintain their own spending on public welfare at 75 percent of their 1994 level or 80 percent if they failed to put enough public welfare recipients to work.

♦ States cannot penalize a woman on public welfare who does not work because she cannot find day care for a child under six years old.

♦ States are required to deduct benefits from welfare mothers who refuse to help identify the fathers. States may deny Medicaid to adults who lose welfare benefits because of a failure to meet work requirements.

♦ A woman on public welfare who refuses to cooperate in identifying the father of her child must lose at least 25 percent of her benefits.

♦ Future legal immigrants who have not yet become citizens are ineligible for most federal welfare benefits and social services during the first five years in the United States. SSI benefits and food stamp eligibility end for non-citizens, including legal immigrants, receiving benefits in 1996.[69]

At the time of this writing, states were in the process of designing and implementing their welfare systems within the federal guidelines for the Personal Responsibility and Work Opportunity Reconciliation Act. It is too early to determine the long-term effects of this act. An initial positive result was that the number of Americans on cash assistance plummeted in the first year of the program by 1.7 million, by far the biggest one-year decline in the history of welfare.[70] The new laws' tough provisions may be chasing away recipients who can more or less afford to leave public assistance (at least temporarily) because they have undisclosed income—from friends, family, or under-the-table jobs. Glastris notes, "Far from living in royal luxury, however, most of these 'cheaters' have been struggling to make ends meet."[71]

Many unanswered questions remain about this 1996 welfare reform act. Will the program be successful in getting adult welfare recipients into decent paying jobs that will enable their families to leave being on public assistance? Even if adult welfare recipients obtain employment, will their children be cared for in healthy child-care arrangements while the parents are working? How difficult will it be for single parents with one or more of the following issues to obtain gainful employment—lack of a marketable job skill, a drug habit, a chronic medical problem, a child at home with a mental or physical disability, a lack of convenient transportation, being in a violent domestic relationship, failure to have a strong work ethic, and having a chronic emotional or behavioral problem? Will some states design a punitive welfare system that cuts welfare benefits to the minimum allowed by federal guidelines in order to accomplish two things: to avoid becoming magnets for the poor, and to minimize state taxes?

Will the new legislation result in increases in the number of homeless persons—when adult recipients are forced off public assistance when they reach the limit on the number of years they are eligible to receive public assistance without obtaining employment? Will this program add extensive additional stress to the lives of adult recipients, and thereby result in increased incidents of child abuse (that is, will some adult recipients take out their frustrations and feelings of stress on their children)? If rates of child abuse and neglect increase, will more children be placed into the expensive foster-care system? Will some adult recipients who reach their term eligibility limits on public assistance without obtaining a decent paying job turn to prostitution or to theft? How can jobs be found or created in geographic areas having high unemployment rates?

AFDC was originally created to provide a stable, safe, and healthy living environment for the children of single unemployed parents. What assurance is there that the 1996 welfare reform act will continue to seek to provide a stable, safe, and healthy living environment for the children in these families? The 1935 Social Security Act created a social safety net of programs for children and others in need. Has the 1996 welfare reform act punctured major holes in this social safety net?

## PROPOSED WELFARE ALTERNATIVES

If the 1996 welfare reform act becomes recognized as a failure, what other systems may be enacted? This section will examine three proposals: offering family allowances, guaranteeing a basic annual income, and eliminating or reducing the causes of poverty.

*Family Allowance* The United States is the only Western industrialized country without a family allowance program. Under a family allowance program the government pays each family a set amount based on the number of children in the household. If payments were large enough, a program like this could aid in eliminating poverty, particularly in large families.

There are some strong criticisms of family allowance plans. If payments were made to all children, the program would be very expensive and much of the money would go to nonpoor families. This problem could be solved (as Denmark has done) by varying the family allowance payments with income and terminating payments after a certain income is reached. (However, such an approach would then involve a means test and continue to stigmatize recipients.) A second criticism is that such a program would provide an incentive to increase the birthrate at a time when overpopulation is a major concern. A final criticism is that it would not provide payments to single individuals and childless couples who are poor.

*Guaranteed Annual Income* A variety of proposals to guarantee every American a certain annual income have been put forth, including proposals by Presidents Nixon and Carter. The base level could conceivably be set slightly above the poverty line and adjusted each year to account for inflation. Such a proposal, if implemented, would eradicate poverty.

Practically all guaranteed-income proposals are based on the concept of a "negative income tax." That is, persons earning above a certain level would pay income tax, whereas those earning below that level would receive a grant—the negative tax—to bring their income up to the guaranteed level. Most negative-income-tax plans also contain an incentive-to-work provision that allows recipients to keep a proportion of their earnings above the guaranteed base level.

Many variations of the negative income tax are possible, and some have been tested by the federal government. The minimum-income guarantee for a

# Case Example: Will Welfare Reform End The Poverty Trap?

Elaine Johnson, age thirty-five, has recently become a grandmother. Her oldest daughter, Sylvia, is a sixteen-year-old unmarried mother. Today, October 13, 1997, is a significant day in their lives because Elaine and Sylvia are applying at Milwaukee's Public Welfare Office to place baby Tony's name on America's welfare rolls. He will represent the third successive generation in the Johnson family to receive public assistance benefits.

Elaine's parents migrated from Mississippi to Milwaukee in 1962, shortly after Elaine's birth. Her father got a job as a janitor in the school system, and her mother has been a part-time nurse's aide at a hospital. Elaine started high school and received above-average grades. She had hopes of getting a student loan to go to college. She wanted to get out of the inner city where she was being raised.

At the age of seventeen, however, Elaine became pregnant. Her parents talked her out of an abortion, and she gave birth to Sylvia. Two months after the birth, she signed up for AFDC at the urging of her parents and friends. It would only be temporary, she thought, until she could get a better handle on her life. She found going to school and caring for a baby to be too much work, so she dropped out of high school in her senior year. She no longer had the same interests as her former friends who did not have children. At times Elaine found it a joy to care for Sylvia, and at other times she found caring for the baby frustrating. Elaine went out as much as she could, when she had a little extra money and when she could find someone to babysit for her. Over the next fifteen years, Elaine had three other children. Only one of the four different fathers married her, and that marriage lasted only two and a half years. The husband left home one day, complaining about children and responsibilities. He never returned, and Elaine has never heard from him.

Elaine has tried a variety of jobs while on AFDC—nurse's aide, dishwasher, waitress, and service station attendant. But the costs of transportation, uniforms, and babysitting left her no better off financially than if she stayed home and received her monthly AFDC checks. Life has been hard for Elaine. Because she is on welfare, she feels like a second-class citizen and a "charity" case. She has had to pinch pennies all her life to try to make ends met. Countless days she has fed her children on beans and rice. She sharply regrets not being able to give her children the material things that many other kids have. While some parents are buying computers for their children, she takes her kids to Goodwill's clothing store to try to find bargains on secondhand sneakers, shirts, jeans, and jackets.

She is living in a deteriorated inner-city neighborhood and is alarmed that her oldest son, Marvin, is experimenting with cocaine and other drugs. The school system is another concern: A high percentage of students drop out, the windows in the buildings are boarded up, vandalism is frequent, physical attacks on teachers sometimes occur, and the educational quality is known to be inferior.

When Elaine discovered that Sylvia was sexually active at fifteen, she pleaded with her daughter not to make the mistake she had made. Elaine even took her to Planned Parenthood to get birth control pills. Elaine's remaining dream is that her children will have a better life than hers. Tears often come to her eyes when she sees her children getting caught in the same poverty trap that she is in. Sylvia took her pills for several months. When the supply ran out, she never got around to going back to Planned Parenthood to get her prescription refilled.

Yes, today is a significant day for Elaine. Upon entering the welfare office she is informed she must immediately enter work training and will soon be expected to be searching for employment. She also is informed of the 1996 welfare reform act, and that all public assistance benefits for her will be terminated in a few years. Furthermore, Sylvia and Elaine are informed that Sylvia must continue to attend high school in order to be eligible to receive public assistance benefits. Sylvia is also informed there now is a maximum lifetime limit of five years for which she and Tony will be eligible to receive public assistance benefits. Elaine is overwhelmed and starts to cry. Her life is already in disarray. Now she is informed that both she and Sylvia have only a few years of eligibility left for public assistance, and that both of them must immediately start working on: learning a marketable job, making child-care arrangements for Tony for when they are receiving training or looking for a job, getting their lives in order, finding ways to help Marvin with his drug experimentation, finding efficient forms of transportation, and finding decent paying jobs within a year or two. Elaine is clueless how all this can be accomplished.

Will the 1996 welfare reform legislation help Elaine and Sylvia and their family members escape the cycle of poverty? Or, will the 1996 welfare reform legislation result in increased stress for their family, and gradually result in further family deterioration?

family of four, for example, could be set at the poverty line, and the incentive-to-work factor (the tax-back rate) could range widely. But such plans could be very expensive.

Using a hypothetical example, with a guaranteed base level of $16,000 for a family of four and the tax-back rate at 50 percent—allowing a family to keep $50 out of every $100 earned—the family would receive subsidies until the break-even point of $32,000. The mathematics of this guaranteed base level and tax-back rate can be illustrated as follows:

| If Your Annual Income from a Paying Job is: | Then Your Annual Income from the Government Is: | So Your Total Income Is: |
|---|---|---|
| $   0 | $16,000 | $16,000 |
| 5,000 | 13,500 | 18,500 |
| 10,000 | 11,000 | 21,000 |
| 15,000 | 8,500 | 23,500 |
| 20,000 | 6,000 | 26,000 |
| 25,000 | 3,500 | 28,500 |
| 30,000 | 1,000 | 31,000 |
| 32,000 | 0 | 32,000 |

There are a number of advantages to negative-income-tax plans. They would shift the focus of income maintenance programs from "charity" to a "right" of entitlement to a guaranteed income. The stigma of being a recipient would be sharply reduced. Such programs would be relatively simple to administer, as eligibility would be based on income-tax returns. Furthermore, such a program would serve everyone who is poor, if the base level is at the poverty line, poverty would be eradicated. Another advantage would be to reduce equity problems that have occurred under present programs, in which nonworking people are eligible for several types of benefits (for example, food stamps and Medicaid) and may be able to achieve a higher standard of living than a low-income employed person who is eligible for few, if any, benefits. A negative-income-tax plan could also replace practically all other public assistance programs and thereby reduce the expense and complexity of administering a variety of programs.

Several unanswered questions, however, have been raised about a negative-income-tax plan:

♦ Such plans are based on the filing of income-tax forms. If a family has little or no income (and no assets), must they wait nearly a year until their tax form is filed before being eligible for benefits?

♦ Will a guaranteed income destroy the incentive to work?

♦ The cost of living varies greatly between urban and rural areas and among different parts of the country. Should financial adjustments be made for this?

♦ Perhaps the biggest problem with a negative-income-tax plan involves what has been called the "unholy triangle"—that is, developing a plan that:

1. Has an adequate guaranteed base level.

2. Allows low-income workers to keep a sufficiently high percentage of their earnings above the guaranteed base level so that the incentive to work is not destroyed.

3. Is not exorbitantly expensive, so that our national economy is not severely affected.

The federal government in the past showed considerable interest in negative-income-tax programs, as evidenced by the passage in 1973 of the Supplemental Security Income (SSI) program, which has a guaranteed income base. But proposed negative-income-tax plans for unemployed, impoverished adults with children have not received much support in Congress. Liberals argued that the guaranteed base level of payments was too low and would not move families above the poverty line. Conservatives objected that the plans would be too costly and would provide financial payments to many more poor families than do current public assistance programs. Conservatives also opposed the plans because they feared they would destroy the incentive to work and would provide "something for nothing."

***Eliminate or Reduce Causes of Poverty*** As noted earlier, a number of factors cause and perpetuate poverty. Another way of combating poverty is to develop and expand programs to alleviate its major causes.

Laws to end racial and sex discrimination can be more vigorously enforced. Programs to curb alcohol and drug abuse can be expanded to reach out and serve more of those who are addicted. Higher-quality educational programs (and more resources) are needed in pockets of poverty (for example, urban inner cities) to inspire students, to help them stay in school, and to help them achieve higher academic levels. Sex education and family planning services need to be provided to more teenagers and young adults to teach responsible sexuality and prevent unwanted pregnancies, which play a role in locking young people into poverty. Family planning services also need to be expanded to help couples who do not want, and cannot afford, large-sized families. An expanded public housing program is needed to provide adequate living quarters for the poor. A national health insurance program is needed to pay for unusually high medical bills, which at present wipe out the savings of some families and plunge them deep into debt.

Some families need financial counseling to help them more effectively manage and spend within the limits of their financial resources. Many middle-aged adults need educational programs to teach them to plan for their retirement years—what lifestyle they want, how to remain healthy, and how to prepare financially.

Provision of jobs for able-bodied workers is a key to reducing the number of people in poverty. In recent years high unemployment rates have forced many of the unemployed and their families into poverty. A variety of suggestions have been advanced to progress toward a full-employment society.

Able-bodied adults who do not have marketable job skills (perhaps because their skills have become obsolete) need to receive training for jobs that are available. (In Germany adults are paid by the government during the weeks or months they are receiving job training or job retraining.) Our government should have a program to financially assist workers and their families to relocate from areas of high unemployment to booming areas where jobs are readily available. Many areas need more quality day-care centers that charge reasonable rates so that single parents (and also two-parent families) can work. For the unemployed able-bodied, the government could be a "last resort" employer. In many other countries the government offers tax incentives to industries to locate in depressed areas. Another suggestion is to encourage industries to hire workers who have been unemployed for a long time by reimbursing the employers for a portion of the new workers' salaries.

## THE FUTURE

With the passage of the 1996 welfare reform act, our country is embarking on a critically important new course. The people that will be most affected by this new legislation will be the adult recipients and their children who are in this program. Will most of these families be successful in making this shift from welfare to work? Even if the adult recipients are successful in attaining employment, will their children be placed in quality child-care arrangements so that their lives are not adversely impacted?

Past experiences with the enactment of a major new social program suggest that, at first, there are apt to be significant difficulties that require some adjustments in the design of the program. For example, the 1935 Social Security Act has been amended numerous times to adjust to human needs that have become evident. It appears our political leaders will give considerable attention to making the 1996 welfare reform program viable for a variety of reasons. The general public strongly supports the concept of welfare-to-work for unemployed single parents. Both Republican and Democratic political leaders have agreed this is the welfare program that should be provided in this country for unemployed parents with children; and these political leaders are committed to making the changes that need to be made in order to make the program viable. Yet another reason that our political leaders will give considerable attention to making this program viable is because alternative programs for combating poverty (such as a family allowance program or a guaranteed-income program) are much more expensive. Other countries, such as Sweden, who have similar programs that assist public assistance recipients in obtaining employment have been able to make their programs viable.[72]

Make no mistake, however, we will soon be hearing heartbreaking stories about families who will be adversely impacted by this program. Adjustments will have to be made to alleviate these adverse effects.

Currently, the United States is experiencing social welfare changes as profound as those that occurred in the 1930s, when the Social Security Act inaugurated federally funded public assistance programs. At the present time there is a "devolution revolution" occurring in regard to the provision of human services in our society. The term *devolution revolution* refers to the fact that decisions about the provision of key social welfare programs are being transferred from the federal government to state and local governments. The replacement of the AFDC program with the 1996 welfare reform legislation is an example of this devolution revolution.

It is clear that local communities will play increasingly important roles in developing programs and services for the poor and for other vulnerable populations.

Churches, civic clubs, and other institutions in the local community are being asked to "take up the slack" that is being created by the federal government downsizing its support for social welfare programs. Healthy communities are those that are able to respond to social problems by providing a web of support for families and individuals in order to fill the holes in the social service safety net that are occurring due to the devolution revolution.

Poverty is interrelated with most other social problems. Therefore, it may well be that, if the poverty problem intensifies, there will be rate increases in crime, emotional disorders, infant mortality, inadequate health care, inner-city problems, substandard housing, alcoholism, the school dropout rate, malnutrition, child neglect, and suicide. If the 1996 welfare reform act fails, the poverty problem will be intensified, and there will be an escalation in severity of many other problems!

## Summary

About 14 percent of our population lives below the poverty line. Poverty is relative to time and place. An agreed on definition of poverty does not exist. The usual definitions are based on a lack of money, with annual income most commonly used to gauge who is poor. Income is defined using either an absolute approach or a relative approach. The pain of poverty involves not only financial hardships but also the psychological implications that being "poverty stricken" has for a person.

Huge income and wealth gaps exist between the highest fifth and lowest fifth in our society. Social mobility (movement up the social status ladder) occurs rarely in our society. Wealth perpetuates wealth, and poverty perpetuates poverty. The ideology of individualism and the Protestant ethic still stigmatize the poor in our society.

Those most likely to be poor include female heads of households, children, people of color, the elderly, large-sized families, those with limited education, the unemployed, and those living in pockets of poverty and high unemployment.

The causes of poverty are numerous. Poverty is interrelated with all other social problems. Therefore almost every social service, to some extent, combats poverty. Some researchers have noted that the poor have a set of values and attitudes that constitute a culture of poverty. There is now considerable controversy about whether this culture *perpetuates* poverty or is simply an *adaptation* to being poor.

Poverty, to some extent, is functional for society. For this and other reasons, some decision makers are not actively seeking to eradicate it.

The major income maintenance programs to combat poverty were created by the 1935 Social Security Act. The federal government's role in providing social insurance programs and public assistance programs was initiated by this act.

Social insurance programs (which are consistent with the institutional view of income transfers) receive less criticism than public assistance programs (which are consistent with the residual view of income transfer). There are many negative myths about public assistance programs, especially the now-defunct AFDC program. A danger of punitive, stigmatized public assistance programs is that poverty and dependency may be passed on to succeeding generations.

In 1996, welfare reform legislation was enacted that focuses on putting adult public assistance recipients with children to work. In 1935, when the AFDC program was enacted, it was thought that it was best for single mothers to stay at home to raise their children. The 1996 welfare reform act maintains that single mothers (and fathers) must work.

# CHAPTER 10

## Family

*T*he family is a social institution found in every culture. One common definition of a family is "A group of people related by marriage, ancestry, or adoption who live together in a common household."[1] It should be noted that such a definition does not cover a number of living arrangements in which the members consider themselves to be a family. Some of these arrangements are

♦ A husband and wife raising two foster children who have been in the household for several years.

♦ Two lesbians in a loving relationship who are raising children born to one of the partners while in a heterosexual marriage that ended in divorce.

♦ A family unit in which one of the spouses is living away from home—perhaps because of military service in a foreign country or because of incarceration.

♦ A man and a woman who have been living together for years in a loving relationship but who have never legally married.

Following a short introduction to various family forms throughout the world, this chapter:

♦ Presents a brief history of changes in the American family since colonial days

♦ Describes current problem areas in the American family

♦ Describes biomedical reproductive technological advances that are impacting families

♦ Summarizes new family forms (such as contract marriages) that will affect the family of the future

A wide diversity of family patterns exist in the world. Families in different cultures take a variety of forms. In some societies, husband and wife live in separate buildings. In others, they are expected to live apart for several years after the birth of a child. In many societies, husbands are permitted to have more than one wife. In a few countries, wives are allowed to have more than one husband. Some cultures permit (and a few encourage) premarital and extramarital intercourse.

Some societies have large communes where adults and children live together. In some communes the children are raised separately from adults. In some cultures without communes, surrogate parents raise the children. Certain societies encourage certain types of homosexual relationships, and a few recognize homosexual as well as heterosexual marriages.

In many cultures, marriages are still arranged by the parents. In a few societies, an infant may be "married" before birth (if the baby is of the wrong sex, the marriage is dissolved). Some societies do not recognize the existence of romantic love. Some cultures expect older men to marry young girls. Others expect older women to marry young boys. Most societies prohibit the marriage of close relatives, yet a few subcultures encourage marriage between brothers and sisters or between first cousins. Some expect a man to marry his father's brother's daughter, whereas others insist he marry his mother's sister's daughter. In some societies a man, upon marrying, makes a substantial gift to the bride's father, and in others the bride's father gives a substantial gift to the new husband.

There are indeed a number of variations in family patterns. People in each of these societies generally feel strongly that their particular pattern is normal and proper; many feel the pattern is divinely ordained. Suggested changes in their particular form are usually viewed with suspicion and defensiveness, and are often sharply criticized as being unnatural, immoral, and a threat to the survival of the family.

Despite these variations, sociologists have noted that practically all family systems can be classified into two basic forms: the extended family and the nuclear family. An *extended family* consists of a number of relatives living together, such as parents, children, grandparents, great-grandparents, aunts, uncles, in-laws, and cousins. The extended family is the predominant pattern in preindustrial societies. The members divide various agricultural, domestic, and other duties among themselves.

A *nuclear family* consists of a married couple and their children living together. The nuclear family emerged from the extended family. Extended families tend to be more functional in agricultural societies where many "hands" are needed; the nuclear family is more suited to the demands of complex, industrialized societies, as its smaller size and potential geographic mobility enable it to adapt more easily to changing conditions—such as the need to relocate to obtain a better job.

It should be noted that in the United States and a number of other countries a third family form is gradually emerging: the *single-parent family*. One-parent families are created in a variety of ways: an unmarried person adopts a child; an unmarried mother gives birth to a child; a married couple divorce and one parent (usually the woman) assumes custody of the children.

Single-parent families now comprise nearly 25 percent of all families in the United States.[2]

## The American Family: Past and Present

xxxxxxxxxxxxxxxxxxxx

We often view the American family as being a stable institution in which few changes have occurred. Surprisingly, a number of changes have taken place since colonial and frontier days.

## PREINDUSTRIAL SOCIETY

Prior to the 1800s, the economy in our country was predominantly agricultural. The majority of people lived on small farms in rural areas. In preindustrial society, transportation was arduous, and travel was constricted. The family was nearly self-sufficient; most of what it consumed was produced on the farm. The house and the farm were the center of production. The most common family type was the extended family. Each family member had specific roles and responsibilities. Because there were many tasks to be performed on small farms, the extended family form was functional, as it contained a number of family members to carry out the tasks.

Economic considerations influenced a variety of family patterns. Marriage was highly valued, and so was having a number of children. A large family was needed to do the wide variety of tasks involved in planting and harvesting crops and in raising cattle and other animals. With more children, a married couple could cultivate more acreage, thereby making the farm more profitable. Children were therefore important economic assets. Parents wanted their sons to marry robust, industrious women who could substantially contribute to the work that needed to be done.[3]

John F. Cuber et al. have noted that preindustrial American society developed a *monolithic code* of cultural beliefs, which were accepted by most people during this era.[4] (A monolithic code permits only one acceptable pattern of behavior.) Components of this code were:

- Adults were expected to be married. Women were expected to marry in their teens or early twenties. (Women who delayed marriage or did not marry were referred to as "old maids" and "spinsters.")
- Marriage was considered to be permanent, for life. Divorce was rare and highly disapproved.

- An individual was expected to place the welfare of the family unit ahead of his or her own preferences. (For example, an individual's preferences about whom to marry were considered less important than the parents' notions about what was best for the family as a unit.)
- Sexual relations were to be restricted to marriage. (There was a double standard, however, as women who had premarital or extramarital affairs were more harshly criticized and stigmatized than men.)
- Married couples were expected to have children. (Children were not only an economic asset but were also viewed as a religious obligation, based on the biblical charge, "Be fruitful and multiply.")
- Parents were expected to take care of their children, whatever the cost. Children were expected to be obedient to their parents and to honor them. Children were expected to care for aging or infirm parents.
- The father was the head of the family and made the important decisions. Women and children were expected to be subordinate to him. There were numerous advantages to being male. Women left their parents' home upon marriage and moved into their husband's home (usually near or in his parents' home). Male children were more highly valued than female children, partly because male children remained home after marrying. American preindustrial society was clearly patriarchal, as the father was viewed as the family head.
- The woman's place was in the home; she was expected to do the cooking, washing, cleaning, and a variety of other domestic tasks.

These beliefs were so strongly held by most people that they were thought to be the morally decent way to live. To violate these beliefs was viewed as going against nature and against God's will. As we shall see, remnants of this code still remain in American society.

## INDUSTRIAL SOCIETY

The Industrial Revolution, which began roughly two hundred years ago, has greatly changed family life. Factories and large-scale businesses have replaced the small family farm as centers of economic production. Most people now live in urban and semiurban areas.

Urbanization has accompanied industrialization. Products produced on small family farms or in small family shops are no longer competitive with products that are mass produced on assembly lines or by complex equipment and technology.

With the advent of the Industrial Revolution, the family gradually began losing its economic/productive function. Fewer people were needed in families to fill essential economic roles. There was a sharp decline in the economic need for extended families. In fact, smaller families became more functional for industrialized societies, as these families could more readily relocate to fill employment openings.

Gradually there was a shift toward individualism. A key component of individualism is the belief that the desires of the individual should take precedence over those of the family. As part of individualism and the loss of the economic productive function, it became increasingly recognized that the choice of a mate should be based on personal preference.

Also, with the loss of the economic productive function, children came to be viewed as economic liabilities; that is, they did nothing to increase family income but still had to be clothed, fed, and sheltered. In response, parents began having fewer children.

There have been numerous other changes. As noted in Chapter 8, no longer is the wisdom of the elderly as highly valued, as children are now trained and educated in educational settings. In a rapidly changing industrial society, the job skills of older workers often become obsolete. As a result, the elderly no longer are regarded with the esteem they once were.

Gradually, females won the right to vote, and in the past three decades the feminist movement has called into question the "double standards" of sexual morality. Women are also seeking equalitarian relationships with males. An increasing number of women are entering the labor force and seeking employment in settings that were once considered appropriate only for men (such as police departments). Sexuality is now more openly discussed, and there has been an increase in the rate of sexual relations outside marriage.[5] However, concern about AIDS appears to be a factor in decisions by individuals to reduce the number of sexual partners they have. (The chances of acquiring AIDS increase with the number of sexual partners.)

Still, remnants of the old monolithic code remain today. Some people think there is something "morally wrong" in a married couple's decision not to have children. Those who obtain a divorce are still stigmatized by some people. Those who decide never to get married are looked at as being "strange" by some. Becoming pregnant while single still is somewhat stigmatized.

In 1938 sociologist William Ogburn[6] noted the American family had undergone a number of changes in family functions as a result of industrialization and technological advances:

♦ The economic/productive function has been lost. In most families the financial resources are now acquired outside the home.

♦ The protective function has been lost and is now being met by agencies such as police departments, hospitals, insurance companies, and nursing homes.

♦ The educational function has been sharply reduced. Schools, day-care centers, and Head Start programs have taken on much of this function.

♦ The family is less likely to be the center for religious activity.

♦ The recreational function has largely been reduced. Each family member is now more apt to join recreational groups outside the home.

♦ The status recognition function has been sharply reduced. Individuals now receive recognition through their own achievements in organizations outside of the family, such as at school, at work, and in social and religious groups.

♦ The family has retained its affectional function. Family members receive social and emotional gratification from the family and have many of their companionship needs met by the family.

Most authorities agree with Ogburn's assessment that many functions of the American family have been lost or sharply reduced. It has been noted, however, that the modern family retains certain functions Ogburn overlooked.[7] Families in modern industrial societies perform the following essential functions that help maintain the continuity and stability of society:

♦ *Replacement of the population.* Every society has to have some system for replacing its members. Practically all societies consider the family as the unit in which children are to be produced. Societies have defined the rights and responsibilities of the reproductive partners within the family unit. These rights and responsibilities help maintain the stability of society, although they are defined differently from one society to another.

# Romantic Love versus Rational Love

Achieving a gratifying, long-lasting love relationship is one of our paramount goals. The experience of feeling "in love" is exciting, adds meaning to living, and psychologically gives us a good feeling about ourselves. Unfortunately, few people are able to maintain a long-term love relationship. Instead, many encounter problems, including falling in love with someone who does not love them, falling out of love with someone after an initial stage of infatuation, being highly possessive of someone they love, and having substantial conflicts with the loved one because of differing expectations abut the relationship. Failures in love relationships are more often the rule than the exception.

The emotion of love, in particular, is often viewed (erroneously) as being a feeling over which we have no control. A number of common expressions imply that love is a feeling beyond our control: "I fell in love," "It was love at first sight," "I just couldn't help it," and "I was swept off my feet." It is more useful to think of the emotion of love as being primarily based on our self-talk (that is, what we tell ourselves) about a person we meet.

Romantic love can be diagramed as follows:

*Event*

Meeting or becoming acquainted with a person who has some of the overt characteristics you desire in a lover.

*Self-talk*

"The person is attractive, personable; has all the qualities I admire in a lover/mate."

↓

*Emotion*

Intense infatuation, being romantically in love, a feeling of ecstasy.

Romantic love is often based on self-talk that stems from intense unsatisfied desires and frustrations rather than on reason or rational thinking. Unsatisfied desires and frustrations include extreme sexual frustration, intense loneliness, parental and personal problems, and extensive desire for security and protection.

A primary characteristic of romantic love is to idealize the person with whom we are infatuated as a "perfect lover"; that is, we notice this person has some overt characteristics we desire in a lover and then conclude that all the desired characteristics are present.

A second characteristic is that romantic love thrives on a certain amount of distance. The more forbidden the love, the stronger it becomes. The more social mores are threatened, the stronger the feeling. (For example, couples who live together and then later marry often report living together was more exciting and romantic.) The more effort necessary to be together (e.g., traveling long distances), the more intense the romance. The greater the frustration (e.g., loneliness or sexual needs), the more intense the romance.

---

- *Care of the young.* Children require care and protection until at least the age of puberty. The family is a primary institution for the rearing of children. Modern societies have generally developed supportive institutions to help in caring for the young—for example, medical services, day-care centers, parent training programs, and residential treatment centers.

- *Socialization of new members.* To become productive members of society, children have to be socialized into the culture. Children are expected to acquire a language, learn social values and mores, and dress and behave within the norms of society. The family plays a major role in this socialization process. In modern societies, there are a number of other groups and resources

involved in this socialization process. Schools, the mass media, peer groups, the police, and literature are important influences in the socialization process. (Sometimes these different influences clash by advocating opposing values and attitudes.)

- *Regulation of sexual behavior.* Failure to regulate sexual behavior would result in clashes between individuals due to jealousy and exploitation. Unregulated sexual behavior would probably result in the birth of large numbers of children outside marriage—children for whom no fathers could be held responsible for raising. Every society has rules that regulate sexual behavior within family units. Most societies, for example, have incest taboos, and most disapprove of extramarital sex.

The irony of romantic love is that, if an ongoing relationship is achieved, the romance usually withers. Through sustained contact, the person in love gradually comes to realize what the idealized loved one is really like—simply another human being with certain strengths and limitations. When this occurs, the romantic love relationship either turns into a rational love relationship, or the relationship is found to have significant conflicts and dissatisfactions and ends in a broken romance. For people with intense unmet desires, the latter occurs more frequently.

Romantic love thus tends to be temporary and based on make-believe. A person experiencing romantic love never loves the real person—only an idealized imaginary person.

Rational love, in contrast, can be diagrammed in the following way:

*Event*

While being aware of and comfortable with your own needs, goals, identity, and desires, you become well acquainted with someone who fulfills, to a fair extent, the characteristics you desire in a lover/spouse.

↓

*Self-talk*

"This person has many of the qualities and attributes I seek in a lover/spouse. I admire this person's strengths, and I am aware and accepting of his or her shortcomings."

↓

*Emotion*
Rational love.

The following are ingredients of a rational love relationship:

♦ You are clear and comfortable about your desires, identity, and goals in life.
♦ You know the other person well.
♦ You have accurately and objectively assessed the loved one's strengths and shortcomings and are generally accepting of them.
♦ Your self-talk about this person is consistent with your short- and long-term goals.
♦ Your self-talk is realistic and rational, so that your feelings are not based on fantasy, excessive desires, or pity.
♦ You and this person are able to communicate openly and honestly, so that problems can be dealt with when they arise and the relationship can continue to grow and develop.
♦ Rational love also involves giving and receiving, being kind, showing affection, knowing and doing what pleases the other person, communicating openly and warmly, and so on.

Because love is based on self-talk that causes feelings, it is we who create love. *Theoretically*, it is possible to love anyone by making changes in our self-talk. On the other hand, if we are in love with someone, we can gauge the quality of the relationship by analyzing our self-talk to determine the nature of our attraction and to determine the extent to which our self-talk is rational and in our best interests.

*Source:* Charles Zastrow, *You Are What You Think: A Guide to Self-Realization* (Chicago: Nelson-Hall, 1993), 56–60.

♦ *Exchange of affection.* Spitz, like Ogburn, demonstrated that humans need affection, emotional support, and positive recognition from others (including approval, smiles, encouragement, and reinforcement for accomplishments).[8] (As noted above, Ogburn identified this function as the primary one that remains in modern families.) Without such affection and recognition, a person's emotional, intellectual, physical, and social growth is stunted. The family is an important source for obtaining affection and recognition, as family members generally regard each other as among the most important people in their lives and gain emotional and social satisfaction from family relationships.

## *Problems in the Family*

Our brief sketch of American family history shows that a number of changes have occurred; yet the family retains several important functions. We will now examine four problem areas: the family is presently experiencing: divorce, empty-shell marriages, family violence, and births outside of marriage.

### DIVORCE

Our society places a higher value on romantic love than most other societies. In societies where marriages are arranged by parents, being in love generally has no role in mate selection. In our society, however, romantic love is a key factor in forming a marriage.

Children are socialized from an early age to believe in the glories of romantic love where, it is asserted, "love conquers all." Movies, TV programs, magazines, and books continually portray "happy-ending" romantic adventures. All of these breathtaking romantic stories suggest that every normal person falls in love with that one special person, gets married, and lives happily ever after. However, "happily ever after" is an ideal that rarely happens. Now one out of two marriages ends in divorce.[9] This high rate has gradually been increasing, whereas prior to World War I, divorce seldom occurred.

Divorce usually leads to a number of difficulties for those involved. First, divorcing parties face a number of emotional concerns such as a feeling of failure, concern over whether they are able to give and receive love, a sense of loneliness, the stigma attached to divorce, the reactions of friends and relatives, whether they are doing the right thing by parting, and whether they generally can make it on their own. Many people who part or are considering parting feel trapped, as they believe they can neither live *with* nor apart from their spouse. Dividing up the personal property between the two is another area that frequently leads to bitter differences of opinions. If there are children, there are concerns about how the divorce will affect them.

Other issues also must be decided. For example, who will get custody of the children? (Joint custody is now an alternative, where each parent has the children for part of the time.) If one parent is awarded custody, controversies are apt to arise over visiting rights and how much (if any) child support should be paid. Both spouses often face the difficulties of finding a new place to live, making new friends, doing things alone in our couple-oriented society, trying to make it financially on one's own, and fearing the hassles of dating.

Studies show that people going through a divorce are less likely to perform their jobs well and more likely to be fired during this period.[10] Divorced people have a shorter life expectancy.[11] Suicide rates are higher for divorced men.[12]

Divorce per se is no longer automatically assumed to be a social problem, although some of its consequences still are. On the other hand, there is increasing recognition that in some marriages where there is considerable tension, bitterness, and dissatisfaction, divorce is sometimes a solution: it may be a concrete step that some people take to end the unhappiness and to begin leading more productive and gratifying lives. It is also increasingly being recognized that a divorce may be better for the children because they may no longer be subjected to the tension and unhappiness of a marriage that has gone sour.

The rising rate of divorce does not necessarily mean that more marriages are failing. It may simply mean that more people are dissolving, instead of tolerating, unhappy marriages.

***Reasons for the Rising Divorce Rate*** There are many reasons for marital breakdown. Some obvious causes are alcoholism, economic strife, incompatibility, infidelity, jealousy, verbal or physical abuse, and interference from relatives and friends. But these factors have been around for centuries. How do we explain the recent rise in the number of divorces?

As noted earlier many people marry because they believe they are romantically in love. If this romantic love does not grow into rational love, the marriage is apt to fail. Unfortunately, young people are socialized in our society to believe that marriage will bring them continual romance; resolve all their problems; be sexually exciting, thrilling, full of adventure, and always as wonderful as the good moments of the courtship. (Most young people only need to look at their parents' marriage to realize such romantic ideals are seldom attained.) Unfortunately, living with someone in a marriage involves carrying out the garbage, washing dishes and clothes, being weary from work, putting up with one's partner's distasteful habits (for example, belching), changing diapers, and dealing with conflicts over such things as finances and differences in sexual interests. To make a marriage work requires that each spouse puts considerable effort into that marriage.

Another factor contributing to an increasing divorce rate is the unwillingness of some men to accept the changing status of women. Many men still prefer a traditional marriage where the husband is dominant and the wife plays a supportive (subordinate) role as child rearer, housekeeper, and emotional comforter. Many women no longer accept such a status and demand an equalitarian marriage in which major decisions, domestic tasks, raising the children, and bringing home paychecks are shared responsibilities.

Today, about two-thirds of American women with children under eighteen work outside the home.[13] Women who work outside the home are no longer as heavily reliant financially on their husbands. Women who are able to support themselves financially are more likely to seek a divorce if their marriages go sour.[14]

Another factor contributing to divorce is the growth of individualism. Individualism is the belief that people should seek self-actualization, be happy, develop their interests and capacities to the fullest, and seek to fulfill their own needs and desires. People in our society have increasingly come to accept individualism as a way of life. In contrast, people in more traditional societies and in extended families are socialized to put the interests of the group first, with their own individual interests being viewed as less important. In extended families, people view themselves as members of a group first and as individuals second. With America's growing belief in individualism, people who conclude they are unhappily married are much more apt to dissolve the marriage and seek a new life.

Growing acceptance of divorce in our society contributes to its rise. With less of a stigma attached to a divorce, more people who are unhappily married are now ending the marriage.

Finally, modern families no longer have as many functions as traditional families. Education, food production, entertainment, and other functions once centered in the family are now largely provided by outside agencies. Kenneth Keniston notes:

> In earlier times, the collapse of a marriage was far more likely to deprive both spouses of a great deal more than the pleasure of each other's company. Since family members perform so many functions for one another, divorce in the past meant a farmer without a wife to churn the cream into butter or care for him when he was sick and a mother without a husband to plow the field and bring her the food to feed their children. Today, when emotional satisfaction is the bond that holds marriages together, the waning of love or the emergence of real incompatibilities and conflicts between husband and wife leave fewer reasons for a marriage to continue. Schools and doctors and counselors and social workers provide their support whether the family is intact or not. One loses less by divorce today than in earlier times, because marriage provides fewer kinds of sustenance and satisfaction.[15]

Box 10.2 identifies variables that predict whether a marriage will or will not last.

***Divorce Laws*** In the past, society attempted to make the breakup of marriages almost impossible. One way it did this was by having laws that made divorce difficult to obtain. Once one of the spouses petitioned the court for a divorce, long waiting periods ensued before a divorce could be obtained. Divorce courts also followed "adversary" judicial procedures in

***

which the spouse seeking the divorce had to document that the other spouse was guilty of some offense such as adultery, desertion, or cruel and inhuman treatment. In many cases, the actual reasons for the divorce (such as no longer finding the relationship satisfying) bore little relationship to the grounds on which the court allowed the divorce. Often the marital partners contrived a story to accommodate the legal requirements for divorce.

In most divorces, both partners contribute to a marital breakdown. Yet traditional divorce laws erroneously assumed that one partner had to be the guilty party and the other the innocent party. Traditional divorce laws intensified the trauma that both partners were undergoing. Not only did it pit partners against each other, the process was highly expensive.

Because of these difficulties, most states have passed "no fault" divorce laws, which allow the couple to obtain a divorce fairly rapidly by stating to the court that they both agree their marriage has irreparably broken down. (The adversary process is still available for any spouse who chooses it.)

Issues still often contested between parties in divorce proceedings involve the division of property, alimony (or maintenance), child support, and child custody. In the past, the court invariably awarded the mother custody of the children, child-support payment, and alimony (particularly if she was not employed). Many men failed to make their child-support and alimony payments, which left former wives in dire financial traits.

Changes in sex roles and the rise of working women are restructuring divorce settlements. Most states have enacted legislation allowing courts to require that the woman pay alimony to her former husband, although few courts have as yet issued such orders. Custody of the children is still generally given to the mother, although this assignment is no longer automatic. More fathers are requesting custody of their children and expressing resentment toward the sexist bias of courts that assume a mother automatically to be better qualified to raise children.

A critical fact of divorce is that when it occurs, many costs of a family's shattered life are paid by society. In families of average income or less, the burden of divorce-related poverty falls on society as a whole. Divorced women with children who have limited incomes usually apply for public assistance programs. Additional expenses are incurred when lower-income people divorce. Costs include subsidized housing, public sector make-work jobs, and payments to lawyers who are involved in collecting support for women and children.

The willingness now of courts to consider giving custody to the father is creating a hidden cost to society. Fathers can and do threaten a protracted court battle. As a result, mothers who want custody without a fight are routinely forced to barter custody in exchange for reduced child-support payments. Because such payments are so low, these women and their children then qualify as welfare recipients. Richard Neely, a state supreme court justice notes:

> Most of us begin with a political conviction that women *ought* to be equal to men economically, and then leap to a conclusion that they *are*. It then logically follows that women can support children as well as men and that whoever wants the children can pay for them.
>
> The fact is that women are much poorer than men, and this pattern appears highly resistant to change.[16]

Custody battles between father and mother are currently becoming more common in divorce cases. Typical custody battles proceed through the courts at a snail's pace. The process may take as long as two years. It is common for parents to spend thousands of dollars on attorneys, expert witnesses, and court costs. During this process some parents may use the children as pawns against each other by bribing them with large allowances, relaxing discipline, and indulging outrageous whims. At the same time they may seek to turn children against the other parent by bad mouthing him or her. Custody battles are not only costly but also emotionally damaging to mother, father, and children.

In many states children over fourteen are allowed to select the parent with whom they wish to live if that parent is fit. To avoid custody battles, and the process in which women barter reduced child-support payments for custody, Neely recommends that for children under age fourteen, custody be awarded to the primary caretaker parent, defined as:

> the parent who: (1) prepares the food; (2) changes the diapers, dresses, and bathes the child; (3) takes the child to school, church, and other activities; (4) makes appointments with a doctor and generally watches over the child's health; and (5) interacts with the child's friends, the school authorities, and other adults engaged in activities that involve the child. It is not surprising that the "primary caretaker" is usually the mother, but that need not be the case.[17]

In 90 percent of divorce cases, the mothers are awarded custody of the children.[18] Upon divorce, the mother's standard of living sharply declines, but the father's standard of living generally increases as he now has fewer financial responsibilities.[19] Women are awarded alimony in only 15 percent of divorce cases.[20] When there are children, the fathers are usually required to pay child support, but the amounts awarded are generally insufficient to meet the financial needs of the children. In addition, 50 percent of divorced fathers fail to pay the full amount of child-support payments, and 24 percent make no court-ordered child-support payments.[21] As a result, the income for the divorced mother and her children often plunges below the poverty level. In many cases taxpayers wind up supporting the mother and her children through the welfare system.[22]

In an effort to combat these problems, Congress mandated in the late 1980s that states enact legislation to withhold child support from the paychecks of all noncustodial parents (generally fathers). For example, Wisconsin passed legislation that the noncustodial parent pay a set percentage (based on the number of children) of his gross income for child support—the percentage ranges from 17 percent for one child to 35 percent for five or more children. These child-support payments are sent by the employer to the court that handled the divorce, and the court then sends a check to the custodial parent. Additional mechanisms that have been created to pressure the noncustodial parent to pay child support include: withholding of the noncustodial parent's income-tax refunds; reporting of child support arrearages to consumer credit agencies; reporting the names of delinquent noncustodial parents in newspapers; and placement of liens on delinquent noncustodial parents. Such mechanisms have reduced rates of failure of the noncustodial parent to make child-support payments—which increases the chances that the custodial parent (generally the mother) will have a steady income from child support.

## EMPTY-SHELL MARRIAGES

In empty-shell marriages the spouses feel no strong attachments to each other. Outside pressures keep the marriage together, rather than feelings of warmth and attraction between the members. Such outside pressures include business reasons (for example, an elected official wanting to convey a stable family image); investment reasons (for example, husband and wife may have a luxurious home and other property that they do not want to lose by parting); and outward appearances (for example, a couple living in a small community may remain together to avoid the reactions of relatives and friends to a divorce). In addition, a couple may believe that ending the marriage would harm the children or that getting a divorce would be morally wrong.

John F. Cuber and Peggy B. Harroff have identified three types of empty-shell marriages.[23] In a *devitalized relationship*, husband and wife lack excitement for or real interest in their spouse or their marriage. Boredom and apathy characterize this marriage, and serious arguments are rare.

In a *conflict-habituated relationship*, husband and wife frequently quarrel in private. They may also quarrel in public or put up a facade of compatibility. The relationship is characterized by considerable conflict, tension, and bitterness.

In a *passive-congenial relationship*, neither partner is happy with the marriage, but both are generally content with their lives and very seldom quarrel. The partners may have some interests in common, but these interests add very little excitement or romance to the relationship. The spouses contribute little to each other's real satisfactions.

The number of empty-shell marriages is unknown—it may be as high or higher than the number of happy marriages. Empty-shell marriages hold little fun or laughter and members do not share their problems or experiences with each other. There is seldom any spontaneous expression of affection or sharing of a personal experience. In such families children are often starved for love, or they receive the love that would otherwise go to the spouse. Sometimes the children, embarrassed about the way their parents interact, are reluctant to have friends over.

Empty-shell couples enjoy few activities together and seldom display pleasure in being in one another's company. Sexual relations between the partners, as might be expected, are rare and generally unsatisfying. Visitors note that the partners (and often the children) appear insensitive, cold, and callous toward each other. However, the members are highly aware of each other's weaknesses and vulnerable points, as they manage to mention these areas frequently in order to hurt one another.

William J. Goode compares empty-shell marriages to marriages that end in divorce:

> Most families that divorce pass through a state—sometimes *after* the divorce—in which husband and wife no longer feel bound to each other, cease to cooperate or share with each other, and look on one another as almost a stranger. The "empty-shell" family is in such a state. Its members no longer feel any strong commitment to many of the mutual role obligations, but for various reasons the husband and wife do not separate or divorce.[24]

Although the number of empty-shell marriages ending in divorce is unknown, it is likely that a fair number eventually do. Both spouses have to put considerable effort into making a marriage work to prevent an empty-shell marriage from gradually developing.

## VIOLENCE IN FAMILIES

We tend to view the family as a social institution in which love and gentleness abound. Sadly, the opposite is often true, because violence is pervasive in American families.

Beatings, stabbings, and assaults are common in many families. The extent of violence in families is largely unknown, as much of the violence is unreported. It is estimated that child abuse, spouse abuse, and other physical violence occur in more than half of all U.S. households.[25] An estimated 50 million people fall victim annually to physical harm at the hands of another family member.[26] Studies show that in 20 percent of child-abuse cases, a spouse is also abused.[27]

Violence in families is not limited to child abuse and spouse abuse. The number of children who assault their parents is greater than the number of children who are abused by their parents.[28] *Elder abuse* is increasingly receiving attention. This term refers to "the physical or psychological mistreatment of the elderly."[29] The perpetrator may be the son or daughter of the elderly victim, a caregiver, or some other person. Lewis and Joanne Koch provide one case example:

> In Chicago, a 19-year-old woman confessed to torturing her 81-year-old father and chaining him to a toilet for seven days. She also hit him with a hammer when he was asleep: "I worked him over real good with it. Then after I made him weak enough, I chained his legs together. After that I left him and rested. I watched TV for a while."[30]

The varied forms of mistreatment of the elderly are typically grouped into the following four categories:

♦ *Physical abuse,* the infliction of physical pain or injury, including bruising, punching, restraining, or sexually molesting.

♦ *Psychological abuse,* the infliction of mental anguish, such as intimidating, humiliating, and threatening harm.

♦ *Financial abuse,* the illegal or improper exploitation of the victim's assets or property.

♦ *Neglect,* including deliberate failure or refusal to fulfill a caretaking obligation, such as denial of food or health care, or abandoning the victim.[31]

Violence between children is also common. Some children even use a weapon (such as a knife or a gun) when having conflicts with their siblings.

Patterns of family violence appear to be learned in families. If a child is abused, that child (when he becomes an adult and a parent) is more likely to abuse his children. Also, if an adult was abused as a child by his parents and then becomes the primary caregiver for those parents, he is more likely to abuse his elderly parents.

The victims of family violence—battered children, battered parents, and battered wives—have common disadvantages. They are generally smaller in size, have less physical strength, and usually feel helpless in relation to the aggressors (primarily because they depend on their aggressors for physical, financial, and emotional support).

Before the 1960s little attention was given to violence in families, partly because the family was viewed as a sacred institution and a private domain: What went on within families was viewed as a personal concern and the responsibility of family members alone—not outsiders. Over the past four decades there has been an increasing awareness that violence in families is a major social problem.

Family fights constitute the largest single category of calls to police. The highest rate of police fatalities arise from response to disturbance calls, and domestic violence cases make up a large proportion of such calls.[32] Suzanne Steinmetz and Murray Straus have noted: "It would be hard to find a group or an institution in American society in which violence is more of an everyday occurrence than it is within the family."[33] Violence not only causes physical harm in families; each incident also weakens the loyalty, affection, and trust among members that are basic to positive family functioning.

One explanation of why family violence occurs is based on the theory that frustration often provokes an aggressive response. A husband or wife who is frustrated at work may come home and take out that frustration on the spouse or the children. A young child frustrated by the action of a sibling may take a poke at him or her. Steinmetz and Straus observe: "In a society such as ours, in which aggression is defined as a normal response to frustration, we can expect that the more frustrating the familial and occupational roles, the greater the amount of violence."[34]

In another explanation, John O'Brien has noted that family members often use physical force to gain an advantage.[35] A parent spanks a child for disciplinary

reasons. A sister may shove her brother out of the way to attempt to obtain something they both want. O'Brien suggests that family members are likely to resort to physical force when other resources are non-existent, diminished, or exhausted. Thus an alcoholic husband who feels he has lost the respect of his family may resort to physical abuse as a last-ditch effort to assert his authority.

*Spouse Abuse*  Spouse abuse, particularly wife beating, was, unfortunately, tolerated for many years but has now become an issue of national concern. The problem leaped into the spotlight in 1994 following the death of Nicole Brown Simpson, who was savagely stabbed to death, and her former husband (O. J. Simpson) was charged with the murder. At least eight times prior to her death, police had been called to the Simpson home after Nicole claimed she was being battered by O. J.[36] (Two years later in a civil trial, O. J. was found responsible for the causing the deaths of his former wife and Ronald Goldman.)

It is not just wives who are abused. Husbands are slapped or shoved with about the same frequency as are wives.[37] The greatest physical damage, however, is usually suffered by women. Studies show that men cause more serious injuries, largely because they are physically stronger.[38] More than 10 percent of all murder victims are killed by their spouses.[39] It should be noted that women also tend to endure cruelty and abuse much longer than men, at times because they feel trapped due to unemployment and financial insecurity. Spouse abuse is sometimes precipitated by the victim, that is, the recipient of the abuse may be the first to use verbal or physical violence in the incident.[40] However, the dominant theme in American spouse abuse is the systematic use of violence and the threat of violence by some men to "keep their wives in line." That is to say, there is a traditional belief held by some segments of our society that husbands have a right to control what their wives do and to force them to be submissive.

Domestic violence from husbands, male partners, or other family members happens so often that violence is the major cause of injury to women.[41] Injuries from woman battering are more common than those from rape, mugging, or even auto accidents.[42]

Incidents of physical abuse between spouses are not isolated, but tend to recur frequently in a marriage. Spouse abuse occurs as often among the well educated as among the less educated.[43]

Most wives who are severely beaten by their husbands do not seek to end the marriage. Wives are more likely to remain in the home if (1) the violence is infrequent, (2) they were abused by their parents when they were children, or (3) they believe they are financially dependent on their husbands.[44]

Many authorities believe spouse abuse is related to a norm of tolerating violence in American families. Straus notes:

There seems to be an implicit, taken-for-granted cultural norm which makes it legitimate for family members to hit each other. In respect to husbands and wives, in effect, this means that the marriage license is also a hitting license.[45]

Several studies have found that a sizable number of both men and women believe it is appropriate of a husband to hit his wife "every now and then."[46]

Men batter women for a variety of reasons. Many have a poor self-image; they are insecure about their worth as breadwinners, fathers, and sexual partners. They tend to have a stereotyped view of their wives as playing a submissive role and as needing to be controlled. Many men use alcohol and other drugs to excess and are much more likely to be violent when intoxicated or high.

In battered-spouse families a cycle of violence tends to be continually repeated, as follows: A battering incident occurs, and the wife sustains injuries. The husband feels remorse, but he also fears his wife may leave or may report the abuse to the police, so he tries to "honeymoon" her into thinking he is a good husband who won't abuse her again. (He may even send flowers, buy expensive gifts, or be overly attentive.) Gradually the "honeymoon" efforts on his part cease, and tensions about work or family matters again begin to build inside him. As the tension builds, a minor incident sets him off, often while he's intoxicated, and he again batters his wife. The battering/honeymoon/tension-building/battering cycle tends to be repeated again and again.

Abusive husbands often isolate their spouses and make them dependent. They try to make their wives sever ties with relatives and friends. They ridicule their wives' friends and relatives, and they usually create an embarrassing scene when the wife is with those friends or relatives. The wife then ends contact with friends and relatives in order to "keep peace." Abusive husbands make their wives dependent on them by continually ridiculing them, which lowers the women's self-esteem and leads them to play a submissive role. Husbands also create financial dependency, such as by creating barriers that prevent their wives from seeking high-paying employment.

A surprising number of battered women do not permanently leave their husbands. There are a variety of reasons for this. Many are socialized to play a subordinate role to their husbands, and the husbands use violence and psychological abuse to make them feel too inadequate to live on their own. Some women believe it is their moral duty to stick it out to the end—that marriage is forever, for better or for worse. Many hope (in spite of the continuing violence) that their husbands will change. Some fear that, if they try to leave, their husbands will retaliate with even more severe beatings. A fair number do not view leaving as a viable alternative because they feel financially dependent. Many have young children and do not believe they have the resources to raise children on their own. Some believe the occasional beatings are better than the loneliness and insecurity connected with leaving. Some dread the stigma associated with separation or divorce. These women are captives in their own homes.

Fortunately, new services in recent years have been developed for battered women. Shelter homes for battered women and their children have been established in many communities. These shelters give abused women an opportunity to flee from their abusive situation. The women also generally receive counseling, assistance in finding a job, and legal help. Services to battered women now include "safety planning," which is an empowerment approach to help women develop a repertoire of resources to maintain their safety. In some areas programs are also being established for the husbands. These programs include group therapy for batterers, anger management programs for batterers, marriage counseling for both spouses, and twenty-four-hour hotlines that encourage potential spouse abusers to call when they are angry. (Unfortunately, many batterers refuse to participate in such programs.) Many communities also have public information programs (for example, short television announcements) to inform battered women that they have a legal right not to be abused and that there are resources to stop the abuse.

In an effort to treat domestic abuse as seriously as crimes between strangers, many states have enacted a domestic abuse law that requires police to make an arrest (of either spouse, but usually the husband) if physical abuse has occurred and injury or threat of further harm exists. Police face criminal or civil penalties under the law if they do not make a mandated arrest.[47]

As services for battered wives become more widely available, we may expect an increasing number of these women to flee from their homes and to refuse to return until they have some guarantee of their safety.

***Child Abuse and Neglect***   Although definitions of child abuse and neglect vary somewhat from state to state, Alfred Kadushin and Judith Martin summarize the kinds of situations as including:

- ◆ Physical abuse.
- ◆ Malnourishment; poor clothing; lack of proper shelter, sleeping arrangements, attendance, or supervision. (Includes "failure to thrive" syndrome, which describes infants who fail to grow and develop at a normal rate.)
- ◆ Denial of essential medical care.
- ◆ Failure to attend school regularly.
- ◆ Exploitation, overwork.
- ◆ Exposure to unwholesome or demoralizing circumstances.
- ◆ Sexual abuse.
- ◆ Somewhat less frequently, the definitions include emotional abuse and neglect involving denial of the normal experiences that permit a child to feel loved, wanted, secure, and worthy.[48]

The consequences of child abuse and neglect can be devastating. Gelles notes:

> Researchers and clinicians have documented physical, psychological, cognitive, and behavioral consequences of physical abuse, psychological abuse, sexual abuse, and neglect. Physical damage can range from death, brain damage, and permanent disabilities to minor bruises and scrapes. The psychological consequences can range from lowered sense of self-worth to severe psychiatric disorders, including dissociative states. Cognitive problems range from severe organic brain disorders to reduced attention and minor learning disorders. Maltreated children's behavioral problems can include severe violent and criminal behavior and suicide as well as inability to relate to peers.[49]

*Physical Abuse.* In the past forty years there has been considerable national concern about the "battered-child syndrome." The Children's Division of the American Humane Society conducted a nationwide survey of newspaper reports on child abuse and concluded:

> The forms or types of abuse inflicted on these children are a negative testimony to the ingenuity and inventiveness of man. By far the greater number of injuries resulted from beatings with various kinds of implements and instruments. The hairbrush was a common implement used to beat children. However, the same purpose was accomplished with deadlier impact by the use of bare fists, straps, electric cords, TV aerials, ropes, rubber hoses, fan belts, sticks, wooden shoes, pool cues, bottles, broom handles, baseball bats, chair legs, and, in one case, a sculling oar. Less imaginative, but equally effective, was plain kicking with street shoes or with heavy work shoes.

> Children had their extremities—hands, arms, and feet—burned in open flames as from gas burners or cigarette lighters. Others bore burn wounds inflicted on their bodies with lighted cigarettes, electric irons, or hot pokers. Still others are scalded by hot liquids thrown over them or from being dipped into containers of hot liquids.

> Some children were strangled or suffocated by pillows held over their mouths or plastic bags thrown over their heads. A number were drowned in bathtubs, and one child was buried alive.

> To complete the list—children were stabbed, bitten, shot, subjected to electric shock, were thrown violently to the floor or against a wall, were stamped on, and one child had pepper forced down his throat.[50]

The survey went on to report that these abused children incurred various kinds of injuries:

> The majority had various shapes, sizes, and forms of bruises and contusions. There was a collection of welts, swollen limbs, split lips, black eyes, and lost teeth. One child lost an eye.

> Broken bones were common. Some were simple fractures; others compound. There were many broken arms, broken legs, and fractured ribs. Many children had more than one fracture. One five-month-old child was found to have 30 broken bones in his little body.

> The grimmest recital of all is the listing of internal injuries and of head injuries. The head injuries particularly were a sizable group. Both the internal injuries and the head injuries were responsible for a great many of the fatalities. In this group, we find damage to internal organs such as ruptured livers, ruptured spleens, and ruptured lungs. Injuries to the head were concussion or skull fractures, with brain hemorrhage and brain damage a frequent diagnosis.

> This is indeed a grim, sad, sordid, and horror-filled recital of what happens to children in communities in almost every state of the Union.[51]

Physical abuse involves beating a child to the point at which some physical damage is done. The line between physical abuse and harsh parental discipline is difficult to define. Silver et al. note:

> If a parent punishes a child with a belt, is it after the fourth slash with the belt that parental rights end and child abuse begins; is it after the belt raises a welt over two millimeters that it becomes abuse versus parental rights?[52]

Definitions of abuse vary. Some are narrow in scope, restricting abuse to actual serious injury sustained by the child; broader definitions include intent to harm the child and verbal abuse.

## Case Example: A Case of Physical Abuse and Murder

Chicago—Jody Marie Olcott lived only 102 days. She died on November 16, 1994. The coroner's report showed she had suffered more injuries than most people who live into later adulthood. Charged with second-degree murder in her death is her father, Malcom Olcott, age thirty-four.

Jody Marie was born on August 5, 1994. Her unmarried parents lived together. Her mother, Judy Forbes, worked as a waitress. Her father was unemployed and felt considerable pressure about being unemployed and having parental responsibilities.

Jody's first two months were normal. Her pediatrician saw her early in October and reported she had gained nearly two pounds and appeared in good health. Shortly after that, Jody's nightmare began. The pathologist who examined Jody's body noted that she suffered at least five broken ribs, caused about a month previously by kicking or by punching with a fist.

The pathologist noted that about ten days before her death Jody received bruises to her head, chest, and left elbow. At about the same time she received burn marks on her buttocks and her head. The district attorney acknowledged that Mr. Olcott had admitted at the time of his arrest setting Jody on top of a space heater.

The pathologist's report also noted that one of Jody's knees was broken and the other was badly sprained, possibly resulting from the child being picked up by her legs and then her legs being snapped. At the time of her death Jody's weight had dropped to six pounds—one pound less than when she was born.

The blow that caused Jody's death occurred during the night of November 15, while Ms. Forbes was at work. The district attorney stated Mr. Olcott was feeling on edge because of his financial and family responsibilities. He began drinking. Jody was crying as she had done for the past several days (probably from the pain from all of her injuries). Mr. Olcott stated he just couldn't take the incessant crying. He grabbed Jody and tossed her about ten feet—hoping she'd land on the sofa. Jody missed the sofa and landed on her head on a hardwood floor. Mr. Olcott told the police that during the next few hours Jody stopped crying but appeared to have trouble breathing and sometimes vomited. When Ms. Forbes came home that evening, she found that Jody did not appear to be breathing. She called for an ambulance. Jody was pronounced dead on arrival; the cause of death was a blood clot caused by a skull fracture. Ms. Forbes was asked by the police why she did not report the violence occurring to Jody over the past several weeks. Ms. Forbes stated, "Malcom told me if I went to the police, he would leave me and have nothing more to do with me."

---

In the late 1960s, in response to a growing national concern about child abuse, all states adopted child-abuse and neglect-reporting laws. Such laws are essentially a case-finding device. They require professionals (such as physicians, social workers, counselors, hospital administrators, school administrators, nurses, and dentists) to report suspected cases of child abuse to certain specified agencies, such as the local police department and the county welfare department.

The true extent of child abuse is unknown. Accurate data are difficult to get, for two reasons: the failure of citizens and professionals to report suspected cases and the reluctance of abused children to talk. Many battered children, believing their punishment is deserved, keep mute when interviewed by those who might help, and they develop negative self-images.

A significant result of child abuse is that violence breeds violence. George C. Curtis reports evidence showing that abused children may "become tomorrow's murderers and perpetrators of other crimes of violence."[53] When they become parents, there is also a high probability they will become abusive parents.[54] Theoretically, abuse generates an unusually high degree of hostility, which, in future years, may well be channeled into violence. A disproportionate number of rapists, murderers, robbers, and spouse abusers were child-abuse victims when they were younger. Abused children are high risks to become runaways, which exposes them to other kinds of victimization and sometimes results in their being involved in criminal activity, such as shoplifting, theft, or prostitution.

Although in rare cases abuse is nonrecurrent, generally it is repeated. Nonrecurrent abuse is usually difficult to document, as the abuser can contrive a plausible explanation for the one-time injuries received by the child.

Gelles reviewed studies on the characteristics of parents and caretakers who are most at risk of abusing their children, and found:

♦ Abuse was more likely to occur among parents with limited education and employment skills, among nonwhite families, and among mother-headed, single-parent families.

♦ In many of the families there was evidence of "family discord" and stress due to limited financial resources. (It is possible that the higher incidence of abuse in the lower classes may partly result from the fact that middle- and upper-class parents are in a better position to conceal the abuse.)

♦ Mothers are more likely to abuse their children than fathers. The reasons for this gender difference is probably related to the fact that mothers tend to spend more time with children, and mothers in our society are considered more responsible for the children's behavior than are fathers.

♦ Most abused children (over two-thirds) are permitted to remain in their homes by protective services even after abuse is determined. (Protective services are described later in this section.)[55]

*Physical Neglect.* In contrast to child abuse, child neglect is more a problem of omission than of commission. Specific types of physical neglect include (1) child abandonment; (2) environmental neglect—letting a child live in filth, without proper clothing, unattended, unsupervised, or without proper nourishment; (3) educational neglect, in which a child is allowed to be excessively absent from school; and (4) medical neglect, in which no effort is made to secure needed medical care for the child. Although child neglect has received less national attention than child abuse, it is the most common situation in which protective service agencies must intervene.

In rare cases, such as child abandonment, the parent rejects the parental role. In most child-neglect cases, however, the parent inadequately performs the role. Kadushin and Martin define a typical neglectful mother as being physically exhausted, mentally impoverished, emotionally deprived, and socially isolated.[56] Parental neglect is more likely to be found among those who are poverty stricken or who live on marginal incomes.

Vincent De Francis provides the following description of what a social worker encountered in investigating a neglect complaint:

What I saw as I entered the room was utter, stark disorganization. The room was a combined kitchen-dining room. At the other end of the room, two scrawny, owl-eyed, frightened children—a girl of about four and a boy of three—stared silently at me. Except for thin cotton undershirts, they were stark naked. They had sore crusts on their legs and arms. They were indescribably dirty, hair matted, body and hands stained and covered with spilled food particles. Sitting on a urine-soaked and soiled mattress in a baby carriage behind them was a younger child—a boy about two.

The floor was ankle-deep in torn newspapers. There were feces in about a half-dozen spots on the floor, and the air was fetid and saturated with urine odor.

There were flies everywhere. What seemed like giant roaches were crawling over the paper-strewn floor. The kitchen sink and gas stove were piled high with greasy and unwashed dishes, pots, and pans.[57]

*Emotional Neglect.* Meeting a child's affectional needs is as important to normal growth and development as meeting his or her physical needs. Yet emotional neglect is difficult to define and document in the precise terms required by law.

The National Clearinghouse on Child Neglect and Abuse defines emotional neglect as:

. . . failure to provide the child the emotional nurturing or emotional support necessary for the development of a sound personality, as for example, subjecting the child to rejection or to a home climate charged with tension, hostility, and anxiety-producing occurrences which result in perceivable problems in children.[58]

Interpreted broadly, the problem with this definition is that practically every parent at times is guilty of such neglect. Other definitions of emotional neglect encounter the same problem. Nevertheless, there is solid agreement that some children do suffer from emotional neglect—even when they are adequately cared for physically.

Emotional neglect is very difficult to document in court (see Box 10.4). When emotional neglect is accompanied by physical neglect, protective service agencies make a case based on the physical neglect.

*Abusive and Neglectful Parents.* Why do some parents abuse or neglect their children? Abuse and neglect cover a wide variety of behaviors that have diverse effects on children. No single cause can fully explain why parents abuse or neglect their children. Available research indicates abusive and neglectful parents may have little in common. The following factors[59] have been found to be associated with parents who abuse their children:

Box 10.4 ◆◆◆◆◆◆◆◆◆◆◆◆◆◆◆◆◆◆◆◆◆◆◆◆

# Case Example:
# Is This Emotional Neglect?

The following case example raises a number of yet unanswered questions surrounding emotional neglect.

Gary, age nine, was the only child of Mr. and Mrs. Jim N. The N. family lived in a suburb of a metropolitan area, and Gary's physical needs were adequately met. Yet Gary was not doing well in school. He repeated the first grade and now is repeating the third grade.

Gary was referred for psychological testing and was found to have a very low self-concept. His self-concept was so negative, he refused to study math for fear of failing and would not participate in any competitive games with peers. He instead preferred to play by himself, with toys appropriate to five-year-olds.

A home study found that Mr. N. was a stoic, unaffectional person who was seldom at home, as he spent long hours operating a service station he owned. Mrs. N. had such an obnoxious personality and disposition that she was unable to hold a job and had no close friends. Below average in intellect, she only completed the ninth grade. In her interactions with Gary, she was observed to have a low tolerance level, would frequently berate and criticize him, and call him "stupid" and "an idiot." Gary appeared somewhat fearful of her and tried to avoid interacting with her. Both parents refused to take parent effectiveness training or to receive counseling.

◆ Are Gary's personal problems (negative self-image) a result of interactions with his parents or due to some other factors (e.g., school environment, a past traumatic experience, or an inherited disposition)?

◆ Even if it is assumed his problems are due to his parental interactions, how could this be proved in court?

◆ Would his personal problems be reduced or intensified if he were placed in a foster home?

◆ Many abusive parents were themselves abused as children. If not abused, they generally had a lack of stable love relationships in their childhood and inadequate gratification of early emotional needs.

◆ Although abuse, like neglect, is more heavily concentrated among lower classes, it is more randomly distributed than neglect throughout the population.

◆ Frequently, one child is singled out to be the target of the abuse. A variety of reasons appear to account for this. The child may be viewed as mentally "slow" or a potential delinquent. Where there is marital conflict, one child may be chosen as the victim because of a resemblance to the disliked spouse. One child may cry more, be hyperactive, or be more demanding of parental care. The child may be punished because he or she was conceived prior to marriage or is the result of an unwanted pregnancy.

◆ In some cases, the abused child contributes to the selection process by making greater than normal demands on parental patience: by having severe temper tantrums; by having feeding, speech, or toilet-training problems; and/or by being restless, negative, unresponsive, listless, whiny, or fussy.

◆ The victimized child may, in disturbed families, be essential for the psychic stability of the family. It appears some disturbed families need a "whipping boy" or "scapegoat" to maintain an equilibrium within the family. Sometimes when an abused child is removed, another is selected to be the victim and thereby fulfills this "stabilizing" role.

◆ Abusive parents often show an absence of guilt, have a tendency toward social isolation, have a high level of overall aggressiveness, are prone to impulsivity, tend to have emotional problems, have feelings of inadequacy, and have a low tolerance of criticism.

◆ Environmental stress factors (e.g., marital problems), economic pressures, and social isolation sometimes help trigger abuse.

◆ Abusive parents tend to believe in strict discipline and view misbehavior by their children as willful, deliberate disobedience. Also they are characterized as having a high demand for the child to perform to gratify the parent.

◆ Alcohol/drug abuse plays an important contributing role in some cases.

The following factors[60] have been identified to be associated with child neglect:

◆ The preponderance of families come from the lower socioeconomic classes. Financial deprivation is a major contributing factor. Many also have inadequate housing.

- A high percentage (60 percent in some studies) are one-parent families, generally headed by a female.

- Neglectful parents have also been found frequently to have an atypically large number of children.

- A fair number of neglectful mothers are below normal in intellectual capacity.

- Neglectful parents (particularly the mothers who have most contact with children) are physically and emotionally exhausted; have health problems; are socially withdrawn or isolated, frustrated, apathetic, and lack hope. Such factors lead them to be indifferent toward their children.

- Neglectful parents tend to have been emotionally deprived during childhood. Similar to abusive parents, they failed to have stable affectionate relationships when they were young. Such early childhood experiences appear to lead to current emotional inadequacies and then, when combined with severe financial and environmental stress, result in physical and emotional exhaustion.

- Neglectful families are not without intrapsychic distress but are generally less emotionally disturbed than abusive parents. Similar to abusive parents, they tend to be socially isolated.

*Protective Services.*    Under the concept of *parens patriae,* the state is ultimately a parent to all children. If the natural parents neglect, abuse, or exploit a child, the state has the legal right and responsibility to intervene. This right to intervene is delegated to a protective services agency. (In many states protective services agencies are located within public welfare departments.) These agencies provide specialized social services to neglected, abused, exploited, or rejected children and their parents. The focus of the service is preventive and nonpunitive and is geared toward rehabilitation.

Case finding is almost always through a complaint referral. Complaints generally are filed by neighbors, relatives, public health nurses, physicians, school authorities, police, or another social agency. A complaint is a report of a possible neglect or abuse situations that needs exploration; the complainant may remain anonymous. Once a complaint is received, protective services then investigates whether there is evidence of abuse or neglect. (Occasionally, unfounded complaints are made to harass a parent.)

If abuse or neglect exists, parents are advised that the focus of protective services is to prevent further neglect or abuse and to alleviate the factors that now endanger the child. Because many families charged with abuse or neglect have several problems, services may be far ranging (for example, health, education, financial help, housing, counseling, assistance in finding employment, parent effectiveness training, homemaking assistance, day care, and so on).

If there is no evidence of neglect or abuse, the case may be closed after the initial interview. For families with serious problems, continued services may be provided for years.

If the child is clearly in danger (for example, repeated severe abuse) or if the parents are unable or unwilling to make changes essential for the long-term well-being of the child, the child may have to be removed from the home. Protective services agencies view court action as "a means of protecting the child rather than of prosecuting the parents."[61]

Protective services cannot withdraw from the situation if it finds the parents are uncooperative or resistant. Protective services is one of the few social services where participation is involuntary (probation supervision is another). Because protective services are involuntary and because provision of services is based on an "outside" complaint, the recipients are apt to view the service as an invasion of privacy. The initial conflict by a protective services worker is therefore likely to arouse hostility, be viewed as a threat to family autonomy, and perhaps raise some guilt about past incidents of mistreatment of the children. Having one's functioning as a parent questioned and explored arouses anger and guilt. Although the focus of protective services is rehabilitative and nonpunitive, at least one study has found that former clients generally viewed the service as being punitive and investigatory.[62]

Some recipients of protective services remain hostile and resistant throughout the time services are provided. Others come around to form a productive, working relationship with the agency, with positive changes being much more apt to occur. A few cooperate from the beginning, perhaps because they recognize their family needs help.

Major problems remain unresolved in the area of child abuse and neglect. Physical abuse is difficult to distinguish from harsh discipline. Emotional neglect has not been adequately defined. Many cases of abuse and neglect go unreported. Resources of protective services in many communities are limited, so that effective intervention with abusive or neglectful parents frequently does not occur.

Box 10.5 ◆◆◆◆◆◆◆◆◆◆◆◆◆◆◆◆◆◆◆◆◆◆◆◆◆

# Parents Anonymous (PA)

Parents Anonymous (PA) is a national self-help organization for parents who have abused or neglected their children. Because self-help organizations (including Alcoholics Anonymous, Parents of Gays and Lesbians, Overeaters Anonymous, and Weight Watchers) have had considerable rehabilitative success, PA will be described in this section. It is one of several approaches that can be used in helping parents who abuse their children.

PA (originally called Mothers Anonymous) was established in 1970 in California by Jolly K., who was desperate to find help to meet her needs. For four years she had struggled with an uncontrollable urge to punish her daughter severely. One afternoon, desperate after attempting to strangle her daughter, she sought help from the local child guidance clinic and was placed in therapy. When asked by her therapist what she could do about this situation, she developed an idea. As she explained, "If alcoholics could stop drinking by getting together, and gamblers could stop gambling, maybe the same principle would work for abusers, too."[a] With her therapist's encouragement, she therefore formed Mothers Anonymous and started a few local chapters in California. Now the organization has local chapters in most areas of the United States and Canada, and the name has been changed to Parents Anonymous, because fathers who abuse their children are also eligible to join.

PA, which uses some of the basic therapeutic concepts of Alcoholics Anonymous, is a crisis intervention program that offers two main forms of help:

◆ A weekly group meeting in which members share experiences and feelings and learn to control their emotions better

◆ Personal and telephone contact among members during periods of crisis, particularly when a member feels a nearly uncontrollable desire to take his or her anger or frustration out on a child

Parents may be referred to PA by a social agency (including protective services) or be self-referrals as parents who are aware they need help.

Cassie Starkweather and S. Michael Turner describe why some parents who abuse their children would rather participate in a self-help group than receive professional counseling:

It has been our experience that most [abusive] parents judge themselves more harshly than other more objective people tend to judge them. The fear of losing their children frequently diminishes with reassurance from other members that they are not the monsters they think they are.

Generally speaking, PA members are so afraid they are going to be judged by others as harshly as they judge themselves that they are afraid to go out [to] seek help. Frequently, our members express fears of dealing with a professional person, seeing differences in education, sex, or social status as

---

*Family Preservation Programs.* With the implementation of mandatory child abuse and neglect reporting in the 1960s, the number of reports of suspected abuse and neglect skyrocketed. In many cases where abuse or neglect was determined to be occurring, the maltreated children were placed in temporary placements—typically foster homes. By the end of the 1960s, there was increasing concern about the number of children in foster care and the cost. There was widespread questioning of both the need to remove so many children from their biological homes and the effectiveness of foster care as a means of dealing with children who were being abused or neglected. As a result, intensive family preservation programs were developed as a mechanism of protecting children and preserving families.

Family preservation is a model of intervention developed specifically for work with families in which

the placement of one or more of the children is imminent. Gelles describes family preservation services as follows:

The essential feature is that family preservation services are intensive, short-term, crisis interventions. Services are provided in the client's home, although social workers do not actually move in. The length of a home visit is variable—it is not confined to the "50-minute" clinical hour. Services are available 7 days a week, 24 hours a day, not just during business hours Monday through Friday. Caseloads are small—two or three families per worker. Soft services, such as therapy and education, and hard services, such as food stamps, housing, a homemaker, and supplemental Social Security, are available.[63]

Family preservation services are time-limited, typically four to six weeks.

basic differences that would prevent easy communication or mutual understanding.

Members express feelings of gratification at finding that other parents are "in the same boat." They contrast this with their feelings about professionals who, they often assume, have not taken out the time from their training and current job responsibilities to raise families of their own.[b]

PA emphasizes honesty and directness. In the outside world, parents prone to child abuse learn to hide this problem, as society finds it difficult to stomach. In contrast, the goal in PA is to help parents admit and accept the fact that they are abusive. The term *abuse* is used liberally at meetings. PA has found that this insistence on frankness has a healthy effect. Parents are relieved, as finally they have found a group of people who are able to accept abusive parents for what they really are. Furthermore, once they are able to admit they are abusive, only then can they begin to find ways to cope with this problem.

During PA meetings, parents are expected to say why they believe they are beating their child, and the members challenge each other to find ways to curb the abuse. Members also share constructive approaches that each has found useful, and efforts are made to help each other develop specific plans for dealing with situations that have resulted in abusive episodes in the past. Members learn to recognize danger signs and then to take the necessary action to curb the potential attack.

PA stresses protecting members' anonymity and confidentiality. This protection permits group members to discuss their experiences and asocial thoughts without risk of public disclosure. The fact that they are sharing their experiences with other parents who have abused children ensures their being able to "confess" without danger of humiliation, recrimination, or rejection.

Group members develop a sense of oneness and often the group becomes a surrogate family. Each member is given the phone numbers of all others in the group and is urged to reach for the phone instead of the child when feeling distressed. Members are gradually transformed into "lay professionals" who are able to help other abusers and who perceive themselves skilled at this because they have, at one time, been child abusers.

The group leader or chapter chairperson is always a parent who at one time abused a child. Members can identify more readily with such a person than they can with a professional therapist. Among the reasons PA is successful is that it diminishes the social isolation of abusive parents and provides them with social supports.

a. Phyllis Zauner, "Mothers Anonymous: The Last Resort," in *The Battered Child*, ed. Jerome K. Leavitt (Morristown, NJ: General Learning Press, 1974), 247.

b. Cassie L. Starkweather and S. Michael Turner, "Parents Anonymous: Reflections on the Development of a Self-Help Group," in *Child Abuse: Intervention and Treatment*, ed. Nancy C. Ebeling and Deborah A. Hill (Acton, MA: Publishing Sciences Group, 1975), 151.

Initial evaluations of intensive family preservation programs were uniformly enthusiastic. They were initially claimed to be successful in protecting the children involved, and saving costs by reducing placement of children outside the home. In recent years, however, there has been an increasing level of criticism of family preservation programs. Gelles concludes: "To date, no evaluation study that uses a randomly assigned control group has found that intensive family preservation programs reduce placement, costs or the risk of maltreatment."[64] There is a danger that failing to remove children who are being abused in a home actually places those children at risk of re-abuse or even fatal abuse.

Patrick Murphy describes one family preservation case that ended in tragedy:

In December 1991, the aunt of a 3-year-old girl told the family services department that her sister and her sister's

lover had physically abused the child. State investigators confirmed the abuse: the child had bruises and rope burns on her body. Instead of bringing the case to court the department provided a housekeeper and a social worker who between them went to the home a total of 37 times over the next 90 days. The housekeeper helped the mother clean up and make dinner. The social worker took her out for meals and shopping.

On March 7, 1992, the aunt telephoned the family services agency again, pleading that the child was still being abused. The agency ignored her. On March 17, the agency closed the case with a glowing report on how well the family was doing. Several hours later, the girl was dead. An autopsy revealed that boiling water had been poured on her genitals and that she had been struck on the head with a blunt instrument. Her body was covered with 43 scars, bruises and rope burns, most of which had been made in the previous few weeks. She weighed 17 pounds.[65]

*Rights of Children versus Rights of Parents.* Earlier in American history the law guarded the rights of parents but gave little attention to the rights of children. In recent years, defining and protecting the rights of children has received national attention, as indicated by a variety of child advocacy efforts and the specification of various "bill of rights for children" proclamations. Protective services, particularly in contested court cases, encounter the problem of defining the respective rights of parents and children. The balance of rights between parents and children varies from community to community.[66]

Some of the situations in which this balance becomes an issue are the following:

♦ If, for religious reasons, parents are opposed to their child receiving medication for a serious health problem, should the state intervene?

♦ Should the state intervene where an unmarried parent is exposing the child to the parent's sexual promiscuity but still is meeting the child's basic physical and emotional needs?

♦ Should the state intervene where a child is being raised in a homosexual environment or in a commune where lifestyles and mores are substantially different from the norm in American society?

♦ Should the state intervene in families where a child has serious emotional problems and the parents refuse to seek professional help?

♦ Should the state intervene in certain ethnic or minority settings where educational needs are not being met?

♦ Should intervention occur when a father uses harsh discipline by whipping a child two or three times a week?

♦ Should the state intervene in families where there is long-term alcoholism and serious marital discord?

♦ Should the state intervene where a child is living in filth, has ragged clothing, and seldom bathes but where the child's emotional and social needs are being met?

Different workers, different judges, and different communities would probably disagree on what should be done. The reluctance to intervene may have tragic consequences, as indicated in the following case:

In 1953, a boy of thirteen was referred to a children's court because of chronic truancy. A psychiatric examination established the fact that the boy was "drawn to violence" and represented "a serious danger to himself and to others." Psychiatric treatment was recommended by the psychiatrist and social workers concerned with the boy's situation. The mother refused to accept the recommendation and refused to bring the boy back for treatment. Should the mother have been forced to accept treatment for the boy? This is the question of limits of protective intervention. Nothing was done. Ten years later, the boy, Lee Harvey Oswald, assassinated President Kennedy.[67]

## BIRTHS OUTSIDE OF MARRIAGE

Women between the ages of fifteen and twenty-four constitute about 40 percent of the total population of women of childbearing age—yet they account for roughly 70 percent of births outside of marriage.[68] More than a million teenage women become pregnant each year. Most of these pregnancies are unplanned and unwanted and result from misinformation or lack of access to birth control. Roughly 60 percent of these teenagers have babies, with the remainder ending the pregnancy through abortion or miscarriage.[69] Two of every five American women giving birth to their first child were not married when they became pregnant.[70] Four out of five teenage marriages end in divorce; many of these marriages were preceded by a pregnancy.[71] For those who are unmarried when the child is born, more than 90 percent decide to keep the baby rather than give it up for adoption.[72]

About 70 percent of AfricanAmerican babies are born to single women.[73] African-American women have a substantially higher rate of births outside of marriage than white women.[74] Coleman and Cressey give the following reasons for the high birthrate among single African-American women:

Although the causes are not entirely clear, several factors stand out. First and foremost, blacks are much more likely to be poor than whites, and the illegitimacy rate is much higher among poor people from all ethnic groups. Second, the prejudice and discrimination that have been aimed at blacks for so many years have hit particularly hard at black males from poor homes. The extremely high rate of unemployment among this group makes it much harder to live up to the expectations of fatherhood, and fathers who feel inadequate to meet the needs of their families are far more likely to withdraw and leave their support to the welfare department. Third, the pattern of early pregnancy and single-parent homes has been passed down from one generation to the next in the black underclass.[75]

The higher birthrates among single nonwhite women do not necessarily mean that unmarried nonwhites are more likely to be promiscuous. It may simply mean that nonwhites have less access to contraceptives, or they may be less likely to seek an abortion, or they may be less likely to marry the father before the birth of the child.

Although teenage women represent roughly 25 percent of the population of childbearing age, they account for over 45 percent of all births outside of marriage.[76] These statistics emphasize that birth outside of marriage is a problem that is disproportionately faced by adolescents. Teenagers who marry when pregnant are nearly as likely to be single parents sometime in the future (due to divorce) as are those who are unmarried at the time of birth.

Many adolescents are not adequately informed about the reproductive process and tend not to use contraceptives. Some teenage women think that, if they take a birth control pill once a week, they're OK; some believe it's safe to have sex standing up; some are afraid birth control will harm them or their future babies.[77]

Many unmarried mothers are simply not prepared, by education, work experience, or maturity, to undertake the dual responsibility of parenthood and economic support. As a result, society inevitably must contribute to the support of these children through public assistance payments and social welfare services.

Fifty years ago both premarital intercourse and births outside of marriage were considered immoral in our society. (In fact, children born outside of marriage were labeled "illegitimate" and were usually stigmatized as much as the mother. The terms *illegitimate* and *illegitimacy* persist today, even though they stigmatize innocent people.) In the 1940s, Alfred Kinsey found, however, that high percentages of the population had experienced premarital intercourse.[78] Since the Kinsey studies, attitudes toward premarital intercourse have become more tolerant; today, few people are virgins when they marry.

Attitudes toward birth outside of marriage have also become somewhat more tolerant. Few parents now send their pregnant daughter off to a maternity home to avoid "disgracing" the family. However, we sometimes see the unusual situation in which parents tolerate premarital intercourse yet, if their daughter becomes pregnant, they are highly disapproving.

Why are births outside of marriage seen as a social problem by most Americans? There are many answers to this question. Some parents still feel "disgraced" if their daughter becomes pregnant. Some single pregnant women (and their parents) view it as a problem because difficult decisions need to be made about whether to end the pregnancy. If it is decided not to have an abortion, decisions need to be made about adoption, continued education or employment, a possible marriage, living arrangements, and perhaps welfare assistance. The father of the child must make decisions about his role and the extent to which he will seek to provide emotional and financial support.

Some people see birth outside of marriage as a social problem—a sign of a breakdown in the traditional family and a symptom of moral decay. Others assert that it is a problem mainly because the great majority of these children are born to women who are simply not yet prepared—by experience, education, or maturity—to be a parent or to provide for a family financially. Authorities who view birth outside of marriage as a problem for this reason are concerned about the effects on the child of being raised by a mother who is in many ways merely an older child herself. They are also concerned about the effects on the mother of trying to maintain a one-parent family with limited financial and personal resources. Finally, some authorities view birth outside of marriage as a problem because of the high cost to society of having to make welfare payments to large numbers of single-parent families (see Chapter 9).

Is the social stigma attached to birth outside of marriage functional? Certainly it is not to either the child or the mother. On the other hand, some authorities have argued that the stigma is functional to society because it discourages births outside of marriage, and thereby helps perpetuate the nuclear family, which provides a structure for the financial support and socialization of children. In response to this view, it can be argued that this punitive approach may not be the optimal way to reduce the incidence of births outside of marriage. The Sex Information and Education Council of the United States (SIECUS) asserts that a more effective approach would involve quality educational programs about responsible sexuality. SIECUS asserts the goals of sex education should be:

1. *Information* To provide accurate information about human sexuality, including: growth and development, human reproduction, anatomy, physiology, maturation, family life, pregnancy, childbirth, parenthood, sexual response, sexual orientation, contraception, abortion, sexual abuse, HIV/AIDS and other sexually transmitted diseases.

2. *Attitudes, values, and insights*   To provide an opportunity for young people to question, explore, and assess their sexual attitudes in order to develop their own values, increase self-esteem, develop insights concerning relationships with members of both genders, and understand their obligations and responsibilities to others.

3. *Relationships and interpersonal skills*   To help young people develop interpersonal skills, including communication, decision-making, assertiveness, and peer refusal skills, as well as the ability to create satisfying relationships. Sexuality education programs should prepare students to understand their sexuality effectively and creatively in adult roles. This would include helping young people develop the capacity for caring, supportive, non-coercive, and mutually pleasurable intimate and sexual relationships.

4. *Responsibility*   To help young people exercise responsibility regarding sexual relationships, including addressing abstinence, how to resist pressures to become prematurely involved in sexual intercourse, and encouraging the use of contraception and other sexual health measures. Sexuality education should be a central component of programs designed to reduce the prevalence of sexually-related medical problems, including teenage pregnancies, sexually transmitted diseases including HIV infection, and sexual abuse.[79]

Even with more than one million teenagers becoming pregnant each year, the question of whether to provide sex education is still a controversial issue in many school systems. Apparently, many people believe sex education will lead to promiscuity and to teenage pregnancies. Advocates of sex education argue that such programs reduce the number of teenage pregnancies.

Health clinics located in or near high schools appear to be particularly effective in reducing the number of teenage pregnancies. Such clinics provide birth control information and also prescribe contraceptives for sexually active people.[80] Critics of this approach assert that making birth control information and contraceptives more readily available will simply increase sexual activity. The response of the health clinics to this criticism is that learning accurate information about human reproduction in an educational setting is more desirable than the alternative: receiving largely inaccurate information from peers on the street.

In recent years the peril of AIDS has given sex education in schools a major boost. The best way of stopping the transmission of AIDS is through quality sex education programs that provide accurate information on safe sex practices.[81]

One motivation for the passage of the 1996 Welfare Reform Act was the desire to change policies that conservatives claim reward early childbearing by single mothers. The Welform Reform Act defines public assistance payments to teenage mothers, except under the following conditions—states can provide payments to unmarried teenage parents only if a mother under eighteen is living at home or in another adult-supervised setting and attends high school or an alternative educational or training program as soon as the child is twelve weeks old.

The underlying reason behind denying welfare payments to most teenage mothers is to send a message to teenagers that having babies will not be financially rewarded; that is, conservatives hope this will discourage teenage women from seeking to become pregnant.[82] Most authorities who study this issue believe this reasoning is flawed; if the "welfare incentive" theory is accurate, then one would expect to find higher teenage birthrates in the states with the highest welfare payments, but this has never been true.[83]

## Social Change and the Future of the American Family

Americans generally view the family as being one of our most stable institutions. Yet our family system has undergone a number of changes over the years. Two hundred years ago marriages were often arranged by parents, with economic considerations being the most important determinant of who married whom. Two hundred years ago divorce was rare; now one out of two marriages ends in divorce or annulment.[84] Two hundred years ago women did not work outside the home (or outside the family farm), and children were an economic asset; now, about 60 percent of married women work outside the home,[85] and children are deemed a financial liability.

In viewing the future of the American family, some authorities foresee the family as racing toward extinction. Psychoanalyst William Wolf, for instance, asserts, "The Family is dead except for the first year or two of child raising. This will be its only function."[86] Carle

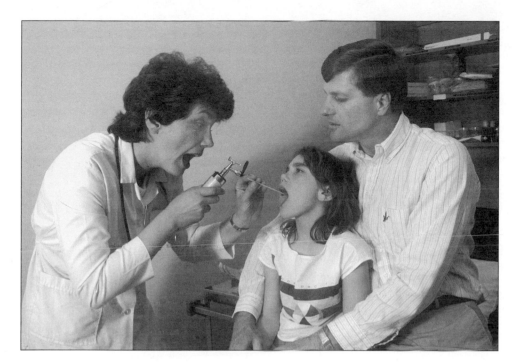

Zimmerman, a sociologist, was a pioneer of the *social disorganization approach* to the modern family.[87] He argued that the modern family was becoming *atomistic;* that is, he saw it as breaking up, becoming less integrated, and losing its capabilities to perform important social functions (such as socializing children into the traditional culture). He believed hedonism (seeking pleasure as the chief goal in life) and individualism (putting individual preferences ahead of family welfare) were running rampant and resulting in higher divorce rates, youth problems, childlessness, and a loss of interest in preserving the institutions of marriage and family.

Family optimists, on the other hand, predict that the family is entering a Golden Age— an era where the members will have more leisure time to spend with each other and will derive considerable enjoyment from family activities.[88] Most sociologists, however, do not agree with either the pessimists or the optimists; instead, they argue that the family is experimenting with a number of novel types and forms, many of which will probably be discarded, but some likely to be found satisfying and functional and gradually becoming "typical."

In our fast-paced society the family is likely to change even more dramatically in the future. As in the past, the family is likely to be affected significantly by technological changes.[89] Labor-saving devices in the home (for example, electrical appliances) have in the past been, and currently are, an important factor in making it possible for both spouses to work outside the home. Birth control devices have undoubtedly been an important factor in leading to an increase in premarital sexual relationships and in extramarital affairs.[90] Abortions now are often used to end unwanted pregnancies. The increased use of abortions has been a factor in sharply reducing the number of children available for adoption. A number of adoption agencies have suspended taking applications from couples desiring healthy white infants. Now, an ethically questionable business has developed where women are paid to deliver and give up their babies for adoption in order to meet the demands of infertile couples who want a child. Women willing to bypass the normal adoption channels may sell an unwanted infant for as much as $20,000.[91]

In the future the American family is likely to be substantially affected by technological breakthroughs in biology and medicine. A few illustrations of scientific developments in these areas will be presented—developments that are as alarming as they are intriguing.

## BIOMEDICAL TECHNOLOGY

*Artificial Insemination* There are thousands of babies born annually in the United States through the

**D**r. Cecil Jacobson is credited with introducing amniocentesis in the United States to diagnose defects in unborn babies. For many years he operated an infertility clinic in Virginia. In March, 1992, a federal jury found him guilty of fifty-two counts of fraud and perjury. He was charged with defrauding patients by artificially inseminating them with his own sperm while claiming to use other donors'. He also was charged with tricking patients into believing they were pregnant when they were not. The prosecution alleged that Jacobson may have fathered as many as seventy-five children through artificial insemination. Dr. Jacobson was sentenced to five years in prison, ordered to pay $116,805 in fines and restitution, and required to serve three years' probation after release from prison. This case example illustrates that the new biomedical reproductive technology can be used unscrupulously.

*Cecil Jacobson*

---

process of artificial insemination, with the usage expected to continue to increase in the future.[92] Artificial insemination is used widely in livestock breeding because it eliminates all the problems that can be associated with breeding. A breeder can transport a prized animal's frozen sperm across the world and raise a whole new herd of animals almost effortlessly.

Human sperm can be frozen for long periods of time (the length of time has not been determined; it is generally acknowledged that five years would be safe with close to 100 percent assurance). The sperm can then be thawed and used to impregnate a female. This new technology has led to the development of a unique new institution, the private sperm bank. The sperm bank is usually a private institution that has a couple of functions. It collects and maintains sperm of private citizens for a fee, depending on length of time. Usually, the sperm is withdrawn at some later date to impregnate (with a physician's assistance) a woman.

The sperm used in artificial insemination may be the husband's (called AIH). There may be several reasons for using AIH. It is possible to pool several ejaculations from a man with a low sperm count and to inject them simultaneously into the vaginal canal of his spouse, thus vastly increasing the chance of pregnancy. AIH may also be used for family planning purposes; for example, a man might deposit his sperm in

the bank, then receive a vasectomy, and then later withdraw the sperm to have children. High-risk jobs (such as a danger of being exposed to radioactive material) might prompt a man to make a deposit in case of sterility or untimely death.

A second type of artificial insemination is called AID and involves the donor of the sperm being someone other than the husband. AID has been used for several decades to circumvent male infertility. It is also used when it is known that the husband is a carrier of a genetic disease (for example, a condition such as hemophilia). In recent years, an increasing number of single women who want a child but do not (at least for the near future) want a husband are requesting the services of a sperm bank. The usual procedure involves the woman requesting the general genetic characteristics she wants from the father and the bank then trying to match such requests from the information known about donors.

A third type of artificial insemination is of recent origin and has received considerable publicity. Some married couples, in which the wife is infertile, have contracted another woman to be artificially inseminated with the husband's sperm. Under the terms of the contract this "surrogate mother" is paid and is expected to give the infant to the married couple shortly after birth. (Surrogate motherhood is discussed in greater detail in the next section.)

There have been a number of ethical, social and legal questions raised about artificial insemination. There are the objections from religious leaders that this practice is wrong, that God did not mean for people to reproduce in this way. In the case of AID, there are certain psychological stresses placed on husbands and on marriages, as the procedure emphasizes the husband's infertility and involves having a baby that he has not fathered. On a broader scale, artificial insemination raises such questions as: What are the purposes of marriage and of sex, and what will happen to male/female relationships if we do not even have to see each other to reproduce?

There have also been some unusual court cases that suggest new laws will have to be written to resolve the questions that are arising. For instance, there is the case of Mr. and Mrs. John M. Prutting. Mr. Prutting was medically determined to be sterile as a result of radiation exposure received at work. Without her husband's knowledge, Mrs. Prutting was inseminated. After the birth of the baby, he sued her for divorce on the grounds of adultery.[93]

In another case, a wife was artificially inseminated with the husband's consent by AID. The couple later divorced. When the husband requested child visiting privileges, his wife took him to court on the grounds that he was not the father and thus had no such right. In New York, he won; but she moved to Oklahoma, where the decision was reversed.[94]

And finally, there was a reported case of an engaged couple whose mothers were discovered to have had the same artificial insemination donor and were thus biologically half brother and sister. The marriage would have been incestuous and was therefore canceled.[95]

There are other possible legal implications. What happens if the AIH sperm at a bank is not paid for? Would it become the property of the bank? Could it be auctioned off? If a woman was artificially inseminated by a donor and the child was later found to have genetic defects, could the parents bring suit against the physician, the donor, or the bank? Does the child have a right to know the identify of the father?

Sperm banks can also be used in genetic engineering movements. In the spring of 1980, it was disclosed that Robert Graham had set up an exclusive sperm bank to produce exceptionally bright children. Graham stated that at least five Nobel Prize winners had donated sperm to inseminate women. A number of women have already given birth through the services of this bank.[96] This approach raises questions about whether reproductive technology should be used to produce "superior" children and what characteristics should be defined as superior.

*Surrogate Motherhood*    Thousands of married couples who want children but are unable to reproduce because the wife is infertile have turned to surrogate motherhood. With this type of motherhood, a surrogate gives birth to a baby conceived by artificial insemination, using the husband's sperm. (Often the surrogate mother is paid a fee for her services.) At birth, the surrogate mother terminates her parental rights, and the child is then legally adopted by the sperm donor and his wife.

Couples using the services of a surrogate mother are generally delighted with this medical technique and believe it is a highly desirable solution to their personal difficulty of being unable to bear children. However, there are other groups who assert that surrogate motherhood raises a number of moral, legal, and personal issues.

A number of theologians and religious leaders firmly believe God intended conception to occur only among married couples through sexual intercourse. These religious leaders view surrogate motherhood as ethically wrong because the surrogate mother is not married to the sperm donor and because artificial insemination is viewed as "unnatural." Some religious leaders also assert that it is morally despicable for a surrogate mother to accept a fee (often from $5,000 to $10,000). They maintain that procreation is a blessing from God and should not be commercialized.

Surrogate motherhood also raises complicated legal questions that have considerable social consequences. For example, surrogate mothers usually sign a nonbinding contract stipulating that the mother will give up the child for adoption at birth. What if the surrogate mother changes her mind shortly before birth and decides to keep the baby? Women who have been surrogate mothers usually report that they become emotionally attached to the child during pregnancy.[97]

Most surrogate mothers to date are married and already have children. A number of issues are apt to arise. How does the husband of a surrogate mother feel about his wife being pregnant by another man's sperm? How does such a married couple explain to their children that their half brother or half sister will be given up for adoption to another family? How does such a married couple explain what they are doing to relatives, neighbors, and the surrounding community?

If the child is born with a severe mental or physical disability, who will care for the child and pay for the expenses? Will it be the surrogate mother and her husband, the contracting adoptive couple, or society?

In 1983 a surrogate mother gave birth in Michigan to a baby who was born with microcephaly, a condition in which the head is smaller than normal and mental retardation is likely. At first, neither the surrogate mother nor the contracting adoptive couple wanted to care for the child. The adoptive couple refused to pay the $10,000 fee to the surrogate mother. A legal battle ensued. Blood tests were eventually taken that indicated the probable father was not the contracting adoptive father but rather was the husband of the surrogate mother. Following the blood tests, the surrogate mother and her husband assumed the care of the child. (This case example illustrates another problem with the surrogate motherhood approach: if the surrogate mother engages in sexual intercourse with her partner/husband at about the same time that artificial insemination occurs, the genetic father of the child that is conceived may be the partner.)

In 1986 Mary Beth Whitehead was a surrogate mother who gave birth to a child. She refused to give up the baby for adoption by the genetic father and his wife, even though she had signed a $10,000 contract in which she agreed to give up the child. The genetic father, William Stern, took the case to court, requesting Whitehead to honor the contract she had signed. Whitehead claimed she was the mother of the child and therefore had maternal rights to the child. The case received national attention. In April 1987, in the nation's first judicial ruling on a disputed surrogate contract, the judge ruled the contract was valid because just as men have a constitutional right to sell their sperm, women can decide what to do with their wombs.[98] Whitehead appealed this decision to the New Jersey State Supreme Court. In 1988 this court ruled that the contract between Whitehead and the Sterns was invalid because it involved the sale of a mother's right to her child, which violates state laws that prohibit child selling. This decision voided the adoption of the baby by Mrs. Stern; Mr. Stern was given custody, and Whitehead was granted visitation rights. Whether this decision will become the legal guideline for disputed surrogate contracts will be determined by future court decisions about surrogate contracts.

## Embryo Case Gains International Attention

A South American-born couple, Elsa and Mario Rios, amassed a fortune (several million dollars) in real estate in Los Angeles. In 1981 they enrolled in a "test tube baby" program at Queen Victoria Medical Center in Melbourne, Australia, after their young daughter died. Several eggs were removed from Mrs. Rios and fertilized by her husband's sperm, which had been collected in a laboratory container. One of the fertilized eggs was implanted in Mrs. Rios's womb, but she had a miscarriage ten days later. The two remaining embryos were frozen so that doctors could try implantation at a later time.

On April 2, 1983, the couple was killed in the crash of a private plane in Chile. Since doctors have successfully thawed and implanted frozen embryos (which have resulted in births) a number of social and legal questions rise:

◆ Should the embryos be implanted in the womb of a surrogate mother in the hope that they will develop to delivery?

◆ Are the embryos legal heirs to the Rios's multi-million-dollar estate?

◆ Does life legally begin at conception: If a surrogate mother carries the embryo to birth is she legally the mother, and is she entitled to some of the inheritance?

◆ Do embryos conceived outside the womb have rights? If so, what rights? Should these rights be the same as those accorded humans? (An Australian court ruled in 1987 that the embryos must be thawed and carried to term if a volunteer surrogate can be found. However, the offspring will not be viewed as legally entitled to inherit their biological parents' estate.)

This case highlights how the rapid advance of in vitro fertilization (fertilization outside the human body) has outstripped attitudes and laws.

*Source:* "Embryo Case Opens New Debate," *Wisconsin State Journal,* June 19, 1984, 1–2; Stephen Budiansky, "The New Rules of Reproduction," *U.S. News & World Report,* April 18, 1988, 66–67.

---

*Test-Tube Babies* In England, on July 25, 1978, Mrs. Lesley Brown gave birth to the first "test-tube baby." An egg taken from Mrs. Brown's reproductive system had been externally artificially impregnated using AIH and then implanted in Mrs. Brown's uterus to complete the normal process of pregnancy. The technique is called embryo transfer and was developed for women whose fallopian tubes are so damaged that the fertilized egg cannot pass through the tubes to the womb as is necessary for it to develop and grow until birth. Following the announcement of this birth, there was a surge of applications from thousands of childless couples to fertility experts asking for similar implants.[99]

Another breakthrough in this area occurred in 1984 when an egg donated by one woman was fertilized and then implanted in another woman. Australian researchers in January 1984 reported the first successful birth resulting from a procedure in which an embryo was externally conceived and then implanted in the uterus of a surrogate.[100] This type of surrogate motherhood is a modern-day twist on the wet nurse of earlier times. An unusual application of this new technology occurred in 1987 in South Africa when a grandmother, Pat Anthony, gave birth to her own grandchildren. The daughter was infertile, so her daughter's eggs (which had been fertilized in the lab) were implanted into Ms. Anthony. Several months later Ms. Anthony gave birth to triplets.[101]

This type of surrogate motherhood differs from the earlier type in which the surrogate mother contributes half of the genetic characteristics through the use of her egg. Here, the surrogate contributes neither her own egg nor any of the genetic characteristics of the child.

Surrogate pregnancies can, on one hand, be seen as the final step in the biological liberation of women. Like men, women can "sire" children without the responsibility of pregnancy and childbirth.

However, surrogate pregnancies promise to create a legal nightmare. Do the genetic mother and father have any binding legal rights? Can the genetic parents place reasonable restrictions on health, medical care, and diet during the pregnancy? Can the genetic parents require the surrogate mother not to smoke or drink? Could the genetic parents require the surrogate to abort? Could the surrogate abort without the genetic parents' consent? Whose child is it if both the

# Mr. Mom: Men Can Give Birth

Scientists indicate the technology now exists to enable men to give birth! Male pregnancy would involve fertilizing a donated egg with sperm outside the body. The embryo would then be implanted into the bowel area, where it could attach itself to a major organ, such as a kidney or the wall of the large intestine. In addition, to achieve pregnancy men would have to receive hormone treatment to stimulate changes that occur naturally in women during pregnancy. Because the embryo creates the placenta, the embryo theoretically would receive sufficient nourishment. The baby would be delivered by cesarean section.

Any attempt at male pregnancy would carry risks (perhaps some as yet unknown risks) for both the man and the embryo. Will some men try it? If people risk their lives climbing Mr. Everest, someone is apt to try this. The "Mr. Mom" technology is depicted in the 1994 movie, *Junior*, in which actor Arnold Schwarzenegger portrays a researcher who becomes pregnant and gives birth to a baby boy.

genetic mother and the surrogate mother want to be recognized as the legal mother after the child is born? Will low-income women tend to serve as "holding tanks" for upper-class women's children? Legal experts see far-reaching changes in family law, inheritance, and the concept of legitimacy if laboratory fertilization and childbearing by surrogate mothers become accepted practices.

In August 1990, surrogate mother Anna Johnson filed legal papers seeking parental rights to a child created from the sperm and egg of Mark and Crispina Calvert in California.[102] Ms. Johnson gave birth to the child, under a $10,000 surrogacy contract. She was the first surrogate mother to seek custody of a child not genetically related to her. In October 1990, the judge handling the case ruled that Ms. Johnson had no parental rights under California law. The judge assigned permanent custody of the child to the child's genetic parents. If the judge's ruling stands, it could lead to a new definition of motherhood in which genetics is the primary criterion for determining parentage in cases in which a surrogate carries a child genetically unrelated to her.

Human embryo transplants, when combined with principles of genetic selection, would allow people who want "superhuman" children to select embryos in which the resultant infant would have a high probability of being free of genetic defects and would also allow parents to choose, with a high probability of success, the genetic characteristics they desired—such as the child's sex, color of eyes and hair, skin color, probable height, probable muscular capabilities, and probable IQ. A superhuman embryo would be formed from combining the sperm and egg of a male and female who are thought to have the desired genetic characteristics. This breakthrough will raise a number of personal and ethical questions. Couples desiring children may be faced with the decision of having a child through natural conception, or of preselecting superhuman genetic characteristics through embryo transplants. Another question that will arise is whether our society will attempt to use this new technology to control human evolutionary development. If the answer is affirmative, decisions will need to be made about which genetic characteristics should be considered "desirable," and questions will arise about who should have the authority to make such decisions. Although our country may not want to control human evolutionary development in this manner, will we not feel it necessary to do so if a rival nation begins a massive evolutionary program? In addition, will parents have the same or somewhat different feelings toward children who result from embryo transplants compared to children who result from natural conception?

*Genetic Screening*   Practically all states now require mandatory genetic screening programs for various disorders. There are about two thousand human disorders caused by defective genes, and it is estimated that each of us carries two or three of them.[103] Mass genetic screening could eliminate some of these disorders. One screening approach that is increasingly being used with pregnant women is amniocentesis, a technique used to determine chromosomal abnormality. Amniocentesis is the surgical insertion of a hollow needle through the abdominal wall and uterus of a pregnant female to obtain amniotic fluid for the determination of chromosomal abnormality. More and more pregnant women are being pressured to terminate the pregnancy of a high-risk or proven genetically inferior fetus. Also, some genetic disorders can be corrected if caught in time.

Genetic screening programs raise serious questions: Which fetuses should be allowed to continue to grow, and which should be aborted? Who shall be allowed to have children? Who shall make such decisions? Is this a direction our country ought to take?

Genetic screening during pregnancy can be used to detect a wide variety of inherited disorders. For example, Huntington's chorea is an inherited disease whose principal symptoms are involuntary movements—either rapid, forcible, and jerky or smooth and sinuous. This disorder is often associated with loss of intellectual abilities. Its onset is usually evidenced during middle age. If a fetus is diagnosed as having the gene for this disorder (which usually results in serious mental and physical deterioration in midlife), the pregnant woman and her partner would then be faced with the heart-wrenching decision of whether it would be best to terminate the pregnancy.

The eugenics (scientific breeding) movement was proposed late in the nineteenth century and embraced by many scientists and government officials. Similar to today, eugenics was designed to improve humanity or individual races by encouraging procreation by those deemed "most desirable" and discouraging it in those judged "deficient." The movement fell into disfavor for a while when Adolf Hitler used it to justify the Holocaust, in which millions of Jews, Gypsies, homosexuals, persons with a cognitive disability, and others were exterminated. Are we headed in a similar direction again?

*Cloning*   This term refers to the process whereby a new organism is reproduced from the nucleus of a single cell. The resultant new organism has the same genetic characteristics of the organism that contributes the nucleus; that is, it is now possible to make biological carbon copies of humans from a single cell. Biologically, each cell is a blueprint containing all the genetic code information for the design of the organism. Cloning has already been used to reproduce frogs, mice, cattle, sheep, and other animals.[104] (See Box 10.9.)

One type of cloning amounts to a nuclear transplant. The nucleus of an unfertilized egg is destroyed and removed. The egg is then injected with the nucleus of a body cell by one means or another. It should then begin to take orders from the new nucleus, begin to reproduce cells, and eventually manufacture a baby with the same genetic features as the donor. The embryo would need a place to develop into a baby—either an artificial womb or a woman willing to supply her own. The technology for a complete artificial womb is not yet in sight. The resultant clone would start life with a genetic endowment identical to that of the donor, although learning experiences might alter the physical development or personality. The possibilities are as fantastic as they are repulsive. With a quarter-

inch piece of skin, one could produce one thousand genetic copies of any noted scientist or of anyone else! Imagine a professional basketball team composed of two Shaquille O'Neals and three Michael Jordans!

In 1993, a university researcher in Washington cloned human embryos, using a technique that is already widely used to clone animal embryos. The process involves taking a single human embryo and then splitting it into identical twins.[105] Since human embryos can be frozen and used at a later date, it is now possible for parents to have a child, and then years later, use a cloned, frozen embryo to give birth to an identical twin. It is now possible with embryo cloning for parents to save identical copies of embryos so that, if their child ever needed an organ transplant, the mother could give birth to a child's identical twin, a perfect match for organ donation.

In 1998, Dr. Richard Seed (a physicist in Chicago) announced he is initiating a program to clone humans, using the same procedures that were used to

Box 10.10

## Will Fetal Tissue Be Used for Medical Treatments?

Pioneering surgery has demonstrated that fetal tissue transplants can be used successfully to replace damaged nerve cells in victims of Parkinson's disease. Parkinson's disease is a neurological disorder that causes severe shaking and eventually death. Transplants of insulin-producing cells from fetuses also show promise in treating sugar diabetes as well.

Would some women seek to abort a fetus so that the tissue could be used for such medical purposes? In January 1988 a woman appeared on Ted Koppel's "Nightline" television show and declared that she wanted to get pregnant for the sole purpose of aborting the fetus so that its tissue could be used to treat her Parkinson's-disease-stricken father.

Many people find this use of reproductive technology to be horrifying. Yet most states have no legal means to stop such activities—or even to prohibit sale of fetal tissue. In 1993 the Clinton administration gave federal approval for allowing the use of fetal tissue in medical research experiments in the United States.

---

clone Dolly (a sheep). Dr. Seed stated human cloning will help infertile couples, and will spur genetic advances that could lead to the cure for diseases such as cancer.

Cloning could, among other things, be used to resolve the ancient controversy of heredity versus environment. On the other hand, there are grave dangers and undreamed-of complications. What is to prevent the Adolf Hitlers from making copies of themselves? Will cloning fuel the population explosion? What legal rights will clones be accorded (inheritance, for example)? Will religions recognize clones as having a "soul"? Who will decide who will be able to have clones made of themselves? Couples may face the choice of having children naturally or raising children who are copies of themselves.

***Breaking the Genetic Code*** Biochemical genetics is the discipline that studies the mechanisms whereby genes control the development and maintenance of the organism. Current research is focused on understanding more precisely the roles of DNA (deoxyribonucleic

acid) and messenger RNA (ribonucleic acid) in affecting the growth and maintenance of humans. When genes, DNA, and RNA are more fully understood, it may be possible sometime in the future to keep people alive, young, and healthy almost indefinitely. It is predicted that aging will be controlled, and any medical condition (for example, an allergy, obesity, cancer, arthritic pain) will be relatively easily treated and eradicated. Such possibilities stagger the imagination.

In January 1989, the National Institutes of Health launched a project to map the *human genome*—that is, to identify and list in order all of the genome's (the full set of chromosomes that carries all of the inherited traits of an organism) approximately 3 billion base pairs. Once completed, this map may permit scientists to predict an individual's vulnerability to genetic diseases, to treat genetically caused diseases, and possibly to "enhance" a person's genetic potential through the introduction of gene modifications.[106] Scientists have already discovered the genes that cause a variety of illnesses, such as cystic fibrosis. With cystic fibrosis, scientists have already demonstrated that gene therapy can be used to correct the underlying defect.[107] The approach uses genetically engineered cold viruses to ferry healthy genes into the body. (Cystic fibrosis results from a mutation in the gene that produces a protein called cystic fibrosis transmembrane conductive regulator. When the protein is missing, thick mucous builds up in the lungs, causing lung damage and eventual death, often by age thirty.) With the potential to break the genetic code and the potential to keep people alive and healthy indefinitely, many legal and ethical issues will arise. Perhaps the most crucial issues will be who will live and who will die and who will be permitted to have children. Such a fountain of youth may occur within our lifetime.

## NEW FAMILY FORMS

Such technological developments hopefully provide a perspective for some of the current and future influences on the American family. Moral and ethical issues currently surrounding technological advances with birth control and abortion may well pale in comparison to issues that could emerge soon.

At the present time the American family is experimenting with a number of new forms, some of which are apt to be found functional and satisfying and to gradually become widely incorporated. These new forms will be mentioned briefly, with the future determining which will endure.

*Childless Couples*   Traditionally, our society has fostered the perception that there is something wrong with a couple who decides not to have children. Parenthood is regarded legally and religiously as one of the central components of a marriage. In some states, deceiving one's spouse before marriage about the desire to remain childless is grounds for an annulment. Perhaps in the future this myth of procreation will be shattered by the concern about overpopulation, and by the high cost of raising children; the average cost of raising a child from birth to age eighteen is estimated to be $161,000 in low-income families, $225,00 in middle-income families, and $315,000 in upper-income families.[108]

*Postponing Parenthood Until Middle Age or Later*
Biological innovations, such as embryo transfers, are now making it possible for women in their fifties and even their sixties to give birth. As a result, couples have more leeway in deciding at what age they wish to raise children. Young couples today are often torn in their time commitments between their children and their careers. In our society most couples now have children at the busiest time of their lives. Deferring raising children until later in life provides substantial activity and meaning to later adulthood. A major question, of course, is whether such a family pattern will lead to an increase in the number of orphans, as older parents have a higher death rate than younger parents. (An increase in the number of orphans would significantly impact adoption and foster-care services.) Additional questions are whether having older parents would lead to even more gaps in values between the older parents and their young children, and whether the older parents would have sufficient energy to keep up with their young children.

*Professional Parents*   Alvin Toffler predicted our society will develop a system of professional, trained, and licensed parents, to whom a number of natural parents (bioparents) will turn to raise their children.[109] The natural parents would of course be permitted frequent visits, telephone contacts, and time to care for the children whenever they desire. Toffler stated: "Even now millions of parents, given the opportunity, would happily relinquish their parental responsibilities—and not necessarily through irresponsibility or lack of love. Harried, frenzied, up against the wall, they have come to see themselves as inadequate to the tasks."[110] The high rates of child abuse, child neglect, and teenage runaways seem to bear out the assertion that in a large number of families the parent/child relationship is more dissatisfying than satisfying. Many parents already hire part-time professional parents in the form of nannies and day-care-center workers.

In our society there is currently a belief system that bioparents should care for their children, even if they find the responsibility unrewarding. Only a tiny fraction of bioparents currently terminate their parental rights. Why? Could it be that many parents who have an unsatisfying relationship with their children are reluctant to give up their parenting responsibilities because of the stigma that would be attached? Two hundred years ago divorces were rare, mostly due to a similar stigma. Now, with increased acceptance of divorce, one out of two marriages is being terminated. Is it not also feasible that a number of parents who cannot choose the characteristics of their children may also find the relationships with some of their children to be more dissatisfying than satisfying? The point is reinforced when it is remembered that a number of pregnancies are unplanned *and* unwanted.

*Serial and Contract Marriages*   Culturally, religiously, and legally speaking, marriages are still expected to be permanent, for a lifetime. Such a view implies that the two partners made the right decision when they married, that their personalities and abilities complement each other, and that their personalities and interests will develop in tandem for the rest of their lives. All of these suppositions (along with the concept of permanency) are being called into question, however.

With the high rates of divorce and remarriage, a number of sociologists have pointed out that a small proportion of our population is entering (perhaps unintentionally) into serial marriages—that is, a pattern of successive, temporary marriages.[111] Serial marriages among celebrities have been widely publicized for a number of years. Viewing marriage as temporary in nature may help reduce some of the embarrassment and pain still associated with divorce and perhaps result in an increase in the number of unhappily married people who will seek a divorce. Divorce per se is neither good nor bad; if both partners find that their lives are happier and more satisfying following legal termination, the end result may well be viewed as desirable.

The growing divorce rate has resulted in the development of extensive services involving premarital counseling, marriage counseling, divorce counseling, single-parent services and programs, and remarriage counseling for spouses and the children involved. If marriage is increasingly viewed as temporary in nature, divorce may become even more frequent and result in an expansion of related social services.

Several sociologists have proposed that the concept of marriage as temporary be legally institutionalized through a contract marriage. For example, a couple would be legally married for a two-year period, and (only in those marriages where there are no children) the marriage would automatically be terminated unless they filed legal papers for a continuation.[112] A closely related type of contract is the prenuptial agreement in which a couple, prior to marriage, specify how their financial assets will be divided if they divorce after they marry. (Prenuptial agreements have been criticized as being a factor in psychologically setting up an expectation that a divorce is apt to occur.)

Another arrangement embodying the temporary concept is "trial marriage," which is increasingly being tested out by young people. They live together on a day-by-day basis and share expenses. Closely related—and perhaps more common—is the arrangement in which the two maintain separate addresses and domiciles but for several days a month actually live together. (Perhaps this latter form is more accurately described as a "serial honeymoon" than a "trial marriage.") Acceptance of trial marriages is currently being advocated by some religious philosophers, and many states no longer define cohabitation as illegal.

Increasingly, courts are ruling that cohabiting couples who dissolve their living arrangements have certain legal obligations to each other quite similar to the obligations of a married couple.

*Open Marriages*   O'Neill and O'Neill contrast traditional marriages with "open marriages," of which they are advocates.[113] A traditional or "closed" marriage, the O'Neills assert, embodies concepts such as (1) possession or ownership of mate; (2) denial or stifling of self; (3) playing of the "couples game" by doing everything together during leisure time; (4) the husband being dominant and out in the world and the wife being domestic and passive and staying at home with the children; and (5) absolute fidelity. An open marriage, in contrast, offers freedom to pursue individual interests, flexible roles in meeting financial responsibilities, shared domestic tasks, and expansion and growth through openness. Such a marriage is based on communication, trust, and respect, and it is expected that one partner's growth will facilitate the other partner's development.

Marriage counselors increasingly report that couples have serious interaction difficulties because one spouse has a traditional orientation whereas the other has an open-marriage orientation. The feminist movement and the changing roles of women have brought the conflict between open and closed marriages into public awareness. Marriage counselors now see large numbers of couples in which the wife wants a career, her own identity, and a sharing of domestic responsibilities, but the husband, traditionally oriented, wants his wife to stay at home and take care of the domestic tasks.

*Group Marriages*   Group marriage provides insurance against isolation. In the 1960s and 1970s, communes of young people flourished. In the later 1970s and in the 1980s most communes disbanded. The goals, as well as the structure, of these communes varied widely, involving diverse social, political, religious, sexual, or recreational objectives.

Interestingly, geriatric communes (which have many of the characteristics and obligations of group marriages) are being advocated by a number of sociologists.[114] Such arrangements may be a solution to a number of social problems of the elderly. They may provide companionship, new meaning, and interest to the participants' lives, as well as an arrangement in which elderly people with reduced functioning capacities can be of mutual assistance to one another. The elderly can thereby band together, pool resources, hire nursing or domestic help if needed, and feel that "life begins at 60." In nursing homes, retirement communities, group homes for the elderly, and assisted living residences, some of the elderly are presently developing relationships that have similarities to a group marriage.

*Homosexual Marriages and Adoptions*   Gay liberation groups seek to inform the public about the "naturalness" of homosexual expression and attempt to change current legislation that defines homosexual behavior between consenting adults as being illegal. England has already rewritten its statutes: Homosexual relations between consenting adults in that country are longer considered a crime. A number of marriages between homosexuals have taken place in churches in the United States, in Europe, and in other countries. (It should be noted, however, that no state in this country yet recognizes homosexual marriages as legal.)

Adoption agencies and the courts are now facing decisions about whether to allow homosexual couples to adopt children. Single people are already being permitted by some agencies and courts to adopt children, so the argument that a child needs both a male and a female figure in the family is diluted.

*Transracial Adoptions* Oriental and Native American children have been adopted by white parents for more than four decades.[115] About 35 years ago some white couples began adopting African-American children. A number of questions have arisen about the desirability of placing African-American children in white adoptive homes. To answer some of these questions, this author conducted a study comparing the satisfactions derived and problems encountered between transracial adoptive parents and in-racial adoptive parents.[116] Transracial adoptions were found to be as satisfying as inracial adoptions. In addition, transracial adoptive children were found to have been accepted by relatives, friends, neighbors, and the general community following placement. The transracial adoptive parents reported that substantially fewer problems have arisen due to the race of the child than even they anticipated before the adoption. They also indicated that they had parental feelings that the child was really their own. They reported becoming "color-blind" following placement—that is, they came to see the child not as African American, but as a member of their family.

Unfortunately, none of the children in the study were older than six. Some observers, a number of whom are African American, have raised questions about whether black children reared by white parents will experience serious identity problems as they grow older. For example, will they experience difficulty in deciding which race to identify with, in learning how to cope with racial discrimination due to being raised in a white home, and in interacting with both whites and blacks due to a (speculated) confused sense of who they are? On the other hand, advocates of transracial adoption respond by asserting that the parent/child relationship is more crucial to identity formation than the racial composition of the members of the family. The question of course is critical, especially since there are a large number of homeless African-American children and a shortage of African-American adoptive parents.

One organization that has been strongly opposed to the adoptive placement of African-American children in white homes is the National Association of Black Social Workers. This group views such placements as "cultural genocide."[117]

In 1971 Rita J. Simon began studying 204 white families who had adopted children of color. Joined later by Howard Altstein and many generations of graduate students, she went back to talk to the families over a period of twenty years.[118] The researchers interviewed the families in 1971, 1979, 1983, and 1991. Most of the children they studied now live away from their parents' homes. The majority of adoptees, despite occasional family conflicts, believe that their parents raised them well. If anything, some felt that the parents had overdone it a bit in trying to educate them about their heritage. African-American adoptees, for example, complained that too many dinnertime conversations turned into lectures on black history. The parents, although also acknowledging occasional conflicts, reported satisfaction with their decisions to adopt across racial lines. Fully 90 percent said they recommended transracial adoption for families who are planning to adopt. The researchers concluded that children of color who grow up in white families do not become confused about their identities, racial or otherwise.

*Comarital Sex* The term comarital sex refers to mate swapping and other organized extramarital relations in which both spouses agree to participate. Comarital sex is distinctly different from a traditional extramarital affair, which is usually clandestine, with the straying spouse trying to hide the relationship.

Although some couples appear able to integrate comarital agreements into their lives successfully, others find their marriages breaking up as a consequence.[119] According to marriage counselors, a major reason why couples drop out of comarital relationships, and sometimes end their marriage, is because of jealousy, competition, and possessiveness.[120]

The interest in comarital sex and extramarital sex raises the age-old question of whether any *one* individual can satisfy all of the intimate, sexual, and interpersonal needs of another. In the future (and perhaps already now) there may be a decrease in comarital and extramarital relationships due to the increasing fear of AIDS.

*Single Parenthood* Although in many people's minds marriage and parenthood "go together," single parenthood is emerging as a prominent form in our society. In many states it is possible for unmarried people to adopt a child. Also, an unmarried pregnant woman can refuse to marry and yet keep her child after it is born. Some unmarried fathers have been

*Portrait of Hispanic blended family around the parents' wedding cake.*

successful in obtaining custody of their child. Today, although the stigma attached to being single and pregnant is not as strong as it once was, this situation is still seriously frowned on by some.

Similar to single parenthood is the one-parent family, in which a person divorces or legally separates and assumes custody of one or more children and chooses not to remarry. Although traditionally the mother has been awarded custody of the children, today the courts are occasionally granting custody to more fathers. Another arrangement is shared custody, wherein both mother and father have the children part of the time.

Do single parents and one-parent families pose a serious problem for society? Are children adversely affected by being raised in a one-parent family? Papalia and Olds summarize some of the problems children face in growing up in one-parent families:

> Children growing up in one-parent homes undoubtedly have more problems and more adjustments to make than children growing up in homes where there are two adults to share the responsibilities for child rearing, to provide a high income, to more closely approximate cultural expectations of the "ideal family," and to offer a counterpoint of sex-role models and an interplay of personalities. But the two-parent home is not always ideal, and the one-parent home is not necessarily pathological.[121]

Research indicates that it is better for children to be raised in a non-tension-laden one-parent family than in a tension-laden two-parent family.[122]

***Blended Families*** Many terms have been used to describe two families joined by the marriage of one parent to another: stepfamilies, blended families, reconstituted families, and nontraditional families. Here we will use the term blended families.

One out of two marriages ends in divorce, and many divorcees have children. Most people who divorce remarry someone else within a few years. Moreover, some individuals who are marrying for the first time may have a child born outside of marriage. Thus a variety of blended families are now being formed in our society.

In blended families one or both spouses have biologically produced one or more children with someone else prior to their current marriage. Often the newly married couple give birth to additional children. In yet other blended families the children are biologically a combination of "his, hers, and theirs."

Blended families are increasing in number and proportion in our society, and the family dynamics and relationships are much more complex than in the traditional nuclear family. Blended families, in short, are burdened by much more "baggage" than are two childless adults marrying for the first time. Blended families must deal with stress that arises from the loss (through divorce or death) experienced by both adults and children, which can make them afraid to love and to trust. Previously established bonds between children and their biological parents, or loyalty to a dead or absent parent, may interfere with the formation of ties to the stepparent. If children go back and forth between two households, conflicts between stepchildren and stepparents may be intensified. Sometimes, divorced spouses continue to feud; in these cases the children are likely to be used as "pawns," thus generating additional strife in the recently formed blended family.

Some difficulties in adjustment for the children are to be expected.[123] Jealousies may arise because the child resents sharing parental attention with the new spouse and with new siblings. Another issue for children is the adjustment to a new parent who may have different ideas, values, rules, and expectations. Sharing space with new people can be a source of stress as well. In addition, if one member of the couple enters the marriage with no child-rearing experience, an adjustment will be necessary by all family members to allow time for the new parent to learn and adapt.

People come into a blended family with ideas and issues based on past experiences. Old relationships and ways of doing things still have their impacts. In discussing blended families, Stuart and Jacobson note that marrying a new partner involves marrying a whole new family.[124] A blended family differs from a traditional family in that more people are involved, including ex-spouses, former in-laws, and an assortment of cousins, uncles, and aunts. The married couple may have both positive and negative interactions with this large supporting cast. If a prior marriage ended bitterly, the unresolved emotions that remain (such as anger and insecurity) will affect the present relationship.

The area of greatest stress for most stepparents is that of child rearing. A stepchild, used to being raised in a certain way, may balk at having to conform to new rules or at accepting the stepparent as a parental figure. Such difficulty is more likely to arise if the stepchild feels remorse over the missing parent. If the husband and wife disagree about how to raise children, the chances of conflict are substantially increased. Stepparents and stepchildren also face the problem of adjusting to each other's habits and personalities. Kompara recommends that stepparents not rush into establishing a relationship with stepchildren; proceeding gradually is more likely to result in a trusting and positive relationship.[125] Kompara also notes

that becoming a stepparent is usually more difficult for a woman because children tend to be emotionally closer to their biological mother and have spent more time with her than with the father.

Three myths about blended families need to be addressed.[126] First, there is the myth of the "wicked stepmother"—the idea that the stepmother is not really concerned about what is best for the children but only about her own well-being. A scene from the children's story "Cinderella" might be brought to mind. Here, the "wicked stepmother" cruelly keeps Cinderella from going to the ball in hopes that her own biological daughters will have a better chance at nabbing the handsome prince. In reality, stepmothers have been found to establish positive and caring relationships with their stepchildren, provided that the stepmothers have a positive self-concept and the affirmation of their husband.[127]

A second myth is that "step is less";[128] in other words, stepchildren will never hold the same place in the hearts of parents that biological children do. The fact is that people can learn to love each other and are motivated to bind members of their new family together.

The third myth is that, the moment families are joined, they will have instant love for each other.[129] Relationships take time to develop and grow. The idea of instant strong love bonds is unrealistic. People involved in any relationship need time to get to know each other, test each other out, and grow to feel comfortable with each other.

Stinnet and Walters reviewed the research literature on stepparenthood and came to the following conclusions: (1) integration tends to be easier in families that have been split by divorce rather than by death, perhaps because the children realize the first marriage did not work out; (2) stepparents and stepchildren come to the blended family with unrealistic expectations that love and togetherness will occur rapidly; (3) children tend to see a stepparent of the opposite sex as playing favorites with their own children; (4) most children continue to miss and admire the absent biological parent; (5) male children tend more readily to accept a stepparent, particularly if the new parent is a male; and (6) adolescents have greater difficulty accepting a stepparent than do young children or adult children.[130]

Berman and Visher and Visher offer the following suggestions to parents in blended families for increasing the chances of positive relationships developing between adults and children:[131]

1. *Maintain a courteous relationship with the former spouse or spouses.* Children adjust best after a divorce when there is a harmonious relationship between former spouses. Problems are intensified when former spouses continue to insult each other and when the children are used as weapons ("pawns") for angry former spouses to hurt each other.

2. *Understand the emotions of children.* Although the newlyweds in a recently blended family may be fairly euphoric about their relationship, they need to be perceptive and responsive to the fears, concerns, and resentments of their children.

3. *Allow time for loving relationships to develop between stepparents and stepchildren.* Stepparents need to be aware that their stepchildren will probably have emotional ties to their absent biological parent and that the stepchildren may resent the breakup of the marriage between their biological parents. Some children may even feel responsible for their biological parents' separation. Others may try to make life difficult for the stepparent so that he or she will leave, with the hope that the biological parents will then reunite. Stepparents need to be perceptive and understanding of such feelings and patiently allow the stepchildren to work out their concerns and take time in bonding.

4. *New rituals, traditions, and ways of doing things need to be developed that seem right and enjoyable for all members of the blended family.* Sometimes it is helpful to more to a new residence that does not hold memories of the past. Leisure time should be structured so that the children spend time alone with the biological parent, with the stepparent, with both, and with the absent parent or parents. In addition, the new spouses need to spend some time alone with each other. New rituals should be developed for holidays, birthdays, and other special days.

5. *Seek social support.* Parents in blended families should seek to share their concerns, feelings, frustrations, experiences, coping strategies, and triumphs with other stepparents and stepchildren. Such sharing allows them to view their own situations more realistically and to learn from the experiences of others.

6. *Provide organization for the family.* Children need to have their limits defined and consistently upheld. One of the difficulties is that children are faced with a new stepparent attempting to gain control when they have not as yet enjoyed many supportive and positive experiences with their new stepparent. It is important, therefore, for this new stepparent to provide nurturance and positive feedback to stepchildren in addition to making rules and maintaining control.

***The Single Life*** In our society women and, to some extent, men are brought up to believe that one of their most important goals is to marry. Women who remain unmarried are labeled "old maids." Elaborate rituals have been developed to romanticize engagement and marriage. Unfortunately, many couples discover after the honeymoon that marriage is not always romantic or exciting. Many people deal with unfulfilled marriages with a series of divorces and remarriages. In the 1970s and early 1980s an increasing number of adults turned away from the responsibilities and restrictions of marriage by remaining single. Temporary and sometimes long-term deep emotional relationships were entered into without the duties and restrictions imposed by a legal arrangement.

At present there appears to be a shift in sexual values. The sexual revolution that began in the 1960s and that glamorized multiple recreational sexual relationships appears to be on the decline. The current renewed interest in sharply limiting the number of sexual partners is largely due to the fear of acquiring AIDS. People are recognizing that the more sexual partners they have, the greater are their chances of being exposed to the AIDS virus.

It is unclear at this point whether the threat of AIDS will lead to a decline in the number of people who choose to remain single. It should be noted that increases in the number of people who remain single has significant implications for social welfare, as statistics show higher rates of depression, loneliness, alcoholism, suicide, drug abuse, and alienation among those who are single.

## Summary

The family is a social institution that is found in every culture; no society has ever existed without this institution. Yet there are substantial variations in family patterns and forms. Most families throughout the world can be classified as either an extended family or a nuclear family. Our culture has moved from an extended family system (prior to the Industrial Revolution) to a nuclear family system. In a number of countries, a third family form—the single-parent family—is now emerging.

No society has ever existed without the institution of the family. Five essential functions performed by the modern family are replacement of the population, care of the young, socialization of new members, regulation of sexual behavior, and an important source of affection.

Four problems in the American family were examined: divorce, empty-shell marriages, family violence, and birth outside of marriage.

Now, one out of two marriages end in divorce. Divorce per se is not a social problem, but the consequences sometimes are. Reasons for the high divorce rate in our society include the extensive emphasis on romantic love, the changing status of women (who are now increasingly more financially independent), the growth of individualism, the growing acceptance of divorce, and the loss of certain functions in the modern family.

In empty-shell marriages the spouses feel no strong attachments to each other. Three types were described: devitalized relationships, conflict-habituated relationships, and passive-congenial relationships. Some empty-shell marriages eventually end in divorce.

Spouse abuse, child abuse, and parent abuse occur in more than half of all U.S. households. In the past thirty years family violence has become recognized as one of our major social problems.

With spouse abuse, the greatest physical damage is usually sustained by women. Although husbands are slapped or shoved with about the same frequency as wives, husbands are not controlled through violence to the extent that battered wives are. Spouse abuse appears to be related to a norm of tolerating violence in American families. A sizable number of men and women believe it is acceptable for a husband to occasionally hit his wife. Services (for example, shelter homes) are increasingly being developed in many communities for battered wives.

Large numbers of children are victims of child abuse or neglect. Physical abuse is dramatic and has received considerable national attention. Child neglect has received less national attention, even though it occurs more frequently than physical abuse. *Physical abuse, physical neglect,* and particularly *emotional neglect* are terms that are somewhat ambiguous and difficult to define precisely. The primary service designed to curb child abuse and neglect is protective services.

Premarital intercourse is fairly common, and is now often tolerated in our society. If a single woman becomes pregnant, however, there is often considerable turmoil within families. Birth outside of marriage has become somewhat more accepted in our society, yet it is still viewed as a social problem. There is considerable variation in the reasons why it is viewed as a problem—ranging from the assertion that it is a sign of the moral decay and collapse of the family, to concern about the difficulties that the single parent and her child will encounter. A disproportionately high number of births outside of marriage occur among teenagers, suggesting a need for quality educational programs about responsible sexuality.

Dramatic changes are now occurring in the American family. Technological developments (particularly in biology and medicine) are beginning to raise a number of ethical, legal, social, and personal questions. Technological advances in biology and medicine that are apt to affect the family include artificial insemination, surrogate motherhood, test-tube babies, genetic screening programs, cloning, and breaking the genetic code.

In addition, many Americans are experimenting with a number of different family forms, which may dramatically alter the central characteristics of future families. Among the forms are childless couples, postponement of raising children until retirement, professional parents, serial and contract marriages, comarital sex, open marriages, group marriages for various age groups, homosexual marriages and adoptions, transracial adoptions, single parenthood, blended families, and remaining single. Technological advances in biology and medicine, along with experimentation with new family forms, will undoubtedly significantly change the style of living for practically all families.

# CHAPTER 11

# *Health Care*

Health is no more a priority of the American health industry than safe, cheap, efficient, pollution-free transportation is a priority of the American automobile industry.

—*Barbara and John Ehrenreich*[1]

Health and happiness are perhaps the highest values in our society. Wealthy people who develop a chronic illness are often heard to say they would relinquish their wealth for a return to health if given a choice. Most Americans consider proper medical care a basic human right for which society should pay when an individual cannot. The view that health is a basic right rather than a privilege is of relatively recent origin. For example, as late as 1967 the president of the American Medical Association still asserted that health care should be available only to those who could afford it.[2] Health care as a right was promoted by former President Richard Nixon in his health message of 1971:

> Just as our National Government has moved to provide equal opportunity in areas such as education, employment, and voting, so we must now work to expand the opportunity for all citizens to obtain a decent standard of medical care. We must do all we can to remove any racial, economic, social, or geographic barriers that now prevent any of our citizens from obtaining adequate health protection, for, without good health, no man can fully utilize his other opportunities.[3]

This chapter:

♦ Provides a brief description of America's health care system

♦ Summarizes specific health care problems (profit orientation, limited attention to preventive medicine, unequal access to health services, unnecessary or harmful care, discrimination against people with a disability, AIDS, health care for the elderly, use of life-sustaining equipment, and high cost of financing of medical care)

♦ Discusses current efforts to resolve these problems and outlines a number of proposals to improve the health care system

## Physical Illnesses and the Health Care System

There are hundreds of thousands of medical conditions, ranging in severity from a minor scratch to a terminal illness. The causes are also diverse: accidents, infections, birth defects, viruses, bacteria, the aging process, stress, diet inadequacies, and so on.

Medical services in this country are organized into four basic components: physicians in solo practice, group outpatient settings, hospital settings, and public health services.

Physicians in *individual* or *solo practice* are proportionately more prevalent in rural areas than urban areas. Such a physician is usually a general practitioner trained to treat the more common medical ailments. Supervision of general practitioners is virtually nonexistent; they are primarily accountable only to the patient. Except through referrals for consultation and occasional use of laboratories and hospitals, a physician in solo practice works in relative isolation from colleagues.

*Group outpatient settings* can be organized in several ways. A group of general practitioners may share facilities, such as a waiting room, examining rooms, and a laboratory. Or, each physician within a group may have a different specialty and complement the skills of the others. Because medical knowledge and treatment techniques have become so vast and diverse, it is now impossible for a physician to have in-depth knowledge in all areas. Another type of outpatient setting is one in which a third party (a university, union, business, or factory) employs a group of physicians to provide medical care for its constituency. Still another type is one in which a group of doctors with the same specialty (for example, neurological surgery) provides services in the same facility.

A third subsystem of health care is the *hospital setting*, which has a wide range of laboratory facilities, specialized treatment equipment, inpatient care facilities, and highly skilled technicians. Hospitals employ a wide range of medical personnel. A hospital is generally the center of a community's medical care system. Due to spiraling hospital costs, many communities have built nursing homes and convalescent homes for those needing extensive medical care but not inpatient hospital attention.

*Public health services* are organized on five levels: local (city or county), regional, state, national, and international. The majority of public health services to a community are provided through local health programs.

Priorities in public health keep changing. As success is achieved in dealing with one problem, other problems emerge demanding attention. Public health services have virtually eliminated a number of communicable diseases in this country, such as tuberculosis, polio, and smallpox. The focus of public health services is primarily preventive in nature. Illustrations of services provided through local health departments include:

♦ Health counseling to families regarding family planning, prenatal and postpartum care, child growth and development, nutrition, and medical care

♦ Skilled nursing care and treatment to the acute and chronically ill

♦ Physical rehabilitation (stroke, arthritis, and similar conditions)

♦ Health services to public and parochial schools and liaison between home, school, and community

♦ Disease prevention and control

♦ Immunization services

♦ Referral

♦ Environmental sanitation, which involves developing and enforcing codes, rules, and regulations designed to maintain and/or improve conditions in the environment that affect health. This activity covers a broad area including air and water pollution, food protection, waste material disposal, and sanitation of recreation facilities

♦ Index maintenance of all area births, deaths, marriages, and current communicable diseases

♦ Public health education and information services

In the United States, the vast majority of health care services are private rather than government administered.

## Problems in Health Care

This section will address a number of problems in the health care system. They include profit orientation, limited attention to preventive medicine, unequal access to health services, unnecessary or harmful care, discrimination against people with a disability, AIDS, health care for the elderly, use of life-sustaining equipment, and high cost of medical care and how it's financed.

Nearly all the money spent on health care in this country goes to treating medical conditions once they arise, with very little being spent on prevention. Many people have considerable difficulty in obtaining access to medical care. Access is particularly difficult in low-income neighborhoods and smaller rural communities, as health care facilities tend to be located in affluent urban and suburban neighborhoods. The late Robert Kennedy described the health care system in America as being "a national failure" that is "providing poor quality care at high costs."[4]

## SERVICE ORIENTATION VERSUS PROFIT ORIENTATION

Most Americans believe that the only focus of health care is to keep people healthy—to prevent diseases, illnesses, and impairments from occurring and to restore to health as rapidly as possible those who do become ill. If this were the only objective, the health care system would not receive very high grades. There are a number of countries that have a higher life expectancy than the United States; these countries include Australia, Austria, Belgium, Canada, France, Italy, Japan, the Netherlands, Spain, Sweden, Switzerland, and the United Kingdom.[5] Life expectancy is highly correlated with the quality of health care in a society. As a population's health improves because of better medical care and improved living conditions, the average age to which its members live rises. (On the other hand, the life expectancy in the United States is more than twice as long as it is in some developing countries. For example, it is seventy-six in the United States, and thirty-four in Uganda.[6])

Another indicator of the quality of health care is the infant mortality rate. Again, many other countries have a lower infant mortality rate than the United States, including Australia, Austria, Belgium, Canada, Denmark, France, Germany, Japan, the Netherlands, Spain, Sweden, Switzerland, and the United Kingdom.[7] The rate at which newborns live in a country is directly correlated with the quality of health care provided to newborns and their mothers. (The infant mortality rate in the United States is, however, much lower than in developing countries; in the United States the infant mortality rate is about eight per 1,000 live births, while in Afghanistan the rate is about 150 per 1,000 live births.[8]) The infant mortality rate is determined by the number of deaths of children under one year of age per 1,000 live births in a calendar year.

The objectives of health care providers in the United States are not only to restore and maintain health but also to make a profit. There are numerous statistics documenting that the system is prospering. Many of our more than 7,000 hospitals are among the most modern in the world. Physicians have the highest median income of any occupational group. They earn several times more than the average wage earner. The mean income of physicians is about $200,000 per year.[9] The average daily cost for a hospital bed has gone from $74 in 1970 to more than $900 in 1997.[10] One of the most profitable small businesses in this country is the private medical practice. Among the most profitable intermediate-sized businesses are nursing homes. The pharmaceuticals industry, involving the manufacture and sale of drugs, has been one of the most profitable large-sized industries in the country.

The United States spends more money on health care (in both absolute and proportionate terms) than any other country. Medical costs constitute 15 percent of our total production of goods and services.[11]

Other industrialized nations regard medical care as a social service, a philosophy based on the premise that the kind of care you receive depends on the kind of illness you have. In contrast, in the United States the kind of medical care you receive depends not only on your illness but also on how much money you are able and willing to spend.

## PREVENTIVE MEDICINE

Most of the major causes of death today in the United States are chronic diseases: heart disease, cancer, cerebrovascular disease (such as strokes), obstructive pulmonary disease, and the like (Table 11.1). Chronic diseases progress and persist over a long period of time. They may exist long before we are aware of them, because often there are no symptoms in the early stages and because we tend to ignore early symptoms. Social, psychological and environmental factors are important influences in the progression of these diseases. Heart disease, for example, is known to be associated with a diet of highly saturated animal fats (beef, butter and cheese), lack of consistent and vigorous exercise, heavy smoking, and stress.

A major problem is that modern medicine is oriented toward crisis medicine, which is geared to treating people *after they become ill*. The crisis approach is effective in coping with some types of medical conditions, such as acute problems (for example, injuries, influenza, or pneumonia). Unfortunately, with chronic diseases, once the symptoms manifest themselves, much of the damage has already been done, and it is often too late to effect a complete recovery. In order to curb the incapacitating effects of chronic diseases, the health care delivery system needs to emphasize the

**Table 11.1**  *Ten Leading Causes of Death in the United States*

| Rank | | Percentage of Total Deaths |
|------|--|----------------------------|
| 1. | Heart disease | 32.0 |
| 2. | Cancer | 23.3 |
| 3. | Stroke | 6.8 |
| 4. | Chronic obstructive pulmonary disease | 4.5 |
| 5. | All accidents | 3.9 |
| 6. | Pneumonia and influenza | 3.6 |
| 7. | Diabetes | 2.6 |
| 8. | Suicide | 1.3 |
| 9. | Chronic liver disease and cirrhosis | 1.1 |
| 10. | Nephritis, nephrotic syndrome, and nephrosis | 1.0 |

Source: U.S. Bureau of the Census, *Statistical Abstract of the United States, 1997* (Washington, DC: U.S. Government Printing Office, 1997), 94

prevention of illness before extensive damage occurs. To date, preventive medicine has had a lower priority than crisis-oriented medicine in terms of research funding, the allocation of health care personnel, and the construction of medical facilities. (There are more profits to be made in treatment programs than in prevention programs.) This emphasis on treatment violates the commonsense notion that "an ounce of prevention is worth a pound of cure."

The kinds of health problems that we have in this country stem largely from our lifestyles. Millions of Americans smoke, drink, or eat to excess. Smoking is a serious health hazard. It has been linked to a long list of diseases, including heart disorders, ulcers, lung cancer, and emphysema. The death rate for heavy smokers (two or more packs a day) is double that for nonsmokers.[12] Some authorities are now asserting that nicotine is more addictive than heroin or cocaine.[13] Secondhand smoke (breathing in the smoke from someone else who is smoking) is now recognized as a dangerous carcinogen.[14]

The health hazards of alcohol abuse are described at length in Chapter 4. The life expectancy of alcoholics is ten to twelve years lower than that of nonalcoholics.[15]

Box 11.1

# Health and Longevity

The following ten health practices have been found to be positively related to good health and longevity:

1. Eating breakfast
2. Eating regular meals and not snacking
3. Eating moderately to maintain normal weight
4. Exercising moderately
5. Not smoking
6. Drinking alcohol moderately or not at all
7. Sleeping regularly seven to eight hours a night
8. Avoiding the use of illegal drugs
9. Learning to cope with stress
10. Leading a healthy sexual life

*Source:* Diane E. Papalia and Sally W. Olds, *Human Development,* 5th ed. (New York: McGraw-Hill, 192), 372–373.

Our diet is another aspect of lifestyle that has a profound impact on health and life expectancy. We eat too many fatty foods (such as red meat), and not enough fruits, vegetables, and whole-grain products. Our sugar consumption should be reduced, and the fiber in our diet increased.[16] In addition, we love high-calorie food and have a major tendency to overeat; both of which cause obesity. Research has found that obesity is associated with a variety of health problems, including high blood pressure, high cholesterol levels, heart disease, and diabetes.[17] One third of all Americans are now estimated to be overweight.[18]

Medical research shows that regular exercise is essential to good health. Exercise reduces significantly the risk of heart disease—which is the leading cause of death in the United States.[19] Regular exercise is one of the best predictors of overall longevity; yet, the majority of Americans do not exercise regularly.[20] An often quoted minimum guideline for exercising is thirty minutes a day at least three or four times per week.

Environmental factors also pose health risks. Our air and water are filled with thousands of toxic chemicals (caused by emissions from autos and factories) that create health hazards, such as cancer and emphysema. The fatality rate from automobile crashes is staggeringly high. Many such accidents are caused by driving while intoxicated.

Physicians often treat the symptoms of chronic illnesses rather than the underlying causes. Patients who are tense or anxious are prescribed tranquilizers rather than receiving therapy to reduce the psychological stress that is causing the tension. Patients who are depressed are prescribed antidepressant medication rather than being counseled to determine the underlying reasons for the depression. Patients with stress-related disorders (for example, ulcers, migraine headaches, insomnia, diarrhea, digestive problems, hypertension) are often prescribed medication rather than receiving therapy to change certain aspects of their lifestyles that would reduce the underlying psychological stress, which is a major factor in producing such problems.

In recent years, holistic programs, which are preventive in nature, have been established in industry, in hospitals, in school settings, in medical clinics, and elsewhere. Holistic medicine recognizes that our thinking processes function together with our body as an integrated unit, and it focuses on both our physical and psychological functions. The major determinants of most illnesses are our lifestyles (including exercise patterns, diet, sleep, and, particularly, stress reaction patterns). Holistic medicine instructs people in proper exercises, proper diet, and techniques to reduce psychological stress in order to maintain health and curb the development of chronic disorders.

Thomas McKeown emphasized the responsibility that each person has (although it is often not recognized) in maintaining good health:

The role of individual medical care in preventing sickness and premature death is secondary to that of other influences, yet society's investment in health care is based on the premise that it is the major determinant. It is assumed that we are ill and are made well, but it is nearer the truth to say that we are well and are made ill. Few people think of themselves as having the major responsibility for their own health. . . .

The public believes that health depends primarily on intervention by the doctor and that the essential requirement for health is the early discovery of disease. This concept should be replaced by recognition that disease often cannot be treated effectively, and that health is determined predominantly by the way of life individuals choose to follow. Among the important influences on health are the use of tobacco, the misuse of alcohol and drugs, excessive or unbalanced diets, and lack of exercise. With research, the list of significant behavioral influences will undoubtedly increase.[21]

## UNEQUAL ACCESS TO HEALTH SERVICES

The use and availability of medical care are directly related to socioeconomic class and race. For example, the average life expectancy for white males is about eight years longer than that for African-American males, and the average life expectancy for white females is about seven years longer than of African-American females.[22] In addition, the infant mortality rates for African Americans is more than twice that for whites.[23] Nonwhites have higher rates of practically every illness than whites;[24] a number of factors help explain this difference, as nonwhites have less access to health care, are exposed to discrimination in a variety of ways, and are apt to receive a lower quality of health care from the health care delivery system.

Membership in a lower social class is also correlated with higher rates of illnesses. The poor are seriously ill more frequently and for longer periods of time. They have higher rates of untreated illnesses and higher mortality rates for almost all illnesses. Contrary to popular belief, the highest rates of heart disease occur among the lowest salaried, not among top-level executives and managers.[25] (Stress levels may in fact be higher among the poor, who continually face psychological stress from financial crises. Differences in diet, exercise, and lifestyle patterns may also be factors.)

Of course, these higher rates of illness among the poor are largely attributable to their inability to afford private, high-quality medical care. Because of the profit motive, health care services are located primarily in affluent urban areas and in suburbs. The poor who live in small rural areas or in urban, low-income regions therefore have much more difficulty in gaining access to medical care, especially if they have transportation barriers. In the United States, health care services are provided on a *fee-for-service* basis. As a result, a two-tier system now exists; the upper tier serves the wealthy with high-quality care, and the lower tier serves the poor with inferior care.

When poor people do decide to seek treatment (often they wait until they are seriously ill), they tend to visit a clinic rather than a private or family physician. At the clinic they may feel self-conscious about their appearance. Frequently they must wait for hours in crowded waiting rooms and generally receive impersonal care. A trusting relationship with a physician is seldom developed. Doctors generally come from the middle and upper classes and therefore may

*Innovative therapy such as the use of pets in hospitals and nursing homes benefits both the animals and the patients. Love and companionship are healing medications that cannot be manufactured.*

face barriers in establishing rapport with low-income and nonwhite patients. Seham notes:

> In general, health professionals have little—if any— understanding of the lifestyle of the poor. For a doctor to advise a patient who is living in poverty to increase his intake of protein, without helping him to work out how to do it, is useless. Similarly, to suggest to a working mother that she come to the clinic for weekly treatments, when the clinic hours coincide with her working hours, is tantamount to not providing treatment at all.[26]

Being poor promotes poor health. The poor cannot afford to eat properly, so inadequate diet makes them more susceptible to illnesses. They are more

# Understanding and Reducing Stress

Miller and Smith document that rational and positive thinking has a major impact in promoting healing and maintaining health, and that irrational and negative thinking is a major determinant of stress-related illnesses. (Thinking is irrational if it does one or more of the following: is inconsistent with objective reality, hampers you in protecting your life, hampers you in achieving short- and long-term goals, causes significant trouble with other people, and leads you to feel unwanted emotions.) Stress-related physiological and psychological disorders have now become our number one health problem.[a]

A simplified description of the effect of our thinking processes in creating stress-related illnesses is outlined as follows:

Stressor
{
*Events or experiences*
↓
Certain kinds of *self-talk*
(e.g., "This is a very dangerous situation.")
}
↓

Stress
{
*Emotions*
(Such as tenseness, anxiety, worry, alarm)
↓

*Physiological reactions*
The alarm stage of the general stress reaction will occur. The physiological changes of this alarm stage include an accelerated heart and pulse rate, shallow respiration, perspiring hands, tenseness of the neck and upper back, a rise in red blood count for fighting infection, increased metabolism, and secretion of proinflammatory hormones.[b] The physiological reactions that most students experience prior to giving a speech before a group illustrate the components of this alarm stage.
}
↓

*Stress-related disorders*
(If the emotional and physiological reactions are intensive and long term, a stress-related disease is apt to develop—such as an ulcer, migraine headache, diarrhea, heart problems, digestive problems, cancer, hypertension, bronchial asthma, hay fever, arthritis, enuresis, certain skin problems, constipation.) According to the above formula, there are two components of a "stressor": (1) the event, and (2) the self-talk that we give ourselves about that event. *Stress* is the emotional and physiological reaction to a *stressor*.

---

likely to live in the most polluted areas, so they are more susceptible to cancer, emphysema, and other respiratory diseases. They cannot afford proper housing, have less heat in the wintertime, and are more exposed to disease-carrying rodents and garbage. Their lives are more stress filled, particularly with respect to financial concerns. They are less likely to know about and use preventive health approaches. They are less likely to seek early treatment that would prevent a serious disorder from developing. Because they are sometimes treated with hostility and contempt by physicians and other medical personnel, they are likely to avoid seeking medical help.

## UNNECESSARY OR HARMFUL CARE

As indicated earlier, one of the objectives of the health care system is to make a profit. All too often this happens by using unnecessary diagnostic and treatment approaches—ordering diagnostic tests that are unnecessary, prescribing drugs and other medications that are unnecessary, and performing unneeded operations.

The poor and nonwhites, as noted earlier, are more apt to be victimized by inferior care. Another group that is apt to be victimized by inferior care is women. The health care industry is male-dominated, with men holding most of the prestigious, high-paying, and powerful positions. Men make up 78 percent of today's physicians, for example, whereas 94 percent of the registered nurses are women.[27] Almost all dentists are men, whereas practically all dental hygienists and dental assistants are women.[28] The health care system in the United States is clearly dominated by men in authority positions who tell women supportive staff what to do. In recent years the number of cesarean births has grown from 5 percent to 25 percent of all births, giving the United States the highest rate of such births.[29] Sullivan notes:

Self-talk plays a key role in producing stress. The self-talk approach enables us to understand how positive (as well as negative) events can lead to a stress reaction. For example:

Positive event

Receiving a promotion

↓

Self-talk

"I now will have additional responsibilities that I may or may not be able to handle."

"If I fail at these new responsibilities, I will be fired and will be a failure. My career plans will never be realized."

"This promotion will make others in the office jealous."

"I'm in big trouble."

↓

Emotion

Worry, tension, anxiety

↓

Physiological reaction

Alarm stage of the general stress reaction

↓

Stress-related disorder

After a prolonged period of self-talk worries, a stress-related illness—such as ulcers or high blood pressure—develops.

Stress can be reduced in three primary ways. One way is to identify irrational and negative self-talk and then give yourself rational self-challenges (see Chapter 3 for examples of this approach). A second way is to become involved in activities that you enjoy, which will lead you to stop your irrational thinking and instead focus on events you view more positively. For example, if you enjoy golf, playing golf will lead you to stop thinking about your day-to-day problems and instead lead you to think about the enjoyable experiences associated with golfing. Activities that are likely to stop your irrational thinking include hobbies, entertainment events, jogging and other exercise programs, biofeedback programs, muscle relaxation exercises, and meditation.[c] A third way to reduce stress is to change the event that is producing it (for example, taking a job that you view as having less pressure).

a. Lyle H. Miller and Alma D. Smith, *The Stress Solution* (New York: Pocket Books, 1993).

b. Hans Selye, *The Stress of Life* (New York: McGraw-Hill, 1965).

c. These stress-reducing techniques are described in Charles Zastrow, *The Practice of Social Work*, 6th ed. (Pacific Grove, CA: Brooks/Cole), 1999.

Some cesareans, of course, are medically justified, but there is much suspicion that some are performed for the convenience of medical personnel, to protect against malpractice suits, or because doctors and hospitals are reimbursed more for surgical births. In any event, the mother loses control of the birth process when it becomes overly medicalized. Over the years, then, male dominance in medicine has meant that men have been the "authorities" telling women about their own bodies, and what the men told the women sometimes did more to bolster inaccurate stereotypes or line the pockets of physicians than to benefit the health of women.[30]

The medical procedure that is among those most likely to be performed unnecessarily is a hysterectomy, which is, of course, only performed on women. It is estimated that one-third of all hysterectomies over the years were medically unnecessary.[31]

In regard to unnecessary, and even harmful, care, Susan Dentzer notes:

Experts estimate that up to one third of all medical services performed in the U.S. are of questionable value and may even be harmful. In effect, as much as $200 billion spent on health last year could have been poured down a rat hole, and 50,000 Americans may have died from procedures they didn't need.[32]

Thousands of deaths and hundreds of thousands of hospitalizations occur annually from reactions to antibiotics and other prescribed drugs. A large number of people each year become addicted to tranquilizers and to pain-killing drugs prescribed by physicians. Thousands of people die each year from complications after undergoing unnecessary surgery. No surgery is without its risks. Even with such a simple operation as a tonsillectomy, two out of every 1,000 patients die.[33]

Why does harmful treatment occur? One reason is that physicians make a profit from prescribing unnecessary treatment—and such treatment sometimes leads to complications. Another reason is that it is conservatively estimated that about 10 percent of the nation's physicians are incompetent and should have their licenses revoked.[34] Unfortunately, most patients are unable to judge the professional competence of their doctors.

Suing has become a national pastime, particularly in the case of malpractice suits in the medical field. The large number of successful suits documents the common existence of harmful treatment. At the same time, the possibility of a malpractice suit arising from failure to make a correct diagnosis because an unlikely procedure was *not* used leads many physicians to routinely order more diagnostic tests than are likely to be needed. Such tests are costly.

## DISCRIMINATION AGAINST PEOPLE WITH A DISABILITY

There are an estimated fifty million people with disabilities in the United States—nearly one out of five persons.[35] People with disabilities include those who:

♦ are temporarily injured (severe burns, injuries to back or spine, broken limbs)

♦ have a chronic physical disability (including people who use canes, crutches, walkers, braces, or wheelchairs; the mobility-impaired elderly; and people with severe cardiovascular disorders, cerebral palsy, chronic arthritis, and AIDS)

♦ have a hearing disability

♦ have a visual disability

♦ have a mental disability (including an emotional disorder, retardation, or severe learning disability)[36]

Society's willingness to tend to the needs of those with a disability has always been largely determined by the perceived causes of the disability, existing medical knowledge, and general economic conditions. When the early Greek civilization prospered a few thousand years ago, the Greeks held a philosophy of unity of body and soul; a blemish on one signified a blemish on the other.[37] This philosophy led to a negative attitude toward those with a disability. The extreme application of this doctrine was found in Sparta, where many adults who were not self-sufficient were put to death.[38] Centuries later Romans also put to death some people who had a disability as they were considered to be "unproductive."[39] In ancient times there were almost no organized efforts to meet the needs of persons with a cognitive disability. (Because the term *mental retardation* has negative connotations, the term *persons with a cognitive disability* is used instead.) In early Greece and during the period of the Roman Empire, those with a mental illness were thought to be possessed by demons, so exorcism was the primary treatment.[40]

During the Middle Ages, disability was seen either as the result of demonic possession or as God's punishment.[41] Modern values of charity and humanitarian treatment were generally absent during this period, partly as a result of adverse economic conditions. About the only employment for people with a disability was provided by feudal lords, who hired them as court jesters, a position also considered suitable for persons with a cognitive disability.[42] The mentally ill continued to be viewed as being possessed by demons, and cruelty was advocated and used to punish and drive out the demons.

Our culture places a high value on having a beautiful body. There are a number of physical fitness and health clubs, and Americans spend large proportions of their budgets on clothes, cosmetics, exercise programs, and special diets to look more attractive. Beauty is identified with goodness and physical ugliness with evil. Movies, television, and books usually portray heroes and heroines as being physically attractive and villains as being ugly. Children are erroneously taught that being physically attractive leads to the good life, while having unattractive features is a sign of being inferior. Richardson found that young children rated people with a disability as being "less desirable" as persons than people without a disability.[43]

Unfortunately, this emphasis upon the body beautiful has subjected those with a disability to being objects of cruel jokes and has occasionally led to their being either shunned or treated as inferior. Often, people with a disability are stigmatized as losers, freaks, and partial persons. According to Cooley, if people who have a disability are related to as if they are inferior, second-class citizens, they are apt to come to view themselves as being inferior and to have a negative self-concept.[44] Our society needs to reassess its values about the perfect physique. Other traits ought to weigh more—honesty, integrity, personality, being responsible, kindness, and helpfulness.

Wright has noted that the emphasis on the body beautiful has led society to believe also that people who have a disability "ought" to feel inferior. Wright has coined the term "the requirement of mourning" for this expectation of society. An able-bodied person

*Rick Green, confined to a wheelchair, owns and operates a successful camera repair shop in Daytona Beach, Florida.*

I'm in church with my father, and my father is standing beside me, and I'm in a wheelchair. I'm relatively intelligent, but I'm disabled. I'm sitting there like anyone else. And somebody comes up to my father, and [he's] about as far away from me as from him, and [he says] to my father, "How's he doing?" [or they say] "Well he's looking pretty good." And I just want to kick him in the stomach.[47]

Unfortunately, relating to people who have a disability as if they are socially and mentally retarded may lead them to believe they are less intelligent and less effective in social interactions.

Studies have found that people also end interactions sooner with people with a disability.[48] Many people are uncomfortable when a person with a disability is near, because they are uncertain what is appropriate and inappropriate to say. They fear saying something that may offend the person. They do not want to make any direct remarks about the disability; yet, if they try to ignore the disability, they may make impossible demands upon the person. (For example, they may arrange a meeting or a social event in a building that is nonaccessible to the person.) People show their discomfort in a variety of ways—abrupt and superficial conversations, fixed stares away from the person with a disability, compulsive talking, or an artificial seriousness. People with a disability are sensitive to such actions. Fred David (who has a disability) describes his reactions to some of these interactions:

I get suspicious when somebody says, "Let's go for a uh, ah . . . [confused and halting speech] push with me down the hall," or something like that. This to me is suspicious, because it means that they're aware, really aware, that there's a wheelchair here, and that this is probably uppermost with them. . . . A lot of people in trying to show you that they don't care that you're in a chair will do crazy things. Oh, there's one person I know who constantly kicks my chair, as if to say, "I don't care that you're in a wheelchair. I don't even know that it's there." But that is just an indication that he really knows it's there.[49]

People detest being treated differently socially simply because they have a physical disability.

Those with a disability have been discriminated against in a variety of ways. Some schools do not have elevators, so those in wheelchairs are unable to attend. Some public transportation facilities (buses for example) are not equipped to transport those in wheelchairs. Many sports stadiums cannot accommodate wheelchairs. Socially, people who have a disability face many barriers in making friends, arranging dates, and

who spends a great deal of time, money, and effort to be physically attractive psychologically wants a person with a disability to mourn having a disability, because the able-bodied person needs feedback that it is worthwhile and important to strive to have an attractive physique.[45]

Another consequence of the "body beautiful" cult is that persons with disabilities are sometimes pitied and given sympathy as being less fortunate. People with a disability decry receiving pity and being patronized. They seek to be treated as equals.

There is also a tendency in our society to conclude that, because a person has a disability in one area, she or he probably has disabilities in other areas. Weinberg has noted that people talk louder in the presence of someone who is blind, as it is (erroneously) assumed that people who cannot see also have hearing problems.[46] Often, adults with a disability are treated like children. People with a physical disability are at times erroneously assumed to be mentally and socially retarded. A twenty-two-year-old college student in a wheelchair describes one example of this tendency:

being accepted into organizations. Because employers are reluctant to hire people with a disability, they have the highest rate of unemployment of any group. One estimate is that more than 50 percent of persons with a disability who are able to work are not employed.[50] Those employed often are underemployed (have lower paying and lower level jobs than those for which they are qualified), as employers are reluctant to offer them challenges.

When people with a disability are hired, they usually refute negative stereotypes, proving for the most part to be conscientious, capable, reliable workers who have a lower than average turnover rate. Their absentee rate is only slightly higher than the norm. They have excellent safety records, are as productive as other workers, and work as fast as other workers.[51]

During World War II, there was a severe labor shortage, which provided work opportunities for people with a disability. They successfully demonstrated to thousands of employers that if placed in an appropriate job they could perform well. This growing realization led to the establishment in 1945 of the President's Committee on Employment of the Handicapped.[52] After World War II, a number of federal programs underscored society's growing belief that those with a disability could be productive workers and should be given the opportunities and training to demonstrate their work capacities.[53]

Spurred by the civil rights movement in the 1950s and 1960s, a new minority group began to be heard in the late 1960s and in the 1970s. Persons with a physical disability began speaking out and demanding equal rights. They have been seeking through legislation and lawsuits an end to job discrimination, limited educational opportunities, architectural barriers, and societal discrimination. In 1973 Congress passed the Vocational Rehabilitation Act, one section of which prohibits discrimination against persons with a disability by any program or organization receiving federal funds. Included in this nondiscriminatory policy is an affirmative action policy (described in Chapter 6) in which employers who receive federal funds must demonstrate extensive efforts to hire those with disabilities.

In 1990 the Americans with Disabilities Act was signed into law. The act prohibits discrimination against people with a disability in employment or by limiting access to public accommodations, such as restaurants, stores, museums, and theaters. Advocates of the law call it the most significant civil rights legislation since the 1964 act prohibiting discrimination based on race. Then-President Bush indicated the law would be implemented cautiously. For example, the act provides that new buildings must be accessible to people with a disability but barriers to access in existing public buildings will be removed only if it can be accomplished without much difficulty or expense.

The twentieth century has seen the development of numerous programs and technological advances to help people with a disability. Yet, much remains to be done to change society's attitudes toward people with a disability and to help them live satisfying and productive lives.

## AIDS

Acquired immune deficiency syndrome (AIDS) is a contagious, presently incurable disease that destroys the body's immune system. AIDS is caused by the human immunodeficiency virus (HIV), which is transmitted from one person to another primarily during sexual contact or through the sharing of intravenous drug needles and syringes.

AIDS made national headlines in 1985 when it was revealed that actor Rock Hudson had contracted the disease. (Hudson died a few months after public release of the story.) National concerns about this disease were spurred again in 1991, when Magic Johnson (a prominent basketball player) announced that he had tested HIV positive (see Box 11.3).

A virus is a protein-coated package of genes that invades a healthy body cell and alters the normal genetic apparatus of the cell, causing the cell to reproduce the virus. In the process the invaded cell is often killed. The HIV virus falls within a special category of viruses called *retroviruses,* so named because they reverse the usual order of reproduction within the cells they infect. HIV invades cells involved in the body's normal process of protecting itself from disease, and it causes these cells to produce more of the virus. Apparently HIV destroys normal white blood cells, which are supposed to fight off diseases invading the body. As a result, the body is left defenseless and can fall prey to other infections. The virus devastates the body's immune or defense system so that other diseases occur and eventually cause death. Without a functioning immune system to combat germs, the affected person becomes vulnerable to bacteria, fungi, malignancies, and other viruses that may cause life-threatening illnesses, such as cancer, pneumonia, and meningitis.

In recent years it has become clear that more than one virus is linked with the development of AIDS. The first virus to be identified, and the one that causes the largest number of AIDS cases, has been designated as human immunodeficiency virus type 1 (HIV-1). This virus appears to be the most virulent member of the growing family of AIDS and AIDS-related viruses. HIV is a formidable enemy in that it is constantly changing, or mutating, and is present in multiple strains. To simplify our discussion of AIDS in the following pages, we refer to the infectious agent simply as HIV.

HIV is a tiny delicate shred of genetic material. As far as scientists know, it can live only in a very limited environment. It prefers one type of cell—the T-helper cell in human blood. Outside of blood and other bodily fluids, the virus apparently dies.

Documented ways in which the AIDS virus can be transmitted are: by having sexual intercourse with someone who has HIV, by using hypodermic needles that were also used by someone who has the virus, and by receiving contaminated blood transfusions or other products derived from contaminated blood. Babies can contract the AIDS virus before or at birth from their infected mothers and through breast milk.

HIV has been isolated in semen, blood, vaginal secretions, saliva, tears, breast milk, and urine. Only blood, semen, vaginal secretions, and to a much lesser extent, breast milk have been identified as capable of transmitting the AIDS virus. Many experts doubt whether there is enough of the virus present in tears and saliva for it to be transmitted in these fluids. Experts rule out casual kissing or swimming in pools as a means of contracting AIDS. Sneezing, coughing, crying, and shaking hands also have not proven to be dangerous. Only the exchange of body fluids (for example, through anal, oral, or genital intercourse) permits infection. The virus is very fragile and cannot survive long without a suitable environment; nor is it able to penetrate the skin. In sum, evidence has not shown that AIDS can be spread through any type of casual contact. You cannot get AIDS from doorknobs, toilets, or telephones. Also, it does not appear that HIV can be transmitted by blood-sucking insects such as mosquitos or ticks.

Few lesbians have contracted AIDS. Lesbians are at low risk unless they use intravenous drugs or have unsafe sexual contact with people in high-risk groups. Female-to-female transmission is possible, however, through vaginal secretions or blood.

Women who use sperm from an infected donor for artificial insemination are also at risk of infection. Donors should be screened by licensed sperm banks as a preventive measure.

◆ Box 11.3 ◆◆◆◆◆◆◆◆◆◆◆◆◆◆◆◆◆◆◆◆◆◆

## Magic Johnson, an American Hero, Joins the Battle Against the AIDS Virus

On November 18, 1991, millions of people throughout the world were stunned when Earvin "Magic" Johnson announced at a news conference that he had contracted the AIDS virus. He also announced his retirement from the Los Angeles Lakers and the National Basketball Association after twelve superb seasons. He added, "I will now become a spokesman for the HIV virus."

Thirteen years earlier, Magic Johnson made his first appearance in the public eye by leading Michigan state, as a sophomore, to the NCAA (National Collegiate Athletic Association) championship. At 6 feet 9 inches, he could play every position, including center.

In his twelve years with the Los Angeles Lakers, he led the Lakers to five world championships, and in the process acquired three Most Valuable Player awards. Magic Johnson is not only one of the most talented individuals ever to play basketball, he is also charismatic and has an appealing smile. A few days after the news conference Johnson indicated he believes he became infected with the virus from sexual intercourse with a female. He further acknowledged that over the years he has had a large number of female partners.

A few days after Johnson's news conference, he appeared on the *Arsenio Hall Show* and stated, "You don't have to feel sorry for me because if I die tomorrow, I've had the greatest life." His main message to Hall's audience and to the general public: "Practice safe sex, start using condoms and be aware. . . . Please put your thinking caps on and put your cap on down there" (gesturing below his belt).

In 1991, fears about the disease ran rampant. Johnson triggered a storm of criticism when he tried to stage a comeback in 1992, for possibly endangering the health of his teammates and other players. In February 1996, Johnson ended his retirement, and returned to play for the Los Angeles Lakers. His comeback unleashed bearhugs from his teammates, and an avalanche of support from across the country. The change in public opinion about his comeback in 1996 versus 1992 is a remarkable sign of growing compassion and understanding by the public of persons infected by HIV. (Johnson retired at the end of the 1996 season "on his own terms.")

After an individual is exposed to the virus, it usually becomes inactive. Once it is in the body, it apparently needs help to stay active. Such help might include the person's history of infections with certain other viruses, generally poor health, the abuse of certain recreational drugs (such as butyl nitrite), malnutrition, and genetic predisposition. For those who do develop AIDS, the mortality rate is very high.

In the early 1980s the AIDS virus was transmitted in some cases through blood transfusions. Today blood that is used in transfusions is tested for the presence of antibodies to the AIDS virus, making it unlikely that the virus could be transmitted in this way. Because antibodies do not form immediately after exposure to the virus, a newly infected person may unknowingly donate blood after becoming infected but before his or her antibody test becomes positive.

Most people infected by HIV will eventually develop AIDS. The length of time between initial infection of HIV and the appearance of AIDS symptoms is called the incubation period for the virus. The average incubation period (prior to the development of recent drugs) used to be estimated to be seven to eleven years.[54] There is considerable variation in this incubation period, ranging from a few months (particularly for babies who are HIV positive) to twenty years or more.

The drug called AZT (azidothymidine) has been found to delay the progress of the disease in some people. First synthesized in 1964 and initially developed as a cancer drug. AZT helps to extend life and provide hope. It does not cure AIDS and there are some serious difficulties with the drug. AZT or Retrovir (its brand name) must be taken every four hours both night and day. People often experience very uncomfortable side effects. These include nausea, headaches, anemia, lowered white blood cell counts, liver function changes, kidney effects, and bone marrow damage. The longer the drug is taken, the more likely the person is to experience side effects with increasing severity. Additionally, the drug is very difficult to manufacture, involving seventeen chemical steps plus six more steps to make it marketable. The result is scarcity and high costs. Nonetheless, the existence of a drug that at least can delay the effects of such a devastating disease has provided hope and has fought the black curtain of pessimism which has shrouded AIDS.

Other drugs to combat the AIDS virus are being developed. In 1991, the Food and Drug Administration approved DDI (didanosine) for treatment of adults and children with advanced AIDS who cannot tolerate or are not helped by AZT.[55] In 1995 and 1996 the Food and Drug Administration approved several drugs called protease inhibitors, which fight HIV by snipping an enzyme the virus needs to be able to infect human blood cells. Researchers see signs that combining AZT with some of these protease inhibitors is delaying substantially the progression of AIDS in people who are HIV infected.[56]

A major health problem involves people who are HIV positive but have no symptoms of AIDS. Most of these individuals have not been tested for the AIDS virus and therefore are unaware they have it. They may then infect others, although they experience no life-threatening symptoms themselves. The following is a summary of high-risk factors in contracting AIDS:

- Having multiple sex partners without using safe sex practices (such as using condoms). The risk of infection increases according to the number of sexual partners, male or female. In considering the risks of acquiring AIDS, a person should heed the assertion "When you have sex with a new partner, you are going to bed not only with this person but also with all this person's previous sexual partners."

- Sharing intravenous needles. HIV may be transmitted by reusing contaminated needles and syringes.

- Having anal intercourse with an infected person.

- Having sex with prostitutes. Prostitutes are at high risk because they have multiple sex partners and often are intravenous drug users.

Sexually active, heterosexual adolescents and young adults are increasingly becoming a high-risk group for contracting HIV. Persons in this age group tend to be sexually active with multiple sex partners. The risk of male-to-female transmission through sexual intercourse is higher than that of female-to-male. As noted, the risk of woman-to-woman transmission through sexual contact appears to be low. Although multiple exposures to HIV infection through sexual intercourse are not necessary for transmission, multiple sexual partners increase the likelihood that transmission will occur.

Lloyd describes the ways in which sexual transmission of HIV can be prevented or reduced:

Only two methods of completely preventing sexual transmission have been identified: (1) abstaining from sex or (2) having sexual relations only with a faithful and uninfected partner. The risk of infection through sexual intercourse can be reduced by practicing what has been called "safe sex," which is using a condom for all sexual penetration (vaginal, oral, and anal) whenever there is any doubt about a sexual partner's HIV status; engaging in nonpenetrative sexual activity; limiting the number of sexual partners; and avoiding sexual contact with people such as prostitutes who have had many partners.[57]

Many people believe that any contact with someone who is HIV positive will guarantee illness and death. Such fears are not justified. Body fluids (such as fresh blood, semen, urine, and vaginal secretions) infected with the virus must enter the bloodstream in order for the virus to be transmitted from one person to another. Male homosexuals account for so many AIDS cases because they're likely to engage in anal intercourse. Anal intercourse often results in a tearing of the lining of the rectum, which allows infected semen to get into the bloodstream. Sharing a needle during mainlining a drug with someone who is carrying the virus is also dangerous because it involves transmission of blood. A small amount of the previous user's blood is often drawn into the needle and then injected directly into the bloodstream of the next user.

At the present time there is no evidence that the virus can be spread by "dry" mouth-to-mouth kissing. There is a theoretical risk of transmitting HIV through vigorous "wet" or deep tongue kissing, as infected blood may be transmitted from one person to the other.

Several tests have been developed to determine if a person has been exposed to the virus. These tests do not directly detect the virus—only the antibodies a person's immune system develops to fight the virus. Two of the most widely used tests are called the ELISA and the Western blot. ELISA stands for Enzyme-Linked Immunosorbent Assay. ELISA can be used in two important ways. First, it can screen donated blood to prevent the AIDS virus from being transmitted by blood transfusions. Second, individuals who fear they may be carriers of the virus can be tested. For a person who has been infected with HIV, it generally takes two to three months before enough antibodies are produced to be detectable by the test.

ELISA is an extremely sensitive test and is therefore highly accurate in detecting the presence of antibodies. It rarely gives a negative result when antibodies are present. However, it has a much higher rate of false positive. That is, it may indicate that antibodies are present when in reality they are not. Therefore, it is recommended that positive results on the ELISA be confirmed by another test called the Western blot or immunoblot. This latter test is much more specific and less likely to give a false positive. Since the Western blot is expensive and difficult to administer, it can't be used for mass blood screening, as can the ELISA.

It must be emphasized that neither test can determine if a person already has AIDS or will actually develop it. The tests establish only the presence of antibodies that indicate exposure to the virus.

The origin of AIDS is unknown, although there have been a variety of speculations. (We probably never will be able to identify the origin, particularly now that AIDS has spread throughout the world.)

Persons with the AIDS virus are now classified as being either HIV asymptomatic (without symptoms of AIDS) or HIV symptomatic (with symptoms of the syndrome). HIV particularly invades a group of white blood cells (lymphocytes) called T helper cells or T-4 cells. These cells in turn produce other cells, which are critical to the body's immune response in fighting off infections. When HIV attacks T-4 helper cells, it stops them from producing immune cells that fight off disease. Instead, HIV converts T-4 cells so that they begin producing HIV. Eventually the infected person's number of healthy T-4 cells is so reduced that infections cannot be fought off.

Once a person is infected with HIV, several years usually go by before symptoms of AIDS appear. Initial symptoms include dry cough, abdominal discomfort, headaches, oral thrush, loss of appetite, fever, night sweats, weight loss, diarrhea, skin rashes, tiredness, swollen lymph nodes, and lack of resistance to infection. (Many other illnesses have similar symptoms, so it is irrational for persons to conclude they are developing AIDS if they have some of these symptoms.) As AIDS progresses, the immune system is less and less capable of fighting off "opportunist" diseases, making the infected person vulnerable to a variety of cancers, nervous system degeneration, and infections caused by other viruses, bacteria, parasites, and fungi. Ordinarily, opportunistic infections are not life threatening to people with healthy immune systems, but they can be fatal to people with AIDS, whose immunological functioning has been severely compromised.

The serious diseases that afflict persons with AIDS include Kaposi's sarcoma (an otherwise rare form of cancer that accounts for many AIDS deaths), pneumocystic carinii pneumonia (a lung disease that is also a major cause of AIDS deaths), and a variety of other generalized opportunistic infections, such as shingles (herpes zoster), encephalitis, severe fungal infections that cause a type of meningitis, yeast infections of the throat and esophagus, and infections of the lungs, intestines, and central nervous system. The incidence of tuberculosis, a disease once nearly eradicated in the United States, has escalated in recent years due largely to the epidemic of HIV infection and AIDS.

Initially, HIV infection was diagnosed as AIDS only when the immune system became so seriously impaired that the infected individual developed one or more severe, debilitating diseases, such as Kaposi's sarcoma or pneumocystic carinii pneumonia. However, on April 1, 1992, the Centers for Disease Control broadened its definition of AIDS; now any one who is infected with HIV and has a helper T-cell count of 200 cells per cubic millimeter of blood or less is said to have AIDS, regardless of other symptoms that person may or may not have. (Normal helper T-cell counts in healthy people not infected with HIV range from 800 to 900 per cubic millimeter of blood.)

AIDS as a syndrome is not any one specific disease. It simply makes those infected by the virus increasingly more vulnerable to any disease that might come along. The process of AIDS involves a continuum whereby those affected become more and more vulnerable to devastating diseases.

In some patients AIDS may attack the nervous system and cause damage to the brain. This deterioration, called AIDS-dementia complex, occurs gradually over a period of time (sometimes a few years). Several specific intellectual impairments may result from AIDS. These include inability to concentrate, forgetfulness, inability to think quickly and efficiently, visuospatial problems that make it difficult to get from place to place or to perform complex and simultaneous tasks, and slowed motor ability. It is interesting that language capacity and the ability to learn, difficulties that characterize people with Alzheimer's disease, do not seem to be affected.

Contrary to popular belief, people who are HIV positive can live for an indeterminately long time. Gavzer summarizes the characteristics that long-term AIDS survivors tend to have:

♦ They are realistic and accept the AIDS diagnosis but do not take it as a death sentence.

♦ They have a fighting spirit and refuse to be "helpless-hopeless."

♦ They are assertive and have the ability to get out of stressful and unproductive situations.

♦ They are tuned in to their own psychological and physical needs, and they take care of them.

♦ They are able to talk openly about their illness.

♦ They have a sense of personal responsibility for their health, and they look at the treating physician as a collaborator.

♦ They are altruistically involved with other persons with AIDS.[58]

There are a fortunate group of HIV-infected persons—some scientists call them long-term nonprogressors—who show no measurable signs of AIDS for ten or more years and who have a stable, near-normal count of T-cells. Only about 5 percent of HIV-infected people fit this description.[59] Do their immune systems have a way of combating HIV? If a combative agent is identified, might such an agent be replicated, and then given as a treatment to others who are HIV infected? Scientists are now investigating these important questions.

As noted, at this time there is no cure for AIDS, and there are a multitude of hurdles to overcome in combating the disease. AIDS is caused by a form of virus. Even with modern technology, we don't know how to cure a virus. The common cold is also caused by a virus; although pharmaceutical companies have spent millions of dollars on research in the hopes of finding an effective treatment for colds, none has yet been found. Currently, extensive research is being undertaken to better understand, prevent, and fight AIDS.

Prevention can be pursued in two major ways. First, people can abstain from activities and behaviors that put them at risk for contracting the disease. Second, scientists can work on developing a vaccine to prevent the disease, just as there are vaccines that prevent polio or measles. A vaccine might either block the virus from attacking a person's immune system or bolster the immune system so that HIV is unable to invade it.

Former Surgeon General C. Everett Koop makes the following recommendations to avoid getting the AIDS virus.

The most certain way to avoid getting the AIDS virus and to control the AIDS epidemic in the United States is for individuals to avoid promiscuous sexual practices, to maintain mutually faithful monogamous sexual relationships and to avoid injecting illicit drugs.[60]

It is advisable to use a condom when having sexual intercourse with a new partner until you are certain the person is not HIV positive. You cannot acquire AIDS from someone who is not infected by HIV.

In June 1998 the U.S. Supreme Court ruled that people infected by HIV (including those having AIDS) are covered by the 1990 Americans with Disabilities Act which protects those with a disability against discrimination in jobs, housing and public accommodations.

## HEALTH CARE FOR THE ELDERLY

As noted in Chapter 8, the proportion of the elderly in our society is increasing dramatically, and the "old old age" (age eighty-five and over) is the most rapidly growing age group. Today there is a crisis in health care for the elderly. There are a variety of reasons for this crisis.

The elderly are much more apt to have long-term illnesses. In the 1960s the Medicare and Medicaid programs were created to pay for much of their medical costs. Due to the high costs of these programs, there have been cuts in recent years in eligibility for payments and limits set for what the government will pay for a variety of medical procedures.[61]

Physicians are primarily trained in treating the young and generally less interested in serving the elderly. As a result, when the elderly become ill they often do not receive high-quality medical care. For example, TV anchor Hugh Downs described the case of an eighty-two-year-old woman who was shuffled from one hospital to another over a three-month period and finally dumped in a county hospital where she eventually died of a single grossly neglected bedsore.

> The revolution of longer life has produced a new complex of critical medical needs, needs this nation does not yet seem prepared to meet. For example, there seems little prospect that there will be anything like the numbers of geriatricians needed to care for the elderly. It's a field still avoided by young doctors. Because of the complicated problems of the aging, there is a need for more health evaluation services and more psychiatric and rehabilitation assistance. Even for the limited efforts we now make, funding has always been meager.
>
> The new era of the longevity revolution is already bringing with it multiplying health problems to which our society remains largely blind . . . and within this nation's vast medical complex, many old who could be helped are left adrift, trapped, their needs unrecognized.[62]

Medical conditions of the elderly are often misdiagnosed, as physicians receive little special training in their unique medical conditions. Many seriously ill elderly do not get medical attention. One of the reasons physicians avoid treating the elderly is the problem of reimbursement. The Medicare program sets reimbursement limits on a variety of procedures that are provided to the elderly. As a result, most physicians prefer to work with younger patients where the fee-for-service system is much more profitable.

Hospital payments have also been restricted under Medicare. In the past, the payment system covered whatever the expenses came to. To curtail rampant costs, the federal government in the early 1980s set flat payments for each category of illness, called diagnostic-related groups (DRGs). A perverse and unintended consequence of DRGs is that many seriously ill elderly patients are being discharged prematurely.[63] With the DRG system, hospitals that have a social conscience and continue to treat the elderly beyond the length of time allowed by the DRG regulations must cover the expenses themselves, and thereby risk facing bankruptcy.

In addition, the elderly who live in their community often have transportation difficulties in getting medical care. Those living in nursing homes sometimes receive inadequate care as some health professionals, assuming such patients no longer have much time to live, are less interested in providing high-quality medical care. Medical care for the elderly is becoming a national embarrassment.[64]

## USE OF LIFE-SUSTAINING EQUIPMENT

Medical technology has made dramatic advances this century. Technology is able to keep alive for months, and in many cases years, people who in the past would have died.

Even after a person's brain has stopped functioning, technology can keep the respiratory processes, the heart, the liver, and other vital organs functioning for months. The lives of those who are terminally ill can be prolonged for substantial periods of time, but they may experience considerable pain and will be in a deteriorated condition. Many controversial issues have arisen about the use of life-sustaining technology. How should death now be defined, since vital functions can be kept going even when the brain is dead? Some lawsuits have already arisen in organ donor cases in which it is charged that organs have been removed before the donor was deceased. Should

*Son visits his mother who has Alzheimer's disease in a private care facility in Northern California.*

the lives of the terminally ill be prolonged when there is practically no hope for recovery and the patients are in severe pain? Should society seek to keep alive people who are so severely and profoundly retarded that they cannot (and will never be able to) walk or sit up? Should abortion be mandatory if major genetic defects are detected in the fetus? When should life-prolonging efforts be used, and when should the patient be allowed to die? If a terminally ill person who is in severe pain wants to end his life by suicide, should he be legally allowed to—and should others (such as physicians and close relatives) be legally allowed to assist in such suicides?

Because of the adverse consequences of being kept alive indefinitely when there is no hope of recovery, an increasing number of people are signing "living wills." In a living will a person states that if a situation arises in which there is no reasonable expectation of recovery from physical or mental disability involving a life-threatening illness, she or he requests to be allowed to die and not be kept alive by artificial means. A living will is not binding, but it conveys a patient's wishes to those (such as relatives and attending physicians) who must make a decision about whether to use life-sustaining equipment. To complement living wills, a number of states have enacted legislation making it possible for adults in these states to authorize (by filling out a Power of Attorney for Health Care form)

other individuals (called health care agents) to make health care decisions on their behalf should they become incapacitated.

The President's Commission for the Study of Ethical Problems in Medicine and Biomedical and Behavioral Research recommended in 1981 that all states define death as occurring when either of the following are judged to have taken place: (a) the irreversible cessation of circulatory and respiratory functions (this is essentially the definition used in the past) or (b) irreversible cessation of all functions of the entire brain, including the brain stem (this is a new definition). In adopting the "whole brain concept," the commission rejected a more controversial argument that death should be deemed to occur when "higher-brain functions" (those controlling consciousness, thought, and emotions) are lost. Patients who have lost higher-brain functions but retain the brain-stem functions can persist for years in a chronic vegetative state. Many states have now incorporated this definition of death into their statutes.

## THE HIGH COST OF MEDICAL CARE

Health care costs have risen dramatically in the past thirty-five years. Expenditures on health care as a percentage of this country's total production of goods and services increased from 5.6 percent in 1960 to 14.6 percent in 1996.[65] These high costs are now recognized as a matter of national concern. There are many reasons why health expenses are so high and continue to increase more rapidly than the rate of inflation.

First, as we've seen, one of the objectives of the health care system is to make a profit. There are few controls designed to keep fees and prices down. Although the United States uses a marketplace approach to health care, ill consumers are not in a position to shop around for medical treatment. If they are suffering, their priority is to feel better, so they are willing to pay whatever a doctor chooses to charge. Most patients are not even informed before receiving treatment what the physician will charge. Fees for doctors' services are not advertised and therefore are not subjected to the competition that exists elsewhere in marketplace systems. Physicians have successfully established a public image in which they are so revered that most patients will sit for an hour in a waiting room without complaining and will be reluctant to ask questions about charges before receiving treatment. (The same individuals don't hesitate to voice their frustrations about having to stand in line for five minutes at a checkout counter in a store.)

Another factor in the high cost of health care is dramatic technological advances in life-saving treatment interventions. New equipment, along with the cost of highly skilled personnel to operate it, is expensive. Thirty-five years ago we did not have cobalt machines, heart pacemakers, artificial heart valves, and microsurgical instruments that enable doctors to perform surgery under a microscope. Coleman and Cressey note that there are huge profits to be made in developing new medical procedures and new drugs, and as a result attention has been diverted away from less expensive (and often more effective techniques) of preventive medicine.[66] Klein and Castleman assert "The processes that drive medical research toward expensive treatments also turn it away from preventive measures that do not hold the promise of corporate profit."[67]

Yet another reason is the increased life span of Americans. Now a larger proportion of our population is old, and the elderly require more health care than younger people. Many technically and professionally trained groups (such as nurses and physical therapists) are demanding salaries consistent with their training and responsibilities. These higher salaries are reflected, of course, in the overall costs of medical treatment.

Another contributor is the fact that third-party financing is increasingly paying medical bills. Historically, medical bills were primarily charged to and paid by consumers. Now, most bills are charged to and paid by third parties, including private insurance companies and the public Medicare and Medicaid programs. Physicians are more likely to recommend expensive diagnostic and treatment procedures if they feel such procedures will not be a financial burden to the patient. Third-party payments also tempt some physicians to perform surgeries that may be unnecessary.

The increase in malpractice suits is also a contributing factor. Juries in many cases have awarded large settlements when malpractice is judged to have occurred. Physicians are required by law to carry malpractice insurance, with annual premiums ranging from $5,000 to more than $90,000, depending on a variety of factors—including geographic area and field of practice. (Neurosurgeons and anesthesiologists are often charged the highest rates, because their fields are considered to be "high risk.") These premium costs are, of course, passed on to consumers.

The tendency toward increased specialization by doctors is another factor. At present about 90 percent of physicians have a specialty.[68] The growth of medical knowledge has encouraged specialization; it is impossible today for a physician to be an expert in all medical areas. However, specialists charge more than general practitioners in order to receive compensation for their additional training and expertise. Specialization also raises costs because patients often are required to consult with (and pay) two or more physicians for each illness that they have. (A serious additional problem caused by specialization is that medical care becomes impersonal, dehumanized, and fragmented because patients now rarely establish a trusting, long-term relationship with one physician.)

Hospital care is extremely expensive. Hospitals compete with one another to offer the most prestigious and expensive equipment, which often leads to a duplication of expensive and seldom-used technology. And hospitals, similar to physicians, are not subjected to fees set by consumers on a supply-and-demand basis. Patients generally are not able to shop around for the hospital they want to go to.

Hospitals, physicians, nursing-home operators, and drug companies are politically powerful. Health care providers are represented by such influential organizations as the American Medical Association, the Pharmaceutical Manufacturers Association, the

## How Much for Health Care?

Fiscal conservatives argue our economy cannot afford to use medical technology to prolong the lives of those who will not be productive in the future. They point to cases such as that of Geri D., a case they say documents the fact that too much money is already being spent in some areas.

At age five months, Geri D. is residing in a residential facility for persons with a severe developmental disability at an annual cost of more than $100,000. She has severe medical problems, including cardiovascular dysfunctions. She has a profound cognitive disability—she will never be able to sit up, a developmental milestone that children of average intelligence achieve at six months of age. Geri was born prematurely, with multiple medical problems. Life-saving technology kept her alive. Already, more than $250,000 has been spent in keeping her alive. By the time she becomes a young adult, more than $2 million will have been spent on keeping her alive. Most of this cost will be borne by the government under the Medicaid program.

With medical advances, our society will face increasingly difficult issues regarding where financial resources should be used. With high medical costs, as in this case, our government simply does not have the funds to pay the medical expenses of everyone who could be kept alive with life-saving technology.

American Hospital Association, and the American Association of Medical Schools. Health care providers appear, at least at present, to have the political clout to prevent changes in health care that would sharply restrict their profits.

## FINANCING MEDICAL CARE

Medical expenses are paid for by private insurance, through governmental programs, and by direct payments from the individual to the health care provider. In 1996 private insurance paid 34 percent of the total costs for health care, the consumer paid 22 percent, and the government paid 44 percent.[69] Most of the 44 percent of the federal government's

health care bill is paid through Medicaid and Medicare. (The government also participates in the health insurance of federal employees, provides medical programs for families of members of the armed forces, and supports Veterans Administration hospitals.)

*Medicaid*    This program was established in 1965 by an amendment (Title XIX) to the Social Security Act. Medicaid provides medical care primarily for recipients of public assistance. It enables states to make direct payments to hospitals, doctors, medical societies, and insurance agencies for services provided to those on public assistance. The federal government shares the expense with states, on a 55 percent to 45 percent basis. Medical expenses that are covered include diagnosis and therapy performed by a surgeon, physician, and dentist; nursing services in the home or elsewhere; and medical supplies, drugs, and laboratory fees.

Under the Medicaid program, benefits vary from state to state. The original legislation encouraged states to include coverage of all self-supporting people whose marginal incomes made them unable to pay for medical care. However, this inclusion was not mandatory, and "medical indigence" has generally been defined by states to provide Medicaid coverage primarily to recipients of public assistance.

Although the stated purpose of Medicaid was to assure adequate health care to the nation's poor and near-poor, the program actually covers less than half of all poor families.[70] This is because the federal government has restricted eligibility in order to cut costs. In the past, hospitals supported the uninsured by charging paying patients more. But, after years of soaring costs, government and private insurers have rebelled against "costshifting" by setting limits on what they will pay for services provided in hospitals. Many hospitals, unable to support the cost of indigent care, are turning these patients away. *A two-tiered system of health care is emerging in this country, based on ability to pay.*[71]

*Medicare*    The elderly are most afflicted with illnesses yet least able to pay for medical care. People over age sixty-five now make up 13 percent of the population, and the percentage is increasing each year. Over four times as many dollars are spent per capita on health care for the elderly as for younger people, mostly for hospital or nursing care.[72]

Therefore, in 1965 Congress enacted Medicare (Title XVIII of the Social Security Act). Medicare helps the elderly pay the high cost of health care. It has two parts: hospital insurance (Part A) and medical insurance (Part B). Everyone age sixty-five or older who is entitled to monthly benefits under the Old Age, Survivors, and Disability Insurance program gets Part A automatically, without paying a monthly premium. Practically everyone in the United States age sixty-five or older is eligible for Part B. Part B is voluntary, and beneficiaries are charged a monthly premium. Disabled people under age sixty-five who have been getting Social Security benefits for twenty-four consecutive months or more are also eligible for both Part A and Part B, effective with the 25th month of disability.

*Part A*—hospital insurance—helps pay for time-limited care in a hospital, in a skilled nursing facility (home), and for home health visits (such as visiting nurses). Coverage is limited to 150 days in a hospital and to 100 days in a skilled nursing facility. If patients are able to be out of a hospital or nursing facility for sixty consecutive days following confinement, they are again eligible for coverage. Covered services in a hospital or skilled nursing facility include the cost of meals and a semi-private room, regular nursing services, drugs, supplies, and appliances. Part A also covers home health care on a part-time or intermittent basis if beneficiaries meet the following conditions: They are homebound, in need of skilled nursing care or physical or speech therapy, and services are ordered and regularly reviewed by a physician. Finally, Part A covers up to 210 days of hospice care for a terminally ill Medicare beneficiary.

*Part B*—supplementary medical services—helps pay for physicians' services, outpatient hospital services in an emergency room, outpatient physical and speech therapy, and a number of other medical and health services prescribed by a doctor, such as diagnostic services, X-ray or other radiation treatments, and some ambulance services.

Each Medicare beneficiary has the choice of choosing from an "alphabet soup" of health plans which plan he or she will be in. The variety of plans include preferred provider organizations, provider service organizations, point-of-service plans, private fee-for-service plans, and medical savings accounts. (It is beyond the scope of this text to give detailed descriptions of these plans.)

*The elderly are dependent upon Medicare to help pay the high cost of health care. Here, demonstrators show their objections to decreased Medicare coverage for individuals.*

*Private Insurance* All health care costs are rapidly rising, including the costs of health insurance. People who are not covered through group plans at their place of employment are increasingly finding it difficult to purchase private health insurance. An estimated 40 million Americans do not have health insurance.[73] Kornblum and Julian note:

Contrary to what many people in the United States believe, the majority of the uninsured are full-time and part-time workers and their children. The very poor who are out of the labor force qualify for Medicaid, and the elderly are eligible for Medicare. Young people who are subject to frequent periods of unemployment, and minority workers who are employed at jobs with no health benefits, are especially likely to be uninsured.[74]

## Proposed Programs to Combat Health Care Problems

ⓍⓍⓍⓍⓍⓍⓍⓍⓍⓍⓍⓍⓍⓍⓍⓍⓍⓍⓍ

There are two ways to cure our health care ills. One is to come up with an entirely new program, such as the National Health Service of Great Britain; the other is to change and improve our present system. First, we'll take a look at the British system.

## THE BRITISH SYSTEM: A COMPARISON

About five decades ago, Great Britain created a health care system that has become known as socialized medicine. We will briefly examine this system to show that there are other ways to providing health care than our marketplace, for-profit system.

The British system, in contrast to ours, provides medical care as a public service, similar to the provision of elementary and secondary education in the United States. Most physicians are employed by the British government, which owns and operates the clinics, hospitals, and other facilities. The British health care system thus is financed through taxes.

In the British system, every individual selects and registers with a physician. Most physicians are general practitioners who see patients at their offices and who, when needed, make house calls. Physicians receive a basic salary paid by the government and an additional small annual fee based on the number of patients on their registers. (This fee is the same whether a person sees a physician fifty times a year or not at all.) Doctors' incomes, then, depend on the number of people who register with them and not on the amount or kind of treatment they provide. There are also some government-paid specialists in Britain to whom general practitioners may refer cases for consultation and treatment. General practitioners earn on the average less than half of what physicians earn in this country.[75]

British physicians are allowed to take private, fee-paying patients if they desire; a few physicians choose to serve only private patients. In addition, some individuals (generally the wealthy) choose to receive private physician and hospital care, for which of course they pay. The quality of public care is generally about the same as private care, although in private care, patients often obtain an appointment sooner for nonemergency medical care; and private hospital rooms are, in general, more spacious and pleasant in appearance.

The British system provides free medical care to any person in the country—including visitors who have a medical emergency. Practically all costs (physician visits, surgery, hospital rooms and meals, ambulance services, diagnostic tests, and essential medical supplies such as eyeglasses and wheelchairs) are paid by the government. There is a small charge for drug prescriptions even though the actual cost may be many times higher. There is also a small charge for each dental visit. (Those over sixty-five and those under sixteen are excused from these fees.) Individuals have to pay for purely cosmetic services such as face-lifts or gold fillings.

British opinion polls show around 80 percent of the public approves of the National Health Service. Health care in Britain is the most highly rated government service. The service is also supported by the medical profession and both political parties. On the basis of cost, the system appears to be more efficient than ours. The per-person cost of health care in Britain is less than half of what it is in the United States.[76] Britons also appear to be healthier than Americans on a number of indicators—they live longer, have a lower infant mortality rate, and spend less time in hospitals.[77]

The main complaint that Britons have about this public health care system is the long waiting lists—days, even months—for treatment of nonemergency medical problems. Emergencies (such as a heart attack or a broken arm) receive immediate attention.

Britain's historical tradition in health care is different from ours. The primary focus of their system is service, whereas ours has both a service and a profit orientation. It is uncertain whether their system would work in our country. The medical profession has considerable vested interest in maintaining its high profits and perhaps would be successful in preventing the establishment of a similar system in this country. Also, the administrative problems and costs for a country the size of the United States would be stupendous. Finally, many Americans are offended by the concept of socialized medicine, as well as the impersonal assembly-line treatment often associated with such government-sponsored medical programs.

## IMPROVING THE CURRENT SYSTEM

Practically everyone agrees that the rising costs of medical care are a threat to a family's financial security and, on a broader scale, are a threat to the economic stability of our society. Yet there is no general consensus about specific measures that should be taken to hold down costs and to resolve the other problems that have been identified in this chapter. Some of the specific suggestions that are being advocated by authorities in the field will be briefly summarized.

### Holding Down Costs

A number of proposals to hold down health care costs have been suggested:

♦ Increase the number of admissions to medical schools in order to train more doctors. Increasing the number of doctors may reduce difficulties in gaining access to health care and also lead to competition between physicians to attract patients and thereby lead to reductions in fee charges.

♦ Expand outpatient facilities (such as emergency care facilities that are open not only during the day but also during evening hours and on weekends) so that illnesses can be detected and treated early, thereby preventing the development of more serious and costly medical conditions.

♦ Permit doctors to advertise their services and fees. Other professionals, such as attorneys and dentists, are increasingly doing this. Such competition may result in fee reductions.

♦ Encourage (through fellowships and scholarships) medical students to become general practitioners rather than specialists.

♦ Expand outpatient treatment facilities so that more illnesses could be treated without hospitalization.

♦ Train more physician assistants and paramedics to handle treatments for common routine illnesses (for example, flu and colds), to provide preventive services, and to service geographical areas without physicians.

♦ Encourage patients to seek a second opinion before consenting to an operation, in order to reduce unnecessary surgeries. Many insurance programs are now paying for the costs of a second opinion.

♦ Expand and encourage the use of generic drugs. Generic drugs are nonpatent drugs that have the same chemical composition as patent drugs. The main differences between generic and patent drugs are that the latter carry a trade name and cost considerably more.

### Preventive Medicine and Managed Care

Prevention programs might also be cost saving in the long run. Specific suggestions for an increased focus on preventive medicine are:

*Educational programs* should be expanded in schools and to inform the general public that it is our lifestyles (diet, handling of stress, exercise patterns, amount of sleep, hygiene habits) that primarily determine when we will become ill and what illnesses we will develop. Educational programs are also needed to help people recognize that, when they become ill, they are important participants in the treatment process, as their attitudes, emotions, diet, and hygiene patterns will greatly influence treatment results. Most Americans unfortunately believe that physicians have nearly magical powers to treat medical conditions that arise. Patients generally rely upon a physician to cure them.

The federal government is encouraging *Health Maintenance Organizations (HMOs)* as an alternative to other private insurance plans. The present health care system is primarily curative in focus, as it concentrates upon illness and injury rather than upon prevention. At the present time, most private health insurance policies do not cover periodic screening examinations but only provide coverage when a person is actually sick or injured. Such a model rewards providers of health services for treating illnesses but not for preventing illnesses.

HMOs, in contrast, are prepaid health care insurance plans that emphasize prevention. Subscribers pay a fixed annual sum, usually in installments, and, in return, receive comprehensive care. HMOs vary in size and structure but generally include physicians (both general practitioners and specialists) who provide a wide range of services—diagnosis, treatment, and hospital and home care. An HMO program operates similarly to an insurance program. Subscribers pay a fee (the fee is often paid by the subscriber's employer), and the HMO pays for all of the medical expenses that occur. Because HMO revenues are fixed, their incentives are to keep patients well, for they benefit from patient well-days, not sickness. Their entire cost structure is geared toward preventing illness and failing that, to promoting a rapid recovery through the least costly services consistent with maintaining quality. In contrast to pay-for-service insurance plans, the HMO's financial incentives tend to encourage the least utilization of high cost forms of care and also tend to limit unnecessary procedures.

In comparison to fee-for-service health insurance plans, HMO plans have been found to: (a) reduce the use of inpatient hospital care from 15 to 40 percent; (b) lower overall health care costs by 15 to 20 percent; and (c) provide quality of care that is better, or at least equal.[78]

It is crucial that incentives be found throughout the health care system to focus on prevention and cost reduction, as HMOs do. Numerous public and private employers have chosen to provide HMO programs for their employees. HMOs have been successful in reducing overall health care costs per patient, partly because they emphasize prevention.

HMOs, Medicare, and Medicaid compose the system of managed care in the United States. The growth in managed care programs has been phenomenal; in 1970 there were about thirty different plans, there are now over 1,500.[79] The majority of Americans with health insurance are now covered by a managed care program.[80] Managed care, in one sense, has turned the system upside down, from one in which payments tempted doctors to do too much, to a system in which payments tempt them to do too little. Under the old system, patients did their doctor a favor by being sick, as the doctor was paid for providing treatment. In the new economics of managed care and HMOs, the relationship has been reversed, as most plans pay physicians a fixed fee per registered member, regardless of how much treatment each patient needs. As a result, a chronically sick person is a liability for the HMO and the physician.[81]

HMOs have recently been criticized for the following practices and procedures:

♦ The twenty-four-hour limits on hospital maternity stays.

♦ The "gag clauses" prohibiting doctors from speaking freely about the range of treatments available to their patients.

♦ The huge corporate bonuses paid to HMO executives.

♦ Sensational cases of patients being denied care. (For example, a young mother in California died because her HMO did not approve a referral to a specialist.)

♦ Patients having to jump through bureaucratic hoops to receive authorized care. (For example, an elderly man in Florida was presented with a $30,000 bill by his HMO because he failed to get emergency room authorization for care for his wife who suffered a cerebral hemorrhage—she later died from the cerebral hemorrhage.)

♦ Patients having fewer choices among doctors and hospitals.

♦ Doctors being required to prescribe medicines from lists of cheaper drugs.

♦ Patients having to battle the HMO bureaucracy to get the treatment they feel they need, as HMOs have utilization review panels that review patients' records and decide which treatments the health plan will cover.

♦ Doctors being frustrated as the utilization review panels occasionally mandate a different treatment program for some patients than what the attending physician believes is optimal.[82]

As the system of managed care expands in the United States, the merits and shortcomings of this system will increasingly be debated.

*Proposals in Other Areas*   Suggestions for taking action to resolve some of the other problems that were identified follow:

♦ Incentives need to be developed to encourage physicians to practice in rural areas and in low-income urban areas. One approach is to give stipends that would help pay the expenses of medical students in exchange for a requirement that recipients practice for a few years in areas currently underserved by physicians.

♦ More nonwhite students should be admitted to medical schools. Such students after graduation tend to serve nonwhite communities.

♦ More female students need to be admitted to medical schools and dentistry schools, in order to counter our health care system being dominated by males.

♦ Further guidelines need to be established regarding when heroic life-sustaining measures should be used and when "the plug should be pulled." The high cost of keeping alive people who will never again be productive is raising some national concerns about euthanasia—so-called "mercy killing." The issues surrounding assisted suicide also need to be resolved.

♦ Colleges and universities need to expand existing programs and develop new programs to meet the emerging health care needs of the elderly. Physicians and other health care professionals

- (nurses, social workers, physical therapists, and so on) should receive training in diagnosing and treating the medical conditions of older citizens. Incentives need to be developed to encourage health care professionals to work with the elderly.

♦ Sex education and AIDS education must start at the lowest grade possible as part of any health and hygiene program. People need to be informed of the importance of safer sex (such as using condoms).

♦ Offices, factories, and other work sites should develop a plan for educating the work force and accommodating people with AIDS. Employees who are HIV positive, and those who have AIDS, should not be discriminated against but should be dealt with as are any other workers with a chronic illness.

### Establishing a U.S. National Health Insurance Program

This country does not as yet have a national health insurance program. Canada, Great Britain, and many other countries have such a plan in which public tax dollars are used to pay for medical care for all citizens. In the past three decades, a number of congressmen and organizations have pressed for a public health insurance program. Now, many families receive partial coverage of costs through subscribing to private insurance plans, which are primarily available to employed persons and their families. Those who are either marginally employed or unemployed are generally not covered by health insurance.

There are multiple reasons why a national health insurance plan is needed. The rapid rise in health and insurance costs makes it impossible for the poor, those of marginal income, and even middle-class families to pay for insurance or extensive medical bills. The poor who are not covered by Medicaid are unable to pay for even moderate medical expenses; thereby, they often forego early treatment and develop more serious medical conditions. Medicare covers short-term hospitalization expenses for the elderly but not long-term expenses. Extensive medical treatment can wipe out substantial savings and force a family deeply into debt, thereby changing dramatically its standard of living and lifestyle.

Hospitals cannot survive without assured income when services are provided. Physicians, as well, need to be paid for their services. Starting with Franklin Roosevelt, every president except Ronald Reagan and George Bush has proposed a national health insurance program, without any being passed. The result is that the United States is the only industrialized nation lacking a comprehensive national medical insurance system.[83] A variety of national health insurance programs have in the past been advanced by Democratic and Republican legislators, administration officials, organized labor, representatives of private insurance companies, and the American Medical Association. President Clinton in 1993 proposed a national health insurance program that would provide universal coverage for all Americans. Clinton assigned the highest priority of his administration to the passage of a national health insurance plan that would provide universal coverage. The proposal was hotly debated by Congress in 1994, and several other alternative plans were proposed by members of Congress and also intensely debated. However, no proposal received sufficient support to attain congressional passage.

The main objection to a national health insurance program has been the cost to taxpayers and the effect such an expensive new program would have on the economy. There is concern that such a program would escalate the costs of health care, similar to what has happened with Medicare and Medicaid.

### Summary

A number of problems beset our health care system. In contrast to other industrialized countries in which health care is viewed as a service, the health care system in the United States has the dual (and sometimes conflicting) objectives of service and profit. The system is indeed prospering. The United States is now spending substantially more on health care per capita than other industrialized nations. Yet a number of other countries have lower infant mortality rates and longer life expectancies. Such statistics suggest other countries are providing lower-cost health care that is as good as or better than ours.

There are other problems in the health care system. The system is focused on treating people *after* they become ill, with little attention being given to preventing illnesses from occurring. It is increasingly being recognized that lifestyle (including exercise, diet, sleep patterns, and stress-reduction patterns) largely determines whether illness will occur and influences the recovery process. People need to realize that they, not their physicians, have the major responsibility for their own health.

The poor and racial minorities have higher rates of illnesses and shorter life expectancies. Largely because of the profit motive, urban low-income areas and rural areas are generally underserved by health care services.

The profit motive has also led to unnecessary diagnostic and treatment approaches being used, including diagnostic tests, medication and drugs, and surgical operations. A more devastating problem is harmful care; it is estimated that 10 percent of practicing physicians are incompetent.

Health care for the elderly is becoming a national disgrace. Many of the elderly lack access to high-quality care and their medical conditions are often misdiagnosed and their treatment is often inadequate.

Individuals with a physical disability are discriminated against in a variety of ways. They are the object of cruel jokes, treated as inferior, and sometimes assumed to be mentally and socially retarded. They have been excluded from public schools, hampered by architectural barriers, and bypassed by employers.

AIDS has emerged as a major health problem. The two primary ways in which it is transmitted from one person to another is through sexual contact and through sharing of intravenous needles. Many misconceptions surround AIDS that have caused those identified as having the HIV virus and those who have AIDS to be shunned and discriminated against.

The use of life-sustaining medical equipment has raised a number of moral, ethical, and legal questions. Should such equipment be used to prolong the life of someone who is terminally ill and in considerable pain? How should death be defined? Should society seek to keep alive people who have such a severe cognitive disability that they will never be able to walk or even sit? Can society afford to continue to expand the use of such costly life-sustaining equipment? Should assisted suicide be legalized for persons who assist the terminally ill to end their life by suicide?

The high costs of medical care, which are still rapidly increasing, have become an issue of national concern. Illnesses now can threaten a family's financial stability. The high costs are also a threat to the economic stability of our country. There are a variety of reasons why medical expenses are so high: the profit motive, high costs of technological advances, increasing life span, third-party financing, inadequate health care planning, increase in malpractice suits, and increased specialization by doctors.

A number of possibilities are available to resolve each of these problems. Some suggestions include increasing admissions to medical schools, permitting doctors to advertise their services and fees, training more physician assistants and paramedics, expanding use of generic drugs, encouraging patients to seek a second opinion before consenting to an operation, developing more preventive medical programs, expanding the use of health maintenance organizations, and developing a national health insurance program.

CHAPTER 12

*Education*

In 1957 the United States and Russia were in an unofficial race to be the first to place a satellite in orbit. The race became a symbol of international honor and prestige. Russia won when it successfully placed *Sputnik I* into orbit. Why did the United States lose? There were numerous reasons; however, the general public blamed the American educational system for neglecting subjects that were vital to national survival. For example, one outspoken critic, Max Rafferty, stated, "Instead of offering a four-year program of studies in mathematics, history, foreign languages, and other disciplines, high schools encouraged students to divert themselves with ceramics, stagecraft, table decorating, upholstering, and second-year golf."[1] The American educational system was called on to provide greater emphasis on mathematics, natural sciences, and other courses that would enable our country to compete successfully with Russia.

The educational system has frequently been called on to resolve or alleviate social problems. For example, it is currently being called on to reduce racism and sexism by developing new curricula designed to change the attitudes of school-age children. It is expected to provide students of low-income families with the education and job training skills that will enable them to escape a life of poverty. The educational system has a function of identifying and referring for treatment those children who have emotional problems and those who abuse alcohol and other drugs. It is a mechanism for conveying antidelinquent values and it is required to refer children suspected of being physically abused, neglected, or sexually abused to protective services agencies.

Education, which in the past has frequently been called on to solve other social problems, is now recognized as a social problem itself, because it is not meeting the expectations of society. Education is in a crisis of controversy and indecision. The self-confidence, morale, and motivation of teachers are down. Schools have been accused of perpetuating, rather than alleviating, social inequality for the poor and for minorities. Although some recent improvements have occurred, student scores on achievement tests are substantially lower than they were thirty-five years ago.[2] Some inner-city schools are so victimized by vandalism and violence that students and teachers are more concerned with survival than with education. This chapter:

♦ Summarizes problems school systems currently face.

♦ Presents proposals for improving education.

♦ Presents proposals for improving educational opportunities for low-income children and minority children.

## Problem Areas in Education

A number of crises and problems surround education. This section will examine specific problems, concerning the quality of education, equal access of minorities and the poor to adequate education, confusion as to the goals of education, and intolerable working conditions for teachers in some school settings.

### THE QUESTION OF QUALITY

A number of indicators raise questions about the quality of education in the United States. Mean SAT (Scholastic Aptitude Test) scores on the verbal-reasoning section and on the mathematics-reasoning section of today's high-school students are lower than they were thirty-five years ago. The SAT is taken annually by about 1 million high-school students who aspire to college. From the mid-1950s to the mid-1960s the scores were fairly constant, ranging from 472 to 478 on the verbal-reasoning section, and from 495 to 502 on the mathematics-reasoning section. In the second half of the 1960s, both scores began to decline and continued to do so until around 1980, when the mean verbal score was 424 and the mean mathematics score was 466. Since 1980 there has been a slight increase, although scores are still significantly below what they were thirty-five years ago.[3]

In 1996 the U.S. Department of Education released the results of the Third International Mathematics and Science Study.[4] This study compared forty-one industrialized nations according to math and science tests taken by eighth graders. American eighth graders ranked twenty-eighth in math tests and seventeenth in science tests. (The top three in math were Singapore, Korea, and Japan; and the top three in science were Singapore, Czech Republic, and Japan.)

It is estimated that at least 3 million adult Americans cannot read or write at all.[5] Furthermore, more than ten times that number are "functionally illiterate"; that is, they cannot perform many of the reading, writing, and math tasks necessary to satisfactorily function in an industrial society.[6] The increasing need for an educated work force in our increasingly complex technological society has accentuated the problem of illiteracy.

In tests of geographic knowledge, students in the United States rank dead last among students tested who live in industrialized nations.[7] In a recent study, young people (ages eighteen to twenty-four) from Canada, France, Germany, Japan, Mexico, and Sweden knew more about the U.S. population than young Americans did.[8]

In 1993 the U.S. Department of Education released the results of a survey showing that nearly half of all adult Americans read and write so poorly that they have trouble holding decent jobs.[9] The survey found that nearly half of all Americans over age fifteen cannot write a short letter explaining a billing error or use a calculator to figure out the difference between a sale price and a regular price.

The National Commission on Excellence in Education summarized the educational problem in the United States as follows: "The educational foundations of our society are presently being eroded by a rising tide of mediocrity that threatens our very future as a nation and a people."[10]

Two explanations have been offered for the decline in student achievement in the United States, neither of which has been proven. One holds the school systems responsible, whereas the other places the cause in societal changes.

The first explanation asserts that school systems responded to the protests of the 1960s by changing their curriculum. At that time there were nationwide protests against racial inequality, the Vietnam War, and the role of traditional institutions (such as education) in our society. In response, many school systems reduced the number of required courses and gave students greater choice in course selections. As a result, for many students there was a decline in the amount of time spent in courses designed to teach basic skills. Such softening of the school curriculum, it has been asserted, led to the decline in achievement scores.

The second explanation focuses on societal changes since the mid-1960s. Students now spend much more time watching television—more time, in fact, than at any other activity except sleeping. Because children watch television more, they spend less time reading books and therefore do not read or write as well. Furthermore, with the advent of the computer age, youngsters are spending much of their time playing computer games and thereby devoting

*even less* time to reading and writing. There have also been changes in the family. The proportion of single-parent families has risen dramatically. Also, in two-parent families *both* parents are now more likely to be employed outside the home. Thus parents may be less involved with the school system and may not monitor their children's homework assignments as closely. A similar assertion (not yet proven) is that there has been an increase in the proportion of dysfunctional families. Being raised in a dysfunctional family not only adversely impacts academic performance but also generates personal problems that sometimes lead to anger, violence, or substance abuse.

Whatever the reason or reasons, there is considerable pressure on school systems to make changes so that students will improve their basic skills of reading, writing, and arithmetic.

## EQUAL ACCESS

An equalitarian society has a responsibility to provide equal opportunity for a high-quality education of all its citizens. Our society has generally failed to meet this responsibility, especially with respect to minority groups and the poor.

A number of studies have found social class to be the single most effective predictor of achieving in school.[11] Students from the middle and upper classes tend to achieve higher grades, stay in school longer, and get higher scores on standardized achievement tests. There are two primary explanations for this relationship—one focuses on family background and the other on school systems.

The family background explanation ascribes the inequality to the fact that lower-class children live in a very different environment from middle- and upper-class children. The theory asserts that lower-income homes tend to have fewer magazines, newspapers, and books. Parents tend to have less education and thus children are less apt to be encouraged to read, as their parents are less likely to act as role models to encourage reading. Because lower-class families tend to be larger in size and are more apt to be headed by a single parent, it is said, their children are likely to receive less guidance and educational encouragement. Because of such factors, poor children may be less likely to view education as a means to achieving in society and less likely to develop educational goals. Also, poor children are more apt to be hungry and undernourished, which tends to inhibit their motivation to learn. In contrast, middle- and upper-class families tend to a place a higher value on education and therefore tend to put more time and effort into helping their children do homework so as to do well in school.

School systems are primarily geared for educating middle- and upper-class students. Students who live in wealthy tax districts benefit from more money spent on their education than students who live in poorer districts. Nearly 50 percent of the funds for public schools in this country come from local school district taxes.[12] Because most of this money comes from property taxes, school districts with numerous expensive homes have much more revenue for their schools. (Roughly 40 percent of public school revenues come from state taxes, and 10 percent come from federal taxes.)[13]

In Illinois, for example, the richest districts spend about six times as much per student as the poorest districts.[14] In New York state, the richest districts spend nearly eight times as much as the poorest.[15]

Ironically, those who live in poorer school districts generally pay a higher percentage of the assessed value of their property in taxes than people who live in wealthier districts. One study on education concluded:

> It is unconscionable that a poor man in a poor district must often pay local taxes at higher rates for the inferior education of his child than the man of means in a rich district pays for the superior education of his child. Yes, incredibly, that is the situation today in most of the fifty states.[16]

Most teachers have middle-class backgrounds, which may mean they are better able to establish relationships with middle- and upper-income children, as they have more in common. There is also evidence that teachers expect less of poor children academically and behaviorally than they expect of middle- and upper-class children. In turn, low-income students tend to respond to such expectations by underachieving and misbehaving.[17] Thus the expectation of low achievement and misbehavior becomes a self-fulfilling prophecy (see Box 12.1).

Many school systems place students in one of several different tracks or ability groups. In high school, the so-called most promising are placed in college preparatory courses, whereas others go into "basic" or vocational classes. Lower-class and students of color are much more likely to be placed in the basic or vocational track[18] and are not exposed to college-oriented math, science, and literature.

In addition, because such students have little contact with college-bound students, they are less apt to aspire to a college education or if they do, to graduate. Without a college education, they have very limited opportunities to obtain high-paying jobs.

The small proportion of low-income and students of color who do pursue a college education generally do not have the financial resources to attend prestigious colleges and universities. Also, they have more difficulty competing academically with wealthier students, partly because they have to work (at least part-time) to offset some of their expenses.

Students of color are particularly apt to have inferior educational opportunities. Until 1954 blacks attended segregated schools in the South that were markedly inferior to those attended by whites. In 1954 the U.S. Supreme Court in *Brown v. Board of Education*, ruled that racial segregation in public schools was unconstitutional. Although *de jure* (legal) segregation ended, *de facto* (actual) segregation remained in many communities with significant proportions of nonwhites. Schools in such communities tend to remain segregated because of a pattern of de facto segregation in housing. To deal with this problem, the Supreme Court ruled that school districts must seek racial balance in schools. In many school districts school busing is used to attain a racial balance. Studies indicate segregation has been reduced *within* school districts but has increased *between* districts.[19] This increase is largely due to "white flight," that is, whites leaving the inner cities and moving to suburbs. In some communities, courts have ordered busing between school districts, and some whites have responded by sending their children to private schools. Chicago's public schools are a classic example of de facto segregation. Although these schools are now improving, some authorities have called this the worst school district in the country. The city's public school system is about 90 percent non-white, whereas the private school system is primarily white.[20]

Ironically, today there is less racial segregation of schools in the South than in other parts of the United States, and the North has become the most heavily segregated region in the country.[21] Much of northern segregation is due to housing segregation.

Surveys have found that most Americans now favor school integration, but most African Americans and whites are opposed to busing programs to achieve school integration.[22] In many large cities (such as Baltimore, Chicago, Cleveland, and Detroit) public schools are approaching 90 percent minority enrollment.[23]

Three decades of school busing have failed to deliver all the benefits its boosters hoped for and its critics demanded. Scores of studies generally agree that white students do not suffer academically from school integration via busing.[24] Integration via busing appears to improve the academic performance of African-American students, but mainly in the primary grades, not in junior high or high school.[25]

There have been other benefits of integration via busing. African Americans who attended elementary and high schools with whites are substantially more likely to attend white-majority colleges, get jobs in desegregated workplaces offering higher pay, and have white friends as adults.[26] Also, African-American students who go to integrated suburban schools rather than segregated city ones are less likely to drop out of high school, get in trouble with the police, drop out of college, or bear a child before age eighteen, and they are more likely to have white friends and live in integrated neighborhoods.[27] Whites also benefit from attending school with African-American students, because they learn more about diversity and tend to more thoroughly confront their racial stereotypes.[28]

Are the benefits of school busing worth the costs? This is a very complex issue, and as yet there is no definitive answer. The financial costs of busing children from one school district to another are high. Many authorities in both white and nonwhite neighborhoods are now increasingly arguing it would be better to use the money currently spent on busing to improve school facilities. Critics of busing also note that busing is inconsistent with the concept of neighborhood schools (in which the schools in the neighborhood become centers for educational, social, and recreational interaction for residents in a community). Critics also assert that busing for integration purposes almost always becomes a major obstacle for parental involvement in the school system, due to the long distances created between the location of the schools and the residences of the parents. (Extensive parental involvement is associated with higher quality educational achievement of students; parental involvement leads to teachers, parents, and school administrators working together to improve school facilities and to develop innovative programs to instruct students.[29]) As noted in Chapter 6, African-American leaders, recent U.S. presidents, and prominent educational authorities are moving away from advocating busing to achieve integration.

## Box 12.1

## The Pygmalion Effect

According to Greek mythology, Pygmalion was a king of Cyprus who made a female figure of ivory that was brought to life for him by Aphrodite (the Greek goddess of love and beauty). Robert Rosenthal and Lenore Jacobson performed an intriguing experiment to demonstrate that teachers' expectations of students can increase students' IQ scores. They called this self-fulfilling prophecy the Pygmalion Effect.

These experimenters began by giving a standard IQ test to students in eighteen classrooms of an elementary school. (The teachers were told the test was the Harvard Test of Inflected Acquisition—no such test exists.) The researchers then randomly selected 20 percent of the students and informed their teachers that the test results showed these students would make remarkable progress in the coming school year. When the students were retested eight months later, those who had been predicted to be remarkable achievers showed a significantly greater increase in IQ scores than the others. The researchers concluded this increase was due to the higher expectations of the teachers, and to the teachers then working more intensively with these students. If the expectations of teachers do indeed affect student achievement, lower-class and minority students may well be at a disadvantage as most teachers are white, from middle-class backgrounds, and have a tendency to expect less from lower-class and minority students.

*Source:* Robert Rosenthal and Lenore Jacobson, *Pygmalion in the Classroom* (New York: Harper and Row, 1969).

Have desegregation programs decreased racial prejudice? Research shows mixed results. Some studies show a decrease in prejudice, whereas others show that prejudice remains the same or even intensifies.[30] In communities in which desegregation takes place in an atmosphere of cooperation and good will, prejudice tends to be reduced. However, desegregation programs that are court ordered in an atmosphere of antagonism and misunderstanding are unlikely to reduce prejudice. In recent years the Supreme Court appears to be less aggressive in mandating that busing be used to achieve desegregation. For instance, the Court has stated that there must be proof that schools

*Multi-ethnic high school students work at computers at a magnet school.*

are intentionally discriminating against minority students before busing is ordered.

In 1991 the Supreme Court declared that busing to achieve integration, when ordered, need not continue indefinitely, although the Court did not say precisely how long is enough. The ruling allows communities to end court-ordered busing if they can convince a judge they have done everything "practicable" to eliminate "vestiges of past discrimination" against minorities. In many inner cities, minority students continue to be segregated in dangerous, crowded, and inferior schools.

Urban Latinos and African Americans are not the only ones who have inferior educational opportunities: Native Americans, Alaskan Eskimo, and migrant workers also lack access to high-quality schools. Many Native Americans attend reservation schools, which are inferior in quality.

For Latinos, bilingual/bicultural education is an issue of intense debate. (There is also controversy about whether black English should be taught in inner-city schools that have high proportions of African-American students.) With bilingual/bicultural education, students are taught wholly or partly in their native language until they can speak English fairly fluently, and in some cases longer. One side asserts that preserving the culture and language of minorities is a worthwhile (or essential) goal of public education. The opposing side asserts that minority students will be best prepared to compete effectively in American society if they are "immersed" in English-language instruction; moreover, bilingual (using black English or Spanish) education is expensive and reinforces separateness, because it is a factor in keeping people of color living in ethnic communities.

Given all the above factors, it is not surprising that there are significant differences in educational achievement between whites and African Americans, and between whites and Latinos. Latinos and African-American students are substantially more likely to drop out of high school as compared to whites.[31] Latinos and African Americans (as compared to whites) have substantially higher rates of being functionally illiterate—that is, unable to read or write a simple sentence in any language.[32] (There are very few jobs in our society for the functionally illiterate.)

## CONFUSION AS TO THE GOALS OF EDUCATION

There is agreement that school systems should teach the basic skills of reading, writing, and arithmetic. However, considerable controversy exists over what other values, knowledge, and skills schools should teach.

- Feminists criticize school systems for teaching and perpetuating sexism—for example, by discouraging females from pursuing careers in science and math (technologically oriented college majors often lead to the highest-paying jobs in our society).

- Schools have been criticized for helping to perpetuate the class system.

- There is considerable disagreement about the extent to which sex education should be taught in the school system.

- There is disagreement on whether prayers should be allowed in public schools, even though the Supreme Court has ruled that prayers in public schools violate the principle of separation of Church and State.

- There is disagreement about the emphasis that should be placed on teaching such subjects as music, sports, and home economics.

- There is disagreement on the extent to which school systems should be used to combat racism, stop drug abuse, prevent unwed pregnancies, help people with a disability, and reduce delinquency.

- There is controversy over whether schools should focus more on developing the creative thinking capacities of students or on teaching academic content.

- Now that the threat of AIDS has arisen, there is controversy over whether school systems should offer information on contraceptive methods that help to prevent AIDS.

- There is controversy regarding what school systems should teach about homosexuality.

In recent years there has been a conservative trend in our society which in school systems has been expressed in a "back to basics" movement. Educational conservatives are opposed to schools being experimental, to schools being custodial institutions of the emotionally disturbed, to schools being recreational facilities, to "frill" and elective courses, and to "social services" such as sex education. This movement is calling for the establishment of clear standards of achievement for students, "criteria mastery" as the basis for grade promotion, participation by students in varsity sports only when certain grade levels are achieved, increased attention to academic subjects and to the teaching of "core values," more testing and homework, longer school hours, and sterner discipline. The movement also urges that teachers receive salary increases based on merit rather than seniority. (The underlying assumption is that such a system would motivate teachers to do a better job in the classroom.)

Within the "back to basics" movement are controversies. Are goals such as "learning to get along with others" and "communicating effectively" components of a "basic" education? Are "the basics" the same for all students?

A variety of other questions have been raised about education. Should private schooling be financially supported by refunding to those families who send their children to private schools the amounts they spend on public education through taxes? Should public colleges and universities collect more of their funds through higher student tuitions (which makes it more difficult to students of low-income families to attend)? What changes in curriculum need to be made in order for schools to do a better job in training students for the high technology jobs that are opening up in our society? Clearly there is a need for increased consensus on the priorities and goals in education.

## INTOLERABLE WORKING CONDITIONS FOR SOME TEACHERS

In surveys, half of all teachers say that, if they had the opportunity to choose careers again, they would not select teaching.[33] Many factors contribute to disenchantment with teaching: low pay, low prestige, inadequate preparation, increased alternative job opportunities for women, and intolerable working conditions. College graduates can earn substantially more money in many other areas: accounting, engineering, computer science, or sales, for example.

Intolerable working conditions in school systems include some teachers in secondary schools being threatened by students, and even being physically attacked. In some schools, teachers spend as much time at trying to keep peace and order (babysitting) as they do at teaching. There are high rates of drug and alcohol abuse among students, and teachers are forced to confront this issue, often without much preparation. Many school districts have insufficient instructional supplies. High student-to-teacher ratios are another concern—the more students, the more difficult it is for teachers to give individualized instruction.

A 1998 study of violence in schools found that 20 percent of American middle schools and high schools reported at least one serious crime (such as rape or robbery) in 1997. Public schools nationwide experienced (in 1997) more than 11,000 fights in which weapons were used, 4,000 rapes and other sexual assaults, and 7,000 robberies.[34]

Many teachers do not feel adequately prepared to teach protective behavior (such as how to protect oneself against sexual assaults), alcohol and drug abuse education, and similar topics.

An amazing statistic is that fewer than one in five new teachers is still in the profession after ten years; many leave because of the distressing working conditions. The United States ranks last of all the major industrialized nations in how generously it compensates its teachers.[35]

## *Improving Education*
xxxxxxxxxxxxxxxxxxxxx

Michael Rutter and his associates evaluated a number of high schools and concluded what most parents already know: "Schools do indeed have important impact on children's development, and it does matter what school a child attends."[36] Rutter found that the best schools required more homework, maintained high academic standards, had well-understood and well-enforced discipline standards, and yet created a comfortable and supportive atmosphere for students.[37] This section will examine four proposals for improving the school system: increased incentives for teachers, improving the curriculum, parental choice of schools, and extending the school year.

## INCREASED INCENTIVES FOR TEACHERS

Perhaps the only way to encourage more high-quality college students to enter the teaching profession, and to raise the morale of existing teachers, is to increase incentives for teaching. Such incentives include increased pay, expanded in-service training, provision of sufficient school supplies, increased availability for classroom use of high-tech equipment (such as computers, film and videotape equipment), and improved working conditions.

A controversial recommended incentive is the creation of a "master teacher" rank that would recognize and reward ability and dedication to teaching. There now is growing evidence that superior teaching can have immense positive effects on students. Pedersen and Faucher found evidence of a high correlation between outstanding first-grade teaching and later adult success of students, all of whom came from an inner-city neighborhood.[38] Master teachers would be paid substantially more and have added responsibilities, such as curriculum design and supervision of new teachers.

The proposal to create a master teacher rank has become highly controversial. Teachers' unions have generally oppose the concept, fearing that criteria other than ability and dedication (such as favoritism) will be used in making such selections. Unions tend to also be opposed to higher pay and promotion based on merit, as the merit concept conflicts with the preferred union concept of basing pay on seniority.

## IMPROVING THE CURRICULUM

If few new resources are required, practically everyone is in favor of this proposal. However, a major question is: In what directions should the curriculum be improved? As noted earlier, considerable confusion exists as to the goals of a quality education. In the 1960s and early 1970s there was criticism of the rigidity and authoritarianism in schools, which led to increases in the number of electives in high schools and colleges, and a reduction in the number of basic

*The "reading buddies" system, in which an older student tutors a younger one with the same school, is used in many reading programs involving bilingual education.*

"academic" classes. Alternative schools were created for students who found traditional schools to be "stifling." Content was included in history and social studies classes about significant contributions made by Native Americans, African Americans, Hispanics, and other minority groups. New courses were developed that attempted to make schoolwork more relevant to the lives of minority students.

In the 1980s and 1990s concern has shifted to focus on the decline in academic achievement and school systems are returning to stiffer academic programs; in fact, many of the requirements for basic academic courses that were dropped in the 1960s and early 1970s have been reinstated. In the 1980s and 1990s there has been a move toward teaching basic skills (reading, writing, and arithmetic) and a move away from electives (sociology, psychology, or specialized areas of literature and history). As part of this movement, children are also taught to respect authority, be patriotic, and lead moral lives. Some schools have reestablished strict dress codes and sought to curb unconventional behavior.

At the same time, a critical-thinking movement is taking place, which focuses on developing the thinking capacities of students. This approach encourages students to make observations and to critically analyze issues. It stresses class discussions and downplays lectures, it emphasizes critical analysis over rote learning, and asserts critical thinking is best assessed by students analyzing an issue or concept in essay form (rather than through the use of objective tests). In some ways the critical-thinking movement conflicts with the back-to-basics movement. The latter places greater emphasis on learning and remembering facts, whereas the former asserts memorization is much less important than developing thinking capacities.

In 1994 the Goals 2000 Educate America Act was passed by Congress and signed by President Clinton. The law was a sweeping reform program that established the first-ever national goals in the United States for education. The act was intended to make American students more competitive in the world economy, and give parents a way to define educational excellence and measure their local school systems. Participation by states was voluntary, but the act provided powerful incentives in the form of educational grants for school systems that seek to upgrade their classrooms. The eight national goals to be met by the year 2000 are:

1. All children in America will start school ready to learn.

2. The high school graduation rate will increase to at least 90 percent.

3. American students will leave grades 4, 8, and 12 having demonstrated competency in English, math, science, history and geography. Every

school in America will ensure that all students learn to use their minds well so they will be prepared for responsible citizenship, further learning, and productive employment.

4. American students will be first in the world in science and math.

5. Every adult will be literate.

6. Every school in America will be free of drugs and violence and will offer a disciplined environment.

7. Schools will encourage parental involvement in education.

8. Schools will promote professional training for teachers.[39]

Very little progress (if any) has been made in implementing these goals. Conservatives attacked the goals as a "federal power grab" and "an attempt to have government determine official knowledge."[40] Local school boards (who have considerable control over what is taught in their school systems) have a tradition of wanting to set their own policies of what is taught. For all practical purposes, there are now few initiatives to achieve the Goals 2000. Americans agree that our educational system needs to be improved, but there is vast disagreement on what the curriculum goals should be.

## PARENTAL CHOICE OF SCHOOLS

Under a parental choice system, not only are parents entitled to enroll their children in public schools outside their geographical district, but also the state tax dollars go to the system that wins the enrollment. By creating market incentives, the thinking goes, academically superior schools should thrive, while inferior schools would have to either improve their performance or face bankruptcy. A voucher system is usually used for implementing a "parental choice system." The voucher system is a program in which the government gives vouchers to students that may be used to pay for education at any school that they or their parents choose.

Parental choice of schools is currently being tried in a number of states, including Minnesota, Iowa, Nebraska, and Arkansas. Initial findings indicate that the reasons parents and students opt out of one school and for another are often unrelated to academics.[41] In some cases the parents select schools with lower educational standards in order to increase the chances that their son or daughter will graduate—or will graduate with higher grades. Other parents pick schools near their work for convenience reasons. Some parents select schools that will increase the chances of their son or daughter playing on a varsity sports team. In many cases transportation problems force parents to select the school located closest to their home.

A major problem with parental choice of schools is that it has the potential to undermine the neighborhood-school concept. This concept asserts that the neighborhood school should be a center of community living, with its facilities being used by both youngsters and adults for a variety of purposes: education, recreation, leisure activities, social gatherings, sporting events, and community meetings. If parents in a neighborhood send their children to a variety of different schools, the neighborhood school will not become a center of community life.

Another drawback of parental choice is that many children are not in a position to travel to far-away schools. Such children (some of whom are already educationally disadvantaged) may then be "left behind" in the worst districts, which become further impoverished as money follows students to better-financed schools.

## EXTENDING THE SCHOOL YEAR

Elementary and secondary schools in the United States are in session an average of 180 days a year. In contrast, Japan's schools are in session an average of 240 days a year. On average, as a result, Japanese students attending twelve years of school receive the equivalent of sixteen years of schooling in America.[42] Comparisons with other advanced nations show a similar disparity.[43]

In 1994, the National Education Commission on Time and Learning found that high schools in the United States require students to spend barely 41 percent of classroom time on academic subjects.[44] Little notes:

> The typical high school student's schedule—"1st period: Driver's ed; 2nd period: AIDS awareness; 3rd period: Counseling"—is looking less and less like a classical education.[45]

The National Education Commission on Time and Learning found that high school students in the United States spend only three hours a day on

**Table 12.1**  *Time Required for Academic Subjects in High School Classrooms (over Four Years)*

| Country | Average Hours |
|---------|---------------|
| Germany | 3,528 |
| France | 3,280 |
| Japan | 3,170 |
| U.S.A. | 1,460 |

(The academic subjects were defined to be English, science, mathematics, civics, languages, and history.)

*Source:* Rod Little, "The Endangered Summer Vacation," *U.S. News & World Report,* May 16, 1994, 12.

English, science, math, civics, languages, or history—half of what is spent on academic courses in Germany, France, and Japan.[46] In 1994 this Commission recommended boosting class time on these basic academic subjects to an average of 5.5 hours per day, and the Commission strongly recommended extending the nation's school year.[47]

A strong case can be made for this suggestion. In a review of one hundred research projects, Toch found that in nine out of ten instances student achievement rises with the amount of time in class.[48] Toch notes:

> A 1989 study of students taking an international math test found that Japanese students had studied 98 percent of the precalculus and calculus topics on the test, while their U.S. counterparts had been taught only 50 percent. Half of the Japanese performed as well as the top 5 percent of Americans.[49]

Research also reveals that students lose a lot of ground educationally while letting their minds lie fallow during the summer. Teachers spend on average the first month of the fall semester reteaching material forgotten over the summer.[50] The problem is particularly acute for students from impoverished families because they often have fewer opportunities to learn during summer. One study found that affluent students gain an average of one month of knowledge during the summer, while disadvantaged students lose three to four months.[51]

Extending the school year into the traditional summer break would also assist working parents who have younger children with child-care arrangements during the daytime.

## Toward Equal Educational Opportunity

As noted earlier, educational opportunities for minorities and the poor are inferior in this country. Nearly everyone agrees that there should be equal educational opportunity for all. But there is considerable disagreement on how this can be achieved. Three proposals for progressing toward equal educational opportunity are:

1. Reforming school financing to spend an equal amount of money on each student's education.
2. Establishing special compensatory educational programs for disadvantaged students.
3. Integrating students from different ethnic backgrounds into the same school.

### REFORMING SCHOOL FINANCING

Schools in wealthy districts tend to receive considerably more money per student than schools in poor districts. At the present time, a majority of the revenues for school districts in practically all states comes from local property taxes. Decaying inner cities are especially hard-pressed to finance school systems, and many schools in these areas are inferior.

There is growing opposition in the United States to using property tax dollars as the primary source of revenue for funding school systems. Property tax payers on fixed incomes (such as the retired elderly) are increasingly unable to pay the annual large increases on their property tax bills. Taxpayers in Michigan in 1993 voted to abolish using property tax revenues to fund the public school system in that state. In 1994 voters in Michigan approved a constitutional amendment to raise the state sales tax and cigarette tax as the primary sources of supporting the state's schools. One result of this action in Michigan is a movement towards equalizing among school districts the amount of money spent on each student's education.[52] Will other states follow this approach?

Another suggestion to equalize the amount of money spent on each student's education is for the federal government to pay for all primary and secondary education, giving the same amount of money per student to each school. Critics of this approach assert that schools in this country have excelled because of local control and involvement. If the funding shifted to the federal government critics say,

Box 12.2

## Schools Without Failure

In 1969 William Glasser wrote *Schools without Failure* (New York: Harper & Row), which has had considerable impact on improving teaching. Glasser's concepts are as relevant today as they were two decades ago. The major concepts of Glasser's approach are summarized as follows.

Glasser asserts that a major problem of school systems is that they are organized in such a way that most students experience failure. He is critical of schools for a variety of reasons. Getting an A is considered the paramount goal in schools; because only a few students get a majority of A's, most do not feel successful. Memorizing is more highly valued than developing thinking capacities. (He believes education is the process of developing thinking capacities.) Glasser asserts that thinking (including creative, artistic, and fun uses of students' brains) is drastically downgraded in schools. Also, schools do not deal with real-life problems faced by children. Relevance is frequently absent from the curriculum; as a result, children do not transfer classroom learning to problem solving outside of school and thus do not gain the motivation to learn.

Glasser notes:

Unless we can provide schools where children, through a reasonable use of their capacities, can succeed, we will do little to solve the major problems of our country. We will have more social disturbances, more people who need to be kept in jails, prisons, and mental hospitals, more people who need social workers to take care of their lives because they feel they cannot succeed in this society and are no longer willing to try [p. 6].

For a child to succeed in this world, she or he has to develop a positive identity (sense of self). Children who develop a failure identity are unlikely to succeed. Instead, they are likely to become angry, depressed, alienated, lonely, or hostile and may express their failure identity through delinquency, withdrawal, or development of emotional disturbances.

Glasser theorizes that there are two needs that must be met for establishment of a positive or success identity: love and self-worth. If these two needs are unmet, then the child will develop a failure identity. If these two needs are met, the child will develop a success identity and will pay off society many times over by being a responsible, contributing citizen.

Because home conditions in many families are less than desirable, many children do not receive the love or the sense of self-worth that they need. When they

---

the result would be greater federal control and increased "red tape," as a huge federal bureaucracy would undoubtedly evolve.

## COMPENSATORY EDUCATION

Many authorities believe that special programs and extra assistance would improve achievement levels of the poor and minorities. A variety of programs already exist.

Project Head Start gives preschool instruction to disadvantaged children. Evaluations of the results of Head Start indicate students who attend are better prepared for starting first grade than disadvantaged students who do not attend Head Start.[53] Unfortunately, the benefits of the program tend to diminish after the students no longer receive services. Coleman and Cressey indicate disadvantaged students continue to benefit when they continue to receive extra help from programs such as Title I of

the Elementary and Secondary Education Act.[54] Coleman and Cressey conclude:

> Don't stop the programs after only a few years. Disadvantaged students should continue to receive help as long as they need it, which in many cases would probably be until their final years of high school. . . . It would certainly take a lot more money to provide help for all the students in all grades who need it, but such an investment would pay enormous dividends in terms of a healthier, more competitive economy, lower rates of crime and welfare dependency, and, most important, a more just society.[55]

More school districts have Pupil Services departments that seek to assess the academic, social, and emotional needs of children who are not progressing well in school. Once an assessment of a child is completed, programs are developed to meet the unique learning needs of the child. A wide variety of services may be provided, depending on the identified needs. There are special classes for the emotionally disturbed

cannot fulfill their needs at home, Glasser asserts, they must have the opportunity to do so at school or they will develop a failure identity. Because every child attends school, schools are in a unique position to identify children who are starting to develop a failure identity.

Teachers need to be better trained in identifying children with failure identities. Colleges of education should provide more content on identifying these children and also should put greater emphasis on developing the relationship capacities of education majors.

Glasser asserts that perhaps the greatest strength of a quality teacher is to be able to form positive relationships with students. Teachers need to be able to convey that each student has a sense of self-worth. Teachers must also be able to convey that they sincerely care about the well-being of each student. Those students identified as beginning to develop a failure identity need to be referred to Pupil Services for help, or the teacher needs to find a way to make the classroom a success experience for these (and all other) students.

Glasser recommends that more emphasis be placed on the teaching of personal development: being assertive, learning to solve life's problems, improving relationships, handling unwanted emotions, learning to express one's sexuality responsibly, learning to handle stress, and so on.

Group problem-solving meetings should be held daily in classes. Such meetings would focus on identifying alternatives for solving the problems that students are encountering at school and in their lives. The topics to be discussed would often be brought up by the students themselves (for example, relationship difficulties they are having with someone). Such discussions should take place in a supportive, positive atmosphere. Blaming and fault finding should be minimized or eliminated entirely. The atmosphere needs to be one in which everyone's opinion is equally valued.

According to Glasser, students should not be separated into tracts, because those placed in lower-level tracts are likely to view themselves as failures. He also recommends abolishing the current grading system of A-B-C-D-F and replacing it with a system of competence criteria for each course. For example, in a mathematics course, a student would have to be able to perform a predetermined level of mathematical computations in order to pass the course. Students who achieve these standards would receive a P (for pass) on their report card. Students who do superior work and who help other students who are not doing as well may be awarded an S (for superior work). Students who do not achieve the standards would not receive any grade, and no records would be kept of classes that students do not pass. For basic academic courses, students would be required to repeat the classes until they successfully achieve the established competency levels.

and for those with learning disabilities. Counseling is sometimes provided. Some students are referred for drug abuse, and some are referred for visual or hearing difficulties. Pupil Services departments are staffed by a variety of professionals—school psychologists, social workers, and guidance counselors. In 1975 Congress passed the Education for All Handicapped Children Act, now known as PL 94–142. This law addresses the numerous physical, developmental, learning, and social-emotional problems that hamper the education of children. In sweeping legislation, the law mandated that all school districts identify students with these problems and then develop specialized programs to meet their needs. Unfortunately, many low-income school districts, because of financial constraints, have not been able to meet the objectives of this bill.

In many states programs are being developed to prevent children from dropping out of school. Some school districts have dropout rates approaching 50 percent, and the national average is over 10 percent.[56] Dropping out represents an enormous loss to those individuals and to society because of lost potential productivity. The estimated lifetime earnings of high school graduates are over $200,000 higher than those of dropouts.[57] Programs for "at-risk" students are a response to the need to help high school students stay in school and learn practical job skills.

Some elementary and secondary school systems now have reading, writing, and arithmetic programs during the summer for students who need assistance in these areas. A variety of compensatory educational programs have been established at the college level as well. These include noncredit courses in English and mathematics, tutoring, and various testing programs. Many colleges have special provisions for the admission of minority students who do not meet standard admission requirements, and such students are encouraged to utilize the educational opportunity

*Native American children participate in a Head Start program in Acoma Pueble, New Mexico.*

programs that are available. (Students who attended inferior elementary and secondary school systems in inner cities are often two to four grade levels behind in reading, writing, and arithmetic and therefore need educational opportunity programs to have a chance to succeed in college.)

Educational opportunity programs have become an accepted part of most colleges and universities. A stickier question involves special admissions of minority students to graduate and professional schools. Supporters assert that these affirmative action admissions are attempts to compensate for the inferior school systems and other discriminations that minorities have been subjected to in the past. On the other hand, because competition is intense for the limited admissions into these schools, white students complain that they are the victims of reverse discrimination—that they are being rejected even though their entrance exam scores are higher than those of some minority students who are accepted. The legal status

of this affirmative action policy has not as yet been fully resolved.

## EFFECTIVE INTEGRATION

As discussed earlier, school busing has been used to attempt to integrate students within school districts. Many whites in large cities have responded by moving to suburbs or sending their children to private schools. Some big cities, through court orders, are experimenting with merging suburban school districts within inner-city school districts and then busing children within each district. The extent to which such merging will occur is questionable. There is a major problem with distance, as some suburban communities are so far from inner cities that students would have to spend a large part of their day on a bus. Most white parents in suburbs would not raise serious objections to a small number of inner-city children being bused to their schools in the suburbs. However, most suburbanites (fearing potential violence and a lower-quality education) would object to their children being bused to inferior school systems in inner cities. Many white parents, if faced with such a court order, would probably respond by placing their children in private schools.

The ideal way to integrate neighborhood schools is through integration of residential areas, so that neighborhood schools are then automatically integrated. Such integration would provide ongoing opportunities for interracial cooperation and friendships for children and for adults. The chances of this proposal working, however, are minute. People of different ethnic and racial groups generally are reluctant to live together in the same neighborhood. In addition, many members of minority groups cannot afford to live in affluent neighborhoods, and white residents of such neighborhoods object to having low-cost housing built in their communities.

Another possible avenue toward integration is through the use of "magnet" schools in cities. Magnet schools are ones that offer special courses, programs, or equipment. Examples would be a fine arts middle school or high school and a school emphasizing curriculum in the area of computer science. Proponents of magnet schools hope that placing such schools in inner-city areas would draw students from suburbs because of the excellent educational opportunities they could offer.

The prospects of significant federal help for inner-city schools in the near future are not bright. In this era of trying to reduce the federal deficit through budget cutbacks, the chances of the enactment of a bold new federal program to channel resources to financially distressed school districts are remote.

John E. Farley summarizes the significance to all Americans of providing equal educational opportunities for minorities and the poor:

> If the overall effectiveness of the educational system is poor, American productivity will suffer, and our standard of living will likely fall in our increasingly competitive world. Likewise, if we fail the large and growing proportion of our young people who are African American, Hispanic, or from low-income homes of any race, the result will be the same. Failing to educate those who account for such a large and growing share of the future labor force will have a similar destructive impact on America's productivity and its standard of living.[58]

## Summary

▨▨▨▨▨▨▨▨▨▨▨▨▨▨▨▨▨▨▨▨▨▨▨

Education, which in the past has been called on to resolve a variety of social problems, is now recognized as a social problem itself. Education is currently facing a variety of crises and problem areas.

A number of indicators raise questions about the quality of education in this country. For example, scores on the Scholastic Aptitude Test that is annually taken by high school seniors are significantly lower than they were thirty-five years ago.

A second problem area is that school systems are providing inferior educational opportunities for the poor and for members of minority groups. Much less money is spent per student on education in low-income school districts and in school districts in which high proportions of minority students live. In our society, achieving in school is highly correlated with socioeconomic status.

A third problem area is the confusion as to the goals of education. There is agreement that schools should teach the basic skills of reading, writing, and arithmetic. However, considerable controversy exists among different interest groups as to the other learning goals that education should strive to attain.

A fourth problem area is intolerable working conditions for teachers in some school settings. Intolerable conditions include low pay, low prestige, confronting drug and alcohol abuse among students, physical threats from students, insufficient instructional supplies, high student-to-teacher ratios, and physical attacks from some students.

Four proposals of improving education in this country are increased incentives for teachers, improved curriculum, parental choice of schools, and extending the school year. One of the controversial proposed incentives for teaching is the creation of master teacher positions that would reward excellence in teaching. A major problem with seeking to improve the curriculum is lack of agreement as to what that curriculum should include. Parental choice runs counter to the neighborhood school concept.

Three proposals were presented for seeking to work toward equal education opportunities for low-income and minority students: (1) reform school financing to spend an equal amount of money on each student's education, (2) establish special compensatory educational programs for disadvantaged students, and (3) integrate students from different ethnic and racial backgrounds into the same schools.

# CHAPTER 13

# Big Business, Technology, and Work

*I*n 1993 Walt Disney Chair Michael D. Eisner was paid an astounding $197 million. (Much of this amount was in stock options that were financed by the corporation.)[1] That works out to an average pay of nearly $4 million per week, and over $750,000 per day of a five-day work week. ($750,000 is more than the total that many workers in the U.S. earn in their lifetime.) Although Eisner's earnings are exceptional, the twenty-five highest paid corporate executives in the United States earn more than $4 million a year.[2] In 1996 Microsoft Corp. Chairman Bill Gates earned in one year (through his company and by investing) $20 billion—a rate of $400 million per week![3] The average American worker is dwarfed by the sheer size and power of big business. Technological advances— at an all-time historical high—have been a major spur to the growth of large corporations.

This chapter:

♦ Describes the impact of big business on our lives and examines the relationships between big business and government.

♦ Summarizes how technological changes benefit and endanger our lives.

♦ Describes three work-related problems (alienation, unemployment, and occupational health hazards).

♦ Presents proposals to combat problems related to big business, technology and work.

## *Big Business*

XXXXXXXXXXXXXXXXXXXXX

This chapter will cover three separate but interrelated areas: big business, technological advances, and work problems.

### BRIEF HISTORY OF THE GROWTH OF CORPORATIONS

Large-scale corporations began to evolve after the Civil War when there was a burst of industrial activity. At first an evolving corporation was owned and controlled by an individual or by a family. At the turn of the century big business was dominated by business magnates who came to be known as *robber barons*— among them John D. Rockefeller, J. P. Morgan, and Andrew Carnegie. Robber barons exploited workers with long hours, low pay, and unsafe working conditions. They engaged in cutthroat competition and certain business practices that laws since have been enacted to prevent (bribery of governmental officials and collusion to set high market prices).

Since the turn of the twentieth century, corporations have continued to grow in size through expansion and mergers with other companies. Legal ownership of most corporations has been dispersed among thousands (and in some cases millions) of shareowners. Complex and sophisticated bureaucracies have evolved to administer such corporations. Because it would be too expensive and cumbersome for all stockholders to be involved in important corporate decisions, the stockholders elect a board of directors to set general policies and to monitor the running of the corporation. Corporations also employ executives and managers to make day-to-day business decisions.

### IMPACT OF BIG BUSINESS

Our country's economy has changed dramatically since two hundred years ago when most people earned a living by working on small farms. Now, only 2 percent of the workforce are farmers.[4]

Today our economy is dominated by national and multinational corporations. *National corporations* are large corporations that confine their business activities primarily to the country in which they are headquartered. *Multinational corporations* are economic enterprises that are headquartered in one country and extensively pursue business activities in one or more foreign countries. Examples of multinational corporations include General Motors, International Telephone and Telegraph (ITT), and Texaco. The annual sales of some multinational corporations, such as General Motors, exceed the Gross National Product (GNP) of many nations—not only Third World countries but even some highly industrialized countries such as Switzerland.[5]

The United States is headquarters for the largest number of multinational corporations, but many other countries (Japan and Britain) also headquarter multinational corporations. Examples of foreign-based multinational corporations that do considerable business in this country are Toyota Corporation and Swiss Nestlé Company.

The size of corporations can partly be grasped by realizing that if all the world's largest enterprises (including governments) were ranked according to size, one-half would be corporations.[6] Some corporations, such as Exxon and Ford, have assets worth billions of dollars.

Antitrust laws prohibit single corporate giants from monopolizing an entire industry. To get around such laws some corporations have expanded into related fields, buying out distributors and suppliers. Others have become *conglomerates,* large firms that own businesses in many areas. Some conglomerates are composed of businesses in unrelated areas—Philip Morris (a tobacco company), for example, owns Oscar Mayer (a meat-processing company), and General Electric owns NBC.

Although monopolies are prohibited, oligopolies have emerged for many important products. An *oligopoly* is created when a few producers dominate the market. Automobile manufacturing in the United States, for example, is dominated by General Motors Corp., Ford Corp., and Chrysler Corp. About 60 percent of all the goods and services produced in the United States (excluding those produced by the government) are made in industries dominated by such oligopolies, ranging from automobiles and gasoline to beer and aspirin.[7] In many oligopolies, one giant is often much larger and stronger than others. General Motors, for example, produces more automobiles than all other American car manufacturers combined.

The danger of oligopolies is that they can easily set market prices rather than allow prices to be set by the principles of competition. The largest corporation in an industry frequently becomes the *price setter,* that is, it sets the prices for its products, and other corporations set theirs at a similar level.

Some oligopolies have *interlocking directorates.* Because it is illegal for a member of a board of directors of one large firm to sit on the board of a competing firm, directors of competing companies sometimes serve on the board of a *third* firm in a *different* industry. This arrangement allows powerful individuals to sit on boards of several giant corporations exchanging plans and ideas with other corporate leaders. Powerful members of boards of competing firms also communicate over dinner and at other social occasions, as they tend to be members of the same country clubs and social registers.

The lives of American workers are directly affected by the actions of large corporations. Employees are affected by salary plans, salary increases, level of job satisfaction, promotion policies, and medical and pension plans. Many workers are also investors and shareholders of companies, so the financial status of such companies affects the pocketbooks of those workers who invest. Because workers also buy and use the goods and services provided by large corporations, the price and quality of the products affect workers as consumers. Workers' environment is also affected by pollution-control practices of corporations.

Large corporations have the power to influence the lives of people throughout the world in a variety of ways. By opening a new plant in an area, a corporation can provide jobs and revitalize the economy. By closing a plant and relocating, it can throw thousands of employees out of work. It can pollute the air or spoil a river or lake with industrial pollution.

## VOICES IN CORPORATE MANAGEMENT

A modern corporation is a complex and vast financial network. Numerous interactions and relationships are involved between a corporation and: competitors, stockholders, directors, managers, workers, subcontractors, unions, local and national governments, and the surrounding communities. These relationships are complex and frequently changing. All of these groups have a voice in how a corporation will run.

Wealthy stockholders have a strong voice in corporations. Although many Americans own stock, most stock is owned by a small group of wealthy individuals and families. It is estimated that the wealthiest one-half of 1 percent of the American people own about half of all privately held stock.[8] How can an individual or family control a corporation by owning a small percentage of its stock? All corporations are controlled by their investors—the stockholders—and the investors who own the largest blocks of stock have the most power in the corporation. Thus, someone who owns only 20 percent of a corporation's stock but is the largest stockholder can effectively control the corporation; in essence, the largest stockholder's real power is equal to the corporation's total value, because his or her wishes can determine company policy. Institutional stockholders (banks, investment companies, and insurance companies) also hold major blocks of shares, which enables them to have a voice in the general directions a corporation will take.

Stockholders who own small amounts of shares generally do not have the knowledge or power to have a voice in directing a corporation. Such stockholders usually vote (often by mail-in ballot) only for or against the recommendations made by the current management. The technical knowledge needed to make productive and profitable decisions is usually beyond the grasp of small stockholders.

Many corporate decisions about policy directions are made by corporate managers, who have become

known as the *corporate technostructure*. These corporate managers are largely anonymous executives and managers who devote their entire careers to developing the technical skills and knowledge to manage a corporation. The security of their jobs is determined largely by profit-loss statements. High profits result in huge bonuses and large salary increases for such executives. Declining profits are the major reason corporate presidents lose their jobs.[9]

## BIG BUSINESS: BENEFITS AND ABUSES

The existence of powerful multinational corporations has generated considerable controversy. Some observers commend these corporations as being innovators and as having developed the technological advances (such as televisions, automobiles, computers, and telephones) that have markedly improved our living standards. The United States economically is the most influential country in the world, largely because of multinational corporations. Multinational corporations are commended for producing high-quality products for consumers at low costs. They also provide millions of jobs in this country and in foreign countries. Some people see the growth of such corpo-

rations as a step toward world unity; through linking the economies of the world, it is claimed they are laying the foundations for increased cooperation among governments. They also are credited with helping to expose other countries to the benefits of our culture and to the merits of a democratic, free-enterprise system of government. Worldwide, perhaps the most envied characteristic of the United States is its economic power, which has been largely achieved by national and multinational corporations.

Critics of multinational corporations have a very different view. They view such corporations as lawless "international bandits" who exploit small countries through paying low wages to workers and through depleting their natural resources (minerals, oil, and forest resources). In small countries such corporations have an image of making substantial profits, and often an image of bribing government officials and the wealthy elite, with the masses receiving no benefits. Reliance on foreign technology decreases political and economic independence. Economic decisions in small nations are often heavily influenced by foreign corporate executives. Such decisions generally result in foreign corporations profiting, often at the expense of the masses. Corporate executives are viewed as being motivated to make profits for their corporations rather than improving living conditions for the masses.

One of the most blatant abuses of corporate power occurred in Chile in the 1960s. International Telephone and Telegraph used its international influence to attempt to stop Salvador Allende (a Marxist) from being elected to power. ITT's efforts failed, as Allende was elected. Allende confiscated a number of Chilean-based American commercial holdings, including those of ITT in Chile. After the election, ITT conspired with the U.S. Central Intelligence Agency to create economic turmoil and overturn Allende's government. Partly as a result of this conspiracy, Allende and many of his supporters were assassinated in a military coup. A military dictatorship took over, which soon became notorious for its brutality and oppression.[10]

In all countries critics assert that corporations pollute the air and water and despoil the land. Corporations are also criticized as having too much influence on politicians, with political decisions often being made to benefit corporations rather than the masses.

Recently there have been charges that major multinational corporations are hiring children at extremely low wages. For example it has been claimed that the Nike Corporation subcontracts with local employers in Asia to hire about 75,000 Asian workers to make Nike shoes. In some cases children as young as eleven years old, who earn about $2.20 a day, are producing sneakers at a cost of about $6 a pair. The sneakers are then sold in stores in the United States for $80 or more per pair, and are advertised by celebrities like Michael Jordan, who earns about $20 million a year for making Nike commercials.[11]

Corporations are primarily motivated by the profit motive, and there have been numerous well-publicized instances of corporations being involved in criminal and unethical practices. There are frequent reports of multinational corporations paying bribes to government officials in foreign countries in exchange, for example, for contracts to build tanks and jet planes.

In 1970 Ford Corporation hastily developed the Pinto to compete with the popular foreign compact cars. In preproduction crash tests, Ford discovered that the fuel tank would rupture and explode when rear-end collisions occurred. Ford had a safer gas tank but decided not to use it because it would cost $11 more per car. From 1971 to 1976 the Pinto was marketed with the unsafe gas tank. More than five hundred people burned to death after rear-end collisions in Pintos during this time period and thousands more were severely injured in car burnings. Although Ford was well aware of the danger, it did not install a safer tank until 1977. In 1978, the U.S. Department of Transportation finally ordered a recall of all 1971 to 1976 Pintos so that a metal shield could be installed to protect the gas tank. It was the most expensive recall in automobile history. Ford was so embarrassed that it dropped a line from its radio advertisements, which read, "Pinto leaves you with that warm feeling."[12]

Collusion by several companies to set uniformly high prices, called *price fixing,* is common. It is definitely illegal, but it is so common that in 1959 some businessmen in a price-fixing arrangement wrote a letter to the U.S. Attorney General's office inquiring what could be done about one of their associates who was *not* complying with a price-fixing arrangement. It could well be that price fixing costs consumers more than any other single crime.

One of the most publicized price-fixing cases involved Westinghouse, General Electric, and McGraw-Edison in the heavy electrical equipment industry. Corporate officials of these companies admitted they had met secretly for years to set prices. They made a point of not associating in public, had a secret code, and used only public telephones. The conspiracy was estimated to have cost the public more than $1 billion.[13]

In 1994 it was charged that tobacco companies suppressed evidence from their research studies for more than thirty years that indicated smoking was a major health hazard. In 1997 and 1998 some executives of tobacco companies acknowledged such evidence had been suppressed.

Many companies have used a variety of illegal tactics to get ahead of their competitors, or even to drive them out of business. One tactic is industrial espionage, which involves a variety of strategies. Bugging offices and telephones to obtain confidential information on what competitors are doing is one approach. Bribing an employee of a competing company for confidential information is another. Using computers to gain access to data stored in computers of competing companies is yet another approach. Some big businesses seek to bankrupt small competitors by selling a product at a loss; once the competition goes out of business, the price can be substantially raised to more than recover the losses incurred when the price was low. Another way of bankrupting small competitors that are buying essential raw materials from a giant corporation is for the giant corporation to stop selling the materials or charge exorbitant prices for them.

## Is There a Power Elite?

In 1956 C. Wright Mills' *The Power Elite*[a] was published, a book that has generated one of the most heated debates in the social sciences.

Mills' thesis is that in the United States there is a small unified ruling class, which he named the *power elite*. Mills asserted that this power elite is composed of a coalition of people in the highest ranks of the economy, the government, and the military.

A major source of the unity of this power elite is the common social background of the members. They are born and raised in upper-class and upper-middle-class white families living in urban areas. They attend Ivy League colleges where they get to know each other. Through such common backgrounds they come to have similar attitudes about the world and their influential roles. They are members of social clubs and frequently socialize with each other, which further ties them together. They seek and secure leadership roles in corporations, the military, or the government. The older generation, which holds leadership positions, assists the younger generation in obtaining similar leadership positions. This power elite does not represent some great conspiracy, but its members frequently meet socially and professionally, which results in a coordination of their activities.

Mills identified two other levels of people in a hierarchical structure that are largely guided by the power elite. At the bottom of the ladder are the masses viewed as being ill informed, unorganized, and virtually powerless. Between the masses and the elite is the "middle level" of power. Mills viewed Congress as an illustration of a middle level of power. Mills asserted that at the middle level of power there is some true competition between interest groups. Those at the middle levels of power usually refrain from making decisions that would antagonize the power elite.

More recent advocates of the elitist school accept most of Mills' observations, but reject his inclusion of the military leadership in the power elite.[b] They recognize the importance of the military, but view the crucial decisions as being made by the economic-political elite.

About the same time that Mills was advocating his view, David Riesman arrived at very different conclusions.[c] His view, called *pluralism*, recognized there is a large mass of people who have little power. But he argued that critical decisions are not made by a power elite, but are decided in a contest between many competing groups. He viewed interest groups as "veto groups," as he asserted their main objective is to seek to block policies that threaten their interests. While Mills saw growing concentration of power, Riesman saw growing dispersion of power. While Mills saw common interests among powerful groups, Riesman saw divergence.

Current pluralist thought generally agrees with Riesman, except for his view that the main objective of interest groups is to stop unacceptable proposals. Current pluralists hold that interest groups not only seek to stop threatening proposals but also actively seek to present favorable proposals and are taking action on their own behalf.

In the continuing controversy between pluralism and power elitism a major point of difference is how unified or competitive those in power positions are. Elitists view them as being quite unified, and pluralists view them as being basically competitive.

a. C. Wright Mills, *The Power Elite* (New York: Oxford University Press, 1956).

b. John E. Farley, *American Social Problems* 2d ed. (Englewood Cliffs, NJ: Prentice-Hall, 1992) 484–85.

c. David Riesman, *The Lonely Crowd*, abridged edition with a 1969 preface (New Haven: Yale University Press, 1969).

## RELATIONSHIP BETWEEN BIG BUSINESS AND GOVERNMENT

The United States, Canada, and other countries have capitalist economies. In addition, a number of countries that used to advocate communism (a philosophy firmly opposed to capitalism) are now incorporating elements of capitalism into their economies. Such countries include Russia, Czechoslovakia, and Romania. A capitalist economy has three essential components:

1. Private or corporate ownership of capital goods (such as factories)

2. Investments that are determined by private decision rather than by government

3. Competition in a free market that determines the prices, distribution, and production of goods

The classic statement of how an ideal free-market capitalist society should operate was made by Adam Smith in 1776.[14] The theory that became known as the invisible hand theory asserted that individuals who work for personal profit will be motivated to work hard and to produce as much as possible. Significantly, private greed will be transformed into public good as workers seek to produce what consumers desire most. What is needed for this to occur is a free market (which functions as an "invisible hand"). The profit motive will motivate manufacturers to produce the goods the public demands, and competition will ensure that those goods are reasonably priced. According to Smith, the government should not interfere with the market, which will function best if left alone to be regulated by the law of supply and demand. Smith's ideas were adhered to by many governments.

However, there have been many changes in how big business has evolved since Smith's era. Rather than compete with one another, some producers found it to their advantage either to agree to set high prices or to limit the supply of goods so that prices would rise. Some businesses found it to their advantage to dispose of waste materials by dumping them into rivers and lakes. Others took no action to prevent deadly fumes and toxic chemicals from being spewed into the air. Many big businesses profited from requiring workers to work long hours at low pay in relatively unsafe conditions. Some businesses obtained tariffs, patents, tax breaks, and other special privileges from the government to reduce free competition. In addition, trade associations, chambers of commerce, and other organizations were formed that encouraged businesses to cooperate, rather than compete, with one another.

Governments of all nations have therefore found it necessary to enact laws and standards to regulate businesses. Environmental laws prohibit industrial pollution, antitrust legislation discourages the formation of monopolies, and fair trade laws prohibit bribery, false advertising, and selling products below cost.

Governments also regulate the amount of money in circulation and the interest rates on loans. By increasing the money supply and lowering interest rates, a government can stimulate an economy so consumers can buy more. An adverse consequence of such actions is that the rate of inflation may increase. Restricting the money supply and raising interest rates help reduce inflation, but also slows down economic growth and increases unemployment.

The government also taxes corporations. Higher taxes usually reduce economic growth, whereas lower taxes usually stimulate economic growth. However, lowering taxes usually results in the government having to cut back on its services, as there are lower tax revenues. Interestingly, governments rather than corporations are now viewed (rightly or wrongly) by the public as being responsible for the growth or decline of an economy.

When giant corporations are on the verge of bankruptcy, governments have sometimes stepped in to keep these corporations solvent. For example, Lockheed Corporation received a special loan in the 1970s from the federal government; so did the Chrysler Corporation in the early 1980s.

The government has also created a number of agencies to regulate various aspects of businesses—for example, the Federal Trade Commission and the Food and Drug Administration. Although these agencies have the function of regulating businesses in the public interest, they often end up helping the industries rather than serving the public interest. They often become an ally of the industries they are supposed to regulate and may provide such services as protecting existing businesses from new competition. This alliance has been created partly by the government's hiring policies. Governmental regulator agencies frequently hire former employees of the businesses they are supposed to regulate. (The government defends this practice on the grounds that the personnel have an in-depth knowledge about how such businesses operate.) After serving in a regulatory agency, many of the personnel are hired (or rehired) by the industries they regulated. If a regulatory agent anticipates future employment in an industry she or he is regulating, the regulator is apt to perform in a way that will please the industries being regulated.

Another area of concern about the relationships between large corporations and governments is the enormous political power wielded by major corporations. In the United States, millions of dollars are spent by practically every viable candidate for Congress. Where do candidates obtain such funds? Much of their campaign funds are obtained from contributors associated with major corporations. Once elected, many politicians feel an obligation to "repay" these large contributors by proposing legislation and voting for legislation that is requested by the major contributors. If the elected politicians fail to "repay" their major contributors, the major contributors will throw their support behind someone else in the next election. Some observers assert many elected officials are "owned" by their major contributors.

# The Military-Industrial Complex

In his farewell address to the nation in 1960, President Dwight D. Eisenhower warned against the growing influence of what he called the military-industrial complex. Hundreds of companies (such as Lockheed, General Dynamics, and Rockwell International) do most of their business with the military, through government contracts. As a result, military-business industries and the armed forces have many interests in common. In fact they are highly interdependent. For example, many former military officials currently work in military-business industries.

Military-business industries often charge exorbitant amounts to the military. For one thing, much of the military's budget is classified as "secret," so it is difficult to know how the money is spent. Also, Congress generally gives generous allocations to the military because they are heavily lobbied and do not want to appear unpatriotic. Finally, senators and representatives from states with high concentrations of defense industries or military bases generally are vigorous supporters of military appropriations, because their constituency back home benefits from such appropriations.

The military, military-business industries, and organized labor all have influential lobbyists in Washington, who lobby for military spending. Military spending has always had a high priority in federal spending, and little is done to punish military-business industries that charge exorbitant amounts—to do so would also make the Defense Department look bad.

It is nearly impossible to accurately determine the true costs of building nuclear submarines, sophisticated tanks, and aircraft carriers. Such equipment is highly complex, has classified parts and functions, and has hundreds of thousands of components. What is known, however, is that the military has paid:

- $748 for $7.61 pliers
- $100 for 25-cent compressor caps
- $387 for 10-cent washers
- $37 for 5-cent screws
- $114 for 9-cent batteries
- $511 for 60-cent lamps
- $110 for 4-cent electronic diodes
- $435 for $17 clay hammers
- $2,043 for 13-cent nuts
- $9,606 for 12-cent Allen wrenches
- $1,118 for 31-cent plastic covers for toilets
- $714 for $46.68 electrical bells
- $75 for 57-cent metal set screws

Every nation has to choose between guns (military spending) and butter (social welfare spending). In most presidential administrations, guns have a higher priority than butter. President Eisenhower, a highly decorated five-star general, warned that the military-industrial complex could dominate the nation.

*Source:* Daniel J. Curran and Claire M. Renzetti, *Social Problems*, 3rd ed. (Boston, MA: Allyn and Bacon, 1993), 121; Jack Anderson, "We Can Help End Government Waste," *Parade Magazine*, Jan. 20, 1985, 14–15; Robert A. Kittle, "Pentagon Bogs Down in Its War on Waste," *U.S. News & World Report*, June 4, 1984, 73–75; Julia Malone "No Bargains: Military Buys Pricey," *Wisconsin State Journal* March 19, 1998, 2A.

## *Technology*

Technology is a double-edged sword. Every major technological innovation has both freed humans from previous hardships and created new, unanticipated problems. Technology can be defined as the totality of means employed to provide objects necessary for human comfort and sustenance. Bell defines *technological change* as "the combination of all methods (apparatus, skills, organization) for increasing the productivity of labor and capital."[15]

Technological innovations are causing major changes in the types of work available to Americans. Blue-collar and agricultural jobs are declining, whereas high-tech jobs—computers and communications for example—are increasing.[16] In this century, the nature of the U.S. economy has shifted from manufacturing to services. People laid off or discharged in declining industries (such as the steel industry) face immense obstacles in obtaining employment that pays comparable wages. On the other hand, people trained for high-tech positions have excellent career opportunities. Technological advances are a boon for some and a disaster for others. For example, automobile executives welcome the use of robots in assembly lines to cut production costs, whereas unemployed assembly-line workers with mortgages curse their use.

A growing concern among many educational, political, and civil rights leaders is that, as our society

# Technological Disasters

In addition to solving problems technology has also created a lot of disasters. Following are some of the most publicized technological disasters in the past four decades.

1958—An accident occurs at a plutonium weapons facility in the Soviet Union that contaminates 1,500 square kilometers with radioactive debris.

1961—More than 2,500 deformed babies are born to European women who used the drug thalidomide to relieve discomfort during pregnancy.

1967—A fire erupts during prelaunch tests and kills the three-man crew of what was to have been the first U.S. *Apollo* flight.

1971—The cabin of *Soyuz II* (a Soviet satellite) decompresses upon reentry and kills the three crew members.

1976—A Swiss-owned chemical plant near Milan, Italy, explode and spews into the air a cloud of the highly toxic gas dioxin, which kills tens of thousands of birds and animals and results in over 500 children developing skin rashes.

1978—Residents of Love Canal, a suburb of Niagara Falls, learn that their neighborhood was a dumping ground for over 20,000 tons of toxic waste in the 1940s and 1950s. Studies find high rates of cancer and birth defects among residents. More than 2,000 residents relocate in the next three years.

1979—An accident at a nuclear reactor at Three Mile Island in Pennsylvania releases a cloud of low-level radioactive gas into the environment.

1984—A chemical storage tank explodes at a Union Carbide plant (owned by a U.S. corporation) in Bhopal, India. A cloud of lethal methlyisocyanate gas is released, killing more than 2,000 and injuring tens of thousands.

1985—More than 2,000 people are killed worldwide in plane crashes.

1986—U.S. space shuttle *Challenger* explodes after takeoff, killing the crew of seven, including the first teacher in space.

1986—An explosion at a Soviet nuclear reactor at Chernobyl spews lethal radioactive debris over Russia and Europe. Twenty-five die within a few weeks, and tens of thousands may have their lives shortened due to exposure to radiation.

1987—On September 28, Air Force Captain Lawrence Haskell loses control of a $280 million B-1 bomber when it runs into a pelican in the air above Colorado. The plane crashes, and three of its six crew members are killed.

1989—In March, 10.8 million gallons of crude oil spill into Prince William Sound in Alaska when the petroleum tanker *Exxon Valdez* runs aground. It is the worst, and most expensive, oil spill in our nation's history. Exxon spends $2 billion in an attempt to clean up the crude oil, and recovers only 5 to 9 percent of the oil spilled. Millions of birds, mammals, fish and other living things are killed. Local fishing industries (and many other businesses) are ruined.

1994—In September, an Estonian ferry carrying passengers from Estonia to Sweden capsizes, killing over 900 people, in one of history's worst ferry disasters.

1996—On July 17, Flight 800 left John F. Kennedy International Airport, soon exploded, and all 230 passengers and crew were killed. The exact cause of the explosion has not as yet been determined.

*Sources:* William L. Chaze, "Living Dangerously," *U.S. News & World Report*, May 19, 1986, 19–25; William Kornblum and Joseph Julian, *Social Problems*, 6th ed. (Englewood Cliffs, NJ: Prentice-Hall, 1989), 404; Matti Huuhtanen, "Death Toll Surpasses 900," *Wisconsin State Journal*, Sept. 30, 1994, 11A.

---

comes to depend more on computers and on other high technology, only a select portion of the population will have the skills needed to function well in our society. Those who lack such skills may find themselves trapped in lower social class positions.

In some ways technological advances are gradually making the world a "global village," a term coined by futurist Marshall McLuhan.[17] Through advances in communications (television, satellites, the Internet, telephone networks, fax machines), people on this planet are tied more closely. People all over the world can watch the same sporting events or hear the same political speeches. Will this closeness increase our sense of world citizenship? Or will the distraction of television lead to a decline in reading skills, and will calculators and computers lead to a decline in mathematical skills?

Technological advances have contributed to the growth of large industries and corporations and vastly increased efficiency and productivity. But, as will be expanded on later, such advances are again a double-edged sword, as they have led many workers to feel alienated from their jobs.

## FUTURE SHOCK

In his book *Future Shock* prominent futurist Alvin Toffler advanced the thesis that technological advances are occurring at a much faster pace than at any other time in human history.[18] These advances are radically changing lifestyles and are also creating tremendous social and psychological stress for individuals. Former values and traditional customs are being destroyed, with few meaningful values replacing them. Toffler views technological advances as being out of control, as occurring so rapidly that people cannot adjust to them. Toffler asks, "Can one live in a society that is out of control? That is the question posed for us by the concept of future shock."[19] According to Toffler, future shock is a general sense of confusion and anxiety about the present and the future, brought about by rapid technological changes. As compelling as Toffler's argument is, there is little concrete evidence that rapid technological change leads to a sense of confusion and anxiety.

## CULTURAL LAG

One of the most prominent theories involving technology is cultural lag. According to William F. Ogburn, "A cultural lag occurs when one of two parts of culture which are correlated changes before or in greater degree than the other part does, thereby causing less adjustment between the two parts than existed previously."[20] Many examples of cultural lag can be cited. All of the following technologies have been developed, but are they desirable? Embryo transfer techniques make it possible for a woman to be a biological mother without being pregnant. Artificial insemination has led to surrogate mothers. The technology for abortion is available. The technology to sterilize rapists and persons with a cognitive disability is available. The technology is available to sustain the life of comatose, terminally ill individuals even though virtually no hope exists for return to a life of quality. The technology to clone a human is available.

According to Ogburn, the development of social welfare services sometimes lags behind technological advances. For example, despite advances in health care that enable the elderly to live longer, our society has been slow in developing meaningful social welfare services to meet their needs. Also, robots and other forms of automation are rapidly displacing many blue-collar workers, but our society has been slow in developing retraining programs for the unemployed whose skills are now obsolete.

Ogburn notes there also may be "technological lags." For example, our society has come to depend on the availability of relatively inexpensive fossil fuels. Crude oil resources are rapidly being depleted. As a result, technological breakthroughs are needed to maintain the supply of low-cost energy. Former Presidents Reagan and Bush convinced many Americans that it is feasible to develop a Star Wars defense system against an attack by nuclear missiles, but technological breakthroughs are needed to make this happen.

## *Work*

"What do you do for a living?" is a question commonly asked when two strangers meet. Work is a central focus of our lives. Work not only enables a person to earn money to pay bills; it can also help develop a sense of self-respect, provide a circle of colleagues and friends, and be a source of self-fulfillment. A challenging job can help a person to grow intellectually, psychologically, and socially. Work also largely determines a person's place in the social structure. We have considerable choice in the vocations we select, and vocational choice is a key factor in determining our social status. We are largely defined by our work.

Our society values the "work ethic"; that is, we consider work to be honorable, productive, and useful. Unemployed able-bodied persons are often looked down on.

## A BRIEF HISTORY OF WORK

Work was not always esteemed. The ancient Greeks viewed work as a curse imposed on humanity by the gods. They regarded it as an unpleasant and burdensome activity that was incompatible with being a citizen. Citizens sought to have extensive leisure time so they could further develop their minds. The Greeks therefore justified slavery on the basis that it freed citizens to spend their time in philosophic

## Max Weber and the Protestant Ethic

In 1904 German sociologist Max Weber published what has become one of the most provocative theories in sociology. In *The Protestant Ethic and the Spirit of Capitalism*,[a] Weber asserted that the Protestant ethic encouraged and made possible the emergence of capitalism. Weber theorized that the ideas of Puritanism (advocated by Martin Luther and John Calvin) provided the value system that led to the transformation from traditional society to the Industrial Revolution.

Weber noted that Puritan Protestantism embraced the doctrine that people, divinely selected for either salvation or damnation, could do nothing to alter their fate. People never knew for sure whether they were destined for eternal salvation or eternal damnation. However, they looked for signs from God to suggest their fate. Because they also believed that work was a form of service to God, they concluded success at work (making profits) was a sign of God's favor. They therefore worked very hard to accumulate as much wealth as possible.

Because the Protestant ethic viewed luxury and self-gratification as sinful, the profits acquired were not spent extravagantly, but instead were reinvested into new ventures to increase incomes. Such new ventures included building factories and developing new machines. Thus, according to Weber, the Industrial Revolution began, and capitalism was born.

_____

a. Max Weber, *The Protestant Ethic and the Spirit of Capitalism* (New York: Scribners, 1958).

Early Christians took a slightly more positive view of work. Like the ancient Hebrews, they accepted the idea of work as penance for original sin. But they also believed people needed to work to make their own living and to be able to help those in need. They also thought work had spiritual value, as they associated it with purification and self-denial. Later, certain Christian monks believed that for them work was degrading; that it was morally better for them to beg than to work.

The Protestant Reformation, which began in the seventeenth century, brought about profound changes in social values concerning work. For the first time, work became highly valued. Martin Luther, a Protestant reformer, asserted that labor was a service to God. Since the time of Luther, work has continued to be viewed as honorable and having religious significance.

Another Protestant reformer, John Calvin, had an even more dramatic effect on changing the views toward work. Calvin preached that work is the will of God. Hard work, good deeds, and success at one's vocation were taken to be signs that one was destined for salvation. Calvin preached that God's will was for people to live frugally and to invest profits from work in new ventures, which in turn would bring in more profits for additional investments, and so on. Hard work and frugality came to have great value; idleness or laziness came to be viewed as sinful. The religious group most influenced by Calvin's teachings was the Puritans, who also developed an ascetic lifestyle; that is, they denied worldly pleasures as demonstration of their commitment to their religious beliefs. Calvin's teachings were widely accepted and formed a new cultural value system, which became known as the Protestant ethic. This ethic had three core values: hard work, frugality, and asceticism.

The values of hard work and saving advanced by the Protestant ethic have continued throughout our history. For example, Benjamin Franklin praised these values by noting in several adages:

◆ "A penny saved is a penny earned."

◆ "Remember that time is money."

◆ "After industry and frugality, nothing contributes more to the raising of a young man than punctuality."

◆ "He who sits . . . idle throws away money."

◆ "Waste neither time nor money; an hour lost is money lost."[22]

---

contemplation and cultural enrichment. Aristotle remarked, "No man can practice virtue who is living a life of a mechanic or laborer."[21]

Although the Romans viewed commercial banking as acceptable employment, practically all other occupations were considered vulgar and demeaning. Ancient Hebrews viewed work ambivalently: on one hand, they regarded work as a drudgery and a grim necessity; on the other hand, they saw it as a penance for "original sin." (The Bible asserts that original sin began with Adam and Eve disobeying God in the Garden of Eden.)

Former President Nixon declared in a speech on welfare reform that labor had intrinsic value, that it had a strong American tradition, and that it was consistent with religious teachings. Nixon added, "Scrubbing floors and emptying bedpans have just as much dignity as there is in any work done in this country—including my own. . . . Most of us consider it immoral to be lazy or slothful."[23]

Although we no longer value the frugal, ascetic lifestyle of Puritanism, we still believe strongly in the ethic of hard work. To gain approval from others, an able-bodied person is expected to be employed (or at least receiving job training). People on welfare are often looked down on. There still remains a strong link between amount of income and personal worth; the more people are paid, the more highly they are regarded by others, and the more highly they regard themselves.

People in low-status jobs are generally unable to form a satisfying identity with their jobs. Having an assembly-line job, for example, often leads workers to view themselves as being personally insignificant. They routinely perform the same task day in and day out—such as attaching nuts to bolts. Many such workers feel embarrassed about not having a better job.[24]

Because the status of our work immensely affects our self-concept, a job perceived to be degrading, boring, and dehumanizing can adversely affect our psychological well-being. We judge ourselves not only by how much our job pays but also by whether the job is challenging and satisfying and helps us grow and develop.

## TRENDS IN THE AMERICAN WORKFORCE

Since the turn of the twentieth century, unions have generally been growing in power in this country, which has led to significant pay increases and fringe benefits for employees. Since 1980, however, the power balance between unions and management has shifted more toward management. In a number of businesses, management has been asking that employees take zero wage increases (or even pay cuts), with the threat of moving the business elsewhere or closing the doors permanently. Employees have generally chosen, with considerable reluctance, to accept management's offers rather than to strike and risk losing their jobs.

In the twentieth century the nature of work and the composition of the workforce have changed radically in our society. Seven changes seem especially prominent: the increase in white-collar workers, the emergence of an employee society, specialization, changes in the sex and age composition of the workforce, the emphasis on intrinsic rewards, the growth of low-paying jobs, and outsourcing in a global factory.

*Increase in White-Collar Workers* In colonial times most people made a living working on small farms, either their own or someone else's. We have since moved from an agricultural economy to a modern industrial economy.

In 1990, 27 percent of the labor force were farm workers, and 18 percent were white-collar workers. In 1995, only 2 percent were farm workers, and 58 percent were white-collar workers.[25] The immense productivity of our industrial system has made it possible for 2 percent of the workforce to feed all of us! Farm workers (farmers, farmhands, and farm managers), once the largest occupational group, are now one of the smallest.

White-collar workers (professionals, clerical personnel, sales personnel, managers), once the smallest occupational group, are now the largest. This group surpassed blue-collar workers in terms of numbers in 1956.[26]

Work in industrial societies can be grouped into three categories: primary, secondary, and tertiary.

Primary industry is the gathering or extracting of undeveloped natural resources, such as farming, mining, or fishing. In the early stages of industrialization most workers are employed in this category.

Secondary industry involves turning raw materials into manufactured goods, such as processed food, steel, and automobiles. In the middle stages of industrialization most workers are employed in this category. Most of these workers are blue-collar workers.

Tertiary industry involves service activities of one kind or another, such as dental care, medical services, automobile maintenance, sales, and pest control. In advanced societies such as ours, most workers are employed in service activities, primarily in white-collar jobs. Now, more than 60 percent of our workforce is employed in tertiary industry.[27] Work in this category is generally cleaner and more pleasant than work in primary and secondary industries.

*An Employee Society* No longer are Americans likely to be self-employed, as they generally were in colonial

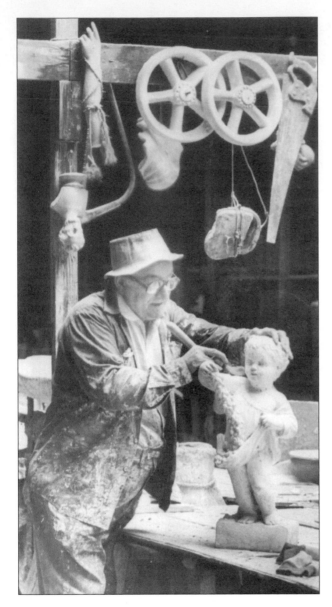

*As work in our society becomes more mechanized, the role of the craftsperson is ever more valued, and the opportunity to earn a living by making something oneself is rare.*

majority of workers are employed by someone else: large corporations, the government, and so forth. Even physicians, who once were largely self-employed as general practitioners, now generally work for a medical clinic or some other organization.

*Specialization* The 1850 census listed a total of only 323 distinct job titles in the United States.[29] There are now more than 35,000 job titles—more than 100 times as many different occupations.[30] Some of the unusual jobs one can choose for a career are clock winder, tea taster, and water smeller. With this extensive specialization, production of goods is now fragmented into repetitive and monotonous tasks, with each worker contributing only a small portion of the final product. A worker on an assembly line commented:

> The assembly line is no place to work, I can tell you. There is nothing more discouraging than having a barrel beside you with 10,000 bolts in it and using them all up. Then you get a barrel with another 10,000 bolts, and you know every one of those 10,000 bolts has to be picked up and put in exactly the same place as the last 10,000 bolts.[31]

Specialization has contributed substantially to the development and provision of highly sophisticated products and services. But it has also created problems. Workers find it difficult to take pride in their work when they realize they are merely a replaceable adjunct to a machine or a process and when they contribute only a small part to the final product. Such specialization often results in job dissatisfaction. Those who are trained for a single, narrowly defined job that later becomes obsolete are often without marketable skills for other openings. Specialization has also created problems of worker cooperation and coordination for managers of organizations. Our society has become highly interdependent because of specialization. With interdependence, disruption in one work area may gravely affect the whole economy. In 1997, for example, employees of United Parcel Services (UPS) went out on strike for about a week, seriously disrupting the U.S. economy which is heavily dependent on products being transported by mail.

*Sex and Age of the Labor Force* The labor force consists of people sixteen years of age and over who are employed or who are actively seeking work (the

times. Less than 10 percent of the workforce now classify themselves as self-employed.[28] A few small-business owners, small family-owned farms, independent shopkeepers, and independent carpenters and artists still remain. But small, owner-operated businesses increasingly are finding it difficult to compete against well-organized corporations and businesses. The vast

unemployed). There have been some significant trends in the composition of the labor force.

Older men are becoming less likely to be in the labor force. In 1954, 40 percent of males over age sixty-five were in the labor force, but by 1995 only 16 percent in this category were in the labor force.[32] Employers are reluctant to hire older workers when younger workers with more recent training are available at lower salaries. Job obsolescence and myths about the unproductivity of older workers also make it difficult for unemployed older workers to be hired.

Women are increasingly entering the labor force. In 1900 only 20 percent of all adult women were in paid employment, compared to over 55 percent at present.[33] Women, however, still tend to be employed in the less prestigious, lower-paying positions (as is discussed further in Chapter 7).

Two groups that have historically had high rates of unemployment or received low pay if employed have been minority-group workers and teenage workers. Unemployment rates are particularly high for non-white teenagers; in some cities more than 50 percent of people in this category are unemployed.[34] Women who work full time are paid, on the average, only about two-thirds of what men who work full time are paid.[35] Nonwhite women, subjected to double discrimination, earn even less.

### Emphasis on Intrinsic Rewards

Intrinsic rewards are rewards that come from the nature of the work itself. Work that offers intrinsic rewards is fulfilling and challenging, helps one grow socially and emotionally, contributes to physical fitness, promotes a sense of accomplishment through the use of one's talents, generates a feeling of self-respect, provides interest and enjoyment, offers an opportunity to meet new friends, and so on. In the past, people took a job primarily for its extrinsic rewards—a paycheck that would enable them to pay their bills. In the last thirty years workers have become increasingly concerned about the intrinsic rewards prospective jobs will provide.[36]

### More Low-Paying Jobs

Despite the increase in the total number of jobs in the American economy in the 1980s and 1990s, average wage and salary income (adjusted for inflation) declined in most industries.[37] A major reason for this trend has been the extensive growth in low-wage jobs. For example, there has been extensive expansion of minimum-wage-paying jobs in the fast-foods industry. There has also been significant expansion of part-time employment, that is, jobs offering less than thirty-five hours of work per week. More part-time jobs are now being created each month than full-time jobs.[38] Employers are also more likely now, as compared to two decades ago, to hire temporary employees (for example, for limited term positions).[39] By hiring part-time employees and temporary employees, employers avoid paying many fringe benefits (such as paying for health care insurance and paying into retirement plans). Another reason for the growth in low-paying jobs is a continued shift of the labor force out of manufacturing and into service jobs. As plants have closed and manufacturing jobs have been exported to less-developed countries, displaced workers have been forced to accept jobs in services and trade, which have twice the proportion of low-wage jobs as the manufacturing sector.[40] Many manufacturing corporations in the 1990s emphasized *downsizing* the number of their full-time employees.

### Outsourcing in a Global Factory

Multinational corporations (corporations that are headquartered in one country and that pursue business activities in one or more foreign countries) are transforming the world's economy with "global factories." Such corporations are no longer confined to producing their products in just one country. High-speed transportation enables such corporations to get raw materials and finished products from one location to another anywhere in the world. Such transportation systems enables multinational companies to take advantage of the supply of cheap labor in developing countries. For example, U.S. baseball manufacturers send the materials for their product—yarn, leather covers, cement, and thread—to Haiti, where baseballs are assembled for wages far below those paid for similar work anywhere in the United States.

Outsourcing is the practice of locating plants that produce products for American markets in Third World nations where the corporation can take advantage of lower wage rates. Outsourcing in effect "exports" manufacturing jobs from the United States to the Third World. (Some authorities have referred to this phenomenon as deindustrialization in the United States.)

# Problems with Work

XXXXXXXXXXXXXXXXXXXXX

## ALIENATION

*Alienation* has a specific sociological meaning: *the sense of meaninglessness and powerlessness that people experience when interacting with social institutions they consider oppressive and beyond their control.* The term "worker alienation" was originally used by Karl Marx. (Perhaps because Marx has been associated with Communism, the subject of worker alienation has tended to be neglected in our country.) Marx suggested that worker alienation occurs largely because workers are separated from ownership of the means of production and from any control over the final product of their labor. They thus feel powerless and view their work as meaningless. Marx described alienation as follows:

> In what does this alienation consist? First, that work is external to the worker, that it is not part of his nature, that consequently he does not fulfill himself in his work but denies himself, has a feeling of misery, not well-being, does not develop freely a physical and mental energy, but is physically exhausted and mentally debased. . . . His work is not voluntary but imposed, forced labor. . . . Finally, the alienated character of work for the worker appears in the fact that it is not his work but work for someone else, that in work he does not belong to himself but to another person.[41]

According to Marx, specialization is a major cause of alienation. With specialization workers are forced to perform an unfulfilling task repeatedly. Because people use only a fraction of their talents, work becomes an enforced, impersonalized activity rather than a creative venture.

Marx believed that worker alienation would eventually lead to such discontent that the workers would band together and revolt against owners. Another reason workers would revolt is that they would realize they were being exploited by the dominant class, who prosper from their toil.

Marx's prediction of a class revolution has not come true in the United States. Marx did not foresee the effectiveness of collective bargaining and new technology in improving the conditions of workers during the twentieth century. Interestingly, even workers in such socialist countries as China and Cuba experience considerable alienation. (Marx had predicted that there would be less alienation in socialist countries.)

It may be that much of the alienation that Marx attributed to capitalistic societies was really caused by industrialism. Workers in this country, contrary to what Marx predicted, continue to have basic trust and faith in the American capitalistic system. Many workers have made financial investments in stocks, bonds, real estate, savings, and so forth. To a significant extent, they are also part of the dominant class. Marx saw only a struggle between two classes—owners and workers. He did not foresee considerable overlap occuring between these classes, nor did he foresee the development of a large middle class that tends to include both investors and workers. Because of Americans' faith in our system and their disdain of Communism, it is highly unlikely that there will be a class revolution in our country in the foreseeable future.

In fact, the working class has not successfully staged a socialist revolution in any industrialized country. The socialist revolutions that have occurred—in the former Soviet Union, China, Cuba, and so forth—have all taken place in developing or preindustrial countries. It is important to note that even China and, especially, Russia are increasingly using the profit motive (a key component of capitalism) as an incentive to work and as a method to stimulate their economies.

In addition, it appears that Marx's theories about the evils of a capitalistic economy are being rejected by many of the societies (such as the former Soviet Union and Poland) that tried to establish economic systems based on Marxist principles. These countries have concluded that, unless they use capitalistic incentives, they cannot motivate their citizens to produce at desired rates. Some authorities are now asserting that Marx's theories about economic production have been tried and tested and have been found to have failed miserably. In terms of productivity, the economies of Eastern Europe that have been based on Marx's theories have fallen far behind those of Western Europe (which have been using capitalistic incentives). In 1990, posters of Karl Marx bearing the caption "Workers of the World! Forgive me" were selling widely in eastern Germany.[42] (Marx had coined the slogan "Workers of the World! Unite.")

***Sources of Alienation*** Alienation has many sources. Specialization has led workers to feel that they have meaningless jobs and are contributing insignificantly to the business. It is difficult, for example, for assembly-line workers to take pride in producing an automobile when they only attach an ignition wire.

Working for a large business or corporation and knowing that you can readily be replaced leads to feelings of powerlessness and lowered self-esteem. Not being involved in the decision-making process and being aware that supervisors do not want workers to "make waves" also lead to feelings of powerlessness and meaninglessness.

In some businesses, machines have been developed to do most of the work. This automation (for example, assembly lines in the auto industry) has led workers to feel they are insignificant cogs in the production process. Even the pace at which they work is controlled by the assembly-line machinery. Jobs that offer little opportunity to be creative also contribute to alienation. Such jobs include typist, receptionist, janitor, garbage collector, assembly-line worker, or telephone operator. Most American workers do not hold jobs they had planned for; they are doing what they do for such reasons as "simple chance" or "lack of choice." As a result, many people feel trapped in their jobs.[43]

Alienation also derives from jobs that do not provide: opportunities to learn, a sense of accomplishment, or the chance to work with compatible people. Many authorities believe that alienation leads to acts of disruption in the production process—work of poor quality, high rates of absenteeism, and vandalism or theft of company property.

*Job Dissatisfaction* Dissatisfaction with one's job is a useful indicator of alienation at work. Studies on job satisfaction show wide differences, according to vocation, in worker satisfaction with their jobs. Many jobs are simply dull. For workers who already earn enough to live adequately, additional income cannot always offset the meaningless of such jobs.

## UNEMPLOYMENT

This section will review the costs of unemployment, identify the groups having high unemployment rates, examine the reasons for high unemployment, and review factors that affect the unemployment rate.

*The Costs of Unemployment* As illustrated in Case Example 13.6 unemployment can have devastating effects. Most obviously, it reduces (sometimes to be low poverty levels) the amount of income that a family or single person receives. Short-term unemployment, especially when one receives unemployment compensation (described in Chapter 9), may have only minor consequences. But long-term unemployment inflicts numerous problems.

Harold Wilensky found that long-term unemployment often leads to extreme personal isolation. Work is a central part of many people's lives. When unemployment occurs, work ties are severed. As a result, many of the unemployed see friends less, cease participating in community life, and become increasingly isolated.[44]

D. D. Braginsky and B. M. Braginsky found that long-term unemployment causes attitude changes that persist even after reemployment.[45] Being laid off (or fired) is often interpreted by the unemployed as a sign of being incompetent and worthless. Self-esteem is lowered, they are likely to experience depression, and they feel alienated from society. Many suffer deep shame and avoid their friends. They feel dehumanized and insignificant and see themselves as an easily replaced statistic. They also tend to lose faith in our political and economic system, with some blaming the political system for their problems. Even when they find new jobs, they do not fully recover their self-esteem.

Harvey Brenner found a strong association between unemployment and emotional problems. During an economic recession, mental hospital admissions increase. The suicide rate also increases, indicating an increase in depression. Also higher during times of high unemployment are the divorce rate, the incidence of child abuse, and the number of peptic ulcers (a stress-related disease).[46] Just the threat of unemployment can lead to emotional problems.

In many cases the long-term unemployed are forced to exhaust their savings, sell their homes, and become public assistance recipients. A few turn to crime, particularly the young. The unemployed no longer enjoy the companionship of their fellow workers. They often experience feelings of embarrassment, anger, despair, depression, anxiety, boredom, hopelessness, and apathy. Such feelings may lead to alcoholism, drug abuse, insomnia, stress-related illnesses, marital unhappiness, and even violence within the family. The work ethic is still prominent in our society: When people lose their jobs, they devalue themselves and also miss the sense of self-worth that comes from doing a job well.

As more and more women have entered the labor force, the consequences of unemployment for single women with children have assumed ever-greater importance. Newman found that middle-class women who experience divorce "typically have to make do

# Case Example: Job Dissatisfaction

Mary and Robert Buyze met in college and were married shortly after Mary graduated in 1991. Bob had graduated a year earlier. Bob majored in history and Mary in psychology. Both shared the American dream of having a home in the suburbs, a motorboat, and two cars. Because both had graduated from college, they were optimistic that they were well on their way. They fantasized about taking a yearly trip to such places as Acapulco, Europe, Jamaica, and Hawaii.

It is now six years later. Bob is twenty-nine and Mary is twenty-eight. They have yet to take a trip and now have two young children. They are deeply in debt, having tried to buy much of their dream with credit. They purchased a run-down "starter" home with two bedrooms that was advertised as a "fixer's delight." Unexpected repairs to the furnace, the roof, and the plumbing have plunged them even deeper into debt, as have medical expenses, food, and clothing for the family.

What is even sadder is that they both have jobs they dislike. Bob has been a life insurance salesman for a small company for the past three and a half years. Bob states:

I took the job because I couldn't find anything else. There were no job openings for historians when I graduated, so I took a variety of odd jobs, none of which I enjoyed. I was a truck driver, manager of a pizza place, taxicab driver, car salesman—and much of the time I was unemployed.

I hoped when I took this job that I would finally be able to make good money. It just hasn't worked out. I hate selling insurance. Most of the time I randomly call people from the telephone directory and urge them to buy a policy. It's like begging for money for a charity. I absolutely despise having to put myself in a position of peddling policies—and being nice and charming to people who at times end up slamming the phone down and hurting my eardrum. But I have no choice, I've got so many bills to pay that I can't afford not to work. I also have to see Mary having to work with the kids

being so young. But, again we have no choice. What really hurts is that both of us are slaving away at jobs we don't like. Yet, with all the bills we have to pay, we hardly are able to buy Christmas presents.

Mary is a clothing store clerk. She also was unable to get a job in her field (psychology). After graduating, she worked for two years as a typist, which paid about the same as her present job—slightly above the minimum wage. She quit being a typist shortly before their first child (Rob) was born; she disliked secretarial work even more than her present job. A few months after Rob's birth, she began working part time in the job she now holds full time.

Mary states:

When I was in college, I guess I was too idealistic. I expected to get a challenging job that would help me grow as a person and also pay well. That just hasn't happened. What I earn now is very little, especially after having to pay the babysitter. This job at times is boring, especially during the months when business is slow. November and December are just the opposite—we're running all the time, and I'm exhausted by the end of the day. It's feast or famine. But my day doesn't end when I leave the store. I've got cooking, washing, and cleaning to do—plus trying to find time to spend with the children. The last four years since the kids were born have been a nightmare—changing diapers, getting up in the middle of the night, taking care of sick kids. Don't get me wrong—I wouldn't trade them in, but some days I really wonder where I went wrong. What really hurts is that we have almost nothing to show for our efforts.

I tell you, some mornings I'm so worn out when I get up and so unhappy with work that tears roll out of my eyes when I drive to work. What's just as bad is that I know that Bob hates his job as much as I do. Increasingly, when he has a bad day, he drinks too much—and that is worrying me more and more. I'm in a dead-end job with no chance for advancement, and I can't afford to give it up. Is this all there is to life?

with 29 to 39 percent of the family income they had before divorce."[47] When these women are in the labor force and experience unemployment, it is often difficult for them to support their families while looking for new jobs. Typically they had interrupted their careers for marriage and child rearing, and they now find themselves less competitive in the labor market than men who have been working more or less continuously.

Widespread unemployment also sharply cuts government tax revenues. When tax revenues are reduced, federal departments are forced to cut services at a time when the services are most needed. Such cuts further add to alienation and despair.

High unemployment also leads to high rates of underemployment. Underemployment occurs when people are working at jobs below their level of skill. College graduates, for example, may be forced to take unskilled road construction work or become clerical workers.

*The Unemployed* In the past two decades, the national unemployment rate has ranged from 4 percent to 11 percent. Official statistics are compiled by the Bureau of Labor Statistics. The bureau, usually monthly, makes a survey of households randomly selected from the total population.

Virtually all of us will be unemployed at some point during our working years. There is some variation from time to time in the groups that are most vulnerable to unemployment. In the late 1970s and early 1980s, unemployment was particularly high among steel workers and automobile workers. In the mid-1970s PhDs in the liberal arts and social sciences had high unemployment rates. In the early 1980s the housing industry was in a slump, and there were high unemployment rates among carpenters and construction workers. In the middle and late 1980s there were high rates of unemployment among workers in the petroleum production industry. In the 1990s businesses and corporations were downsizing their workforces, including administrative positions; as a result, there were high unemployment rates among middle-level managers.

Some groups have chronically high unemployment rates. These groups include African Americans and Latinos, teenagers, women, older workers, the unskilled, the semiskilled, and persons with a disability.

High unemployment among African Americans and Latinos is partly due to racial discrimination. Unfortunately, there is truth in the cliché that minori-
ties are "last to be hired, first to be fired." Another reason for high unemployment is due to their lower average level of educational achievement, which leaves them unqualified for many of the available jobs. (Lower educational levels and lack of marketable job skills are largely due to *past* discrimination.)

High unemployment among women also stems partly from discrimination. Many employers (most of them men) are still inclined to hire a man before a woman, and many jobs are still erroneously thought to be "a man's job." Women have also been socialized to seek lower-paying jobs, to not be competitive with men, and to believe their place is in the home and not in the workforce. (See Chapter 7 for a fuller discussion.)

Myths about older workers—age forty and over—make it more difficult for them to obtain a new job if they become unemployed. They are *erroneously* thought to be less productive, more difficult to get along with, more difficult to train, clumsier, more accident prone, less healthy, and more prone to absenteeism than younger workers (see Chapter 8 for a further discussion of these myths, along with a review of research studies that refute these stereotypes). An additional problem for unemployed older workers is that younger people are often available at salaries far below what the older applicants were paid at their last job.

Unemployment is high for teenagers and young people. This is partly because many of them have not received the training that would provide them with marketable skills.

Employers are willing to hire unskilled workers when they have simple, repetitive tasks to be performed. But unskilled workers are the first to be laid off when there is a business slump. These workers can readily be replaced if business picks up. Highly skilled workers are more difficult to replace. Also, employers have much more invested in skilled workers, as they have spent more time in training them.

Blue-collar workers are more affected by economic slumps than white-collar workers. Industries that employ large numbers of blue-collar workers—housing, road construction, manufacturers of heavy equipment such as tractors, the auto industry—are quickly and deeply hit by recessions and often forced to lay off workers. As noted earlier, the number of blue-collar jobs is decreasing, whereas white-collar jobs are increasing. A major reason for this decline is *automation,* whereby the system of production is increasingly controlled by means of self-operating

Box 13.6

## Case Example: American Dream Becomes Economic Nightmare Through Unemployment

Lorraine and Jim Dedrick thought they had it made. They had a five-bedroom, stone-foundation home on a lake, a landscaped yard, two well-behaved children, a car, a van, a motor-powered boat, and a sailboat. The home, the vehicles, and the boats were bought on time payments. Because both were working, they were confident that they could easily make the monthly payments. Mrs. Dedrick describes what happened.

> My husband worked at Dana Corporation (a car and truck-axle manufacturing plant). He was a crew supervisor and was making over $37,000 a year. I was, and still am, a legal secretary.
>
> When the layoffs started in spring 1993, we didn't think it would touch Jim. He had six years of seniority. But by March of 1994 we knew a layoff was inevitable. Dana Corporation was not doing well financially. When the layoff came in June of 1994, we weren't surprised.
>
> At first we weren't worried. Jim thought it would be nice to have a summer off and looked forward to doing some fishing and some fixing up around the house. Because he was 39 years old and had worked steadily since he was 18, I also thought a few months' break would do him good. He was of course able to draw unemployment benefits, and with my salary I was certain we could get by. Surely Dana Corporation would recover, and he would be called back in the fall.
>
> In late summer, however, a rumor started and quickly spread throughout the plant that Dana was going to close its plant. In September they announced the plant was going to close.
>
> Both of us immediately became alarmed. Jim started looking for other work in earnest. Unfortunately, there were no comparable jobs in the area.
>
> Jim applied at many different jobs but had no luck. I know of nothing worse than to see a once-proud, secure person come home each evening with the look on his face that he has once again been rejected. Jim began developing stomach problems from the rejections, and I started having, and still have, tension headaches. We used to go out a lot, laugh, and have a good time. Now, we not only cannot afford it, we no longer have an interest.
>
> Jim grabbed at every straw. He even went to apply for jobs in Milwaukee and Chicago. In the last year he appears to have aged ten years.
>
> In February of 1995 his unemployment benefits ended. Bill collectors began hounding us. We soon

---

machinery. Examples of automation include the automobile assembly line and direct-dial telephone (which displaced thousands of telephone operators). Robots are now replacing workers in a number of industries, particularly for doing simple, repetitive tasks.

Persons with a disability have very high unemployment rates. There are many stereotypes that contribute to these high rates. There is a tendency in our society to conclude that because a person has a disability in one area, that he or she also has other disabilities. For example, those with a physical disability are sometimes thought to be less intelligent and less effective in social interactions. Numerous studies have found that when people with a disability are hired, they usually dispel all of the negative myths that surround them.[48] Kornblum and Julian conclude: "An overwhelming majority prove to be dedicated, capable workers; they have only a slightly higher than average absentee rate, and their turnover rate is well below average. They are neither slower nor less productive than other workers and have excellent safety records."[49]

At times recent graduates from college and other categories of people seeking employment are susceptible to *under*employment. (Underemployment is a condition in the labor force in which people are working at jobs below their level of skill.) It is crucial that college students (if they want a job in their major field of study) select a major that helps prepare them for desired job opportunities. Admittedly, this is difficult to do. For one reason, job prospects fluctuate. In 1980, for example, there were substantial openings in social service positions. However, after Ronald Reagan was elected president and severe cuts were made in social service positions, the job market in social service programs from 1981 to 1985 was poor. With such rapidly changing job prospects, it is difficult to predict at the time when students are selecting a major what the job prospects will be like when graduation occurs in three or four years. This is one reason why a general

depleted all our savings. We got so many calls from bill collectors that we took out an unlisted telephone number. Never before were we unable to pay our bills.

The months since February have been hell. Increasingly we have gotten into arguments. Whenever I bring my check home, Jim has a pained look on his face, as he feels he's not doing his share. I try to tell him that it's not his fault, but whenever we talk about it he appears hurt and becomes angry.

At the end of February he began to advertise by word of mouth that he was an independent carpenter. He's good with his hands. Unfortunately, the few jobs he got have as yet not even paid for the extra tools he's had to buy. It has only gotten us deeper into debt.

When I drive to work, the tears often fall. It's my only time alone. Driving home I often cry as I think about our situation and know I'll have to face Jim's sad look.

We don't associate much with friends now. They either pity us or have that arrogant "I told you so" look in response to our optimism when Jim was first laid off.

It just doesn't look like Jim is going to be able to get a job in this area. Next week he's going to go to Atlanta—we've heard there are a lot of job openings there.

Dennis, our twelve-year-old son, is alternately sad and angry about the possibility of leaving this area. He's got a lot of friends and loves to go boating, fishing, and sailing. Having to take your son away from something he really loves is one of the most difficult things I'll probably ever have to do.

Karen, our daughter who's fifteen, really had a bad year at school. Her grades fell, and, when we asked her why, she said "What's the use in studying—won't help in getting a job." That remark hurt deeply, probably because it may have a ring of truth in it.

It looks like we're gong to have to give up our dream house on this lake. (Tears came to Mrs. Dedrick as she spoke.) We've lived here for the past five years and really loved it. This is our first real home. We've added on a patio, a bedroom, and enlarged the living room. We also spend a lot of time in painting and fixing it up. It's really become a part of us. If Jim gets a job in Atlanta, we'll be forced to sell. We checked what market prices are, and there's no way we're going to get what we put into this house.

A few years ago we thought we were starting to live the American dream. This past year and a half has been hell. Here we are broke, unhappy, and about to lose our home. At our age starting life over is almost more than we can take.

or liberal arts education, though appearing less relevant to future employment in the short run, may be more useful in the long run. Students who have a solid general education tend to adapt more readily to changing job conditions than students who have had a more narrow, technical education.

*The Reasons for High Unemployment* In recent years, the official unemployment rate has generally ranged from 4 to 11 percent. Why is the unemployment rate so high in this country? The reasons are numerous and complex. First of all, it should be noted that, even when a society has "full employment" there will always be some people capable of working who are temporarily unemployed: there will be some people who are changing jobs; there will be some recent graduates (and recent high-school or college dropouts) who have not as yet found a job; and there will be some people who have had a prolonged illness or other career absence (such as child rearing) who are now

starting to look for a job. It is for these reasons that most countries generally consider they have full employment when the unemployment rate does not exceed 2 or 3 percent of the workforce.

In many areas of the country there are more people in the workforce than there are available jobs. Automation in many industries has reduced the number of workers needed and made certain job skills (such as blacksmith) obsolete. Planting and harvesting machines in agriculture, for example, have drastically reduced the number of people needed in producing food. Picking beans, digging potatoes, and picking cotton and corn once required large numbers of workers, but much work is now done by machines.

From the end of World War II until around 1965 there was a "baby boom," when large numbers of children were born. For the past thirty-five years these baby-boom children have been growing up and entering the labor force in large numbers. The last few decades have also seen women being liberated from the cultural expectations that they should remain at home. Millions of females are now employed or seeking full- or part-time work. This increase in the number of workers seeking employment has added to the unemployment rate.

As discussed earlier, outsourcing in a global factory is exporting manufacturing jobs from the United States to the Third World. For example, global sportswear companies headquartered in the United States are paying young girls and women in Indonesia less than $2.00 *per day* to assemble shoes that will be exported and sold in the United States.[50]

We now have a structural unemployment problem that could linger for years. Large numbers of people are looking for work, but they are not trained for the positions that are open. For example, there are a number of jobs available in high technology areas, such as computers, but there are not enough skilled people in these areas. And, as people become trained for current positions, the employment needs of our economy will continue to shift so that there will continue to be disharmony between skills needed for vacant positions and skills held by unemployed people.

*Factors That Increase Unemployment*  Businesses and governments in many other countries take a much more paternalistic approach to employees and to assuring there will be jobs available for those who are unemployed. When an economic slump occurs in the United States, businesses usually lay off workers. In Japan, in contrast, businesses are much less likely to lay off workers; they seek to have their employees spend their entire working lives with the same company. Governments in many other countries attempt to create jobs for those who are unemployed when there is an economic slump. Germany, for example, pays its unemployed to receive work training.

Economic slumps are not the only reason for an increase in the unemployment rates. A decrease in orders for American products by foreign countries forces American companies to cut back their production and often to lay off workers.

In the 1970s oil-producing countries sharply increased the cost of a barrel of oil. Because practically all companies are dependent on oil for energy and many depend on it for manufacturing their products, the price of most products increased. Because consumers could no longer afford them, demand slackened. Thus companies had to reduce production, and layoffs occurred.

Excessively dry summers in our country sharply reduce the amount of food produced, and the law of supply and demand therefore drives up the price of available food. With more of their money going for groceries, consumers are less able to buy other products. Companies are then forced to cut back production and lay off workers.

High interest rates can make it too costly for consumers to purchase homes, automobiles, and other expensive items normally purchased with a loan. When this happens, the demand for such items goes down; again businesses have to cut back production and lay off workers.

*Factors That Reduce Unemployment*  Many factors increase the number of jobs and thereby reduce the unemployment rate. Lower interest rates encourage consumers to purchase more items through loans and with credit. Consumers buy more, stimulating companies to produce more to meet the demand and thus to hire more people. Lower interest rates have a direct effect on businesses. Companies often borrow money to purchase capital items (for example, additional machinery to produce their goods or buildings to expand the business) in order to increase production. When interest rates are lower, businesses borrow more money to increase production—which usually creates additional jobs.

Wars almost always reduce the unemployment rate. Some workers are drafted to fight as soldiers. Their former jobs are then available for people who are unemployed. In addition, it takes many additional jobs to provide the military with the products needed to fight a war—bullets, bombs, tanks, fighter planes, food, medicine, and so on.

The development of new products opens up many new jobs. The invention of the automobile, airplane, television, computer, hair dryer, and refrigerator created jobs not only for factory workers but also for managers, repair personnel, sales personnel, insurance personnel, and so on.

In the early 1980s, the economy was in a slump, with a high unemployment rate and a high inflation rate. President Reagan stimulated the economy through a tax cut to individuals and to businesses. The tax cut gave individuals more buying power and businesses additional money to reinvest to increase production. Reagan's plan worked: The economy was stimulated, production increased, more jobs were created, and the unemployment rate went down.

Reagan's plan also included immense cuts in federal spending for social welfare programs and for educational programs. The cuts were designed to reduce the inflation rate. (Big spending by the federal government has often been blamed as a major contributor to inflation.) For the most part, Reagan's plan worked. The economy was again stimulated, and the rates of unemployment and inflation were cut nearly in half. Unfortunately, massive tax cuts (along with sharp increases in military spending) led to other problems: a huge federal deficit that threatens to increase the inflation rate in the future and cuts in social programs that have increased the rates of poverty, homelessness, hunger, and a variety of other social problems.

Economics is a complicated and complex area. Certainly it is a mistake to assume that tax cuts will always stimulate the economy and lead to reductions in unemployment and inflation. For example, a case can be made that high rates of inflation and unemployment in the 1970s were due to rising oil prices, and drops in these rates in the 1980s were due not to tax cuts but to declining oil prices. Petroleum is the major source of energy in producing practically all goods. When the price of petroleum goes up, the cost of production increases, which raises the price of all commodities and results in inflation. With inflation, the public cannot buy as much, which results in an oversupply of goods. Industries then lay off workers, which increases the unemployment rate. When the price of petroleum goes down, the cost of producing goods goes down, which reduces prices and thereby reduces the rate of inflation. Also, the public can purchase more goods at lower prices, which reduces the supply of available goods. Industries are then stimulated to produce more goods, which they do by hiring more employees—thus reducing the unemployment rate.

## OCCUPATIONAL HEALTH HAZARDS

A number of occupational health hazards affect workers. These health hazards include: on-the-job accidents and work-related illnesses and job stress.

### On-the-Job Accidents and Work-Related Illnesses

Every year in the United States about 5,000 workers are killed on the job, and more than 3 million suffer disabling injuries from work accidents.[51] Proponents of occupational health have widened their focus to include illnesses as well as accidents, and they have also concentrated on preventing work-related diseases rather than merely treating or compensating workers for them. More than 100,000 Americans die of job-related diseases each year.[52]

Occupations that have high rates of injuries from accidents (some of which are fatal) are shipbuilding and repairing, meat packing, mobile-home construction, timber cutting and logging, aviation, asbestos insulation, structural metal work, electric power line and cable installation and repair, mining, firefighting, roofing, farming, and law enforcement.

An example of a hazardous work site is farming. Farmers, their families, and the workers they employ operate a wide range of heavy equipment. Often they are not carefully trained in the safe operation of that equipment. As a result, we hear frequent reports of people who are fatally injured when a tractor overturns. On-the-job accidents are common on farms. An even graver danger for farmworkers comes from pesticides and herbicides that are misused or overused. More farmworkers are poisoned by chemicals than are injured in farm accidents.[53]

Other industries also have serious health hazards. Cotton dust levels are a threat in the textile and cottonseed-oil industries. Continued inhalation of cotton dust in the mill air causes brown-lung disease or byssinosis, which is irreversible and fatal. Although brown-lung disease was recognized in the eighteenth century, it was not until 1968 that it was officially classified as an occupational illness. (Company owners did not want official recognition of the disease, because they did not want to pay compensation for those workers who became ill.) Even after official recognition, it took another eight years of pressure from labor groups (such as the Amalgamated Clothing and Textile Workers Union) to force the government to set standards for allowable levels of cotton dust. Company owners were reluctant to have standards set because of the cost of remodeling buildings and purchasing the necessary equipment to meet these standards. They also argued that it might be more profitable for them to close the plants and relocate in foreign countries where governments are less safety conscious and they could hire workers at much lower wages.

Currently, one of the most controversial occupational hazards is the use of nuclear power for energy purposes. A number of nuclear power plants have already been built. In 1979, an accident at the nuclear

*Asbestos is now recognized as a serious health hazard. It was a component in many products, including fireproof suits.*

about the dangers of using nuclear power plants to produce electricity.

A serious problem involving occupational hazards is that some substances take years before their deadly effects appear. Asbestos is a prime example. Asbestos is a mineral that has multiple uses, from construction to beer brewing. It has been handled by workers in a wide range of industries. Two decades ago it was discovered that employees who had worked extensively with asbestos later became high risks to develop cancer. It was not only the workers who were in danger, but also their spouse and children who were being exposed to clinging asbestos particles on the worker's clothes. The government is now advising persons who have been exposed to asbestos to undergo periodic medical examinations for early detection and treatment of cancer.

Asbestos workers die from lung cancer at a rate more than seven times that of the general public.[54] Mesothelioma was once a rare form of cancer; it attacks the abdominal organs and the lining of the lungs and is usually fatal. This type of cancer has now become relatively common among asbestos workers. Manufacturers and insurers had known for half a century that asbestos workers were dying prematurely from mesothelioma, but it was not until the mid-1970s that this became public knowledge.

Asbestos may be only the tip of the iceberg. There are over 2,400 suspected carcinogens (cancer-causing substances). Only a few of them have been so designated and regulated by the government.[55]

Rubber workers are exposed to a variety of carcinogens and are dying of cancer of the prostate, cancer of the stomach, and leukemia and other cancers of the blood and the lymph-forming tissues.[56]

Steelworkers, especially those handling coal, are becoming victims of lung cancer at excessive rates. Workers exposed to benzidine and other aromatic amines (often used in producing dyestuffs) have excessively high rates of bladder cancer. Dry cleaners, painters, printers, and petroleum workers are exposed to benzene, which is a known leukemia-producing agent. Miners of iron ore, uranium, chromium, nickel, and other industrial metals fall victim to a variety of occupationally related cancers. Insecticide workers, farmworkers, and copper and lead smelter workers are exposed to inorganic arsenic, a carcinogen that results in high rates of lymphatic cancer and lung cancer.

One of the gravest health dangers involves the chemical industry. This industry was born amid the

power plant at Three Mile Island in Pennsylvania caused small amounts of radioactive particles to be released into the air. Although thousands of people in the surrounding area were evacuated, authorities feared there was a serious threat of substantial amounts of radioactivity being released. This accident demonstrated that nuclear energy is a potential hazard for plant workers and for people living in the surrounding area. In 1986 an accident at the nuclear power plant in Chernobyl, Russia, released massive amounts of radioactivity into the atmosphere. More than twenty people died within a few days and thousands now face the possibility of an early death due to radiation exposure. This accident has raised a worldwide concern

technological innovations of World War II and has been rapidly growing ever since. Chemicals are now involved in the manufacture of practically every product we use—our clothing, the processed food we eat, the soaps we wash with, our televisions, and our automobiles. A number of these chemicals have been found to cause certain diseases, such as cancer, birth defects, heart problems, nervous disorders, weight loss, and sterility. (DDT will be described in Chapter 17; it is a chemical that has been found to be a carcinogen.) There is some evidence that saccharin (used in the past in diet soft drinks) may be a carcinogen. Because new chemicals are being introduced at the rate of one every twenty minutes,[57] it is extremely difficult to determine the hazards of all the chemicals currently in use, not to mention those that will be discovered and used in the future.

It is extremely difficult to prove that a substance causes cancer. Scientists disagree about how much evidence is needed to document a causal relationship. In addition, cancer, as well as certain other diseases (such as respiratory disorder), can take several years to appear after exposure. When a segment of the population has a high incidence of cancer, it is often difficult to identify the cancer-causing substances they were exposed to years earlier.

Simply documenting that certain chemicals are hazardous does not automatically mean they will be taken off the market. For example, there is solid evidence that tobacco is a health hazard, yet many Americans continue to smoke.

When given the choice of being unemployed or working in an industry that is a recognized health hazard (such as coal mining or the textile industry) people often elect to work. Because of the high cost of meeting safety standards, businesses commonly drag their feet in complying with government regulations and sometimes threaten to relocate to other countries when the government applies pressure on them. In many occupational areas, such as textile mills, there is considerable controversy regarding what should be considered "safe" levels of exposure to substances.

*Job Stress*  Most standard textbooks in medicine attribute anywhere from 50 percent to 80 percent of all diseases to stress-related or psychosomatic origins.[58] One of the main sources of stress is job pressures. Practically any job has stresses. Some of the more stressful jobs are air traffic controller, police officer, surgeon, firefighter, coaching professional sports,

| Table 13.1 | *Most Stressful Jobs: Rank Ordered* |
|---|---|
| 1. | Inner-city school teacher |
| 2. | Police officer |
| 3. | Air traffic controller |
| 4. | Medical intern |
| 5. | Firefighter |
| 6. | Waiter/Waitress |
| 7. | Assembly-line worker |
| 8. | Customer-service representative |
| 9. | Securities trader |
| 10. | Newspaper editor |
| 11. | Advertising executive |
| 12. | Public relations specialist |
| 13. | Middle-level manager |
| 14. | Salesperson |
| 15. | Attorney |
| 16. | Urban bus driver |
| 17 | Roofer |
| 18. | Real estate agent |
| 19. | Politician |
| 20. | Banker |

Source: "Stressed Out?" *Wisconsin State Journal*, Sept. 3, 1996, 2C.

labor arbitrator, prison warden, and administrator of a large agency. (See Table 13.1.) Stress is further described in Chapter 11. The list of stress-related illnesses includes bronchial asthma, peptic ulcer, ulcerative colitis, mucous colitis, hay fever, arthritis, hyperthyroidism, enuresis, hypertension, alcoholism, insomnia, cancer, migraine headache, impotence, atopic dermatitis, amenorrhea, and chronic constipation. As described in chapter 3, stress is also one of the causes of emotional disorders.

Employers are increasingly becoming aware of the costs of stress to employees and to their businesses: absenteeism, low productivity, short- and long-term stress-related illnesses, job alienation and job dissatisfaction, marital difficulties, and emotional disorders. Therefore, many companies are sponsoring stress-management programs to help their employees learn to reduce stress through such techniques as meditation, relaxation approaches, hypnosis, exercise programs (such as jogging), time management, biofeedback, and hobbies.[59]

## Regulating Big Business and Technological Development

x x x x x x x x x x x x x x x x x x x x x x x x x

At issue for every presidential administration is the extent to which the government should regulate big business and technological development. Basically this issue involves a continuum from a laissez-faire approach to a planning approach.

### LAISSEZ-FAIRE APPROACH

In the 1980s the Reagan administration deliberately weakened regulatory agencies such as the Occupational Safety and Health Administration (OSHA), the Federal Trade Commission (FTC), and consumer protection programs. It also decided not to pursue antitrust actions against AT&T and IBM. The Reagan administration moved the federal government close to laissez-faire in its relationship to big businesses. The Reagan administration also promoted deregulation. George Bush, elected president in 1988, continued the economic policies of the Reagan administration. To a large extent, the goal was to shift control of the economy from the government to the private sector. To some extent, Reagan and Bush's position was similar to the position advocated by Adam Smith when he asserted the public will benefit best if private enterprise has little interference from the government.

Presidents Reagan and Bush believed the private sector will prosper best if it is less regulated by government. It is then in a better position to develop new markets, increase its productivity, and thereby create new job opportunities.

Reagan and Bush's approach has been called supply-side economics, as it focuses on economic growth through a strategy of increasing the supply of goods. (Most prior presidential administrations sought to stimulate economic growth through increasing the demand for goods.) Supply-siders seek to reduce excessive government regulation of business in such areas as consumer product safety and environmental pollution. Supply-siders have also sought to stimulate economic growth through sharp across-the-board reductions in taxes. With tax cuts, businesses have additional money to reinvest to increase production. Also, with tax cuts, individuals are able to buy more. The economy is thus stimulated, production increases, and more jobs are created. With a more productive economy, it is hoped that government tax revenues will gradually increase to make up for the money lost in the original tax cuts.

Critics point out that supply-side economics primarily benefits the rich, as they have reductions in their income taxes, which enables them to further increase their wealth through investing in productive business ventures. Tax cuts, combined with reductions in social welfare services, widen the gap between the rich and the poor. Supply-side economists seek to counter such criticism with the *trickle down theory*. According to this theory, governmental action taken to assist business or wealthy people will stimulate economic growth and provide jobs for the unemployed and the poor. Critics of the trickle down theory point to evidence showing that the proportion of poor families tends to increase whenever the government cuts both taxes and social welfare services.[60]

### PLANNING APPROACH

The main alternative to a laissez-faire approach calls for increased planning and regulation by the federal government. Many successful economic competitors of the United States (such as Japan, Sweden, and Germany) have governments which are much more involved in planning and regulating the economies of their countries. The governments own many more businesses in these countries. They also work more closely with private industry and labor unions to spur the economy.

Advocates of the planning approach assert that our federal government needs to develop a comprehensive plan that identifies areas of economic strengths and weaknesses, and that analyzes what kinds of new business ventures would be profitable for private industry and government to cooperatively pursue. Following are some suggestions: A federal bank or financial corporation could be established to provide low-interest loans to high-growth industries and to assist old industries in modernizing their production capacities to become more competitive. For example, it appears that computers, communications, and other high-tech fields will be foremost in the world's growth industries in the future. The government could encourage such growth through special tax breaks, low-interest loans, and outright subsidies. If our country does not take the lead in developing such technology, other countries (such as Japan) will. In recent years Japan has emerged as a prominent leader in developing, producing, and marketing high-tech products.

Another proposal is for the government to develop a plan and spend the resources to revitalize the educational system to teach students the skills needed in a high-tech society. Yet another proposal is for the government to assist workers (perhaps through loans) in taking over the ownership of financially troubled industries. Employees who take over ownership generally are willing to accept necessary cuts in wages, and work harder when they are working for themselves.

A variety of groups are urging the federal government to take an increased role in planning and regulating big business activities. The textile industry is urging the government to set higher tariffs on clothing imports from foreign countries—as textile manufacturers in foreign countries are able to produce lower-cost clothing through paying substantially lower wages. Environmental groups want the government to enact and enforce stricter pollution statutes and standards. Antidiscrimination organizations urge the government to take a more active role in enforcing statutes that prohibit job discrimination against women, racially diverse groups, the elderly, people with disabilities, and gays and lesbians. Other organizations urge the government to hold corporations more responsible for finding jobs for workers who are discharged from work due to automation, use of robots, and plant closings in order to pursue more attractive business ventures elsewhere.

The Clinton administration has taken more of a planning approach to stimulate the economy than did the Reagan and Bush administrations. In 1993 the Clinton administration was successful in passing a budget that increased taxes on the wealthy and on corporations, with the additional tax revenues to be used for a variety of purposes, including: reducing the federal deficit, giving tax breaks to employers in ninety-five designated high-poverty communities, and giving tax credits to employers who hire economically disadvantaged youths and persons with a disability.[61] The Clinton administration has also successfully worked on developing "free-trade" treaties with Mexico, Canada, and a number of other countries, which eliminate or reduce tariffs. (Tariffs are charges imposed by a government on imported goods.) It is hoped that such treaties will stimulate the economies of the countries entering into the agreements by increasing trade—and thereby increasing the demand for products, which will eventually create more jobs. In 1998 President Clinton asserted his economic policies are working very effectively as the economy is robust, and Clinton was able to advance the first balanced federal budget (that is, no deficit spending) in decades.

Critics of an increased governmental role in the economy argue that the more deeply involved the government becomes, the more inefficient and wasteful the economy becomes. Supporters of increased government involvement assert that past problems with government involvement were caused by special interest groups that used the programs to serve their own narrow interests.

## Current and Proposed "Solutions" to Work Problems

This section will present approaches that have been tried or proposed to reduce alienation and job dissatisfaction. We will also look at recommendations of reducing unemployment and for confronting health hazards.

### CONFRONTING ALIENATION AND JOB DISSATISFACTION

One of the best-known efforts to increase worker satisfaction and productivity was that of Hawthorne Works, a division of Western Electric Company in Chicago. The results were surprising, as described in Box 13.7.

Many employers have become aware that job dissatisfaction often reduces efficiency and productivity. There are a number of ways to increase job satisfaction. The first step is to find out precisely what the workers are dissatisfied with and then seek to make changes. In one job setting, workers may be most concerned about safety conditions (as in coal mining); in another, they may be most concerned about boring, repetitive work (as on an assembly line); in another, it may be wages (as of jobs that only pay at or barely above the minimum wage); in another, it may be lack of recognition (as of clerical workers who make their supervisors look good); and so on.

A wide variety of changes can be made to improve job satisfaction. The following list is far from exhaustive:

♦ Find ways to make the work challenging and interesting.

♦ Provide opportunities for career advancement.

# Case Example:
# The Hawthorne Effect

In 1927 the Hawthorne Works of the Western Electric Company in Chicago began a series of experiments designed to discover ways to increase worker satisfaction and worker productivity. Hawthorne Works primarily manufactured telephones, with the plant operating on an assembly-line basis. Workers needed no special skills for this production process and performed simple, repetitive tasks. The workers were not unionized, and management sought to find ways to increase productivity. It was thought that the employees would work more efficiently (and thereby increase productivity) if ways were found to increase job satisfaction.

The company tested a number of factors to examine their effects on productivity. These factors included rest breaks, better lighting, changes in the number of work hours, changes in the wages paid, improved food facilities, and so on.

The results were surprising. Productivity increased as expected with improved working conditions; but it also increased when working conditions worsened. One way that working conditions were worsened was by substantially dimming the lighting. The finding that productivity increased when working conditions worsened was unexpected and led to additional study to find an explanation.

The investigators discovered that participation in the experiments were extremely attractive to the workers. They felt they had been selected by the management for their individual abilities and so they worked harder, even when working conditions became less favorable. There were additional reasons. The workers' morale and general attitude toward work improved, as they felt they were receiving special attention from management. By participating in this study, they were able to work in smaller groups and also become involved in making decisions. Working in smaller groups allowed them to develop a stronger sense of solidarity with their fellow workers. Being involved in making decisions decreased their feelings of meaninglessness and powerlessness.

The results of this study have become known as the Hawthorne effect in sociological and psychological research. The Hawthorne effect holds that subjects who know they are participants in a study may behave differently and thus substantially influence the results of the study.

*Source:* Fritz J. Roethlisberger and William J. Dickson, *Management and the Worker* (Cambridge, MA: Harvard University Press, 1939).

---

◆ Provide in-service training about aspects related to the work—for example, stress-management programs.

◆ Increase wages, salaries, and fringe benefits, such as on-site day care.

◆ Involve workers in the decision-making process.

◆ Have social get-togethers to help increase group morale.

◆ Give workers a share of the profits through a profit-sharing program.

◆ Establish a reward system to recognize significant contributions made by workers.

◆ Establish employee policies that generate a sense of job security.

◆ Establish policies that allow workers to have some control over the hours they work—flexitime for example.

◆ Allow workers to have some control over their schedules—for example, through flexitime.

Workers are more satisfied in jobs in which they feel they have some decision-making responsibilities and some control over their work schedules. They don't like punching a time clock, whereas flexitime is appealing. The idea behind flexitime is to have most workers present during the busiest time of the day but to leave the remaining hours up to the discretion of the workers. Those who want to start earlier, so they can leave earlier, can do so. Those who want to come in later and stay later also have this option. In some places it is possible with flexitime to work four days a week (ten hours per day) and thereby have an extra day off. Many government agencies and private companies are now on flexitime. Although supervisors have found it is more difficult to coordinate work schedules when using flexitime, absenteeism declines and productivity increases under such a program.

◆ Make the work setting as free of hazards as possible.

- Have promotion-from-within policies, training programs, personnel policies that assure equal opportunity for advancement and education, and good physical facilities and conveniences (lounges, cafeterias, gyms, and the like).

A variety of programs involve employees in *participative management*. For example, in *consultive management,* managers consult with their employees (either individually or in small groups) in order to encourage them to think about job-related issues and contribute their own ideas before decisions are made. *Democratic management* goes even further; it systematically allows employee groups to make a number of major decisions. An example of democratic management is the practice of allowing work teams to hire, orient, and train new employees.

*Self-managing teams* are a subcategory of democratic management; they are autonomous work groups that are given a high degree of decision-making authority and are expected to control their own behavior and work schedules, with compensation usually being based on the team's overall productivity. *Quality circles* are work-improvement taskforces in which managers and employees meet regularly to allow employees to air grievances (which in itself has a ventilating effect in reducing job dissatisfaction), to identify problems that hinder productivity, and to offer suggestions for alleviating these concerns.

*Suggestion programs* are formal procedures to encourage employees to recommend work improvements, often in writing; in many companies employees whose suggestions result in cost savings receive monetary awards. *Stock trusts* allow employees to buy or receive stock in the company, thereby becoming partial owners; a benefit of stock trusts is that they act as an incentive for higher productivity among employees. *Employee ownership* occurs when employees provide the capital to purchase control of an existing company; employee ownership generally increases employee interest in the company's financial success and acts as an incentive for workers to remain with the company.[62]

A number of American companies have increased productivity by conducting "climate surveys," in which workers are asked to vent their concerns and to criticize their jobs. Sometimes such surveys identify problematic situations that can be improved through relatively minor changes. Even when the problems cannot be resolved, work tensions are often temporarily reduced just by allowing workers to let off steam.

Theory Y-type managers have been found to substantially improve productivity and job satisfaction, as compared to Theory X-type managers. (See Box 13.8.)

## CONFRONTING UNEMPLOYMENT

Economists agree that the ideal way to cure unemployment is with increased economic growth. Economists, however, are in sharp disagreement about the causes of a sluggish economy and about the best ways to stimulate growth.

Although rapid economic growth would probably reduce the rate of unemployment substantially, it is a mixed blessing. Rapid economic growth historically has had adverse effects on the natural environment and has always led to more rapid consumption of scarce resources (see chapter 17). These adverse effects illustrate again the principle that a solution to one problem often creates or aggravates another problem; that is, in sociological terms, the solution has both functional and dysfunctional aspects.

Some of the proposals advanced for reducing unemployment will be reviewed briefly. As mentioned previously, President Reagan used tax cuts to stimulate the economy and create more jobs in the private sector.

Those unemployed and unable to find employment in the private sector could be hired by the government, a last resort employer. The work performed ideally would be useful to society—for example, building and repairing highways, planting trees, and providing services in social service agencies (such as recreational services to youths in high delinquency areas). Working for the government in such capacities would also provide workers with job skills that would increase their opportunities to be hired in the private sector.

Another proposal is for the government to subsidize private companies to maintain their payrolls during economic recessions. A number of foreign governments do this.

Throughout our history there have been geographic areas of high unemployment as well as boom areas that want more workers. The government could take a more active role in identifying boom areas, publicizing jobs available, and providing assistance with relocation expenses for unemployed workers willing to move from areas of high unemployment.

Another proposal is for the government to expand its role in providing job training to the

## Theory Y: Improving Productivity and Job Satisfaction

Douglas McGregor categorized management thinking and behavior into two types—Theory X and Theory Y.

*Theory X managers* view employees as being incapable of much growth. Employees are perceived as having an inherent dislike for work, and it is presumed that they will attempt to evade work whenever possible. Therefore, X-type managers believe they must control, direct, force, or threaten employees to make them work. Employees are also viewed as having relatively little ambition. Theory X managers believe employees seek to avoid taking on new responsibilities, and prefer to be directed. X-type managers therefore spell out job responsibilities carefully, set work goals without employee input, use external rewards (such as money) to force employees to work, and punish employees who deviate from established rules. Because Theory X managers reduce responsibilities to a level at which few mistakes can be made, work usually becomes so structured that it is monotonous and distasteful. The assumptions of Theory X are, of course, inconsistent with what behavioral scientists assert are effective principles for directing, influencing, and motivating people.

In contrast, *Theory Y managers* view employees as wanting to grow and develop by exerting physical and mental effort to accomplish work objectives to which they are committed. Y-type managers believe that internal rewards, such as self-respect and personal improvement, are stronger motivations than external rewards (money) and punishment. A Y-type manager also believes that, under proper conditions, employees will not only accept responsibility but seek it. Most employees are assumed to have considerable ingenuity, creativity, and imagination for solving the organization's problems. Therefore, employees are given considerable responsibility in order to test the limits of their capabilities. Mistakes and errors are viewed as necessary phases of the learning process, and work is structured so that employees can have a sense of accomplishment and growth.

Employees who work for Y-type managers are generally more creative and productive, experience greater work satisfaction, and are more highly motivated than employees who work for X-type managers. Under both management styles, expectations often become self-fulfilling prophecies.

*Source:* Douglas McGregor, *The Human Side of Enterprise* (New York: McGraw-Hill, 1960).

---

unskilled and semiskilled and to those workers whose skills have become obsolete. As mentioned earlier, Germany not only provides more work training than this country, but usually pays workers during their period of training.

Critics of government as a last-resort employer, payroll subsidization, worker relocation, and paid job training argue that extensive efforts in any of these areas would sharply increase government spending and increase the rate of inflation. They also maintain that government-supplied jobs would merely be a stopgap measure that would not solve the overall problem of joblessness and that government should not be in the business of creating make-work jobs.

## CONFRONTING HEALTH HAZARDS

The federal government in recent decades has become increasingly concerned about occupational illnesses. In 1970 it passed the Occupational Safety and Health Act, which established two new organizations to combat occupational hazards. The Occupational Safety and Health Administration (OSHA) was created in the Department of Labor to establish health standards for industry. The National Institute for Occupational Safety and Health (NIOSH) was created in the Department of Health and Human Services to research occupational hazards. In 1976 the government enacted the Toxic Substances Control Act, which established systems and guidelines for screening and controlling dangerous substances. With the rapid development of chemicals and other substances, OSHA and NIOSH face formidable tasks in testing the effects of all of these substances and in setting and enforcing safety limits for substances found to be health hazards.

Big business and big government are sometimes in collusion to find ways to avoid making the extensive changes required to meet governmental regulations. It is safe to predict that the following cycle will continue. Industry will continue to develop new chemicals and other substances, some of which are health hazards. After some years, the government or some

*The 1986 Chernobyl accident aroused international concern about the dangers of nuclear power. Here, a year after the incident, vehicles are screened for radiation in the vicinity of the nuclear power plant.*

private organization will eventually identify the health hazards. There will be pressure put on the producing companies to make changes to minimize the hazards. During this time period, a number of workers will have been adversely affected.

## Summary

Today our economy is dominated by national and multinational corporations. The annual sales of some multinationals are larger than some countries' gross national product. Monopolies have been prohibited by antitrust laws, but oligopolies have emerged for many important products, and can relatively easily set market prices.

An important question is whether major economic, political, and military decisions are made by a power elite, or decided in a contest between competing groups. Large corporations have benefited societies by producing needed goods, developing new technologies, and providing jobs. Some large corporations, however, have also abused their power by fixing prices, polluting the environment, meddling in governmental decisions, and exploiting the masses.

Big business and government are interrelated in a variety of ways. Regulatory agencies are often allies of the industries they regulate. Political decisions are often influenced by big business. An example of this interdependence is the military-industrial complex.

Technology is a double-edged sword, as every major technological innovation has both freed humans from prior hardships and created new problems. Alvin Toffler theorizes that rapid technological changes have led to future shock, which involves a general sense of confusion and anxiety about the present and the future. William Ogburn theorizes that there is often a cultural lag in developing values about the desirability of some new technological advances, and a lag in determining how some advances should be used. Ogburn also indicates there is often a cultural lag in developing social welfare services to meet emerging human needs that are brought about by technological advances.

Two main approaches have been advanced for the government's role in regulating big business and technological development. The laissez-faire approach calls for the government to reduce its role, and predicts all of society will benefit. In contrast, the planning approach urges increased regulation and planning by the government.

Work is highly esteemed in our society. Prior to the Protestant Reformation, work was denigrated and even considered a curse by some societies. Under the influence of the Protestant ethic, work has become a moral obligation. It is also a source of self-respect, an opportunity to form friendships, and a potential source of self-fulfillment and an opportunity to use one's talents. To a large extent, our work determines our social status.

There have been significant changes or trends in the nature of work and the composition of the workforce in the past few decades. There is an increase in white-collar workers and a decrease in farmers and blue-collar workers. Most workers are now employees rather than self-employed. Work is increasingly becoming specialized, and considerable automation is occurring. More women are entering the labor force, and older male workers are increasingly becoming unemployed. Workers are increasingly seeking intrinsic rewards, rewards that come from the nature of the work itself. In the past two decades, there has been an extensive growth in low-paying jobs. There has also been a trend to outsource manufacturing jobs to Third World countries (some authorities have referred to this phenomenon as deindustrialization in the United States).

Alienation appears to be a serious problem for many workers. Sources of alienation include specialization, automation, lack of involvement in the decision-making process, routine and repetitive tasks, and lack of opportunity to be creative or to use one's talents fully. Alienation may lead to poor-quality work, absenteeism, job turnover, and low productivity.

Job dissatisfaction is one measure of worker alienation. Available studies indicate conflicting results about how satisfied American workers are with their jobs. Sources of workers' satisfaction with their jobs include: participative management, interesting work, enough help and equipment to get the job done, enough information and authority to get the job done, good pay, opportunity to develop special abilities, job security, seeing the results of one's work, pleasant work settings, some decision-making responsibilities, and promotion-from-within policies.

There is a question about whether the traditional work ethic is declining. Some authorities suggest that specialization and automation are leading to a decrease in workers' interest in doing their best.

In the past two decades, the unemployment rate has generally ranged between 4 and 11 percent, which is considered alarmingly high. Long-term unemployment has serious adverse effects: depletion of savings, loss of self-respect, financial crises, loss of friends, isolation, and feelings of embarrassment, anger, despair, depression, anxiety, boredom, hopelessness, and apathy. It can be a factor in emotional problems, suicide, alcoholism, and stress-related illnesses.

Groups that have chronically high rates of unemployment are: people of color, teenagers, women, older workers, the unskilled, the semiskilled, and persons with a disability. There are a variety of reasons for high unemployment among these groups: racial and sexual discrimination, low educational level, lack of marketable job skills, and age discrimination. The reasons of the high unemployment rate among the total workforce include automation, dramatic increases in the number of baby boomers entering the labor force, a higher proportion of women seeking work, lack of trained people for available jobs, and a sluggish economy.

Economists agree that the ideal way to cure unemployment is with rapid economic growth. Economists, however, are in sharp disagreement about the causes of a sluggish economy and about the best ways to stimulate it. Proposals for reducing the unemployment rate include a tax-cut plan to stimulate the economy, government as last-resort employer, government subsidization of private companies to maintain their payrolls during economic recessions, government aid in worker relocation, and government job training programs.

There are three main occupational health hazards: on-the-job accidents, working conditions that lead to physical diseases, and job stress that leads to stress-related illnesses. The growing number of untested chemicals being used poses one of the biggest health dangers for the future. Many chemical substances have a delayed reaction, as is the case with cancer, that often first appears several years after exposure. The federal government has become more concerned about occupational illnesses and has established organizations (such as the Occupational Safety and Health Administration) to combat occupational hazards. Many companies are now sponsoring stress-management programs and employee assistance programs for employees with chemical substance abuse problems.

CHAPTER **14**

# *Violence, Terrorism, and War*

Violence is as American as cherry pie.

—*H. Rap Brown*[1]

Two of the tallest, most impressive, skyscrapers in the United States are the twin towers of the World Trade Center in New York City. On February 26, 1993, terrorists set off a bomb in the underground parking garage connecting the two buildings. The explosion killed six people, injured more than a thousand others, and caused hundreds of millions of dollars worth of damage. Four men, all militant Muslims from Arab countries, were convicted of the bombings, and sentenced to life imprisonment with no chance of parole. For a long time, international terrorism had been the bane of other parts of the world, but the United States had been largely exempt. The Trade Center bombing shockingly demonstrated that the United States is also vulnerable to violence from international terrorism.

Americans hold ambivalent attitudes toward violence. We say we deplore violence and at the same time we glorify those who use it "in the name of the law." Violence is commonplace, not only in our country but worldwide.

This chapter:

♦ Summarizes ways in which violence is expressed (such as terrorism and war)

♦ Presents theories on violence and describes some of its causes

♦ Suggests ways to reduce violence and combat terrorism, war, and nuclear war

## *Types of Violence*

Violence is expressed in a variety of ways: war, nuclear war, terrorism, violent protest, violent crime, suicide, family violence, violence against minorities, police brutality, and violence among youths.

### WAR

Ours is a nation of war. Shortly after the earliest European settlers arrived, they fought with the Native Americans, gradually taking away their lands.

The American Revolution (1775–1783) lasted more than seven years and took an estimated 4,435 American lives.[2] Americans justified this war as being necessary to achieve liberty, freedom, and self-determination from the injustices and oppression of the British. The British, on the other hand, viewed the Revolution as civil disorder by rebels who lacked appreciation of the help the colonies had received from the British Empire. This help included food and supplies during times of famine, medicine, and soldiers during war with the Indians and other foes. (Any war ever fought is viewed very differently by the two sides.)

Mexico's objection to the annexation of Texas by the United States led to the Mexican War (1846–1848). Although the United States suffered 17,000 casualties,[3] it was victorious. Mexico not only lost Texas in the settlement, but also a large portion of land that is now Arizona, California, New Mexico, Nevada, Utah, and much of Colorado.

The Civil War (1861–1865) was one of the bloodiest ever fought by America. An estimated 300,000 Americans were killed.[4] The economy of the Confederate states was devastated, and the harmful effects of the war on life in the South lasted many decades.

According to the American government, the Spanish-American War (1898) was fought to liberate Cuba from Spain. Again the United States was victorious and in the process acquired Guam, Puerto Rico, and the Philippines. Some 2,500 Americans were killed.[5]

World War I (1914–1918) was supposedly fought to make the world "safe for democracy." Germany was defeated, and the United States became recognized as a world power. The number of Americans killed totaled 53,400.[6]

World War II (1939–1945) was fought against Germany, Japan, and Italy. An estimated 400,000 Americans were killed. Worldwide, 30 million people were estimated to have been killed, including soldiers and civilians.[7] During this war, the United States exploded the first two atomic bombs. The first was on August 6, 1945, on Hiroshima, in Japan; the second was on Nagasaki, three days later. Nearly 200,000 people were killed by these two bombs.[8] The use of nuclear power now is a threat to the survival of civilization.

A few years after World War II, the United States became involved in the Korean War (1950–1953). American political leaders said its purpose was to stop the spread of communism in Asia. Nearly 55,000 Americans lost their lives.[9] China unofficially sent multitudes of troops into Korea to battle the Allied troops (which largely consisted of American and South Korean soldiers).

The Vietnam War was fought in the 1960s and early 1970s. Nearly 60,000 Americans were killed.[10] Its supposed purpose was the containment of communism. This undeclared war was a war that America was unable to win. North Vietnam used guerilla war tactics to demoralize the South Vietnamese and the Americans. The war led to widespread violent protests in the United States. Dissent was so extensive on college campuses that many colleges were forced to suspend classes and call out the National Guard. Dissent became so extreme that some observers feared the American political system was endangered. This war, and the protests on campuses, ended for the United States in the early 1970s, when a truce was reached between South and North Vietnam. A few months after America pulled out, North Vietnam militarily took over South Vietnam.

The last war that the United States was involved in was the Persian Gulf War in 1991. The United States, along with about thirty other countries, fought Iraq. Saddam Hussein (the president of Iraq) initiated the conflict by invading and taking over Kuwait in 1990. In this war, Iraq was no match for the Allied Forces. The war lasted only six weeks, and fewer than 200 Americans were killed in combat. An estimated 75,000 to 100,000 Iraqi soldiers died.[11]

The United States indeed has a history of fighting internal and external wars. Yet the United States is not unique. Most other countries also have a history of conflict.

The history of generally successful warfare in the United States has been a factor in the development of beliefs that encourage violence and aggression. Violence is believed to be permissible if it helps achieve a desired goal. History shows rewards go to the violent and the strong. When conflicts arise among groups, the result is often settled in terms of who has the most power, rather than in terms of fairness and justice.

The costs of war and of military defense are extremely high. Not only are many soldiers and civilians killed, but billions of dollars are spent.[12] By any standard, the twentieth century has been the deadliest in human history. Tens of millions of soldiers and civilians have been killed. For every person killed, more are wounded and require medical care for months or years. Many are so badly injured that they are unable to hold a job or return to a normal way of life.

War also takes a psychological toll for soldiers through exposure to the threat of death, seeing friends and fellow soldiers die, the hardships of life on the battlefield, the value conflicts involved in killing others, and the inability to control one's own actions. Upon returning home, many soldiers suffer for years afterward; they are depressed, alienated, irritable, and have flashbacks and nightmares of war experiences. Such emotional suffering is now clinically known as *post-traumatic stress disorder.*

There are other costs of wars. Wars disrupt the lives of civilians. Buildings, roads, bridges, homes, offices, and schools are destroyed and need to be rebuilt. Wars lead to mass migrations of people who want to escape danger, oppression, or persecution; others are forced to migrate to look for new job opportunities. Even less quantifiable is the impact of war on how people think. After World War I, for example, many Europeans were disillusioned about traditional values, alienated from their former way of life, and pessimistic about the future of civilization.[13]

Wars are fought for a variety of reasons. For example, the Civil War was fought because the North and South disagreed on whether slavery should exist. The United States entered World War I ostensibly to make the world safe for democracy. The United States entered the Korean War and the Vietnam War to stop the spread of communism. Many wars have been fought over religious differences, as were the Crusades in the Middle Ages. Hitler was a key figure in starting World War II, as he wanted to rule the world. Many wars are fought for economic reasons; European kings in the seventeenth, eighteenth, and nineteenth centuries often waged war to gain land, prestige, and other benefits. Many former colonists have fought a revolutionary war (including the United States against England) to establish home rule and become independent. Some wars are caused by political leaders stirring up an international conflict to divert their citizens' attention from domestic troubles, as citizens of a country almost always rally to support their political leaders whenever the citizens perceive their country is being attacked (or is apt to be attacked) by another country.

It should be noted that probably no war has been fought for just one reason. A variety of contributing factors increase the probability of war. Having a large, well-equipped military force makes it easier for political leaders to choose war rather than negotiation to settle international disputes. A strong feeling of nationalism also increases the chances for war. (*Nationalism* is a sense of identification with and devotion to one's nation—with an emphasis on promotion of its culture and interests above those of all other nations.) In democracies, governmental leaders are

Box 14.1

# My Lai

The atrocities committed by Americans in Vietnam are unparalleled in our history. (These atrocities are partly explainable by the atrocities committed by the other side—it *was* a two-way street.) The United States used chemical warfare to force enemy soldiers out into the open, where they were then shot. Bullets were used that expand upon entering the body. Huge amounts of napalm were used. (Napalm burns and melts human flesh and also removes oxygen from the air so that those who escape being burned die of suffocation.) White phosphorus was also used. (It continues to burn its victims from within the body.) In addition, the United States did extensive bombing from the air and tortured prisoners of war.

Although American soldiers officially were supposed to "win the hearts and minds" of the people, their actions showed that many of them generally viewed the South Vietnamese as "slant-eyed gooks" and "commies." A number of the fighting men had the view that "there are no good Vietnamese except dead ones." Many American soldiers held highly racist attitudes, a situation partly resulting from the war itself. (Our military leaders urged our soldiers to hate the enemy in order to make it easier to kill them.)

With these attitudes, it is not surprising that many massacres took place in Vietnam. The most noted massacre occurred in the village of My Lai on March 16, 1968. More than five hundred civilians—women, men, and children—were methodically killed. These deliberate murders were carried out by sixty to seventy soldiers in a battalion of the United States Army.

One sergeant who refused to participate described the massacre:

> They [the infantrymen] would get the people together and gather them in groups. Then they would shoot them with rifles and machine guns. Going through the village, I saw a lot of bodies in these things that looked like bomb craters. I actually saw them shoot some of them. I saw them shoot a group in ditch, about twenty of them.[a]

---

a. Quoted in Alphonso Pinkney, *The American Way of Violence* (New York: Random House, 1972), 66.

---

more apt to choose war when they believe the public is supportive of the tactic. The perception that one is more powerful and can easily win a war also increases the chances for military conflict. A nation is also more apt to go to war if its citizens are socialized to believe that violence is one of the best ways to settle disputes. Romanticizing war (as our country has done with the American Revolution and World War I) increases the chances of future wars. Warfare is also more likely to occur when a nation views war and combat as a heroic show of strength, and when young people view it as a path to personal fame and fortune. If military leaders and arms manufacturers have considerable influence on a government, war is more likely to occur, as such groups tend to benefit from war.

## NUCLEAR WAR

On the morning of August 6, 1945, adults in Hiroshima, Japan, were preparing to go to work. An American bomber was spotted overhead. Seconds later, an atomic bomb was dropped, which exploded 2,000 feet above the center of the city. The destruction was devastating. The heat and force of the blast killed tens of thousands of people almost instantly. It also released radiation, which eventually killed more than 100,000 more.[14] Numerous bombs have since been built that are 1,600 times more powerful than the one that destroyed Hiroshima.[15]

Perhaps the greatest danger to the survival of civilization is a nuclear war. Many authorities believe a nuclear war could end human civilization. Russia and the United States have the nuclear capacity to destroy each other several times over. Many other nations now possess nuclear bombs or are seeking to develop or purchase nuclear warheads.[16]

If a nuclear war occurred, those located near where the bombs struck would be killed instantly. Those who initially survived would face death from exposure to cancer-causing radiation and a variety of other fatal medical conditions. Some scientists predict that survivors would face a "nuclear winter" in which a cloud of soot would block the sun over much of the earth, which would push temperatures far below freezing and prevent the growth of most foods. Another worry is that the ozone layer would break down. This layer protects the earth from the full power of the sun's rays. Breakdown of the ozone layer would result in intense sun rays penetrating humans and animals, causing skin cancer and other disorders.

Another danger is that crops would be affected by radioactivity and would be potentially dangerous as food sources. It could well be that the initial survivors would face a slow, painful death. Their quality of life could slip into a new age in which they would grub out a brutish, barely human existence. The quality of life for survivors would drastically decline due to the unraveling of the social infrastructure: that is, the industrial, educational, agricultural, transportation, health care, political, and communication systems would cease to function. Those who did survive would also face intense psychological stress from grief, despair, disorientation, hopelessness, and anger.[17]

The United States is still the only country that has used nuclear bombs in a war. In addition, the United States has threatened to use nuclear weapons on at least eleven occasions since 1946, including during the Berlin crisis of 1961, the Cuban missile crisis of 1962, and twice during the Vietnam War.[18] Fortunately the rejection of communism by Russia and its movement towards democracy in recent years has resulted in improved relationships between the United States and Russia. These two countries have most of the world's nuclear weapons. Improved relationships between these two superpowers have eased somewhat the fears and trepidations of a nuclear war occurring. However, serious nuclear war dangers continue, as noted by Kornblum and Julian:

> The United States, Russia, and Ukraine have agreed to dismantle or otherwise disable their missiles, but vast destructive nuclear capabilities remain in place around the globe. The possibility that nuclear bombs will be obtained by nations in unstable areas of the world such as Southeast Asia, North Korea, and the Middle East keeps the threat of nuclear war alive. Even a limited nuclear war would create human catastrophes on a scale not hitherto experienced, to say nothing of the environmental damage and destruction such wars would cause for years afterward, even in regions beyond the boundaries of the original conflict. These concerns, as well as the possibility that nuclear weapons could be used by terrorists, suggest that it is premature to celebrate the end of the threat of nuclear war. Experts in the field agree that efforts to control the proliferation of nuclear weapons are as vital today as they ever were.[19]

In May 1998, India set off five underground nuclear test explosions in an effort to further develop nuclear weapons. The danger of such testing is that it may serve as a catalyst for neighboring countries (such as China and Pakistan) to expand the development of their nuclear weapons.

## TERRORISM

Terrorism is a serious threat to world stability. Terrorism is similar to traditional warfare in that it kills or seriously disables many people, including innocent civilians. It wastes both human energy and money, destabilizes economies and governments, and interferes with efforts to resolve social problems.

In contrast to war, which is overt, terrorism is covert. It seeks to influence the masses through fear and coercion. Common terrorist acts include the kidnaping or assassination of politicians and business leaders, airline hijackings, blackmail, bombings, arson, and the taking of hostages. Terrorist acts have rapidly increased in frequency in the twentieth century.[20]

In recent decades, the United States has been spared the large number of terrorist acts that have occurred in Northern Ireland, Israel, Iraq, Iran, Italy, and Germany. The United States, however, has not escaped terrorist attacks completely. In 1977, a dozen Hanafi Muslims forcefully took over three federal buildings in Washington and held 132 hostages for nearly two days. None of the hostages was connected with the cause of the Black Muslims, whom the Hanafi Muslims opposed.[21]

On November 4, 1979, Iranian students rushed the American embassy in Tehran, Iran. Fifty-two hostages were held in captivity in Iran for fifteen months, largely with the concurrence and assistance of the Iranian government. The students and the Iranian government demanded the return of the deposed Shah, the return of the Shah's financial assets, and an apology from the United States for supporting the alleged criminal acts carried out by the Shah when he was in power. The United States did not comply with any of these demands.

On December 21, 1988, Pan Am flight 103 exploded. A bomb killed 259 people aboard and 11 on the ground. Many of the passengers were Americans living abroad, who were returning to the United States for Christmas. Several months later ABC television reported that the bomb was planted by a terrorist group that was paid $10 million by Iran to avenge a U.S. downing of a commercial Iranian airliner with 290 people aboard earlier in July. (Our military had mistakenly assumed the Iranian jet was going to attack a U.S. ship in the Mediterranean Sea.)

As noted at the beginning of this chapter, on February 26, 1993, the World Trade Center in New York City was bombed, causing several deaths and extensive damage.

## The Specter of Germ Warfare

The United States, and a number of other countries, have had a long history of experimentation with germ warfare on unwitting human subjects. A few countries and some terrorist groups have already used biological and chemical weapons. A few examples of the experimentation and use of these weapons will be summarized.

In 1900 a U.S. doctor doing research in the Philippines infected a number of prisoners with the Plague (a deadly disease). He continued his research by inducing Beriberi (another potentially deadly disease) in another twenty-nine prisoners. The experiments resulted in two known fatalities.

In 1931 Dr. Cornelius Rhoads, under the auspices of the Rockefeller Institute for Medical Investigations, purposely infected subjects with cancer cells. Thirteen of the subjects died.

In a crash program in the 1940s to develop new drugs to fight malaria during World War II, doctors in the United States infected nearly 400 prisoners with the disease. The prisoners were not adequately informed that they were participants in a malaria study.

In 1950 the U.S. Navy sprayed a cloud of bacteria over San Francisco. The U.S. Navy was experimenting with a simulated germ warfare attack. Many San Francisco residents became ill with pneumonia-like symptoms, and one is known to have died.

In 1965 seventy volunteer prisoners at the Holmesburg State Prison in Philadelphia were subjected to tests of dioxin, the highly toxic chemical contaminant in Agent Orange. The testers were studying how dioxin leads to the development of cancer.

In 1968–1969 the CIA experimented with the possibility of poisoning drinking water by injecting a chemical substance into the water supply of the Food and Drug Administration in Washington, D.C. None of the human subjects in the building were ever asked for their permission.

In 1981 more than 300,000 Cubans were stricken with Dengue fever. It has been suggested the outbreak was the result of a release of infected mosquitoes by Cuban counterrevolutionaries.

In September 1984, a religious cult (whose leader was Bhagwan Shree Rajneesh) spread Salmonella bacteria on salad bars in four restaurants in The Dalles, Oregon. The bacteria had been grown in laboratories on the cult's ranch. About 750 people became sick.

Although the production and use of biological warfare agents was banned by President Nixon in 1972, the Department of Defense was forced to reveal in 1987 that it still operated 127 chemical and biological warfare research programs in the United States.

In 1996 the U.S. Department of Defense acknowledged that at least 20,000 U.S. service personnel may

---

In May 1995 the Alfred P. Murrah Federal Building in Oklahoma City was blown up, killing 168 people. In 1997, Timothy McVeigh was sentenced to death for deliberately bombing this building. An accomplice, Terry Nichols, was sentenced to life imprisonment for his part in assisting in preparing the bomb.

Some observers have asserted that the U.S. government at times has engaged in acts that may be interpreted as terrorism. For example, in April 1986, President Reagan ordered jet fighters to attack the Libyan cities of Tripoli and Bengazi. The raids killed thirty-seven people and wounded ninety-three others. President Reagan stated the raids were carried out in retaliation for Libya's alleged sponsorship of a bombing of a discothèque in West Berlin, in which two American servicemen and a Turkish woman were killed, and 229 others were wounded.[22]

In the 1980s, the Reagan administration gave millions of dollars in military assistance to revolutionary forces in Nicaragua who were trying to overthrow the government headed by Daniel Ortega. The Ortega government undoubtedly viewed such assistance as terrorist support.

In 1993 there was a standoff between the FBI and David Koresh, the leader of the Branch Davidian cult (located near Waco, Texas). The FBI eventually attacked the compound, setting off a major fire—which destroyed the cult compound, killing many cult members.

Most terrorist acts can be classified as either revolutionary or repressive. *Revolutionary terrorism* is used by groups seeking to bring about major political changes in a particular government. In contrast, *repressive terrorism* has the goal of protecting an existing political order. Terrorist acts by government officials are usually done to quiet dissidents and to serve as a warning to the masses, not to publicly express opposition to the government. Adolph Hitler's Nazi regime sent large numbers of civilians (most of whom were

have been exposed to chemical weapons during operation "Desert Storm" in 1991. The exposure came as a result of the destruction of a weapons bunker in Iraq.

On March 20, 1995, a religious cult in Japan, Aum Shinrikyo ("Supreme Truth"), released the nerve agent *Sarin* in the Tokyo subway system. Twelve people were killed, and 5,500 were injured. A tiny drop of sarin can kill within minutes after skin contact or inhalation of its vapor.

There are numerous biological agents that can be used in germ warfare. Some are amazingly deadly. For example, the Ebola virus kills an estimated 90 percent of its victims in less than a week. For Ebola, there is no known cure or treatment. Even the manner in which it spreads is unclear—perhaps close contact with victims and their blood, or other bodily fluids, or even by just breathing the surrounding air.

According to sources cited in 1995 by the office of Technology Assessment at U.S. Senate Committee hearings, seventeen countries have been named as being suspected of developing biological weapons. These countries include Iran, Iraq, Libya, Syria, North Korea, Taiwan, Israel, Egypt, Vietnam, Laos, Cuba, Bulgaria, India, South Korea, South Africa, China, and Russia. In addition, there is increasing interest by terrorist groups in developing biological weapons.

Is the danger of germ warfare attacks more likely than that of a nuclear attack? Definitely. Building a nuclear capability would cost $1 billion or more, require more than 1,000 scientists, and take years. Developing biological weapons would cost less than $100,000, require only a few biologists and one room, and take just a few weeks. The equipment that is needed is readily available almost anywhere in the world. One can cultivate trillions of bacteria at relatively little risk to one's self with gear such as the following—a beer fermenter, a protein-based culture, a gas mask, and a plastic overgarment.

A large population cannot, at the present time, be protected against a biological attack. Vaccines can prevent some diseases, but only if the causative agent is known in advance. With many biological weapons, the causative agent is first discovered a few days after its release—when a number of people become identified as being ill. In this era of biotechnology, novel organisms can be engineered against which vaccines or antibodies are useless. In addition, certain micro-organisms can persist indefinitely in an environment. For example, Gruinard Island, off the coast of Scotland, remained infected with anthrax spores (which causes the potentially deadly anthrax disease) for forty years after biological warfare tests were carried out there in the 1940s. Those infected with anthrax disease experience high fever, vomiting, joint ache, labored breathing, internal and external bleeding lesions, and possible death.

*Source:* Leonard A. Cole, "The Specter of Biological Weapons," *Scientific American*, December 1996, 60–65.

Jews) to concentration camps, where an estimated 6 million were exterminated. Mao Tse-tung of China, Joseph Stalin of Russia, and Idi Amin of Uganda imprisoned and executed hundreds of thousands of dissidents. Since the end of World War II, the most extreme example of repressive terrorism occurred in Cambodia (officially Democratic Kampuchea). In the mid-1970s Cambodia's government killed about 2 million of its citizens in less than four years.[23] In the past few decades government-backed death squads, a fixture in many Latin American countries, have assassinated numerous political opponents of the governments.

The most common form of terrorism is revolutionary terrorism. Some revolutionary groups believe that periodic terrorist acts will create such chaos that the government they oppose will either meet their demands or fall. Some groups hope that their acts of violence will make the public aware of their cause, enabling them to build popular support and to recruit more members. Sophisticated terrorists openly seek media attention by granting special interviews or releasing prepared statements to the press. Some revolutionary terrorists receive the help of foreign governments that support their goals and objectives.

Most revolutionary terrorist recruits are young, well educated, and have a middle- or upper-middle-class background.[24] They want to save the world, although their vision of what the world should be is tailored to their own inflexible beliefs, which justify whatever methods they use. As a result, the lives of innocent victims are often sacrificed. Evolutionary terrorists seek to punish society for its shortcomings and to intimidate the masses into accepting their demands. Victims are often viewed as being responsible and accountable for society's wrong and therefore generally given little compassion.

Victims may be grouped into two types.[25] *Random victims* are those who find themselves in the wrong place at the wrong time; for example, many

*Theodore Kaczynski looks around as he is led by U.S. Marshals into the federal courthouse in Helena, Montana, on April 4, 1996. Kaczynski admitted that he mailed 16 bombs during a 17-year period that killed three people and injured more than 20 others.*

Israeli citizens have been killed in the past four decades by terrorist attacks of Arab groups who do not recognize Israel as a country. *Selected victims* are chosen because of their prominence. In 1978, for example, Italian Prime Minister Aldo Moro was kidnapped by the Italian Red Brigade, which hoped to win concessions from the Italian government. When that failed, they executed their hostage as a sign of their commitment to their demands.

The specific beliefs and goals of revolutionary terrorists are sometimes only vaguely understood. Some terrorists use violent acts to gain publicity for their causes, to demonstrate their ability to avoid arrest and prosecution, and to encourage others who are discontented with the government to join with them to create a revolution. Some terrorists seek to start a revolutionary war to overturn the government.

Many terrorists unaffiliated with a recognized government agree with radical Marxist theory that armed revolution by the exploited working class is the only way to achieve significant political change. Although only a minority of terrorists hope to set up a communist state, most believe in the necessity of armed revolution.[26] Revolutionary terrorist groups are generally not isolated factions. Although they vary in their goals and beliefs, there is evidence of substantial cooperation and mutual protection by divergent groups. Claire Sterling has noted that there is a vast underground network beyond the reach of national and international law that assists terrorist groups in transporting stolen arms, provides cadet training camps, helps in forging and stealing documents, and provides protection for members wanted by the law.[27] Many revolutionary terrorist organizations finance their activities through illegal activities such as forgery, bank robbery, and kidnapping and ransom.

With the development of nuclear technology and germ warfare, there is increasing concern that a revolutionary terrorist group may acquire such weapons to blackmail a country into releasing political prisoners, paying a financial ransom, or giving political power to the terrorist group.

## VIOLENT PROTEST

Violent protests are closely related to terrorism. Some countries—including Northern Ireland, Israel, and Bosnia—are presently experiencing a number of violent protests.

From 1965 to 1970 the United States was subjected to violent protests. In inner cities thousands of African Americans took to the street and protested living conditions through looting, shooting, and the burning of inner cities in Detroit,

Newark, Washington, Los Angeles, Chicago, and elsewhere. These young African Americans were frustrated and angry over many civil rights promises of the early 1960s that were not fulfilled.

Following the eruption of our inner cities during this period, college students began protesting the Vietnam War en masse. Students took control of campus buildings and disrupted classes. When police tried to evict them, some resisted with force. The violence escalated on many campuses. Buildings were set ablaze, and stores surrounding campuses were looted and vandalized. On some campuses, the National Guard was called out. Clashes between students and the National Guard led to bloodshed in Chicago, at Kent State University in Ohio, and in Washington, DC. In the late 1960s, our country became sharply divided between those who supported and those who opposed the Vietnam War. Our nation's confidence in the "establishment" was considerably weakened during those years.

Protests that sometimes turn into violence have continued on a smaller scale. Examples include employee strikes at businesses for higher pay and improved working conditions, clashes between pro-choice and pro-life advocates, clashes between opponents and proponents of nuclear power, and so on.

## VIOLENT CRIME

Big city newspapers and national weekly news magazines are filled with blood-curdling stories of senseless and bizarre murders. For example, in January 1998, Ted Kaczynski (the Unabomber) pleaded guilty to thirteen federal charges, involving the deaths of three people and the injury of two others. They resulted from five bombings—sent through the mail. This Unabomber also admitted that he placed or mailed an additional eleven bombs that led to twenty-one more injuries. Mr. Kaczynski mailed such bombs, over a seventeen-year period, to protest (at least in his mind) the movement toward high technology in our society. Mr. Kaczynski pleaded guilty in return for a sentence of life in prison.[28]

In addition to murder, other violent crimes commonly committed include aggravated assault, armed robbery, forcible rape, kidnapping, hijacking, and arson (see Chapter 2).

Americans have learned that anyone can become a victim of violent crime. In the late 1970s, the mayor of San Francisco was shot and killed by a disgruntled

◆ Box 14.3 ◆◆◆◆◆◆◆◆◆◆◆◆◆◆◆◆◆◆◆◆◆◆◆◆◆

## Lorena and John Bobbitt: A Bizarre Domestic Violence Case

On January 22, 1994, Lorena Bobbitt was acquitted by reason of temporary insanity on the basis of the "irresistible impulse" that had supposedly compelled her to cut off her husband's penis several months earlier. She claimed her four-year marriage to John Bobbitt was a "reign of terror" in which she was verbally, sexually, and physically abused by her husband.

In a separate trial several months earlier, John Bobbitt was acquitted of marital sexual assault for allegedly raping Lorena Bobbitt shortly before she mutilated him. (After mutilating him, Lorena Bobbitt threw his penis into a cornfield. Police officers found it, and doctors then surgically reattached it to John Bobbitt.)

Lorena Bobbitt spent a few weeks receiving treatment in a Virginia mental hospital and was then released after being evaluated as "recovered" from her temporary insanity. John Bobbitt has since been arrested a few times on domestic abuse charges in which he allegedly abused a few other women that he dated following his divorce from Lorena Bobbitt.

member of the city council. In 1980 John Lennon of the Beatles was assassinated outside his home in New York City. In 1981 both President Ronald Reagan and Pope John Paul II were severely injured by would-be assassins. In 1981 Anwar Sadat, president of Egypt, was assassinated. In August 1981 both the prime minister and president of Iran were killed in a bomb blast. On November 4, 1995, Israeli leader Yitzhak Rabin was assassinated by an Israeli citizen who disagreed with Mr. Rabin's political views. Political leaders assassinated in the 1960s and 1970s in the United States included John F. Kennedy, Martin Luther King, Jr., Malcolm X, and Robert Kennedy. With rapes, muggings, aggravated assault, and armed robberies much more common than murder, Americans' fear of becoming a violent-crime victim is realistic.

The fear of becoming a violent-crime victim has led many Americans to fear walking the streets at night; some fear to venture out even during the daytime. In many big cities, bus drivers are not permitted

## Fear of Involvement and Apathy Toward Strangers

One evening in 1964, Kitty Genovese was walking outside her apartment building in a middle-class section of Queens, New York City. A man stalked her, grabbed her, and began stabbing her. She broke away and let out some blood-curdling screams. Thirty-eight residents in the area began watching from their windows as Miss Genovese yelled and screamed and continued for thirty-seven minutes to fight off her attacker. Most of the witnesses looked on as if they were watching a television thriller. No one rushed to help. No one called the police during this thirty-seven minute ordeal. Had they called, she probably could have been saved.[a] Why didn't the witnesses do something?

A major reason of noninvolvement appears to be that witnesses of violent crime fear the attacker will go after them if their identity becomes known.[b] Fear of getting involved may be a major reason why no one rushed to intervene. But why did the onlookers not call the police anonymously? One explanation is that they may be unconcerned about the well-being of strangers in a big city. If so, this explanation raises questions about how much the traditional value of "lending a helping hand to those in need" still exists.

a. Robert B. Toplin, *Unchallenged Violence: An American Ordeal* (Westport, CT: Greenwood Press, 1975), 15–17.

b. Ibid., 17.

---

to carry change for passengers for fear of robberies. Some churches have been robbed during services; a few have hired security guards to protect their collection plates. Millions of Americans now arm themselves with rifles, shotguns, or handguns.

Armed civilians present a dangerous situation, because the presence of a gun sometimes leads to spur-of-the-moment violence. For example, in the small community of Janesville, Wisconsin, a father verbally chastised his ten-year-old son one evening in April 1994. The son thought the disciplining was unfair. After his father fell asleep on the sofa, the boy took a loaded rifle from his father's gun case, pointed it at his dad's head, and pulled the trigger. After killing his father, the boy walked to the nearest police station and informed the police of his actions.

## SUICIDE

Over 30,000 suicides occur every year, making suicide one of the top ten causes of death in the United States.[29] Suicide can occur during almost any time of life. Why do people decide to terminate their own lives? Is it because life is unbearable, painful, hopeless, or useless?

Patterson et al. cite various risk factors that are related to a person's actual potential of carrying through with a suicide.[30] They propose the following instrument, called the SAD PERSONS scale, for evaluating suicide potential.

Each letter corresponds to one of the high-risk factors.

**S** (Sex)

**A** (Age)

**D** (Depression)

**P** (Previous Attempt)

**E** (Ethanol Abuse)

**R** (Rational Thinking Loss)

**S** (Social Supports Lacking)

**O** (Organized Plan)

**N** (No Spouse)

**S** (Sickness)

It should be emphasized that any of the many available guidelines to assess suicide potential are just that—guidelines. Any person who actually threatens to commit suicide should be believed. The very fact that they are talking about it means that they are thinking about actually doing it. This means that there is some chance that they may kill themselves. However, the following variables are useful as guidelines for determining risk, i.e., how high is the probability that they actually will attempt and succeed at suicide.

*Sex* Among adolescents, females are more likely to try to kill themselves than males; however, males are more likely to succeed in their attempts.[31] Adolescents of either gender may have serious suicide potential. However, greater danger exists if the person threatening suicide is a male. One reason for this is that males are more likely to choose a more deadly means of committing suicide.

*Age*   Although a person of almost any age may attempt and succeed at suicide, the risks are greater for some age groups than for others. Statistics indicate that people who are nineteen or younger, or forty-five or older are in the high-risk groups. The group that has the highest suicide rate in the United States is elderly males.[32]

*Depression*   Depression contributes to a person's potential to commit suicide. Depression doesn't involve simply feeling bad. Rather, it involves a collection of characteristics, feelings, and behaviors that tend to occur in conjunction with each other. People experiencing this collection are referred to as being depressed. These characteristics and feelings include a general feeling of being unhappy, a low level of physical energy, problems in relating to and interacting with others, guilt feelings, feelings of being stressed and burdened, and various physical problems such as sleep disturbances, headaches, and loss of appetite.[33]

*Previous Attempt*   People who have tried to kill themselves before are more likely to succeed than people who are trying to commit suicide for the first time.[34]

*Ethanol Abuse*   Ethanol abuse is abuse of alcohol. Alcoholism is related to suicide. A person who is an alcoholic is much more likely to commit suicide than one who is not.[35] People who attempt or complete suicide are often intoxicated at the time.

*Rational Thinking Loss*   People who suffer from mental or emotional disorders, such as depression, are more likely to kill themselves. Hallucinations, delusions, extreme confusion, or anxiety all contribute to an individual's risk factor. If a person is not thinking realistically and objectively, emotion, and impulsivity are more likely to take over, and a person is more likely to act in a desperate manner.

*Social Supports Lacking*   Loneliness and isolation are primary elements contributing to suicide. People who feel no one cares about them may begin to feel useless and hopeless. Suicide potential may be especially high in cases where a loved one has recently died or deserted the individual who's threatening suicide.

*Organized Plan*   The more specific and organized an individual's plan regarding when and how the suicide will be undertaken, the greater the risk. Additionally, the more dangerous the method, the greater the risk. A plan involving placing the loaded

*Popular cable talk show host Larry King interviews Dr. Jack Kevorkian.*

rifle you have hidden in the basement to your head this evening at 7:00 P.M. is more lethal than a plan of somehow getting some drugs and overdosing sometime. There are several questions which might be asked when evaluating this risk factor. How much detail is involved in the plan? Has the individual put a lot of thought into developing the specific details regarding how the suicide is to occur? How dangerous is the chosen method? Is the method or weapon readily available to the individual? Has the specific time been chosen for when the suicide is to take place?

*No Spouse*   People who have no spouse have a greater likelihood of committing suicide than people who are married.[36] People who are single, divorced, widowed, or separated are included in this high-risk category. Members of this group have a greater chance of being lonely and isolated.

*Sickness*   People who are ill are more likely to commit suicide.[37] This is especially true for those who have long-term illnesses that place substantial limitations on their lives. Perhaps in some of these instances, their inability to cope with the additional stress of sickness and pain eats away at their overall coping ability; they then simply give up.

*Other Symptoms*   There are other characteristics that operate as warning signals for suicide. For example, drug abuse other than alcohol can affect suicide potential.[38]

Rapid changes in mood, behavior, or general attitude are other indicators that a person is in danger of committing suicide. A potentially suicidal person may be one who has suddenly become severely depressed and withdrawn. On the other hand, a person who has been depressed for a long period of time and suddenly becomes strikingly cheerful may also be in danger. Sometimes in the latter instance, the individual has already made up his/her mind to commit suicide. In those instances, the cheerfulness may stem from relief that the desperate decision has finally been made.

Suddenly giving away personal possessions that are especially important or meaningful is another warning signal of suicide potential. It is as if once the decision has been made to commit suicide, giving things away to selected others is a way of finalizing the decision. Perhaps it's a way of tying up loose ends, or of making certain that the final details are taken care of.

### Adolescent Suicide

One high-risk group for suicide is adolescents. Suicide among adolescents is especially upsetting because it is usually sudden and unexpected; family members and friends generally do not have an opportunity for *closure* to the relationship (resolution of conflicts and saying goodbye are not accomplished). Survivors often feel guilty that they did not recognize the severity of the adolescent's emotional pain and that they did not intervene to prevent the adolescent from completing suicide. The survivors also deeply regret that the adolescent's life has been drastically shortened, and that the adolescent will no longer have the opportunity to live a full and gratifying life.

### Causes of Adolescent Suicide

Freese discusses five variables that seem related to adolescent suicide.[39]

*Feeling Helpless and Hopeless*  As adolescents struggle to establish an identity and function independently of their parents, it's no wonder that many feel helpless. They must abide by the rules of their parents and schools. They suffer from peer pressure to conform to the norms of their age group. They seek acceptance by society and a place where they will fit in. At the same time, an adolescent must strive to develop a unique personality, a sense of self that is valuable for its own sake. At times such a struggle may indeed seem hopeless.

*Loneliness*  Feelings of isolation and loneliness also tend to characterize adolescents who attempt suicide. Jacobs and Teicher studied adolescents who attempted suicide and determined that they became increasingly detached and isolated from their relationships with others.[40] Four variables were found to characterize this isolation. One was a long duration of various problems in their lives. The second was a sharp increase prior to the suicide in the number of problems experienced. Third, these adolescents underwent a gradual diminishment of their ability to cope with stress, which resulted in isolating themselves even more. Fourth, there seemed to be a chain-reaction breakdown of one relationship after the other right before the suicide attempt.

*Impulsivity*  Impulsivity, or a sudden decision to act without giving much thought to the action, is yet another variable related to adolescent suicide. Confusion, isolation, and feelings of despair may contribute to an impulsive decision to end it all.

*Lack of a Stable Environment*  Many times, turbulence and disruption at home contribute to the profile of an adolescent suicide. Lack of a stable home environment contributes to the sense of loneliness and isolation. It also eats at the base of a person's social support. Adolescents who attempt suicide are more likely to be alienated from their parents, in addition to having experienced more problems in childhood that escalate in adolescence.[41]

*Increased External and Internal Pressures*  Teeagers today express concern over the many pressures they have to bear. To some extent, these pressures might be related to current social and economic conditions. Many families are breaking up. Pressures to succeed are great. Many young people aren't even certain they will find a job when they get out of school. Peer pressures to conform and to be accepted socially are constantly operating. Suicidal adolescents may simply lose their coping powers and give up.

Rohn et al. studied sixty-five adolescents who tried to commit suicide.[42] Subjects were selected from an inner-city suicide prevention program. They were primarily African American and came from backgrounds characterized by lower socioeconomic status. Three-quarters of the subjects were females. The youngest subject was seven, and the oldest nineteen; the median age was sixteen. Findings revealed that these young people were troubled, isolated, and victimized by numerous pressures. About half of the subjects were labeled "loners." Over half lived in single-parent homes. Approximately one-quarter lived in homes without their own parents. Almost one-third had at least one alcoholic parent. Approximately three-quarters of the subjects had academic difficulties. Over one-third either did not attend school at all or frequently were truant.

## FAMILY VIOLENCE

Steinmetz and Straus note, "It would be hard to find a group or institution in American society in which violence is more of an everyday occurrence than it is within the American family."[43] Violence is perhaps as common in families as is the expression of love and understanding. Spouse abuse, child abuse, sibling abuse, and other examples of physical violence occur in more than half of all U.S. households.[44] (The extent, nature, and causes of family violence were discussed in Chapter 10.)

## VIOLENCE AGAINST PEOPLE OF COLOR

People of color have been subjected to extensive violence by whites in our society. (It has been a two-way street as a number of whites have been subjected to violence by people of color.)

During the second half of the nineteenth century, there were frequent massacres of Chinese mining and railroad workers in the West. For example, during a railroad strike in 1885, white workers stormed a Chinese community in Rock Springs, Wyoming, murdering sixteen persons, and burned all the homes to the ground. No one was arrested. In 1871 a white mob raided the Chinese community in Los Angeles, killing nineteen persons and suspending fifteen of them from scaffolds to serve as a warning to survivors.[45]

Alphonso Pinkney comments about the treatment of black slaves by their white owners:

> Few adult slaves escaped some form of sadism at the hands of slaveholders. A female slaveholder was widely known to punish her slaves by beating them on the face. Another burned her slave girl on the neck with hot tongs. A drunken slaveholder dismembered his slave and threw him piece by piece into a fire. Another planter dragged his slave from bed and inflicted a thousand lashes on him.[46]

Slave owners often used a whip made of cowskin or rawhide to control their slaves. An elaborate punishment system was developed for linking the number of lashes to the seriousness of the offenses with which slaves were charged.

Shortly before the Civil War, roving bands of whites commonly descended on black communities and terrorized and beat the inhabitants. Slaves sometimes struck back and killed their owners or other whites. During the Reconstruction years following the Civil War, it is estimated that five thousand blacks were killed in the South by white vigilante groups.[47]

Following the Civil War, white mobs began lynching blacks, a practice that continued into the 1950s. Blacks were lynched for peeping into a window, attempting to vote, making offensive remarks, seeking employment in a restaurant, arguing with a white person, and expressing sympathy for another lynched black. Arrests for lynching black people were a rarity. Lynch mobs included not only men but sometimes women and children. Sometimes lynchings were publicly announced and the public invited to participate. The public often appeared to enjoy the activities and urged active lynchers on to greater brutality.

Race riots have been commonplace since the Civil War. During the summer of 1919, for example, there were twenty-six major race riots; the most serious that summer was in Chicago. The riot lasted from July 27 to August 2. Fifteen whites and twenty-three blacks were killed, 537 were injured, and over one thousand were left homeless.[48]

Since the Pilgrims arrived, Native Americans have been subjected to kidnapping, massacres, conquest and forced assimilation, and murder. Some tribes have been completely exterminated. The treatment of Native Americans by whites stands as one of the most revolting series of violent acts in history.

Extermination of Native Americans began when the early Christian Pilgrims initiated a policy of massacre and extermination. In 1636 the Massachusetts Bay Puritans sent a force to massacre the Pequot, a division of the Mohegans. The dwellings were burned, and six hundred inhabitants were slaughtered.[49]

In 1642 the governor of New Netherlands offered bounties for Native American scalps. A year later, this same governor ordered the massacre of the Wappinger tribe. Pinkney describes the massacre:

> During the massacre, infants were taken from their mothers' breasts, cut in pieces, and thrown into a fire or into the river. Some children who were still alive were also thrown into the river, and, when their parents attempted to save them, they drowned along with their children. When the massacre was over, the members of the murder party were congratulated by the grateful governor.[50]

A major motive for this violence was that the European settlers were land hungry, and it was difficult to obtain land without confronting the original occupants, the Native Americans. The deliberate massacre and extermination of Native Americans continued from the 1600s throughout most of the 1800s. The whites made and broke treaties and ended up taking

Box 14.5 ◆◆◆◆◆◆◆◆◆◆◆◆◆◆◆◆◆◆◆◆◆◆◆◆◆◆◆

## Battered Woman Arrested in Stabbing Death of Her Husband

**M**rs. Toni Soltis, twenty-eight, [names and other identifying information have been changed], was arrested for killing her husband, Hilton, on August 27, 1998, in Milwaukee, Wisconsin. The Milwaukee County Coroner's office determined the death was caused by a knife piercing the jugular vein. Authorities indicated they considered filing manslaughter charges against Mrs. Soltis.

Mrs. Soltis called police from a Stop and Go convenience store about 3:30 A.M. and said her husband had beaten her. She stated:

> My husband came home after a night of drinking. He was so drunk he had trouble standing up straight. He started yelling at me for the way I keep house. I tried to explain that, with two kids, it's hard to keep the house clean, especially with my working part time. He then ordered me to make him supper and said it better be good. I mentioned we only had TV dinners left and asked him what kind he wanted. He followed me into the kitchen and started yelling and knocking me around.

Mrs. Soltis said she had twice left her husband and gone to a shelter for battered women, as he had often beaten her in the past. She stated she had always returned to her husband, as she couldn't financially raise her children alone and didn't want to be on welfare. She added that when her husband was sober, he was really nice to her and to their two daughters, ages three and five.

Police records showed she filed reports on two of the beatings but did not follow through with formal charges. She received treatment in December 1997 at St. Luke's Hospital after her husband knocked her unconscious. In February she received emergency treatment at St. Luke's for a serious burn to her lip after her husband held the burning end of a cigarette to her lips. Mrs. Soltis said she often was battered by Hilton while he was drunk. When he sobered up the next day, he would not remember the beatings.

Mrs. Soltis went on to describe the present incident:

> When we were in the kitchen, he slapped his hand against my face, and I fell backward against the wall. He then kicked me a couple of times in my side. I suggested one of us should leave so I wouldn't get hurt. He grabbed me and shook me while yelling, "I should kill you right now so you won't ever be able to leave me." He kept yelling at me and slamming me around. I was crying and could no longer fight back. Finally, he got tired of torturing me and left me lying on the dining room floor. I was nearly unconscious.
>
> He left and went into the bedroom, where he soon drifted off to sleep. Gradually, I stopped moaning, and my strength slowly came back. I knew that he would never leave me alone, even if I tried to get a divorce. He'd come after me if I did and kill me. I just couldn't take it anymore. I got up, got a butcher knife, and went into the bedroom. He was lying on his back, snoring. I jabbed it into his throat. I knew if I missed, he'd kill me. When I saw blood, I fled and ran out of the house.
>
> I ran out into the street, expecting him to follow me. I kept looking back.

Police reported Mrs. Soltis ran barefoot into the street and flagged down a car, which took her to the convenience store. Police investigated and found Mr. Soltis had died in the bedroom. Mrs. Soltis was taken to St. Luke's Hospital, where she was treated for a broken rib, a fractured jaw, and numerous cuts and bruises.

After carefully reviewing the facts of this case, the district attorney decided her actions were taken in self-defense and did not press charges. Law enforcement officers in a number of other jurisdictions in the country have struggled with the question of whether similar actions by other wives who are battered should be prosecuted or viewed as self-defense.

most of their land and sharply reducing their population. For example, in 1838 during a forced march, an estimated four thousand Cherokees died from cold and exhaustion.[51] Native Americans were considered savage beasts, and whites felt "the only good Indian is a dead one." Native Americans were exterminated because, it was felt, they impeded economic progress.

Today racial clashes among certain groups still occur on a smaller scale on the street and in schools. Still active in many areas of our country are Skinheads, the Ku Klux Klan, the American Nazi party, and other "white supremacy" groups. Demonstrations by these organizations have led to several bloody clashes. The worst in recent years was a

1979 shoot-out in Greensboro, North Carolina, in which five anti-Klan protestors were killed.

## POLICE BRUTALITY

There have also been a number of accusations of unnecessary violence by police officers. Several examples follow.

In the early morning of December 4, 1969, fifteen police officers (armed with revolvers, submachine guns, and shotguns) stormed an apartment in Chicago occupied by members of the Black Panther party. (The Black Panthers sought to end racial discrimination and sometimes resorted to violent actions.) Evidence indicates the inhabitants were sleeping. No evidence was found that the Panthers fired at all. Two Panthers were shot and killed, and four more were wounded.

On September 4, 1968, three members of the Brooklyn chapter of the Black Panther party appeared at a preliminary hearing in Brooklyn Criminal Court. They had been arrested on charges of assaulting police officers and resisting arrest. Eight or nine other Panthers came to view the hearing. When this group left the courtroom, they were attacked by approximately fifty off-duty white police officers in the corridors of the courthouse. The officers clubbed them with blackjacks and kicked them for several minutes. No arrests of police officers were ever made.

The 1968 Democratic National Convention was held in Chicago from August 26 through August 30. Anti-Vietnam demonstrators came to protest U.S. involvement in the Vietnam War. Police used tear gas, mace, and excessive violence to disperse demonstrators. During that week more than eleven hundred civilians suffered injuries at the hands of the Chicago police. Some innocent individuals were attacked by police as they walked home from work. A thirty-three-year-old schoolteacher who was peacefully demonstrating was knocked to the ground by police. His girlfriend rushed to help him, and she was repeatedly struck by six police officers with police clubs. True, the police were frequently provoked by the demonstrators, but their response was grossly excessive. A study team of the National Commission on the Causes and Prevention of Violence concluded:

> [O]n the part of the police, there was enough wild club swinging, enough cries of hatred, enough gratuitous beating to make the conclusion inescapable that individual policemen, and lots of them, committed violent acts far in excess of the requisite force for crowd dispersal or arrest.[52]

American police officers are six times more likely to kill than be killed. In Europe, far fewer police officers are killed, and officers are much less apt to kill civilians.[53]

Occasionally, we still hear of individuals who are brutally beaten, even killed, following an arrest by police. On May 17, 1980, an all-white jury acquitted four white police officers accused of bludgeoning to death Arthur McDuffie, an African-American insurance salesman in Miami, Florida, who had sped through red lights on a motorcycle. Angry African Americans took to the streets in Miami charging that this was only one of many incidents in which police escaped punishment for brutalizing African-American citizens. Three days of racial rioting ensued, in which nine African Americans and six whites were killed. Damage from fires and looting was estimated at nearly $200 million.[54]

In 1977 three Houston patrolmen killed a Mexican American and threw him into a bayou. The officers were placed on probation by a local court.[55] In 1979, Eulia Love, an African-American woman, was killed in Los Angeles by two white police officers after she resisted attempts to turn off her gas service. The officers were exonerated by the police department's Shooting Review Board.[56]

Police brutality received national attention again in 1991 when an African-American motorist, Rodney King, was stopped and beaten by four club-wielding, white police officers in Los Angeles. The beatings were videotaped by a bystander. Mr. King received more than fifty blows from clubs and sustained eleven skull fractures, a broken ankle, and a variety of other injuries.

The National Advisory Commission on Criminal Justice Standards and Goals found that more than 50 percent of those killed by police are African American, even though African Americans comprise only 12 percent of the population.[57]

However, it is a serious mistake to stereotype all police officers as brutal. Most carry out their duties with reasonable professionalism. Henry Singer notes that the image of a police officer as a brutal borderline criminal is erroneous:

> During the last four years, I have worked with many policemen, and I have found some who conform to this stereotype. But I have also discovered many more who are among the most dedicated, hard-working, committed individuals I have ever met.

*Summer school teacher breaks up a scuffle between two students in the cafeteria of a public elementary school in Northern California.*

The job of a policeman in our society is by far one of the most frustrating, enervating, distressing, and least financially rewarding of any municipal function. . . . The policeman is one of the few agents of society who is required to perform the unpleasant tasks that none of us would do for three or four times his salary.[58]

Robert Toplin adds:

Even with extraordinary police reform, however, police abuses, violence, and difficulties with the community are likely to remain serious problems until the dangers of violence against police can be reduced greatly. In view of the threats that many officers face daily, it is understandable that many have turned increasingly nervous and trigger-happy. . . . We can imagine what ran through the minds, for example, of three Chicago police officers who found themselves trapped in the elevator of a housing project for more than an hour while some residents tried to set the elevator afire with Molotov cocktails. Policemen deserve greater public sympathy for the extremely difficult and often thankless job they perform.[59]

## VIOLENCE AMONG YOUTHS

On March 24, 1998, Mitchell Johnson (age thirteen) and Drew Golden (age eleven) ambushed a group of classmates and teachers at their school in the small town of Jonesboro, Arkansas. Four students and a teacher were shot to death, and ten others were injured. Mitchell Johnson was reportedly upset over being romantically rejected by an eleven-year-old girl at school.[60] This incident highlights the growing rise in youth violence. In some cases police have arrested youths as young as seven for rape, robbery, and assault. Eight- and nine-year-olds have been arrested for murder.

There are more than 200 million guns in the United States, nearly one gun for every citizen.[61] Youths have obtained access to guns in large numbers. Many of today's schools and city streets have the appearance of war zones. Youths have joined gangs in larger cities in increasing numbers. Gangs are a menace in most large cities, and many smaller communities are also now experiencing violent gang activities.

Many schools, like prisons, have now become schools of crime and violence, with atmospheres that provide training for robbery, vandalism, gang warfare, and defiance. School bombings and arson occur frequently. Teachers often fall victim to robberies, sometimes being held up by intruders who appear in front of packed classrooms. Teachers also fall victim to aggravated assaults, and female teachers fear being raped. One authority noted, "Kids carry guns to school like we used to carry cigarettes."[62] When newspapers speak of mugging, vandalism, robbery at knifepoint, assault, and rape, they do not refer to the underworld but to our schools, our children.

A sixteen-year-old casually and without remorse explains the senseless murder he committed:

> We were just driving down the street, and we saw some guy in a blue pickup truck. We looked at him. We didn't know who he was. We weren't too sure. We figured we knew who he was. We drove up next to him, and we looked. We still couldn't—we weren't too sure. I looked over to someone in the car, and he said to go ahead. I just pointed the gun out of the car and shot him, right under the ear. The reason is just—we were kind of high. I don't know if it was for the fun of it or what. We just decided to do it.[63]

Some youths achieve status and self-esteem by joining a gang, where displays of toughness help them counter insecurity during adolescent years. By committing crimes and showing a willingness to fight, unskilled, unemployed school dropouts can feel successful in the eyes of friends. Today's gangs engage in violence of greater severity than did gangs of past years.[64] During the 1950s, gangs fought with bottles, clubs, chains, knives, and fists; now they fight with handguns, revolvers, assault weapons, and shotguns. Coleman and Cressey note:

> The primary motivation of the "fighting gang" is to control their "turf" (territory) and defend their honor, sometimes to the death. Some gangs have long histories, going back thirty or forty years, and gang fights and killings have been a fact of life in some urban neighborhoods for generations.[65]

The enormous popularity of cocaine and other illegal drugs has created serious problems both for law enforcement and for the communities in which drug users live. A major aspect of this problem is that many juvenile gangs are involved in drug trafficking and using drugs, and many cities have experienced a series of gang wars with groups trying to expand and protect their lucrative drug business.

## *Causes of Violence*

At least three main categories of theories seek to explain violence: biological theories, frustration-aggression theory, and control theory. There has also been research on specific sources of violence, including socialization processes, effects of language, and media influence.

## BIOLOGICAL THEORIES

With violence so prevalent, some social scientists have argued that humans, like animals, have a built-in aggressive instinct. Sigmund Freud theorized that humans have a death wish that leads them to enjoy hurting and killing others and themselves.[66] Robert Ardrey suggests that humans have an instinct to conquer and control territory, which often leads to violent interpersonal conflict.[67]

Konrad Lorenz asserts that aggression and violence are useful to survival. Aggressive humans and animals are more apt to reproduce and survive, whereas the less-aggressive ones are likely to die off. Aggression helps ensure that the stronger males will mate, thereby increasing the strength of the species. Aggression also helps establish a system of dominance, thereby giving structure and stability to groups.[68]

Other social scientists have been highly critical of the notion that violence and aggression are inherited. As yet there is no decisive evidence that violence is or is not inherited. Critics of instinctual theories note that aggression and violence are not necessarily the same thing. If humans do have an aggressive drive, it does not necessarily mean they also have an instinct for violence. Furthermore, even if some animals do have territorial or aggressive instincts, this does not mean humans must also, as human behavior tends to be far less instinctive than animal behavior. Finally, it is argued that people reared in some cultures show very little aggressiveness or violence, which suggests humans may not have an aggressive or violent instinct.[69] The Tasaday, a Stone Age tribe in the Philippines, do not even have words in their language to express violence or aggression.

It is widely recognized that males are more aggressive and violent than females. Some biological theories hypothesize that male sex hormones cause more aggressive behavior. Learning theorists, on the other hand, theorize such differences in aggressive behavior are primarily due to socialization differences between boys and girls (see Chapter 7). The question becomes,

Is violence socialized *into* a society that would otherwise be *non*violent, or is violence socialized *out* of societies that would otherwise be *violent*?

## FRUSTRATION-AGGRESSION THEORY

Frustration-aggression theory explains violence as a way to release tension produced by a frustrating situation. The theory results from the commonsense notion that a frustrated person often becomes involved in an aggressive act. The frustrated person may lash out at the source of frustration or may displace the frustration elsewhere. A teenager, for example, who is taunted by others may retaliate, similarly to a pet that is teased. Residents of impoverished neighborhoods who are promised a better life may displace their frustration through rioting when the promises are not fulfilled. An unemployed husband unable to find a job may beat his wife and children.

A major problem with this theory is that it does not explain why frustration leads to violence in some people and situations but not in others. In addition, much aggression and violence seem unrelated to frustration. For example, a professional killer or armed robber does not have to be frustrated to commit an offense.

Although frustration-aggression theory was largely developed by psychologists, some sociologists have applied it to large groups (macro theory). They note that inner-city slums have substantially higher rates of violence. They then argue that poverty, lack of opportunity, and other injustices in these areas are highly frustrating to the residents. Inhabitants want all the material goods they see other citizens enjoy but have no legitimate means of obtaining them. As a result, they become frustrated and lash out against others. This theory provides a reasonable explanation of high rates of violence in inner city slums. A shortcoming is that the theory fails to explain why many frustrated poor people display little or no violence.

## CONTROL THEORY

Closely related to the frustration-aggression theory is control theory. This theory holds that people whose relationships with others are unsatisfactory or inadequate are apt to resort to violence when their attempts to relate to others are frustrated. The theory holds that people who have close relationships with significant others are better able to control or restrain impulsive behavior, as they tend to be more aware and concerned about how their acts of violence may adversely impact others.

Support for this theory is observed in a study by Travis Hirschi, who found that teenage boys with a history of physically aggressive behavior generally lack close relationships with others.[70] Also cited in support of the theory is the fact that violence is significantly higher among ex-convicts and those estranged from friends and family than among Americans in general.

Control theory provides one explanation for the increase in violence. Because traditional socializing factors (church, close family relationships, and being raised in a small community) are declining, control theory suggests violence will increase as people become increasingly isolated.

Some sociologists have taken a different approach to control theory.[71] They picture violence as a human instinct that is expressed when society fails to place tight enough restraints on its members. These control theorists view group norms that discourage violence as being the initial set of restraints. Additional controls include integrated families, the church, and other primary groups. A final set of controls is the police and the fear of arrest, prosecution, and sentencing. When all these controls fail then violent behavior is expressed.

## CULTURE AND SUBCULTURE OF VIOLENCE

Many sociologists believe violence is learned or acquired through the process of socialization. This theory holds that violence is most likely to occur in cultures and subcultures that accept or encourage violent acts.

American culture as a whole seems especially tolerant of, and even encourages, aggression, particularly in males. (Some companies advertise in job announcements that they are looking for "aggressive" executives.) Pinkney noted in 1972:

> My theme is that the United States is an unusually violent society, that such behavior has characterized this society both domestically and in its relations with other countries throughout its history, and that violence thrives in America because the social climate nurtures and rewards it. From the massacre of Indians and the enslavement of blacks in the early years of the nation's history, to the assault on the populations of Hiroshima and Nagasaki in the middle of the twentieth century, to the present-day slaughter of Indo-Chinese peasants and members of the Black Panther Party, American society

has clearly demonstrated its propensity for human destruction.[72]

A Harris poll found further evidence that violence is largely accepted in our society. The poll showed a large majority of Americans agreed with statements such as:

- [As] a boy grows up, it is important he have a few fist fights.

- Human nature being what it is, there will always be wars and conflict.

- Justice may have been a little rough and ready in the days of the Old West, but things worked out better than they do with all the legal red tape.[73]

Learning to be violent may occur in the family, in a subculture such as a street gang, in schools, through watching television, and in a variety of other ways. The learning processes themselves are varied. Aggressive actions are often rewarded by peers. Television and movies often portray that being tough and aggressive leads to respect from others, material success, and exciting romances. Violent habits are also acquired through imitation and modeling. Children who observe adults displaying physical aggression will imitate this aggression in later play activities. Children who are physically abused are much more likely to abuse their own children. Frederick Ilfeld concludes:

> [P]hysical punishment by parents does not inhibit violence and most likely encourages it. It both frustrates the child and gives him a model to imitate and learn from. The learning of violence through modeling applies to more than just parental behavior. It is also relevant to examples set by the mass media, one's peers or other reference groups, and local and national leaders.[74]

It appears that many families teach their children to be violent in certain situations in much the same way that they pass on religious values and practices.

Certain subcultures in America encourage violence more than other subcultures. Subcultures that encourage considerable violence to get what one wants include young working-class males, street gangs, organized crime, militant groups such as the neo-Nazis and the Ku Klux Klan, and terrorist groups.

The tolerance—and even glorification—of violence in our society is pervasive. Our national anthem is a battle song that highlights "bombs bursting in air." We have popular war chants, such as Patrick

Henry's "Give me liberty or give me death," or "I have not yet begun to fight" (made by a U.S. naval commander when asked to surrender). Our history books glorify the wars Americans have fought and won. During the Vietnam War, the Defense Department tried to stir pride for fighting by weekly listing low Allied death counts and high body counts for the enemy. Millions praised Lt. William Calley as a "war hero" after an army court found him guilty of murdering twenty-two Vietnamese men, women, and children at My Lai (during the Vietnam War).

Many people go to stock-car races primarily to see major accidents. Contact sports (football, hockey, boxing, and wrestling) are popular, as Americans enjoy watching and participating in violent activities.

Another aspect that encourages violence in our culture is the idolization of a tough, machismo image. The term *machismo* derives from the Spanish word *macho*, meaning "in a manly style." To be macho is to assert one's masculinity by being tough, brave, and virile; by defending one's honor; by not backing down from a challenge or fight; by putting others in their place. Although men of all ages are influenced by the machismo image, it is young males who usually seek to play the role to the fullest. As part of the machismo role, personal slight (even the most trivial, such as being accidentally bumped on a street) is seen as a direct insult requiring a violent reaction. Coleman and Cressey note that wives have been badly beaten or even killed because their macho husbands felt insulted by a discourteous glance or a laugh at the wrong time.[75] Not only Latin American males but most American males have adopted at least some aspects of the machismo image.

Max Lerner comments on the relationship between machismo and murder:

> We have the wrong picture of most killers. It is not the tough who kill. It is more often the weak who kill, out of fear—yearning to be tough, afraid to face the dismal fact of their weakness, panicking when the moment of test comes. The strong are confident and can live and let others live. They don't have to prove anything.[76]

Lerner's description of killers matches closely the typical profile of assassins of noted national leaders. Assassins and would-be assassins are generally weak individuals who lack friends, have below-average stature, are introverted, and failing their occupational efforts. Through killing a prominent figure, they hope to be recognized as a "great man" in history.[77]

Box 14.6

# Violence in Our Society Is Reflected in Our Language

Language is a mirror of our personality and culture as it reflects a group's dominant concerns and interests. Language is also a molder of personalities and cultures, as it plays an important role in socializing youth as well as adults. Many people are acutely aware of the importance of carefully choosing their words in order to convey their message. Language is very effective in changing attitudes, in arousing wants and emotions, and in inducing changes in behavior. Language also makes possible the growth and transmission of cultures.

Aggressive words and phrases are used extensively in advertising, by the news media, in sports, in entertainment programs on television and movies, in everyday conversation, and in many other areas. To illustrate, the author noted everyday conversations over three consecutive weeks and made the following list of phrases that are aggressive or have aggressive undertones:

- I could wring her neck.
- I could break her neck.
- I could beat the tar out of her.
- She lost her head.
- Get off my back.
- He was fighting mad.
- Sock it to me.
- When he said that, I nearly died.
- I'll get that SOB.
- We'll do her in this time.
- He beat (clobbered, smashed, murdered, mauled, etc.) them.
- He's always chewing me out.
- Well, I'll kick his ass.
- I hate her guts.
- He fights like a tiger.
- Sure as shootin'.
- I'll body-slam him.
- Wait until I see that runt.
- I'll beat her brains out.
- I'll cut her into ribbons.
- She clipped me.
- If she stands in my way, I'll run right over her.

The language used in describing sports events is also highly violent and aggressive. Sportscasters, for example, describe plays as "The halfback 'exploded,' 'sliced,' 'plunged,' 'ploughed,' 'cut,' 'knifed,' or 'punched' through the line," when in fact, all the ball carrier did was to run through an opening. Newspapers describe upcoming games as a "battle," "shootout," "grudge match," or "duel." If one team loses by a large margin, that team is said to have been "mauled," "conquered," "devastated," "mangled," "smothered," "destroyed," "disposed of," "demolished," "annihilated," "crushed," "smashed," "crunched," or "wiped out."

Not only are sports described in aggressive terms, the names of teams also suggest bravery, fierceness, and violence:

Detroit Tigers

Pittsburgh Pirates

Denver Broncos

San Francisco Giants

Detroit Lions

St. Louis Rams

Oakland Raiders

Kansas City Chiefs

Atlanta Braves

Cleveland Indians

Boston Bruins

Chicago Bears

In referring to the consumption of alcoholic beverages it is interesting to note the numerous aggressive idioms applied to having been intoxicated: "got smashed," "bombed," "blitzed," "stoned," "bent out of shape," "blew my mind," "run over by a hippopotamus/herd of buffalo/German tank," or "sniper got me."

Through the continued use of such aggressive expressions in our communications, patterns of aggression are being conveyed and incorporated into attitudes, emotions, behavior, personalities, and our future culture. When channeled into constructive activities, such aggression can be beneficial. When channeled into violence, however, it can generate serious problems.

## MEDIA INFLUENCE

*Taxi Driver,* a violent film portraying an assassination attempt, influenced John Hinckley, Jr., to shoot President Reagan on March 30, 1981. Sixteen people shot themselves to death in 1980 after they saw the film *The Deer Hunter,* which depicted scenes of Russian roulette (taking a handgun containing one bullet, spinning the chamber, pointing it at the head, and pulling the trigger).

A San Francisco mother filed suit against NBC for showing *Born Innocent,* a made-for-TV movie featuring a graphic jailhouse rape with a broom handle. This mother claimed the film influenced five youths to rape her nine-year-old daughter with a pop bottle. The 1994 film *Natural Born Killers* led to several actual copycat murders in the United States.[78] Violent video games, such as Mortal Kombat, have been found to raise levels of aggression and hostility in children and adults who play them frequently.[79]

Such incidents have led a number of people to conclude that violent movies and TV cause violent action. Others disagree, claiming that violent programs may actually reduce violence, as they theorize it is a passive way to release pent-up tensions.

Television violence is common. It is estimated that by age eighteen, a youngster in the United States will have seen 200,000 acts of violence on TV, including 40,000 murders.[80] Youths spend more time watching television than they spend in school or in any other activity except sleep. There is no doubt the mass media is flooded with fictional violence. The crucial question is how it affects our lives.

Since the 1950s, when the viewing of television became widespread, its impact on viewers has received considerable study. After reviewing this evidence, Leo Bogart concludes:

> [T]he overwhelming weight of evidence from this research supports the thesis that exposure to filmed or television violence tends to lead young children to a state of heightened excitability and to an increase in subsequent displays of aggression.[81]

In the late 1960s, a national commission examined the effects of television violence. This Task Force on Mass Media and Violence of the National Commission on the Causes and Prevention of Violence concluded: "Exposure to mass media portrayals of violence over a long period of time socializes audiences into the norms, attitudes, and values contained in those portrayals."[82] The task force also concluded that viewing television violence leads viewers to perform violent acts when they encounter a situation similar to that portrayed, when they anticipate being rewarded for such behavior, or when they do not observe disapproval of the portrayed violence from a fellow viewer.[83]

Timothy Hartnagel et al. have asserted that watching TV violence may have both direct and indirect effects.[84] It may directly lead viewers to engage in violence as it portrays that violence is an acceptable and often gratifying way to get what one wants. Indirectly it may lead viewers to become calloused by overexposure to such programming and therefore make them more tolerant of violence in others.

The extent of TV violence is shown by the results of a study by Richard L. Tobin that monitored three major networks for eight hours a day for one week:

> We marked down ninety-three specific incidents involving sadistic brutality, murder, cold-blooded killing, sexual cruelty and related sadism. . . . We encountered seven different kinds of pistols and revolvers, three varieties of rifles, three distinct brands of shotguns, half a dozen assorted daggers and stilettos, two types of machetes, one butcher's cleaver, a broadax, rapiers galore, a posse of sabers, an electric prodder, and a guillotine. Men (and women and even children) were shot by gunpowder, burned at the stake, tortured over live coals, trussed and beaten in relays, dropped into molten sugar, cut to ribbons (in color), repeatedly kneed in the groin, beaten while being held defenseless by other hoodlums, forcibly drowned, whipped with leather belt.[85]

Tobin's research included reviewing cartoons, recognized as containing the most violence.

A report in May 1982 by the National Institute of Mental Health stated that "violence on television does lead to aggressive behavior by children and teenagers who watch the programs." The report noted that, in a five-year study of 732 children, "several kinds of aggression—conflicts with parents, fighting, and delinquency—were all positively correlated with the total amount of television viewing."[86]

Laboratory studies have shown that viewers are affected by seeing violent movies, at least for a brief period of time. For example, in one study a group of college students was shown a violent movie, and a second group was shown a nonviolent movie. Then both groups were given an opportunity to punish a fellow student with electric shock. Those who watched a violent movie were more likely to punish the student than those who viewed a nonviolent movie.[87]

Leonard Berkowitz, a psychologist who has conducted extensive studies on aggression states:

> I think the link is there. I think it is safe to say that somebody will act more aggressively after seeing a violent movie, for instance. Even if it is only one person in 100,000, that's 100 more violent acts if 10 million people see the movie.[88]

Children imitate television actors in play and both children and adults imitate them in everyday conduct and language. It is certainly plausible that television and movies teach people how to resolve interpersonal conflicts and disagreements. Watching violent programs is likely to increase the chances that viewers will use violence to resolve disputes.

Robert Toplin cites several violent movies shown on TV that have directly elicited violent actions. One of these was *Fuzz*.

> A television movie called . . . *Fuzz* . . . became directly associated with serious acts of violence. The movie contained a scene in which a person was doused with gasoline and set aflame. Shortly after the film's airing on Boston television in 1973, six city youths attacked a twenty-four-year-old woman, forced her to pour gasoline over herself, then struck a match to her body. The charred woman died a short time after reporting the incident. A few weeks alter, another apparently related incident occurred involving four teenage boys who laughingly set a homeless derelict afire.[89]

It is not only fictional TV programs that portray violence. News programs and news magazine programs show considerable real-life violence through reporting accounts of rapes, murders, assassinations, arsons, armed robberies, racial conflicts, gang conflicts, violent disputes between nations, kidnappings, and acts of terrorism. Such real-life violence is apt to suggest to at least some viewers that violence is a common way to settle disputes and disagreements. It has been charged that the news media distort the facts by stressing the violent aspects of news events. It has also been charged that the presence of news media at potentially violent situations (such as protests) increases the chances of violence occurring, as some protestors are aware that violence in front of the media will obtain increased publicity for their cause. Finally, it has been asserted that media coverage of acts such as bomb scares, prison riots, and assassinations is "contagious," as it inspires others to attempt dramatic acts.

Studies are compounding that show a link between TV violence and real-life violence. Yet some authorities still claim media violence has little effect or may actually reduce real-life violence. Some psychiatrists claim watching someone being hurt provides an outlet for pent up tensions and hostilities and thereby reduces the need to express hostility directly in real-life violence.

Leonard Wolf, author of books about Dracula, Frankenstein, and Bluebeard, states he does not believe news media violence produces violent actions:

> I don't buy the notion that TV produces any of this stuff. For every child who commits some form of crime after watching a television program, several million others watch it with no effect. If you look back in history, there were an overwhelming number of horrors before the invention of TV or film. Bluebeard never saw a movie. Hitler never saw TV. . . .
>
> A psychotic does not need TV to turn him loose. His private pressures are sufficient.[90]

Most authorities, however, now agree with Joan Beck's conclusion about the life-imitates-art theory:

> There is no longer any real doubt that watching televised violence can be a direct cause of aggressive behavior in youngsters, or that it teaches them aggression is a powerful, socially acceptable and routine technique for getting their own way. . . .
>
> It's increasingly obvious that we will voluntarily have to give up some dubious pleasures of televised violence as entertainment or be faced with enduring an increasing level of crime in real life.[91]

One study found that children who watch a lot of TV violence at eight years of age have a higher propensity to commit violent crime by age thirty, including beating their own children.[92]

It is an oversimplification to conclude that any portrayal of violence will always tempt viewers to act out what they have just seen. The desire to imitate what is seen on the movie screen or TV partly depends on how it is presented. Characteristics of viewers will also predispose them to react to what they see in different ways. For example, youths with high morals who are well adjusted are apt to react with repulsion while viewing a scene of a juvenile gang laughingly setting fire to an elderly woman doused with gasoline, whereas unhappy youths who feel oppressed and trapped by "the system" may be inspired by this scene to make a similar real-life attempt.

Media violence assuredly is not the single cause of violence. Others include family influence, boredom, poverty, neighborhood environment, peer influence, and psychological maladjustment, to name just a few.

However, because media content is perhaps easier to change than many other contributing factors, it has rightfully drawn considerable attention in an effort to reduce brutality and violence.

## UNIQUE AND VARIED CAUSES FOR EACH VIOLENT ACT

The preceding discussion covered a variety of general factors that contribute to violence. Yet it should be remembered that each individual violent act has unique, specific causes. The reasons the Vietnam War was fought differ from the reasons World War II was fought. The causes of arson differ from gang violence. Every homicide has a set of unique determining factors. The uniqueness of each violent act will be illustrated by presenting some factors that contribute to one of the violent acts in our society —rape.

There is no "typical" profile of a rapist. Rapists vary considerably in motivation for committing the rape: prior criminal record, education, occupation, marital status, and so on.

To further understanding of the diversity in personalities and motivations of rapists, M. L. Cohen et al. developed a typology for categorizing rapists.[93] The typology focuses on the motivation of the rapists, particularly whether motivation is aggression or sex. Four types were established: the aggressive-aim rapist, the sexual-aim rapist, the sex-aggression-fusion rapist, and the impulse rapist.

The *aggressive-aim rapist* seeks to hurt his victim. These rapists may painfully insert objects into the woman's vagina or try to damage the genitals or breasts; sexual satisfaction is not the goal. Often, vaginal intercourse does not even occur. Victims are usually strangers, and the rapist is often angry. Rapists in this category tend to have a so-called macho occupation, such as construction worker or truck driver. Often they are married and have a history of violent relationships with women.

The *sexual-aim rapist* seeks sexual gratification. He uses a minimum amount of aggression, only what is needed to obtain his sexual goal. During the rape he is highly sexually aroused. He has fantasized the rape many times, so the act is not impulsive. He fantasizes that the woman first protests, then submits, and finally falls in love with him because he is such a great lover. (Sad to say, television and films often portray date rape scenes that reinforce the notion that a woman will "fall in love with" a male date who forces

her to engage in sexual intercourse.) In reality, he has a history of poor sexual adjustment; adequate sexual behavior is present only in his fantasy. In childhood and early adolescence he is apt to have been shy, lonely, and passive. He has low self-esteem and has few mature relationships.

The *sex-aggression-fusion rapist* seeks violence to experience sexual excitement. Some rapists of this type are unable to attain an erection unless the victim resists. These rapists, who appear motivated by sadism, use violence only until they are aroused, although a few proceed to murder their victims. This type tends to have a history of antisocial behavior, a noncaring attitude toward others, a lack of stable relationships, no guilt over their behavior, and little control over their impulses. Some have a history of marriage and divorces, with little commitment to any of the marriages. Rapists in this category tend to be the rarest, although also the most dangerous.

The *impulse rapist* commits rape on impulse because the opportunity is available. For example, while robbing an apartment he may find it unoccupied except for one sleeping woman. Seeing the opportunity, he rapes her. This type of rapist has also been called the *predatory rapist*.

In addition to these explanations of rape, there are a variety of others. Feminist theorists deemphasize the sexual motives for rape and instead view rape as a learned expression of power and dominance by men over women. The act of rape is theorized to be learned through gender-role socialization practices in our culture.[94]

## Approaches to Reducing Violence

Many suggestions about how to reduce crime are widely debated. Some of the major ones are instituting gun control, reducing media violence, changing socialization practices, combating violent crimes, and proposing social reform.

### GUN CONTROL

There are more than 200 million firearms in the United States, one for almost every man, woman, and child.[95] Of these guns, one-fourth are handguns, primarily used for target practice or committing crimes such as armed robbery or murder. More than

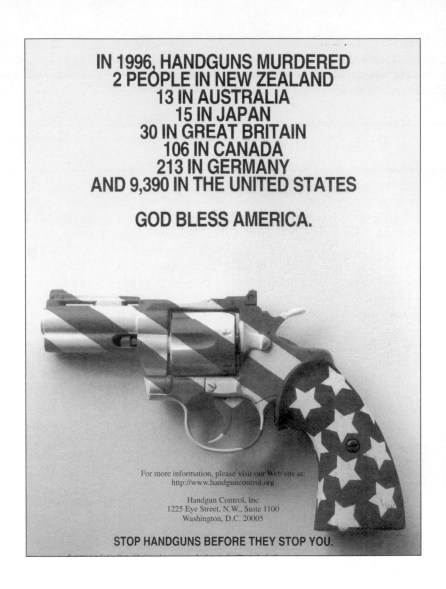

IN 1996, HANDGUNS MURDERED
2 PEOPLE IN NEW ZEALAND
13 IN AUSTRALIA
15 IN JAPAN
30 IN GREAT BRITAIN
106 IN CANADA
213 IN GERMANY
AND 9,390 IN THE UNITED STATES

GOD BLESS AMERICA.

For more information, please visit our Web site at:
http://www.handguncontrol.org

Handgun Control, Inc
1225 Eye Street, N.W., Suite 1100
Washington, D.C. 20005

STOP HANDGUNS BEFORE THEY STOP YOU.

60 percent of all murders in this country are committed with a firearm.[96] Homicide involving a firearm is the leading cause of death among African-American males between the ages of fifteen and twenty-four.[97] A 1998 study found that the United States has the highest rate of any nation of gun deaths—murders, suicides, and accidents.[98]

Regulatory gun laws now vary considerably among states. In practically all states, guns are relatively easy to obtain. The rifle Lee Harvey Oswald used to shoot President Kennedy was bought through the mail for $21.45.[99]

Proponents of stricter gun-control laws argue that restricting guns would reduce the number of homicides. It has been found that the fatality rate for attacks with a gun is five times higher than for attacks with a knife (the second most commonly used weapon in fatal attacks).[100]

Robert Toplin gives an example indicating guns are much more lethal than knives:

A glimpse at Martin Luther King, Jr.'s experiences with violent attacks illustrates the significant difference between the lethality of two kinds of weapons. In 1958, a deranged woman plunged a Japanese letter opener into King's chest while he was signing autographs in a department store. The knife-like object barely missed his aorta, and King recuperated. A decade later, James Earl Ray fired a single shot at King from a considerable distance, killing the civil rights leader immediately. Had the frenzied woman used a gun in her assault ten years before, perhaps American society would have been denied the services of one of its greatest twentieth-century figures just as he was beginning the most active part of his career.[101]

FBI statistics also show the lethal impact of guns. Although guns are used in only one-quarter of all assaults, over two-thirds of all murders involve the use of a gun. In addition, a pistol in a family is six times more likely to be used against a family member than against an intruder.[102] Thus it is argued that stricter gun-control laws would sharply reduce the number of gun-related killings.

Proponents also argue that stricter laws would reduce the number of assaults. That is, people would be less likely to fight if (without a gun) they are less certain to win and there is a greater chance they would suffer injury. It takes only a split second to decide to fight with a gun and pull a trigger. Trying to get the best of someone without using a gun takes more planning and may provide the time for second thoughts.

It is also argued that stricter laws would cut down the number of accidental injuries and deaths by gunshot. Annually, thousands of Americans are injured or killed from accidental discharges from guns.

It is also argued that countries with strict gun control laws, such as Japan and England, have sharply reduced the number of guns held by private citizens, which has resulted in very low gun-murder rates.[103] England, for example, passed a Firearms Act in 1937, which required every gun owner to obtain police certification. This law along with later legislation, established a system allowing gun possession for hunters and target shooters, and farmers plagued by wild animals. Every transaction involving guns and ammunition has to be registered. Gun licenses are given only to those who pass extensive police investigations after filing an application. These licenses have to be renewed every three years with the chief police officer of the area.

Public opinion polls repeatedly show that a substantial majority of Americans favor strategic gun-control laws.[104] Yet this majority preference is being thwarted, mainly by the National Rifle Association (NRA), which can send out as many as 500,000 opposing letters on request. The NRA, called the most effective lobby in the capital, is often joined in lobbying efforts by manufacturers and distributors of firearms.

In the late 1960s the National Commission on the Causes and Prevention of Violence recommended a modest gun-control law. It asked that ownership or possession of handguns be prohibited except for people who received a license after proving they had a special need for such a gun. (Handguns, called "Saturday night specials," are used in a majority of homicides involving guns.) Owners of shotguns and rifles would merely have to obtain identification cards that would be granted to anyone over age eighteen who is not mentally incompetent or a convicted felon. The NRA was largely responsible for lobbying efforts to prevent its enactment.

Opponents of gun control often use catchy phrases to summarize their arguments. The slogan, "Guns don't kill people; people kill people" argue that people and their motives are the problem, not guns. If killers and other felons were locked up (the argument goes), there would be no need for gun-control laws. Proponents of gun control counter this cliché with "People with guns kill people."

Another catchy slogan used by gun-control opponents is "When guns are outlawed, only outlaws will have guns." This phrase suggests that law-abiding citizens need guns to protect themselves from criminals. Proponents counter this argument with statistics showing only a tiny fraction of crimes are aborted by citizens with guns. They add that numerous accidents and emotional shootouts occur when guns are present in homes.

Opponents of gun control also argue that guns help protect the country. They assert that, if an attack by a foreign country occurs, citizens would need guns to fight back. Proponents counter this argument by stating that, if such an unlikely attack did occur, citizens would need much more than pistols, shotguns, and rifles to fight an invading force that has jet fighter planes, bazookas, hand grenades, tanks, and nuclear weapons.

Opponents assert that government control of private firearms would violate the Second Amendment to the Constitution: "A well-regulated Militia, being necessary to the security of a free state, the right of the people to keep and bear arms shall not be infringed." However, proponents note that the courts have already interpreted this amendment to mean that it applies to collective military preparedness, and not to individual gun ownership.[105]

Opponents and proponents of stricter gun-control laws have argued for decades. Yet we still have ineffective gun-control laws and considerable violence occurring through the use of guns. However, there has been movement in the past decade in enacting stricter gun-control laws in the United States. In

1993 the Brady Law was enacted. (This law is named after Jim Brady, who was shot in the head during the assassination attempt on President Reagan in 1981.) The law requires that handgun buyers must wait five business days before obtaining their firearms and also requires that local police agencies must make a reasonable effort to check buyers' backgrounds.[106] In 1994 Congress passed and President Clinton signed, a crime bill banning nineteen types of assault-style firearms; critics asserted the main use of such firearms is to rapidly kill a number of people.

## REDUCING MEDIA VIOLENCE

Although the final verdict is not in, the weight of the evidence discussed earlier suggests movie and TV violence leads to increased real-life violence and aggression in at least some viewers. Many observers, particularly religious leaders, have urged that the focus on violence in television and movies be replaced with programs promoting the ethic of nonviolence. The more our society encourages nonviolence and penalizes violence, the more peaceful our society will be.

But what should be done about the potential influence media violence has on violent behavior? To date, relatively little has been done. TV spokespersons have pledged to reduce violence on television, yet it is still commonly portrayed. A few programs open with warnings that the content may be disturbing to some members of the audience. The movie industry and the TV industry have voluntarily revised rating systems designed to give the public some idea of the level of violence and sex in movies and in TV programs.

A major reason producers have not sharply reduced the level of violence is that violence sells. In the highly competitive entertainment business, producers are much more concerned about ratings than values.

Because the media industries have failed to effectively regulate themselves with respect to violence, some authorities are now urging a federal regulation system. Critics argue that such regulation would violate the First Amendment, which guarantees freedom of speech. Critics further argue federal intervention would be the first major step in the federal government's attempting to control individuals' thoughts through the media. Yet proponents assert the government is already involved in licensing TV stations. It also regulates content by disallowing TV advertisements for cigarettes and alcoholic beverages stronger than wine or beer, by limiting the number of hours network programs can be shown during prime-time evening hours, and by prohibiting the use of vulgarity.

Proponents request guidelines that would significantly reduce media brutality. They ask for guidelines that would sharply limit depictions of killings, painful beatings, and torture of human beings.

The most recent policy effort to address the increase in televised violence is the controversial V-chip. This computer chip is designed to allow parents to program their TV sets so that children cannot watch certain channels or programs while the parents are away from home. The Clinton administration has approved legislation that requires manufacturers to equip new TV sets with the chip. This computer chip approach will undoubtedly face court challenges on the ground that it restricts freedom of expression.

## CHANGES IN SOCIALIZATION PRACTICES

As described in Chapter 7, boys in our society are socialized to be tough and aggressive. Boys are socialized to believe the way to get what they want is by being aggressive, including in male-female relationships. If the goal is considered important, they are urged "to fight for it." Boys are given toy pistols, toy machine guns, and toy tanks to play with. They are urged not to cry or express their insecurities but instead to put forth a facade of toughness and competitiveness. They are urged to excel in violent contact sports like football, wrestling, and hockey.

Girls, on the other hand, are urged to be feminine—passive and nonviolent. They are socialized to be less aggressive, more nurturing, and less competitive than males. (As also noted in Chapter 7, such sex stereotyping and socialization practices are changing, largely due to the women's movement.)

With such traditional socialization practices, it is not surprising that males commit most homicides, armed robberies, rapes, acts of terrorism, aggravated assaults, acts of police brutality, acts of racial clashes, and rioting. Societal leaders are increasingly recognizing that training boys to be macho and girls to be feminine has destructive effects on males, on females, and on society as a whole.

It would seem more reasonable to allow both boys and girls the freedom to choose a wide variety of ways to express themselves—to let them choose the roles, careers, and lifestyles they desire rather than those defined by traditional sex-role stereotypes. It would also seem that the macho role for boys should be deemphasized, that violence should be discouraged rather than glorified, that the virtues of nonviolence should be emphasized, and that peaceful and civilized ways of settling interpersonal disputes should be taught and encouraged more. Some school districts are moving in this direction by using professional mediators to help settle disputes between students. These mediators also instruct students in using the process of mediation to resolve their own disputes.

## COMBATING VIOLENT CRIME

As described in Chapter 2, there have been many suggestions for reducing the rate of violent crimes. These recommendations can be grouped into three major categories: control approaches, punitive approaches, and reformative approaches.

*Control approaches* involve recommendations to improve the effort to arrest, prosecute, and sentence those who commit violent crimes. Such recommendations include:

- Increase the number of police officers
- Improve the training of police officers
- Establish programs to encourage citizens to report violent crimes and to provide information to police departments to help identify violent-crime offenders
- Establish programs to speed up the prosecution of suspected offenders
- Increase expenditures for additional technical equipment (e.g., computers to analyze data) for police departments to use in their efforts to arrest offenders

*Punitive approaches* seek to increase the amount of punishment given to convicted offenders in order to remove them from society and to deter others from committing such crimes. Punitive recommendations include:

- Longer sentences
- Decreased opportunities for probation and parole
- More extensive use of capital punishment
- Harsher prison living conditions

*Reformative approaches* see to rehabilitate convicted offenders, the assumption being that society will be better off if convicted offenders are rehabilitated before being returned to society. Reformative programs seek to change the views of offenders so

that they become law-abiding citizens. Reformative recommendations include:

- Increased use of probation and parole
- Expansion of counseling programs
- Expansion of efforts to educate and provide work training for offenders
- Increased use of victim restitution with a reduction of sending offenders to prison
- Use of halfway houses to help inmates in the process of returning to society
- Use of halfway houses in place of sending offenders to prison
- Use of electronic monitoring in place of sending offenders to prison

(Obviously, as noted in Chapter 2, many of the punitive and rehabilitative recommendations conflict.)

Many of these recommendations have been tried, yet the rate of violent crimes committed per one thousand persons has not shown a significant decrease. Because crime rates have not decreased does not necessarily mean that past and present efforts to curb crime are ineffective. It could be that many efforts are successful but worsening social conditions are counteracting those efforts. Such worsening conditions may include increased exposure to media violence, increased access to guns, increased breakup of American families, less respect for traditional values that discourage violence, schools increasingly becoming battlegrounds for violence, higher unemployment rates, and increased dissatisfaction by the poor with the amount of money the rich have.

## SOCIAL REFORM

A number of sociologists have urged that social programs be developed and expanded to reduce social conditions that are causative factors of crime and violence. Such social conditions include high unemployment, racism, poverty, poor-quality education, alcoholism, drug addiction, and urban ghettos. Former Attorney General Ramsey Clark emphasizes the need for social reform:

> In every major city in the United States, you will find that two-thirds of the arrests take place among about two percent of the population. Where is that area in every city? Well, it's in the same place where infant mortality is four times higher than in the city as a

whole; where the death rate is 25 percent higher; where life expectancy is ten years shorter; where common communicable diseases with the potential of physical and mental damage are six and eight and ten times more frequent; where alcoholism and drug addiction are prevalent to a degree far transcending that of the rest of the city; where education is poorest—the oldest school buildings, the most crowded and turbulent schoolrooms, the fewest certified teachers, the highest rate of dropouts, where the average formal schooling is four to six years less than for the city as a whole.[107]

If resources were available, hardly anyone would be against expanded social programs. The problem is that resources are limited. Government has to decide where and how to allocate limited funds. In the 1980s the Reagan administration severely cut back federal funding for social welfare programs. Many of these programs had the objectives of reducing poverty, illiteracy, poor housing, and alcoholism and drug abuse—all contributing factors in crime and violence. At the present time the rates of crime and the number of people sentenced to prison are increasing. Our prisons are currently bulging with inmates, and many states are forced to build new ones that cost millions of dollars.[108] It appears federal cutbacks in the 1980s have contributed to the increase in crime and violence and to prison crowding.

## COMBATING TERRORISM

A variety of strategies have been suggested to respond to terrorist aggression. Although they have potential payoffs, most also have some negative consequences.

One strategy is negotiation. For example, if a prominent person is kidnapped, a government or private party may seek to meet some or all demands of the terrorists, in exchange for the release of the kidnapped victim. With such a strategy, the hostage or hostages are usually freed. The adverse consequence is that such a strategy encourages further kidnappings and hijackings as terrorist groups are more likely to believe that future ransom demands are apt to be met. In 1987 American citizens were shocked when informed that a year earlier, the Reagan administration had traded military arms to Iran (whose government has been involved in terrorist activities) for Iran's help in releasing American hostages held by terrorist groups in the Middle East.

Some governments have rigidly rejected terrorists' demands in the hope of discouraging future attacks. A few governments even refuse to meet or discuss terrorists' demands. Such a policy endangers the lives of hostages, as terrorists may carry out the threat of disposing of their victims if their demands are unmet. The payoff of this strategy is that non-negotiation sends a message that terrorists' ransom demands are unlikely to be met.

Another strategy is based on "an eye for an eye," an approach often used by Israel. When a Palestinian terrorist group commits terrorist acts (such as bombing) against Israeli civilians, the government usually retaliates with similar actions against Palestinian civilians to inflict similar pain. An adverse consequence of this approach is that each side is apt to build up intense hostility toward the other, which then lessens chances for a negotiated peaceful resolution.

Yet another strategy is to seek to reduce the effects of terrorism. This might be accomplished by: improved intelligence networks better able to identify terrorist groups and to monitor their activities; improved physical defenses, such as better security systems, specialists in hostage negotiations, and police trained in responding to terrorist acts; and improved crisis response, for example, specially trained SWAT teams to free hostages.

Another strategy is directed at governments, such as Libya and Cuba, that support terrorist activities. The United States and its allies sometimes retaliate against countries that support terrorist activities by imposing political and economic sanctions such as refusing to trade goods and services.

An ideal way to end terrorism is for the nations of the world to agree (perhaps in the United Nations) that they will not support terrorist activities, that they will aggressively seek to arrest terrorists who hide in their countries, and that they will not permit known terrorists to enter their countries.

In the past two decades a major political revolution has occurred in many countries that formerly advocated communism. Such countries as Russia, Poland, and Czechoslovakia have now rejected communism in favor of a more democratic form of government. With improved relationships among the Western powers (such as the United States) and Eastern powers (such as Russia), there is also increasing efforts among the major powers to work together to combat terrorism.

## STRATEGIES TO PREVENT WAR AND INTERNATIONAL CONFLICT

A world without war has been a dream of many idealists for centuries. The frequency of past and present international conflicts suggests such as dream may never come true. Even if war cannot be eliminated, certainly for the survival of human civilization its frequency and scope can be reduced. A nuclear war, for example, has the potential of annihilating civilization. This section will examine the following strategies to curb war and international conflict: maintaining a balance of power, disarmament, establishment of an effective world court, peace education, and a worldwide movement toward democracy.

*Balance of Power*    Many authorities (including many military and political leaders) assert the best way of preventing a world war is to maintain a balance of power in which the military strength of the world's most powerful nations is roughly equalized. The assumption is that no nation is apt to strike first if no single nation (or bloc of nations) has military superiority. It has been argued that such a balance of power has prevented the outbreak of a nuclear war between capitalist and communist countries. (The recognition that an all-out nuclear war would probably destroy civilization has also been a factor in preventing a nuclear holocaust.) The balance-of-power concept is not new. The city-states of ancient Greece used it, as have many other societies in the past.

Although the balance-of-power concept has had some success, it also has some limitations. First, it is very difficult to assess the military strength of the enemy. New weapons are continually being developed, and it is difficult to assess, without combat, the effectiveness and efficiency of weapons (such as tanks and fighter planes) of one country against another. As a result, an arms race often develops with a balance-of-power concept. For example in the past the United States wanted to make certain it had military strength at least equal to that of the Soviet Union, which led our country to continually produce more weapons and to develop new ones. The Soviet Union observed us expanding our arsenal and expanded its arsenal. We responded by expanding even more, and so it went for decades. Although the balance-of-power concept appears useful in limiting major confrontations, it does seem to encourage limited conflicts that become games of bluff and counterbluff. For example, the United States and the Soviet Union bluffed each other in the Berlin crises of the 1950s, the Cuba missile crisis in the early 1960s, in Vietnam, and in a variety of other crises.

The balance-of-power concept cannot be counted on as a strategy to maintain international peace. It already has broken down twice in this century, when World War I and II were fought. The strategy is based on fear, not cooperation. If other strategies could be found to curb war successfully, there would be substantially more financial resources available to combat social problems.

*Disarmament*    Advocates of disarmament recommend a balance of power based on fewer weapons or, ideally, on the elimination of all military weapons. Most advocates of disarmament call for a gradual reduction in arms. They assert that a gradual reduction (in which there are inspection systems as well as agreements for the reduction of military weapons and forces) will gradually lead to increased trust and cooperation between powerful nations. They assert a major problem of the balance-of-power strategy is that it leads to distrust. If there are two military superpowers in the world (as there were from about 1950 to 1990—the United States and the Soviet Union), each superpower is apt to believe the other will cheat on any disarmament agreement that is reached by keeping weapons hidden for a surprise attack. From roughly 1960 to 1990 the United States and the Soviet Union debated disarmament plans but were unable to come to an agreement, largely because of distrust. For years the two superpowers were unable to agree on the specifics of an inspection plan. As a result, both countries built and stockpiled nuclear weapons and eventually achieved the capacity to destroy each other several times over.

Only after the Soviet Union rejected communism and started to move toward a democratic form of government around 1990 were the two superpowers willing to sufficiently trust each other and begin to make serious progress toward reducing their nuclear warheads. In 1993 Russia and the United States signed the START (Strategic Arms Reduction Treaty) agreement, which reduces U.S. and Russian stockpiles of long-range nuclear missiles to about one-third of the previous levels.[109] With the disarmament agreement, the chances for an all-out nuclear war between the two superpowers were substantially reduced. A major reason for the more cooperative relationship between

Russia and the United States in recent years was the easing of the mutually hostile ideologies. Once Russia moved toward democratization and away from a state-controlled economy, it became less ideologically opposed to the United States. At the same time, the move toward democratization by Russia led the United States to no longer view Russia as "the evil empire." (This term was used, in reference to Russia, by President Reagan in 1984.)

*World Court* An alternative to settling conflicts by military means is to establish an effective world court. Just as citizens go to court to settle civil disputes, a world court could be used to settle conflicts among nations.

Two essential components are needed in establishing an effective world court. First, a common international law would have to be established. Similar to criminal law, international statutes would need to state what actions constitute international aggression and then specify punishments for offenses. The second essential component is the establishment of an international organization for enforcing the law. This component would involve the establishment of a court system to decide whether or not an accused country has violated the law, and the establishment of a system to administer penalties against countries found guilty.

An elementary framework for international law already exists in the United Nations. The United Nations has a rather vague definition of national aggression:

> The threat or use of armed force across an internationally recognized frontier, for which a government, *de facto* or *de jure,* is responsible because of act or negligence, unless justified by necessity for individual or collective self-defense, by the authority of the United Nations to maintain international peace and security, or by consent of the state within whose territory armed force is being used.[110]

With such a definition, there have been heated debates when countries have brought their disputes to the United Nations as to who started the conflict, and as to whether aggressive actions were performed in self-defense. The United Nations has helped restore peace in three wars between the Arabs and Israelis, in the Greek civil war, in the Korean conflict, and in other conflicts.

The United Nations, however, has generally failed to resolve clashes involving the superpowers. The problem is that Russia, the United States, and other major nations are generally unwilling to give up some of their power to the United Nations or to any other organization. The United Nations has been most effective when its most powerful members (particularly Russia and the United States) agreed on a course of action. Such agreement puts tremendous pressure on less-powerful countries to comply with the agreement. When the superpowers disagree, the United Nations has been ineffective, as it has no power of its own.

One of the difficulties in setting up a more effective world court system is finding an unbiased "jury" to hear the case. The United Nations has been a highly political organization, with individual nations tending to vote with the political blocs they are aligned with rather than in terms of the merits of issues they are dealing with. Despite these complexities, it is essential (perhaps for the survival of the human race) for nations to work toward resolving their differences through peaceful mechanisms rather than through war.

*Peace Education* Pacifists and peace workers have made progress throughout the world informing school-children and the general public about the dangers of war (particularly nuclear war) and the importance of using nonviolent mechanisms for settling disputes. Their activities include offering peace studies courses in schoolrooms, teaching children gentleness and nonviolence in everyday life, and offering courses and conferences on the causes and consequences of war. Content has also been provided on using mediation and arbitration to settle disputes. The peace movement has gradually developed into a loosely organized, worldwide movement that continues to generate peace symbols and curricular content that emphasizes nonviolent approaches to settle disputes—between individuals, between groups, and between countries.

*Worldwide Movement toward Democracy* Future historians may record the political changes taking place in the Eastern European bloc in the late 1980s and 1990s as being the most important political revolution in the twentieth century. The following countries have rejected communism and are moving to establish democratic processes: Russia, Poland, Romania, East Germany (now merged into Germany with West Germany), Bulgaria, Albania, Czechoslovakia, and Hungary. Other countries are also moving toward incorporating, to a greater extent, democratic principles in their political processes, countries such as Nicaragua and China. All of these countries have basically concluded that communism (which has involved state ownership of practically all industries and businesses) does not provide sufficient incentives for its citizens to be economically productive. These countries have concluded not only that Western nations have advanced much more with capitalistic incentives and democratic processes, but also that communism and its Marxist principles have failed.

This movement toward democracy will have far-reaching effects. Here are a few speculations/observations:

- The cold war between the United States and Russia has ended. With similar forms of government the two superpowers are beginning to work cooperatively on resolving international social problems.

- The chances of an all-out nuclear war occurring have been reduced.

- There is significant political and social unrest in some of the countries undergoing substantial political changes. For example, the former country of Yugoslavia has been divided into several small countries; and one of these countries (Bosnia) is experiencing extensive internal conflict between rival factions. Throughout history, when major political changes occurred, substantial social unrest almost always followed.

- The major superpowers are spending less on defense and thereby have more funds available to support educational and social welfare programs.

- Future conflicts among countries may be increasingly centered on economic and ethnic issues rather than differences in political philosophies—as used to exist between the opposing philosophies of communism and democracy. An international crisis that was largely based on economic reasons did occur in 1990 when Iraq invaded Kuwait. A major objective of Iraq was to take control of Kuwait's highly profitable oil fields. The United States, Russia, and other superpowers worked together for the first time in the twentieth century to resolve an international crisis. After the Persian Gulf War was over (with Iraq being soundly defeated) President Bush asserted that the war was an excellent example of a New World Order that is emerging. The New World Order involves the superpowers working together to resolve international disputes between countries.

- Ethnic conflicts in recent years have erupted in Iraq, Bosnia, Kosovo, and Rwanda.

- Countries such as Cuba, Libya, and Iran may seek to establish improved relationships with the United States. In the past, these countries were openly antagonistic to, and suspected of supporting terrorist activities against, the United States. (They engaged in such activities in part because they presumed they had the support of Russia.) With improved relations, Russia is less apt to be supportive of terrorist activities against the United States.

## Summary

Violence is commonplace not only in our society, but worldwide. The incidence of violence has increased considerably over the past decades. America has a history of violence, beginning when the colonists massacred Native Americans.

Violence is expressed in a variety of ways: war, nuclear war, terrorism (acts by terrorist groups and by governments), violent protest, violent crime (homicide, assault, armed robbery, rape, arson), suicide, family violence (spouse abuse, child abuse, sibling abuse, elder abuse), violence against people of color, police brutality, and violence among youths.

Many theories seek to explain violence. Biological theories assert violence is due to built-in aggressive instinct. Frustration-aggression theories explain violence as a way to release tension produced by a frustrating situation. Control theories view violence as resulting from the lack of development of internal controls. Culture-subculture theories believe violence is learned or acquired through socialization processes and assert that the learning of violence results from many factors: our aggressive language, glorification of the machismo image, peer and family influences, the violence that occurs in many of our schools, neighborhood environment, sex-role socialization patterns, and violent TV and movie programs.

There has been considerable controversy over the relationship between violence in television programs/movies and real-life violence. The weight of the evidence suggests violent media programs contribute to real-life violence.

Each violent act also has unique, specific causes. For example, each homicide has a unique set of determining factors, and the reasons murder in general is committed differ somewhat from the determinants of other violent acts.

Approaches for reducing violence include stricter gun-control laws, decreasing media violence, and changes in socialization practices that would reduce the glorification of machismo and violence in males. Three major approaches for reducing violent crimes are expansion of control efforts, increased punitive measures for convicted offenders, and expansion of reformative efforts to rehabilitate offenders. Social reform efforts seek to reduce violence by alleviating some of the breeding grounds of violence, such as poverty, racism, unemployment, low-quality education, and impoverished inner cities. It appears that federal cutbacks in funding social programs in the 1980s may have been a contributing factor in leading to a worsening of these determinants—which may be a reason why higher rates of violence are now occurring.

Numerous strategies have been suggested to combat terrorism. If hostages are taken, negotiating with terrorists about their ransom demands is one strategy to attain release of hostages. (This strategy has the drawback of encouraging further terrorist activities.) Refusing to negotiate is a second strategy, which is designed to curb future terrorist acts. Endorsing the philosophy of an "eye for an eye" is another strategy used by some governments. Improving intelligence networks, physical defenses, and crisis responses to terrorist activities is yet another strategy. An ideal way to combat terrorism is a mutual agreement among all nations to aggressively fight terrorism. The chances for such an agreement have increased in recent years with the improvement in relationships between Russia and the United States.

Strategies to prevent war and international conflict include maintaining a balance of power, disarmament, establishment of an effective world court, peace education, and a worldwide movement toward democracy. The chances of an all-out nuclear war occurring between the superpowers appears to have lessened in recent years, primarily because of the improvement in relationships between Russia and the United States.

CHAPTER 15

*Urban Problems*

City dwellers differ from rural dwellers in a number of ways. City dwellers have higher levels of income and education, greater social mobility, smaller families, greater diversity, less-stable marriages, and higher reported rates of alcoholism, drug addiction, suicide, and mental illness. This chapter:

♦ Provides a brief history of the development of cities

♦ Summarizes contemporary sociological theories on the effects of urbanism on city dwellers

♦ Summarizes serious problems encountered by central cities

♦ Presents proposals for combating problems in central cities

**Table 15.1**   *Population of the Ten Largest U.S. Cities*

| | | |
|---|---|---|
| 1. | New York | 7,333,000 |
| 2. | Los Angeles | 3,449,000 |
| 3. | Chicago | 2,732,000 |
| 4. | Houston | 1,702,000 |
| 5. | Philadelphia | 1,524,000 |
| 6. | San Diego | 1,152,000 |
| 7. | Phoenix | 1,049,000 |
| 8. | Dallas | 1,023,000 |
| 9. | San Antonio | 999,000 |
| 10. | Detroit | 992,000 |

*Source:* U.S. Bureau of the Census, *Statistical Abstract of the United States, 1997* (Washington, DC: U.S. Government Printing Office, 1997), 45–47.

## History of Cities

Large cities are a relatively recent phenomenon. True, ancient history tended to revolve around cities such as Athens, Rome, Jerusalem, and Constantinople. But compared to today's urban centers, they would be viewed as small. For example, in 1400 London was the largest city in Europe, with only about thirty-five thousand inhabitants.[1] Today, New York City has over 7 million people, and if surrounding suburbs are included, greater New York contains over 20 million people.[2]

The proliferation of cities in the United States emerged from the Industrial Revolution. Until the nineteenth century, the United States was primarily an agricultural country, with most people living and working on small farms. The few existing cities were mainly market towns.

In the eighteenth, nineteenth, and twentieth centuries the Industrial Revolution flourished in Europe and America. Mainly this was due to technological advances, such as development of the steam engine.

Prior to the Industrial Revolution there were few communities in Europe or America with populations larger than a few thousand. One of the consequences of the revolution was the development of large urban areas located close to factories. Because employment opportunities were limited in rural areas, many workers moved to cities. With such movement, family and kinship ties were broken, and those who were unable to adapt faced a loss of community identity, alienation, and social breakdown.

Technological innovations (such as the invention of the elevator and the use of cast iron in building construction) made it possible for cities to expand vertically. Other inventions, such as railroads and automobiles, have made it possible for cities to expand horizontally as well. The railroad was also important in the westward expansion in urban development. Railroads helped tie the country's regions together by providing rapid transportation of people and goods. Many towns were built along railroad lines and some evolved into major cities.

In the past two centuries there has been a dramatic movement of people from rural to urban areas. In 1780, 90 percent of the U.S. population lived in rural areas, mostly on small farms. Now, more than 77 percent of the U.S. population resides in urban areas.[3] Populations of the ten largest U.S. cities are shown in Table 15.1.

The rapid growth of cities has led to a variety of social problems, some of which have been solved. For example, at the beginning of this century, when horses were a major mode of transportation, there was serious concern that horse dung would despoil city life and spread disease. The invention of the automobile resolved this problem but created new problems of air pollution, traffic deaths, and traffic jams. Prior to the twentieth century, cities had much higher death rates than rural areas. These problems were resolved in the early part of this century by the development of adequate waste disposal and water supply systems. Innovations in sanitation and medicine in this century have also improved urban living conditions. Yet, as will be discussed later, many urban problems remain unresolved, some of them intensifying in severity.

## Urban and Rural Areas Defined

XXXXXXXXXXXXXXXXXXXXX

Some definitions of terms may be useful. The Census Bureau uses a set number of people in a community to separate urban from rural. The bureau defines a community as being *urban* when twenty-five hundred or more inhabitants live in an incorporated city, village, borough, or town. A community with fewer than twenty-five hundred inhabitants is classified as *rural*.

The term *megalopolis* refers to areas in which one large city fuses with others. The largest megalopolis in the United States is the stretch of cities and suburbs (largely unbroken) along the East Coast from Boston to Miami Beach. On the West Coast the urban areas from San Diego to San Francisco may also be considered a megalopolis.

It is increasingly difficult in some communities to accurately distinguish rural areas from urban areas. In the past, farming was considered the epitome of rural life. Today, many rural areas demonstrate some urban characteristics. For example, in rural areas near urban centers, many people who work in cities have built homes in the country. A number of grocery stores, service stations, and other small businesses have relocated to such areas, which are gradually becoming semirural-semiurban. In addition, in many rural areas large-scale farming operations (called agribusinesses) are gradually replacing small farms. Agribusinesses have some characteristics of urbanism.

## An Urbanizing World

XXXXXXXXXXXXXXXXXXXXX

The move to living in an urban area is a worldwide phenomenon. By the year 2010 it is projected that more than half of the world's population will live in an urban area.[4] Some urban areas are growing much faster than others. In 1950, the New York metropolitan area was the largest in the world. At the present time two other metropolitan areas in the world are larger (Mexico City and São Paulo), and according to U.N. population projections it will be in about eleventh place by 2015, outstripped by Tokyo, Bombay, Lagos, Shanghai, Jakarta, São Paulo, Karachi, Beijing, Dhaka, and Mexico City.[5]

While some of the consequences of this urban transformation are positive for those who move to urban areas, there are also a number of adverse conditions in large urban areas—such as crowding, deterio-

rated housing, threats of gangs and violence, high rates of crime, and high rates of homelessness. In addition, urban infrastructures (water systems, sewage disposal, transportation, lighting, and medical facilities) are often inadequate to serve a rapidly increasing population. (In India, for example, only eight of the more than 3,000 cities and towns have sewage treatment plants.[6]) The World Resources Institute estimates that 90 percent of the raw sewage from urban areas in developing nations is seeping into rivers and streams.[7]

The size of the urban population of many developing nations is much higher than would be expected from their overall level of industrialization. These countries are "overurbanized," as more people live in the cities than can reasonably be supported by the infrastructures.

*Aerial view of Tokyo, showing the expanse of one of the world's largest cities.*

Because the less developed countries have more than double the population growth rate of the industrialized nations and only a fraction of their wealth, urban problems in these countries are staggering in severity.[8] In many such urban centers shantytowns have developed. Coleman and Cressey describe living conditions in shantytowns:

> These shantytowns are more than just overcrowded: They lack the basic services necessary for a decent life. The streets are unpaved, there is little fire or police protection, clean water is scarce, and proper sewage facilities are often nonexistent. As a result, health conditions are deplorable, death rates are high, and disease runs rampant. Urban squatters have no legal rights to the land they live on, and they are in constant danger of losing their homes. If the government decides it needs the land or that the squatters are an eyesore or a source of political unrest, they can simply be moved out.[9]

## Theories on the Effects of Urbanism

Do city dwellers have a unique way of looking at life? What are the effects of urbanism on city residents? We will examine the theories of Georg Simmel, Louis Wirth, Herbert Gans, and Claude Fischer.

### GEORG SIMMEL

Georg Simmel was a German sociologist who published his classic thesis "The Metropolis and Mental Life" in 1903.[10] Simmel observed that urban people are constantly bombarded by "nervous stimulation," through traffic, noise, the rapid pace of life, numerous advertisements, crowds, and many other stimuli. These stimuli tend to overload city dwellers, who cannot attend to everything that goes on around them.

Consequently, they become indifferent to their surroundings; they lose interest in the well-being of strangers and acquaintances. Although the city offers greater anonymity and freedom to be unconventional, it also increases the chances that inhabitants will be isolated and lonely.

## LOUIS WIRTH

Louis Wirth reached conclusions that were similar to Simmel's about the psychological impact of urban life.[11] Wirth, who was in the sociology department at the University of Chicago, published his theory in 1938. Wirth identified the unique characteristics of cities as being their density, size, and the social diversity of their populations. Wirth's basic theory is that cities increase the incidence of personality and social disorders.

Wirth agrees with Simmel that the overabundance of stimulation leads urban dwellers to become unconcerned about the well-being of strangers and acquaintances. City dwellers become aloof, impersonal, and brusque in interactions with others. Such estrangement loosens the bonds that unite rural people. In some cases, the bonds are completely severed, and such "victims" then express their feelings of alienation and loneliness through acting out their fantasies. Such people are without emotional support or societal restraint, and as a result they are more apt to either be creative (in innovations) or turn to antisocial behavior—including suicide, delinquency, crime, and emotional and behavioral disorders.

City life contributes to the loosening of social restraints and interpersonal relationships in another way. The city emphasizes economic competition and division of labor. Being highly specialized in their work, people are more apt to know one another only superficially. That is, they interact in their roles as barber, bank teller, store clerk, or bus driver and seldom get to know one another in a caring and intimate way. As a result, city dwellers are less likely to have close emotional ties and more apt to feel isolated and lonely in the midst of vast crowds. City dwellers learn to accept instability and insecurity as a way of life.

There are other factors that loosen social bonds. City dwellers are forced daily to assume many different roles in interactions with neighbors, coworkers, customers, merchants, friends, and family. The multiplicity of people and places weakens social bonds. In addition, as people spend considerable time interacting with others at work and in unique leisure activi-

ties, the family becomes less important. Many urban dwellers feel alienated and have a sense of anomie. (*Anomie,* as described in Chapter 2, is a condition in which individuals no longer have an interest in being guided by norms that govern acceptable social behavior.) According to Wirth, all these factors lead to a decline in moral values, encourage greater social disruption, and promote personality disorders.

## HERBERT GANS

Not all urban sociologists are as pessimistic about urban life as Wirth. Herbert Gans asserts that Wirth's view represents an antiurban bias and reflects rural America's dislike of cities.[12] Gans asserts Wirth overlooks many urban dwellers who have a strong sense of community. Gans identified five types of city inhabitants, and asserted only the last two of these types suffer from social isolation (and experience urban life as described by Wirth):

1. *Cosmopolites* (writers, artists, intellectuals, entertainers, and professionals) choose to live in cities because of their cultural activities.

2. *Childless people* choose to live in cities because of nearness to job opportunities and because of the social life.

3. *Ethnic villagers* desire to live in self-contained ethnic communities, which enable them to maintain their cultural and kinship patterns.

4. *Deprived people* who live in cities include those with disabilities, the poor, and minorities who are victimized by discrimination.

5. *Trapped people* are sliding down the socioeconomic scale or are retired and unable to leave their decaying neighborhoods, as they are living on fixed incomes.

Gans asserted the first three categories live in the city because of the benefits it offers, and because they are in a supportive subculture. Gans also found that social class and age have a greater effect on urban lifestyles than does city living itself.

## CLAUDE FISCHER

Clause Fischer developed a theory of urbanism that became known as *subculture.*[13] Fischer agrees with Wirth that cities produce major social and psychological effects. However, Fischer asserts these effects are not the result of existing social groups breaking down, but instead are due to the creation of new social groups, which cities foster.

According to Fischer, cities foster the development of diverse subcultures—Chinese Americans, college students, drug cultures, homosexuals, artists, and juvenile gangs, for example. Fischer believes that people in cities have meaningful lives that partially result from membership and participation in subcultures. Urbanism encourages subcultures, as cities are more likely to attract a sizable proportion of a given subculture (due to a larger critical mass) than a smaller community. This subcultural process is true not only for ethnic and racial groups, but also for a wide variety of other subcultures—academians, corporate executives, welfare recipients, criminals, physicians, computer programmers, dentists, pharmacists, and so on. Some subcultures develop values and take actions that benefit a community; for example, charity work done by the Zor Shriners. Other subcultures, such as juvenile gangs, develop values and take actions that are destructive in a community.

## Problems Confronting Central Cities

Central cities are being confronted with a variety of problems that are so severe and pervasive that they appear nearly unresolvable. This section will examine the following problems: inner-city distressed neighborhoods, deconcentration and financial crises, lack of planning and coordination, housing, crime, transportation, and anti-urban bias.

### INNER-CITY DISTRESSED NEIGHBORHOODS

A variety of negative adjectives have been used to describe the dismal living conditions in distressed neighborhoods. The following are examples: *decaying, inhuman, dreadful, distasteful, shocking,* and *degrading.* Distressed neighborhoods are primarily inhabited by the poor, the elderly, and by people of color, particularly African Americans and Latinos. Many distressed neighborhoods have an ethnic concentration, such as African Americans, Mexican Americans, Cubans, or Puerto Ricans.

Distressed neighborhoods have high rates of crime, illiteracy, births outside of marriage, single-parent households, mental illness, suicide, drug and alcohol abuse, unemployment, infant mortality, rape, aggravated assault, and delinquency. High proportions of the residents are on public assistance, and many city services are inferior. Schools are inferior. Streets are narrow and often filled with potholes. Police and fire protection are inadequate.

The housing is crowded, decaying, and much of it is substandard. Heat in winter is often inadequate, and many units lack adequate plumbing. Broken windows and doors and peeling paint are common sights. People of color inhabit much of this substandard housing because most cannot afford an alternative, and because discrimination makes relocation difficult even for those whose incomes would enable them to move.

One factor leading to the decline of inner cities is the sharp decline of blue-collar jobs. Many blue-collar jobs are unskilled or semi-skilled and therefore require less training and education than white-collar and service jobs. In the past the employable in inner cities have largely held blue-collar jobs. For a neighborhood to resist deterioration, a minimal economic base must be maintained. As blue-collar jobs decline and the quality of municipal services (such as transportation and public schools) deteriorates, faith in community restoration and revitalization fades.

Distressed neighborhoods are a national disgrace. Our country is the richest and most powerful in the world, yet we have been unable to improve living conditions in our distressed neighborhoods.

Our country has tried a variety of approaches to improve distressed neighborhoods. Programs and services include work training, job placement, financial assistance through public welfare, low-interest loans to start businesses, Head Start, drug and alcohol treatment, crime prevention, housing rehabilitation, day-care services, health care services, and public health services.

One of the most comprehensive undertakings to assist distressed neighborhoods was the Model Cities Program, which was part of the War on Poverty in the 1960s. The program involved tearing down dilapidated housing, and then building comfortable living quarters. Salvageable buildings were renovated. Several inner cities were targeted for this massive intervention. In addition to housing, these Model City projects offered a variety of programs that provided job training and placement, health care services, social services, and educational opportunities. The results were more than depressing. The communities have again become distressed neighborhoods. Living conditions are as bleak, or bleaker, than at the start of the Model City interventions.[14]

To date, most programs implemented have had, at best, only short-term success. Distressed neighborhoods continue to be characterized by abysmal living conditions. Since the early 1980s the federal government appears to have given up trying to improve living conditions in inner cities, as federal programs in inner cities have either been eliminated or sharply cut back. Poverty and dependence on public assistance have become a lifestyle for large numbers of residents in distressed neighborhoods.

Our society, for better or worse, is a materialistic society. The two main legitimate avenues for acquiring material goods arise through a good education and a high-paying job. It appears many residents of distressed neighborhoods realize the prospects are bleak for them to obtain a good education (when only inferior schools exist in their areas) or a high-paying job (when they have few marketable job skills). As a result, many are turning to illegitimate ways to get material goods (shoplifting, drug trafficking, robbery, con games). Many have also turned to immediate gratifications (sex and drugs). A value system is developing based on resignation, dependence on public assistance, and a substandard lifestyle.

In spite of the dismal living conditions in distressed neighborhoods, a significant proportion of the residents find a way to have a happy and productive life (see Box 15.2).

## DECONCENTRATION AND FINANCIAL CRISES

Deconcentration is the flight from cities to the suburbs by middle- and upper-class families. The trend toward suburbanization began with the introduction of commuter railways several decades ago. Commercial institutions (grocery stores, hardware stores, banks) soon followed. With the introduction of automobiles in the 1920s, the trend toward suburbanization accelerated. Court-ordered busing for school integration in the 1970s also accelerated the flight of middle class whites to suburbs. The federal government in the 1960s and 1970s indirectly encouraged the suburban trend in at least two ways. First, the construction of expressways made it easier for people who could afford a home to live in suburbs and travel to the city to work. Also, low-interest mortgages made available by the Federal Housing Authority (FHA) and Veterans Administration (VA) made it easier for middle-income people to buy homes in the suburbs. Because a large proportion of mortgage payments is interest which is tax deductible, federal Internal Revenue Service policies also encouraged people to buy a home.

With the exodus of middle- and upper-class families to suburbs, those who remained living in inner cities included primarily the poor, the elderly, the homeless, the chronically unemployed, and people of color.

Box 15.2 ◆◆◆◆◆◆◆◆◆◆◆◆◆◆◆◆◆◆◆◆◆◆◆◆◆

# Playing a Poor Hand Well

**M**any adults who currently are enjoying a happy and productive life grew up under very difficult and stressful conditions. They may have been raised in a high-crime, distressed neighborhood. They may have been abused physically, sexually, or emotionally by a family member. They may have been raised in a series of foster homes. They may have significant physical disabilities, or a learning disabilities. Some of these individuals have managed to escape serious emotional damage entirely. Others struggled as children and teenagers with school and had emotional and behavioral difficulties, but then turned their lives around in their twenties.

What turned things around for them? Why were they able to play a poor hand well—while many others in similar situations succumbed, and lived a life full of despair? Mark Katz asserts in *On Playing a Poor Hand Well* that through identifying why some people have learned to play a poor hand well, we will then learn to provide avenues through which turning point experiences and second-chance opportunities can occur for those experiencing severe adversity.

Katz summarizes evidence that a variety of *protective influences* are key to helping a young person find a way to enjoy a happy and productive life. Some of these protective influences are the following. A close-knit family living in a distressed neighborhood can be protective; children may not feel safe on the street, but they feel safe at home. Homeless mothers who see their prime necessity to be insuring that their child was outside waiting for the school bus each morning have been a protective influence for some homeless children.

Parents advocating for a child with special needs, trying to insure that those needs are met, provide protection. The protective influence may be an older brother or sister helping a younger family member understand a parent's illness; or it may be an aunt or uncle or grandparent helping to raise a child because the child's parents may be unable to do so. A school that offers smaller class sizes, that can address each child's unique learning needs, and highlight each child's special strengths, talents, and interests, can be protective. Also protective are high-quality recreational programs in distressed neighborhoods that children and teenagers go to after school, and stay at for hours.

Mentors and special role models whom children get to know at school, during after-school activities, or through involvement in church or youth groups, are protective. Those who overcome childhood adversities often identify a special person in their lives—a teacher, coach, parent, or counselor—who was always there when needed the most.

Protection can also come from within. Some children have qualities that draw others toward them in times of need. They may be sparkly. They may excel at developing safety nets for themselves; when adversity arises, their safety net is there to catch them. Some children are strong academically, or very skilled socially, so that success in the neighborhood and in school comes fairly easily. Some children are more resilient, having the capacity to withstand the effects of exposure to known risk factors; for example, having the tendency to reframe adversities as being challenges that they know they have the capacities to overcome.

*Source:* Mark Katz, *On Playing a Poor Hand Well* (New York: W. W. Norton, 1997).

---

Many suburbanites utilize municipal services without having to pay taxes to support these services. They come to cities to work, visit city museums, enjoy outings in parks, while at the same time taking for granted the use of a variety of services that the city pays for, such as police and fire protection, transportation, and sanitation facilities. The result is that city residents (who often have limited financial resources) are forced to finance services used tax free by wealthier suburbanites.

Due to the exodus of the middle and upper classes and due to the movement of many commercial and industrial businesses to suburbs the tax base in inner cities has largely been depleted. Sadly, the remaining population is most in need of public services, but the revenues of central cities are contracting. Deconcentration has greatly contributed to urban decay and blight.

Many suburbs have now become self-contained communities. Some suburbanites who do not work in the city never travel to the central city. More than twice the nation's commuters journey from suburb to suburb now, compared to suburb to central city.[15] A study of suburbanites in the Detroit metropolitan area found that one-third never visit the city for any purpose.[16] Many suburbs have a full range of services: schools, parks, department stores, places of worship, medical services, libraries, nightclubs, counseling services, automobile repair shops, bus transportation, and so on.

In the past thirty years there has also been a tremendous shift of the workforce from the Snowbelt cities of the East and North to the Sunbelt cities of the West and South—cities such as Phoenix, Dallas, Atlanta, San Antonio, and Orlando. This shift has also contributed to the urban decay of central cities in the North and East.

Having seen the advantages of suburban relocation, many manufacturers have moved. By relocating near expressways they have reduced their transportation and freight costs. Land is also less expensive there than in the city. Manufacturers who already lived in the suburbs have relocated their businesses closer to their homes. Their move away from cities has sharply reduced the number of jobs in central cities, reduced the tax base and contributed to urban decay.

Property taxes provide cities with their major source of revenues. With the exodus of white middle- and upper-class city dwellers to suburbs, the tax base has contracted even more. The increased concentration of the poor, the elderly, and the unemployed in central cities has resulted in greater demands for public assistance programs and other services. In a very real sense, central cities are in competition with suburbs for the relocation of businesses and for housing that will attract middle- and upper-class families. To compete, central cities must undertake large-scale redevelopment and physical rehabilitation projects. Otherwise, they will lose more businesses and residents. With a contracting tax base, however, central cities find it very difficult to undertake such projects. In fact, some cities experiencing financial difficulties are forced to channel funds away from mass transportation, sewage and water systems, streets, libraries, and other essential services to meet daily operating costs and finance their current debts.[17] Such cities are further diminishing their chances to rebound in the future. The economic gap between healthy suburbs and distressed cities continues to worsen.[18] In many central cities public transportation, highway systems, bridges, and buildings are severely deteriorating, as cities are generally unable to fund the costs of repairs or replacement.

In the 1970s the federal government sought to help cities by giving federal grants to state and city governments. Between 1970 and 1980, the amount of money allocated to state and city governments nearly quadrupled—from $24 billion to $91 billion.[19] This money was used by most cities to finance basic services, even though such expenditures were never the purpose of federal aid. Sizable proportions of paychecks to municipal employees were paid with these federal funds. In the 1980s, the government sharply reduced these federal grants. Cities (which had become dependent on the grants) experienced severe financial strains and were forced to reduce expenditures for public housing, education, and mass transit. In more affluent states, such as California and New York, state governments have offset some of the loss by increasing state aid to cities. Other states, particularly in the Midwest, have not sought to replace the cuts in federal funding. In these states the federal cutbacks have accelerated the deterioration of central cities.

With the suburban flight of middle- and upper-income classes, cities cannot rely on property taxes to pay their bills. They have turned, therefore, to city sales taxes, city income taxes, and city automobile taxes. The more these taxes increased, the more those who could pay the taxes (including businesses) moved to suburbs.

## LACK OF PLANNING AND COORDINATION

In the past century the growth of cities has been explosive. Much of this growth was unplanned. The central areas of many cities were built with narrow streets and with houses closely packed together. When satellite cities and suburbs sprang up, they established their own local governments and services, while largely disregarding the need for coordinating services with the central city. In many ways metropolitan areas became fused into one big unit, through fusion of highways, bus systems, taxi services, air service, and communication systems, yet the areas failed to fuse politically. Each suburb ran its own affairs with little regard for neighboring areas. (In extreme cases, a suburb would dump sewage into "its" river, with little concern that it was polluting the drinking water of the urban areas downstream.)

As a result of largely unplanned growth, today's metropolitan areas tend to have a confusing network of fragmented local governments and overlapping service districts. Such areas tend to have dozens of fire chiefs, police chiefs, school superintendents, and department heads. This overlap and duplication of services is not only costly but also inefficient and creates coordination problems.

## New York City and Washington, DC, Teeter on the Brink of Bankruptcy

In 1975 New York City (the Big Apple) nearly went bankrupt on several occasions, as it was close to defaulting due to shortages of funds to pay its debts. The reasons for the near-bankruptcy were numerous: deconcentration, high pay to city employees, the provision of services beyond the tax base, and lack of sound financial planning by politicians and the city government. In each of these financial crises in 1975, either the state government or the federal government provided the resources that prevented a default. The near-bankruptcy of the nation's largest city illustrates the financial crises many large cities are facing.

In May 1994, the city government of Washington, DC, indicated it was nearly bankrupt. The reasons were very similar to those that precipitated the 1975 financial crisis in New York City. (The federal government has provided the resources that prevented a default in the nation's capital.)

## HOUSING

A majority of the poor in the United States live in cities, and a majority of the poor also live in substandard, deteriorated housing. This housing has been rejected by higher-income families, many of whom have moved to the suburbs. In central cities the deteriorated housing is now largely inhabited by the elderly poor and by people of color, particularly African Americans and Latinos. Most cannot afford an alternative. Problems include inadequate heat in the winter, broken light fixtures, leaking toilets, rats, cockroaches, overcrowded rooms, and broken windows.

A recent study found that one-third of all Americans (about 78 million people) are "shelter poor."[20] This means that they are obliged to pay so much for housing that they no longer have enough money for food, medical care, and clothing. Social scientists estimate that a household that pays more than 25 percent of its income for housing is shelter poor and does not have enough money left to pay for other basic needs.[21] It should be noted many poor families and households that pay 25 percent or less for housing are also shelter poor because their incomes are so low that even with lower rents or lower housing costs they cannot afford to buy other essentials.[22] One consequence of shelter poverty can be homelessness. A high percentage of Americans who are shelter poor reside in distressed neighborhoods.

Many cities in the 1960s and 1970s, and to a lesser extent in the 1980s and 1990s, have tried to resolve the deteriorated housing problem by urban renewal projects. It was hoped that urban renewal projects would help low-income residents. Governmental agencies bought up decaying central-city areas and relocated the residents. They sold the land to private developers, who were expected to build apartments for people with low and moderate incomes. But because the developers were not required to build inexpensive housing, they generally aspired to the greater profits in building office buildings and luxury apartments. Because the former residents could not afford this housing, they moved to other deteriorating areas of the city. In the process of relocating, their sense of community was even more severely weakened. They often felt they were pawns and victims of a huge uncaring municipal system. Many were uprooted from friends, family, schools, and churches they had psychologically adopted as part of "their world." Many who were uprooted moved to nearby areas that are apt to be demolished in future urban renewal projects.

The federal government responded in some cities by building public housing units, usually apartment complexes. Federal policy usually has restricted public housing to the poorest poor. Often the working poor earn too much to meet eligibility guidelines for living in these housing projects. Many public housing projects quickly turn into distressed neighborhoods, inhabited by people on public assistance, single-parent families, and people with disabilities. Choldin describes these housing projects as containing "large concentrations of people with the greatest number of problems and the least amount of success in overcoming them."[23]

Probably the only thing worse than substandard housing is no housing. As described in Chapter 3, there has been a large increase in the number of homeless people in central cities. The homeless wander through public places and sleep on the street, in parks, or in subways. Temporary shelters are woefully inadequate to meet their needs. In the wintertime some homeless live in cardboard boxes on streets!

*The historical start of suburbia—row upon row of tract housing—promised an escape from the problems of the city.*

Efforts to build more shelters are often stymied by the protests of citizen organizations who do not want them in their communities.

Historically, governmental programs to improve housing have benefited middle- and upper-income classes. Most federal housing assistance has gone directly or indirectly to entrepreneurs and to the middle and upper classes.

In 1983 the Reagan administration decided the country would be best served if federal funding for additional low-income housing was cut by 94 percent, from $8.6 billion to $515 million. The remaining 6 percent was to be used only for housing for people with disabilities and for the elderly.[24] Low-income housing for the poor was cut completely. Since 1983 only limited federal funds for low-income housing have been made available—at a time when the growing number of homeless has become a national disgrace.

## CRIME

Crime is primarily an urban problem. In rural areas, because everyone tends to know everyone else's business, illegal activities are much more difficult to hide.

When apprehended, rural offenders face much more ostracism. As described earlier, the process of urbanization weakens social restraints against committing crime. Statistics show big cities have four times as much violent crime as suburbs, and over six times as much as rural areas. Property crimes are also much more prevalent in big cities.[25]

Not surprisingly, fear of becoming a crime victim is more common in cities. Many city dwellers arrange their daily activities to reduce their chances of being mugged, conned, robbed, or raped. One survey found that half of big-city residents are afraid to walk outside at night, compared to only about 20 percent of suburbanites.[26]

A study showed that nearly one in four young African-American men currently is in jail or prison or on probation or parole.[27] In contrast, the study found one in ten young Latino men and one in sixteen young white men are under control of the criminal justice system. The study focused on twenty- to twenty-nine-year-olds. Another astounding finding was that the number of young African-American men in the criminal justice system was greater than the total number of all African-American men enrolled in college.[28] The researchers trace the high proportion of young African-American men in the criminal justice system to "the last thirty years during which inner-city youngsters who are denied opportunities for decent educations and jobs just fell into the criminal justice system."[29]

## TRANSPORTATION

Sixty-five percent of the land in U.S. cities is dedicated to cars—if one includes the space for streets, highways, parking lots, garages, gas stations, repair shops, and other uses.[30] Americans are fascinated by cars. Owners often seek the kind of car that will best express their personality. It is not uncommon for suburbanites to drive fifty to sixty miles to and from work.

An influx of automobiles has created tremendous problems for central cities. Downtown Manhattan in New York has a perpetual traffic jam during daylight hours. Similar problems exist during rush hours in many other cities. Exhaust from automobiles is the major source of air pollution and contributes substantially to smog problems. Double-parking is another problem in many cities.

Drivers can spend more time hunting for a parking spot than the time it takes to drive to their destination. Backups from street repair projects are a common frustration for city motorists. City drivers also have substantially higher accident rates than rural drivers. Expressways are usually constructed in the poorer areas, where the costs of demolition and land are lower. Such construction uproots residents, usually forcing those in the distressed neighborhood where the expressway is built to move to another distressed neighborhood.

Automobiles are the most convenient, but also the least efficient, form of transportation. In one hour a single traffic lane can move twenty-four hundred people in automobiles, nine thousand in buses, forty thousand in subway trains, and sixty thousand in express subway trains.[31]

Highways were expected to bring shoppers *from* suburbs *to* the central city. Instead they have been a major factor in encouraging middle- and upper-class families, along with businesses, to relocate to suburbs.[32] Although city dwellers suffer from the congestion and air pollution caused by automobiles, many do not have the funds to buy and maintain their own cars. Forced to rely on public transportation (buses or subway systems) they often experience frustrating delays in city travel. Poor public transportation systems also are obstacles to employment and educational opportunities for city dwellers who do not have access to a car.

Public officials are struggling with how they can make mass transportation attractive enough for current motorists to ride. As private passenger cars increase, mass transportation is dwindling. Mass transportation systems (such as subways, commuter railroads, and buses) are deteriorating and in many cities are being used less. One reason is that urban areas are becoming decentralized. Suburbs are developing commercial centers with shopping centers and business districts. Shopping centers and business districts are also evolving in diverse areas rather than being concentrated downtown. As a result, people desire to travel more randomly in cities, rather than from outlying areas to the central business district. When this happens, public transportation becomes even more difficult to develop and maintain.

## ANTI-URBAN BIAS

There has always been an anti-urban sentiment in the United States. Thomas Jefferson, for example, wrote: "The mobs of great cities add just so much to the support of pure government, as sores do to the strength of the human body."[33] American literature often glamorizes the virtues of the self-sufficient farmer, depicted as being in an agricultural paradise, living a happy, relaxed, and uncomplicated life. The truth is, farming is a laborious vocation, often a seven-day-a-week job. Presently, many farmers are going bankrupt. Only about 2 percent of our workforce is now engaged in farming.[34]

The city frequently is pictured as inconsistent with the "natural" relationship between humans and their environment. A Lou Harris poll found that two-thirds of those living in large urban areas would prefer to live elsewhere.[35] A Gallup poll asked a similar question: "If you could live anywhere you wanted, would you prefer a city, a suburban area, small town, or farm?" Again, cities did not fare well: small town, 32 percent; suburb, 31 percent; farm, 23 percent, and city, 13 percent.[36] Living in the country evokes a trouble-free, peaceful, and virtuous image. In the country, people are thought to be able to live in harmony with nature. Cities have an image of being stressful and as having high rates of crime and other social problems.

Cities are viewed as generating impersonal interrelationships, cutthroat competition, loneliness, apathy, and uncaring attitudes toward others. Despite these images, most Americans live in or near large urban areas because of job opportunities and cultural advantages.

A major sociological question is, "To what extent do the negative images of cities become self-fulfilling prophecies?" For example, if city inhabitants believe that drug use, crime, suicide, apathy toward neighbors, public assistance, and cutthroat competition constitute a way of life in cities, are such inhabitants more apt to act accordingly?

## Strategies to Improve Urban Areas

As discussed earlier in this chapter, problems that exist in urban areas are much more severe in central cities than in the surrounding suburbs. Suburbs do experience many of the same problems as central cities: crime, housing deterioration, and transportation delays—but to a lesser extent. Furthermore, suburbs have a much stronger economic base and therefore are more apt to have the financial resources to combat such problems. The problems of our inner cities appear to be much more unresolvable. They appear so severe to many people, that some have despaired and given up hope that conditions will ever improve.

It is important to remember that the living conditions of people in inner cities are substantially better than those in the impoverished Third World countries. (Many of the poor in Third World countries are living in shantytowns and earn less than $500 per year.) It is a mistake to give up hope that conditions in our inner cities will improve. There are strategies available to improve inner cities.

This section will present several proposals: urban renewal, Great Society programs, Model Cities programs, school busing, laissez-faire, setting limits on the size of cities, governmental reorganization, population control, the welfare-to-work program, and grassroots organizations.

The objective in presenting these proposals is to indicate that there are alternatives for combating the problems in our inner cities.

### URBAN RENEWAL

A major effort to improve inner cities in the past has been urban renewal, as described earlier in this chapter. Under urban renewal, governmental agencies buy up deteriorated housing and relocate the residents. Such agencies then contract with private developers, who demolish the old buildings and build shopping centers, office space, and housing for middle- and upper-income individuals and families. Such new hosing is sufficiently attractive to some middle- and upper-income suburbanites that they decide to relocate to these renewal projects, as they are closer to their jobs and to the cultural attractions of the city.

Of course, the major problem with urban renewal is that it does not benefit the poor. Often it intensifies the problems of the poor, as they are uprooted from their former neighborhood and forced to relocate. They relocate, generally, in nearby decaying areas, which accelerates the deterioration of these areas. In the long run, urban renewal accomplishes very little in resolving the problems of low-income residents of distressed neighborhoods.

### GREAT SOCIETY PROGRAMS

In the 1960s President Johnson launched an ambitious campaign to improve living conditions for all Americans. Antipoverty programs were significant components of the Great Society concept. For inner-city residents, such programs included a variety of social and educational programs that had the goals of eliminating poverty and improving the living conditions of residents in distressed neighborhoods. There were a variety of programs—Head Start, day-care services, work-training programs, job placement programs, health care programs, drug and alcohol treatment programs, programs to assist people in getting a high-school and college education, financial assistance, parenting programs, sex education, and the formation of a variety of self-help groups (such as programs for neighborhood residents to work together to renovate their homes). Such programs were successful in helping some lower-income residents get an education, obtain a good-paying job, and move into the middle and upper-middle classes. Those who progressed generally relocate to suburbs.

However, the vast majority of residents in distressed neighborhoods did not progress. Some critics have charged that social welfare programs had the adverse consequence of making residents in distressed neighborhoods more dependent on the government for their livelihood and less self-reliant. The Reagan administration in the 1980s became disenchanted with the provision of social welfare services and made sharp cutbacks in such services to distressed neighborhoods.

The administrations that followed Reagan (Bush and Clinton) have not restored these cutbacks.

## MODEL CITIES PROGRAMS

As part of the War on Poverty, the Johnson administration in the 1960s experimented with a complex of services (called Model Cities programs) that involved massive interventions into inner-city areas. Deteriorated buildings were demolished, and quality housing units were built. Inner-city dwellers were moved into these units, with the federal government subsidizing much of the monthly rent. In addition, these areas were provided with a variety of social, educational, and work training programs. The results have been discouraging. Today these areas have deteriorated and again are distressed neighborhoods.

## SCHOOL BUSING

In the 1970s there was an intensive effort by the federal government and the courts to promote equal educational opportunities for inner-city residents through busing. Such busing was promoted as a way to achieve racial integration. An additional underlying objective was to prepare inner-city children to obtain good-paying jobs and become productive citizens. Unfortunately, in many cities busing accelerated white flight to suburbs and also led some whites to send their children to private schools. Because of a variety of problems with school busing (including the high costs and the disadvantages of busing children long distances) the federal government and the court system in the 1980s and 1990s became less enthusiastic about promoting busing. There is little evidence, one way or another, as to whether busing inner-city children to quality schools will enable them, when they become adults, to obtain high-paying jobs and become productive citizens. (School busing for integration objectives is described in Chapter 6.)

## LAISSEZ-FAIRE

*Laissez-faire* may be defined as a philosophy or practice characterized by an abstention (usually deliberate) from direction or interference. Such a description appropriately describes the approach taken by the Reagan and Bush administrations in the 1980s and early 1990s. Both administrations adopted a policy of sharp cutbacks in federal support for social welfare programs and for educational programs. The Clinton administration was elected in 1992; it set a high priority on reducing the size of the federal deficit—as a result, it has asserted federal funds are simply unavailable to restore the cutbacks in federal support for social welfare programs that occurred in the 1980s. Inner-city areas have been particularly hard hit by these federal cutbacks as they had grown accustomed to (and dependent on) such programs.

The results of such cutbacks are becoming obvious. Inner-city areas are deteriorating at a faster pace. More people are homeless and hungry. Buildings and bridges are increasingly becoming eyesores, and roads have more potholes. Traffic is becoming more congested. The optimism in the 1960s and 1970s for a better life has been replaced with a sense of despair, and a sense that everything possible has been tried and has failed—and therefore living conditions will only get worse. At the present time, inner-city residents have high rates of illiteracy, suicide, crime, violence, drug and alcohol abuse, teenage pregnancies, and unemployment.

## LIMIT ON THE SIZE OF CITIES

Advocates of setting limits on the size of a city assert limits can be set without infringing on personal liberties. New water and sewer hook-ups can be restricted. Tax breaks can be created for businesses that locate in smaller towns, which would encourage a slow redistribution of the population without coercion. (China and Russia seek to contain, partially, the size of their cities by policies which allow no more immigrants into their cities than the number set by government planners.) Advocates of size limits assert overcrowding in cities has resulted in serious problems—air, water, and land pollution. This crowding, combined with the anonymity of city life, has also weakened social controls that normally provide direction and guidance. As a result, there are high rates of crime, delinquency, suicide, and a host of other social problems. Such advocates assert the elimination of urban growth would give cities time to find solutions to their problems without having to cope with the additional problems of an increasing population.

Critics of setting limits on the size of cities assert that there is no way to set limits without violating personal rights and freedoms. Rezoning land so that current and future owners cannot build on it takes away their right to use their property as they chose. Preventing people from living where they wish would violate freedom of choice. Policies against housing expansion would increase the demand for existing housing and thereby result in an increase in rent and property values, which would be an increased financial burden for renters, particularly the poor. In addition, no-growth policies would sharply reduce creative development, as cities have always been centers of cultural development and change. The ideas that have fostered technological advances have primarily been generated by city dwellers. The safe comforts of conventional small town life are not as conducive to creative change. The diversity of expanded growth in cities also generates new ideas and creative advances.

## GOVERNMENTAL REORGANIZATION

Authorities note that suburbanites utilize the services of central cities without paying property taxes to support these services. Some planners suggest that cities and suburbs be merged politically and economically into a metropolitan or regional government, which would increase the tax base of cities.

Others propose that only some units of government be regionalized, such as school districts, sewage districts, and water districts. A disadvantage of regionalizing only some services is that government then becomes more complex, with services administered by a variety of governmental units. The use of special districts creates more governmental agencies, which increases administrative expenses and complicates coordination of services and community-wide planning.

Annexation of suburbs, or the merging of two or more units of government, is the easiest and most uncomplicated form of reorganization. However, voters in suburban areas are generally unwilling to merge with nearby cities. They moved to suburbs to avoid the problems of central cities and are opposed to their property taxes being increased to provide improved services to residents of distressed neighborhoods.

## POPULATION CONTROL

China urges its citizens to have only one child.[37] Women who become pregnant after having one child are urged to seek an abortion. There are considerable financial incentives for families to have only one child, such as increased taxes for families who have more than one child. India, for a short time in the 1970s, had a policy of involuntary sterilization of any male or female of reproductive age who was a biological parent to three or more living children.[38] The objective of such policies is to reduce the size of the population. By slowly decreasing the population, more resources will become available to provide a higher quality of life.

A strategy for combating problems in large cities is population control. Residents of large cities could be encouraged to have only one child. Sex education programs in schools could be expanded to teach responsible sex behavior. Free birth-control information and devices could be provided by the government. Increased taxes might be levied for those who had more than one or two children. If such a program failed to reduce the size of the population in large cities, involuntary sterilization (perhaps after the birth of a third living child) might be considered.

There are a number of criticisms of population control policies. There is a strong value in our country that holds that every person has a right to be a natural parent to as many children as he or she desires. Some religious institutions, such as the Roman Catholic church, strongly object to birth control. Involuntary sterilization violates freedom of choice. Attempts to impose control on the size of families would violate established civil rights in our society.

Our society has tried a variety of programs in the past to combat the problems faced by residents of distressed neighborhoods. These programs have largely failed to improve our distressed neighborhoods. At the present time our federal government has a laissez-faire approach, and conditions are deteriorating in many of our inner cities. Will our country try an unpopular program, such as reorganization of governmental boundaries, or population control? Or are there other workable alternatives?

## WELFARE-TO-WORK PROGRAM

As noted in Chapter 9, Charles Murray asserted in 1986 that the Aid to Families with Dependent Children Program provided an incentive for single women to want to have children in order to receive welfare payments.[39] He also asserted that increases in crime and drug abuse, poor educational performance in schools, and deteriorating conditions in inner cities stem largely from the increase in single-parent families, which he attributed to government programs that support such families. He asserted that being on welfare has become a way of life for many of those on AFDC. His solution to improving distressed neighborhoods (and also combating crime, drug abuse, births outside of marriage, and poor educational performance in schools) is to eliminate the AFDC program.

*A billboard in Kunming (Yunnan Province), China, exhorts Chinese families to support China's one-child only campaign.*

In 1996 Congress and President Clinton passed the Personal Responsibility and Work Opportunity Reconciliation Act. It eliminated AFDC, and it limits public welfare assistance in individual households to five years in an attempt to prevent "chronic" welfare dependency. The primary focus of the program is to put able-bodied adults to work, instead of being on welfare. By working, it is hoped these individuals will have an improved self-image, be much less involved in using alcohol and other drugs, be less apt to commit crimes, be better role models for their children, and become tax-paying citizens. Furthermore, it is hoped that these individuals will become more involved in improving their communities, and thereby all communities (including distressed neighborhoods) will gradually improve.

Will such lofty objectives be obtained by this welfare-to-work program? It is too early to tell. Critics point out (as noted in Chapter 9) that many unanswered questions have arisen. Will the program be successful in getting adult welfare recipients into decent-paying jobs that will enable their families to leave being on public assistance? Even if adult welfare recipients obtain employment, will their children be cared for in healthy child-care arrangements while the parents are working?

How difficult will it be for single parents with one or more of the following issues to obtain gainful employment—lack of a marketable job skill, a drug habit, a chronic medical problem, a child at home with a mental or physical disability, a lack of convenient transportation, being in a violent domestic relationship, failure to have a strong work ethic, and having a chronic emotional or behavioral problem? Will some adult recipients who reach their term eligibility limits on public assistance without obtaining a decent-paying job turn to prostitution or to crime? How can jobs be found or created in geographic areas having high unemployment rates? Rather than improving distressed neighborhoods, there is a danger that the welfare-to-work program may result in greater despair among the program participants, and eventually lead to further deterioration of distressed neighborhoods.

## GRASS-ROOTS ORGANIZATIONS

The efforts of some grass-roots organizations at times have positive, long-lasting effects. Grass-roots organizations are composed of community residents who work together to improve their community. (It may be that lasting changes can be made in a neighborhood only when the residents are inspired, in some way, to improve their community.) The following description is an illustration of a successful grass-roots effort in Cochran Gardens, St. Louis, Missouri.[40]

Cochran Gardens, a low-income housing project, was typical of many deteriorating housing projects in large urban areas. It was characterized by rubbish, graffiti, broken windows, frequent shootings, crime, drug trafficking, and angry and fearful people.

Bertha Gilkey grew up in this housing project. If it had not been for her efforts this neighborhood would have continued to deteriorate. At a young age, Gilkey believed the neighborhood could improve if residents worked together. As a teenager she attended tenant meetings in a neighborhood church. When she was twenty years old, she was elected to chair this tenants' association. The neighborhood has since undergone gradual yet dramatically positive changes.

Gilkey and her group started with small projects. They asked tenants what they really wanted that was realistic to achieve. There was a consensus that the housing project needed a usable laundromat, because previous laundromats had all been vandalized and the only working one in the project had no locks. In fact, the entry door had been stolen. Bertha and her group requested and received a door from the city housing authority. The organization then held a fund-raiser for a lock and another fund-raiser for paint. After the organization painted the laundromat, residents were pleased to have an attractive working laundromat, which increased their interest in joining and supporting the tenants' association. The association then organized to paint the hallways of the housing project, floor by floor. Everyone who lived on a floor was responsible for being involved in painting the floor's hallway. Gilkey states:

> Kids who lived on the floor that hadn't been painted would come and look at the painted hallways and then go back and hassle their parents. The elderly who couldn't paint prepared lunch, so they could feel like they were a part of it too.[41]

The organization continued to initiate and successfully complete new projects to spruce up the neighborhood. Each success inspired more and more residents to take pride in their neighborhood and to work toward making improvements. While improving the physical appearance of this housing project, Gilkey and the tenants' organization also reintroduced a conduct code for the project. A committee formulated rules of behavior and elected monitors on each floor. The rules included no loud disruptions, no throwing garbage out the windows, and no fights. Slowly residents got the message, and living conditions improved, one small step at a time.

The building was renamed Dr. Martin Luther King, Jr., Building. (Symbols are important in community development efforts.) The organization also held a party and a celebration for each successfully completed project.

Another focus of Gilkey's efforts was to reach out to children and adolescents. The positives were highlighted. The young people wrote papers in school on "What I Like about Living Here." In art class they built a cardboard model of the housing project that included the buildings, streets, and playground. Such efforts were designed to build the self-esteem of the young people, and to instill a sense of pride in their community.

Today Cochran Gardens is a public housing project with flower-lined paths, trees, and grass—a beautiful and clean neighborhood filled with trusting people who have a sense of pride in their community. The high-rises have been completely renovated. There is a community center, tennis courts, playgrounds, and town house apartments to reduce density in the complex. Cochran Gardens is managed by the tenants. The association (now called Tenant Management Council) has ventured into owning and operating certain businesses: a catering service, day-care centers, health clinics, and a vocational training program.

The Cochran success has been based on the principles of self-help, empowerment, responsibility, and dignity. Gilkey states:

> This goes against the grain, doesn't it? Poor people are to *be* managed. What we've done is cut through all the bullshit and said it doesn't take all that. People with degrees and credentials got us in this mess. All it takes is some basic skills. . . . If we can do it in public housing, it can happen anywhere.[42]

Such successes suggest it is desirable for our federal, state, and city governments to seek to improve inner-city conditions by encouraging and supporting (including financially) grass-roots efforts.

# Summary

Large cities are a relatively recent phenomenon accelerated by the Industrial Revolution. Two centuries ago most people in the United States lived in rural areas; now most live in urban areas. Most sociological theories of the effects of urbanism seek to explain why city dwellers are more apt than rural residents to display personality and social disorders.

The problems confrontating urban areas, particularly central cities, are serious and of immense proportions. The problems seem so severe for residents of distressed neighborhoods that some observers have despaired and concluded there is no hope for improvement.

Living conditions in distressed neighborhoods are a national disgrace. Such neighborhoods are primarily inhabited by the poor, the elderly, and by people of color. Distressed neighborhoods have high rates of crime, births outside of marriage, single-parent households, mental illness, suicide, drug and alcohol abuse, unemployment, infant mortality, rape, and aggravated assault.

The term *deconcentration* refers to the flight to the suburbs by middle- and upper-class families. Suburbanites now use many services without having to contribute (through property taxes) to the financing of such services. Partly due to deconcentration, central cities are experiencing severe financial crises. The financial problems for some central cities are so serious that they have come close to declaring bankruptcy.

In the past century, the growth of cities and suburbs has been nearly explosive. Such growth has largely occurred with little planning. Partially as a result of unplanned growth, metropolitan areas tend to have a confusing network of fragmented local governments and overlapping service districts. Such fragmentation and overlapping have led to severe coordination problems.

Housing in many areas of central cities is decaying and crumbling. The problem in recent years has intensified. An increasing number of poor people in distressed neighborhoods are being forced to move from substandard housing and are now homeless.

Higher rates of crime occur in central cities as compared to rural areas and suburbs. Big-city residents are much more afraid to walk outside at night than are suburbanites.

The increasing use of automobiles in large cities is creating a variety of problems, including: air pollution, traffic jams, traffic accidents, and parking problems. Mass transportation systems are decaying in many central cities.

Throughout American history there has been an anti-urban bias. There is a question as to the extent to which negative beliefs about living in large cities contribute to their becoming self-fulfilling prophecies.

A variety of strategies have already been tried to improve living conditions in inner cities. These strategies include urban renewal, Great Society programs, Model City programs, school busing, and laissez-faire. These strategies have, in general, failed to improve living conditions in inner cities. A program that has recently been enacted is welfare-to-work; it is too early to determine whether this program will have a positive impact (or a negative impact) on distressed neighborhoods. Possible strategies that as yet have not been tried include governmental reorganization (merging suburbs and central cities into one large metropolitan government), setting limits on the size of central cities, and population control. One approach that at times has positive, long lasting effects is the efforts of some grass-roots organizations.

*Population*

*P*roblems associated with worldwide overpopulation seriously threaten to reduce the quality of human life. These problems are so serious that some nations are contemplating enacting compulsory sterilization laws.

This chapter:

♦ Considers the problems associated with rapid population growth throughout the world, presents a theory explaining this rapid growth, and describes two countries' reactions to their own overpopulation

♦ Summarizes current efforts to curtail the growth of the world's population

♦ Outlines proposals that have been advanced for population control in the future

**Table 16.1**  *Doubling Times of the World's Population*

| Date | Estimated World Population | Number of Years Required for Population to Double |
|---|---|---|
| 8000 B.C. | 5 million | |
| A.D. 1650 | 500 million | 1,500 |
| 1850 | 1 billion | 200 |
| 1930 | 2 billion | 80 |
| 1975 | 4 billion | 45 |
| 2015 | 8 billion | 40 |

*Source:* Paul R. Ehrlich and Anne H. Ehrlich, *The Population Explosion* (New York: Touchstone, 1990).

## *Rapid Population Growth and Overpopulation*

There are now about 6 billion people living on earth.[1] In 1930 there were 2 billion. The world's population is increasing at the rate of 185 people a minute, 11,100 an hour, 266,400 a day, and 97.2 million a year[2] (see Table 16.1). The dangers of runaway population growth can be viewed in historical perspective by looking at the world population in units of 1 billion people. It took all of human history until 1850 for the world's population to reach 1 billion, but the next unit of 1 billion was added in only 80 years (1850–1930); the unit after that in 30 years (1930–1960), and the next in 15 years (1960–1975). Since 1975, 2 billion people have been added.[3]

Assuming a continued doubling rate of 40 years, by 2040 there will be 12 billion people. If this growth continued for 900 years, there would be 60 *million billion* people! This would mean that there would be about 10 people for each square yard of the earth's surface, including both land and water.[4]

### DOUBLING TIME AND POPULATION GROWTH

The rate at which population doubles has immense consequences. This section will describe population growth rates and examine their effects.

Doubling time is based on the extent to which the birthrate exceeds the death rate. Doubling times have a compound effect. Just as interest dollars earn interest, people added to the population produce more people. Table 16.2 shows the relationship between the annual population growth rate and the doubling time of the population.

Thus what seems a small population growth rate of 1.9 percent per year (the current rate in the world), leads to a dramatic doubling time of forty years. With an annual growth rate of 1.9 percent, more than 95 million people are being added to the world's population annually.[5]

### DOUBLING TIME AND DEVELOPING COUNTRIES

The countries experiencing the most severe doubling time problems are the "developing countries" (also called the Third World nations). These countries are beginning to industrialize. Sadly, population growth is most severe in the countries that can least afford increases; that is, the countries that need to spend their resources on improving their economic conditions. Developing countries account for over two-thirds of the world's population and have doubling times of about twenty to thirty-five years.[6] People in these countries are hungry; many are starving. Developing countries tend to have primitive and inefficient agriculture, small gross national products, and high illiteracy rates. The bulk of the population spends most of its time trying to meet basic subsistence needs.

Developing countries are characterized by high birthrates and declining death rates. In the past, when a

**Table 16.2** *Rate of Population Growth and Doubling Time*

| Average Rate of Increase (per year) | Doubling Time (in years) |
|---|---|
| 1.0% | 70 |
| 2.0% | 35 |
| 3.0% | 24 |
| 4.0% | 17 |

*Source:* Paul R. Ehrlich and Anne H. Ehrlich, *The Population Explosion* (New York: Touchstone, 1990).

country began to industrialize, the death rate dropped (people lived longer) whereas the birthrate tended to remain high for a substantial period of time. The result was a rapid population growth rate. Unfortunately, developing countries, where living conditions most need improvement, are precisely the countries whose populations are increasing so rapidly that most people are scarcely better off than they were a generation ago. Nine out of every ten people added to the world's population are born in developing countries.[7] Developing countries are much more likely than industrial countries to have a population explosion.

The population crisis in the world today is not due to families having more children than they did in the past, as families are no larger than they were in the past. However, more people are living to the age of fertility and beyond. In effect, more babies are growing to maturity to produce babies themselves. This change is due to several factors: advances in medicine, sanitation, and public health, and increased capacity to reduce the effects of famines, floods, droughts, and other natural disasters.

Lee Rainwater has noted that "the poor get children."[8] There is a vicious circle involving rapid population growth and poverty. Rapid population growth places an increasing strain on a nation's ability to feed and clothe its growing masses. Thus, rapid population growth strains resources, which lead to poverty. Poverty, in turn, leads to a high birthrate, which leads to further population growth. Former World Bank President Robert S. McNamara warned: "Short of thermonuclear war itself, rampant population growth is the gravest issue the world faces over the decades ahead."[9]

Developed or industrialized countries have doubling times in the 50- to 200-year range.[10] In the United States in recent years the birthrate has steadily decreased and is nearing a zero-population-growth rate (an average of two children per family). The basic reason the doubling time in developed countries is longer is that people decide to have fewer children (for financial and other reasons). The average cost of raising a child from birth to age eighteen in the United States is estimated to be $161,00 in low-income families, $225,000 in middle-income families, and $315,000 in upper-income families.[11] Developed nations are characterized by both low birthrates and low death rates.

The slower doubling times in industrialized countries in no way indicate that these countries are not part of the problem. If one looks at consumption rates of raw materials, these countries are the major culprit. The United States, for example, uses about one-third of all the raw materials consumed each year but has less than 1/15 of the world's population.[12] Americans are therefore using five times their "fair share" of raw materials. People in the United States also consume, on the average, four times as much food per person as inhabitants of developing countries.[13]

Werner Fornos noted in 1987 that most of the population growth in the future will occur in the urban centers of the developing (Third World) countries:

> The population of the Third World as a whole is increasing by a significant 2.1 percent each year, but the population of the Third World's cities is growing by a swift 3.5 percent annually—fully three times as fast as the industrialized world's urban centers. Africa's cities are growing fastest, at a runaway 5 percent each year. The slum squatter settlements associated with these centers are growing at twice the rate of the cities themselves.[14]

In many developing countries, families average seven or eight children.[15] As a result, these countries are increasingly populated by the young. Figure 16.1 indicates that one result of this younger population is the developing countries are much more likely than industrialized countries to have a population explosion.

## An Optimal Population Size

A frequent question is, "What is the capacity of the world to support people?" Asserting that a country's population is too large or too small implies there is an optimal size. Such a conception may be in error; probably no exact figure can be precisely determined for the optimum population for the world.

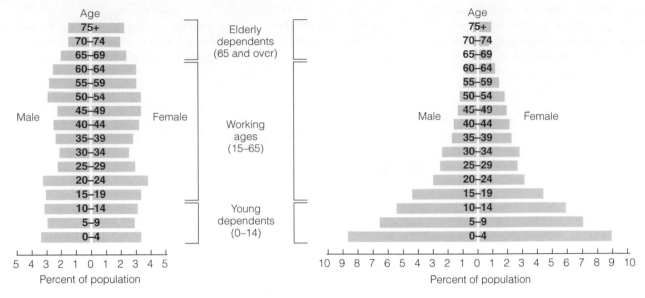

Industrial countries (left) have three or four adults of economically productive ages for each dependent child. When an industrial country's children grow up and reproduce, the population structure will change only a little. Developing countries (right) have one (or less) adult of economically productive age for each dependent child. When the developing country's children grow up and reproduce, a population explosion will occur.

**Figure 16.1**    *Age-Sex Population Pyramids: Industrial and Developing Country Models*

Many variables and values would enter into specifying an optimal world population size, including preservation of a certain standard or quality of life, rate of consumption of nonrenewable raw materials, future technological breakthroughs in finding new energy sources and new food sources, maintenance of "safe" levels of clean air and water, and public acceptance of the government's role (perhaps compulsory) in population control. The industrialized nations, with their high consumption and high waste economies, are using up more of the earth's raw materials and generating more pollution than developing countries. Because of consumption rates, adding 1 million people to industrialized countries is comparable to adding 30 million people to developing countries.[16]

In regard to the question of whether the earth is already overpopulated, Ehrlich and Ehrlich note:

The key to understanding overpopulation is not population density but the numbers of people in an area relative to its resources and the capacity of the environment to sustain human activities; that is, to the area's *carry-*

*ing capacity.* When is an area overpopulated? When its population can't be maintained without rapidly depleting nonrenewable resources (or converting renewable resources into nonrenewable ones) and without degrading the capacity of the environment to support the population. In short, if the long-term carrying capacity of an area is clearly being degraded by its current human occupants, that area is overpopulated.

By this standard, the entire planet and virtually every nation is already vastly overpopulated.[17]

## PROBLEMS OF OVERPOPULATION

A wide range of problems are associated with overpopulation. We will examine a number of these problems, including too little food, too little water, economic problems, international terrorism, crowding, and immigration.

***Too Little Food***    An estimated half-billion people today are undernourished—that is, slowly starving—and another billion are malnourished.[18] Malnourishment during childhood years can have devastating effects. It delays physical maturity, impairs brain development, reduces intelligence, and may produce dwarfism. An undernourished adult is listless, apathetic, and is unable to work as vigorously as a well-fed adult. There are a number of diseases caused directly by dietary deficiency, including beriberi, rickets, and marasmus. Malnutrition also lowers resistance to disease, so the undernourished are likely to have a number of other health problems. The danger of epidemics is always high in overpopulated areas where people are malnourished. In addition, the damage of malnutrition is passed on from one generation to the next, as babies born to malnourished mothers are weaker and in poorer health than the babies of well-fed mothers.[19]

Even in the United States many people are undernourished, with some dying of starvation.[20] In approximately the time it takes to read this sentence, four people will die (three of them children) from malnutrition.[21] The brain of an infant grows to 80 percent of its adult size within the first three years of life. If supplies of protein are inadequate during this period, the brain stops growing, and the damage is irreversible; such children suffer permanent cognitive disabilities.[22]

More than 200 years ago (in 1798), Thomas Malthus asserted that population growth, if left unchecked, would outstrip the food supply.[23] Malthus theorized that uncontrolled population growth increases in powers of 2: 1, 2, 4, 8, 16, 32, 64—that is, in a geometric ratio. In contrast, the food supply cannot possibly increase that fast. At best, the food supply increases in a steady additive fashion: 1, 2, 3, 4, 5, 6, 7—that is, in an arithmetic ratio. Inevitably, according to Malthus, population growth overtakes the growth in food supplies. Therefore, either population has to be controlled by society, or starvation, hunger, and poverty will be the unavoidable fate of most of the world's people. The fact that widespread starvation and poverty are indeed common in many countries today provides some evidence of the validity of the Malthus theory.

There has been an ongoing, heated controversy among scientists over whether technology will be able to substantially increase the world's food supply. Some scientists claim that we have already reached the limit at which technology is no longer able to increase the food supply to meet the needs of even a slowly growing world population. Others are predicting that future technology will provide food for a population ten times as large as our current one.[24]

Which side is right? The verdict is not yet in. A few decades ago a technological breakthrough led to a dramatic improvement in much more food being produced per acre by new strains of wheat and rice. This "green revolution," however, requires increased use of fertilizers and water. Fertilizers are becoming scarce and increasingly expensive, and many of the developing countries cannot afford costly irrigation systems.

Research on increasing the food supply is also taking other approaches. One effort is to investigate the feasibility of cultivating the tropical rain forests of Africa, South America, and Indonesia. Such areas have large amounts of sunshine and water but poor soil (requiring large quantities of fertilizer) and severe insect infestations. Another effort is geared to finding new ways to harvest fish and plant life from the sea. The sea contains huge quantities of food, much of which is currently distasteful. Not only does more food need to be produced, but food distribution systems must be improved. In the United States it is more than ironic that farmers are producing more food than Americans can consume, yet an estimated 30 millon people in the country do not have enough to eat.[25]

***Too Little Water***   Somewhat surprisingly, fresh water is also in short supply in the world. Ninety-seven percent of the world's water is salt water; only 3 percent is fresh water.[26]

Developed nations are using substantially more water per person than developing nations. It has been estimated that an African uses 0.8 gallons of water a day compared to 270 gallons for a New Yorker.[27]

Water is also needed in large quantities to produce food. If irrigation efforts are expanded in the world to grow food, fresh water resources will obviously be depleted at a faster rate. Removing salt from water (desalinization) is now being done on a small scale, but it is so expensive that it is currently only being used for drinking purposes.

***Economic Problems***   In industrialized countries, rapid population growth reduces the standard of living and the quality of life because rapid growth reduces the average per capita income.[28] Because birthrates are consistently higher among the lower-income groups, there are additional social and economic strains. Some authorities openly express alarm that high birthrates among the lower-income groups may lead to a reduction in average educational achievements among the population and may provide a threat to the values held and espoused by the middle and upper classes. Rapid population growth also leads to other problems: not enough jobs, air and water pollution, traffic jams, inadequate and insufficient housing, and so on.

Economic problems are even more serious in developing nations. Economic progress tends to be canceled out by the increased population. For poor countries to industrialize requires that the inhabitants invest (either through public or private funds) in capital items such as factories, tractors, and industrial equipment. Many developing nations simply do not have the funds even to provide adequate food for their people. Being unable to invest in capital items practically guarantees they will be unable to improve their people's standard of living.

Lack of funds also creates educational and political problems. Developing countries have a high proportion of school-age children. Generally, such countries do not have the resources to provide enough schools. For example, Dr. Benson Morah describes the situation in Nigeria: "You have schools with seventy children in the classrooms, there are children sitting in the windows, children carrying their chairs to school."[29]

As a result, in many countries, a majority of children do not attend school. Being illiterate and poorly trained further locks the inhabitants into poverty.

In addition, people who are poorly housed, hungry, and miserably clothed are apt to view the government as protectors of the rich and oppressors of the poor. Such conditions often lead to political unrest, political revolutions, and civil wars—as have been common in Africa, Asia, and South America.

The gap between the living standards of the industrialized and developing countries is wide and growing wider. In 1997, for example, the average per capita gross income was about $20,000 in the United States, and in some developing nations it was less than $500.[30]

*International Terrorism*   Rapid population growth is a factor that contributes to civil unrest, violence, and international strife. Rapid population growth intensifies poverty and feelings of hopelessness. Overpopulation leads to higher unemployment, rapid urbanization, declining public health, environmental degradation, economic stagnation, and a large youthful population. Young people in Third World countries are in destitute poverty and have little hope for a better future; yet, at the same time they have a gnaw-

ing awareness that people in industrialized nations are much more affluent. Such conditions and awareness create an "Aspiration Bomb." Many such young people see violence and terrorism as the only avenue for themselves and others in their country to achieve a better life.

In a report on population, the U.S. National Security Council noted:

> Recent experience, in Iran and other countries, shows that this younger age group, frequently unemployed and crowded into urban slums, is particularly susceptible to extremism, terrorism, and violence as outlets for frustration. On balance, these factors add up to a growing potential for social unrest, political stability, mass migrations, and possible conflicts over control of land and resources.[31]

Werner Fornos makes the following comments about the perils of the aspiration bomb:

> Fully 60 percent of the Third World is under twenty years of age; half are fifteen years or less. These population pressures create a volatile mixture of youthful aspirations that when coupled with economic and political frustrations help form a large pool of potential terrorists.
>
> The "Aspiration Bomb" may well present a greater threat to U.S. security than the atomic bomb. This is because while there is always the hope that mutual deterrence or common sense will preclude the use of nuclear weapons, there is no such countervailing influence against the violence and frustration embodied in the Aspiration Bomb.[32]

It was noted in Chapter 14 that the rejection of communism by many Eastern European countries may reduce the threat of terrorist activities by those revolutionary terrorist groups who adhere to Marxist principles. The current chapter presents a conflicting view that terrorist activities may increase due to the perils of the aspiration bomb. Which view is most accurate will unfold in the next few decades. (It is possible that terrorist activities by Marxist groups may decline, whereas overall terrorist activities may increase due to the aspiration bomb.)

*Crowding*   Crowding is a person's subjective judgment that he or she has insufficient space. There have been a number of studies investigating the effects of crowding on animals. John Calhoun placed rats in laboratory pens and allowed them to breed until their number rose far beyond that found in their natural environment. A number of behavioral changes took

*Rush-hour in Tokyo brings such severe crowding that professional "subway pushers" are employed to load the subway cars.*

place. Many females became infertile, others began to abort, and some to whom offspring were born did not adequately care for their young.[33]

In other studies, overcrowding among animals has led them to become irritable, overly aggressive, nervous, inattentive to grooming, and messy, with some even resorting to cannibalism. In many cases, such negative behaviors continued to occur when the animals were returned to a normal environment.[34]

Although animal research is suggestive, it is not necessarily applicable to humans. The effects of crowding on humans have not been sufficiently researched. Some authorities believe it is a factor in leading to crime, emotional problems, incest, child abuse, suicide, violence, dirty streets, and polluted air. Other authorities believe increases in these behaviors are not due to overcrowding but to poverty and to the breakdown in traditional values. Nonetheless, we should remember that a delicate balance often exists between a population and an environment, which can be drastically changed by a slight increase in a population. For example, adding one or two fish to a fully populated aquarium may result in a shortage of oxygen and kill most of the fish.[35]

***Immigration Problems*** Overpopulation also intensifies problems related to immigration. To *immigrate* means to come into a country of which one is not a native for permanent residence. Throughout the world people living in poor nations dream of moving to richer nations. Immigration to the United States has reached levels unmatched since early in the twentieth century. Other affluent countries have also experienced an influx of people from poorer nations.

It is often said that the United States is a nation of immigrants. Since the earliest days of European settlement, North America has attracted people from all over the world. Some, like black slaves from Africa, were brought against their will. Most other groups came in search of freedom from oppression and for economic opportunities. In the past two centuries, millions of immigrants of different religions, races, cultures, and political views have come to the United States. This diversity is one of the attributes and strengths of American culture. The immense variety of dress, diet, and music in our society can be traced to the contributions of immigrants from many different cultures and nations.

Immigration has also contributed to some of the social problems plaguing American society. Immigration has resulted in ethnic and racial conflict, exploitation of illegal aliens, competition among different nationality groups for a "piece of the pie," and the stresses and costs associated with educating and caring for new arrivals.

The presence of illegal aliens (also called undocumented immigrants) is one of the most severe social problems associated with immigration. The number of undocumented immigrants in the United States is unknown. Also unknown is the number of new arrivals each year. By far, the largest percentage of undocumented immigrants are Mexicans and Central Americans.

The effects of illegal residents on the economy of the United States has been a topic of heated debate for decades. Some authorities argue they take jobs away from native-born residents. Other authorities assert they are a boon to our economy as they perform distasteful work that U.S. citizens are reluctant

*Cuban refugees beg for water as they float in homemade rafts on the high seas about 45 miles south of Key West, Florida. Hoping to reach the United States, they had been at sea for at least two days.*

to do—such as harvesting garden crops on their knees. They also maintain some industries by accepting lower wages and inferior working conditions. The survival of such industries stimulates growth in associated services, thereby creating more jobs. During economic recessions, undocumented immigrants are generally laid off or discharged more readily than citizens; they thereby help cushion the native-born population from economic uncertainty.

A highly controversial issue related to immigration is whether people who test positive for the HIV virus should be allowed into the United States. As of this writing, individuals who are HIV positive are allowed to enter the United States. (For most of the 1980s, and part of the 1990s, they were prohibited from entering.)

Undocumented immigrants are easily exploited by ruthless individuals who know that the immigrants cannot complain to authorities when they have been victimized. (If they went to the authorities, their illegal status might be discovered, which would subject them to deportation.) Although many undocumented immigrants are working in the United States, their employment is now illegal. In 1986 Congress passed the Immigration Reform and Control Act, under which employers are subject to civil penalties ranging from $250 to $10,000 for each illegal alien they hire.

The vast majority of the immigrants who arrive in the United States settle in only a few cities and regions, such as the metropolitan areas of New York City, Los Angeles, Miami, and Chicago. The phenomenon of *chain migration* is the primary cause of this urban concentration. The term refers to the tendency of immigrants to migrate to areas where relatives and others from their home communities are already living. These relatives and acquaintances share the immigrants' culture and language (or dialect) and are available to help the immigrants adjust to the new surroundings. The clusters of immigrants in large cities greatly add to the costs of services in these areas, such as education, health care, job training, public housing, and adult English-language classes.

Now, as in the past, much of the opposition to immigration is based on racial and ethnic prejudice, because most of the immigrants to the United States in recent decades have been people of color and non-Europeans. But there is a legitimate question as to whether immigrants raise the unemployment rate by adding to the competition for a limited number of jobs.

Sudden surges of political refugees or illegal immigrants may create special problems. For example, in 1980 Fidel Castro released a number of prisoners and residents of mental hospitals in Cuba; many of these individuals fled to southern Florida, particularly Miami. The influx taxed governmental services in southern Florida and also spurred several serious outbreaks of racial violence in the area during the 1980s.

In 1997, the respected National Academy of Sciences/National Research Council released a landmark report entitled *The New Americans: Economic, Demographic and Fiscal Effects of Immigration*. The report concluded immigration has a very small impact on the U.S. economy, "The costs to native-born workers are small, and so are the benefits."[36] The report found that immigrants have no negative effects on the wages of most Americans. There is one exception: the very low skilled workers with less than a high school degree (who represent about 15 percent of the workforce) earn wages that are somewhat lower (about 5 percent) than they would without competition from low-skilled immigrants. The study found that the other losers are taxpayers in California, Florida, Texas, and a few other states where most immigrants live. Taxpayers in those states end up paying more in taxes for the government services (primarily health care and public schools) used by the newcomers. The study also found that immigrants generate a growing share of taxes the longer they are here; the study concluded each additional immigrant and his or her descendants provide $80,000 in extra tax revenues over their lifetimes.[37] (See Figure 16.2.)

## THEORY OF DEMOGRAPHIC TRANSITION

The rate of population growth is highest in developing countries. Researchers on population growth have observed that growth rates tend to decrease and then stabilize after a fairly high level of industrialization. This observation is assumed to be true about population growth in general, and the assumption is called the theory of demographic transition. This transition is thought to take place in three stages:

1. *Preindustrial, agricultural societies.* In this stage, there is a fairly stable population size, as the societies have both high birthrates and high death rates.

| Impact on state and local treasuries | Impact on federal treasury | Total impact |
| --- | --- | --- |
| −$25,000 | +$105,000 | +$80,000 |

These figures are arrived at by adding the taxes that an immigrant and his or her descendants are likely to pay over their lifetimes, while subtracting the costs of the government services they are likely to use. The result: each immigrant produces a net revenue gain to government, with the federal government getting most of the benefit, and state and local treasuries losing. In addition, immigrants with higher education are a greater benefit to government treasuries—as indicated below:

| Less than high school | High school graduate | More than high school | Overall |
| --- | --- | --- | --- |
| −$13,000 | +$51,000 | +$198,000 | +$80,000 |

**Figure 16.2** *The Bottom Line on Immigration*

*Source:* National Academy of Sciences/National Research Council, *The New Americans* (Washington, DC, 1997).

2. *Developing societies beginning to industrialize.* Birthrates remain high, but death rates drop, leading to a rapid increase in the population growth rate. The death rates drop because these societies have the medical capacities to extend the average life span.

3. *Developed industrial societies.* Such societies have both low birthrates and low death rates, resulting once again in a stable population. The low birthrates are thought to be due to people voluntarily limiting the number of children they have. Parents have fewer children to maintain a higher standard of living for themselves and their children.

The theory of demographic transition gives hope that as developing countries continue to industrialize, their high population growth rates will eventually decrease and then stabilize. It should be noted, however, that the concept of demographic transition is merely a theoretical model, a summary statement of what happened in the United States and in many other industrialized nations. Because some past societies have had this demographic history does not necessarily mean that current developing nations will repeat the same process.

*Would-be immigrants crawl under the wall running along the border between the United States and Mexico in Tijuana, to try to cross to the other side.*

A variety of factors, including religious and cultural values, can greatly affect the rate of population growth. In Japan, for example, certain values rapidly accelerated the passage of the second stage in the demographic transition. At the end of World War II, Japan was a developing nation and had a high birthrate. Two variables speeded Japan into the third stage of demographic transition. First, there was a general consensus that population control was needed. Second, abortion was not considered immoral (as it was in Western societies). As a result, from 1947 to 1957, Japan's birthrate dropped from thirty-four children per one thousand to fourteen per one thousand, one of the sharpest declines on record. During this decade, half the conceptions were terminated by abortion.[38] It is doubtful that such a rapid transition could be achieved in countries with cultural traditions that encourage large families.

In regard to stabilizing population growth, Robertson notes:

> The question is not whether population will stabilize—it will. If the global population exceeds the carrying capacity of the earth, death rates will rise and

halt population growth. The issues are whether stability will result from a decrease in birth rates or an increase in death rates, how long it will take before stability occurs, and how many people will be here when this finally happens. The prospect of a demographic transition offers the hope that if certain preconditions are met, population growth rates in the developing world will be reduced by a decline in birth rates rather than the grim alternative.[39]

It is unfortunate, however, that most developing countries have become lodged in a holding pattern in the middle stage of demographic transition, with high birthrates and lowered death rates.[40] The longer these countries remain in this stage, the more their populations will swell and the more difficult it becomes for them to industrialize and to complete the demographic transition.

*Problematic Attitudes and Values* The Roman Catholic Church still objects to using any birth-control approach except the rhythm method. In many countries, widely accepted values encourage parents to have large families. Abortions are still a controversial issue in our society. Many Americans still believe population growth is *not* a major issue requiring immediate attention.[41] With such attitudes and values, it is clear that Americans as yet do not recognize that overpopulation is one of our most serious problems.

In regard to attitudes toward the use of birth control, Ehrlich and Ehrlich note:

> We shouldn't delude ourselves: the population explosion will come to an end before very long. The only remaining question is whether it will be halted through the humane method of birth control, or by nature wiping out the surplus. We realize that religious and cultural opposition to birth control exists throughout the world; but we believe that people simply don't understand the choice that such opposition implies. Today, anyone opposing birth control is unknowingly voting to have the human population size controlled by a massive increase in early deaths.[42]

## TWO COUNTRIES WITH SEVERE POPULATION PROBLEMS

India and China are two countries having immense problems associated with overpopulation. We will briefly look at these problems. If the population growth rate in the world is not curbed, most countries will in the future be facing similar problems.

*India*   With an area about one-third the size of the United States, India has a population more than three times the size of ours; it is approaching 1 billion people.[43] About 25 million babies are estimated to be born in India each year.[44]

India is also one of the world's poorest nations, with a per capita income of $250 per year.[45] Many of its citizens are malnourished and starving. The average Indian has a daily food intake of about 2,000 calories. (The minimum requirement for staying healthy is about 2,300 to 2,500 calories.) In some states in India, more than 100 out of each 1,000 babies die due to inadequate antenatal care and delivery services, low levels of immunization among children, and a substantial proportion of high-risk births.[46]

In 1952, India became the first country in the world to adopt a public family-planning program to reduce the birthrate. At first the program was poorly funded. In 1956, for example, total expenditures amounted to 1¢ per year for every 20 people. The principal contraceptive method that was promoted was the rhythm method—one of the least effective

*A CARE family-planning worker supervises a community health worker as she describes one of the methods available, the intrauterine device (IUD).*

approaches. In the 1960s, vasectomies and the intrauterine device (IUD) were added to the techniques used. At the end of the 1960s oral contraceptives were also added, although vasectomies and IUDs remain the preferred methods.

Although the birthrate has declined somewhat in India, birth-control devices have not reduced the rate to the zero-growth level. A major reason is that most people using birth-control techniques decide to do so only after they already have a large family.[47]

In 1976 the Indian government under Indira Gandhi decided to promote a more aggressive population-control strategy. Public educational programs were developed to try to persuade Indians that their main problem was not too little food but too many people. The federal government threatened to dismiss civil service employees who had more than three children. Individual states were asked to pass bills requiring compulsory sterilization of parents after the birth of their third child. One state, Maharashtra, passed such a law and began compulsory sterilization.

In 1977, however, Mrs. Gandhi received a crushing electoral defeat, partly because of her government's record on civil liberties and partly because of the unpopularity of the population-control programs. Following her defeat, the compulsory sterilization law in Maharashtra was rescinded.

At India's current growth rate of 1.7 percent annually India's population will soon exceed 1 billion.[48] India's population is projected to surpass China in population size by the year 2050, as India's growth rate is substantially higher than China's.[49]

More than 80 percent of all Indians are Hindus. Hindu husbands frequently will not permit their wives to use contraceptives until they have produced at least two sons.[50] An additional 11 percent of the population are Muslims. Some Muslim religious leaders denounce birth control of any kind, but especially sterilization, because cutting the body is a violation of religious law.[51] The obsession for sons is so strong in India that, in order to prevent abortions of unwanted female fetuses, national law prohibits physicians from telling a pregnant woman the sex of the unborn child.[52]

Will India continue to race toward starvation and famine, or will it find politically acceptable approaches to controlling its population growth and begin to raise the standard of living for its citizens? Answers to such questions are of vital significance to all developing countries (and will also have substantial consequences for the rest of the world).

*China*  In terms of sheer size, China's population surpasses that of India. China already has more than 1 billion people—nearly one-fifth the world's entire population.[53]

China's attitude about population growth has varied over the years. For many years the government considered its huge population an important military resource in any conflict with the former Soviet Union or the United States. Furthermore, it urged other developing nations to take the same view. As is common with many developing nations, China's standard of living is low, and much of the farming and factory work is done by hand.

Poor harvests and resulting food shortages (along with changes in the top leadership and a closer relationship with the United States) have convinced the Chinese government that population control is essential. These leaders are now promoting the view that limiting family size will improve the health and living conditions of all its citizens and will also liberate women from traditional restrictions. Propaganda posters advertise that an education and a good career are more easily attained with a small family.

Prior to the present policies on family size, Chinese women averaged three children each.[54] In 1980 China's government established a one-child-per-family policy. It raised the minimum legal age for marriage by two years, to 22 for men and 20 for women. In some higher-density areas, this minimum age is even higher; in Beijing it is 28 for men and 25 for women.[55] (A higher minimum age of marriage is correlated with a smaller average family size.[56]) To have a large family is now regarded as disrespectful to the Communist party and to the country.

Women who become pregnant after the birth of their first child are sometimes pressured to have an abortion. China has also established a number of economical social incentives for couples to have no more than one child, including income bonuses, priority consideration in urban housing assignments, subsidies in health care, promises of higher pensions, and private vegetable gardens for city residents. For couples who have more than two children, there are also disincentives, such as possible wage deduction to fund welfare programs.

China has greatly slowed its growth rate with these policies. China's current growth rate is down to about 1.1 percent—an extremely low rate for what is still a poor agricultural nation.[57] It is clear that China is now committed to an all-out effort to stabilize the size of its population, which is good news for the future of China (and for the rest of the world).

Yet, new problems have emerged. Some fears have surfaced about the possibility of an emerging generation of spoiled and self-centered only children. Also, if the one-child policy were fully achieved, China would become a society without brothers, sisters, uncles, or aunts.[58] Chinese peasants have traditionally placed a high value on having sons, who live with the extended family throughout their lives. Daughters, on the other hand, are expected to move in with their husband's family and are therefore considered more of a burden than an asset. Having a son is also viewed as vitally important in continuing the family's name and heritage. As a result, the one-child policy has caused a startling increase in female infanticide, because couples then are able, without government opposition, to attempt another pregnancy in the hope of having a male child. The pace of childbearing in China has decelerated faster than in any other large developing country.[59]

Another problem related to female infanticide in China is that today there are nearly three men for every two women in China.[60] This tendency poses some obvious problems for unmarried Chinese men.

In recent years, China has opened its doors to the West, inviting tourists and Western technology and investments. Undoubtedly there will be rapid techno-logical, social, cultural, and lifestyle changes. History suggests that such changes will be accompanied by political turmoil. (For example, in the 1970s the Shah of Iran established governmental policies and pro-grams to facilitate industrialization, using funds from the sale of its crude oil to foreign countries. These rapid changes led to political unrest, civil war, and the eventual ouster of the shah.) The future changes in China will have immense implications for the rest of the world.

Will coercive population-control policies such as those in India and China eventually be needed in the United States? Ehrlich and Ehrlich note:

> We must hope that our government doesn't wait until it too decides that only coercive measures can solve America's population problem. One must always keep in mind that the price of personal freedom in making childbearing decisions may be the destruction of the world in which your children or grandchildren live. How many children a person has now has serious social consequences in all nations, and therefore is a legiti-mate concern of society as a whole.[61]

## CONFRONTING OVERPOPULATION

This chapter highlights national and international problems associated with overpopulation: food short-ages, starvation and malnourishment, shortage of water reserves, crowding, international terrorism, and economic problems. This section will summarize a number of recommendations for confronting over-population.

Limiting population growth will have a major pos-itive impact on all of the problems discussed in this chapter. If the world population growth rate is reversed to head toward a zero-growth rate, and even to go negative, it may give us the time necessary to find solutions to the other problems that have been discussed. Limiting population growth is a key factor in maintaining our current quality of life.

Dr. Paul Ehrlich provides the following sugges-tions for limiting the population. Being the most affluent and influential superpower, the United States should become a model for population control by first setting a goal of a stable optimal population size for our country and demonstrating our determination to achieve this goal rapidly and then by reversing our government's current "reward" system for having children. Specific measures include:

- No longer allowing income tax deductions for children
- Placing a luxury tax on layettes, diapers, cribs, expensive toys, and diaper services
- Rewarding small families by giving "responsibility prizes" to each man who has a vasectomy after having two children
- Subsidizing adoptions and simplifying adoption procedures
- Guaranteeing the right of any woman to have an abortion
- Enacting a federal law requiring sex education in schools, sex education that includes material on the need for regulating the birthrate and the techniques of birth control
- Developing new contraceptives that are reliable, easy to use, and do not have harmful side effects[62]

Bernard Berelson compiled a list of other proposals to control population:

- Adding temporary sterilants to water or food sup-plies, with doses of an antidote being carefully rationed by the government to produce the desired population size (such sterilants are not as yet in existence)
- Compulsory sterilization of men with three or more living children
- Raising the minimum age for marriage
- Providing benefits (money, goods, or services) to couples not bearing children for extended time periods
- Requiring foreign countries to establish effective population-control programs before *any* foreign aid is provided[63]

Some of these proposals appear "too radical" for most Americans to accept and may conflict with moral and ethical values of many U.S. citizens. But will we reach such an overpopulation crisis that they may be necessary in the future?

As mentioned previously, many developing nations now provide sex education and family planning programs to their people, which (at least temporarily) are showing evidence of lowering birthrates. We hope that the population-control measures recommended by Berelson can be avoided.

A developing country that has had success in reducing the rate of population growth is Indonesia. It first launched its national family-planning program in the 1960s. Initially Indonesia focused its effort on informing its people (including the country's conservative religious leaders) of the problems associated with overpopulation and the advantages of a smaller family. The government's next effort shifted to making contraceptives available to everyone who wanted them. This effort was careful to respect the conservative sexual attitudes of most Indonesians. (For example, there was very little effort to promote the use of condoms because most Indonesians associate them with prostitution.)

The government now offers incentives for the long-term use of contraceptives, including subsidies for government employees, valuable agricultural products, and even expense-paid trips to Mecca (the holiest site of the Islamic religion). As a result of such efforts, Indonesia's birthrate has declined by about 45 percent in the last two decades.[64] Its current annual growth rate is now about 1.6 percent, which is significantly lower than most other developing countries.[65]

Ehrlich, Ehrlich, and Holdren provide an elegant summary of the need to establish a worldwide vision of the future of the human race:

> Perhaps the major necessary ingredient that has been missing from a solution to the problems of both the United States and the rest of the world is a goal, a vision of the kind of Spaceship Earth that ought to be and the kind of crew that should man her. Society has always had its visionaries who talked of love, beauty, peace, and plenty. But sometimes the "practical" men have always been there to praise smog as a sign of progress, to preach "just" wars, and to restrict love while giving hate free rein. It must be one of the greatest ironies of the history of the human species that the only salvation for the practical men now lies in what they think of as the dreams of idealists. The question now is: can the self-proclaimed "realists" be persuaded to face reality in time?[66]

### The Abortion Controversy

If the world's population continues to grow at or near its present rate, the current debate over voluntary abortions may pale compared to controversies that will be generated if compulsory population-control measures are needed.

The abortion controversy has been going on for two decades, but it was heightened in January 1973, when the U.S. Supreme Court, in a 7-2 decision, overruled state laws that prohibited or restricted a woman's right to obtain an abortion during the first three months of pregnancy. Suing under the assumed name of Jane Roe, a Texas resident argued that her state's law against abortion denied her a constitutional right. The Court agreed that the right of personal privacy includes the right to decide whether to have an abortion. However, the Court held that such a right is not absolute and that states have the authority to impose restrictions after the third month. This decision, known as *Roe* v. *Wade,* also allowed states to prohibit abortion in the last ten weeks of pregnancy (a time when there is a good chance that the fetus will live), except when the life or health of the mother is endangered.

In 1977 Congress passed, and President Carter signed into law, the so-called Hyde Amendment (named for its original sponsor, Representative Henry Hyde from Illinois). This amendment prohibits Medicaid spending for abortions except when a woman's life would be endangered by childbirth or in cases of promptly reported rape or incest. In June 1980 this amendment was upheld as constitutional in a 5-4 vote by the U.S. Supreme Court. The ruling means that the federal government and individual states do not have to pay for most abortions for women on welfare.

The Hyde Amendment is significant because more than one-third of the legal abortions performed in the United States between 1973 and 1977 were for women on welfare.[67] The passage of the amendment illustrates the strength of the anti-abortion forces in this country. Is it fair for middle- and upper-class women to have more access to abortions than lower-income women?

With the election of President Reagan in 1980, there was a move toward conservatism in our society. Certain groups, such as the Catholic Church and right-to-life groups, have been strongly urging that a constitutional amendment be passed to prohibit abortions, except in cases where the woman's life is endangered.

During the Reagan and Bush administration from 1980 to 1992, some liberal Supreme Court judges retired and were replaced by more conservative judges. As a result, the Supreme Court gradually assumed a more conservative (pro-life) position on the abortion issue. The waning of the Supreme Court majority recognizing a woman's right to an abortion became clear in a 1989 decision, *Webster* v. *Reproductive Health Services.* The Supreme Court upheld a restrictive

Missouri law that (1) prohibited state employees from assisting in abortions and prohibited abortions from being performed in state-owned hospitals, and (2) banned abortions of *viable* fetuses. (The Missouri law viewed fetuses as viable if the woman was believed to be 20 weeks or more pregnant and a viability test showed the fetus could live.) The broader effect of the Court's decision was to throw the hot-potato issue of abortion back to state legislatures, many of which debated a variety of abortion bills.

In 1992 Bill Clinton was elected President. He had adhered to a pro-choice position on the abortion issue. President Clinton has had the opportunity to appoint a few liberal judges to the Supreme Court. As of the late 1990s, it appears that the Court is likely to continue to uphold the basic provisions of *Roe* v. *Wade*.

Waldman, Ackerman, and Rubin summarize significant information on abortions in the United States. Roughly 1.4 million women have abortions each year. About 80 percent are unmarried or separated. More than 40 percent have had at least one previous abortion. Catholic women have them at a higher rate than do Protestant women. It is estimated that 43 percent of women in the United States will have an abortion in their lifetime.[68]

The major objection to permitting abortions is based on perceptions of moral principles. The Roman Catholic Church views the abortion issue as one of the most important current moral issues. This church and "right-to-life" groups condemn abortion as being synonymous with murder. They assert that life begins at conception and point out that there is no phase during pregnancy in which there is a distinct, qualitative difference in the development of the fetus. The Catholic Church views abortion as acceptable only when it is done to save the physical life of the mother. This type of abortion is justified on the principle of "double effect," which holds that a morally evil action (an abortion) is allowable when it is the side effect of a morally good act (saving the life of the mother).

There are numerous arguments that have been advanced for permitting abortions:

- If abortions were prohibited again, women would seek illegal abortions as they did in the past. Performed in a medical clinic or hospital, an abortion is a relatively safe operation; but performed under unsanitary conditions, perhaps by an inexperienced or unskilled abortionist, the operation is extremely dangerous and may even imperil the life of the woman. If abortions were again prohibited, some women would attempt to self-induce abortions. Attempts at self-induced abortions can be extremely dangerous. Women have tried such techniques as severe exercise, hot baths, and pelvic and intestinal irritants and have even attempted to lacerate the uterus with such sharp objects as hatpins, nail files, and knives.

- Recognizing abortions as being legal helps prevent the birth of unwanted babies; such babies have a higher probability of being abused or neglected.

- Permitting women to obtain an abortion allows women to have greater freedom, as they would not be forced to raise a child at a time when they had other plans and commitments. Feminists argue that women must be free and autonomous to make an abortion decision in order to have equality with men. They assert if the right to abortion were taken away from women, women's lives and lifestyles would be substantially determined by men and impregnation.

Opponents of abortion argue that the "right to life" is the basic right that everyone has and should in no way be infringed on. Proponents of abortion seek to counter this view by arguing that there may be a more basic right than the right to life, that is, the preservation of the quality of life. Given the overpopulation problem and given the fact that abortion appears to be a necessary population-control technique (in some countries the number of abortions is approaching the number of live births), some authorities are asserting that abortion is a necessary measure (although less desirable than contraceptives) to preserve the quality of life.[69] Unless life has quality, the right to life is meaningless. Table 16.3 presents arguments both for and against legal abortion.

***Family-Planning Services*** Family-planning services obviously are essential for preventing unwanted pregnancies. Such services provide birth-control information and contraceptives; pregnancy testing; HIV testing and counseling; testing and counseling about other sexually transmitted diseases; sex education, abortion counseling, and abortions; counseling on child spacing, sterilization information and operations; and infertility counseling. Family planning includes helping couples who desire children to have children. It also helps couples to prepare for parenthood.

**Table 16.3**    *Legal Abortion: Arguments Pro and Con*

| Against Legal Abortion | In Favor of Legal Abortion |
| --- | --- |
| Human life begins at conception; therefore, abortion is murder of a person. Even scientists have not reached a consensus on any other point in fetal development that can be considered the moment the fetus becomes a person. Life is a matter of fact, not religion or values. | The belief in personhood at conception is a religious belief held by the Roman Catholic Church. Most Protestant and Jewish denominations regard the fetus as a potential human being, not a full-fledged person and have position statements in support of legal abortion. When the unborn becomes a person is a matter of religion and values, not absolute fact. |
| We must pass a constitutional amendment to protect unborn babies from abortion. To say the law will not be followed and should not be made is like saying people still get murdered so laws against murder should be repealed. | No law has ever stopped abortion and no law ever will. The issue is not whether abortions will be done, but whether they will be done safely, by doctors, or dangerously, by back-alley butchers, or by the women themselves. History has shown that anti-abortion laws are uniquely unenforceable, as they do not prevent abortions. |
| Medicaid should not pay for abortion. It is wrong to try to eliminate poverty by killing the unborn children of the poor. Tax money should not be used for the controversial practice of aborting unwanted children. The decision not to have children should be made before getting pregnant. | The original intent of Medicaid was to equalize medical services between the rich and the poor and to help the poor become independent and self-sufficient. To make them ineligible for abortion defies justice, common sense, and rational policy. Women burdened by unwanted children cannot get job training or go to work and are trapped in the poverty/welfare cycle. Neither abortion nor childbirth should be forced on poor women. |
| If you believe abortion is morally wrong, you are obligated to work for the passage of a "human life" amendment to the Constitution. | Many people who are personally opposed to abortion, including most Roman Catholics, believe it is wrong to impose their religious or moral beliefs on others. |
| The right of the unborn to live supersedes any right of a woman to "control her own body." | In order for women to have equality with men, women must be free and autonomous to make an abortion decision. If women lose the right to have an abortion, their lives and lifestyles would substantially be determined by men and impregnation. |
| The "abortion mentality" leads to infanticide, euthanasia, and killing of retarded and elderly persons. | In countries where abortion has been legal for years, there is no evidence that respect for life has diminished or that legal abortion leads to killing of any persons. Infanticide, however, is prevalent in countries where the overburdened poor cannot control their childbearing and was prevalent in Japan before abortion was legalized. |
| Abortion causes psychological damage to women. | The Institute of Medicine of the National Academy of Sciences has concluded that abortion is not associated with a detectable increase in the incidence of mental illness. The depression and guilt feelings reported by some women are usually mild, temporary, and outweighed by |

Table 16.3    *continued*

| Against Legal Abortion | In Favor of Legal Abortion |
|---|---|
| | feelings of relief. Such negative feelings would be substantially lessened if anti-abortion advocates were less vehement in expressing their beliefs. Women choosing abortion should be informed of the risks and benefits of the procedure and should decide for themselves what to do. |
| Women have abortions for their own convenience or on "whim." | Right-to-life dismisses unwanted pregnancy as a mere annoyance. The urgency of women's need to end unwanted pregnancy is measured by their willingness to risk death and mutilation, to spend huge sums of money, and to endure the indignities of illegal abortion. Women have abortions only when the alternative is unendurable. Women take both abortion and motherhood very seriously. |
| In a society where contraceptives are so readily available, there should be no unwanted pregnancies and therefore no need for abortion. | No birth-control method is perfectly reliable, and for medical reasons many women cannot, or will not, use the most effective methods. Contraceptive information and services are not available to all women, particularly teenagers, the poor, and rural women. |
| Abortion is not the safe and simple procedure we're told it is. | Before the 1973 Supreme Court rulings, illegal abortion was the leading cause of maternal death and mutilation. Having a legal abortion is medically less dangerous than childbirth. |
| Doctors make large profits from legal abortions. | Legal abortion is less costly and less profitable than illegal abortion was. Many legal abortions are done in nonprofit facilities. If it's not improper to "make money" on childbirth, it is not wrong to earn money by performing legal abortions. |
| Parents have the right and responsibility to guide their children in important decisions. A law requiring parental notification of a daughter's abortion would strengthen the family unit. (Many states have now passed parental laws that are consistent with this argument.) | Many teenagers voluntarily consult their parents, but some simply will not. Forcing the involvement of unsympathetic, authoritarian, or very moralistic parents in a teen's pregnancy (and sexuality) can damage the family unit beyond repair. Some family units are already under so much stress that knowledge of an unwed pregnancy could be disastrous. |
| Pro-abortionists are anti-family. Abortion destroys the American family. | The unwanted child of a teenaged mother has little chance to grow up in a normal, happy American home. Instead, a new family is created: a child and her child, both destined for a life of poverty and hopelessness. Legal abortion helps women limit their families to the number of children they want and can afford, both emotionally and financially, and reduces the number of children born unwanted. Pro-choice is definitely pro-family. |

Box 16.1

# RU-486: An Abortion Pill

RU-486, a pill that induces abortion early in pregnancy, was developed and introduced in France. This pill is now being widely used in France, Britain, Sweden, and China to induce abortions. RU-486 acts by impeding a hormone (progesterone) that is necessary for a fetus to stay implanted in the uterus. In 85 percent of cases, this pill works until seven weeks after conception. For its effectiveness to reach 96 percent, it must be followed by a dose of prostaglandin, a substance that induces uterine contractions. Proponents envision a day when a woman who wants to end a suspected pregnancy can merely take a pill in the privacy of her own home, avoiding demonstrators outside abortion clinics.

A small percentage of users experience some adverse side effects of RU-486, including heavy bleeding and nausea. (Surgical abortions also pose some risks—from anesthesia, infections, and damage to the cervix and uterus.)

RU-486 is also a highly effective morning-after pill. RU-486 appears to prevent implantation of the fertilized egg in the wall of the uterus. RU-486 may also be effective in treating breast and ovarian cancer (two of the biggest killers of women). It may prove useful in treating endometriosis, a leading cause of female infertility.

The right-to-life movement was successful in the late 1980s and early 1990s in keeping RU-486 from being distributed legally in the United States. The Food and Drug Administration banned the drug in 1989 after being pressured by anti-abortion groups. The anti-abortion movement has said it will call for boycotts against any company that seeks to market it in the United States.

The U.S. government announced in 1994 that an agreement had been reached with France's Roussel Uclaf, the company that originally patented the drug, that would lead to testing of the drug on two thousand U.S. women. Will the drug be licensed for use in the United States?

*Source:* Lauran Neergaard, "Agreement Clears Way for Abortion Drug in U.S.," *Wisconsin State Journal*, May 17, 1994, A.

---

*Governmental Programs* National family-planning programs are governmental efforts to lower birthrates by funding programs that provide birth-control information and services. With family-planning programs, families voluntarily decide whether to limit the number of children they have. Most countries, including developing and developed nations, now have official family-planning programs. This is a remarkable achievement, since forty-five years ago no developing country had a governmental family-planning program. (In fact, forty-five years ago, several countries had programs with the opposite objective—to increase the birthrate and the rate of immigration.) This indicates that concern about world population growth is a recent phenomenon.

In spite of these advances, only a few countries have established population-control policies. Two countries that have are India and China, as described earlier in this chapter. (Population control is the deliberate regulation of the size of the population by society. Family planning, in contrast, is the regulation of births by individual families.) As we noted, India's population control program launched in 1976 included a sterilization policy that was soon retracted after the party that passed the legislation failed to be reelected. Whether India will attempt to enact another population-control policy is unclear; future population growth may be a decisive factor in India's determining whether population control is necessary.

Until President Lyndon Johnson's 1965 State of the Union Address, family planning was not considered a proper concern for our government. In his address, President Johnson stated that $5 spent on family planning was worth $100 invested in some other area of world economic development. In 1966, the federal government developed regulations that, for the first time, allowed federal funds to provide family-planning services to welfare clients on a voluntary basis. The avowed purpose of this policy (which was widely criticized) was not phrased in terms of family-planning goals but instead had the objectives of reducing the welfare burden by lowering the illegitimacy rate and of breaking the poverty cycle by decreasing the transmission of poverty from one generation to another.

The National Center for Family Planning Services was established by the passage of the Family Planning

Services and Population Research Act of 1970. This act recognized that family planning was part of the delivery of comprehensive health services for all. In 1972, Congress mandated that family-planning services must be provided to all welfare recipients who desired them. At that time, contraceptive policy changes were also made, lifting restrictions on marital status and age for receiving birth-control information and devices.

*Private agencies* In the United States, most family-planning services have in the past been provided by private agencies and organizations. The largest and best-known organization is Planned Parenthood. This organization was founded in 1916 by Margaret Sanger, with the opening of the first birth-control clinic in Brooklyn. The organization now has clinics located throughout the nation. Planned Parenthood now offers (a) medical services—physical examinations, Pap smear tests, urine and blood tests, screening for sexually transmitted diseases, all medically approved methods of contraception, and pregnancy testing; (b) counseling services—infertility, premarital, contraceptive, pregnancy, and sterilization for males and for females; and (c) educational services—sex education, contraceptive information including effectiveness and side effects of the varied approaches, and breast self-examinations. (Table 16.4 shows a ranking of the effectiveness of various contraceptives in preventing pregnancies.)

Family-planning services are now available in practically all areas in the United States from a variety of public and private organizations, including health departments, hospitals, physicians in private practice, Planned Parenthood affiliates, and other agencies such as community action groups and free clinics.

**The Future** Violence against abortion clinics and family planning clinics has escalated in recent years. Anti-abortion groups have picketed clinics, with the objective being to stop patients from using the services of the clinics. Clinic physicians and other staff often receive threatening phone calls and have their own homes picketed. Abortion clinics, staff, and patients have been subjected to a number of incidents of violence involving bombings, arsons, vandalisms, burglaries, assaults, death threats, kidnappings, and stalkings. Violent tactics by anti-abortion supporters have even included incidents of shooting and killing staff at abortion clinics. It is ironic that some fringe elements of the right-to-life movement have resorted

**Table 16.4** *Ranking of Effectiveness of Birth-Control Methods in Preventing Pregnancies*

| Method | Number of Pregnancies per 100 Women during One Year of Use |
|---|---|
| 1. Abstinence | 0 |
| 2. Norplant implant | .09 |
| 3. Depo-Provera | .3 |
| 4. Sterilization | .4 |
| 5. IUD | .8 |
| 6. Condom | 12 |
| 7. Diaphragm | 18 |
| 8. Cervical cap | 18 |
| 9. Withdrawal | 19 |
| 10. Natural Family Planning (rhythm) | 20 |
| 11. Contraceptive foam and suppositories | 21 |
| 12. Vaginal pouch (female condom) | 21 |

*Note:* After the first five listed methods, the risk of pregnancy for sexually active users is sharply increased. (Sterilization for women, tubal ligation, is nearly 100 percent effective, although in very rare cases the tubes may rejoin themselves.)

*Source: Facts About Birth Control* (New York: Planned Parenthood Federation of America, 1997).

to murder to seek to force their views on others. Will such violence continue to escalate in the United States in the future?

On a policy level, the United States needs to resolve a number of family-planning issues in order to have an effective national policy on family planning. Currently there is considerable controversy about a number of issues associated with family planning: sex education in schools, provision of birth-control information and devices for teenagers, approaches to prevent HIV and other sexually transmitted diseases, and abortions (including the issue of whether the federal government should pay for abortions for those who cannot afford them).

A number of authorities are predicting dire consequences for the future of the world unless population-control measures are implemented immediately. Other authorities discount overpopulation concerns and predict that technological advancements will prevent cataclysmic effects from rapid population growth. If the latter authorities are mistaken, we may be forced in a few years to apply population-control measures that now seem unethical and "inhumane."

Werner Fornos strongly urges that the United States fund international programs that are designed to slow population growth in developing countries:

> If Americans now feel anguish over witnessing the recent human suffering and needless deaths in Ethiopia, just imagine a world in which virtually the entire Third World will be wracked by vast poverty and human misery. . . .
>
> And if Americans are now troubled by the specter of instability, revolution, and authoritarianism in the Third World, they have only to imagine the consequences of inaction, because the fragile seed of democracy cannot survive long in societies with escalating misery, crippled economies, and dying environments.
>
> In shaping the federal budget, the U.S. Congress must ask not only how much it will cost to fund population programs, but also what will be the cost of *not* funding them.[70]

## Summary

Problems associated with overpopulation are very serious and may have an adverse, dramatic effect on the quality of life in the future. The world's population has tripled in size since 1930. About six billion people now live on Earth. At current growth rates, the population will again double in size in the next forty years. Already we are experiencing resource crises. Some of the problems associated with overpopulation are:

- *Too little food.* At present, a large proportion of the people in the world are undernourished, and many are starving.

- *Too little water.* Fresh water is in short supply.

- *Economic problems.* Overpopulation lowers the average per capita income, reduces the standard of living, and often leads to political turmoil.

- *International terrorism.* Rapid population growth is a factor that contributes to civil unrest, violence, and international strife.

- *Crowding.* There is evidence that the subjective feeling of insufficient space may be a factor in leading to such problems as crime, emotional problems, suicide, violence, incest, and child abuse.

- *Immigration problems.* Immigration has resulted in ethnic and racial conflict, economic competition among different nationality groups, exploitation of undocumented immigrants, and the stresses and costs associated with educating and caring for new arrivals.

Unless the size of the world's population is brought under control, these problems are apt to intensify. A number of proposals have been advanced to curtail the growth of the world's population, some of which, if implemented, would radically change current lifestyles. Proposals include: subsidizing adoptions, expanding sex education programs in schools, developing safer contraceptives, compulsory sterilization, raising the minimum age for marriage, no longer allowing tax deductions for children, making birth-control information and devices more available, and making abortions more accessible. If nations are not successful in controlling the birthrate with voluntary family-planning programs, pressure will mount for countries to adopt population-control programs.

CHAPTER 17

*Environment*

Sometimes the environment is despoiled by human accidents. The worst and most expensive oil spill for the United States occurred in March 1989 in Prince William Sound in Alaska. The petroleum tanker *Exxon Valdez* struck rocks, puncturing a huge hole in the vessel. Nearly 11 million gallons of crude oil spilled into the water. Exxon spent $2 billion to clean up the crude oil, but recovered only 5 to 9 percent of the oil spilled. Millions of birds, animals, fish, and plants were killed. Local fishing industries, along with many other industries that depend upon ocean commerce in this area, were ruined.[1]

Sometimes the environment is intentionally despoiled by humans. Prior to being forced out of Kuwait in 1991 during the Desert Storm war, President Saddam Hussein of Iraq ordered his military forces to set six hundred oil wells in Kuwait on fire. Billions of dollars of oil reserves were destroyed, skies were blackened for months, and the smoke and fire—which lasted for many months—had severe adverse effects on the quality of life for humans and wildlife in the region.

These incidents are among the most dramatic of the many events that are despoiling the environment. This chapter:

♦ Summarizes current environmental problems

♦ Describes efforts to combat environmental problems

♦ Outlines proposals advanced to protect our environment and to create new forms of energy

♦ Provides suggestions for what all of us can do to save Earth

## *Environmental Problems*

◊◊◊◊◊◊◊◊◊◊◊◊◊◊◊◊◊◊◊◊◊◊

In this section we will examine the following problems: despoiling the land, radioactive wastes, solid waste disposal, toxic wastes, air pollution, water pollution, acid rain, general pollutants, too little energy, and nonrenewable resources.

### DESPOILING THE LAND

The scenic beauty of our land (and often its long-term economic value) is being spoiled by a variety of short-term human efforts: strip mining of coal, oil drilling, clearing of trees and forests, building high-ways, constructing oil pipelines, overgrazing by cattle and sheep, dumping garbage, littering, and erecting highway billboards. In nature, there is often a delicate balance of elements: fertile land needs trees and grass to retain moisture and fertility; grass-eating animals need grass to survive; carnivorous animals need the grass-eating animals; some birds need seeds and insects; other birds feed on the carcasses of dead animals; all are in need of water. Upsetting this balance often leads to devastating destruction. Dinosaurs once ruled the earth but died out from some as yet unknown environmental change. Less than two thousand years ago the Sahara Desert was a luxuriant forest. Overgrazing by domesticated sheep and goats and clearing of the forests were major factors in destroying the area.[2]

Deforestation is caused almost entirely by humans who log trees to get lumber and fuel, and intentionally destroy the forests to make room for the farms and cities demanded by a growing population. Every year the world loses an area of tropical forest land that is comparable to the size of Wisconsin.[3] At this rate, virtually no tropical forests will be left in thirty or forty years.[4] If the rain forests are destroyed, over a million unique species of animals and plants will die with them.[5]

Paul and Anne Ehrlich describe what happens when forests are cleared:

> Numerous animals that depend on the trees for food and shelter disappear. Many of the smaller forest plants depend on the trees for shade; they and the animals they support also disappear. With the removal of trees and plants, the soil is directly exposed to the elements, and it tends to erode faster. Loss of topsoil reduces the water-retaining capacity of an area, diminishes the supply of fresh water, causes silting of dams, and . . . flooding. . . . Deforestation . . . reduces the amount of water transferred from ground to air by the trees in the process known as "transpiration." This modifies the weather downwind of the area, usually making it more arid and subject to greater extremes of temperature.[6]

Some areas of the world are losing several inches of topsoil each year because of poor management that exposes the land to water and wind erosion. This is particularly alarming in light of the fact that it takes 300 to 1,000 years to produce one inch of topsoil under favorable conditions.[7] Each year 25 billion tons of topsoil are lost, primarily by erosion and by being washed into the sea.[8]

Forests, water, and soil are renewable resource systems that have "carrying capacities"—that is, levels at which they can provide maximum yields without injuring their capacity to repeat those yields. We can chop down only a certain number of trees in a forest each year without destroying the forest's capacity to replace those trees. Human populations in many parts of the world have grown so large that they are beginning to exceed the "carrying capacities" of their environments.[9]

## WASTE DISPOSAL

As yet our country does not have a safe way to dispose of radioactive waste material. We will look at this problem and also examine solid waste disposal problems.

*Radioactive Wastes*   America now has more than one hundred nuclear power plants, with plans to build more in the future.[10] A danger is that nuclear power plants generate radioactive nuclear wastes, and disposing of radioactive wastes is a major problem. In large doses, radiation from these wastes can cause death, whereas small doses may lead to cancer or birth deformities. These wastes are particularly hazardous because they remain radioactive for many years—as long as 300,000 years. The Nuclear Regulatory Commission (NRC) has considered various proposals for disposing of these wastes: firing them into space by rockets, burying them at sea, burying them in solid rock formations, and burying them in the deepest abandoned mines that can be found. No ultimate solution has been found. Such wastes generally are put in concrete tanks and buried underground. A serious danger is that these tanks are built to last for only a couple of hundred years.

Because radioactive wastes remain boiling hot each day for years, leakage from some of these tanks has already occurred. In 1974, one leak continued for fifty-one days and raised the radiation count substantially above the maximum acceptable level.[11] With our current way of disposing of nuclear wastes, are we creating a lethal problem for the future?

*Solid Wastes*   So much public concern is focused on radioactive waste disposal that we sometimes overlook the serious disposal problems of old-fashioned junk. Each year Americans produce billions of tons of wastes: food, glass, paper, plastics, cans, paints, dead animals, abandoned cars, old machinery, and a host of other things. We are often referred to as a "consumer society"; it is more accurate to say that we are a throwaway society.

Solid wastes are ugly, unpleasant, and odorous. They pollute water that circulates through them and provide breeding grounds for rats and other noxious pests.

The two principal methods of solid waste disposal are in landfills (that is, burying in the ground) and through incineration. Many of the garbage dumping

## Nuclear Power Plant Explosion in Chernobyl, Russia

In spring 1986, there was an explosion and fire at a nuclear power plant in Chernobyl, Russia. The explosion blew the top off the reactor and sent a radioactive plume across large parts of the Soviet Union and much of Eastern and Western Europe. The four-thousand-degree (Fahrenheit) fire burned in the reactor's graphite core for more than a week before it was extinguished. Within a few weeks after the disaster, twenty-five people died from massive doses of radiation. It is feared that exposure to lesser amounts of radiation will result in early deaths for tens of thousands of people from cancers of the bone marrow, breast, and thyroid.

The disaster happened at a highly vulnerable place; eighty miles from the site is the city of Kiev, which has a population of more than 2 million. Chernobyl is also near the breadbasket area of Russia, as nearly half of the country's winter wheat is grown in this area. Much of the grass and animal feed in the area was contaminated with radioactive particles. Two hundred thousand people were relocated from their homes, and a thousand square miles of agricultural land was rendered unusable. Now (several years after the accident), it is still uncertain when some of the land can be used again, though clearly it will not be for many years. Already, increased rates of cancer and birth defects have been observed. The rate of leukemia in Kiev is four times higher than normal. The head of the scientific team in charge of the evacuation zone around the remains of the plant estimated in 1991 that there had already been seven to ten thousand deaths (mainly among the cleanup crew) due to the effects of massive radiation exposure. The economic losses have been staggering—an estimated $358 billion—and the destruction of 20 percent of the farmland of the entire republic of Byelorussia. An estimated 4 million people are still living on contaminated ground in the area. This disaster startled the world and raised serious questions about whether the energy produced by nuclear power plants is worth the dangers.

*Source:* Scripps News Service, "Tragedy of Chernobyl Keeps on Building in Byelorussia," *San Luis Obispo Telegram-Tribune,* March 27, 1991, D1; Associated Press, "Mystery Ailments Plague Chernobyl," *San Luis Obispo Telegram-Tribune,* April 22, 1991, A1, A12; Michael Parks, "Chernobyl," *Los Angeles Times,* April 23, 1991, H1, H6; Scripps News Service, "Chernobyl Worse Than Earlier Feared," *San Luis Obispo Telegram-Tribune,* April 28, 1991, A1; William Kornblum and Joseph Julian, *Social Problems,* 9th ed., Upper Saddle River, NJ: Prentice Hall, 1998, 509.

---

areas, particularly in small towns, do not meet the sanitary standards set by the federal government.[12] In addition, improperly designed municipal incinerators are major contributors to urban air pollution.

*Toxic Wastes*   Toxic wastes, or residues, are a major problem. Toxic wastes result from the production of pesticides, plastics, paints, and other products. These wastes have typically been buried in pits or ditches. The famous case of Love Canal, near Niagara Falls (see Box 17.1), arose when toxic residues that had been dumped into the unfinished canal seeped into the surrounding area and contaminated both the soil and the water.

## AIR POLLUTION

Air pollution is most severe in large and densely populated industrial centers. Some cities (such as Los Angeles) occasionally have such dense smog that even on clear days there is a haze over the city. Moreover, it is not only city air that is polluted; the entire atmosphere of the earth is affected to some degree.

Air pollution rots windshield wiper blades and nylon stockings, blackens skies and clothes, damages crops, corrodes paint and steel, *and kills people*. Death rates are higher when and where smog occurs—especially for the very old, the very young, and those with respiratory ailments. Pollution contributes to a higher incidence of pneumonia, emphysema, lung cancer, and bronchitis. A 1952 smog disaster in London was directly linked to some four thousand deaths. Although devastating, such disasters are of substantially less significance than the far-reaching effects of day-to-day living in seriously polluted cities. For example, every day New York City residents inhale enough cancer-producing substances to equal two packs of cigarettes.[13] Also, poor visibility caused by smog is recognized as a major factor in both airplane and automobile accidents.

The air is hazardous to one's health in many large metropolitan areas.

Tons of the following pollutants are being released into the air annually in the United States: carbon monoxide, hydrocarbons, oxides of nitrogen, oxides of sulfur, soot, and ashes. Although cars emit much of these pollutants, industrial centers (particularly pulp and paper mills, petroleum refineries, chemical plants, and iron and steel mills) add a large share, as do burning trash and burning fuel for heating homes and offices.[14]

Air pollution is believed to contribute to the deaths of at least 50,000 Americans every year.[15] Valleys and closed air basins are more likely to have air pollution than are plains and mountains where the air can circulate freely. Air quality can become especially bad when a layer of warmer air moves over a layer of cooler air and seals in pollutants that would ordinarily rise into the upper atmosphere. This condition is known as *temperature inversion*.

*Air Pollution and Environmental Changes* Air pollution may also be breaking down the earth's protective ozone layer. The ozone layer surrounds the earth from an altitude of eight to thirty miles above sea level and screens out many of the harmful rays from the sun. Some studies suggest that chlorofluoro-carbon gases (commonly used in refrigeration systems and spray cans) maybe destroying this ozone layer.[16]

If the ozone layer is breaking down, it is predicted there will be sharp increases in skin cancer, crop failure, and also changes in the world's climate. When these studies became public knowledge, the use of fluoro-carbon spray cans by American consumers dropped sharply (demonstrating that individuals acting in the same direction make a difference). Manufacturers responded to this drop in sales by developing spray cans that do not use fluorocarbons. However, fluorocarbons are still being used in coolants in refrigerators and air conditioners, for making plastic foams, and as cleaning solvents for micro-electronic circuity. Under certain conditions these compounds escape into the atmosphere, rise high into the stratosphere, and set off chemical reactions that rapidly destroy ozone.[17]

Air pollutants have the potential to alter the earth's atmosphere and climate in other ways as well. For example, some scientists are concerned that a buildup of carbon dioxide in the atmosphere could produce a "greenhouse" effect; that is, the carbon dioxide could trap heat near the earth's surface, raising the average temperature. Such overheating, even just a few degrees, could melt much of the polar ice caps and lead to incredible flooding around the world. Other scientists predict the opposite may occur; that is, air pollutants may deflect sun rays away from the

*The Cuyahoga River near downtown Cleveland was so polluted that it caught fire in November 1952.*

earth. The earth would then become cooler and perhaps enter into a new Ice Age.

The greenhouse effect is largely due to the burning of fossil fuels (such as coal and petroleum), which emits carbon dioxide into the atmosphere. There has been some evidence in the past decade that the world's climate is getting warmer—about which some scientists have expressed grave concern.[18] Changing temperatures could also change the pattern of rainfall, which could turn the American Midwest and other major agricultural areas into dust bowls.

***Radioactive Leaks from Nuclear Power Plants*** We have mentioned one of the problems associated with nuclear energy, that of radioactive wastes. Another nuclear energy problem is the potential for radioactive leaks into the air.

Numerous malfunctions at U.S. nuclear power plants have resulted in the release of minor amounts of radioactivity into the air from the power plants.[19]

In 1979 more than 200,000 residents had to be evacuated from the area surrounding the power plant at Three Mile Island, Pennsylvania. Radioactive leakage from a damaged reactor caused fear that an explosion might occur. In 1986 an explosion did occur at a nuclear power plant in Chernobyl, Russia.

Such accidents have alerted the public to the dangers of nuclear power plants and have slowed the use of nuclear energy. Whether to expand or curtail the development of nuclear power plants is an international issue in our energy-hungry world. This issue illustrates the complexity of trying to decide between energy needs and physical safety—especially when experts are in sharp disagreement about the technological risks. If given a choice, those exposed to radioactivity in Chernobyl undoubtedly would choose less energy than the reality that they are more apt to develop cancer and that any children they give birth to are more apt to have birth defects.

## WATER POLLUTION

Over two-thirds of the world's surface is covered by water. Water is continually cleansing itself by evaporating, forming clouds, and raining back to the earth. Unfortunately, people are contaminating the water supply faster than it can cleanse itself. As the population grows in a particular area, so does industry, which pours into the water a vast array of contaminants: detergents, sulfuric acid, lead, hydrofluoric acid, ammonia, and so on. Increased agricultural production also pollutes water from insecticides, herbicides, and nitrates (from fertilizers). The result is the spread of pollution in creeks, streams, and lakes; along coastlines; and—most seriously—in groundwater, where purification is almost impossible. Water pollution poses the threat of epidemics of diseases such as hepatitis and dysentery, as well as poisoning by exotic chemicals. Some rivers and lakes are now so polluted that they cannot support fish and other organisms that require relatively clean, oxygen-rich water. Such lakes and rivers are accurately described as "dead."

The United States has the dubious distinction of being the only country in the world with a river that has been called a fire hazard. So many industrial chemicals, oils, and other combustible pollutants have been dumped into the Cuyahoga River in Ohio that it has twice caught on fire.[20]

Human waste is also a major contributor to water pollution. The sewage from New York City alone produces 5 million cubic yards of sludge a year, which is dumped into the ocean and now covers over 15 square miles of ocean bottom.[21] An even bigger source of pollution is water from oil refining, food processing, animal feedlots, textile and paper manufacturing, and other industries. Of the world's rural populations, 86 percent, or more than 2 billion people, lack adequate clean water.[22]

A study by the Natural Resources Defense Council concluded that 20 percent of the drinking water in the United States is not adequately treated for bacteria, toxic chemicals, parasites, and other pollutants. The study also found that 14 percent of the U.S. population drinks from water systems that have been caught violating federal water standards within the previous three years.[23]

*Acid Rain* There is a growing concern over acid rain. Formed from emissions from automobiles and industrial plants, acid rain has become a serious problem in eastern Canada, in the northeastern United States, and in many other countries.[24] It is created when sulfur and nitrogen oxides in emissions combine with moisture in the air to form sulfuric and nitric acids. Acid rain is killing fish in lakes and streams and

This monument in Krakow, Poland, has been destroyed by acid rain.

is reducing the number of plant nutrients in the ground, thereby making soil less fertile. It has also damaged timber and may eventually start affecting synthetic structures, including classic architecture and sculptures. Scientists estimate that 50,000 lakes in the United States and Canada are now so polluted by acid rain that fish populations have been either destroyed or severely damaged.[25]

*General Pollutants* Some substances—such as chlorinated hydrocarbons, lead, mercury, and fluorides—reach us in so many ways that they are considered *general pollutants*. Of the chlorinated hydrocarbons, DDT was used the longest but is now banned. DDT is a synthetic insecticide; chemically it breaks down slowly, and it will last for decades in soil. Unhappily, the way DDT circulates in ecosystems leads to a concentration in carnivores (including humans); that is, it becomes increasingly concentrated as it is passed along a food chain. Following World War II, DDT was widely used as an insecticide until research with laboratory animals showed that it affects fertility, causes changes in brain functioning, and increases the incidence of cancer.[26]

The long-term effects of DDT (and of many other general pollutants) are still unknown. The substance is poisonous and may (or may not) lead to subtle physiological changes. An important question is: Among the thousands of chemicals currently being used, which ones will have unknown toxic side effects?

Radioactive wastes and certain poisons such as DDT also pose serious problems because of biological magnification. With this process (mentioned previously), the concentration of the substance increases as it ascends in the food chain. For example, Richard Curtis and Elizabeth Hogan found in a study of the Columbia River in the western United States that, although the radioactivity of the water was at such low levels that it was nonhazardous, the radioactivity of river-related biological lifeforms was much higher and potentially hazardous:

> . . . the radioactivity of the river plankton was 2,000 times greater; the radioactivity of the fish and ducks feeding on the plankton was 15,000 and 40,000 times greater, respectively; the radioactivity of young swallows fed on insects caught by their parents in the river was 500,000 times greater; the radioactivity of the egg yolks of water birds was more than a million times greater.[27]

The radioactivity was thought to be due to isotopes released into the river from the nuclear power plant at Hanford, Washington.

DDT, many other pesticides, and radioactive material are cumulative poisons; that is, they are retained in the tissues of the organisms that consume them rather than being excreted back into the environment. Thus one never loses the poison of previous exposure, and future exposures compound the potential danger to the individual. In 1984 the National Academy of Sciences released a report stating that little or nothing is known about the effects on humans of 80 percent of the 48,500 different chemicals in use, because very little research has been conducted in this area.[28]

The use of pesticides by American farmers also has a number of adverse consequences. An article in *Newsweek* noted:

It's a bit of a devil's bargain. In exchange for using $3 billion worth of pesticides yearly, American farmers reap $12 billion worth of crops that might otherwise be lost to weeds and insects. Without the chemicals, millions of people might face food shortages. On the other hand, less than 1 percent of the poisons reach their target pests; the rest wind up as contaminants in water, residues on produce and poisonous fallout on farm workers. Worldwide, the compounds fatally poison an estimated 10,000 people a year and injure 400,000 more. Uncounted millions more may be at increased risk for cancer, reproductive problems and birth defects due to low-level, chronic exposure. We can't seem to do without pesticides; but can we live with their consequences?[29]

Chronic lead poisoning is also serious; it leads to loss of appetite, weakness, and apathy. It also causes lesions of the neuromuscular system, the circulatory system, the gastrointestinal tract, and the brain. Exposure to lead comes from a variety of sources: combustion of leaded gasoline, pesticides, lead pipes, and lead-contaminated food and water. Perhaps the most hazardous instance is when children eat paint containing lead. It should be noted that most household paints today do not contain lead, but the danger still exists with older buildings and furniture that were painted with a lead-based paint. Even when these buildings are painted over with lead-free paint, peeling may expose the original lead-based ones.

Exposure to high concentrations of mercury can cause blindness, deafness, loss of coordination, severe mental disorders, or even death. Mercury is added to the environment in many ways. It may leak into the water from industrial processes that produce chlorine; it is emitted by the pulp and paper industry; and it is a primary ingredient of agricultural fungicides. Also, small amounts are released when fossil fuels are burned.

## TOO LITTLE ENERGY

The consumption of energy has doubled every twelve years in our recent history.[30] More than nine-tenths of the world's energy consumption is provided by fossil fuel sources: oil, coal, and natural gas. Natural gas sources are rapidly being depleted. The domestic supply of oil in the United States cannot meet our needs, and therefore this country is heavily dependent on foreign oil sources.

The United States, with less than 5 percent of the world's people, uses a quarter of all the energy consumed each year.[31] All the industrialized nations combined hold only 25 percent of the world's people, but they use an estimated 85 to 90 percent of the energy consumed each year.[32] It has been estimated that world petroleum and natural gas reserves will be substantially depleted within a century from now.[33] New sources of energy that work as well as fossil fuel sources will have to be found.

## OTHER NONRENEWABLE RESOURCES

Mineral resources other than fuels are essential elements for industrial production. Essential elements include copper, lead, zinc, tin, nickel, tungsten, mercury, chromium, manganese, cobalt, molybdenum, aluminum, platinum, iron, and helium. Consumption of such minerals is proceeding so rapidly that reserve sources will eventually be depleted, expensive mining of low-quality ores will have to be undertaken, and substitutes will have to be found. As developing countries continue to industrialize, demand for these nonrenewable minerals will far exceed supply.

## *Confronting Environmental Problems*

Although environmental problems are very serious, it would be a mistake to assume that the environment is headed for catastrophe. It was not until the late 1960s that the public began to realize the seriousness of the environmental problems we face. Dozens of organizations have since been formed (many of them with international memberships) that are now working on such problems as saving wild animals, recycling waste materials, and developing new sources of energy.

Since the 1960s there has been progress in a number of areas. Air quality has improved. Less sewage is being dumped into waterways. Most automobiles have emission control devices. Life expectancy in the United States has been rising, which is an indirect measure that environmental conditions may be improving. Relationships between the United States and Russia have improved, which reduces the chances of a nuclear war. However, much more needs to be done.

Energy development, preserving the environment, and economic growth are interdependent problems. Programs that advance one of these often aggravate the others. For example, the development of nuclear power plants led to an explosion in a nuclear reactor in Chernobyl, Russia, in 1986 that released radioactivity into the air—which may shorten the lives of the tens of thousands of people who were exposed. There are other examples. Devices that clean exhaust from automobiles reduce air pollution but also decrease fuel economy and thereby more rapidly deplete oil reserves. Strip mining of coal increases available energy supplies, but despoils the land. Effective environmental programs in the future need to strike a balance between the competing objectives of preserving the environment, developing energy sources, and fostering economic growth.

Since the late 1960s, environmentalists have been waging a political and educational campaign that has not only increased public awareness of environmental concerns but also won passage of significant legislation to protect the nation's air, land, and water. For example, the Clean Air Act of 1970 established the Environmental Protection Agency (EPA) and empowered it to set and enforce standards of environmental quality. However, since the 1980s political opposition to environmental concerns has intensified. For example, some of the largest corporations in the world have sought to drill oil wells and dig mines in fragile wilderness areas and to get "the government off their backs" when they spew pollutants into the air and water.[34] Such corporations have spent millions of dollars to persuade the government to let them continue their polluting without penalty. Environmentalists have been struggling to preserve the gains made in the 1970s, but they do not have the financial resources that large corporations have. Therefore, it is crucial for those who are concerned about preserving our environment to be aware of political issues in this area and to express their views to political leaders.

It is clear that our environmental problems are not going to disappear on their own. In fact, left alone, existing problems are likely to increase, and new ones will come to the fore. What can be done? First of all, the rate of growth of the world's population has to be reduced. There are now (as discussed in chapter 16) about 6 billion people living on Earth, and the doubling rate of the world's population is currently at forty years. Unless the size of the world's population is stabilized, the quality of the environment will continue to deteriorate. Proposals for stabilizing the world's population are described in chapter 16. Additional actions to improve the environment include changing values from consumption to conservation and developing new sources of energy.

# What You Can Do to Help Save Planet Earth

You can make a difference! If everyone takes small steps, major improvements will occur. The following are simple things that you and your family members can do to help Earth:

♦ Use mugs instead of paper cups, washable cotton towels instead of paper towels, and cloth napkins rather than paper napkins.

♦ Use both sides of a sheet of paper when taking notes.

♦ To avoid wasteful packaging that contributes to garbage, buy products in bulk or those that have the least amount of packaging. Packaging accounts for 50 percent of our trash. America's daily output of garbage weighs 400,000 tons.

♦ At the market, ask for paper bags (which you can recycle) instead of plastic bags. Plastics tend to be nonbiodegradable; they usually do not break down into innocuous products.

♦ Buy products that are recyclable, reliable, repairable, refillable, and/or reusable. Avoid disposables. The new buzz words in waste management are "source reduction"—buy wisely to minimize the consequences of consumption.

♦ Grow some of your own food—organically, when possible. Plant deciduous shade trees (trees whose leaves fall off) that protect south and west-facing windows from sun in summer but allow it in during winter. Plant and maintain trees and bushes. Trees and shrubbery consume carbon dioxide and thereby reduce air pollution.

♦ Reduce use of styrofoam cups, which tend to be nonbiodegradable.

♦ To save water, install faucet aerators and water-efficient showerheads. Such adjustments cut water use up to 80 percent without a noticeable decrease in performance. Repair leaky faucets.

♦ Take showers of less than five minutes instead of a bath.

♦ Do not run water continuously when brushing your teeth or shaving.

♦ Consider ultralow flush toilets, which use 60 to 90 percent less water than conventional models. Conserve water by placing a brick or a jug of water in the water tank of the toilet.

♦ Where possible, use fluorescent bulbs rather than incandescent bulbs. Fluorescent bulbs use considerably less energy.

♦ Buy beverages in returnable containers and then return them.

♦ Use cloth diapers for babies. Disposable diapers annually account for 18 billion tons of trash that, because of plastic content, will take five hundred years to decompose. In addition, disposable diapers in landfills frequently contain fecal matter, which can harbor viruses that cause diseases such as hepatitis that can find their way into water supplies.

♦ Turn down the thermostat at night and when you are away. Close off and do not heat or cool unused rooms. Wear a sweater instead of turning up the heat. Keep windows (especially near thermostats) tightly shut.

♦ Turn the thermostat on the water heater down to 120 degrees Fahrenheit.

♦ When possible, use a clothesline instead of a clothes dryer.

♦ Reduce the use of hazardous chemicals in your home. For example, instead of using ammonia-based cleaners, use a mixture of vinegar, salt, and water for surface cleaning, and baking soda and water for bathroom tile and fixtures.

## CHANGING VALUES

Bigger is not necessarily better. In addressing the need to focus on preserving and conserving, rather than consuming our resources Georg Ritzer notes:

> We need a reorientation of American culture, a reorientation that may already be under way. Basically, we need to move away from a system that values things growing constantly bigger and better. We are no longer able to master and subdue all that surrounds us. Rather, we must learn to live more harmoniously with our environment. We need to learn to value and protect our environment rather than seeing it as something to be exploited, raped and despoiled. Most importantly, we need to accept the idea that we are approaching the limits of what the environment can yield to us. At best, we can expect a steady state, at worst a marked decline in our style of life. . . . We need, in other words, to focus on, and invest in, resources that we can renew rather than the current propensity to exploit such nonrenewable resources as coal and oil.[35]

The move toward resource conservation can be implemented in a variety of ways, a few of which will

- Don't buy motorized or electric tools or appliances when hand-powered ones are available. This includes lawnmowers. (Mowing a lawn with an old-fashioned mower is good exercise.)
- To conserve energy, wash clothes and other materials in warm water and rinse in cold water.
- Open blinds of south and east facing windows during the day to allow heat from the sun to warm the rooms during cold weather, and close them at night to conserve heat. Close blinds during the day in hot weather to reduce air-conditioning costs.
- Bike, walk, carpool, or use public transit. Try to live close to your work, and shop close to home.
- Get a low-cost home energy audit from your utility company for suggestions to conserve energy.
- Check caulking around windows and doors, and add caulking where needed.
- Use latex paints (which are considerably less toxic to the environment) rather than oil-based paints.
- Buy and use cars that are fuel-efficient and keep them well-tuned so that they are fuel-efficient. (Burning one gallon of gasoline produces nearly twenty pounds of carbon dioxide, which is a major cause of the greenhouse effect that contributes to global warming.)
- Avoid use of aerosols and other products containing chlorofluorocarbons (CFC). CFCs are depleting the protective ozone layer in the atmosphere. Such depletion has already led to sharp increases in the rates of skin cancer caused by the sun's rays.
- Reduce food wastes, which are major contributors to garbage. Where possible, compost food wastes and use them in a garden.
- Stop the delivery of junk mail. Your local post office will give you the address and instructions for writing to Direct Mail Marketing Association in New York City to request the stoppage of delivery of junk mail.

- Buy products made of recycled paper. This helps create a market for recycled paper.
- Do not litter.
- Keep the grass of your lawn relatively tall. Short grass requires more water. Water lawns at night or early in the morning rather than during the day. Watering in direct sunlight wastes water as much of the water evaporates.
- Recycle motor oil. Used oil is highly destructive to the environment when dumped, and also is apt to contaminate nearby water supplies.
- Use soap detergents that are low in phosphates. Phosphates are toxic.
- Use dry cleaning sparingly, as it is done with toxic chlorinated solvents.
- Be cautious in using chipboard, plywood, insulation materials, carpeting, and upholstery as they contain or can emit toxic formaldehyde.
- Avoid purchasing products made from parts of endangered animals—ivory from elephants, tortoise shells, and reptile skins.
- Buy eggs in paperboard cartons instead of plastic foam cartons (which tend to be nonbiodegradable).
- Purchase meat, poultry, and other products that are wrapped in paper rather than plastic.
- Buy beverages in aluminum cans or glass bottles, and food in glass containers with metal lids, instead of plastic. Return the bottles, cans, and glass for recycling.
- Do not put toxic waste products into garbage containers. If deposited into landfills, such products can trickle into nearby water reserves.
- Keep fireplace dampers closed (in order to reduce heat loss) unless there's a fire going.

*Source:* "A User's Guide To Saving The Planet" CBS Television, April 19, 1990; "What You Can Do to Help Earth," *Wisconsin State Journal*, April 22, 1990, 1H.

be mentioned here. Garbage can be used as fuel to run mills that recycle paper. Water in communities can be purified continually so it can be reused without being discharged into a river, lake, or ocean. Homes can be better insulated to conserve heat. Smaller cars can be driven at more energy-efficient speeds. People can ride trains and buses instead of driving cars. Newspapers, aluminum cans and other aluminum products, tin, cardboard, magazines, plastic, paper, and glass can be recycled to reduce the amount of solid waste materials. Recycling a four-foot stack of newspapers saves a forty-foot pine.[36] Aluminum recycling saves 95 percent of the energy needed to make new cans from raw materials.[37] Using recycled glass to make new glass reduces the amount of air and water pollution by 50 to 60 percent compared to producing glass from silica.[38] Our society needs to use the conservation measures that are already available. Each of us can make a difference in combating the environmental problems on this planet!

Some advances have been made in recent decades. People in this country appear to be increasingly recognizing that all of us have a responsibility to preserve the environment. There is a growing interest in Earth

In January 1993, the tanker Braer *ran aground in the Shetland Islands, Scotland, spilling its cargo of crude oil into the sea. The spill threatened the local fisheries and marine wildlife.*

Day, which was founded on April 22, 1970, and is annually recognized.[39] The pesticide DDT has been banned.[40] The United States cut sulfur dioxide emissions (from 1970 to 1994) by 28 percent.[41] Auto emissions have been cleaned up dramatically: catalytic converters cut hydrocarbons by as much as 87 percent, carbon monoxide by an average of 85 percent, and nitrogen oxides by 62 percent.[42] Lead has been removed from gasoline. Emissions of lead into the air dropped by 96 percent since 1970, and overall lead levels in the average American's blood dropped by one-third since 1976.[43]

Since the late 1980s, economic and political values have changed significantly in Eastern European countries. These changes have largely been based on former Soviet President Mikhail Gorbachev's concepts of *glasnost* and *perestroika*. Glasnost means greater openness and increased freedoms for people in the Eastern bloc countries. Perestroika means economic, social, and political reforms in these Eastern bloc countries. Based on these principles a number of these countries have rejected communism and are moving toward establishing democracies. There is optimism that such restructuring will lead to improved relationships between Western and Eastern nations. Such improvements

hopefully will lead to fewer funds being allocated to defense. Will the savings lead to more funds being available to combat environmental destruction and overpopulation? Will Western and Eastern nations now work cooperatively to combat the problems that severely impact all inhabitants of this planet? Slow but gradual progress appears to be occurring in these areas.

## FINDING NEW SOURCES OF ENERGY

Reduction of pollution, population, and energy consumption will not alter the fact that much of our current energy comes from nonrenewable fuel sources. Sooner or later, we will have to find new sources of energy. Three possible sources are reviewed in the following sections.

*Nuclear Energy*   Nuclear energy has been one attempt to solve the energy shortage, but concerns about the safety of nuclear power plants have slowed their construction. In March 1979 the near-disaster at Three Mile Island amplified these concerns when radioactive steam escaped and there was danger of a meltdown. A meltdown probably would have killed many in the area from lethal overdoses of radiation. The April 1986 explosion in a nuclear reactor in Chernobyl, Russia, was a much more serious accident. Tens of thousands of inhabitants were exposed to radioactivity, which threatens to shorten their lives. Livestock, plant life, and wildlife were devastated.

These accidents serve to emphasize that safety in a nuclear power plant cannot be taken for granted. Nuclear energy out of control has the potential for large-scale disaster. Is development of nuclear energy worth the risks?

*Synthetic Fuel*   In 1980 the federal government passed legislation to finance and create a synthetic fuel industry. Raw materials for synthetic fuel are found in oil shale formations, coal deposits, and gooey tar sands. The term *synthetic fuel* is a misnomer, because its components have the same carbon base as crude oil. Coal, for example, will become gas if it is pulverized and then mixed with oxygen and steam under extreme heat. Shale is a dark-brown, fine-grained rock that contains carbon. Production problems are considerable, as it is estimated that it takes 1.7 tons of shale to produce one barrel of oil and that it takes 1 ton of coal to produce two barrels of oil.[44]

Whether synthetic fuel is cost effective remains questionable. A few years after the initiation of the synthetic fuel program, a temporary glut of crude oil occurred worldwide. Partly as a result of this glut, synthetic fuel efforts have received very little research and development interest in recent years. If another shortage of crude oil occurs, it remains to be seen whether development programs will again be initiated. On a positive note, it is estimated that the United States has a six-hundred-year supply of the raw materials for synthetic fuel.[45]

***Solar Energy*** Solar energy is another hope. Thousands of U.S. homes and offices get all or part of their heating and cooling from the sun.[46] Even the White House has a solar water-heating system on its roof. Another potential use of sunlight is direct conversion to electricity. Sunlight can be converted directly into electricity with photovoltaic cells, but the process is as yet too expensive to be used widely. Solar energy is really an imitation of nature, because all energy ultimately comes from the sun.

## Summary

This chapter summarizes the following environmental problems:

♦ *Despoiling the land.* Coal strip mining, oil drilling, destroying trees and forests, oil spills, and overgrazing by cattle and sheep are not only unsightly but have devastating environmental effects when the delicate balance between nature's elements is interrupted.

♦ *Radioactive wastes.* As yet we have no way to safely dispose of nuclear wastes, which may create lethal problems in the future.

♦ *Garbage.* Increased consumption means increased throwaways, the disposal of which often leads to air pollution, water pollution, and other undesirable environmental effects.

♦ *Air pollution.* In large industrial centers, air pollution is a health hazard.

♦ *Water pollution.* Some rivers and lakes are so polluted they cannot support fish and other organisms.

♦ *Acid rain.* Acid rain has damaged timber and is killing fish in lakes and streams.

♦ *Radioactive leaks from nuclear power plants.* Nuclear accidents raise the question of whether nuclear energy is worth the risks.

♦ *General pollutants.* We are becoming more aware of the harmful effects of such pollutants as lead, mercury, DDT, and other chlorinated hydrocarbons.

♦ *Too little energy.* Fossil fuel resources (oil, coal, and natural gas), which provide over nine-tenths of the world's energy consumption, are being depleted rapidly.

♦ *Depleted mineral resources.* Essential elements such as copper, zinc, and manganese are becoming less plentiful.

To confront environmental problems, actions are needed on a variety of concerns. Two essential actions are to change values toward conserving resources and to develop new sources of energy. The chapter includes a number of suggestions for all of us to follow to help save Earth.

# Epilogue

Reading about how humans are tragically affected by the social problems covered in this text, you could very easily despair and become depressed. Because some of these problems (such as crime, poverty, and urban problems) appear so difficult to resolve, it is easy to become further discouraged and disheartened. Yet, giving up hope would result in little effort made to resolve these problems, which would almost certainly result in a worsening of present conditions. And there is reason for hope.

A major reason there is hope is because our country has had a history of making progress in resolving social problems. Progress made in the past thirty-five years will document that continued optimism is justified. Spouse abuse, child abuse, and elder abuse have increasingly been recognized as serious problems, and a variety of services have been developed or expanded to combat such problems—including protective services for both children and adults, shelters for battered women, self-help groups (such as Parents Anonymous) and group counseling programs for abusers. The increased use of birth-control devices) including contraceptive pills) and abortions has significantly reduced the birth rate in many countries and gives hope that population size can be controlled without mass starvation and famine. Flexitime and involving workers in decision-making processes have, at least in a number of companies, helped to reduce the problems of worker alienation and unsatisfying work; when these and similar methods become widely accepted among business leaders as helpful to business, it can be assumed they will become even more widely utilized. Air-pollution control measures (including emission-control devices on automobiles) have helped reduce smog problems in many urban areas. Civil rights laws have been enacted and are being enforced, which is helping to reduce overt racism and, more slowly, covert racism. These laws are also helping many African Americans, Hispanics, Native Americans, and other people of color to receive equal opportunities and improve their standard of living. Barriers to female participation in the workforce and society have been recognized, and many have been eliminated, thereby helping women to progress in achieving equality with men. There is increased recognition that the elderly and persons with disabilities have been discriminated against in a variety of ways, and a number of programs have been developed to meet the needs of these groups. Medical breakthroughs (such as open-heart surgery and organ transplants) have improved the health care of many Americans. The stigma attached to receiving therapy for emotional problems has been reduced, and new treatment approaches (such as rational therapy) are having success in resolving emotional problems. Sexual problems are better understood, and sexual treatment programs are highly effective in resolving sexual dysfunctions. Sexual abuse and rape have received more attention, so that a variety of treatment programs serve both victims and perpetrators.

Therefore, hope is realistic and essential. And it is with hope that we will look toward the future. Remember, however, accuracy in predicting the future tends to be very low, as unexpected occurrences substantially influence outcomes. Perhaps the best results in predicting the future come when we base our predictions on past and present conditions. Thus we will review briefly some past and present efforts to resolve social problems.

## The Past and the Present

Our nation's efforts in the past seventy years to resolve social problems are reflected in the policies and social programs of the federal government. These policies and programs are heavily influenced by social movements and interest groups.

In the 1930s we were in the midst of a depression, with millions unemployed and living in poverty. To pull us out of this depression, President Franklin Roosevelt's administration enacted the 1935 Social Security Act, which firmly established for the first time the federal government's role in providing: (a) public health and social services to Americans; (b) social insurance programs, such as Old Age, Survivors, and Disability Insurance; and (c) public assistance programs. The federal government has now become the primary funding source for social programs.

The basic intent of the Social Security Act was to provide a decent standard of living to every American. President Roosevelt believed that financial security (even if provided through public assistance) was not a matter of charity but a matter of justice. He believed every individual in a civilized society has a right to a minimum standard of living. He believed that liberty and security were synonymous. Without financial security, he thought that people eventually would despair and revolt. Therefore, Roosevelt thought the very existence of a democratic society depended on the health and welfare of its citizens.[1]

From the 1930s to the 1980s, there was a gradual expansion in the role of the federal government in providing financial assistance and social programs to Americans suffering from social problems. President Roosevelt's social programs have largely been credited with helping to bring our country out of a depression and with raising the standard of living for many Americans.

The role of the federal government was particularly expanded during the 1960s by President Lyndon B. Johnson's Great Society programs. In his January 1965 State of the Union Address to Congress, President Johnson stated the following specific goals of the Great Society.

> We are only at the beginning of the road to the Great Society. I propose we begin a program in education to insure every American child the fullest development of his mind and skills, . . . begin a massive attack on crippling and killing diseases, . . . [and] launch a national effort to make the American city a better and more stimulating place to live.
>
> I propose we increase the beauty of America and end the poisoning of our rivers and the air we breathe, . . . carry out a new program to develop regions of our country now suffering from distress and depression, . . . make new efforts to control and prevent crime and delinquency, . . . [and] honor and support the achievements of thought and the creations of art.[2]

The Great Society programs helped many Americans. For example, the proportion of the population living in poverty was reduced, and health-care services were improved. Yet, many of the goals have not been achieved. Poverty has not been eradicated, racism still remains, and living conditions in our inner cities have shown little improvement.

During President Jimmy Carter's administration in the late 1970s, there was widespread recognition that the federal government did not have the power (no matter how much money it spent) to cure all the social ills of the country. Instead of an acceptance of the fact that the government could *partially* allay many of the problems, there appears to have been a 180-degree turn; many citizens began despairing and demanding that the government sharply reduce the amount of tax money spent on programs to combat social problems.

In 1980 our domestic economy was in a mess. The rates of both unemployment and inflation were high and the country had been in a recession for several years. Ronald Reagan was elected president that year and proceeded, as he had promised during his campaign, to make a number of changes to revitalize the economy and to strengthen the military. The following changes were implemented:

♦ Taxes were sharply cut for both individuals and corporations. Our economic growth was again stimulated, as described in chapter 13, and both the rates of inflation and unemployment were sharply reduced.

♦ Military expenditures were sharply increased, which resulted in strengthening our armed forces.

♦ Expenditures for social programs were sharply cut. This massive cutback was the first large-scale federal reduction in social welfare expenditures in our country's history.

In 1988 Reagan completed two terms (eight years) as president. George Bush was elected president on a platform to continue the Reagan policies. Our economy prospered throughout most of the 1980s, which is one of the longest periods of sustained prosperity in our country's history. Then, in 1990, the huge federal deficit and rising oil prices initiated a recession. The recession ended in 1993. However, during the presidential election in 1992, voters, concerned about the lagging economy, elected a new president, Bill Clinton. Twelve years of a conservative Republican administration came to an end. Bill Clinton has been characterized as being more moderate or liberal. To reduce the federal deficit, he has gained congressional approval of a tax reform package that increases taxes on the rich. In contrast to Reagan and Bush who were pro-life, Clinton is pro-choice on the abortion issue. Clinton is also cutting the amount of money spent on defense.

In the 1980s the rich became richer, and the financial gap between the rich and the poor widened. We are increasingly hearing alarming stories of people living in poverty. Increasingly, homeless, unemployed people are sleeping in subways or on city streets— even in the winter. Millions of Americans are now going hungry, as they cannot afford to buy enough food. Since 1980, there have been sharp increases in crime rates, with many Americans now identifying crime as our most serious social problem. AIDS cases started appearing in the United States in the 1980s; AIDS has now become an epidemic of monumental proportions throughout the world.

In the 1990s new drugs have been developed (such as AZT and protease inhibitors) that are having

# Explaining the Past Is Far Easier Than Predicting the Future

Predictive studies have a very low rate of accuracy. The major reason is that unexpected occurrences often have dramatic effects on the future. This author, for example, was involved in the mid-1960s in a study in a midwestern state to determine how many beds would be needed in public residential treatment centers (also called colonies) for persons who had a severe or profound cognitive disability. At that time, the state had three centers with a total of 2,400 beds, which were nearly filled. The study examined a number of factors and found that, over the prior thirty years, about 0.4 percent of the population was being placed in long-term care in state residential treatment centers for persons with a severe or profound cognitive disability. The study therefore estimated a population increase for the next five- and ten-year periods and assumed an increase in beds of 0.4 percent of the increased growth would be needed. Because the treatment centers were filled to capacity, it was concluded that a new institution would be needed in four to five years. This projection was accompanied by a recommendation to build another facility.

Shortly after the recommendation, there was a national recognition that it was much better (and less costly) for persons with a cognitive disability to receive services in the local community rather than being placed in state institutions. There was a substantial development of community-based services: sheltered workshops, public school special education programs, group homes, foster homes, halfway houses, and day-care centers for those with developmental disabilities. With this expansion of local services, a much smaller proportion of those with a severe or profound cognitive disability were placed in residential treatment facilities. In fact, many of the residents that were institutionalized at the time of the study were placed in group homes, halfway houses, and foster homes within the next several years. This change was so dramatic that the total population in these three centers fifteen years later was only half as large as it was in the mid-1960s. These three centers have continued to downsize, and will soon be closed—with all persons with a cognitive disability in this state now receiving services in their home community.

The change in attitude to serve persons with a cognitive disability in local communities—and the services that were thus developed—was unexpected and made the recommendation to build a new center look ridiculous. Fortunately, the new center was not built.

---

success in delaying the development of AIDS in persons who are HIV positive. Tremendous strides have been made in communications (for example, in communicating via the Internet). With the end of the Cold War in the 1980s, the world seems, in the 1990s, a safer place to live. The threat of an all-out nuclear war has been reduced. We approach the new millennium with a sense of optimism that the overall quality of life on Earth is slowly improving.

## Changes Occurring in Our Society That Will Affect the Future

Predicting the future is very difficult. Unexpected occurrences will intensify some social problems and reduce the severity of others. There are a number of dramatic changes occurring in our society that will be major determinants of what the future will be:

1. Our society is increasingly developing an economy that emphasizes high technology, such as computers and communication. Automation and robots are now doing more of the work that was previously done by blue-collar workers. Now those who are well-educated, particularly in high technology areas, face a promising future. However, there is growing concern that the unskilled, poorly educated in our society face increased prospects of being trapped in the lower socioeconomic class—perhaps many will be trapped in poverty.

2. For the first time in history a revolution in weaponry has made it possible for the superpowers to obliterate civilization through an all-out nuclear war.

3. The women's movement is resulting in questioning by both females and males of traditional sex role stereotypes. The role of women in our society is changing toward a more equalitarian relationship with men. As the role of women changes, men are also beginning to make gender-role changes.

4. Overt discrimination against racial minorities is declining.

5. The numbers of single-parent families and of blended families are increasing. Also, a higher proportion of women are working outside the home.

6. Living conditions in central cities are deteriorating.

7. Increasingly, our society lives in fear of terrorist attacks—at home and abroad.

8. Some improvements have been made in controlling pollution. Yet acid rain, depletion of the ozone layer, and global warming appear to be emerging problems.

9. There is a graying of our population as the median age of Americans is increasing. The elderly are now the fastest growing age group in society. Our society faces a crisis of developing needed services for the elderly and of helping the elderly to have a meaningful, productive role.

10. Advances in reproductive technology (such as cloning, test-tube babies, genetic testing, and human embryo transplants) are increasingly creating value dilemmas in regard to how such technology should be used.

11. The financial gap between rich and poor in our society is widening. The wealthy are probably better off than they have ever been. They are able to jet around the world on vacations. They are receiving the best health care in history. They are able to utilize sophisticated technological advances for their personal comfort—luxury cars and boats, videotape recorders, central air conditioning, color television, health and fitness clubs, and an ever-expanding area of electrical appliances (such as microwave ovens, garbage disposals, and automatic washers and dryers). Living conditions for the poor and the unemployed have deteriorated in the past two decades. Many of those living in poverty have been plunged deeper into poverty. A two-tier health care system is reemerging in which the wealthy have access to good health care and the poor either lack access or receive inferior care.

12. The size of the world's population continues to grow. About 6 billion people live on this planet. Unless the world's population is stabilized, problems of malnutrition and starvation will intensify.

13. There are increasing concerns about the educational system in the United States, partly because American students are not performing as well on standardized educational tests as students in many other industrialized countries.

14. The social-program safety net that has helped prevent poverty and despair for many Americans has been sharply reduced. No longer is there as much hope for a Great Society and for resolving social problems as there was in the 1960s.

15. Technological changes are occurring at a faster pace now than at any other time in history.

16. AIDS has become a major health problem. It has the potential to kill more people than any other virus in human history. Partly as a result of the fear of the transmission of sexually transmitted diseases, the sexual revolution is ending—for example, recreational sex is no longer popular.

17. The abortion question continues to be a highly controversial social issue in the United States.

18. The question of whether assisted suicide should be legalized in the United States has emerged as a significant social issue.

19. An increasing proportion of our population is being sentenced to prison. Many prisons are overcrowded. State and federal governments are under increasing pressure to build more prisons—each of which costs millions of dollars.

20. We are increasingly aware that energy development, preservation of the environment, and economic growth are interdependent. Programs that advance one of these often adversely affect the others.

## Reasons for Optimism

On a positive note, it should be indicated that technological breakthroughs may contribute significantly to resolving some of our social problems. Throughout our history, technological advances have contributed immensely to raising our standard of living and to resolving social problems. A few of the advances presently being worked upon are as follows:

♦ Cures for AIDS, cancer, and heart diseases are being researched.

*East German border guards look through a hole in the Berlin wall after demonstrators pulled down one segment at the Brandenburg gate. For four decades, the wall had stood as both a physical and symbolic barrier between Eastern and Western Europe.*

♦ New, safe, and easy-to-use contraceptives are being studied for family-planning purposes, which may help reduce the overpopulation problem.

♦ New sources of energy are being developed (such as oil from our vast coal and shale deposits).

♦ A wide range of effective treatment approaches have been developed in recent years to help the emotionally disturbed and people who have a physical disability—continued development of additional approaches is expected in the future.

♦ Robots are now being developed to perform many of the assembly-line jobs in industries that in the past have contributed to high rates of worker alienation.

♦ Techniques are being developed to treat sexual dysfunctions.

♦ Drug abuse programs are being developed to treat more effectively those who are addicted to alcohol and to other drugs.

There is considerable optimism that the changes occurring in Eastern European countries may lead to increased international cooperation in studying and combating social problems. Future historians may record the political changes that took place in the Eastern European countries in the late 1980s and early 1990s as being the most important political revolution in the twentieth century. The following countries have rejected communism and are moving to establish democratic processes: Russia, Poland, Romania, East Germany (which has merged with West Germany to form Germany), Bulgaria, Albania, Czechoslovakia, and Hungary. These countries have concluded that communism (which involves state ownership of practically all industries and businesses) does not provide sufficient incentives for citizens to be economically productive. Western nations have advanced much more with capitalistic incentives and democratic processes. As a result, these countries are rejecting Marxist principles.

This movement toward democracy will have far-reaching effects. Already we are seeing some positive consequences, such as:

♦ The cold war between the United States and Russia is ended. With similar forms of government, the two superpowers are beginning to cooperate on resolving international social problems.

♦ The chances of an all-out nuclear war occurring are lessened.

- The major superpowers are spending less on defense and thereby have more funds available to support educational and social welfare programs.

- The superpowers are beginning to work together to combat worldwide problems, such as overpopulation, despoiling of the environment, poverty, terrorism, and AIDS. Some authorities assert that a New World Order is emerging, one in which the United States and Russia cooperate to combat international crises.

Although our society has many imperfections and problems, there is much to value and appreciate. *Our standard of living and quality of life is one of the highest.* Many social problems have been resolved in the past. Through understanding and attacking our present social problems, we can make life even more fulfilling and humane for future generations. Our ancestors' successes in resolving social problems have given us much for which to be thankful and much about which to be optimistic.

**Absolute definition of poverty**  Determined by setting a minimum amount of goods and services as being essential to an individual's or a family's welfare. Those who do not have this amount are viewed as poor.

**Addiction**  Intense craving for a drug that develops after a period of physical dependence from heavy use.

**Affirmative action**  Programs designed to guarantee equal hiring and admission opportunities (e.g., admission to a medical school) for minority applicants. Affirmative action programs cover groups such as persons of color, women, and persons with disabilities.

**Ageism**  Discrimination and prejudice against the elderly.

**Age structure**  The percentage of a population in each age category.

**Aging**  Social and biological changes that occur in everyone throughout life but at different rates.

**AIDS (Acquired immune deficiency syndrome)**  A disease that destroys the body's natural immunity to infection.

**Alcoholism**  Repeated and excessive intake of alcohol to the extent that it is harmful to interpersonal relations, job performance, or the drinker's health.

**Alienation**  Sense of meaninglessness and powerlessness that people experience when interacting with social institutions they consider oppressive and beyond their control.

**Androgyny**  Taken from the Greek words *andro* (male) and *gyn* (female). Androgyny urges people to explore a broad range of role-playing possibilities and to express emotions and behaviors without regard to sex-role stereotypes.

**Anomie**  A state of society in which normative standards of conduct and belief are weak or lacking. When anomie occurs, social norms are no longer meaningful or effective, which often results in deviant behavior.

**Anomie theory**  A criminological theory that views criminal behavior as resulting when an individual is prevented from achieving the high-status goals in a society. If unable to achieve the goals through society's legitimately defined channels, the individual loses respect for these channels and then seeks to achieve the desired goals through illegal means.

**Assault**  An attack on an individual with the intention of physically hurting or even killing the victim.

**Automation**  Production technique in which the system of production is increasingly controlled by self-operating machinery.

**Baby boom generation**  The portion of the U.S. population born during the years immediately following World War II.

**Bail**  Security (usually money) put up to be forfeited if a person accused of committing a crime does not appear for trial.

**Barrio**  A Spanish-speaking section of a city.

**Biosocial theory**  A theory that holds that much of human behavior (e.g., personality characteristics, deviant behavior, intelligence, and values) is largely due to instincts and other biological influences.

**Birthrate**  The number of births per year per thousand members of a population.

**Blaming the victim**  The tendency to blame the poor, the emotionally disturbed, those raped or otherwise victimized, and others who have personal or social problems as being at least partially responsible for their problems and predicaments.

**Bourgeoisie**   A Marxist term that refers to the class of people who own capital and capital-producing property.

**Bureaucracy**   A form of social organization characterized by a set of formal rules, division of labor, a hierarchy of authority, job security, and impersonal enforcement of rules.

**Capitalism**   An economic system characterized by:
- private ownership of capital goods,
- investments that are determined by private decision rather than by state control, and
- production, prices, and the distribution of goods determined mainly by competition in a free market.

**City**   A relatively large, permanent, dense settlement of socially heterogeneous individuals.

**Class conflict**   Disagreements and conflicts that rise between divergent social classes due to their different economic, political, and social interests.

**Classical criminological theory**   Asserts a person makes a decision regarding whether to engage in criminal activity based on the anticipated balance of pleasure minus pain.

**Communism**   A classless society in which economic goods are distributed according to need. No modern society has ever been organized in this fashion, although many have called themselves Communist.

**Comparable worth**   The idea that pay levels of certain jobs should be adjusted to reflect the intrinsic value of the job; holders of jobs of comparable value would then be paid at comparable rates.

**Conflict theory**   A theoretical approach that views conflicts between different groups as common. Conflict between competing groups is seen as a principal source of social problems and of social change.

**Control group**   The subjects who do not receive the "treatment" in an experiment.

**Control theory**   A criminological theory that asserts that people commit crimes when social norms, social groups, and other social forces no longer constrain them.

**Corporation**   An entity formed and authorized by law to act as a single person although constituted by one or more persons and legally having various rights and duties.

**Crime**   An act committed or omitted in violation of a law.

**Crime-control approach**   A criminal justice model that emphasizes speedy arrest and punishment of law violators.

**Crowding**   A person's subjective judgment that he or she has insufficient space.

**Cultural lag**   A dysfunction in an area of society where some part has not "caught up" with changes elsewhere.

**Culture**   The way people live in a certain geographic area. Culture includes nonmaterial items such as beliefs, norms, patterns of thought, values, languages, political systems, religious patterns, music, and courtship patterns. Culture also includes material items such as type of dwellings, paintings, dishes, cars, buses, factories, business offices, and clothes.

**Culture of poverty theory**   Asserts poverty is sustained in certain subcultures by attitudes, norms, and expectations, which restrict the members' opportunities and prevent their escape from poverty.

**Death rate**   The number of deaths per year per thousand members of a population.

**Deconcentration of cities**   Migration of urban residents from central city areas to suburbs.

**Decriminalization**   Reducing or abolishing the penalties on certain illegal activities (such as possession of marijuana). The term is also used to refer to declassifying an activity (such as prostitution) previously defined as crime.

**De facto discrimination**   Discrimination that actually exists, whether legal or illegal.

**De jure discrimination**   Discrimination permitted by law.

**Demographic transition theory**   Predicts that developing societies will have rapid population growth and that population size will stabilize in industrial societies.

**Demography**   A scientific discipline dealing with the density, distribution, and vital statistics of populations.

**Demonology**   A criminological theory that views crime as being caused by evil spirits.

**Developed country**   A nation that is fully industrialized (e.g., Britain, Japan, and the United States).

**Developing country**   A nation that is moving from a primarily agricultural economy to a modern industrial economy. Developing nations include most of Asian, African, and Latin American countries.

**Deviance**   Behavior that does not conform to recognized social norms, usually those norms held by the dominant culture. Sociologists are careful to avoid making moral judgments when using the term deviance, as deviant behavior may be as (or even more) functional than behavior prescribed by social norms.

**Deviant subculture theory**   A criminological theory that views crime as being due to some groups' developing attitudes, values, and perspectives that support criminal activity.

**Differential association**   A criminological theory that asserts people become criminals because they are exposed to more associations with people who favor crime than with those who are opposed to it.

**Discrimination**   Negative treatment of people because of their membership in a minority group. Groups victimized by discrimination include women, people of color, gays and lesbians, people with disabilities, and the elderly.

**Diversion program**   A program that has as its goal keeping juveniles and adults out of courts.

**Double standard**   A code of behavior that gives men greater freedom than women, including sexual freedom.

**Doubling time**   The length of time it takes for a population to double in size.

**Drug**   A habit-forming substance that directly affects the brain and nervous system. It is a chemical substance that affects moods, perceptions, bodily functions, or consciousness and that has the potential for misuse, as it may be harmful to the user.

**Drug abuse**   The use of illegal drugs and the excessive or inappropriate use of legal drugs with the potential for psychological or physical harm.

**Drug addiction**   Occurs when the user develops a dependence on a drug, leading to an intense craving.

**Drug dependence**   Occurs when the user develops a recurring craving for a drug; may be physical, psychological, or both.

**Drug tolerance**   Occurs when the user has to take increasing amounts of the drug over time to achieve a given level of effect.

**Due-process approach**   A criminal justice model that emphasizes protecting human rights and dignity. This model conflicts with the crime-control approach, which emphasizes punishment.

**Dysfunction**   A situation that has negative rather than positive effects for an individual, or for a system.

**Ecology**   The scientific study of the mutual relationships and interactions among plants, animals and their environment.

**Ecosystem**   A self-sustaining community of organisms in a natural environment.

**Elder abuse**   The physical or psychological mistreatment of the elderly.

**Empty-shell marriage**   A marriage in which the spouses feel no strong attachment to each other.

**Ethnocentrism**   The tendency to view one's own culture and customs as right and superior and to judge other cultures by one's own standards.

**Exhibitionism**   Indecent exposure of one's body.

**Experiment**   A rigorously controlled research approach that traces (usually in a laboratory) the influence of one variable on another.

**Experimental group**   The subjects who receive the "treatment" in an experiment.

**Extended family**   A family system in which a number of relatives live together, such as parents, children, grandparents, great-grandparents, aunts, uncles, in-laws, and cousins.

**Family**   A group of people who live together and are related by marriage, ancestry, or adoption.

**Family-planning services**   Such services include providing birth-control information and contraceptives, pregnancy testing, infertility counseling, sex education, abortion counseling and abortions, counseling on child spacing, sterilization information and techniques, and help for couples preparing for parenthood.

**Family violence**   The occurrence of spouse, sibling, child, or elder abuse in a family.

**Felony**   A serious criminal offense.

**Femininity—achievement incompatibility**   The erroneous notion that one cannot be both feminine and an achiever.

**Flexitime**   A system for making work hours flexible. Workers are present during the busiest time of the day but are allowed to choose the remaining hours and days per week that they wish to work.

**Folkway**   A custom or convention that is not strongly held. Violation of a folkway (e.g., eating with one's fingers rather than a knife and fork) is mildly disapproved.

**Food Stamps**   A program to offset some of the food expenses for low-income people.

**Frustration-aggression theory**   Asserts frustration often provokes an aggressive response. Violence is seen as the releasing of tension produced by a frustrating situation.

**Functionalist theory**   A theoretical approach that sees society as an organized system with each part having a useful function in maintaining stability. These parts are in delicate balance, and it is asserted that social problems arise when some parts become dysfunctional or disorganized.

**Future shock**   A general sense of anxiety or confusion about the future and, at times, the present, caused by the constant need to adapt one's way of life to new ways of doing things.

**Generic drugs**   Nonpatent drugs that have the same chemical composition as patent drugs but are much less expensive.

**Group**   A number of individuals having organized and recurrent relationships with each other. Groups have norms that govern behavior and a purpose or goal—even if it is only to provide opportunities for members to enjoy each other's company.

**Growth rate**   A measure of population growth obtained by dividing the population increase by the total population. This figure is usually expressed as an annual percentage.

**Hawthorne effect**   Asserts that when subjects know they are participants in a study, this awareness may lead them to behave differently and may influence the results of the study.

**Health maintenance organization (HMO)**   A prepaid health care insurance plan that emphasizes prevention.

**Hispanic Americans**   Americans of Spanish origin; includes Mexican Americans (Chicanos), Puerto Ricans, Cubans, people from Central and South America and the West Indies, and others of Spanish origin.

**Homicide**   The killing of a human being.

**Homosexual**   A person whose sexual or erotic orientation is toward members of his or her own sex.

**Homosexual lifestyle**   Adopting a homosexual self-identity, including possibly having frequent homosexual experiences and fantasies and/or participating in a homosexual community.

**Hospice program**   A social program that allows the terminally ill to die with dignity, to live their final weeks as they choose.

**Humanitarianism**   A belief system that ascribes a high value to human life and to benevolently helping those in need.

**Hypothesis**   An idea about reality that is to be tested—or at least that is capable of being tested.

**Ideology**   A set of beliefs and ideas that justifies the perceived interests of those who hold it. For example, during slavery, white landlords viewed African Americans as inferior, which served to justify (to them) their discrimination against African Americans.

**Illegitimate birth**   An unfortunate and outdated term for the birth of a child whose parents are not married to each other.

**Imperialism**   The creation or expansion of an empire.

**Incest**   Sexual intercourse between persons so closely related that they are generally prohibited by law to marry.

**Income**   Amount of money a person earns in a given year.

**Individualism**   The view that one is master of one's own fate. This view asserts the rich are personally responsible for their success and the poor are to blame for their failure to earn a higher income.

**Infrastructure**   Public facilities such as water, sewage, transportation, lighting, and medical care facilities.

**Institutionalized racism**   Discriminatory acts and policies that pervade major institutions of society such as the legal system, politics, the economy, and education.

**Institutional view of social welfare**   Holds that funds and social services should be accepted as a legitimate function of modern society in helping individuals achieve self-fulfillment. Recipients are viewed as entitled to help, and there is no stigma attached to receiving funds or services.

**Jim Crow system**   A system, largely operating in the South after the Civil War, which prescribed how African Americans were supposed to act in the presence of whites. The system asserted white supremacy, embraced racial segregation, and denied political and legal rights to African Americans.

**Juvenile delinquency**   Actions by minors (usually defined as individuals under age eighteen) that are violations of the law.

**Labeling theory**   A theory that holds that branding a person as a deviant is a major factor in initiating and perpetuating the kind of deviant behavior consistent with the label.

**Laissez-faire economic theory**   A theory that asserts the economy and society in general will prosper best if businesses and industries are permitted to do whatever they desire to make a profit.

**Law**   A formal norm enacted by a governmental entity.

**Lesbianism**   Female homosexuality.

**Life expectancy**   The number of years that the average newborn will live.

**Lombrosian theory**   A criminological theory that maintains a criminal is born with certain physical abnormalities or stigmata (such as a distorted nose) that signify that the person is predisposed to a criminal career.

**Looking-glass self theory**   A theory that holds that people develop their sense of self (who they are) in terms of how others relate to them, as if others were a looking-glass or mirror.

**Machismo**   An exaggerated awareness and assertion of masculinity by being tough, brave, defending one's honor, not backing down from a challenge or fight, and "putting others in their place."

**Macrosociological theory**   A theory concerned with explaining the behavior of large groups of people and the workings of entire societies.

**Manslaughter**   The unlawful killing of another person without malice.

**Marxist-Leninist theory**   A criminological theory that asserts all crime results from the exploitation of workers and from severe competition among people.

**Medicaid**   A government public assistance program that pays for medical expenses for low-income people who qualify.

**Medicare**   A public health insurance program designed to help pay the medical and hospital expenses of the elderly.

**Membership group**   A group of which a person is a member, willingly or not.

**Mental illness**   The view that emotional and/or behavioral problems are a disease of the mind.

**Microsociological theory**   A theory concerned with explaining the behavior of small groups.

**Military-industrial complex**   An interlocking network of military chiefs, Pentagon bureaucrats, politicians, and corporation executives that work together in supplying military equipment.

**Minority or minority group**   A group that has a subordinate status and is subjected to discrimination. It is not size, but rather lack of power that is critical in defining a group as a minority. Women, even though in the majority of our society, are a minority according to this definition.

**Misdemeanor**   A minor criminal offense.

**Monopoly**   The situation in which a person or a single corporation has gained control of a market.

**Mores**   Morally binding customs of a group. Mores are strong norms, violations of which are viewed as morally wrong. Many mores are encoded in laws. Punishment is usually severe. Examples of violations of mores in our society include desecrating the flag, murder, punching a priest, and walking nude in public.

**Morphological theory**   A criminological theory that asserts there is a fundamental relationship between the psychological makeup and the physical structure of people. The theory holds certain body types are more apt to be common to criminals.

**Multinational corporation**   An economic enterprise that is based on one country and pursues business activities in one or more foreign countries.

**Negative income tax plan**   A proposal to help alleviate poverty by which persons earning below a set level would receive a grant (the negative tax) to bring their income up to the guaranteed minimum level.

**Norm**   A formal or informal rule that prescribes what is acceptable in a certain situation and what is not. Norms are usually taken for granted. We seldom notice them until they are broken—such as when a person belches loudly in church. Depending on the norm (and the circumstances), punishment for violating a norm ranges from mild disapproval (as for picking one's nose in public) to severe punishment (as for rape).

**Nuclear family**   A family system in which a married couple and their children live together without other relatives.

**Obscene**   Abhorrent to morality or virtue; designed to incite to lust or depravity; repulsive.

**Oligopoly**   The situation that occurs when an industry is controlled by a few large corporations.

**Organized crime**   A system in which illegal activities are carried out as part of a rational plan devised by a large organization that is attempting to maximize its overall profit.

**Outsourcing**   The location of American manufacturing plants that produce goods for American markets in Third World nations, where the manufacturing firm can take advantage of lower wage rates.

**Parents Anonymous**   A national self-help organization for parents who have abused or neglected their children.

**Parole**   Release of an inmate from prison after part of the sentence has been served. The person is then supervised for the duration of the sentence by a parole officer.

**Participant observation**   A research approach in which the researcher participates in the activities of the group being studied.

**Personal interview**   A research approach in which the researcher asks the people being studied about their attitudes or activities.

**Phrenology**   A criminological theory that maintains crime is related to the size and shape of the human skull.

**Plea bargaining**   A practice in which the prosecuting and the defense attorney agree to allow the defendant to plead guilty (usually to a lesser offense) in return for a reduction in charges or for other considerations.

**Population control**   The deliberate regulation of the size of the population by the government.

**Pornography**   Pictorial or written material designed to excite the viewer sexually and having no redeeming social value.

**Poverty line**   The level of income that the federal government considers sufficient to meet basic requirements of food, shelter, and clothing.

**Power**   The capacity to force others to do something whether they want to or not or to protect oneself from being forced by others to do something against one's will.

**Prejudice**   A negative attitude toward a different group considered different and (usually) inferior.

**Preliminary hearing**   A court proceeding during which a judge decides whether evidence against the accused is sufficient to justify further legal proceedings.

**Preventive medicine**   The practice of using good health habits to stay healthy or to reduce the severity of existing medical problems.

**Primary industry**   Economic activity that primarily involves the gathering and extracting of undeveloped natural resources.

**Probation**   The action of suspending the sentence of a convicted offender and giving him or her freedom during good behavior under the supervision of a probation officer.

*Projection*   A psychological defense mechanism of attributing to others characteristics one is unwilling or unable to recognize in oneself.

*Proletariat*   The working class in an industrial society.

*Prostitution*   Paid sexual activity. Prostitution involves using sex to make money rather than as a way to express love or to procreate.

*Protective services*   A specialized social service to neglected, abused, exploited, or rejected children and their parents. Such services are also provided to adults who are unable to protect themselves.

*Protest*   A solemn declaration of opinion, usually involving dissent.

*Protestant ethic*   An ethic that values hard work and acting in one's own self-interest. It emphasizes individualism. An overriding goal often resulting from this ethic is to acquire material goods. With this ethic, people largely are judged by how much wealth they have acquired or inherited.

*Prurient material*   Material that arouses lewd or lustful thoughts and desires.

*Psychoanalysis*   Long term psychotherapy, which seeks to bring to the conscious mind repressed thoughts and emotions. Once this occurs, it is assumed the energy of the disabling emotions will be released and patients can function more effectively.

*Psychosis*   Fundamental mental derangement characterized by defective or lost contact with reality.

*Psychosomatic illness*   A physical illness caused by negative thinking, mental conflicts, or stress.

*Psychotherapy*   Any of a variety of counseling approaches to help clients understand and better handle their emotional and behavioral problems.

*Psychotropic drugs*   Drugs that act upon the mind. These drugs include tranquilizers, antipsychotic drugs (such as thorazine), and antidepressants.

*Puritanism*   Beliefs and practices characteristic of the Puritans. These beliefs and practices emphasized strictness and conformity, especially in matters of religion or conduct.

*Race*   People thought to have a common set of physical characteristics but may or may not share a sense of identity or unity. There are no clearly delineating characteristics of any race. As applied to human beings, race is primarily a social rather than biological concept.

*Racial stereotyping*   Attributing a fixed and usually inaccurate or unfavorable conception to a racial group.

*Rape*   Sexual intercourse without consent and often by deception or force.

*Rational therapy*   A psychotherapy approach that asserts a person's emotions and actions are primarily determined by thoughts. Rational therapy seeks to help clients change unwanted emotions and ineffective actions by challenging and changing negative and irrational thinking.

*Reality therapy*   A psychotherapy approach that seeks to help clients identify their ineffective and irresponsible actions and then attempts to help clients learn to function more effectively and responsibly.

*Recidivism*   Re-arrest and conviction of a person previously convicted of a crime. Sometimes the term is used to refer to the return to prison of someone who has previously been incarcerated.

*Redlining*   The generally illegal practice by some lending institutions of giving few or no loans to certain city areas. Failure to give loans to certain areas is a factor leading to deterioration in the neighborhood.

*Reference group*   A group with whose values and standards an individual identifies and of which he or she wants to be a member.

*Relative definition of poverty*   This approach holds that people are poor if they have significantly less (such as less than one-fourth or one-fifth) income and wealth than the average person in their society.

*Residual view of social welfare*   A view that asserts financial payments and social services should serve only a gap-filling or first-aid role. This view has been characterized as being "charity for unfortunates." Funds and services are not seen as a right but as a gift, with the receiver having certain obligations. With the residual view, there is a stigma attached to receiving services or funds.

**Role**   A set of expectations and behavior associated with a social position. The sociologist's use of the term is very similar to the theatrical definition of the term *role*. The term is closely related to status. The distinction is that a person occupies a status and plays a role. For example, an adult male may be a father (status) and share the roles of disciplinarian, cook, and breadwinner with his wife.

**Sample**   A group of subjects selected for study who are thought to be representative of a larger population.

**Scapegoat**   Anyone blamed for the faults or problems of others.

**Schizophrenia**   A psychotic disorder characterized by loss of contact with the environment and by disintegration of personality expressed as disorder of feeling, thought, and conduct.

**Secondary industry**   Economic activity involving the transformation of raw materials into manufactured goods.

**Self-determination**   Allowing clients (for example, recipients of social services) to make their own decisions.

**Self-talk theory**   Asserts that emotions and actions are primarily determined by thoughts. Applied to criminology, the theory asserts that the reasons for any criminal act can be determined by examining what the offender was telling himself or herself prior to and during the time the crime was being committed.

**Senescence**   The process of advanced aging. Senescence affects different persons at different rates. Visible signs include the appearance of wrinkled skin, graying and thinning of hair, and stooped or shortened posture from compressed spinal discs.

**Sexism**   Prejudice, discrimination, and stereotyping based on gender. In our society, women are frequently subjected to sexism.

**Sex role**   Learned patterns of behavior associated in a society with one or the other sex.

**Sex-role expectations**   Expectations, largely based on stereotypes that define how men and women are to behave and to be treated by others.

**Sex-role socialization**   The process through which people learn the behaviors and attitudes expected of males and females.

**Social class**   A category of people who have similar shares of the items that are valued in a society. The items that are usually valued include social status, power, and money.

**Social Darwinism**   Belief system based on the theory of evolution. This system asserts struggle, destruction, and survival of the fit are essential to progress in human society. In its most inhumane form, it asserts the strong (the wealthy) will survive because they are superior, the weak (the needy) should perish, and it would be a mistake to help the weak survive.

**Social disorganization**   A situation in which society is imperfectly organized to achieve its goals and maintain its stability. When disorganization occurs, the system loses control over its parts.

**Social institution**   A significant practice, relationship, or organization in a society. The term is somewhat abstract. Common institutions in a society include the family, religion, economics, education, and politics. Social institutions tend to have stable patterns of thought and action and focus on the performance of important social tasks. The family, for example, functions to raise children and to provide companionship and emotional support to family members.

**Social mobility**   Movement from one social status or class to another.

**Social movement**   A large number of people who join together to initiate or resist some social or cultural condition.

**Social problem**   A problem that exists when an influential group asserts a certain social condition affecting a large number of people is a problem and may be remedied by collective action.

**Social stratification**   The division of a society into social classes that have varying degrees of access to the rewards the society provides.

**Social structure**   The organized patterns of human behavior and social relationships in a society, including the ways in which social classes, marriage, and family patterns are organized.

**Socialism**   Systems of society in which the means of production are owned or controlled by government, which also administers the distribution of goods. According to Marx, socialism is a transitional stage between capitalism and communism.

**Socialization**   The process through which individuals learn proper ways ("proper" as defined by the society) of acting in a culture. The roles, norms, customs, values, language, beliefs, and most behaviors are learned in the socialization process. Most basic socialization occurs in the early years, but socialization continues throughout life.

**Society**   A community, nation, or broad grouping of people having common traditions, institutions, and collective activities and interests.

**Sociology**   The scientific study of human society and social behavior.

**Status**   A person's position or rank in relation to others. Each person occupies numerous positions in a society—for example, student, woman, daughter, Chicano, Catholic, and so on. Ascribed statuses are inherited from parents, whereas achieved statuses are derived from occupation, accomplishments, and lifestyle.

**Status offenses**   Acts defined as illegal for juveniles, but not if performed by adults. Such offenses include being truant, running away from home, having sexual relations, being ungovernable, and curfew violations.

**Statutory rape**   Sexual contact between a male who is of a legally responsible age (usually eighteen) and a female who is a willing participant but is below the legal age of consent (sixteen in some states and eighteen in others).

**Stereotype**   A fixed mental image of a group that is applied to all its members.

**Stereotyping**   Attribution of a fixed and usually inaccurate and unfavorable conception to a category of people.

**Stress**   Bodily and mental tension caused by physical, chemical, or emotional factors.

**Subculture**   A culture within a culture. A subculture has certain unique material and nonmaterial features, yet is influenced by the larger culture. For example, certain urban areas have subcultures of homosexuals, marijuana smokers, prostitutes, superrich, jet-setters, juvenile gangs, motorcycle riders, and actors and actresses.

**Supplemental Security Income (SSI)**   A public assistance program that provides a minimum income for the blind, disabled, and elderly who are indigent.

**Supply-side economics**   The theory that if the side of the economy that supplies goods and services is stimulated, unemployment will decrease and prices will drop.

**Survey**   A research approach in which the researcher uses personal interviews or questionnaires to ask the people being studied about their attitudes or activities.

**Taboo**   A prohibition against behavior that is considered so despicable it is almost unthinkable. A taboo is the strongest norm. Examples of taboo behaviors in our society are incest, cannibalism, and yelling vulgarities during a church service.

**Terrorism**   The systematic use of unpredictable violence to accomplish some purpose, such as to destabilize a government.

**Tertiary industry**   Economic activity primarily involving the provision of various services.

**Theory**   A statement that seeks to explain a relationship between concepts and/or facts. Competing theories can be sorted out by turning them into hypotheses and testing them through research.

**Underemployment**   The condition in a labor force in which people are working at jobs below their level of skill.

**Urban area**   Any area with more than 2,500 residents as defined by the Bureau of Census.

**Urbanization**   The movement of people from rural to urban areas.

**Urban renewal**   A program, usually financed by the government, intended to upgrade deteriorating city areas.

**Value**   A belief about what is right, good, and desirable.

**Variable**   A characteristic that can change. Age, social class, and religious affiliation are common social variables.

**Victimless crime**   A law violation in which no one suffers except society and perhaps the person who decides to engage in the illegal activity.

**Victimology theory**   A criminological theory that asserts that, in a majority of cases the victim contributes (e.g., through carelessness) to becoming a crime victim. The theory urges individuals to take precautions to prevent becoming a crime victim.

**Violence**   Use of physical force to injure or abuse.

**Voyeurism**   Secretly watching persons while they undress, are in the nude, or are performing a sexual act.

**Wealth**   A person's total assets—real estate holdings, cash, stocks, bonds, and so forth.

**White-collar crime**   Crime committed by people of respectability and high social status in the course of their occupations.

**Worker alienation**   Having an intense sense of job dissatisfaction and feeling that one's contribution to the final product is insignificant. It also involves feeling one has little input into the work decisions made.

**Work ethic**   Viewing work as honorable, productive, and useful.

**Zero population growth**   A stable population size in which the birthrate is equal to the death rate. Zero population growth is roughly equivalent to an average of two children per family.

## Chapter 1

1. William Kornblum and Joseph Julian, *Social Problems,* 9th ed. (Upper Saddle River, NJ: Prentice-Hall, 1998), 243–245.

2. Ibid., 243–245.

3. James W. Coleman and Donald R. Cressey, *Social Problems,* 6th ed. (New York: HarperCollins, 1996), 459–461.

4. *Brown v. Board of Education,* 347 U.S. 483 (1954).

5. Auguste Comte, *System of Positive Philosophy,* trans. H. H. Bridges and F. Harrison (London: Longmans, Green, 1875–1877; original French edition, 1851–1854).

6. Lester Ward, *Applied Sociology* (New York: Ginn, 1906).

7. Saul Alinsky, *Rules for Radicals* (New York: Vintage Books, 1972).

8. Malcolm Spector and John I. Kitsuse, "Social Problems: A Reformation," *Social Problems* 21 (Summer, 1973): 145–149; and Malcolm Spector and John I. Kitsuse, *Constructing Social Problems* (Menlo Park, CA: Cummings, 1977).

9. Ethel Sloane, *Biology of Women* (New York: Wiley, 1980).

10. Coleman and Cressey, *Social Problems,* 168–169.

11. H. J. Eysenck, "The Effects of Psychotherapy," *International Journal of Psychiatry* 1 (Winter, 1965): 97–144.

12. Kornblum and Julian, *Social Problems,* 254–255.

13. Harold Wilensky and Charles Lebeaux, *Industrial Society and Social Welfare* (New York: Free Press, 1965).

14. Ibid., 139.

15. James Midgley, *Social Development: The Developmental Perspective in Social Welfare* (Thousand Oaks, CA: Sage, 1995).

16. Ibid., 25.

17. James Midgley and Michelle Livermore, "The Developmental Perspective in Social Work: Educational Implications for a New Century," *Journal of Social Work Education* 33, no.3 (Fall 1997): 573–585.

18. Ibid., 576.

19. Alexander Liazos, "The Poverty of the Sociology of Deviance: Nuts, Sluts, and 'Perverts,' " *Social Problems* 20 (Summer 1972): 103–120.

20. Oscar Lewis, *La Vida: A Puerto Rican Family in the Culture of Poverty—San Juan and New York* (New York: Random House, 1966).

21. Dorwin Cartwright, "Achieving Change in People: Some Applications of Group Dynamics Theory," *Human Relations* 4 (Nov. 1951): 383.

22. James W. Coleman and Donald R. Cressey, *Social Problems,* 2d ed. (New York: Harper & Row, 1984), 21–22.

23. Charles H. Cooley, *Human Nature and the Social Order* (New York: Scribner's, 1902).

24. Thomas J. Sullivan, et al., *Social Problems* (New York: Wiley, 1980), 27.

25. Thomas Scheff, *Being Mentally Ill* (Hawthorne, NY: Aldine, 1966).

26. Kornblum and Julian, *Social Problems,* 183–184.

27. Ibid., 243–245.

28. Ibid., 61–89.

29. Janet S. Hyde, *Understanding Human Sexuality,* 5th ed. (New York: McGraw-Hill, 1994), 424–426.

30. Kornblum and Julian, *Social Problems,* 191–192.

31. Shere Hite, *The Hite Report on Male Sexuality* (New York: Knopf, 1981), 477.

## Chapter 2

1. Vincent N. Parrillo, John Stimson, and Ardyth Stimson, *Contemporary Social Problems,* 2d ed. (New York: Macmillan, 1989), 127–158.

2. William Kornblum and Joseph Julian, *Social Problems,* 9th ed. (Upper Saddle River, NJ: Prentice-Hall, 1998), 156–181.

3. U.S. Department of Justice, *Crime in the United States: Uniform Crime Report, 1996* (Washington, DC: U.S. Government Printing Office, 1997), 5.

4. Donald Baer, "Guns," *U.S. News & World Report,* May 8, 1989, 20–25.

5. James W. Coleman and Donald R. Cressey, *Social Problems,* 6th ed. (New York: HarperCollins, 1996), 400.

6. Ibid.

7. Kornblum and Julian, *Social Problems,* 174.

8. Ibid., 175.

9. Ibid.

10. *Crime in the United States, 1996,* 224–225.

11. Kornblum and Julian, *Social Problems,* 178.

12. Ibid.

13. Donald Jackson, "Justice for None," *New Times,* Jan. 11, 1974, 51.

14. William Kornblum and Joseph Julian, *Social Problems,* 6th ed. (Englewood Cliffs, NJ: Prentice-Hall, 1989), 175.

15. *Crime in the United States, 1996,* 97–103.

16. Coleman and Cressey, *Social Problems,* 397.

17. Kornblum and Julian, *Social Problems,* 9th ed., 164–166.

18. Ibid.

19. Coleman and Cressey, *Social Problems,* 397.

20. H. E. Pepinsky and R. Quinney, *Criminology as Peacemaking* (Bloomington: Indiana University Press, 1991).

21. Charles Goring, *The English Convict* (London, His Majesty's Stationery Office, 1913).

22. Thomas Szasz, *The Myth of Mental Illness* (New York: Hoeber-Harper, 1961).

23. H. J. Eysenck, "The Effects of Psychotherapy," *International Journal of Psychiatry,* 1 (1965), 97–144.

24. Charles Zastrow and Ralph Navarre, "Self-Talk: A New Criminological Theory," *International Journal of Comparative and Applied Criminal Justice* (Fall 1979), 167–176.

25. Edwin H. Sutherland and Donald R. Cressey, *Criminology,* 8th ed. (Philadelphia: Lippincott, 1970), 10.

26. Robert K. Merton, *Social Theory and Social Structure* (New York: Free Press, 1968), 232.

27. John M. Johnson and Jack Douglas, eds., *Crime at the Top: Deviance in Business and the Professions* (Philadelphia: Lippincott, 1978).

28. Walter B. Miller, "Lower Class Culture as a Generating Milieu of Gang Delinquency," *Journal of Social Issues,* 14 (1958), 5–19.

29. Albert Cohen, *Delinquent Boys: The Culture of the Gang* (New York: Free Press, 1955).

30. Charles Cooley, *Human Nature and the Social Order* (New York: Scribner, 1902).

31. Gary Cavendar, "Alternative Approaches: Labeling and Critical Perspectives," in Joseph F. Shelley, ed., *Criminology: A Contemporary Handbook* (Belmont, CA: Wadsworth, 1995), 185–199.

32. Stewart Powell, Steven Emerson, and Orr Kelly, "Busting the Mob," *U.S. News & World Report,* Feb. 3, 1986, 24–31.

33. Kornblum and Julian, *Social Problems,* 9th ed., 170–171.

34. Ibid.

35. Ibid.

36. Powell, Emerson, and Kelly, "Busting the Mob," 24–31.

37. Ibid.

38. Johnson and Douglas, *Crime at the Top.*

39. Edwin H. Sutherland, *White Collar Crime* (New York: Dryden Press, 1949), 9.

40. Kornblum and Julian, *Social Problems,* 9th ed., 168.

41. Coleman and Cressey, *Social Problems,* 392.

42. Kornblum and Julian, *Social Problems,* 9th ed., 168.

43. Thomas Sullivan, Kenrick Thompson, Richard Wright, George Gross, and Dale Spady, *Social Problems* (New York: John Wiley, 1980), 586.

44. *Crime in the United States, 1996.*

45. Alexander B. Smith and Harriet Pollack, "Crimes without Victims," *Saturday Review,* December 4, 1971, 27–29.

46. Janet S. Hyde, *Understanding Human Sexuality,* 5th ed. (New York: McGraw-Hill, 1994), 483.

47. Kornblum and Julian, *Social Problems,* 9th ed., 166.

48. Coleman and Cressey, *Social Problems,* 386.

49. Ibid., 387.

50. Edwin H. Sutherland, *The Professional Thief* (Chicago: University of Chicago Press, 1937).

51. Charles H. McCaghy and Stephen A. Cernkovich, *Crime in American Society,* 2d ed. (New York: Macmillan, 1987), 245–247.

52. *Crime in the United States, 1996,* 224.

53. Kornblum and Julian, *Social Problems,* 9th ed., 394.

54. Ibid.

55. Ibid.

56. J. F. Longres, "Youth Gangs," in *Encyclopedia of Social Work: 1990 Supplement* (Silver Spring, MD: NASW Press, 1990), 320.

57. A. P. Goldstein, *Delinquent Gangs: A Psychological Perspective* (Champaign, IL: Research Press, 1991).

58. Ibid.

59. Armando Morales, "Urban Gang Violence," in Armando Morales and Bradford W. Sheafor, eds., *Social Work: A Profession of Many Faces,* 5th ed. (Boston: Allyn & Bacon, 1989), 419–421.

60. T. A. Sweeney, *Streets of Anger: Streets of Hope* (Glendale, CA: Great Western, 1980), 86.

61. C. R. Huff, "Gangs in the United States," in A. P. Goldstein and C. R. Huff, eds., *The Gang Intervention Handbook* (Champaign, IL: Research Press, 1993).

62. Longres, "Youth Gangs," 323.

63. Goldstein, *Delinquent Gangs.*

64. Longres, "Youth Gangs," 325.

65. I. A. Spergel, *The Youth Gang Problem: A Community Approach* (New York: Oxford University Press, 1995).

66. Ibid.

67. Coleman and Cressey, *Social Problems,* 408.

68. Ibid., 406.

69. David M. Peterson, "The Police Officer's Conception of Proper Police Work," *The Police Journal,* 47 (London: P. Allen, 1974), 102–108.

70. Coleman and Cressey, *Social Problems,* 406.

71. Ibid., 406–407.

72. Don C. Gibbons, *Society: Crime and Criminal Behavior,* 5th ed. (Englewood Cliffs, NJ: Prentice-Hall, 1987), 439.

73. Coleman and Cressey, *Social Problems,* 407.

74 Alan Neigher, "The *Gault* Decision: Due Process and the Juvenile Court," *Federal Probation,* 31, no. 4 (December 1967): 8–18.

75. George F. Cole, *The American System of Criminal Justice,* 6th ed. (Pacific Grove, CA: Brooks/Cole, 1992), 506–513.

76. Ibid., 532–537.

77. Kornblum and Julian, *Social Problems,* 9th ed., 183–184.

78. Ibid.

79. Coleman and Cressey, *Social Problems,* 408.

80. Ibid.

81. Kornblum and Julian, *Social Problems,* 9th ed., 187.

82. Cooley, *Human Nature and the Social Order.*

83. Sutherland and Cressey, *Criminology,* 354.

84. *Crime in the United States, 1996.*

85. Coleman and Cressey, *Social Problems,* 412.

86. "Guns, Guns, Guns" NBC News Summer Showcase, July 5, 1988.

87. Ibid.

88. Coleman and Cressey, *Social Problems,* 409.

89. Marc Mauer, quoted in "Prison Ratio Highest in U.S.," *Wisconsin State Journal,* Jan. 5, 1991: 3A.

90. Dae H. Chang, "How to Avoid Becoming a Victim of Crime," in Charles Zastrow and Dae H. Chang, eds., *The Personal Problem Solver* (Englewood Cliffs, NJ: Prentice-Hall, 1977), 348–349.

## Chapter 3

1. William Kornblum and Joseph Julian, *Social Problems,* 9th ed. (Upper Saddle River, NJ: Prentice-Hall, 1998), 65.

2. Ibid., 66–67.

3. *DSM-IV (Diagnostic and Statistical Manual of Mental Disorders),* 4th ed. (Washington, DC: American Psychiatric Association, 1994).

4. D. L. Rosenhan and M. E. Seligman, *Abnormal Psychology,* 3d ed. (New York: Norton, 1995), 54.

5. Ibid.

6. Thomas S. Szasz, *The Myth of Mental Illness* (New York: Hoeber-Harper, 1961).

7. Thomas S. Szasz, "The Myth of Mental Illness," in John R. Braun, comp., *Clinical Psychology in Transition* (Cleveland: Howard Allen, 1961), 27.

8. Thomas Scheff, *Being Mentally Ill* (Chicago: Aldine, 1966); David Mechanic, "Some Factors in Identifying and Defining Mental Illness," *Mental Hygiene* (Jan. 1962): 46, 66–74.

9. P. J. Caplan, *They Say You're Crazy* (Reading, MA: Addison-Wesley, 1995).

10. Ibid.

11. Davie L. Rosenhan, "On Being Sane in Insane Places," *Science,* 179 (Jan. 1973): 250–257.

12. Rosenhan and Seligman, *Abnormal Psychology.*

13. Ibid.

14. Charles H. Cooley, *Human Nature and the Social Order* (New York: Scribner, 1902).

15. Thomas S. Szasz, "The Psychiatrist as Double Agent," *Transaction,* 4 (Oct. 1967): 16.

16. Ibid., 17.

17. Scheff, *Being Mentally Ill.*

18. Ibid., 31.

19. Kornblum and Julian, *Social Problems,* 86–88.

20. Ibid.

21. Ibid.

22. Rosenhan and Seligman, *Abnormal Psychology,* 695–703.

23. Ibid., 696–700.

24. The President's Commission on Mental Health, *Report to the President from The President's Commission on Mental Health,* vol. 1 (Washington, DC: U.S. Government Printing Office, 1978)

25. Ibid., 69–72.

26. Rosenhan and Seligman, *Abnormal Psychology,* 695–725.

27. "Psychiatric Testimony Clouds Justice in the Courtroom," *Freedom* (Feb. 1980): 1.

28. Ibid., 4.

29. "Behind Growing Outrage over Insanity Pleas," *U.S. News & World Report* (May 1979): 41.

30. Ibid., 42.

31. "Psychiatric Testimony Clouds Justice in the Courtroom": 4.

32. Kornblum and Julian, *Social Problems,* 85.

33. Rosenhan and Seligman, *Abnormal Psychology,* 722–725.

34. August B. Hollingshead and Frederick C. Redlich, *Social Class and Mental Illness: A Community Study* (New York: Wiley, 1958).

35. William Rushing, "Two Patterns in the Relationship between Social Class and Mental Hospitalization," *American Sociological Review* 34 (Aug. 1969): 533–541.

36. Leo Srole, T. S. Langer, S. T. Michael, M. K. Opler, and T. A. L. Rennie, *Mental Health in the Metropolis: The Midtown Manhattan Study,* rev. ed. (New York: Harper & Row, 1975).

37. Kornblum and Julian, *Social Problems,* 72–75.

38. Ibid.

39. Rosenhan and Seligman, *Abnormal Psychology,* 322.

40. Daniel J. Curran and Claire M. Renzetti, *Social Problems,* 3d ed. (Boston: Allyn & Bacon, 1993), 484.

41. Kornblum and Julian, *Social Problems,* 76–77.

42. Ibid., 77.

43. Ibid., 76.

44. George Rosen, *Madness in Society: Chapters in the Historical Sociology of Mental Illness* (New York: Harper & Row, 1969).

45. Ibid., 172–195.

46. Clifford W. Beers, *A Mind That Found Itself* (New York: Longmans, Green, 1908).

47. H. J. Eysenck, "The Effects of Psychotherapy: An Evaluation," *Journal of Consulting Psychology,* 11 (1955), 319–324.

48. A good summary of these therapies is provided in Raymond Corsini and Danny Wedding, eds., *Current Psychotherapies,* 5th ed. (Itasca, IL: Peacock, 1995).

49. Miriam Siegler and Mumphrey Osmond, *Models of Madness, Models of Medicine* (New York: Harper & Row, 1974).

50. Joseph Mehr, *Human Services* (Boston: Allyn & Bacon, 1980), 88.

51. Erving Goffman, *Asylums: Essays on the Social Situation of Mental Patients and Other Inmates* (New York: Doubleday, 1961).

52. Rosenhan and Seligman, *Abnormal Psychology.*

53. Kornblum and Julian, *Social Problems,* 82–83.

54. Rosenhan and Seligman, *Abnormal Psychology,* 695–726.

55. Ibid.

56. Kornblum and Julian, *Social Problems,* 86–88.

57. Ellis, *Reason and Emotion in Psychotherapy* (New York: Lyle Stuart, 1962), and Maxie Maultsby, *Help Yourself to Happiness* (Boston: Marborough/Herman, 1975).

58. Maultsby, *Help Yourself to Happiness,* 2–23.

## Chapter 4

1. *Webster's New Collegiate Dictionary* (Springfield, MA: Merriam-Webster, 1990).

2. William Kornblum and Joseph Julian, *Social Problems,* 9th ed. (Upper Saddle River, NJ: Prentice-Hall, 1998), 140.

3. Howard Abadinsky, *Drug Abuse: An Introduction* (Chicago: Nelson-Hall, 1989), 90–97.

4. Ibid., 54–58.

5. Ibid.

6. James W. Coleman and Donald R. Cressey, *Social Problems,* 5th ed. (New York: HarperCollins, 1993), 304.

7. Quoted in Earle F. Barcus and Susan M. Jankowski, "Drugs and the Mass Media," *The Annals of the American Academy of Political and Social Science,* 417 (1975): 89.

8. Ian Robertson, *Social Problems,* 2d ed. (New York: Random House, 1980), 438.

9. Leon G. Hunt and Carl D. Chambers, *The Heroin Epidemic* (New York: Spectrum Books, 1976).

10. Alfred R. Lindesmith, *The Addict and the Law* (Bloomington: Indiana University Press, 1965), 228.

11. Joseph Gusfield, *Symbolic Crusade: Status Politics and the American Temperance Movement* (Urbana: University of Illinois Press, 1963).

12. Émile Durkheim, *Suicide: A Study in Sociology,* trans. John Spaulding and George Simpson (New York: Free Press, 1951).

13. Robert Merton, *Social Theory and Social Structure,* 2d ed. (New York: Free Press, 1968).

14. See Charles H. Cooley, *Human Nature and the Social Order* (New York: Scribner, 1902), and Howard S. Becker, *Outsiders: Studies in the Sociology of Deviance* (New York: Free Press, 1963).

15. Edwin H. Sutherland and Donald R. Cressey, *Principles of Criminology,* 7th ed. (Philadelphia: Lippincott, 1966).

16. Kornblum and Julian, *Social Problems,* 132–134.

17. Ibid.

18. Ibid.

19. For a review of these theories, see Abadinsky, *Drug Abuse: An Introduction,* 111–136.

20. Howard S. Becker, "Becoming a Marijuana User," *American Journal of Sociology,* 59 (Nov. 1953): 235–242.

21. Kornblum and Julian, *Social Problems,* 132.

22. "Why Liquor is Quicker for Women," *U.S. News & World Report* (Jan. 22, 1990): 13.

23. The material in this section is summarized from studies that were reviewed in Kornblum and Julian, *Social Problems,* 131–134.

24. Ibid., 129–134.

25. See David J. Armor, J. Michael Polich, and Harriet G. Stambul, *Alcoholism and Treatment* (New York: Wiley Interscience, 1978).

26. Kornblum and Julian, *Social Problems,* 137–140.

27. Ibid., 132.

28. Ibid.

29. Ibid., 132–135.

30. Ibid.

31. Ibid., 134–135.

32. Ibid., 135.

33. John E. Farley, *American Social Problems,* 2d ed. (Englewood Cliffs, NJ: Prentice-Hall, 1992), 237.

34. Kornblum and Julian, *Social Problems,* 135.

35. Ibid., 135–136.

36. Ibid., 135.

37. Ibid., 135–136.

38. Ibid., 136.

39. Sharon Wegscheider, *Another Chance: Hope and Health for the Alcoholic Family* (Palo Alto, CA: Science and Behavior Books, 1981).

40. Kornblum and Julian, *Social Problems,* 136–140.

41. Brenda C. Coleman, "Study Adds to Alcoholism Gene Theory," *Wisconsin State Journal* (Apr. 18, 1990): 1A.

42. Ibid.

43. Brenda C. Coleman, "Alcoholism Gene May Not Be Key," *Wisconsin State Journal* (Dec. 26, 1990): 3A.

44. Wayne W. Dunning and Dae H. Chang, "Drug Facts and Effects," in Charles Zastrow and Dae H. Chang, eds., *The Personal Problem Solver* (Englewood Cliffs, NJ: Spectrum Books, 1977), 177.

45. John Timson, "Is Coffee Safe to Drink?" *Human Nature* (Dec. 1978): 57–59.

46. Abadinsky, *Drug Abuse: An Introduction.*

47. Tony Blaze-Gosden, *Drug Abuse* (Birmingham, Great Britain: David & Charles Publishers, 1987), 99.

48. Abadinsky, *Drug Abuse: An Introduction.*

49. Blaze-Gosden, *Drug Abuse,* 95.

50. Abadinsky, *Drug Abuse: An Introduction,* 90–97.

51. Ibid.

52. Ibid., 14–22.

53. Robertson, *Social Problems,* 450.

54. Abadinsky, *Drug Abuse: An Introduction.*

55. Timothy Noah, "A Hit or a Miss for Mr. Butts?" *U.S. News & World Report* (June 30 1997): 22–24.

56. Ibid., 22.

57. Ibid.

58. Ibid.

59. Ibid.

60. Ibid.

61. Ibid.

62. Lynn Rosellini, "Rebel with a Cause: Koop," *U.S. News & World Report* (May 30, 1988): 55–63.

63. Noah, "A Hit or a Miss for Mr. Butts?"

64. Ibid., 22–24.

65. "About Marijuana," *Hope Health Letter,* 14, no. 4 (Apr. 1991): 7.

66. John Kaplan, *Marijuana: A New Prohibition* (New York: World, 1970).

67. National Academy of Sciences, *Marijuana and Health* (Washington, DC: U.S. Government Printing Office, 1982).

68. Ibid.

69. Warren E. Leary, "Panel Recommends Marijuana Studies," *Wisconsin State Journal* (Feb. 21, 1997): 2A.

70. A. Toufexis, "Shortcut to the Rambo Look," *Time* (Jan. 30, 1989): 78.

71. Ibid.

72. Ibid.

73. Tim Bliss, "Drugs—Use, Abuse, and Treatment," in Charles Zastrow, ed., *Introduction to Social Welfare Institutions* (Homewood, IL: Dorsey Press, 1978), 301.

74. Frank Riessman, "The 'Helper Therapy' Principle," *Journal of Social Work* (Apr. 1965): 27–34.

75. Martin Kasindorf, "By the Time It Gets to Phoenix," *New York Times Magazine* (Oct. 26, 1975): 30.

76. For descriptions of these self-help groups, see Thomas J. Powell, *Self-Help Organizations and Professional Practice* (Silver Spring, MD: 1987).

77. Bliss, "Drugs—Use, Abuse, and Treatment," 314.

78. Kornblum and Julian, *Social Problems,* 131–135.

79. "A Test-Tube War on Drugs?" *U.S. News & World Report* (Mar. 17, 1986): 8.

80. Alvin P. Sanoff, "Baseball's Drug Menace," *U.S. News & World Report* (Mar. 17, 1986): 57.

81. National Commission on Marihuana and Drug Abuse, *Drug Use in America: Problem in Perspective,* Second Report (Washington, DC: U.S. Government Printing Office, March 1973).

82. Kornblum and Julian, *Social Problems,* 151–153.

83. Thomas J. Sullivan, *Introduction to Social Problems,* 4th ed. (Needham Heights, MA: Allyn & Bacon, 1997), 386.

84. Ibid.

85. Ibid.

86. Ibid.

87. Ibid., 387.

## Chapter 5

1. Havelock Ellis, *Sex and Marriage: Eros in Contemporary Life* (Westport, CT: Greenwood Press, 1977).

2. David A. Schulz, *Human Sexuality* (Englewood Cliffs, NJ: Prentice-Hall, 1979), 4.

3. Don Grubin, "Sexual Offending: A Cross Cultural Comparison," in John Bancroft, Clive M. Davis, and Howard J. Ruppel, Jr., eds., *Annual Review of Sex Research,* Vol. 3 (Lake Mills, IA: Society for the Scientific Study of Sex, 1993), 201–217.

4. Janet S. Hyde, *Understanding Human Sexuality,* 5th ed. (New York: McGraw-Hill, 1994), 502.

5. Ibid., 13.

6. Ibid.

7. John Gagnon and Bruce Henderson, *Human Sexuality: The Age of Ambiguity* (Boston: Little, Brown, 1975), 14.

8. Duncan Chappell et al., "Forcible Rape: A Comparative Study of Offenses Known to the Police in Boston and Los Angeles," in James H. Henslin, ed., *Studies in the Sociology of Sex* (Englewood Cliffs, NJ: Prentice-Hall, 1971), 174–175.

9. John E. Farley, *American Social Problems*, 2nd ed. (Englewood Cliffs, NJ: Prentice-Hall, 1992), 164.

10. Hyde, *Understanding Human Sexuality*, 412–415.

11. Gagnon and Henderson, *Human Sexuality*, 16.

12. J. John Palen, *Social Problems* (New York: McGraw-Hill, 1979), 544.

13. Ibid.

14. Hyde, *Understanding Human Sexuality*, 322–324.

15. Ibid., 284.

16. Ibid.

17. Ibid., 224–229.

18. Alfred C. Kinsey et al., *Sexual Behavior in the Human Male* (Philadelphia, PA: W. B. Saunders, 1948).

19. Alfred C. Kinsey et al., *Sexual Behavior in the Human Female* (Philadelphia, PA: W. B. Saunders, 1953).

20. William H. Masters and Virginia E. Johnson, *Human Sexual Response* (Boston, MA: Little, Brown, 1966). For a layperson, an excellent summary is Ruth Brecher and Edward Brecher, *An Analysis of Human Sexual Response* (New York: Signet Books, 1966).

21. William H. Masters and Virginia E. Johnson, *Human Sexual Inadequacy* (Boston, MA: Little, Brown, 1970). For a lay person, an excellent summary is Fred Belliveau and Lin Richter, *Understanding Human Sexual Inadequacy* (New York: Bantam Books, 1970).

22. Gagnon and Henderson, *Human Sexuality*, 14.

23. Hyde, *Understanding Human Sexuality*, 284–286.

24. Ibid., 636.

25. William Kornblum and Joseph Julian, *Social Problems*, 9th ed. (Upper Saddle River, NJ: Prentice-Hall, 1998), 95–99.

26. Hyde, *Understanding Human Sexuality*, 498–499.

27. Ibid., 490.

28. Ibid.

29. A. Nicholas Groth, "The Incest Offender," in *Intervention in Child Sexual Abuse*, ed. Suzanne M. Sgroi (Lexington, MA: Lexington Books, 1982), 215–239.

30. G. G. Abel et al., "Multiple Paraphilic Diagnoses among Sex Offenders," *Bulletin of the American Academy of Psychiatry and the Law*, 16, no. 2 (1988): 153–168.

31. G. G. Abel et al., "Self-Reported Sex Crimes of Nonincarcerated Parapheliacs," *Journal of Interpersonal Violence*, 2, no. 1 (1987): 3–25.

32. Hyde, *Understanding Human Sexuality*, 500.

33. Ibid.

34. Ibid.

35. Blair Justice and Rita Justice, *The Broken Taboo: Sex in the Family* (New York: Human Sciences Press, 1979).

36. Hyde, *Understanding Human Sexuality*, 502.

37. Justice and Justice, *The Broken Taboo*, 177.

38. Judith Siegel et al., "Reactions to Sexual Assault," *Journal of Interpersonal Violence*, 5, 2 (1990): 229–246.

39. Thomas J. Sullivan, *Introduction to Social Problems*, 4th ed. (Boston: Allyn and Bacon, 1997), 329.

40. Hyde, *Understanding Human Sexuality*, 493.

41. Philip Sarrel and William Masters, "Sexual Molestation of Men by Women," *Archives of Sexual Behavior* 11 (1982): 117–132.

42. A. Nichols Groth, *Men Who Rape* (New York: Plenum Press, 1979).

43. Hyde, *Understanding Human Sexuality*, 492.

44. Cindy Struckman-Johnson, "Forced Sex on Dates: It Happens to Men, Too," *Journal of Sex Research*, 24 (1988): 234–241.

45. M. P. Koss et al., "Non-stranger Sexual Aggression: A Discriminant Analysis of the Psychological Characteristics of Undetected Offenders," *Sex Roles* 12 (1985): 981–992.

46. Eugene J. Kanin, "Date Rapists: Differential Sexual Socialization and Relative Deprivation," *Archives of Sexual Behavior* 14 (1985): 219–232.

47. Ann W. Burgess and Lynda Holmstrom, *Rape: Victims of Crisis* (Bowie, MD: Robert J. Brady, 1974).

48. Ann W. Burgess and Lynda Holmstrom, "Rape Trauma Syndrome," *American Journal of Psychiatry* 131 (1974): 981–986.

49. Ibid.

50. Ibid.

51. Abel et al., "Self-Reported Sex Crimes on Nonincarcerated Paraphiliacs," 3–25.

52. Kornblum and Julian, *Social Problems*, 106–110.

53. Kinsey et al., *Sexual Behavior in the Human Male*; and Vance Packard, *The Sexual Wilderness* (New York: McKay, 1968), 509.

54. Joannie M. Schrof, "Sex in America," *U.S. News & World Report*, Oct. 17, 1994, 74–81.

55. Palen, *Social Problems*, 551.

56. Kornblum and Julian, *Social Problems*, 112–113.

57. Ibid.

58. Ibid., 110–111.

59. Freda Adler, *Sisters in Crime: The Rise of the New Female Criminal* (New York: McGraw-Hill, 1976), 76.

60. Kingsley Davis, "The Sociology of Prostitution," *American Sociological Review*, 2 (Oct. 1937): 746.

61. Hyde, *Understanding Human Sexuality*, 515–517.

62. Norman R. Jackman, Richard O'Toole, and Gilbert Geis, "The Self-Image of the Prostitute," *The Sociological Quarterly* 4 (April 1963): 150–161.

63. Quoted in John Gosling and Douglas Warner, *City of Vice* (New York: Hillman, 1961), 82.

64. Jackman, O'Toole, and Geis, "Self-Image of the Prostitute."

65. Davis, "Sociology of Prostitution."

66. Kornblum and Julian, *Social Problems,* 106–112.

67. Ibid., 119–120.

68. Hyde, *Understanding Human Sexuality,* 524.

69. James Leslie McCary, *Human Sexuality,* 2d ed. (New York: Van Nostrand Reinhold, 1973), 379–380.

70. M. Brown, D. M. Amoroso, and E. E. Ware, "Behavioral Effects of Viewing Pornography," *Journal of Social Psychology* 98 (1976): 235–245.

71. Hyde, *Understanding Human Sexuality,* 524–527.

72. Ibid., 521–522.

73. Kornblum and Julian, *Social Problems,* 113–115.

74. Quoted in Palen, *Social Problems,* 570.

75. Ibid., 569.

76. Hyde, *Understanding Human Sexuality,* 526.

77. Ibid., 636.

78. Kinsey et al., *Sexual Behavior in the Human Male,* 639.

79. Thomas Sullivan et al., *Social Problems* (New York: Wiley, 1980), 537.

80. Hyde, *Understanding Human Sexuality,* 424.

81. Ibid.

82. Ibid.

83. Kornblum and Julian, *Social Problems,* 99–104.

84. Ibid.

85. Hyde, *Understanding Human Sexuality,* 426.

86. Ibid.

87. Ibid.

88. Schrof, "Sex in America," 74–81.

89. Kinsey et al., *Sexual Behavior in the Human Male;* and Kinsey et al., *Sexual Behavior in the Human Female.*

90. Hyde, *Understanding Human Sexuality,* 436–438.

91. Ibid., 437–438.

92. Alan P. Bell, Martin S. Weinberg, and Sue Kiefer Hammersmith, *Sexual Preference* (Bloomington: Indiana University Press, 1981).

93. Charlene Crabb, "Are Some Men Born to be Homosexual?" *U.S. News & World Report,* Sept. 9, 1991, 58.

94. William F. Allman, "The Biology-Behavior Conundrum" *U.S. News & World Report,* July 26, 1993, 6–7.

95. Ibid., 6–9.

96. Kim I. Mills, "Was 1993 'The Year of the Queer'?" *Wisconsin State Journal,* Jan. 1, 1994, 4A.

97. Hyde, *Understanding Human Sexuality,* 636–638.

98. "Congress Defines Marriage: 1 Man, 1 Woman," *U.S. News & World Report,* September 23, 1996, 19.

99. Karlein M. G. Schrewrs, "Sexuality in Lesbian Couples: The Importance of Gender," in *Annual Review of Sex Research,* vol. IV, ed. John Bancroft, Clive M. Davis, and Howard Ruppel, Jr. (Lake Mills, IA: Society for the Scientific Study of Sex, 1994), 49–66.

100. Jack H. Hedblom, "The Female Homosexual: Social and Attitudinal Dimensions," in *Deviance: Studies in Definition, Management, and Treatment,* 2d ed., ed. Simon Dinitz, Russell R. Dynes, and Alfred C. Clark (New York: Oxford University Press, 1975), 246.

101. Hyde, *Understanding Human Sexuality,* 453.

102. Ibid., 454.

103. Ibid.

104. Ibid., 631–643.

105. Ibid., 438–456.

106. Timothy F. Murphy, "Redirecting Sexual Orientation: Techniques and Justifications," *Journal of Sex Research* 29 (1992): 510–523.

107. For descriptions of sex therapy, see Fred Belliveau and Lin Richter, *Understanding Human Sexual Inadequacy;* and Lloyd G. Sinclair, "Sex Counseling and Therapy" in *The Practice of Social Work,* 5th ed., ed. C. Zastrow (Pacific Grove, CA: Brooks/Cole Publishing Co., 1995), 487–513.

108. Jack S. Annon, *Behavioral Treatment of Sexual Problems: Brief Therapy* (New York: Harper and Row, 1976); and *Behavioral Treatment of Sexual Problems: Intensive Therapy,* vol. 2 (Honolulu: Enabling Systems, 1975).

109. Lloyd G. Sinclair, "Sex Counseling and Therapy," in *The Practice of Social Work,* 5th ed., ed. by C. Zastrow, (Pacific Grove, CA: Brooks/Cole, 1995), 491.

110. Lloyd G. Sinclair, "Sexual Counseling and Sex Therapy," in *Introduction to Social Welfare Institutions: Social Problems, Services, and Current Issues,* 3d ed., ed. C. Zastrow (Homewood, IL: Dorsey 1986), 213.

111. Jack S. Annon, *Behavioral Treatment of Sexual Problems* (Hagerstown, MD: Harper and Row, 1976), 77.

112. For an extended discussion, see Richard L. Stimmers, "For Men: Controlling Premature Ejaculation," in *The Personal Problem Solver,* ed. C. Zastrow and D. H. Chang (Englewood Cliffs, NJ: Prentice-Hall, 1977), 97–105.

113. Annon, *Behavioral Treatment of Sexual Problems;* Belliveau and Richter, *Understanding Human Sexual Inadequacy;* and Sinclair, *Sex Counseling and Therapy,* 490–493.

## Chapter 6

1. Excerpted from a speech by Abraham Lincoln in Charleston, Illinois, in 1858, as reported in Richard Hofstader, *The American Political Tradition* (New York: Knopf, 1948), 116.

2. James W. Coleman and Donald R. Cressey, *Social Problems,* 6th ed. (New York: HarperCollins, 1996), 565.

3. *Encyclopedia of Sociology* (Guilford, NC: Duskin Publishing Group, 1974), 101.

4. Ibid., 236.

5. Gordon W. Allport, *The Nature of Prejudice* (Reading, MA: Addison-Wesley, 1954), 7.

6. Robert Merton, "Discrimination and the American Creed," in *Discrimination and National Welfare,* ed. Robert M. MacIver (New York: Harper, 1949).

7. Marlene Cummings, "How to Handle Incidents of Racial Discrimination," in *The Personal Problem Solver,* ed. C. Zastrow and D. H. Chang (Englewood Cliffs, NJ: Prentice-Hall, 1977), 200. Permission to reprint obtained from Prentice-Hall.

8. Gunnar Myrdal, *An American Dilemma* (New York: Harper, 1994).

9. Elmer H. Johnson, *Social Problems of Urban Man* (Homewood, IL: Dorsey, 1973), 344.

10. Robert Barker, ed., *The Social Work Dictionary,* 3d ed. (Washington, DC: NASW Press, 1995), 236.

11. Ashley Montague, *Man's Most Dangerous Myth: The Fallacy of Race,* 4th ed. (Cleveland, OH: World, 1964).

12. Johnson, *Social Problems,* 350.

13. Arnold Rose, *The Negro in America* (New York: Harper and Row, 1964).

14. Paul Ehrlich and Richard Holm, "A Biological View of Race," in *The Concept of Race,* ed. Ashley Montague (New York: Free Press, 1964).

15. Montague, *Man's Most Dangerous Myth.*

16. R. J. Herrnstein and C. Murray, *The Bell Curve: The Reshaping of American Life by Differences in Intelligence* (New York: Free Press, 1994).

17. G. R. LeFrancois, *The Lifespan,* 5th ed. (Belmont, CA: Wadsworth, 1996).

18. Johnson, *Social Problems of Urban Man,* 50.

19. T. W. Adorno, E. Frenkel-Brunswik, D. J. Devinson, and R. N. Sanford, *The Authoritarian Personality* (New York: Harper and Row, 1950).

20. Charles F. Marden and Gladys Meyer, *Minorities in American Society* (New York: American Book Co., 1962).

21. Eugene Hartley, *Problems in Prejudice* (New York: King's Crown Press, 1946).

22. Barker, *The Social Work Dictionary,* 189.

23. Ibid., 185.

24. S. Carmichael and C. V. Hamilton, *Black Power: The Politics of Liberation in America* (New York: Vintage Books, 1967).

25. Barker, *The Social Work Dictionary,* 189.

26. William Kornblum and Joseph Julian, *Social Problems,* 9th ed. (Upper Saddle River, NJ: Prentice-Hall, 1998), 272.

27. Jeannette Henry, *The Indian Historian* 1 (December 1967): 22.

28. Kornblum and Julian, *Social Problems,* 261.

29. C. H. Cooley, *Human Nature and the Social Order* (New York: Scribner's, 1902).

30. Coleman and Cressey, *Social Problems,* 199–200.

31. E. Pinderhughes, "Afro-American Families and the Victim System," in *Ethnicity and Family Therapy,* ed. M. McGoldrick, J. K. Pearce, and J. Giordana (New York: Guilford, 1982).

32. Albert Szymanski, "Racial Discrimination and White Gain," *American Sociological Review,* 41 (June 1976): 403–414.

33. Kornblum and Julian, *Social Problems,* 275–279.

34. Richard T. Schaefer, *Racial and Ethnic Groups,* 6th ed. (New York: HarperCollins, 1996), 7.

35. Ibid.

36. Ibid.

37. Charles H. Henderson and Bok-Lim Kim, "Racism," in *Contemporary Social Work,* ed. Donald Brieland, Lela Costin, and Charles Atherton (New York: McGraw-Hill, 1975), 180.

38. Quoted in David Gelman, "Black and White in America," *Newsweek,* Mar. 7, 1988, 19.

39. Schaefer, *Racial and Ethnic Groups,* 238–240.

40. Ibid., 226–228.

41. Ibid.

42. Ibid., 235.

43. Ibid., 235–236.

44. B. B. Solomon, "Social Work with Afro-Americans," in *Social Work: A Profession of Many Faces,* 3d ed., A. Morales and B. W. Sheafor, eds. (Boston: Allyn and Bacon, 1983), 420.

45. J. L. Dillard, *Black English: Its History and Usage in the United States* (New York: Random House, 1972).

46. Schaefer, *Racial and Ethnic Groups,* 252–254.

47. Ibid., 278–298.

48. Ibid., 294.

49. Ibid.

50. Ibid., 294–295.

51. Ibid., 304.

52. Ibid., 320.

53. Johnson, *Social Problems of Urban Man,* 349.

54. Dee Brown, *Bury My Heart at Wounded Knee* (New York: Holt, Rinehart & Winston, 1971).

55. Helen M. Crampton and Kenneth K. Keiser, *Social Welfare: Institution and Process* (New York: Random House, 1970), 104.

56. Schaefer, *Racial and Ethnic Groups,* 161–162.

57. Communication with Mace J. Delosme, Arcata, CA.

58. Schaefer, *Racial and Ethnic Groups,* 185.

59. Ian Robertson, *Social Problems*, 2d ed. (New York: Random House, 1980), 218.

60. Johnson, *Social Problems of Urban Man*, 349.

61. Schaefer, *Racial and Ethnic Groups*, 385–391.

62. Charles Henderson, Bok-Lim Kim, and Ione D. Vargus, "Racism," in *Contemporary Social Work*, 2d ed., ed. Donald Brieland, Lela Costin, and Charles Atherton (New York: McGraw-Hill, 1980), 403.

63. Schaefer, *Racial and Ethnic Groups*, 362–370.

64. Barker, *The Social Work Dictionary*, 362–370.

65. George E. Simpson and J. Milton Yinger, *Racial and Cultural Minorities*, 3d ed. (New York: Harper & Row, 1965), 510.

66. Thomas Sullivan et al., *Social Problems* (New York: Wiley, 1980), 437.

67. Johnson, *Social Problems of Urban Man*, 374–379.

68. Sullivan et al., *Social Problems*, 438.

69. Ibid., 439.

70. Ibid., 439.

71. Jerelyn Eddings, "Second Thoughts About Integration," *U.S. News & World Report*, July 28, 1997, 32.

72. Ibid.

73. Ibid.

74. Allan P. Sindler, *Bakke, DeFunis and Minority Admissions: The Quest for Equal Opportunity* (New York: Longmans, Green, 1978).

75. Henderson et al., "Racism," 403.

76. Kornblum and Julian, *Social Problems*, 283–290.

77. S. V. Roberts, "Affirmative Action on the Edge," *U.S. News & World Report*, Feb. 13, 1995, 32–39.

78. M. B. Zuckerman, "Fixing Affirmative Action," *U.S. News & World Report*, March 20, 1995, 112.

79. Quoted in Cummings, "How to Handle Incidents," 201.

80. Milton Gordon, "Assimilation in America: Theory and Reality," *Daedalus* 90 (Spring 1961): 363–365.

81. Jim Bishop, *The Days of Martin Luther King, Jr.* (New York: Putnam, 1971), 327–328.

## Chapter 7

1. William Kornblum and Joseph Julian, *Social Problems*, 9th ed. (Upper Saddle River, NJ: Prentice-Hall, 1998), 293.

2. Ibid.

3. U.S. Bureau of the Census, *Statistical Abstract of the United States, 1997* (Washington, DC: U.S. Government Printing Office, 1997).

4. Ibid.

5. Ibid., 478.

6. Jean Stockard and Miriam M. Johnson, *Sex Roles* (Englewood Cliffs, NJ: Prentice-Hall, 1980).

7. Joseph H. Fichter and Virginia K. Mills, "The Status of Women in American Churches," *Church and Society*, Sept.–Oct., 1972.

8. Thomas Sullivan et al., *Social Problems* (New York: Wiley, 1980), 452.

9. Francine D. Blair, "Women in the Labor Force: An Overview," in *Women: A Feminist Perspective*, ed. Jo Freeman (Palo Alto, CA: Mayfield, 1979), 272.

10. John Money, J. G. Hampson, and J. L. Hampson, "An Examination of Some Basic Sexual Concepts: The Evidence of Human Hermaphroditism," *Bulletin of the John Hopkins Hospital*. 97 (1955): 301–309.

11. H. L. Rheingold and K. V. Cook, "The Contents of Boys' and Girls' Rooms as an Index of Parents' Behavior," *Child Development* 46 (June 1975): 461.

12. Eleanor Maccoby and Carol Jacklin, *The Psychology of Sex Differences* (Stanford, CA: Stanford University Press, 1974).

13. Ibid.

14. Clarice Stasz Stoll, ed., *Sexism: Scientific Debates* (Reading, MA: Addison-Wesley, 1973).

15. Warren Farrell, *The Liberated Man* (New York: Random House, 1975).

16. Sullivan et al., *Social Problems*, 455.

17. Betty Friedan, *The Feminine Mystique* (New York: Dell, 1963).

18. Kornblum and Julian, *Social Problems*, 309–310.

19. Ibid., 309–310.

20. Paul B. Horton, Gerald R. Leslie, and Richard F. Larson, *The Sociology of Social Problems*, 9th ed. (Englewood Cliffs, NJ: Prentice Hall, 1988), 252.

21. Sullivan et al., *Social Problems*, 475–476.

22. Kornblum and Julian, *Social Problems*, 299–301.

23. Ibid.

24. Ibid.

25. "ERA Stalled, But Women Make Piecemeal Gains," *U.S. News & World Report*, Aug. 20, 1979, 56.

26. Horton et al., *The Sociology of Social Problems*, 261.

27. Amy Saltzman, "Hands Off at the Office," *U.S. News & World Report*, Aug. 1, 1988, 56–58.

28. D. A. Charney and R. C. Russell, "An Overview of Sexual Harassment," *American Journal of Psychiatry*, 151, No. 1, January, 1994, 11.

29. Stockard and Johnson, *Sex Roles*, 133–147.

30. Richard C. Friedman, Ralph M. Richart, and Raymond L. Vande Wiehe, eds., *Sex Differences in Behavior* (New York: Wiley, 1974).

31. Shirley Weitz, *Sex Roles: Biological, Psychological, and Social Foundations* (New York: Oxford University Press, 1977); Betty Yorburg, *Sexual Identity: Sex Roles and Social Change* (New York: Wiley, 1974); and Michael Teitelbaum, ed., *Sex Roles: Social and Biological Perspectives* (New York: Doubleday Anchor, 1976).

32. Ibid.

33. Maccoby and Jacklin, *Psychology of Sex Differences.*

34. Ibid.

35. John Money, Joan Hampson, and John Hampson, "Imprinting and the Establishment of Gender Role," *Archives of Neurology and Psychiatry* 77 (March 1967): 333–336. See also John Money and Anke A. Ehrhardt, *Man and Woman, Boy and Girl* (New York: New American Library, 1974); and Richard Green, *Sexual Identity Conflict in Children and Adults* (Baltimore: Penguin, 1975).

36. Clellan S. Ford and Frank Beach, *Patterns of Sexual Behavior* (New York: Harper and Row, 1951).

37. Margaret Mead, *Sex and Temperament in Three Primitive Societies* (New York: Morrow, 1935).

38. Deborah S. David and Robert Grannon, eds., *The Forty-Nine Percent Majority: The Male Sex Role* (Reading, MA: Addison-Wesley, 1976).

39. Allan Katcher, "The Discrimination of Sex Differences by Young Children," *Journal of Genetic Psychology* 87 (Sept. 1955): 131–143.

40. Lawrence Kohlberg, "A Cognitive-Developmental Analysis of Children's Sex-Role Concepts and Attitudes," in Maccoby and Jacklin, *Psychology of Sex Differences,* 82–173.

41. Ruth E. Hartley, "American Core Culture: Changes and Continuities," in *Sex Roles in Changing Society,* ed. G. H. Seward and R. C. Williamson (New York: Random House, 1970), 140–141.

42. Ibid., 141.

43. Charles H. Cooley, *Social Organization* (New York: Scribner's, 1909).

44. Martina Horner, "Fail: Bright Women," *Psychology Today,* Nov. 1969, 36–38; Vivian Gornick, "Why Women Fear Success," *MS,* Spring 1972, 50–53.

45. Janet S. Hyde, *Understanding Human Sexuality,* 5th ed., (New York: McGraw-Hill, 1994), 385–394.

46. *Statistical Abstract of the United States, 1997,* 412.

47. American Association of University of Women, *How Schools Shortchange Women: The A.A.U.W. Report* (Washington, DC: A.A.U.W. Educational Foundation, 1992).

48. James W. Coleman and Donald R. Cressey, *Social Problems,* 6th ed. (New York: HarperCollins, 1996), 300.

49. Ibid.

50. Myra Sadker, David Sadker, and Susan S. Klein, "Abolishing Misconceptions About Sex Equity in Education," *Theory into Practice* 25 (Autumn, 1986): 220.

51. Coleman and Cressey, *Social Problems,* 302.

52. Janet S. Chafetz, *Masculine, Feminine or Human? An Overview of the Sociology of Sex Roles* (Itasca, IL: Peacock, 1974).

53. Kornblum and Julian, *Social Problems,* 304–305.

54. Sigmund Freud, *A General Introduction to Psychoanalysis* (New York: Boni & Liveright, 1924).

55. Kornblum and Julian, *Social Problems,* 293.

56. Ibid., 299–301.

57. Coleman and Cressey, *Social Problems,* 305.

58. Ibid.

59. Ibid., 304–305.

60. Ann M. Morrison, "Up against a Glass Ceiling," *Los Angeles Times,* Aug. 23, 1987, sec. 1, 3.

61. Kornblum and Julian, *Social Problems,* 299–301.

62. Coleman and Cressey, *Social Problems,* 302–303.

63. Hyde, *Understanding Human Sexuality.*

64. Coleman and Cressey, *Social Problems,* 303.

65. Hyde, *Understanding Human Sexuality.*

66. Horton et al., *The Sociology of Social Problems,* 258.

67. Ibid.

68. Kornblum and Julian, *Social Problems,* 303.

69. Hyde, *Understanding Human Sexuality.*

70. Ibid.

71. Martina S. Horner, "Femininity and Successful Achievement: A Basic Inconsistency," in *Feminine Personality and Conflict,* Judith M. Bardwich, ed. (Pacific Grove, CA: Brooks/Cole, 1970).

72. David and Brannon *The Forty-Nine Percent Majority,* 53–54.

73. Hartley, "American Core Culture," 142.

74. U.S. Bureau of the Census, *Statistical Abstract of the United States, 1997.*

75. Ibid.

76. Carl Glassman, "How Lady Cops Are Doing," *Parade,* July 27, 1980, 4–5.

77. Coleman and Cressey, *Social Problems,* 313.

78. Ibid., 309.

79. *Statistical Abstract of the United States, 1997,* 410–413.

80. Kornblum and Julian, *Social Problems,* 314.

81. Hyde, *Understanding Human Sexuality.*

82. Coleman and Cressey, *Social Problems,* 313–314.

83. Hyde, *Understanding Human Sexuality.*

84. Kornblum and Julian, *Social Problems,* 293.

## *Chapter 8*

1. Gordon Moss and Walter Moss, *Growing Old* (New York: Pocket Books, 1975), 17–18.

2. Colin M. Turnbull, *The Mountain People* (New York: Simon and Schuster, 1972).

3. American Association of Retired Persons, *A Profile of Older Americans: 1996* (Washington, DC: AARP, 1996).

4. Diane E. Papalia and Sally W. Olds, *Human Development,* 6th ed. (New York: McGraw-Hill, 1995), 543–550.

5. Milton L. Barron, "The Aged as a Quasi-Minority Group," in *The Other Minorities,* Edward Sagarin, ed. (Lexington MA: Ginn, 1971), 149.

6. William Kornblum and Joseph Julian, *Social Problems,* 9th ed. (Upper Saddle River, NJ: Prentice-Hall, 1998), 333.

7. American Association of Retired Persons, *A Profile of Older Americans: 1996,* 1.

8. Joan Arehart-Triechel, "It's Never Too Late to Start Living Longer," *New York,* Apr. 11, 1977, 38.

9. Thomas Sullivan, Kenrick Thompson, Richard Wright, George Gross, and Dale Spady, *Social Problems* (New York: Wiley, 1980), 335–370.

10. U.S. Bureau of the Census, *Statistical Abstract of the United States, 1997* (Washington, DC: U.S. Government Printing Office, 1997).

11. American Association of Retired Persons, *Profile of Older Americans: 1996,* 1.

12. Alan S. Otten, "Ever More Americans Live into 80s and 90s, Causing Big Problems," *The Wall Street Journal,* July 30, 1984, 1.

13. Papalia and Olds, *Human Development,* 569.

14. Ibid., 569–570.

15. Eisdor Fer, quoted in Otten, "Ever More Americans Live into 80s and 90s, Causing Big Problems," 10.

16. American Association of Retired Persons, *A Profile of Older Americans: 1996,* 11.

17. Kornblum and Julian, *Social Problems,* 333–337.

18. Ibid.

19. Ibid.

20. F. L. Schick, ed., *Statistical Handbook on Aging Americans* (Phoenix, AZ: Oryz, 1986).

21. R. Bossé, C. M. Aldwin, M. R. Levenson, and D. J. Ekerdt, "Mental Health Differences Among Retirees and Workers: Findings from the Normative Aging Study," *Psychology and Aging* 2, 1987, 383–389.

22. M. P. Lawton, "Leisure Activities for the Aged," *Annals of the American Academy of Political and Social Science,* 438 (1978), 71–79.

23. American Association of Retired Persons, *A Profile of Older Americans: 1996,* 13.

24. Ibid., 14.

25. Ibid.

26. Marilyn L. Flynn, "Aging," in *Contemporary Social Work,* 2d ed., Donald Brieland, Lela Costin, and Charles Atherton, eds. (New York: McGraw-Hill, 1980), 353.

27. American Association of Retired Persons, *A Profile of Older Americans: 1996,* 10.

28. Kornblum and Julian, *Social Problems,* 342–344.

29. American Association of Retired Persons, *A Profile of Older Americans: 1996,* 10–11.

30. Sullivan et al., *Social Problems,* 357–358.

31. *Statistical Abstract of the United States, 1997.*

32. Kornblum and Julian, *Social Problems,* 342–344.

33. Ibid.

34. Ibid.

35. American Association of Retired Persons, *A Profile of Older Americans: 1996,* 3.

36. Moss and Moss, *Growing Old,* 47.

37. American Association of Retired Persons, *A Profile of Older Americans: 1996,* 3–4.

38. Ibid., 3.

39. Ibid.

40. Ibid., 3–4.

41. Ibid., 5.

42. Ibid., 3–5.

43. Janet S. Hyde, *Understanding Human Sexuality,* 5th ed. (New York: McGraw-Hill, 1994).

44. Ibid.

45. William H. Masters and Virginia E. Johnson, "The Human Sexual Response: The Aging Female and the Aging Male," in *Middle Age and Aging,* L. Neugarten, ed. (Chicago: University of Chicago Press, 1968).

46. Ibid., 269.

47. Merlin Taber, "The Aged," in *Contemporary Social Work,* Donald Brieland, Lela Costin, and Charles Atherton, eds. (New York: McGraw-Hill, 1975), 359.

48. Papalia and Olds, *Human Development.*

49. B. M. Newman and P. R. Newman, *Development Through Life: A Psychosocial Approach* (Pacific Grove, CA: Brooks/Cole, 1995).

50. R. C. Atchley, *Social Forces and Aging,* 5th ed. (Belmont, CA: Wadsworth, 1988), 8–10.

51. *Statistical Abstract of the United States, 1997.*

52. Ibid.

53. Ibid.

54. Carol Staudacher, *Beyond Grief* (Oakland, CA: New Harbinger, 1987).

55. Ibid.

56. Sullivan et al., *Social Problems,* 363.

57. *Older Americans Act of 1965, as Amended, Text and History* (Washington, DC: U.S. Department of Health, Education and Welfare), November 1970.

58. American Association of Retired Persons, *A Profile of Older American: 1996,* 4.

59. *Statistical Abstract of the United States, 1997.*

60. Ibid.

61. Kornblum and Julian, *Social Problems,* 340–341.

62. Donald Robinson, "The Crisis in Our Nursing Homes," *Parade,* Aug. 16, 1987, 13.

63. Ibid.

64. Frank Moss, "It's Hell to Be Old In the U.S.A.," *Parade,* July 17, 1977, 9.

65. K. Pillemer and D. W. Moore, "Abuse of Patients in Nursing Homes: Findings From a Survey of Staff," *Gerontologist,* 29, 1989, 314–320.

66. Ibid.

67. Paplia and Olds, *Human Development.*

68. Moss and Moss, *Growing Old,* 79.

69. Quoted in Robert N. Butler, "Why Survive? Being Old in America" (New York: Harper & Row, 1975), 341.

70. Robert C. Atchley, *The Social Forces in Later Life: An Introduction to Social Gerontology,* 2d ed. (Belmont, CA: Wadsworth, 1977), 267.

71. Ibid., 81.

72. Tamar Lewin, "Many Retirees Tire of Leisurely Lives, Seek New Jobs," *Wisconsin State Journal,* Apr. 22, 1990, 1A.

## Chapter 9

1. William Kornblum and Joseph Julian, *Social Problems,* 9th ed. (Upper Saddle River, NJ: Prentice-Hall, 1998), 2.

2. Ian Robertson, *Social Problems,* 2d ed. (New York: Random House, 1980), 176.

3. Lester F. Ward, *Dynamic Sociology,* reprint of 1883 ed. (New York: Johnson Reprint, 1968).

4. Michael Harrington, *The Other America* (New York: Macmillan, 1962).

5. "Poverty Gap Widens, Studies Reveal," *NASW News,* Jan. 1990, 19.

6. Kornblum and Julian, *Social Problems,* 253.

7. Ibid.

8. James W. Coleman and Donald R. Cressey, *Social Problems,* 6th ed. (New York: HarperCollins, 1996), 156–159.

9. Kornblum and Julian, *Social Problems,* 229.

10. Ibid.

11. Ibid., 227–231.

12. Ibid.

13. Quoted in Kornblum and Julian, *Social Problems,* 232.

14. Paul Samuelson, quoted in Kornblum and Julian, *Social Problems,* 230.

15. Coleman and Cressey, *Social Problems,* 162.

16. Robertson, *Social Problems,* 31.

17. James W. Coleman and Donald R. Cressey, *Social Problems,* 4th ed. (New York: Harper & Row, 1990), 161.

18. Randolph E. Schmid, "Census Bureau: Poor Lose, Rich Win," *Wisconsin State Journal,* September 30, 1997, 2A.

19. Kornblum and Julian, *Social Problems,* 227–230.

20. Ibid., 32–35.

21. Ibid.

22. Ibid., 235–237.

23. Schmid, "Census Bureau: Poor Lose, Rich Win," 2A.

24. Second inaugural address of President Franklin D. Roosevelt (Jan. 20, 1937).

25. President's Council on Economic Advisors, *Economic Report of the President* (Washington, DC: U.S. Government Printing Office, 1964), 56–57.

26. Schmid, "Census Bureau: Poor Lose, Rich Win," 2A.

27. U.S. Bureau of the Census, *Statistical Abstract of the United States, 1997* (Washington, DC: U.S. Government Printing Office, 1997), 478.

28. Kornblum and Julian, *Social Problems,* 293.

29. *Statistical Abstract of the United States, 1997.*

30. Kornblum and Julian, *Social Problems,* 240–242.

31. Ibid.

32. *Statistical Abstract of the United States, 1997,* 475.

33. Ibid.

34. *The Future of Children,* Volume 7, no. 1 (Los Altos, CA: Center for the Future of Children, 1997).

35. American Association of Retired Persons, *A Profile of Older Americans, 1996* (Washington, DC: AARP, 1996).

36. R. V. Kail and J. C. Cavanaugh, *Human Development* (Pacific Grove, CA: Brooks/Cole, 1996).

37. *Statistical Abstract of the United States, 1997.*

38. Ibid.

39. Kornblum and Julian, *Social Problems,* 227–232.

40. Ibid.

41. *Statistical Abstract of the United States, 1997.*

42. Ibid.

43. Kornblum and Julian, *Social Problems,* 242–243.

44. Harrington, *The Other America,* 21.

45. Oscar Lewis, "The Culture of Poverty," *Scientific American,* 215 (October 1966), 19–25.

46. Ibid., 23.

47. Eleanor Leacock, ed., *The Culture of Poverty: A Critique* (New York: Simon and Schuster, 1971).

48. Elliott Liebow, *Tally's Corner: A Study of Negro Street-Corner Men* (Boston: Little, Brown, 1967); Ulf Hannertz, *Soulside: An Inquiry into Ghetto Culture and Community* (New York: Columbia University Press, 1969); Leacock, *The Culture of Poverty.*

49. William Ryan, *Blaming the Victim,* rev. ed. (New York: Vintage Books, 1976).

50. Thomas Sullivan, Kendrick Thompson, Richard Wright, George Gross, and Dale Spady, *Social Problems* (New York: Wiley, 1980), 390.

51. Herbert J. Gans, *More Equality* (New York: Pantheon, 1968), 133–135.

52. Harold Wilensky and Charles Lebeaux, *Industrial Society and Social Welfare* (New York: Free Press, 1965).

53. Ibid., 14.

54. Samuel Mencher, "Newburgh: The Recurrent Crisis in Public Assistance," *Social Work* 7 (Jan. 1962): 3–4.

55. Rex A. Skidmore and Milton G. Thackeray, *Introduction to Social Work*, 2d ed. (Englewood Cliffs, NJ: Prentice-Hall, 1976), 111–112.

56. Helen M. Crampton and Kenneth K. Keiser, *Social Welfare: Institution and Process* (New York: Random House, 1970), 73.

57. Coleman and Cressey, *Social Problems*, 6th ed., 162.

58. Charles Murray, *Losing Ground* (New York: Basic Books, 1986).

59. Ibid.

60. Kornblum and Julian, *Social Problems*, 243–245.

61. Ibid.

62. Coleman and Cressey, *Social Problems*, 6th ed., 166–179; Kornblum and Julian, *Social Problems*, 243–245.

63. Kornblum and Julian, *Social Problems*, 243–245.

64. Ibid., 243–245.

65. A. Dale Tussing, "The Dual Welfare System," *Society*, 11 (January–February 1974), 50–57.

66. Eleanor Clift, "Benefits 'R' Us," *Newsweek*, Aug. 10, 1992, 56.

67. Charles Murray, *Losing Ground*.

68. Quoted in David Whitman, "The Next War on Poverty," *U.S. News & World Report*, Oct. 5, 1992, 38.

69. Ralph Dolgoff, Donald Feldstein, and Louise Skolnik, *Understanding Social Welfare*, 4th ed. (White Plains, NY: Longman Publishers, 1997), 217–218.

70. Paul Glastris, "Was Reagan Right?," *U.S. News & World Report*, October 20, 1997, 3.

71. Ibid.

72. James Midgley and Michelle Livermore, "The Developmental Perspective in Social Work: Educational Implications for a New Century," *Journal of Social Work Education*, Vol. 33, No. 3, Fall 1997, 573–585.

## Chapter 10

1. James W. Coleman and Donald R. Cressey, *Social Problems*, 6th ed. (New York: HarperCollins, 1996), 124.

2. Ibid., 126.

3. Philippe Aries, "From the Medieval to the Modern Family" in *Family in Transition*, ed. Arlene S. Skolnick and Jerome H. Skolnick (Boston, MA: Little, Brown, 1971), 90–104.

4. John F. Cuber, Martha Tyler John, and Kenrick S. Thompson, "Should Traditional Sex Modes and Values Be Changed?" in *Controversial Issues in the Social Studies: A Contemporary Perspective*, Raymond H. Muessig, ed. (Washington, DC: National Council for the Social Studies, 1975), 87–121.

5. Janet S. Hyde, *Understanding Human Sexuality*, 5th ed. (New York: McGraw-Hill, 1995).

6. See William F. Ogburn, "The Changing Family," *The Family* 19 (July 1938), 139–143.

7. George P. Murdock, *Social Structure* (New York: Free Press, 1949); William F. Ogburn, "The Changing Family," *The Family* 19 (July 1938), 139–143; William J. Goode, "The Sociology of the Family," in *Sociology Today*, ed. R. K. Merton, L. Broom, and L. J. Cottrell (New York: Basic Books, 1959); and Talcott Parsons and Robert F. Bales, *Family, Socialization and Interaction Process* (Glencoe, IL: Free Press, 1955).

8. Rene Spitz, "Hospitalism: Genesis of Psychiatric Conditions in Early Childhood," *Psychoanalytic Study of the Child* 1 (1945): 53–74.

9. Coleman and Cressey, *Social Problems*, 130.

10. Diane E. Papalia and Sally W. Olds, *Human Development*, 5th ed. (New York: McGraw-Hill, 1992), 457–459.

11. Ibid.

12. Ibid., 514–516.

13. William Kornblum and Joseph Julian, *Social Problems*, 9th ed. (Upper Saddle River, NJ: Prentice Hall, 1998), 359.

14. Ibid.

15. Kenneth Keniston, *All Our Children: The American Family under Pressure* (New York: Harcourt Brace Jovanovich, 1977), 21.

16. Richard Neely, "Barter in the Court," *The New Republic*, Feb. 10, 1986, 14.

17. Ibid., 17.

18. Coleman and Cressey, *Social Problems*, 133–134.

19. Ibid.

20. Ibid.

21. Ibid.

22. Ibid.

23. John F. Cuber and Peggy B. Harroff, "Five Types of Marriage," in *Family in Transition*, Arlene S. Skolnick and Jerome H. Skolnick, eds. (Boston: Little, Brown, 1971), 287–299.

24. William J. Goode, "Family Disorganization," in *Contemporary Social Problems*, 4th ed., Robert K. Merton and Robert Nisbet, eds. (New York: Harcourt Brace Jovanovich, 1976), 543.

25. Richard J. Gelles, *Intimate Violence in Families*, 3d ed. (Thousand Oaks, CA: Sage Publications, 1997).

26. Ibid.

27. Ibid.

28. Ibid.

29. Coleman and Cressey, *Social Problems*, 564.

30. Lewis Koch and Joanne Koch, "Parent Abuse—A New Plague," *Parade,* Jan. 27, 1980, 14.

31. Gelles, *Intimate Violence in Families,* 116.

32. Coleman and Cressey, *Social Problems,* 136.

33. Suzanne K. Steinmetz and Murray A. Straus, *Violence in the Family* (New York: Dodd, Mead, 1974), 3.

34. Ibid., 9.

35. John O'Brien, "Violence in Divorce Prone Families," *Journal of Marriage and the Family,* 33 (November 1971), 692–698.

36. Steven V. Roberts, "Simpson and Sudden Death," *U.S. News & World Report,* June 27, 1994, 26–32.

37. Gelles, *Intimate Violence in Families.*

38. Ibid.

39. Ibid.

40. Ibid.

41. Ibid.

42. Ibid.

43. Ibid.

44. Murray A. Straus, Richard Gelles, and Suzanne Steinmetz, *Behind Closed Doors: A Survey of Family Violence in America* (Garden City, NY: Doubleday, 1979).

45. Ibid.

46. Gelles, *Intimate Violence in Families.*

47. Andrea Saltzman and Kathleen Proch, *Law in Social Work Practice* (Chicago: Nelson-Hall, 1990), 296–307.

48. Alfred Kadushin and Judith A. Martin, *Child Welfare Services,* 4th ed. (New York: Macmillan, 1988), 218–327.

49. Gelles, *Intimate Violence in Families,* 66.

50. Vincent De Francis, *Child Abuse—Preview of a Nationwide Survey* (Denver: American Humane Association, Children's Division, 1963), 5–6.

51. Ibid., 6.

52. Larry Silver et al., "Does Violence Breed Violence? Contribution from a Study of the Child-Abuse Syndrome," *American Journal of Psychiatry* (September 1969), 404–407.

53. George C. Curtis, "Violence Breeds Violence-Perhaps?" in Jerome E. Leavitt, *The Battered Child* (Morristown, NJ: General Learning Press, 1974), 3.

54. Gelles, *Intimate Violence in Families.*

55. Ibid.

56. Kadushin and Martin, *Child Welfare Services,* 243–244.

57. Vincent De Francis, *Special Skills in Child Protective Services* (Denver: American Humane Association, 1958), 11.

58. American Humane Association, *National Analysis of Official Child Neglect and Abuse Reporting* (Denver: Author, 1978), 27.

59. C. Henry Kempe and Ray E. Helfer, *Helping the Battered Child and His Family* (Philadelphia: Lippincott, 1972); Kadushin and Martin, *Child Welfare Services;* Jerome E. Leavitt, *The Battered Child* (Morristown, NJ: General Learning Press, 1974); and Gelles, *Intimate Violence in Families.*

60. Ibid.

61. Kadushin and Martin, *Child Welfare Services,* 218.

62. Edith Varon, "Communication: Client, Community and Agency," *Social Work* 9 (April 1964): 51–57.

63. Gelles, *Intimate Violence in Families,* 152.

64. Ibid., 153.

65. Patrick Murphy, "Family Preservation and Its Victims," *New York Times,* June 19, 1993, 21.

66. Gelles, *Intimate Violence in Families.*

67. Kadushin and Martin, *Child Welfare Services,* 315.

68. U.S. Bureau of the Census, *Statistical Abstract of the United States, 1997* (Washington, DC: U.S. Government Printing Office, 1997), 73–76.

69. Ibid.

70. Ibid.

71. Ibid.

72. Ibid.

73. Ibid., 74.

74. Ibid., 74.

75. James W. Coleman and Donald R. Cressey, *Social Problems,* 4th ed. (New York: Harper & Row, 1990), 136.

76. *Statistical Abstract of the United States, 1997.*

77. C. P. Green and K. Poteteiger, "Major Problems for Minors," *Society* (1978), 10–13.

78. Alfred C. Kinsey, W. B. Pomeroy, and C. E. Martin, *Sexual Behavior in the Human Male* (Philadelphia: Saunders, 1948); and Alfred C. Kinsey, W. B. Pomeroy, C. E. Martin, and P. H. Gebhard, *Sexual Behavior in the Human Female* (Philadelphia: Saunders, 1953).

79. SIECUS, *Guidelines for Comprehensive Sexuality Education,* (New York: Sex Information and Education Council of the United States, 1991).

80. Janet S. Hyde, *Understanding Human Sexuality,* 5th ed. (New York: McGraw-Hill, 1994), 659–674.

81. Joseph P. Shapiro, "Teenage Sex: Just Say 'Wait,' " *U.S. News & World Report,* July 26, 1993, 56–59.

82. Kornblum and Julian, *Social Problems,* 369.

83. K. Luker, *Dubious Conceptions: The Politics of Teenage Pregnancy* (Cambridge, MA: Harvard University Press, 1996).

84. *Statistical Abstract of the United States, 1997.*

85. Ibid.

86. William Wolf, quoted in Alvin Toffler, *Future Shock* (New York: Bantam, 1970), 238.

87. Carl C. Zimmerman, *Family and Civilization* (New York: Harper and Row, 1947).

88. John Edwards, "The Future of the Family Revisited," *Journal of Marriage and the Family* 29 (Aug. 1967): 505–511.

89. W. F. Ogburn and M. F. Nimkoff, *Technology and the Changing Family* (New York: Houghton-Mifflin, 1955).

90. Kingsley Davis, "Sexual Behavior," in *Contemporary Social Problems*, 4th ed., ed. R. K. Merton and R. Nisbet (New York: Harcourt Brace Jovanovich, 1976), 219–621.

91. Kadushin and Martin, *Child Welfare Services.*

92. Hyde, *Understanding Human Sexuality*, 654.

93. L. Rifken, *Who Should Play God?* (New York: Dell, 1977).

94. Ibid.

95. Ibid.

96. Art Caplan, "Superbaby Sperm Bank Morally Bankrupt," *Wisconsin State Journal*, Nov. 28, 1989, 9A.

97. Rita Christopher, "Mother's Little Helper," *Maclean's Magazine*, March 10, 1980, 10.

98. "Dad Wins Custody of Baby M," *Wisconsin State Journal*, April 1987, 1.

99. Hyde, *Understanding Human Sexuality*, 189–190.

100. "Healthy Baby Is Born from Donated Embryo," *Wisconsin State Journal*, Feb. 4, 1984, sec. 1, 2.

101. Stephen Budiansky, "The New Rules of Reproduction," *U.S. News & World Report*, April 18, 1988, 66–69.

102. Susan Peterson and Susan Kelleher, "Surrogate's Loss Could Redefine Motherhood," *Wisconsin State Journal*, Oct. 23, 1990, 4A.

103. Philip Reilly, *Genetics, Law, and Social Policy* (Cambridge, MA: Harvard University Press, 1977).

104. William R. Wineke, "Calves Cloned Successfully in UW Experiment," *Wisconsin State Journal*, Sept. 9, 1987, 1.

105. Gina Kolata, "Human Clones," *Wisconsin State Journal*, Oct. 23, 1993, 3A.

106. Barbara M. Newman and Philip R. Newman, *Development Through Life*, 6th ed. (Pacific Grove, CA: Brooks/Cole Publishing Co., 1995) 142.

107. Daniel O. Haney, "Cystic Fibrosis Therapy Promising," *Wisconsin State Journal*, Oct. 29, 1993, 7A.

108. R. V. Kail and J. C. Cavanaugh, *Human Development* (Pacific Grove, CA: Brooks/Cole, 1996), 363.

109. Alvin Toffler, *Future Shock* (New York: Bantam, 1970), 27.

110. Ibid., 243–244.

111. Ethel Alpenfels, "Progressive Monogamy: An Alternate Pattern?" in *The Family in Search of a Future*, ed. H. Otto (New York: Appleton-Century-Crofts, 1970), 67–74.

112. Ibid.

113. George O'Neill and Nena O'Neill, *Open Marriage* (New York: M. Evans, 1971).

114. Victor Kassel, "Polygamy After Sixty," *Geriatrics* 21 (April 1966).

115. David Fanshel, *Far from the Reservation* (Metuchen, NJ: Scarecrow Press, 1972).

116. Charles Zastrow, *Outcome of Black Children—White Parents Transracial Adoptions* (San Francisco, CA: R & E Research Associates, 1977).

117. David L. Wheeler, "Black Children, White Parents: The Difficult Issue of Transracial Adoption," *Chronicle of Higher Education*, Sept. 15, 1993, A16.

118. Ibid., A9.

119. Hyde, *Understanding Human Sexuality*, 349–350.

120. Ibid.

121. Diane E. Papalia and Sally W. Olds, *Human Development*, 2d ed. (New York: McGraw-Hill, 1981), 326.

122. Diane E. Papalia and Sally W. Olds, *Human Development*, 6th ed. (New York: McGraw-Hill, 1995), 328.

123. C. Janzen and O. Harris, *Family Treatment in Social Work Practice*, 2d ed. (Itasca, IL: Peacock, 1986), 273.

124. R. B. Stuart and B. Jacobson, *Second Marriage* (New York: Norton, 1985).

125. D. Kompara, "Difficulties in the Socialization Process of Step-Parenting," *Family Relations*, 29 (1980): 69–73.

126. Janzen and Harris, *Family Treatment*, 275–276

127. G. L. Shulman, "Myths That Intrude on the Adaptation of the Step-Family," *Social Casework*, 53, no. 3 (1972): 131–139.

128. E. Wald, *The Remarried Family* (New York: Family Service Association of America, 1981).

129. Ibid.

130. N. Stinnet and J. Walters, *Relationships in Marriage and Family* (New York: Macmillan, 1977).

131. C. Berman, *Making It as a Stepparent: New Roles/New Rules* (New York: Bantam, 1981); E. Visher and J. Visher, "Stepparenting: Blending Families," in *Stress and the Family: Vol. I. Coping with Normative Transitions*, ed. H. I. McCubbin and C. R. Figley (New York: Bruner/Mazel, 1983).

# Chapter 11

1. Barbara Ehrenreich and John Ehrenreich, *The American Health Empire: Power, Profits and Politics* (New York: Vintage Books, 1971), vi.

2. Joseph Julian, *Social Problems*, 3d ed. (Englewood Cliffs, NJ: Prentice-Hall, Inc., 1980), 25.

3. Richard Nixon, "Health Message of 1971," Feb. 18, 1971, White House.

4. Quoted in John A. Denton, *Medical Sociology* (Boston, MA: Houghton-Mifflin, 1978), 65.

5. William Kornblum and Joseph Julian, *Social Problems,* 9th ed. (Upper Saddle River, NJ: Prentice-Hall, 1998), 31.

6. Ibid., 29–31.

7. Ibid.

8. Ibid.

9. U.S. Bureau of the Census, *Statistical Abstract of the United States, 1997* (Washington, DC: U.S. Government Printing Office, 1997).

10. Ibid.

11. James W. Coleman and Donald R. Cressey, *Social Problems,* 6th ed. (New York: HarperCollins, 1996), 248.

12. Ibid., 224.

13. Ibid.

14. Ibid.

15. Kornblum and Julian, *Social Problems,* 134.

16. Coleman and Cressey, *Social Problems,* 223.

17. Ibid.

18. Ibid., 224.

19. Ibid., 223.

20. Ibid.

21. Thomas McKeown, "Determinants of Health," *Human Nature,* 1 (April 1978), 66.

22. Kornblum and Julian, *Social Problems,* 9th ed., 34–36.

23. Ibid.

24. Ibid.

25. Ibid.

26. Max Seham, *Blacks and American Medical Care* (Minneapolis: University of Minnesota Press, 1973), 22–23.

27. Thomas J. Sullivan, *Social Problems,* 4th ed. (Needham Heights, MA: Allyn and Bacon, 1997), 146.

28. Ibid.

29. Ibid., 147.

30. Ibid., 147–148.

31. Ibid., 148.

32. Susan Dentzer, "America's Scandalous Health Care," *U.S. News & World Report,* Mar. 12, 1990, 25.

33. Ibid.

34. Larson, *The Sociology of Social Problems,* 10th ed. (Englewood Cliffs, NJ: Prentice-Hall, 1991), 232.

35. *Statistical Abstract of the United States, 1997.*

36. Ibid.

37. G. L. Dickinson, *Greek View of Life* (New York: Collier, 1961), 95.

38. G. L. Dickinson, *Greek View of Life* (New York: Collier Brooks, 1961), 95.

39. S. Nichtern, *Helping the Retarded Child* (New York: Grosset and Dunlap, 1974), 14.

40. J. F. Garrett, "Historical Background," in *Vocational Rehabilitation of the Disabled,* D. Malikan and H. Rusalem, ed., (New York: New York University Press, 1969), 29–38.

41. J. C. Coleman, *Abnormal Psychology and Modern Life,* 3d ed. (Glenview, Ill.: Scott, Foresman, 1964).

42. C. E. Obermann, *A History of Vocational Rehabilitation in America* (Minneapolis, Minn.: Dennison, 1964).

43. S. Richardson et al., "Cultural Uniformity in Reaction to Physical Disabilities," *American Sociological Review* 26 (April 1961): 241–247.

44. C. H. Cooley, *Human Nature and the Social Order* (New York: Scribner's, 1902).

45. Beatrice A. Wright, *Physical Disability: A Psychological Approach* (New York: Harper, 1960), 259.

46. Nancy Weinberg, "Rehabilitation," in *Contemporary Social Work,* 2d ed., eds. Donald Bieland, Lela Costin, and Charles Atherton (New York: McGraw-Hill, 1980), 310.

47. Salvatore G. DiMichael, "The Current Scene," in *Vocational Rehabilitation of the Disabled: An Overview,* David Malikan and Herbert Rusalem, eds.(New York: New York University Press, 1969).

48. Weinberg, "Rehabilitation," 310.

49. R. Kleck, H. Ono, and A. H. Hastorf, "The Effects of Physical Deviance Upon Face-to-Face Interaction," *Human Relations* 19 (Nov. 1966): 425–436.

50. Kornblum and Julian, *Social Problems.*

51. Ibid.

52. Stanford Rubin and Richard Roessler, *Foundations of the Vocational Rehabilitation Process* (Baltimore, Md.: University Park Press, 1978), 30–32.

53. Ibid., 32–45.

54. G. A. Lloyd, "HIV/AIDS Overview." In *Encyclopedia of Social Work,* 19th ed. (Washington, DC: NASW Press, 1995).

55. C. Scanlan, "New AIDS Drug Wins OK by FDA," *Wisconsin State Journal,* October 10, 1991, 3A.

56. S. Brink, "Beating the Odds," *U.S. News & World Report,* February 12, 1996, 60–68.

57. G. A. Lloyd, "AIDS and HIV: The Syndrome and the Virus," *Encyclopedia of Social Work: 1990 Supplement* (Silver Spring, MD: National Association of Social Workers, 1990), 25.

58. B. Gavzer, "Why Do Some People Survive AIDS?" *Parade,* Sept. 18, 1988, 5.

59. Brink, "Beating the Odds," 60–68.

60. C. Everett Koop, *Surgeon General's Report on Acquired Immune Deficiency Syndrome* (Washington, DC: U.S. Department of Health and Human Services, 1987), 27.

61. "Growing Old in America," ABC News Program Transcript (New York: Journal Graphics, Dec. 28, 1985).

62. Ibid., 11.

63. Ibid.

64. Ibid.

65. *Statistical Abstract of the United States, 1997.*

66. Coleman and Cressey, *Social Problems,* 249–250.

67. Jeffrey Klein and Michael Castleman, "The Profit Motive in Breast Cancer," *Los Angeles Times,* April 4, 1994, B7.

68. Coleman and Cressey, *Social Problems,* 250.

69. *Statistical Abstract of the United States, 1997.*

70. Kornblum and Julian, *Social Problems,* 35–36.

71. Ibid., 34–36.

72. American Association of Retired Persons, *A Profile of Older Americans: 1996* (Washington, DC: American Association of Retired Persons, 1996).

73. Kornblum and Julian, *Social Problems,* 29.

74. Ibid., 58.

75. Coleman and Cressey, *Social Problems,* 251.

76. Judith Randa, "Health Services is 30 and British Still Love It," *New York Daily News,* July 5, 1978, 36.

77. Coleman and Cressey, *Social Problems,* 251.

78. Dorothy P. Rice, "Health Care: Financing," *Encyclopedia of Social Work,* 19th ed. (Washington, DC: NASW Press, 1995), 1171.

79. Susan Brink and Nancy Shute, "Are HMOs the Right Prescription?" *U.S. News & World Report,* October 13, 1997, 60–64.

80. Ibid.

81. Ibid.

82. Ibid.

83. Coleman and Cressey, *Social Problems,* 251.

## Chapter 12

1. Quoted in William Kornblum and Joseph Julian, *Social Problems,* 6th ed. (Englewood Cliffs, NJ: Prentice-Hall, 1988), 394.

2. James W. Coleman and Donald R. Cressey, *Social Problems,* 6th ed. (New York: HarperCollins, 1996), 103.

3. Ibid.

4. "The Learning Lag: You Can't Blame TV," *U.S. News & World Report,* December 2, 1996, 16.

5. Coleman and Cressey, *Social Problems,* 103.

6. Ibid.

7. Ibid., 105.

8. Ibid.

9. "If U Cn Reed Thiz Storie . . .," *U.S. News & World Report,* Sept. 20, 1993, 10.

10. Quoted in Coleman and Cressey, *Social Problems,* 105.

11. John E. Farley, *American Social Problems,* 2d ed. (Englewood Cliffs, NJ: Prentice-Hall, 1992), 446–451.

12. "Michigan's Model," *U.S. News & World Report,* March 28, 1994, 16.

13. Ibid.

14. Coleman and Cressey, *Social Problems,* 96.

15. Ibid.

16. Manley Fleischmann et al., *The Fleischmann Report on the Quality, Cost, and Financing of Elementary and Secondary Education in New York State* (New York: Viking, 1974), 57.

17. Farley, *American Social Problems,* 448–455.

18. Ibid., 448–464.

19. Coleman and Cressey, *Social Problems,* 98–100.

20. Jerelyn Eddings, "Second Thoughts About Integration," *U.S. News & World Report,* July 28, 1997, 32.

21. Ibid.

22. Ibid.

23. Ibid.

24. Ibid.

25. Ibid.

26. L. Tye, "Study: U.S. Retreats on Integration," *Wisconsin State Journal,* Jan. 12, 1992, 9A.

27. Ibid.

28. Ibid.

29. Coleman and Cressey, *Social Problems,* 98–101.

30. L. Tye, "Study: U.S. Retreats on Integration," 9A.

31. Coleman and Cressey, *Social Problems,* 100.

32. Ibid., 100.

33. Ibid., 114.

34. Robert Burns, "20% of Middle Schools, High Schools Had at Least One Serious Crime in '97," *Wisconsin State Journal,* March 20, 1998, 2A.

35. Coleman and Cressey, *Social Problems,* 114–115.

36. Michael Rutter and Associates, quoted in W. William Salgank, "British Study Finds Sharp Differences in Schools," *Los Angeles Times,* Nov. 22, 1979, Part VIII, 1–2.

37. Michael Rutter, *15,000 Hours: Secondary Schools and Their Effects on Children* (Cambridge, MA: Harvard University Press, 1979).

38. Eigil Pederson and Therese Annette Faucher, with William W. Eaton, "A New Perspective on the Effects of First-Grade Teachers on Children's Subsequent Adult Status," *Harvard Educational Review,* 48 (1978), 1–31.

39. "Education Reform Signed," *Wisconsin State Journal,* Apr. 1, 1994, 2A.

40. Thomas Toch, "The Case for Tough Standards," *U.S. News & World Report,* April 1, 1996, 52–56.

41. "The Uncertain Benefits of School Choice," *U.S. News & World Report,* Nov. 6, 1989, 79–81.

42. Rod Little, "The Endangered Summer Vacation," *U.S. News & World Report,* May 16, 1994, 12.

43. Ibid.

44. Ibid.

45. Ibid.

46. Ibid.

47. Ibid.

48. Thomas Toch, "The Perfect School," *U.S. News & World Report,* Jan. 11, 1993, 60–61.

49. Ibid.

50. Ibid.

51. Ibid.

52. "Michigan's Model," *U.S. News & World Report,* 16.

53. Coleman and Cressey, *Social Problems,* 109.

54. Ibid., 108–109.

55. Ibid., 109.

56. Coleman and Cressey, *Social Problems,* 100.

57. William Kornblum and Joseph Julian, *Social Problems,* 9th ed. (Upper Saddle River, NJ: Prentice-Hall, 1998), 375.

58. Farley, *American Social Problems,* 480.

## Chapter 13

1. John A. Byrne, "Their Cup Runneth Over—Again," *Business Week,* March 28, 1994, 26–27.

2. William Kornblum and Joseph Julian, *Social Problems,* 9th ed. (Upper Saddle River, NJ: Prentice-Hall, 1998), 414–416.

3. Eric R. Quinones, "Rich Get Richer: Forbes Lists 170 Billionaires," *Wisconsin State Journal,* Nov. 3, 1997, 2A.

4. U.S. Bureau of the Census, *Statistical Abstract of the United States, 1997* (Washington, DC: U.S. Government Printing Office, 1997).

5. Kornblum and Julian, *Social Problems,* 410.

6. James W. Coleman and Donald R. Cressey, *Social Problems,* 6th ed. (New York: HarperCollins, 1996), 30–34.

7. Kornblum and Julian, *Social Problems,* 410–413.

8. Coleman and Cressey, *Social Problems,* 31.

9. David R. James and Michael Soref, "Profit Constraints on Managerial Autonomy: Managerial Theory and the Unmasking of the Corporate President," *American Sociological Review,* 46 (Feb. 1981): 1–18.

10. Anthony Sampson, *The Sovereign State of I.T.T.* (New York: Stein and Day, 1980).

11. Kornblum and Julian, *Social Problems,* 413.

12. Mark Dowie, "Pinto Madness" in *Crisis in American Institutions,* 4th ed., ed. J. Skolnick and E. Currie (Boston, MA: Little, Brown, 1979).

13. Richard Austin Smith "The Incredible Electrical Conspiracy," *Fortune,* May 1961, 161–224.

14. Adam Smith, *An Inquiry into the Nature and Causes of the Wealth of Nations,* (1776; reprint ed., New York: Random House, 1937).

15. Daniel Bell, *The Coming of Post-Industrial Society: A Venture in Social Forecasting* (New York: Basic Books, 1973), 188–195.

16. Kornblum and Julian, *Social Problems,* 417.

17. Ibid., 412.

18. Alvin Toffler, *Future Shock* (New York: Bantam Books, 1970), 27.

19. Alvin Toffler, "The Strategy of Social Futurism" in *The Futurists,* ed. A. Toffler (New York: Random House, 1972), 96.

20. William F. Ogburn, "Cultural Lag as Theory," *Sociology and Social Research* 41 (Jan.–Feb. 1957): 167.

21. Aristotle, *Politics,* Book 3, Sec. V (Jowlett translation).

22. Quoted in Thomas Sullivan, Kenrick Thompson, Richard Wright, George Gross, and Dale Spady, *Social Problems* (New York: Wiley, 1980), 300.

23. Quoted in Ian Robertson, *Social Problems,* 2d ed. (New York: Random House, 1980), 87.

24. Coleman and Cressey, *Social Problems,* 37–41.

25. Kornblum and Julian, *Social Problems,* 417.

26. Ibid.

27. Ibid., 417–418.

28. Coleman and Cressey, *Social Problems,* 36.

29. Seymour Wolfbein, *Work in American Society* (Glenview, IL: Scott, Foresman, 1971), 45.

30. Coleman and Cressey, *Social Problems,* 420.

31. Charles R. Walker and Robert Guest, *Man on the Assembly Line* (Cambridge, MA: Harvard University Press, 1952), 54–55.

32. American Association of Retired Persons, *A Profile of Older Americans, 1996* (Washington, DC: American Association of Retired Persons, 1996), 12.

33. *Statistical Abstract of the United States, 1997.*

34. Coleman and Cressey, *Social Problems,* 38–39.

35. Ibid., 302–304.

36. Kornblum and Julian, *Social Problems,* 417–418.

37. Coleman and Cressey, *Social Problems,* 420.

38. Ibid., 420–421.

39. Ibid.

40. Ibid., 421.

41. Karl Marx, *Selected Writings in Sociology and Social Philosophy,* T. B. Bottomore, trans. (New York: McGraw-Hill, 1964), 47.

42. Charles Fenyvesi, "Trade Marx," *U.S. News & World Report,* Mar. 12, 1990, 23.

43. Karen Ball, "Most Jobs Aren't What We Planned," *Wisconsin State Journal,* Jan. 12, 1990, 1A.

44. Harold L. Wilensky, "Work as a Social Problem," in *Social Problems,* Howard Becker, ed. (New York: Wiley, 1966), 129.

45. D. D. Braginsky and B. M. Braginsky, "Surplus People: Their Lost Faith in Self and System," *Psychology Today* (August 1975), 70.

46. Harvey Brenner, *Mental Illness and the Economy* (Cambridge, MA: Harvard University Press, 1973).

47. K. Newman, *Falling From Grace* (New York: Free Press, 1988), 202.

48. Kornblum and Julian, *Social Problems,* 46–47.

49. Ibid., 47.

50. Thomas J. Sullivan, *Social Problems,* 4th ed. (Needham Heights, MA, 1997), 61.

51. Kornblum and Julian, *Social Problems,* 426.

52. Coleman and Cressey, *Social Problems,* 41.

53. Ibid.

54. Ibid.

55. Kornblum and Julian, *Social Problems,* 426–427.

56. Ibid., 427.

57. Ibid.

58. Brian L. Seaward, *Managing Stress,* 5th ed. (Boston: Jones and Bartlett Publishers, 1994).

59. Ibid.

60. Philip R. Popple and Leslie H. Leighninger, *Social Work, Social Welfare, and American Society* (Boston: Allyn and Bacon, 1990).

61. Robert A. Rankin and Brigid Schulte, "Detailed Look at Budget Plan," *Wisconsin State Journal,* Aug. 8, 1993, 1F.

62. Keith Davis and John W. Newstrom, *Human Behavior at Work,* 8th ed. (New York: McGraw-Hill, 1989), 232–249.

## Chapter 14

1. Quoted in Robert B. Toplin, *Unchallenged Violence: An American Ordeal* (Westport, CT: Greenwood Press, 1975), 100.

2. Alphonso, Pinkney, *The American Way of Violence* (New York: Random House, 1972), 22.

3. Ibid.

4. Ibid.

5. Ibid.

6. Ibid.

7. Ibid., 23.

8. Ibid.

9. Ibid., 24.

10. Ibid.

11. William Kornblum and Joseph Julian, *Social Problems,* 9th ed. (Upper Saddle River, NJ: Prentice-Hall, 1998), 523.

12. John E. Farley, *American Social Problems,* 2d ed. (Englewood Cliffs, NJ: Prentice-Hall, 1992), 355.

13. Kornblum and Julian, *Social Problems,* 524–526.

14. Ibid., 526–527.

15. Ibid.

16. Carla A. Robbins, "The Nuclear Epidemic," *U.S. News & World Report,* March 16, 1992, 40–44.

17. Orr Kelly, "Nuclear War's Horrors: Reality vs. Fiction," *U.S. News & World Report,* Nov. 28, 1983, 85–86.

18. Farley, *American Social Problems,* 363.

19. Kornblum and Julian, *Social Problems,* 527–528.

20. James W. Coleman and Donald R. Cressey, *Social Problems,* 6th ed. (New York: HarperCollins, 1996), 542–543.

21. "The 38 Hours: Trial by Terror," *Time Magazine,* March 21, 1977, 16–20.

22. Kornblum and Julian, *Social Problems,* 537–538.

23. Coleman and Cressey, *Social Problems,* 543.

24. Kornblum and Julian, *Social Problems,* 538.

25. Ibid.

26. Coleman and Cressey, *Social Problems,* 542–544.

27. Claire Sterling, "The Terrorist Network," *Atlantic,* Nov. 1978, 37–47.

28. Gordon Witkin and Ilan Greenberg, "End of the Unabomber," *U.S. News & World Report,* February 2, 1998, 34.

29. U.S. Bureau of the Census, *Statistical Abstract of the United States, 1997* (Washington, DC: U.S. Government Printing Office, 1997).

30. William M. Patterson et al., "Evaluation of Suicidal Patients: The Sad Persons Scale," *Psychosomatics* 24, no. 4 (April 1983): 343–349.

31. Michael L. Jensen, "Adolescent Suicide: A Tragedy of Our Times," *FLEducator,* Summer 1984, 12–16.

32. *Statistical Abstract of the United States, 1997.*

33. Peter M. Lewinsohn, Ricardo F. Munoz, M. A. Youngren and M. Z. Antonette, *Control Your Depression* (Englewood Cliffs, NJ: Prentice-Hall, 1978).

34. Harvard Medical School, "Suicide—Parts I and II," *Mental Health Letter* 2, nos. 2, 3 (Feb. and March, 1986).

35. D. E. Papalia and S. Wendkos Olds, *Human Development,* 5th ed. (New York: McGraw-Hill, 1992).

36. Harvard Medical School, "Suicide."

37. N. L. Farberow and R. E. Litman, "Suicide Prevention" in *Emergency Psychiatric Care,* ed. H. L. P. Resnick and H. L. Ruben (Bowie, MD: Charles Press, 1975), 103–188.

38. Papalia and Olds, *Human Development.*

39. A. S. Freese, "Adolescent Suicide: Mental Health Challenge," (New York: Public Affairs Pamphlets, 1979).

40. J. Jacobs and J. Teicher, "Broken Homes and Social Isolation in Attempted Suicide of Adolescents," *International Journal of Social Psychology* 13 (1967): 139–149.

41. Ibid.

42. R. R. Rohn, R. Sarles, T. Kenny, B. Reynolds, and F. Heald, "Adolescents Who Attempt Suicide," *Journal of Pediatrics* 90, no. 4 (1977): 636–638.

43. Suzanne K. Steinmetz and Murray A. Straus, "The Family as Cradle for Violence," *Society* 10 (Sept.–Oct. 1973): 69.

44. Richard J. Gelles, *Intimate Violence in Families*, 3d ed. (Thousand Oaks, CA: Sage Publications, 1997).

45. Pinkney, *American Way of Violence*, 73.

46. Ibid., 76.

47. Ibid., 79.

48. Arthur I. Waskow, *From Race Riot to Sit-In*, (Garden City, NY: Doubleday, 1967).

49. Pinkney, *American Way of Violence*, 96.

50. Ibid., 97.

51. Ibid., 107.

52. Quoted in Pinkney, *American Way of Violence*, 141–142.

53. George F. Cole, *The American System of Criminal Justice*, 6th ed. (Pacific Grove, CA: Brooks/Cole, 1992), 298–302.

54. David F. Pike, "Rage in Miami: A Warning?" *U.S. News & World Report*, June 2, 1980, 19–22.

55. "Police Brutality Issue Reaches Beyond Miami," *U.S. News & World Report*, June 2, 1980, 23–24.

56. Ibid.

57. Cole, *The American System of Criminal Justice*, 298–302.

58. Quoted in Toplin, *Unchallenged Violence*, 54.

59. Ibid., 76.

60. John C. Henry, "U.S. Seeks Ways to Try Arkansas Boys as Adults," *Wisconsin State Journal*, March 27, 1998, 2A.

61. Ted Gest, "Violence in America," *U.S. News & World Report*, Jan. 17, 1994, 24.

62. Ed. Bradley, "CBS Reports: Murder, Teenage Style," Sept. 4, 1981.

63. Ibid.

64. Coleman and Cressey, *Social Problems*, 394–395.

65. Ibid., 394.

66. Sigmund Freud, *A General Introduction to Psychoanalysis* (New York: Boni and Liveright, 1924).

67. Robert Ardrey, *The Territorial Imperative* (New York: Atheneum, 1967).

68. Konrad Lorenz, *On Aggression* (New York: Harcourt Brace Jovanovich, 1966).

69. Robert Dentan, *The Semai: A Nonviolent People of Malaya* (New York: Holt, Rinehart and Winston, 1968).

70. Travis Hirschi, *Causes of Delinquency* (Berkeley: University of California Press, 1969).

71. Coleman and Cressey, *Social Problems*, 404–405.

72. Pinkney, *American Way of Violence*, xiii.

73. Louis Harris, *The Anguish of Change* (New York: Norton, 1973), 159.

74. Frederick Ilfeld, "Environmental Theories of Violence," in *Violence and the Struggle for Existence*, ed. D. N. Daniels, M. Gilula, and F. Oehberg (Boston, MA: Little, Brown, 1970), 81.

75. Coleman and Cressey, *Social Problems*, 136–137.

76. Max Lerner, *The Unfinished Century: A Book of American Symbols* (New York, 1959), 364–365.

77. James F. Kirkham, Sheldon G. Leuy, and William J. Crotty, *Assassination and Political Violence*, A Report to the National Commission on the Causes and Prevention of Violence (New York, 1970), 79–88.

78. Kornblum and Julian, *Social Problems*, 204.

79. Ibid.

80. Mortimer B. Zuckerman, "The Victims of TV Violence," *U.S. News & World Report*, Aug. 2, 1993, 64.

81. Leo Bogart, "Warning: The Surgeon General Has Determined That TV Violence Is Moderately Dangerous to Your Child's Mental Health," *Public Opinion Quarterly* 36 (Winter 1972–1973): 491–521.

82. *Mass Media and Violence: A Report to the National Commission on the Causes and Prevention of Violence* (Washington, DC: U.S. Government Printing Office, 1969), 367.

83. Ibid.

84. Timothy F. Hartnagel, James J. Teevan, Jr., and Jennie M. McIntyre, "Television Violence and Violent Behavior," *Social Forces* 54 (Dec. 1975): 341–351.

85. Quoted in Arthur Schlesinger, Jr., *Violence: America in the Sixties* (New York, 1968), 54–55.

86. James Mann, "What Is TV Doing to America?" *U.S. News & World Report*, Aug. 2, 1982, 27–30.

87. David N. Rosenthal, "Do Violent Movies, TV Cause Violent Action?" *Wisconsin State Journal*, Aug. 14, 1981, sec. 4, 1.

88. Quoted in Rosenthal, "Violent Movies," 1.

89. Toplin, *Unchallenged Violence*, 197.

90. Quoted in Rosenthal, "Violent Movies," 1.

91. Joan Beck, "TV's Violence Hits Home," *Wisconsin State Journal*, Sept. 15, 1981, sec. 1, 8.

92. Zuckerman, "The Victims of TV Violence," 64.

93. M. L. Cohen, R. Garofalo, R. Boucher, and T. Seghorn, "The Psychology of Rapists," *Seminars in Psychiatry* 3 (1971): 307–327.

94. Janet S. Hyde, *Understanding Human Sexuality*, 5th ed. (New York: McGraw-Hill, 1994), 482–497.

95. Gest, "Violence in America," 24.

96. Kornblum and Julian, *Social Problems,* 206.

97. Ibid., 206–207.

98. Chelsea J. Carter, "U.S. Has Highest Rate of Gun Deaths—By a Huge Margin," *Wisconsin State Journal,* April 17, 1998, 2A.

99. Toplin, *Unchallenged Violence,* 217.

100. Kornblum and Julian, *Social Problems,* 218.

101. Toplin, *Unchallenged Violence,* 217.

102. Kornblum and Julian, *Social Problems,* 217–220.

103. Coleman and Cressey, *Social Problems,* 412.

104. Ibid.

105. Toplin, *Unchallenged Violence,* 234.

106. Ted Gest, "Gun Control's Limits," *U.S. News & World Report,* Dec. 6, 1993, 24–26.

107. Ramsey Clark, *Crime in America* (New York: Simon and Schuster, 1970), 11.

108. Gest, "Violence in America," 27.

109. Barry Schweid, "U.S., Russia Seal Missile Deal," *Wisconsin State Journal,* Jan. 4, 1993, 1A.

110. Quoted in Quincy Wright, *A Study of War,* abridged by L. L. Wright (Chicago, IL: University of Chicago Press, 1964), 186.

## Chapter 15

1. Paul B. Horton, Gerald R. Leslie, and Richard F. Larson, *The Sociology of Social Problems,* 10th ed. (Englewood Cliffs, NJ: Prentice-Hall, 1991), 274.

2. U.S. Bureau of the Census, *Statistical Abstract of the United States, 1997* (Washington, DC: U.S. Government Printing Office, 1997).

3. William Kornblum and Joseph Julian, *Social Problems,* 9th ed. (Upper Saddle River, NJ: Prentice-Hall, 1998), 439–440.

4. Ibid., 439.

5. Ibid., 438.

6. Ibid., 440.

7. Ibid., 439–440.

8. James W. Coleman and Donald R. Cressey, *Social Problems,* 6th ed. (New York: HarperCollins, 1996), 465–467.

9. Ibid., 467.

10. George Simmel, "The Metropolis and Mental Life," in *Neighborhood, City, and Metropolis,* ed. R. Gutman and D. Popenoe (New York: Random House, 1970).

11. Louis Wirth, "Urbanism as a Way of Life," *American Journal of Sociology* 44 (July 1938): 1–24.

12. Herbert J. Gans, "Urbanism and Suburbanism as Ways of Life: A Re-evaluation of Definitions," in Gutman and Popenoe, *Neighborhood, City, and Metropolis.*

13. Claude Fischer, *The Urban Experiences* (New York: Harcourt Brace Jovanovich, 1976).

14. Coleman and Cressey, *Social Problems,* 468–469.

15. Ibid., 463–64.

16. Ibid.

17. Kornblum and Julian, *Social Problems,* 455–456.

18. Ibid.

19. Ibid., 455–457.

20. Ibid., 457–458.

21. Ibid., 457–458.

22. Ibid.

23. H. M. Choldin, "Social Life and the Physical Environment" in *Handbook of Contemporary Urban Life,* ed. D. Street (San Francisco, CA: Josey-Bass, 1978), 372.

24. League of Women Voters, *Report from the Hill,* No. 98, 1–2, March 1983, HR/SP3.

25. Kornblum and Julian, *Social Problems,* 452–458.

26. Coleman and Cressey, *Social Problems,* 459–461.

27. Ibid., 195.

28. Ibid.

29. Ibid.

30. Ibid., 463–464.

31. Horton, Leslie, and Larson, *Sociology of Social Problems,* 285.

32. Kornblum and Julian, *Social Problems,* 455.

33. Quoted in Kornblum and Julian, *Social Problems,* 441.

34. *Statistical Abstract of the United States, 1997.*

35. Kornblum and Julian, *Social Problems,* 441–442.

36. Ibid.

37. Coleman and Cressey, *Social Problems,* 472.

38. Lynn C. Landman "Birth Control in India: The Carrot and the Rod?" *Family Planning Perspectives* 9 (May–June 1977): 102.

39. Charles Murray, *Losing Ground* (New York: Basic Books, 1986).

40. The source for this material is Harry C. Boyte, "People Power Transforms a St. Louis Housing Project," *Occasional Papers* (Chicago, IL: Community Renewable Society, 1989), 1–5.

41. Quoted in Boyte, "People Power," 3.

42. Quoted in Boyte, "People Power," 5.

## Chapter 16

1. Thomas J. Sullivan, *Social Problems,* 4th ed. (Needham Heights, MA: Allyn and Bacon, 1997), 434–435.

2. Ibid.

3. James W. Coleman and Donald R. Cressey, *Social Problems,* 6th ed. (New York: HarperCollins, 1996), 479.

4. Paul R. Ehrlich, *The Population Bomb* (New York: Ballantine, 1971), 4.

5. Sullivan, *Social Problems,* 434–436.

6. Warner Fornos, *Gaining People, Losing Ground* (Washington, DC: Population Institute, 1987), 57.

7. William Kornblum and Joseph Julian, *Social Problems,* 9th ed. (Upper Saddle River, NJ: Prentice-Hall, 1998), 470–474.

8. Lee Rainwater, *And the Poor Get Children* (Chicago: Quadrangle Books, 1960).

9. Quoted in Donald C. Bacon, "Poor vs. Rich: A Global Struggle," *U.S. News & World Report,* July 31, 1978, 57.

10. Fornos, *Gaining People, Losing Ground,* 38–61.

11. R. V. Kail and J. C. Cavanaugh, *Human Development* (Pacific Grove, CA: Brooks/Cole, 1996), 363.

12. Kornblum and Julian, *Social Problems,* 470–474.

13. Paul Ehrlich and Anne Ehrlich, *The Population Explosion* (New York: Simon and Schuster, 1990), 34–36.

14. Fornos, *Gaining People, Losing Ground,* 7.

15. Ibid.

16. Ehrlich and Ehrlich, *The Population Explosion.*

17. Ibid., 38–39.

18. Coleman and Cressey, *Social Problems,* 485.

19. Ibid.

20. Ibid., 485–487.

21. Ehrlich and Ehrlich, *The Population Explosion.*

22. Ian Robertson, *Social Problems,* 2d ed. (New York: Random House, 1980), 41.

23. Thomas R. Malthus, *On Population,* Gertrude Himmelfarb, ed. (New York: Modern Library, 1960), 13–14. (Original edition published 1798.)

24. Coleman and Cressey, *Social Problems,* 485–487.

25. Ibid., 485–487.

26. Paul R. Ehrlich and Anne H. Ehrlich, *Population, Resources, Environment* (San Francisco: W. H Freeman, 1970), 65.

27. "Warning: Water Shortages Ahead," *Time,* Apr. 4, 1977, 48.

28. Fornos, *Gaining People, Losing Ground,* 7–23.

29. Quoted in Fornos, *Gaining People, Losing Ground,* 10.

30. U.S. Bureau of the Census, *Statistical Abstract of the United States, 1997* (Washington, DC: U.S. Government Printing Office, 1997).

31. Quoted in Fornos, *Gaining People, Losing Ground,* 20–21.

32. Fornos, *Gaining People, Losing Ground,* 21.

33. John B. Calhoun, "Population Density and Social Pathology," *Scientific American,* 206 (February 1962), 139–148.

34. Joseph Julian, *Social Problems,* 3d ed. (Englewood Cliffs, NJ: Prentice-Hall, 1980), 502.

35. Ibid.

36. Paul Glastris, "The Alien Payoff," *U.S. News & World Report,* May 26, 1997, 20.

37. Ibid., 21.

38. Irene B. Taeuber, "Japan's Demographic Transition Reexamined," *Population Studies,* 14 (July 1960), 39.

39. Robertson, *Social Problems,* 43.

40. Fornos, *Gaining People, Losing Ground,* 5.

41. Ibid.

42. Ehrlich and Ehrlich, *The Population Explosion,* 17.

43. "25 Million Births in India Each Year," *Popline,* July–August, 1997, 3.

44. Ibid.

45. Ibid.

46. Ibid.

47. Ibid.

48. Ibid.

49. Ibid.

50. "India's Program Stresses Role of Women," *Popline,* vol. 12 (March–April 1990), 3.

51. Ibid.

52. Ibid.

53. Coleman and Cressey, *Social Problems,* 495–497.

54. Ibid.

55. Ibid.

56. Ibid.

57. Ibid.

58. Fornos, *Gaining People, Losing Ground,* 42.

59. Ehrlich and Ehrlich, *The Population Explosion,* 205–209.

60. Coleman and Cressey, *Social Problems,* 495.

61. Ehrlich and Ehrlich, *The Population Explosion,* 207.

62. Ehrlich, *The Population Bomb,* 127–145.

63. Bernard Berelson, "The Present State of Family Planning Programs," *Studies in Family Planning,* 57 (September 1970), 2.

64. Coleman and Cressey, *Social Problems,* 497.

65. Ibid.

66. Paul R. Ehrlich, Anne H. Ehrlich, and John P. Holdren, *Human Ecology: Problems and Solutions* (San Francisco: W. H. Freeman, 1973), 279.

67. "Abortion Foes Gain Victory," *Wisconsin State Journal,* July 1, 1980, sec. 1, 1.

68. Steven Waldman, Elise Ackerman, and Rita Rubin, "Abortions in America," *U.S. News & World Report,* January 19, 1998, 20–25.

69. Fornos, *Gaining People, Losing Ground,* 78–85.

70. Ibid., 106–107.

# Chapter 17

1. David Foster, "Hidden Oil Soils Alaska's Coast," *Wisconsin State Journal*, March 22, 1990, 2A.

2. Paul R. Ehrlich, Anne H. Ehrlich, and John P. Holdren, *Human Ecology: Problems and Solutions* (San Francisco, CA: W. H. Freeman, 1973), 159–160.

3. James W. Coleman and Donald R. Cressey, *Social Problems*, 6th ed. (New York: HarperCollins, 1996), 511.

4. Ibid.

5. Ibid.

6. Paul Ehrlich and Anne Ehrlich, *The Population Explosion* (New York: Simon and Schuster, 1990), 205–209.

7. Werner Fornos, *Gaining People, Losing Ground* (Washington, DC: Population Institute, 1987), 45–46.

8. Ibid.

9. Ibid., 13.

10. Coleman and Cressey, *Social Problems*, 54.

11. Ian Robertson, *Social Problems*, 2d ed. (New York: Random House, 1980), 71.

12. William Kornblum and Joseph Julian, *Social Problems*, 9th ed. (Upper Saddle River, NJ: Prentice-Hall, 1998), 470–474.

13. Joseph Julian, *Social Problems*, 3d ed. (Englewood Cliffs, NJ: Prentice-Hall, 1980), 528.

14. Coleman and Cressey, *Social Problems*, 507–509.

15. Ibid., 508.

16. Ibid.

17. Ibid.

18. Ibid., 509

19. Ibid.

20. Kornblum and Julian, *Social Problems*, 470–474.

21. Coleman and Cressey, *Social Problems*, 510.

22. Vincent Parrilo, John Stimson, and Ardyth Stimson, *Contemporary Social Problems*, 2d ed. (New York: Macmillan, 1989), 501.

23. Coleman and Cressey, *Social Problems*, 511.

24. Ehrlich and Ehrlich, *The Population Explosion*, 123–124.

25. Ibid.

26. Paul Ehrlich, *The Population Bomb* (New York: Ballantine Books, 1971), 4.

27. Richard Curtis and Elizabeth Hogan, *Perils of the Peaceful Atom* (New York: Ballantine Books, 1969), 194.

28. "Chemical Dangers May Be Unknown," *Wisconsin State Journal*, March 3, 1984.

29. "Silent Spring Revisited," *Newsweek*, July 14, 1986, 72.

30. Coleman and Cressey, *Social Problems*, 518.

31. Ibid.

32. Ibid., 518–519.

33. Ibid.

34. Kornblum and Julian, *Social Problems*, 474–476.

35. George Ritzer, *Social Problems*, 2d ed. (New York: Random House, 1986), 556.

36. "Don't Throw a Good Thing Away," *Policyholder News*, 23, no. 1 (Spring 1990): 3.

37. Ibid.

38. Ibid.

39. Steven Thomma, "Some Problems Solved since Earth Day in '70, But Now We Face New Troubles," *Wisconsin State Journal*, April 22, 1994, 1D.

40. Ibid.

41. Ibid.

42. Ibid.

43. Ibid.

44. "Fuels for America's Future," *U.S. News & World Report*, Aug. 13, 1979: 33.

45. Ibid.

46. Ibid.

# Epilogue

1. W. Trattner, *From Poor Law to Welfare State: A History of Social Welfare in America* (New York: Free Press, 1974).

2. Quoted in James M. Hildredth, "Now the Squeeze Really Starts," *U.S. News & World Report*, Oct. 5, 1981, 22–23.

# Photo Credits

# Subject Index

Depression
  causes of, 63
  elderly individuals and, 78, 219–220
  sex roles and, 196
  suicide and, 377
  symptoms of, 219–220
Desoxyn (methamphetamine hydrochloride), 104
Developmental perspective, 16–17
Deviance, 24, 72. *See also* Crime; Violence
Deviant subcultures theory, 37
Devitalized relationships, 267
Devolution revolution, 256
*Diagnostic and Statistical Manual of Mental Disorders* (DSM-IV) (American Psychiatric Association), 66
Diagnostic-related groups (DRGs), 311
Diet. *See* Nutrition/diet
Differential association theory, 37, 93
Disarmament, 395–396
Discrimination
  age, 204–205, 210
  effects and costs of, 165–166
  explanation of, 24, 158
  homosexuals and, 150
  individuals with disabilities and, 304–306
  institutional, 164–165
  job, 150, 193–195, 201, 204
  as majority problem, 160
  oppression and, 159
  racial, 162–164
  sex, 186
  types of, 159
Disease. *See* Illness; *specific conditions*
Disengagement theory, 213
Dissociative disorders, 66
Distressed neighborhoods, 404–405
Diversion programs, 59
Divorce
  actions taken regarding, 13
  factors contributing to, 264–265
  functional vs. dysfunctional views of, 20
  legal aspects of, 265–267
  overview of, 264, 265
DNA (deoxyribonucleic acid), 288
Domestic violence. *See* Family violence
"Don't ask, don't tell" policy, 150
Doubling time, population, 418–419
Driving, alcohol use and, 97, 99, 300
Drug abuse prevention
  British approach and, 121
  curtailment of illegal trafficking across borders and, 118–119
  decriminalization and, 120–121
  educational programs and, 116–118
  employee drug-testing programs and, 119
  stricter laws and enforcement and, 119–120
Drug-related disorders, 66

Drugs. *See also* Alcohol; Alcohol use/abuse; Alcoholism; *specific drugs*
  addiction to, 91, 106
  alcohol combined with other, 98, 102, 103, 106
  anabolic steroids and, 110–111
  dependence on, 91
  depressants as, 94–102 (*See also* Depressants)
  facts and effects of, 95
  hallucinogens as, 108
  legal vs. illegal, 91
  marijuana as, 109–110
  narcotics as, 92, 105–107
  over-the-counter, 90
  overview of, 90
  prescription, 90–91, 98
  psychoactive, 80
  psychotropic, 76
  stimulants as, 103–105
  tobacco as, 108–109
  withdrawal symptoms from (*See* Withdrawal symptoms)
Drug subcultures, 94
Drug-testing programs, 119
Drug trafficking
  gangs and, 94, 383
  of narcotics, 107
  prevention of, 118–119
  trends in, 40
Drug treatment programs
  for alcoholics, 111–114, 116
  codependency and, 116
  employee assistance programs, 112–113
  halfway houses, 113–114
  inpatient, 113
  outpatient, 113
  self-help, 111–113
  therapeutic communities, 113
  using drugs, 114–116
Drug use/abuse
  communal needle use and, 105, 107, 120
  drug subcultures and, 94
  gangs and, 46, 383
  historical background of, 92
  reasons for, 91–92
  as social problem, 4–5
  sociological theories of, 92–93
*Dynamic Sociology* (Ward), 232
Dysfunction, 24
Eastern Europe, 456
Eating disorders
  explanation of, 64, 66
  treatment of, 65
  types of, 64–65
Economic justice
  explanation of, 174
  strategies to advance, 174–179
Economic trends/problems
  employment and, 356–357, 363
  overpopulation and, 421–422

Education. *See also* Schools
  compensatory, 332–334
  curriculum improvements and, 328–330
  effective integration in, 334–335
  equal access to, 323–327
  extending school year and, 330–331
  goals of, 327
  parental choice of schools and, 330
  peace, 396
  poverty and, 239
  in prisons, 53–54
  quality in, 322–323
  school finance reform and, 331–332
  as social problem, 322
  teacher incentives and, 328
  working conditions for teachers and, 327–328
Education for All Handicapped Children Act (PL 94-142), 333
Educators, 327–328
Egoistic suicide, 8
Eighteenth Amendment, 92
Elderly abuse, 220–221
Elderly individuals
  abuse of, 220
  aging process and, 206–207
  Alzheimer's disease and, 216–217
  crime and, 218–219
  death and, 220
  disengagement and, 213
  emphasis on youth and, 213–214
  growing population of, 207–209
  health care and, 311
  health problems and, 214
  housing and, 217–218
  income of, 215
  legislation impacting, 221
  loss of family and friends and, 215–217
  malnutrition and, 219
  mental health and, 78, 212, 219–220
  as minority group, 204–205
  myths and stereotypes of, 205
  nursing home care and, 221–224
  overview of, 204
  as political force, 225
  poverty among, 215, 218, 239
  preparation for becoming, 228
  in primitive societies, 205–206
  programs for, 224, 225
  retirement and, 212–213
  sexuality and, 125–126, 219
  social roles for, 225–228
  social security and, 215
  status of, 210–212
  suicide and, 220
  transportation and, 218
  in workforce, 349
Electroconvulsive therapy, 75
Elementary and Secondary Education Act, 332
ELISA test, 309
Embezzlement, 41–42
Emotional neglect, 273, 274

Pluralism, 341
Police
    criticisms of, 47
    family violence and, 268
    female, 198
    hostility toward, 48
    rape victims and, 137
    role of, 47–48
Polio, 12, 13
Political activism, Civil rights movement.
        *See also* Women's movement
    elderly individuals and, 225
Politics
    of activism, 175
    big business and, 342
    female candidates and, 194, 201
Polls, 23
Pollution. *See* Environmental problems
PONY (Prostitutes of New York), 143
Population
    of elderly individuals, 207–209
    optimal, 419–420
    statistics regarding, 418
Population control
    abortion and, 430–434
    family-planning services and, 431,
        434–435
    future outlook for, 435–436
    methods of, 429–430
    urban improvement and, 413
Population growth
    in China, 427–429
    demographic transition theory of,
        425–426
    in developing countries, 418–419
    doubling time and, 418
    in India, 426–427
    problems related to excessive, 420–425
Pornography
    censorship and, 144–145
    effects of, 143–144
    explanation of, 143
    types of, 143
Post-traumatic stress disorder, 369
Poverty
    African Americans and, 167, 168, 215
    approaches to defining, 237–238
    causes of, 240–242
    conflict perspective on, 243
    crime and, 31, 45
    criminal justice system and, 48, 49,
        165
    elderly and, 215, 218, 239
    females and, 218
    functional perspective on, 242–243
    functions of, 242
    gap between wealth and, 234–235,
        453
    health care and, 301–302
    historical background of, 231–234
    interactionist perspective on, 243–244
    Latinos and, 215
    mental illness and, 77–78
    Native Americans and, 173
    overpopulation and, 418, 422

personal troubles approach to, 17
single-parent families and, 238–239
trends in rate of, 235, 237, 238
Poverty programs. *See* Welfare programs
Power, 24
Power elite, 341
Power rapists, 135–136
*The Power Elite* (Mills), 341
Pregnancy. *See also* Artificial insemination;
        Birth control
    adolescent, 278–280
    alcohol use and, 98–99
    crack use and, 106
    male, 286
    marijuana use and, 110
    tobacco use and, 108
Prejudice
    causes of, 162–164
    against elderly, 210, 225
    explanation of, 25, 158
    historical explanations of, 162–163
    immigration and, 424–425
    socialization patterns and, 163
Prejudiced discriminators, 158
Prejudiced nondiscriminators, 158
Premarital sex, 125
Prescription drugs. *See also* Drug
        use/abuse; Drugs
    abuse of, 90–91
    for AIDS, 308
    alcohol taken with, 98
Presidents
    assassinations and attempted assassina-
        tions of, 3, 36, 57, 75
    social problem identification and, 4
President's Commission on Mental
        Health, 75
Preventive medicine
    contemporary health problems and,
        299–300
    health care reform and, 317–319
    overview of, 299
    trends in, 300
Price fixing, 340
Prisons
    criticisms of, 47
    function of, 51–52
    treatment approaches in, 53–54
Probation, 54–55
Pro-choice movement, 2, 21
Professional parents, 289
Professional thieves, 45
Prohibition, 57, 92
Project Head Start, 332
Projection, 162
Proletariats, 9
Pro-life movement, 2, 21
Proposition 209 (California), 178
Prosecuting attorneys, 48–49
Prostitution
    decriminalization of, 57, 143
    drug use and, 107
    forms of, 140–142
    legalization of, 143

male, 140–141
organized crime and, 40
reasons for, 142
as social problem, 139
trends in, 139–140
Protective services, 275
Protest, violent, 374–375
Protestant ethic, 231, 346
Protestant Reformation, 126, 346
*The Protestant Ethic and the Spirit of
        Capitalism* (Weber), 346
Psilocin, 95, 108
Psilocybin, 95, 108
Psychiatry, 35
Psychoactive drugs, 80
Psychoanalytic theory, 35–36
Psychodynamic problem-solving theory,
        36
Psychological abuse, 268
Psychological dependence, 91
Psychotherapy. *See* Counseling
Psychotropic drugs, 76
Public assistance programs
    features of, 247–248
    types of, 248–253
Public health services, 297–298
Puerto Ricans, 171–172. *See also* Latinos
Punitive approach for criminals, 50–53,
        393
Puritans, 126, 127, 346
Pygmalion Effect, 325
Quaaludes
    alcohol taken with, 98, 102
    facts and effects of, 95, 102
Quality circles, 363
Race
    explanation of, 158
    mental illness and, 78
    as social concept, 160–162
Race riots, 175
Racial discrimination, 162–164. *See also*
        Discrimination
Racial groups. *See also* specific racial groups
    explanation of, 158
    interaction between, 175
    similarities in capacities of, 161–162
    in United States, 166
Racial segregation. *See* Segregation
Racism
    explanation of, 158
    institutional, 164–165
Radioactive wastes, 439, 440, 442, 444
Rape
    categories of, 135–136
    counseling for victims of, 138
    cultural variations and, 125
    date, 103, 136–137
    dowry disputes and, 193
    effects on victims of, 137–139
    explanation of, 135
    fraternity gang, 136
    prevention of, 138
    reporting of, 43

controversy in classifying conditions as, 6
developmental perspective on, 16–17
elements of defining, 2–5
explanation of, 25
historical foundations of studying, 5–8
importance of studying, 3
liberal perspective on, 15–16
microsociological theories and, 17–22
optimistic outlook for, 455–457
progress in dealing with, 452–454
research on, 22–27
role of sociology and social science in
resolving, 8–10
social issues vs., 17
social movements and, 10–12
societal change and, 454–455
Social reality, 22
Social reform, 393–394
Social science, 8–10
Social Security Act of 1935
amendments to, 256
explanation of, 232, 234, 452
Title XIX, 314
Title XVIII, 246, 249, 315
unemployment insurance and, 247
Social Security system, 215, 225
Social stratification, 25, 234–235
Social structure, 25
Social welfare
conservative perspective on, 14–16
developmental perspective on, 16–17
liberal perspective on, 15–16
Socialism, 8, 9
Socialization. See also Sex roles
explanation of, 25
male arrest rate and, 31
prejudice and patterns of, 163
sexism and, 191–193
sex-role differences and, 184–185,
392–393
Societal control theory, 37–38
Society, 25
Socioeconomic level. See also Social class
alcohol use and, 96
health care access and, 301–302
Sociological approach
defining social problems and, 2–5
early illustration of, 8
historical foundations in, 5–8
role of sociology and social science in,
8–10
Sociological research
control group approach to, 26–27
function of, 22–23
participant observation approach to, 23
sample survey approach to, 23, 26
Sociology
explanation of, 2
list of terms used in, 24–25
social problem resolution and role of,
8–10
Solar energy, 449
Solid wastes, 439–440
Somatoform disorders, 66
South American cultures, 125
Spanish-American War, 368

Spouse abuse, 269–270, 375, 380
State Farm Insurance Company, 186
Statutory rape, 43
Stereotypes
changes in sex-role, 198–199 (See also
Sex roles; Socialization)
of elderly, 205, 212
explanation of, 160
racial and ethnic, 160, 178
Steroids, 110–111
Stimulants
amphetamines as, 95, 103–104
amyl nitrate and butyl nitrate as, 95,
105
caffeine as, 103
cocaine and crack as, 95, 104–105
Stockholders, 338
Streetwalkers, 140–142
Stress
health and, 302–303
job-related, 359
Students Against Drunk Driving (SADD), 97
Subculture
drug, 94
explanation of, 25
urban, 403–404
Substance abuse. See Drug use/abuse
Suburbs
crime in, 31
exodus to, 405–406
Suggestion programs, 363
Suicide
adolescent, 376, 378
alcohol use and, 98
assisted, 222–223
barbiturate use and, 102
Durkheim's study of, 8
elderly and, 220
risk factors for, 376–378
types of, 8
Supplemental Security Income (SSI) program, 248, 255
Supreme Court
abortion and, 201, 430–431
affirmative action and, 177, 178
age of justices on, 227
death penalty and, 51
juvenile procedural safeguards and, 49
pornography and, 145
racial segregation and, 3, 167, 177,
324–326
sexual harassment and, 189
Surrogate motherhood
issues related to, 6, 282–285
social problems and, 6
test-tube babies and, 285–286
Symbols, 22
Synthetic fuel, 448–449
Taboo, 25
Teachers, 327–328
Technological advances
artificial insemination, 281–286
breaking genetic code, 288
childbirth, 281–282
cloning, 287–288
cultural lag from, 345

disasters stemming from, 344
effects of, 343–345
future shock from, 345
genetic screening, 286–287
urban development and, 400
Television violence, 385, 387, 388, 392
Terrorism
examples of, 371–372
forms of, 372–373
overpopulation and, 422
strategies to combat, 394
victims of, 373–374
Test-tube babies, 285–286
Theft, 44–45
Theories, 25
Theory X-type managers, 363, 364
Theory Y-type managers, 363, 364
Therapeutic communities, 113
Third International Mathematics and
Science Study, 322
Three Mile Island, 442
Tobacco. See also Drug use/abuse; Drugs
addiction to, 108–109
death rate and, 108
facts and effects of, 95, 108
as legal drug, 91
use of, 90, 92
Tobacco companies, 340
Tobriand Islanders, 125
Toxic Substances Control Act, 364
Toxic wastes, 440
Trait theories, of crime, 34–35
Tranquilizers. See also Drug use/abuse;
Drugs
explanation of, 76
facts and effects of, 95, 102
Transitional programs, 59
Transportation
elderly and, 218
in urban areas, 410
Transracial adoptions, 291
Transvestism, 146
Treatment approach (criminal)
development of, 53
imprisonment and, 52
methods used in, 53–54
Trial marriage, 290
Trickle down theory, 360
Twenty-Seventh Amendment, 186
Underemployment, 354
Unemployment. See also Employment
actions taken regarding, 13
adolescents and, 349, 353
African Americans and, 168, 353
case example of, 354–355
crime and, 31
effects of, 351, 353
efforts to reduce, 363–364
factors increasing, 356
factors reducing, 356–357
females and, 353
individuals facing, 353–355
of individuals with disabilities, 354
poverty and, 239
reasons for, 355–356